DATE DUE

NOV 05 2001		
MAR 07 2002		

Demco, Inc. 38-293

LATINOS AND EDUCATION: A CRITICAL READER

LATINOS AND EDUCATION: A CRITICAL READER

Antonia Darder,
Rodolfo D. Torres, and
Henry Gutíerrez

Editors

Routledge
New York • London

Published in 1997 by

Routledge
29 West 35th Street
New York, NY 10001

Published in Great Britain by

Routledge
11 New Fetter Lane
London EC4P 4EE

Library of Congress Cataloging-in-Publication Data

Latinos and education : a critical reader / edited by Antonia Darder,
    Rodolfo D. Torres, and Henry Gutierrez.
        p.   cm.
    Includes bibliographical references and index.
    ISBN 0–415–91181–8. — ISBN 0–415–91182–6 (pbk.)
    1. Hispanic Americans—Education—Social aspects.   2. Hispanic
Americans—Education—Economic aspects.   3. Hispanic Americans—
Education—History.   4. Language and education—United States.
5. Educational anthropology—United States.   I. Darder, Antonia.
II. Torres, Rodolfo D., 1949–   .   III. Gutierrez, Henry.
LC2669.L39   1996
371.97'68'073—dc20   96–9686
                                                                CIP

To Guido Nunez del Prado, whose love has opened up a whole new world to me and transformed my life.

—Antonia

To Patricia Speier for all her support, love, and understanding.

—Rudy

To Enrique and Ruth Funari Gutierrez in honor of their fiftieth wedding anniversary, for all their encouragement at every phase of my life, and for the loving family they brought me into.

—Henry

Acknowledgements

We would like to express our gratitude and appreciation to the following: To our colleagues at Routledge, Jayne Fargnoli, whose vision founded this project, and David Auburn, for his persistence and dedication in bringing it to completion; to our colleagues at Claremont Graduate School, Cal-State Long Beach, and San Jose State, as well as our friends and other colleagues around the country who provided assistance and support; to Connie Hurston, our loyal friend and researcher whose long hours at the library and computer made this book possible; and most importantly, to the contributors, for their work and dedication to improving the education of Latino students in this country.

Contents

Introduction

Antonia Darder
Rodolfo D. Torres
Henry Gutíerrez

> *The frequent prostitution of democratic ideals to the cause of expediency, political vested interests, ignorance, class, and "race" prejudice, and to indifference and inefficiency is a sad commentary on the intelligence and justice of a society that makes claims to those very progressive democratic ideals. The dual system of education . . . the family system of contract labor, social and economic discrimination, educational negligence on the part of the state . . . all point to the need for greater insight into a problem which is inherent in a "melting pot" society.*
>
> —George I. Sanchez, 1943

Over half a century after George I. Sanchez, one of the first Chicano psychologists in the United States to challenge the educational inequalities faced by Latinos, wrote the above words, educators across the country continue to grapple with the failures of public education to meet the academic needs of Latino students. Even more disturbing is the absence of a critical discourse that engages the historical, political, and economic dimensions that shape public schooling in most Latino communities. This absence is strongly reflected in much of the literature that attempts to address questions related to Latinos and education in the United States.

Yet despite the dearth of critical discourse, there is a growing awareness of the Latino population and the increasing political impact that such a population could potentially have on the future of the United States. Latinos are among the youngest and fastest growing ethnic groups in the country. This, coupled with their concentration in the most populous states and major metropolitan areas, points to the great, but still dormant, political power that exists within Latino communities nationwide. Despite generations of protests, activism, and reform efforts, the historical record and current statistical data confirm the persistence of Latinos among the nation's most educationally disadvantaged and economically disenfranchised groups. Given the growing Latino population and the political potential present, why have the conditions of Latino students changed so little over the last three decades?

To answer this question we must acknowledge and understand the dual nature of public education in this country. On one hand, we have a public institution which supports the agenda of the market economy by reproducing particular class relations of power. This is orchestrated through the recalcitrant structures of public schools and the traditional cultural values and artifacts of classroom life which overtly and covertly shape the consciousness of students. As such, students learn to accept uncritically the existing social and material conditions of inequality—conditions which function to perpetuate social relations of dominance and subordination.

But on the other hand, public schooling is widely upheld as the promise of upward social mobility, individual privileges, economic opportunities, intellectual development, and personal satisfaction. Education is consistently promulgated as the vehicle for social and material success. It is lauded as the greatest example of the democratic process in action—anyone in the United States can become educated and hence, economically successful, if only they work hard and meet the academic standards of public schools. What we have here are blatant contradictions which have often served to obscure the problems faced by Latino students and the best solutions for addressing these problems.

It must also be acknowledged that, despite such contradictions, many Latino educators, parents, and community organizations have worked through various local and regional efforts to support the academic development and achievement of Latino students. These efforts have revealed the importance that members of the community attach to public schooling, as well as the political development necessary to effect meaningful change. It has been through such efforts over the past several decades that Latino teachers, parents, and students have developed their critical capacities and collective consciousness to question the nature of inequality and struggle for educational justice.

Yet in recognizing the counterhegemonic possibilities in such movements, it is essential that we also acknowledge the failure of these efforts to integrate their educational objectives with a larger critique of the structural forms of social and economic inequality in the United States. Too often the demands for a "multicultural" curriculum, bilingual education, and greater participation in school decisionmaking have been made in a context devoid of any critical analysis of the role of public education in a changing political economy. It is becoming more obvious from a historical analysis that educational restructuring cannot be accomplished independently from radical demoractic social and economic reform.

On the basis of such an analysis, it should not be surprising to discover that despite thirty years of educational reforms, Latino students continue to lag behind students from the dominant culture. This disparity is reflected by a variety of measures. On measures of reading and writing proficiency, Latino students are twice as likely as Anglo students to score at below basic levels. The dropout rate remains very high, with over 40 percent of Latinos over the age of nineteen years having no high school diploma. The proportion of Latino students attending segregated schools remains high, particularly in large urban school districts where Latino student enrollments are concentrated. Finally, the proportion of Latino students enrolled in colleges and universities and those who graduate from high school prepared for admission to higher education remains low. As a body of scholarly research begins to evolve, it appears that these conditions have been chronic over at least the past thirty years.

We reject the notion that this persistence of low achievement and failure can be explained primarily by reference to the nature or culture of Latino people. In the past, this had been the most common conclusion that could be drawn from social science research. Too often the culturally deterministic view that engenders such research simply functions to perpetuate racialized perceptions that further disenfranchise Latino students.

More recent historical investigations have revealed not only the persistence of a pattern of discrimination against Latinos in public education, but also patterns of resistance. As the United States established control over and integrated the territories it took from Mexico and Spain in the nineteenth century, Latinos were directly affected. At the end of this period, as public school systems were established, a similar pattern emerged. A poignant example is Mexican Americans in the Southwest who, despite a shared belief in the value of public education, faced major obstacles. As economic conditions permitted, these parents presented their children for enrollment, but often found that their children were either not accepted or segregated and provided an inferior education.

This contradicts the notion that Mexican Americans and other Latino groups willingly accepted these conditions. In fact, the reality is that since at least the 1920s, Latinos have used political pressure and the legal system to struggle for equal treatment in schools. This is significant because it also contradicts the misguided conclusion of much of social science research that asserts the low value on education within Latino communities. So if the situation is actually that Latinos share the belief in the value of education, and if they have acted on this belief to assure their children equal treatment in schools, how then can we approach understanding the persistent problems that Latino students face in public education? In many ways it is this question that is central to the production of this volume.

RETHINKING THE FOUNDATIONS OF
RESEARCH ON LATINOS AND EDUCATION

Much of the theoretical discourse related to Latinos and schooling over the last thirty years has revolved around issues of cultural and linguistic difference. Unfortunately, these discussions have oftentimes been founded on myopic traditional perspectives which have engaged the Latino population in the United States as a monolithic entity. The consequence has been to perpetuate static notions of culture. Such ahistorical and apolitical discussions have generally failed to link notions of culture with a structural analysis of socioeconomic conditions in the United States.

It is important to note that much of the study of Latino populations emerged out of conditions that have been described as academic colonialism—conditions for legitimation which required studies to be formulated along the very traditional social science values and methods which generated many of the problems faced by

Latinos. It was this academic colonialism that was consistently challenged by Chicano/Latino studies programs. These programs called for a new paradigm for academic scholarship in the field that addressed the problems inherent in standards of legitimation and questioned the disciplinary parameters defined by the academic enterprise in general.

One of the central issues in the struggle to reconstruct the foundations of research approaches to the study of Latinos was the need for a new language to describe the phenomenon of subordinate groups. What this coming to a new language implies is the breaking away from disciplinary and racialized categories of difference and structural inequality. For example, if we consider the literature of the civil rights era and the era of multiculturalism, what is consistently reflected are deeply racialized discourses grounded in black and white categories. As such, this has perpetuated a dimension of invisibility with respect to the role of Latino scholarship in the larger debates about educational theory and practice.

In addressing the need for a new language, there are specific elements which this encompasses. First of all, it is a discourse that is recognized as both simultaneously contextual and contested, and which challenges static and essentialized notions of culture, identity, and language. Secondly, it is rooted in the centrality of the political economy as a significant foundation for understanding how issues of cultural change and ethnicity intersect with the broader structural imperatives of late capitalism. Thirdly, it calls for a rethinking of categories such as "race" and "ethnicity" with respect to the manner in which these can either function to obstruct or further the political project for a cultural and economic democracy in this country. And lastly, such a discourse argues for the defining of a "working canon" of Latino education that is grounded in a critical discourse which avoids the analytical pitfalls of traditional discourses of multiculturalism and cultural studies of the past.

UNDERSTANDING THE EDUCATION
OF LATINOS WITHIN A LARGER CONTEXT

In order to address the growing needs of Latino students, Latino educational studies must be placed within the larger context of both the United States and the worldwide political economy. To do this requires that we link educational practice to the structural dimensions which shape institutional life. By doing so, we recognize the manner in which these economic structures are evolving and changing from a Fordist to a post-fordist or "post-industrial" organization of capitalist accumulation, distribution, and labor processes. This points to a fundamental flaw so often present in most of the educational literature on Latinos: there is a failure to engage the linkage between current educational discourse and the changing nature of work in a late-capitalist society.

It is important to note that there also exists a crucial link between economic changes in this country and the economic restructuring that is occurring worldwide. This calls for new efforts to understand the new class structures of "post-industrial" societies and the changing processes of social stratification and mobility. Needless to say, educational policy considerations are central to the above project as they relate to rethinking the deepening globalization of production, the breakup of working class communities, and the limits and contradictions of state intervention in late-twentieth-century capitalism.

While we cannot ignore that the future of schools will be conditioned by social and economic changes, it is by no means predetermined by those changes. A political and ideological battlefield surrounding the role of schools in the changing economy remains. Researchers who are seeking to discover ways to effectively improve the educational conditions of Latino students cannot afford to shy away from entering into this murky realm of contestation that gives shape to the terrain of American public schooling.

Racism, with its perpetuation of racialized social relations within the context of the above changing economic global picture, is another factor that deeply impacts the nature of educational research and schooling practices within Latino communities in this country. Thus, from a historical view of public education what becomes quickly apparent is that racism cannot be confronted outside of the structural imperatives of class relations and the political reality of the nation state (Miles, 1993). Cultural identity and notions of ethnicity are partly politically formed, rather than embedded in the color of the skin or a given nature (Hall, 1990). Hence, it is impossible to comprehend the social construction of Latino identities and the impact of schooling upon Latino students without critically addressing the context of racialized relations that give rise to public education in the United States.

LATINOS AND EDUCATION:
A DESCRIPTION OF MAJOR THEMES

The above discussion on Latinos and education elucidates the guiding principles that inform the construction of this volume. Our primary purpose is to bring together a collection of articles that provides a variety of perspectives on Latinos and education. The different sections address particular themes identified by educators across the country as representative of some of the most important topics related to the education of Latino students. A critical understanding of the relationship between these different but connected themes constitutes the substantive foundation that we believe must inform current and future debates on the nature of educational theories, practices, and public policies related to the public schooling of Latino students in the United States.

The Political Economy

The articles in this section address the need to frame educational discourse, politics, and practice within the evolving economic conditions of today's society. In particular, these articles present a profile of various Latino subpopulations and their relationship to the changing economy. They represent a concerted effort to define the political-economic context that shapes the definitions of class and "race" within traditional institutions, and unveil how these socially constructed definitions function to reproduce an ideology of inequality within public schools. In addressing the economic context of class relations and other characteristics of the Latino population, several of the early writings included here still prove quite relevant in light of the current "Bell Curve" debate on intelligence and I.Q. Overall, this section constitutes an incisive critique of the foundations of right-wing assaults on educational equality and racialized notions of intelligence.

Historical Views of Latinos and Schooling

This section provides a historical perspective of Latinos and schooling in the United States. In particular, historical assimilative dimensions of traditional educational ideology are questioned, and the process of "Americanization" is exposed as a fundamental social mechanism to conserve the political and economic subordination of Latino communities nationwide. The case is also made in several of the readings that educational policy has historically responded to changes in the economy of the marketplace, reinforcing the link between the educational experience of Latinos and the needs of the capitalist economy—a process that must be understood beyond simple reproductive theories so as to engage with the complexity of resistance movements to a capitalist hegemony. Further, by providing a historical overview of ongoing Latino struggles for educational equality in this country, this section debunks the myth that Latino communities have historically neglected the education of their children.

Constructing Latino(a) Identities

The articles in this section present a multidimensional approach to understanding the construction and articulation of Latino identities. This represents an effort to steer educators away from the trap of static, monolithic, and essentialized notions of culture and Latino identity. In particular, these selections speak to a multiplicity of social factors which shape and structure identity formation both in terms of individual identity and a sense of collective consciousness. Latino ethnic identification is understood as situational and political, while class and ethnic struggles are acknowledged as powerful political interpreters of identity formation and Latino ethnicity. The political implications of labels and standardized terminology is also challenged, exposing its tendency to both homogenize and depoliticize the class character of Latino communities. Related to this discussion, the need to engage with the differences derived from the particular conditions of incorporation of each group into the host political economy of this country is emphasized. Lastly, several of the authors interject a postmodern dimension by putting forth notions of multiple identities and borderland existence, and engaging identity formation as shaped by the experience of the diaspora.

The Politics of Language

The articles in this section articulate the impact of linguistic hegemony as a political process in the schooling of Latino students. The central role of language in the construction of a democratic educational process for Latino students is examined. The racialized aspects of educational policy with its implicit economic need to socialize immigrants is addressed. Also key to the articles presented here is the notion that cultural diversity has significant implications for the process of becoming literate in this country. More specifically, the argument is made that both identity formation and literacy development are culturally framed and differently defined within the context of schools and Latino communities. Rather than limiting the discussion of language and Latino students to that of instrumentalized notions of instruction or the discourse of "obstacle to be overcome," this section seeks to broaden the understanding of language and its impact on society and schooling. Most importantly, the authors argue against viewing language in isolation and reinforce the need for educators to consider the social dimensions of language and its contextual construction within conditions shaped by class and racialized identities.

Cultural Democracy and Schooling

The purpose of this section is to bring together articles by educators who are working to develop an educational practice that is fundamentally grounded in the critical dimensions posited in the previous sections. This represents an effort to translate a reconceptualization of education based upon a critical understanding of the political economy of schooling, historical struggles for educational justice, and the manner in which identity issues and language function to establish conditions of cultural democracy in the classroom. More specifically, the articles propose institutional redefinitions to reverse the pattern of Latino student underachievement, and articulate key features intergral to school success with language minority students. In these writings is also an acknowledgement of the potential alliance of schools and community in transforming the nature of public schooling for Latino students.

Latinos and Higher Education

Most studies of Latino education do not extend their scope to include a discussion of higher education, unless this is the singular focus. The inclusion of this section reinforces the connection of higher education to the articulation of a structural view of Latinos and education. In efforts to address the need to democratize education, some of the articles here focus on curricular concerns related to the incorporation of issues pertinent to Latino students, as well as the obstacles inherent in the fundamental enterprise of higher education. The articles in this section also engage the participation of Latinos in higher education and those significant issues that must be addressed. It is not surprising to discover that many patterns of subordination, exclusion, and marginalization found in K-12 educational institutions are repeated in the higher education of Latino students. Given this reality, the authors argue for the importance of deconstructing racism and other forms of discrimination inherent in the traditional enterprise of academia. Fundamentally speaking, the authors call for a new paradigm that links higher education in this country to a vision of social and economic justice.

PUBLIC POLICY CONSIDERATIONS

The different themes, issues, and concerns addressed in this volume point to a long standing need to provide an ideological critique of educational public policymaking and the role of the state in systematically perpetuating inequality. This requires a move to recast, in more critical and contextual ways, public policy debates related to public schooling and the academic achievement of Latino students. By so doing, Latino educational policy discussions related to issues such as bilingual education, immigration, affirmative action, the recruitment and retention of students, curricular politics, teacher education, and English-only initiatives are linked to questions of political power and material conditions.

Furthermore, Latino educational public policy debates cannot be single issue oriented; when we treat educational policy issues in isolation, we are unable to effectively mobilize an agenda that supports educational justice and democratic schooling. Instead, the relationship between a variety of public policy concerns must be addressed contextually with respect to the cultural, historical, and political dimensions directly associated with the structural position of Latinos in the U.S. political economy. What underpins the necessity for such an approach is the recognition that similar hegemonic forces of social control move across all public policy issues. Hence, this reinforces the need for coalition building across cultural/ethnic/ national ties in efforts to address the social inequities inherent in the educational experience of Latino students.

Central to a critical vision of public policy is the reconceptualization of the role of the state in educational reform. The articulation of such a vision means infusing public policy debates with a new set of frameworks from which to embark. More specifically, this points to a political process that can incorporate a politics of social change, political practices and community movements for social justice, structural educational reform goals, and an overall compounding commitment to equity in American society.

Public policy debates must be formulated in conjunction with social change politics. Public policy reforms devoid of a politics of social change and a theory of social movements constitute limited efforts toward democratizing education. Unfortunately, most reform debates are essentially grounded in liberal theories of the state. This inevitably leads to limited reform due to their failure to fundamentally challenge the economic and political practices of elites. Further, despite the contributions of identity politics to rethinking the nature of Latino schooling, public policy informed by decontextual, static, and monolithic views of Latino identity can potentially function as nothing more than an analytical and political trap which ultimately leads to a deadend system of reform.

Unfortunately, the majority of current public policy in the United States is not linked to social justice practice nor community movements for educational change. Instead, most public policy is overwhelmingly driven by the political and economic interests of the existing social order, which most often places it in direct contradiction (or opposition) to social movements striving to democratize public institutions, including public education. Although it can be said that in recent years social movements have indeed led to some minor changes in institutional practices, these reforms have nevertheless failed to change the fundamental nature of structural inequality in the United States. There is no question that the public policy process must be democratized. To accomplish this, public policymakers must acknowledge and incorporate the political concerns and issues of Latino community movements in the articulation and design of public policy. Along the same lines, community social movements must acknowledge the potential centrality of their role in shifting the educational public policy debate from the hands of elite policymakers to a critical process and practice of democratic participation.

The absence of an analysis of class relations with its structural inequalities of income and power represents a serious shortcoming of contemporary public educational policy. Given this absence of analysis, it is imperative that educational public policy be committed to the goals of structural economic reform. An understanding of the political economy of schooling and the historical conditions which inform current educational practice can enable educators to better reconceptualize the role of public policy in the reconstruction of an educational agenda linked to social justice and economic democracy.

Undoubtedly, public policy that would emerge from such a vision would come at an enormous cost and substantial risk to the status quo—but it would carry real potential for enormous gains to economic and democratic reforms in establishing the conditions for educational justice for Latinos in the United States.

REFERENCES

Hall, S. Ethnicity: Identity and Difference in Radical America. Vol 13, No. 4 (1990): 9–20.

Miles, R. *Racism After Race Relations* (London: Routledge, 1993).

Sanchez, G. I. "Pachucos in the Making" *Common Ground* Vol. 4 (1943): 13.

Foreword

Arturo Madrid

"The more things change, the more they stay the same."

As we approach the thirtieth anniversary of the 1968 Los Angeles "school blowouts"—a signal point in the efforts of the Latino community of the United States to improve the educational services being provided to Latino children—it seems that the more things change, the more they stay the same. Notwithstanding intense and sustained struggle on the part of individuals and organizations, the conditions of schooling for most Latinos are in multiple ways as bad as they were thirty years ago. Moreover, all indicators make it clear that the educational status and conditions of Latinos are in fact deteriorating.

And, as was the case in the 1940s when George I. Sanchez (the pioneering Latino educator cited by authors Darder, Gutiérrez, and Torres in their introduction to this volume) was at the height of his challenge to discriminatory policies and practices, the recourse of the apologists for failed policies and practices is to blame Latino culture, Latino families, and Latino students. What is worse is that there are some among us who not only believe that to be the case but who have become prominent exponents of this point of view.

I cannot help but believe that George I. Sanchez, were he alive today, would be dismayed by the low levels of achievement and attainment that Latino students manifest, by the continuing inequities in the delivery of educational services, and by the de facto segregation that persists in American public education. His life's work was one of challenging the ignorance and prejudice of American educators and policymakers. He won significant policy battles in this regard, and in so doing changed both practices and discourse. Thus he would be shocked that despite so much change, much of what he warred against remains unchanged.

I also think, however, that were he still living, he would be bolstered by the fact that so many Latino scholars and educators have taken up his struggle to challenge discourse, practice, and policy that blame Latino children and their families for the failure of institutions. Thus the value of this volume, which by providing history, context, analysis, and options constitutes an antidote to this insidious intellectual virus. What is contained in it is an extraordinary fund of cultural capital, one that can be used over and over again, which continues to grow, and which can never be exhausted. George I. Sanchez would have been pleased to know that his passion and intellect continue to inform this struggle.

I
THE POLITICAL ECONOMY

1

A Theory of Racial Inequality

Mario Barrera

*Do not obtain your slaves from Britain because they
are so stupid and so utterly incapable of being taught
that they are not fit to form a part of the household
of Athens.*

—Cicero to Atticus,
1st century B.C.

Since things are not always what they seem, social phenomena that appear uncomplicated often require considerable theoretical explanation. Racial inequality is no exception. The most widely held ideas about the causes of racial inequality in the United States turn out, on close examination, to be quite unsatisfactory. In order to develop a satisfactory theory, however, it is first necessary to describe and analyze existing theories. These fall into three broad categories, which will be considered in turn: deficiency theories, bias theories, and structural discrimination theories.

DEFICIENCY THEORIES OF RACIAL INEQUALITY

The contention of these theories is that racial minorities occupy an inferior economic, social, and political status because of some deficiency within the minority groups themselves. There are at least three different varieties of deficiency theory, each stressing a particular type of deficiency.

Biological Deficiency Theory

This category encompasses the classic racist theories associated with such writers as de Gobineau, Houston Chamberlain, and Madison Grant, in which racial inequality was attributed to genetic and thus hereditary inferiority on the part of certain races. These theories, while still commanding considerable overt and covert popular support, have been held in scientific disrepute for several decades (Benedict, 1959). Still, some observers have seen a resurgence in recent years, as in the work of the educational psychologist Arthur Jensen. In his lengthy article "How Much Can We Boost IQ and

Scholastic Achievement?" (1969) and in a more recent book (Jensen, 1973), he deals with the question of differences in the measurement of IQ between Blacks and Whites. Jensen speculates that a substantial part of these differences may be due to biological inheritance. Apparently he feels that if a biologically produced intellectual deficiency could be demonstrated, this would contribute to explaining social inequalities between Blacks and Whites (Jensen, 1969, p. 79). In spite of the notoriety that Jensen's work has achieved, it is difficult to take it very seriously as an explanation of generalized minority inequality in the United States. One reason for this is that there are serious methodological problems with his writings, such as the heavy reliance on IQ test scores, universally acknowledged now as very imperfect measures of anything that could be considered general intelligence. (See Block and Dworkin, 1974, for an extended critique.) Another is that even if racial differences in intelligence could be conclusively demonstrated, their effect on social inequalities would still be highly problematic. In fairness to Jensen, it should be noted that he is very cautious and tentative in his speculations, far more than some of his supporters and mass media popularizers.

The problems encountered in Jensen's work are characteristic of the entire field of intelligence measurement, as brought out in a recent survey of the literature by Loehlin, Lindzey, and Spuhler (1975). In addition to the many pitfalls of definition and measurement, attempts to separate out the effects of heredity and environment on test scores have achieved little or nothing that could be considered conclusive, and many studies hopelessly confound such variables as race and class. Some quotes from this survey give an indication of the status of this type of research.

> The studies we have reviewed . . . provide no unequivocal answer to the question of whether the differences in ability-test performance among U.S. racial-ethnic subpopulations do or do not have a substantial component reflecting genetic differences among the subpopulations. [Ibid., p. 133]

> All in all, while the existence of some amount of cultural bias in some IQ tests for some intergroup comparisons can hardly be doubted, we are a long way from being able to assess with confidence the precise importance of such biases for particular group comparisons. [Ibid., p. 71]

> The majority of the variation in either patterns or levels of ability lies within U.S. racial-ethnic and socioeconomic groups, not between them. Race and social class are not very powerful predictors of an individual's performance on tests of intellectual abilities. [Ibid., p. 235]

In general, then, there is no persuasive evidence for the thesis that racial groups differ in intelligence, much less that such purported differences can tell us something about social inequality, and such theories receive little support from the scientific community. Other types of deficiency theories (described below) generally receive considerably wider support.

Theories Based on Deficiency in Social Structure

This type of theory argues that minority racial groups in the United States are held back by problems in the social structure of those groups. One highly influential work which applies this approach to American Blacks is Daniel Moynihan's report, titled *The Negro Family: The Case for National Action* (Moynihan, 1965; reprinted in Lee Rainwater and William Yancey, 1967, which includes a number of critiques; see also Ryan, 1971), written at the height of the public debate on race that took place in the 1960s. Briefly, Moynihan argues that historical factors have created a weak family structure among Blacks and that this weakness creates emotional and attitudinal problems, such as emotional instability and male role confusion. It also brings about a social "tangle of pathology" (drugs, crime, etc.). This situation results in low educational achievement and a general condition of inequality—poverty, unemployment, low-status jobs. A vicious circle is set up, with economic problems reinforcing the weak family structure. Moynihan acknowledges that prejudice and discrimination exist, but he assigns these factors a distinctly secondary and diminishing role. A diagram of this model can be seen in figure 8. (Moynihan does not present his ideas in a formal model, so I have tried to construct one for him by reading his work carefully. The possibility of misinterpretation, of course, exists. It is unfortunate that virtually none of the analysts of racial inequality attempt a rigorous formulation of their ideas.)

A study which falls within this same category of theories and relates specifically to Chicanos is D'Antonio and Form's *Influentials in Two Border Cities* (1965). D'Antonio and Form describe a condition of political powerlessness of the Chicano residents of El Paso, Texas. This powerlessness they attribute to such structural deficiencies among Chicanos as a lack of political organizations, a "low level of social integration," and factionalism.

Cultural Deficiency Theories

These theories find the source of minority inequality in one or more cultural traits of the group in question. The emphasis here is on attitudes and values rather than social structure, although the two types of factors are often linked together in the models. One of the most widely discussed proponents of this view in recent years is Edward Banfield. Banfield draws some inspiration from the "culture of poverty" school to argue, in *The Unheavenly City*, that inequality in the United States is largely attributable to a "lower class culture," consisting of such traits as a present rather than future orientation, a lack of work discipline, and so on. Individuals who share this "culture" do poorly in school, and their low educational attainment creates conditions of poverty and powerlessness, which interact with each other and create a vicious circle to perpetuate educational inequalities. While it is not only racial minorities that participate in the "lower class culture," they are overrepresented there because of historical reasons, including past racial discrimination. Prejudice and discrimination are acknowledged to exist today, but they are not stressed in Banfield's work. An attempt to construct a formal model of Banfield's concepts is presented in figure 9. A critique of Banfield's ideas on grounds of internal inconsistency and lack of evidence can be found in Franklin and Resnik's *The Political Economy of Racism* (1973, pp. 159–72).

Banfield's work, while widely discussed, is not necessarily typical of the cultural deficiency tradition, which has been applied to Chicanos with a vengeance. A more representative and quite influential work is that of Herschel Manuel, who is con-

Figure 1.1. The Moynihan Model

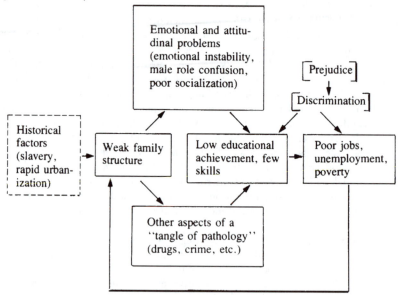

Note: Factors in brackets indicate items given less importance. Factors enclosed in broken lines are characterized as having importance in the past but not the present.

cerned to explain educational nonachievement among Chicano children. It is difficult to present his ideas systematically, since his presentation is rambling and connections are not always explicitly made. In addition, he seems to want to cover his bases by at least mentioning several types of factors. Still, his argument goes something like this:

Cultural deficiencies, including a language handicap and such values and attitudes as fatalism, present rather than future orientation, dependency, and a lack of success orientation lead directly to problems in the schools. At the same time, the low economic level of most Chicano families creates an environment of "cultural disadvantage," a vague term intended to encompass such disparate items as experiential deprivation and a lack of material resources (adequate clothing, books, etc.). Poverty combines with a high incidence of "culture conflict" between Anglos and Chicanos in their communities to produce personality problems such as feelings of inferiority and insecurity. These factors also contribute to poor school performance, which in turn aggravates feelings of inadequacy in another example of a vicious circle (Manuel, 1965, p. 189). This model is set forth in figure 1.3.

Manuel, with many other analysts of Chicano education and psychology, draws inspiration from a long line of writings which picture Chicano culture as highly traditional and nonadapted to the requirements of upward mobility in an industrial society. Perhaps the most influential of these studies has been done by Florence Kluckhohn (Kluckhohn and Strodtbeck, 1961). Her characterization of Spanish-American culture, based on one small village in New Mexico, is often made the basis of sweeping and stereotypical generalizations about Chicano culture, and Manuel's work

Figure 1.2. The Banfield Model

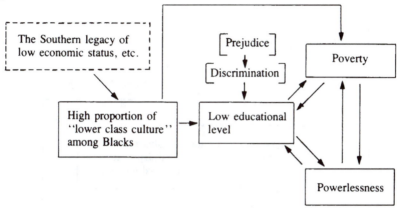

is no exception. For a review of this tradition, see Vaca (1970). The use of the Kluck-holn and Strodtbeck study for this type of interpretation is particularly ironic, since it dealt with possibly the most isolated group of Chicanos in the Southwest, and even here rapid attitudinal change was shown to be taking place in response to changing economic and political conditions (Kluckholn and Strodtbeck, pp. 201, 209, 256–57).

Evaluation of Deficiency Theories

Biological theories of racial deficiency are largely discredited, and recent attempts at revival, such as those based on IQ testing, are embroiled in complex disputes over methods. Even if racial IQ differences could be demonstrated, nothing would have been established with respect to social inequality.

The more popular deficiency theories are based on social structure and culture. The Moynihan model, based on the structure of the Black family, has been subjected to numerous criticisms, such as his use of aggregate statistics rather than ethno-graphic research as a way of characterizing family structure. Critics have pointed out that aggregate statistical measures are crude and provide no means for ascertaining the social meaning of family patterns. Aggregate statistics on "broken" families are taken as an indicator of family pathology, for example, even though a family with a single parent may be as healthy as one with two parents. However, there are more serious methodological problems involved with this approach. Moynihan applies his model only to Black families, and not to Chicano, Native American, or other racial minorities which are also economically disadvantaged but whose family structure is presumed to be "strong" rather than "weak."

As an approach to explaining racial inequality, then, deficiency models based on social structure are inelegant methodologically—different deficiencies have to be found for each racial group. The same is true of the D'Antonio and Form study men-tioned above (for a detailed critique of this study, see Barrera, Muñoz, and Ornelas, 1972). All of these studies are subject to another methodological problem: even if the social structure deficiencies could be established, it could plausibly be argued that

Figure 1.3. The Manuel Model

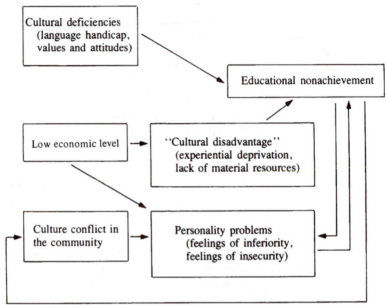

they had succeeded in doing nothing more than identifying certain intervening variables, and that the fundamental causes of racial inequality lie elsewhere. Social disorganization or political fragmentation might as easily be seen as results rather than as causes of the very conditions of racial inequality that these theories seek to explain.

The cultural deficiency models are even more deficient in methodological rigor. The logical process at work seems to go something like this: (1) Here is a group which is disadvantaged socially; (2) the cause of its disadvantage must lie within the group itself; (3) the culture is a likely source of this cause; (4) let us see what we can find in its cultural attributes that would explain its disadvantaged status. A search is then made of the cultural inventory of the group until some presumed traits are discovered that hold the group back from achievement and social mobility. These, then, constitute the explanation.

Given such an approach, it is not difficult to see why the researcher is always able to come up with appropriate explanations. The cultural apparatus of any people is so complex that presumably negative traits can always be discovered, and especially if the researcher relies on cultural stereotypes or on small, atypical samples of the racial minority group. Even if such negative cultural traits could be firmly established, the possibility that there may be offsetting positive cultural traits never seems to enter the minds of cultural deficiency theorists. From a strictly logical standpoint, in order to establish any validity for this approach one would have to take a more or less complete cultural inventory of *both* the disadvantaged group and the majority non-disadvantaged racial group that serves as the basis for comparison. Negative and positive traits would have to be established for both groups. Only if this were done and a clear balance in favor of the more advantaged group emerged could an argument be made with any degree of plausibility. Needless to say, none of the cultural deficiency studies has begun to follow such a procedure, or even an approximation of it. The most sophisticated of these studies, by Kluckholn and Strodtbeck, is marred by the atypicality of the communities studied.

Another argument that can be made against these theories is that the cultural characteristics they point to can in many cases be considered as deficiencies only within a given institutional framework. Let us grant that a monolingual Spanish-speaking child will have difficulty in a monolingual English-speaking school. This is a "deficiency" only because the society has failed to provide a bilingual educational system for that child to attend. Given such an educational system, the "deficiency" here is not in the minority racial group but in the educational system itself.

Furthermore, the cultural deficiency school suffers from the same general methodological problem as the social structural school, that of theoretical inelegance. Different cultural traits have to be found in each cultural group to serve as deficiencies, whether the group be Black, Chicano, Puerto Rican, Filipino, or any of hundreds of Native American groups. It would seem to be rather astonishing that all of these groups should have cultures deficient with respect to Anglo culture. Rather than accept this inelegant approach, it seems far more plausible to consider these theories as legitimizing myths, reflections in the social sciences of the ideologies that have historically served to justify the relationship of inequality between European and Third World peoples. Even though the specifically biological assumptions of the earlier theories have been rejected by most contemporary social scientists, the basic inclination to "blame the victim" (to use William Ryan's phrase) lives on.

If the arguments so far are not sufficiently convincing, one more can be added. Deficiency explanations of racial inequality are superfluous in that all of them assume that equal opportunity exists and has existed for the minority races in American society, and that they have failed to seize the opportunity because of their own deficiencies. Yet such opportunity has not been present for Chicanos. The lack of equal opportunity is so clear and so persistent in the historical record that it seems absurd to have to resort to deficiency arguments to explain racial inequality. Where improved opportunities have existed, even temporarily as during wartime, Chicanos have not been slow to respond. The works cited earlier by Charles Loomis serve to point this out for the very area of the Southwest where one of the most famous cultural deficiency studies was conducted. Margaret Brookshire stated the case quite clearly in her study of Neuces County, Texas:

> There was nothing to support a belief that separate treatment where it occurs is due to unique group response on the part of Mexican-Americans. Indeed, with the exception of the fact that the Mexican-American group continues to be Spanish-speaking, there emerges from this study no distinct group characteristic which might affect the pattern of industrial employment of Mexican-Americans. . . .

> These data . . . support the belief that Mexican Americans generally avail themselves of existing opportunities in the same way that other workers do. [Brookshire, 1954, pp. 270, 271]

BIAS THEORIES OF RACIAL INEQUALITY

The second major category of theories of inequality consists of bias theories. These are theories which focus on prejudice and discrimination as the sources of minority inequality, and thus tend to put the responsibility on the Anglo majority rather than on the minorities. The Kerner Commission's condemnation of "White racism" is the most widely publicized effort in this direction in recent years, although the report also has thrown in a hodgepodge of cultural and social structural deficiency explanations (*Report of the National Advisory Commission on Civil Disorders*, 1968).

The classic work in this area, however, is the still-influential study by Gunnar Myrdal, *An American Dilemma*, published in 1944 (Myrdal, 1962). Myrdal's model is fairly simple in terms of the variables he sees as currently playing an important role, but more complex in terms of historical variables (this model is presented in figure 1.4). Basically, Myrdal explains the unequal status of Blacks as a function of racial discrimination, which in turn is a product of White prejudice. But he places great emphasis on the concept of the vicious circle (the principle of "cumulative causation"), arguing that the disadvantaged condition of Blacks reinforces the prejudice of Whites by confirming their low opinion of Blacks. In the historical section of his massive study, Myrdal argues that the social structure of the American South brought into being a set of interests based on slavery, and that these interests popularized racial ideologies as a means of justifying the subordinate position of Blacks. These racial ideologies are one source of contemporary White prejudice. The other source is also derived from the Southern social structure, and was mediated by a complicated set of notions having to do with sexual relations (Myrdal, 1944, p. 1142). Other factors that enter into Myrdal's theory are the interests that employers in general had in the past in creating divisions among their workers, and the continuing interest that White workers have in limiting job competition with Blacks. These factors are given secondary importance.

Myrdal's study is quite voluminous, and different parts of the work seem to stress different factors in explaining racial inequality. Because of this it is difficult to reduce Myrdal's ideas to a model. In certain passages he appears to stress the interests of Whites, and in others he dwells upon social deficiencies that have been created in Blacks by the long-standing pattern of discrimination to which they have been subjected. He also makes use of the concept of "caste" in describing Black-White relations, although he is not consistent in the way he deals with this concept. Thus by referring to different parts of his work, one might be able to construct several different models of causation. In portraying his core model in the way I have, I have relied on those concepts which seem to be most essential to Myrdal's analysis. Central to that analysis is the idea that discrimination in most of the contemporary United States is primarily due to racial prejudice on the part of Whites, with other factors playing a secondary role.

Kenneth Clark, who was a staff member of the Myrdal study, provides a more recent version of bias theory (Clark, 1972). He also focuses on racial prejudice and discrimination, but he includes a deficiency component consisting of a set of ghetto "pathologies" that are reminiscent of Moynihan. The "pathologies" and the inequalities, both products of discrimination, are then pictured as mutually reinforc-

Figure 1.4. The Myrdal Model

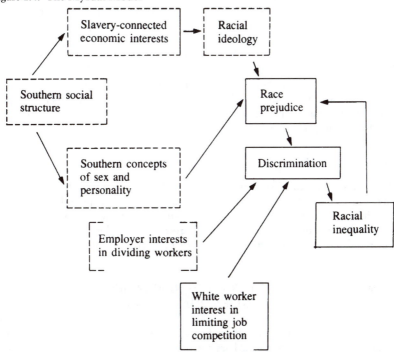

Note: Factors enclosed in solid lines are the major variables. Those enclosed in broken lines operated in the past but not in the present. Factors in solid brackets are minor variables currently operative, while those in broken brackets operated in the past but not in the present.

Figure 1.5. The Clark Model

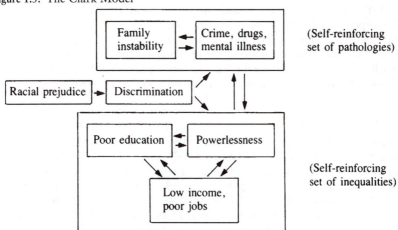

ing. This could be seen as a type of hybrid model, since it includes both bias and deficiency variables, but the bias variables are seen as more fundamental in that the deficiencies are products of discrimination, present as well as past. This model is summarized in figure 1.5.

Another tradition of writing that falls under the general heading of bias theory is that of economists who perceive discrimination in the marketplace as a function of employer and employee "tastes" for discrimination (Becker, 1971; Arrow, 1971). These models will not be discussed further here, since they are relatively technical and operate under assumptions so far removed from the "real world" that their usefulness for my purposes is quite limited.

Evaluation of Bias Theories

While specific bias theories have their problems, the general approach is not so much wrong as incomplete. Generally, these theories begin with racial prejudice and do not inquire further into its origins. Most lack a historical perspective. Myrdal is an exception to this, and there is a great deal of interesting material in his study. His model will be reexamined after the discussion of structural discrimination theories.

STRUCTURAL DISCRIMINATION THEORIES OF RACIAL INEQUALITY

The third major type of theories of racial inequality in the United States can be called structural discrimination theories. These theories locate the source of minority disadvantage in the social structure of the society as a whole. "Structure" here refers to the regular patterns of human interaction in the society. Structures can be either formal, in which case they would be considered institutions, such as schools, government, or corporations, or informal, as in the class structure. "Structure" is thus a broader concept than "institution." The type of theories described in this section consider racial discrimination to be built into the structures of the society. They differ from bias theories in that they do not locate the ultimate source of racial discrimination in the attitudes of prejudiced individuals. Discrimination, for these theorists, can exist quite apart from overt individual prejudice, since it is inherent in the social patterns of the society. The concept of "institutional racism," popularized in recent years, is consistent with the emphasis of these theories. Two major varieties of structural discrimination theory are described below, the caste-class school and internal colonial theory.

The Caste-Class School

Application of the term "caste" to describe American race relations has a considerable history, but it is most closely identified with a series of studies done by W. Lloyd Warner and his associates in the 1930s and 1940s. Perhaps the best representative of this tradition is *Deep South*, published in 1941 (Davis, Gardner, and Gardner, 1941), but Dollard's *Caste and Class in a Southern Town* is also closely linked with this school (Dollard, 1957). The term has also been picked up by other writers, including Myrdal, whose main theoretical thrust was quite different.

Figure 1.6. Warner's Caste-Class Diagram

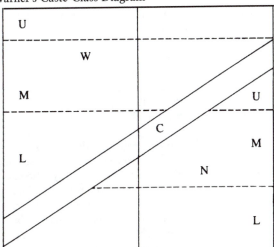

Source: Warner 1936, p. 235. *C* refers to the caste line, *W* and *N* to the White and Negro populations, *U*, *M*, and *L* to upper, middle, and lower classes.

For Warner and his associates, the social structure of the American South could be described as a combination of caste and class. They saw caste and class as both being ways of stratifying people in such a way that privileges, duties, obligations, and opportunities were unequally distributed. Caste, however, was characterized by endogamy (prohibition of marriage outside the caste) and by rigid barriers between the divisions. Class was seen as non-endogamous and as allowing social mobility (Warner, 1936, p. 234; Davis, Gardner, and Gardner, 1941, introduction [written by Warner]).

The writers in this tradition clearly differentiated themselves from those in the bias tradition. Thus, according to Warner:

> One of the terms used in popular currency to express the feelings whites have for Negroes and Negroes for whites is "prejudice". The so-called "more liberal" whites say that certain of their members are "biased" or "prejudiced" against the other group, and some of the "more liberal" Negroes use these same terms when they refer to the attitudes of members of their own group. Both terms refer to the same social phenomena but, while expressive of certain of the attitudes felt by whites and Negroes about the other group, do not adequately represent the whole social situation to which they refer. [Davis, Gardner, and Gardner, 1941, p. 5]

Dollard sees prejudice as an intervening variable:

> We turn now to the mysterious but much discussed theme of race prejudice. In describing caste distinctions we have already indicated the factual mate-

rial related to prejudice against Negroes. The major consideration seems to be that it is a defensive attitude intended to preserve white prerogatives in the caste situation and aggressively to resist any pressure from the Negro side to change his inferior position. [Dollard, 1957, p. 441].

Thus the emphasis on these works was clearly on the social structure and the discriminatory patterns institutionalized in that structure. Warner diagrammed the relationship between caste and class in the South in a much-cited diagram (figure 1.6).

In recognizing that there was considerably more to racial inequality than prejudice, the caste-class school was on the right track. However, its writings are subject to some severe limitations. Part of the problem is definitional. In using the term "caste" to describe race relations, it chose a concept which is closely identified with one particular society, India. Yet in that society caste is a very different phenomenon from anything found in the United States. Each caste, for example, is tied to a particular occupation, and caste lines are not racial or even ethnic in nature. In addition, caste divisions are justified on religious grounds, and have historically been imbued with a high degree of legitimacy. Racial divisions, on the other hand, are typically justified in terms of biology or cultural differences, and are imposed on the subordinate race rather than accepted as legitimate (Simpson and Yinger, 1958, pp. 356–57; Oliver Cox presents an extended discussion of the caste system in India and a critique of the caste-class school in his *Caste, Class and Race*, 1970). Since these distinctions are not of minor importance but have important implications for the dynamics of the system, the use of the concept of caste for the United States is unwarranted.

Secondly, it is difficult if not impossible to construct a model based on these writings, since the lines of causality are unclear. The studies seem to be largely descriptive in nature, and lack of a historical perspective makes it hard to figure out why this system came into existence or why it remains so persistent today. One possibility is that the system of racial division is simply a matter of historical continuity with the social structure that existed under slavery. Another is that the system is actively maintained by Whites because it serves their interest to do so. Dollard, in fact, devotes considerable attention to the ways in which the system benefits the White "middle class," but he does not really say that that is why the system continues in force. The discussion in *Deep South* has a very strong emphasis on the control of sexual relations, but again, it is never actually stated that this is the underpinning of the system.

Finally, this tradition's treatment of class relations is unsatisfactory. Part of the problem is conceptual lack of clarity. Initially, they describe class as a means of unequally distributing the rewards and responsibilities in the society. Elsewhere they state that "'social class' is to be thought of as the largest group of people whose members have intimate access to one another. A class is composed of families and social cliques" (Davis, Gardner, and Gardner, 1941, p. 59n.). Yet in Warner's diagram and in the text generally, class is a matter of how people think of their social status in relation to other people in the society. The other difficulty is that the authors of *Deep South* clearly found their conceptual framework inadequate for describing the workings of Southern society. In chapter 10 they suddenly introduce the concept of the "economic group," which is thought of as a large informal group of persons (1) who exhibit similar attitudes and dogmas with regard to property and money and the distribution of these possessions among the members of society, and (2) whose incomes, economic possessions, and economic functions usually fall within certain limited and characteristic ranges. [Ibid., p. 237]

It seems that the reason for the introduction of this concept is that their class concept does not serve to group people together adequately on the basis of their *interests*, and thus on the basis of their behavior based on the pursuit of their interests. At one point in their study they note the common interests of White and Black employers:

The evidence at hand leaves no doubt that a strong solidarity exists between the leading white and colored business and professional men with regard to the manipulation of the caste sanctions. . . .

A certain amount of co-operation exists . . . between parallel economic groups, across caste lines. This intercaste solidarity is especially strong between the two upper economic groups. [Ibid., pp. 474–75]

This kind of commonality of interests and behavior would never be suspected from an examination of Warner's caste-class diagram, which clearly separates the White upper class and Black upper class. It appears that the authors are groping for, but refuse to embrace, something similar to the Marxist concept of class.

Colonial Theories

During the 1960s a number of factors converged to popularize the idea that the United States could be described as a form of "internal colonialism." These factors were largely political events and trends rather than developments within social theory itself. As Robert Staples has noted, "After assimilation concepts were put to a reality test by the civil rights movement during the sixties and found wanting, a more nationalist orientation emerged" (Staples, 1976, p. 37). One direction that this took was toward the concept of internal colonialism. As the civil rights movement evolved into the Black Power movement, the political imperative switched to organizing along racial and ethnic lines, rather than continuing to work primarily in multiracial groups. From this perspective, it was natural to use the national liberation movements of the Third World as models, and to see racial minorities in the United States as occupying a similarly colonized position.

For this type of organizing to succeed, moreover, it was necessary to develop a different attitude among the minority population. To the extent that deficiency explanations of inequality had been internalized by the minority groups in the United States, a "colonial mentality" existed that had to be broken before effective resistance could become possible. Here, then, was another parallel with colonial situations abroad, and the writings of Fanon and Memmi, with their discussions of the psychology of colonialism, were eagerly seized upon by American political activists (Fanon, 1963; Memmi, 1965).

The decade of the 1960s was also the period of heavy American involvement in the Vietnam War, and as that war dragged on, more and more political activists began to describe the United States as an imperialistic country. If the United States was an imperial power abroad, it was much easier to think of it as an imperial power domestically as well, with its internal Third World colonies. Given this political atmosphere, it is not surprising that many of the early popularizers of this term were writers who were political activists. Stokely Carmichael, Tom Hayden, and Huey Newton wrote articles and books during this period which dealt with American racial minorities, using a colonial framework (Carmichael and Hamilton, 1967; Hayden, 1968; Foner, 1970).

At about the same time, the concept began to be employed by some social scientists. While it is true that the idea of the internal colony had appeared in a few analytic works in the early 1960s (Harold Cruse used it in a 1962 article [reprinted in Cruse, 1968]), it was during the late 1960s that it began to be taken more seriously. Robert Allen made use of the colonial framework in his analysis of Black politics, published in 1969 (Allen, 1969). But it was in the essays of Robert Blauner, the first of which also appeared in 1969, that the concept received its first systematic exposition (these essays are reprinted in Blauner, 1972). Blauner used the concept for several purposes. It became a means of criticizing a number of academic writings which treated America's racial minorities within the same framework as European ethnic immigrants. In this tradition, Blacks were the latest wave of immigrants to arrive in the urban centers of the United States, only this time from the American South rather than from Europe. The assumption was that Blacks, Chicanos, and other racial minorities would fit into the pattern of assimilation and upward mobility that had been established by the White ethnic groups. Blauner argued that the experiences of Third World groups and of White ethnic immigrants were, and would continue to be, significantly different. The Third World groups, Blauner insisted, had been subjected to a system of discrimination which was structurally rooted to a much greater extent than that experienced by European immigrants. Blauner also made use of the colonial framework to explain certain aspects of Black politics in the 1960s, including community control, cultural nationalism, and urban uprisings (ibid., pp. 95–104).

Since the late 1960s the term has been used by a number of writers for different purposes, but my interest in the concept is limited here to its usefulness as a theory of racial inequality. Before dealing with this question, however, it is necessary to consider whether the term "colonial" is appropriately applied to race relations in the United States, and what its connotations might be.

The Nature of Colonialism

The term "colonialism" is applied to a very heterogeneous collection of situations, so that it is difficult to see what, if anything, they have in common. Given this fact, it is not surprising that there is no agreement on the definition of the term. Even if we restrict our attention to European expansion since the fifteenth century, we find very different types of relationships described as colonial. The earliest colonies were founded in the New World and on the coasts of Africa and southern Asia. The British and the French established settlement colonies in North America, pushing out or killing the native inhabitants. The Spanish had "mixed" colonies in the New

World, with a substantial minority of European settlers and relatively large indigenous populations. The Portuguese in Brazil had a large colony, with Portuguese settlers, native Americans, and many slaves imported from Africa. In Africa and Asia, the Portuguese had commercial colonies, restricted to the coastal areas, designed for trade, and with few European settlers and little territory under their direct control (Fieldhouse, 1966, chap. 2).

There was considerable variation in the manner in which the colonies were settled. Originally, most of the colonies were established by private interests, and only later did the European states come to be the main sponsors of colonization. There was variation over time as well. According to Fieldhouse, the first period of European expansion lasted from the fifteenth century to the early nineteenth century, and was centered in America (ibid., p. 100). The second period, beginning later in the nineteenth century and continuing strongly into the twentieth, was largely based on Asia and Africa. The nature of most of the colonies differed in the two major periods.

> The reasons for which a particular dependency is acquired normally determine its character and functions as a colony. The old empire had consisted almost entirely of territories which were occupied by European settlers because they wanted to live there and make use of local resources. They were governed as far as possible as if they were part of the sovereign's European dominions, on the assumption that colonists were full subjects with the same rights and interests as those in the metropolis. [Ibid., p. 75]

> In the last resort, it was neither "mercantilism" nor political subordination that produced the special character of the American colonies, but the fact that they were colonies of European settlement. There were similar colonies in the modern period in Canada, Australia, South Africa, and, with some differences, in Central Africa and Algeria. But apart from these, the modern empires were alien, consisting of colonies which lacked any organic connexion with their metropolitan states. Europe reproduced herself in America as she seldom did again. American colonies were not commercial artifacts but extensions of Europe herself, differing little from the inner ring of European colonies which had been occupied first and had acted as stepping stones to the west—Ireland, the Azores, Canaries, Madeiras and Iceland. All were organic European societies. [Ibid., p. 99]

It is the colonies of the later period that generally come to mind today when we speak of colonialism, since they are the most recent. Even here, there was much variation in the nature of the colonies and in the manner in which they were governed. The British, for example, favored a policy of "indirect rule," in which the traditional political authorities in an area played a central role in governing the colonies. The French also made use of traditional political authorities, but they were much more subordinate to the colonial officers from the European metropolis. Under the French, the colonial subjects were encouraged to assimilate to French culture; the French government's eventual goal was to make French citizens out of the indigenous peoples (Crowder, 1964; see also a number of articles in Cartey and Kilson, 1970).

There is another type of situation which is commonly referred to as colonial, that of neocolonialism. Kwame Nkrumah, in his detailed study of neocolonialism in Africa, defines it this way:

> The essence of neo-colonialism is that the State which is subject to it is, in theory, independent and has all the outward trappings of international sovereignty. In reality its economic system and thus its political policy is directed from outside. [Nkrumah, 1966, p. ix]

Used in this sense, the concept has achieved considerable currency.

Raymond Betts, in his survey of European expansion, notes that

> neo-colonialism is, or has been considered to be, synonymous with what some historians have called the "informal" empire first established by Great Britain in Latin America in the early nineteenth century and then enlarged upon by the United States in the heyday of dollar diplomacy. [Betts, 1968, p. 151]

Stanley and Barbara Stein, in their classic account of the continuity of the colonial heritage in Latin America, illustrate the point clearly:

> The failure of Latin American movements for independence to create the bases of sustained economic growth through balanced agricultural, ranching, and industrial diversification only indicates the continued strength of a colonial heritage of externally-oriented economies linked closely to essential sources of demand and supply outside the new national economies. [Stein and Stein, 1970, p. 135]

> . . . The major consequence of the anti-colonial movements in Latin America between 1810 and 1824, the crushing of the ties of transatlantic empire, led—one is almost tempted to say, inevitably—to neo-colonialism. . . . The absence of an autonomous, self-sustaining economy strengthened the heritage or heritages of colonialism in Latin America after 1824. This is the rationale that Latin Americans and others have evoked in calling post-colonial Latin American economy and society neo-colonial. [Ibid., p. 136–37]

> It is by now obvious that those who profited most in the eighteenth century from west European colonialism in the New World were the English merchants and manufacturers, bankers and shippers. Their greatest harvest came in the nineteenth century when they enjoyed a dominant position in the trade of the area. . . . The English had been the major factor in the destruction of Iberian imperialism; on its ruins they erected the informal imperialism of free trade and investment. [Ibid., p. 154–55]

The use of the term "neocolonialism" is thus well established in the literature. Its use is not intended to denote that the situation referred to is the same as that of "classic" colonialism, but that it is a variety of colonialism which maintains the essential character of colonialism while modifying the form of the relationship. The same relationship is sometimes characterized as the "imperialism of free trade," as in the widely cited article by Gallagher and Robinson (1953). In this article, they argue that it is artificial to treat British imperialism simply in terms of formal control of territory. Adoption of that restricted viewpoint has led some historians to focus on the post-1880 period during which British formal possessions increased rapidly, and to depict the earlier part of the century as anti-imperialist. In fact, Gallagher and Robinson contend, Britain was imperialistic during the whole century in terms of bringing new territories into its economic sphere of control. Where possible, such control was established through the "imperialism of free trade," in which free access to the other territory's economy led to control via British industrial competitive advantage. Only where the local authorities resisted such informal influences and where the political and military situation made it possible did the British exercise direct control.

In reviewing these uses of the term "colonial" it appears that settlement colonies differ fundamentally from all of the others in that only one "people" is involved in those situations, at least in any long-term way. All other situations involve at least two ethnic and/or racial groups, with one being dominant and the other or others subordinate. Because of this and because modern usage generally refers only to the nonsettlement situations, I will use the term to refer only to the second category, in which more than one group is involved. "Presently, in speaking about colonies or colonialism, allusion is made above all to the domination of some people by others" (González Casanova, 1965, p. 29). To do otherwise would be to lump together situations so dissimilar that they would have very little or nothing in common. The term would thus lose all analytic precision.

The only other significant factor that all the nonsettlement colonies have in common is that the relationship was entered into by the metropolitan power because it was felt that it was in its interest to do so. These metropolitan interests could be of various types, but generally they boiled down to economic interests first and political-military interests second. Thus Furnivall notes:

> Ordinarily, the motive of colonial expansion has been economic advantage. Considerations of prestige and military strategy have played their part, but in the main economic considerations have prevailed. [Furnivall, 1948, pp. 3–4]

Fieldhouse lists land and trade as the most important motives for the original European expansion (Fieldhouse, 1966, p. 4). Balandier also assigns primary importance to economic interests (Balandier, 1966, p. 37). Gail Omvedt, in her theoretical treatment of European colonialism, distinguishes two major phases. The first she terms *commercial imperialism* of the mercantile era, in which the motives were precious metals, spices, and other goods for trade, as well as control of labor power for plantations. The second phase she calls *industrial imperialism*: "As European industries developed, their need was no longer for trade control of luxury goods but for a wide-scale procurement of raw materials and markets for the finished products of the new factories, and increasingly outlets for investment" (Omvedt, 1973, p. 2). I believe colonialism in general, then, can be defined as follows:

Colonialism is a structured relationship of domination and subordination, where the dominant and subordinate groups are defined along ethnic and/or racial lines, and where the relationship is established and maintained to serve the interests of all or part of the dominant group.

This definition is similar to that of Gail Omvedt, who sees colonialism as "the economic, political and cultural domination of one cultural-ethnic group by another" (Omvedt, 1973, p. 1).

Certain other characteristics which are sometimes claimed as aspects of colonialism are in fact not universally so. These are:

1. *Formal political domination.* Hans Kohn has this in mind when he states that "a colonial relationship is created when one nation establishes and maintains political domination over a geographically external political unit" (Kohn, 1958, p. 4). As noted above, to base the concept on the formal nature of the relationship is to miss the fact that very similar dynamics are at work in the "imperialism of free trade," or neo-colonialism, and this leads to a misreading of history.

2. *Geographical separation (noncontiguity) of metropolis and colony.* It is difficult to see why the colonial relationship should be dependent on the existence of space between metropolis and colony. At any rate, this is not true of instances cited as neocolonial, for example, the United States and Mexico.

The Nature of Internal Colonialism

On the basis of the preceding discussion, it is possible to advance a definition of internal colonialism:

Internal colonialism is a form of colonialism in which the dominant and subordinate populations are intermingled, so that there is no geographically distinct "metropolis" separate from the "colony."

This definition is similar to that employed by González Casanova: "Internal colonialism corresponds to a structure of social relations based on domination and exploitation among culturally heterogeneous, distinct groups" (González Casanova, 1965, p. 33). Of course, the degree of intermingling can vary considerably from case to case. In Latin American there are many instances of regional concentration of Indian communities, as is also the case in the United States. Chicanos also form majorities in certain regions, such as northern New Mexico. Where the relationship of ethnic/racial subordination coincides with regional concentration, it is easier to see the internal colonial relationship in operation.

The reason for advancing this concept is that there seems to be a clear need for a term to describe a relationship where an ethnic and/or racial group is subjected to systematic structural discrimination within a single society. The widespread use of the term "caste" to describe race relations in the United States and other countries attests to this need. However (as discussed earlier), this term is inappropriate for various reasons. The term "plural society," originally used by Furnivall and later taken up by others, is also sometimes applied in these situations, but it has a disadvantage in that it stresses separateness rather than discrimination in the group relations (Furnivall, 1948; Kuper and Smith, 1971). In the absence of a superior term, the concept of internal colonialism is best suited to designate this kind of relationship. (Other advantages of the term and the model based on it are discussed later in this chapter.)

Two types of objections are generally raised to the use of this concept. The first is that a distinct metropolis and colony are essential to the concept of colonialism. In fact, this has often not been the case in "classic" colonial situations, at least in a formal, legalistic sense. Spain provides one example:

> Perhaps the most interesting feature of Spanish colonial government was that its institutions and concepts so closely resembled those of Old Spain. Spain did not innovate: she adapted. She was fortunate, in that the Spanish Crown already consisted of a multiplicity of kingdoms and provinces linked to Castile only in the person of the King. It was therefore possible and natural to regard the colonies not as dependencies of Old Spain, but as sister kingdoms. [Fieldhouse, 1966, p. 16]

Portugal made no constitutional distinction between her colonies and the metropolis (ibid., p. 31). France considered Algeria to be an integral part of France. Other examples could be cited.

It is true that a distinction between metropolis and colony existed in an informal, sociological sense, even where it did not exist in a legalistic sense. But even here there are ambiguities. While Spain transferred colonial revenues to the Castilian treasury and regulated the colonial economies to serve Castilian interests, these practices were also pursued with respect to the other Spanish kingdoms in the metropolis (ibid., pp. 24–25). One can also cite the presence of metropolitan settlers in the colonies, such as French Algerians or Spanish *peninsulares* in Latin America. These settlers participated in the exploitation of the indigenous people, yet they too were often in a position to feel exploited by the authorities in the old country. Their presence had the effect of blurring the distinction between metropolis and colony. Even if the argument is granted, it serves not to invalidate the concept but simply to justify the designation of these situations as *internal* colonies (the modifier signifies that we are talking about a variety of colonialism and that there is a distinction to be made between it and classic colonialism). Internal colonialism is a variety of colonialism in that it shares with classic colonialism essential characteristics (ethnic/racial subordination, the serving of certain interests) even though there is no clear geographical distinction between metropolis and colony. In the same way, designating a certain relationship as neocolonial does not mean that it is exactly the same as classic colonialism, but only that the same general type of relationship exists. It is as much an analytic error to ignore similarities as it is to pretend there are no differences.

The second type of objection is that in a colonial relationship, the subordinate indigenous population is in a majority. As with the noncontiguity argument discussed earlier with respect to the definition of colonialism, it is difficult to see why this should be considered an essential characteristic. The important thing would seem to be the nature of the relationship, and a dominant-subordinate relationship between racial/ethnic groups can exist regardless of who is in the majority and who is in the minority.

One other point should be clarified with respect to the concept of internal colonialism. In some material written by Latin American authors, the term "internal colonialism" is used to refer to a situation where one region of a country is in a dominant and exploitative relationship with another region of the same country, regardless of ethnicity. One could argue, for example, that the American South has historically been dominated by the Northeast. Such situations are common in Latin America. The term "internal colonialism," as defined here, is not intended to cover such cases, unless ethnic/racial subordination is involved. As Pablo González Casanova has noted, ascriptive criteria (in this case, race and/or ethnicity) make the dynamics of a situation quite different from one in which such criteria are absent (González Casanova, 1965, p. 33). The fact that there is sometimes a strong overlap between regional and ethnic/racial subordination tends to confuse this distinction, but it is important to keep it in mind for analytic purposes. (Stavenhagen, in his article on Mexico, describes a situation involving such an overlap [1965].)

The Internal Colonial Model

The concept of internal colonialism has been used for various theoretical purposes, but has not been systematically applied as a theory of racial inequality. To develop a model along these lines, I have drawn upon Blauner but supplemented his discussion with some additional elements. A diagram of the model is presented in figure 1.7.

The central dynamic role in this model is provided by the concept of interests, which Blauner stresses by way of contrast with bias theories. The interests here are those which originally gave rise to European colonialism, of which internal colonialism is an extension, as well as the contemporary interests of privileged groups (Blauner, 1972, pp. 21–22, 52–53, 58–60). The system of structural discrimination that forms the essence of the colonial relationship exists first of all in the economic realm, but extends into political institutions, the educational system, and all forms of social structures. Blauner gives heavy emphasis to the workings of the labor market in the United States (ibid., pp. 57ff.). The persistence of racial/ethnic inequality in this society is the result of this historic relationship, which continues to operate today.

Figure 1.7. The Internal Colonial Model

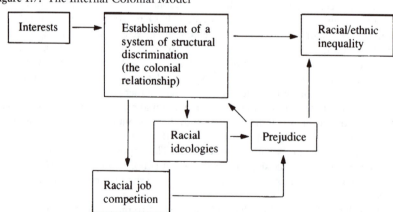

The other important factor in perpetuating this inequality is racial prejudice, both by leading to individual acts of discrimination and by providing support for the structural aspects of discrimination. Prejudice, however, is treated quite differently from bias theories. Although Blauner does not develop the theme, he expresses the belief that racial prejudice is largely a product of racial ideologies that were developed to justify structural discrimination (p. 21). The other mechanism leading to prejudice is not really discussed by Blauner, but I have incorporated it into the model based on other materials. A number of historical works have pointed to job competition between Anglos and racial minorities as increasing racial tension and thus prejudice, and certainly there are numerous instances where this situation prevailed between Anglos and Chicanos. Edna Bonacich has developed this theme in an article on the "split labor market" (Bonacich, 1972). What many writers who have touched on this theme seem to miss, however, is that the antagonism arises because of the institutionalized hiring practices of employers. That is, when employers attempt to undercut the wages of Anglo workers by creating a colonized labor pool, the Anglo workers resist. Anglo workers tend to see this as *unfair* competition, but rather than take their antagonism out on the employers and their manipulations, they often turn their wrath on the more immediate and usually more vulnerable targets, the colonized workers. This dynamic emerges quite clearly from the materials on Chicano economic history.

The theme of racial ideologies and their origins needs to be developed further here, as it is an aspect of racial dynamics that is frequently misunderstood, and it is an important part of the colonial model. First, it should be emphasized that racial ideologies are a modern phenomenon, and do not stretch back into ancient times, as is often claimed. It is true that ethnocentrism, or the belief that one's own ethnic group is superior to others, has been around for a long time. However, this belief has traditionally been justified on cultural grounds, often religious in nature, and not on the idea that the other groups are inherently and biologically inferior. It was not until biological thinking began to displace religious thinking in the eighteenth century that racial distinctions in the modern sense could be made, and it was not until the nineteenth century that full-blown racial ideologies were developed (Benedict, 1959, p. 108; Myrdal, 1962, p. 97; Cox, 1970, p. 329).

When racial ideologies began to emerge in Europe, they were tied in all instances to the advancement of certain interests. These were usually the justification of privilege based on social inequality, but the protection of national interests also played a role. Much of early race theorizing was not aimed at Third World peoples at all, but at Europeans, although contacts with the Third World influenced the general climate of opinion. In Ruth Benedict's words,

> European expansion overseas . . . set the stage for racism dogmas and gave violent early expression to racial antipathies without propounding racism as a philosophy. Racism did not get its currency in modern thought until it was applied to conflicts within Europe—first to class conflicts and then to national. [Benedict, 1959, p. 111]

Racial ideology became one way in which European aristocrats tried to fortify their class position in the face of radical challenges. These ideologies took the position that the aristocrats were descendants of the Germanic peoples (referred to as Teutons and later as Aryans) who had overrun the old Roman Empire. The common people, on the other hand, were depicted as descendants of other, inferior European stocks, including the Romans (ibid., pp. 112ff.). The aristocrats were thus the descendants of a race which had proved its superiority in the distant past, and which had subsequently been responsible for the advance of civilization. By virtue of this inheritance they were ideally suited to rule and to maintain their class privileges. Later on, racist ideologies were transformed in Europe in order to serve the interests of nationalism, as France and Germany struggled for supremacy on the continent (ibid., pp. 129ff.). This tradition of writing was also drawn upon in the twentieth-century United States by American nativists attempting to stem the flow of immigration from southern and eastern Europe. These ideas served to whip up some of the emotion that went into the restrictive immigration legislation discussed in earlier chapters of this book.

In England, the origins of racist ideologies can be traced back to the sixteenth century and the creation of the Church of England (Horsman, 1973). The English sought to persuade themselves, after their break with the Catholic church, that they were returning to a purer form of religion that had prevailed among the early Anglo-Saxon inhabitants of the island. As the English delved more deeply into their past, they began to idealize their past political as well as religious institutions, and to link them historically to the institutions that had existed among the Teutonic people to whom they traced their ancestry. In the early stages this school of thought was not explicitly racial, but seemed to assume that the superiority of the old institutions had simply been transmitted over the generations. In the nineteenth century, however, racial overtones became more characteristic. As Reginald Horsman has noted:

> The flowering of the new science of man . . . gave a firm physical, "scientific" base to the long entrenched ideas of Anglo-Saxon excellence. The work of the early nineteenth-century ethnologists was decisive in giving a definite racial cast to Anglo-Saxonism . . . an essential shift in emphasis occurred when the arguments about the inferiority of other "races" assumed an importance as great or even greater than arguments about the excellence of Anglo-Saxons. [Horsman, 1973, p. 395]

At times the point of reference was broadened to include not just the "Teutons" or "Aryans" identified by researchers on language and history, but the "Caucasian race" identified by researchers on the physical characteristics of humans. Sometimes the concepts were merged, and Anglo-Saxons were held to be the superior branch of the superior race. There also developed a certain exchange of ideas with the United States:

> The development of a belief in the different innate capacities of the various races . . . and of the superiority of the Caucasian race, was considerably helped in the 1830s and 1840s by an influx of ideas from the United States. A country in which a great many were intent on justifying the enslavement of the blacks and the extermination of the American Indians proved a fertile ground for the growth of racism. [Ibid., p. 397]

These ideas were used for various purposes in England. They served in the early period to support English nationalism, but it also appears that they were used to justify English domination of the Celtic peoples of the area, the Welsh, Scots, and Irish, who were sometimes identified with non-Germanic people who had been expelled from continental Europe by the Teutons (ibid., p. 391; Hechter, 1975, p. 342). The concepts of Anglo-Saxon superiority and the broader racial concepts of the period were also important justifications for overseas imperialism, as England and the other European powers divided up the world among themselves.

In the New World, racial ideologies also served to justify exploitative relationships. To the extent that these ideas developed in Latin America, they did so as a means of answering critics of the enslavement and brutalization of the Indians (Cox, 1970, pp. 334–35). It was in the United States that racial theories really flowered, however. As Thomas Gossett puts it,

> Although in the seventeenth century race theories had not as yet developed any strong scientific or theological rationale, the contact of the English with Indians, and soon afterwards with Negroes, in the New World led to the formation of institutions and relationships which were later justified by appeals of race theories. [Gossett, 1965, p. 17]

The delayed nature of the ideological response can be seen in the following manner:

> The importance of Negro slavery in generating race theories in this country can hardly be overestimated, but it must be remembered that there was a minimum of theory at the time the institution was established. The theory of any political or social institution is likely to develop only when it comes under attack. [Ibid., p. 29]

> Institutional arrangements that prove painful or inconvenient to a substantial part of the population are generally called into question, and they are sooner or later justified in a set of popular beliefs. Whenever conspicuous differences of rank lead to embarrassing questions, ideologies emerge to explain the gradation. [Shibutani and Kwan, 1965, p. 241]

This is the essential mechanism that is embodied in the model diagrammed in figure 1.7. Racial ideologies came about in large part because they were useful in justifying classic colonialism and the neocolonial and internal colonial relationships that grew out of it. Of course the process is complex, and many factors enter into it and help determine how strong or how weak the ideology will become. But the essential point is that ideologies develop and are perpetuated because of the interests they serve. Shibutani and Kwan describe the process this way:

> Most ideologies are not deliberately produced artifacts . . . They develop through a selective process, being shaped over a long period through the contributions of thousands of individuals. Students of the sociology of knowledge have pointed out that ideas that tend to support or facilitate the

pursuit of predominant interests tend to be accepted, while other, equally valid ideas pass unnoticed or are rejected. Ideas are not always accepted or rejected on the basis of evidence; in many cases the choice is in terms of their utility. In any situation of inter-ethnic contact thousands of remarks are made; most of them are uttered a few times and are forgotten. But ideas consistent with prevailing interests or justifying deeds that have already been committed seem strangely more appealing and "true." These views tend to be taken more seriously and are repeated... Race ideologies are like other political ideologies; they emerge through a selective process and justify social institutions. [Ibid., pp. 248–49]

The American attitude toward Blacks is a clear case of this process, and is so depicted by Gunnar Myrdal. He notes that "when the Negro was first enslaved, his subjugation was not justified in terms of his biological inferiority" (Myrdal, 1944, p. 84). The origins of a systematic racial ideology in the United States can be traced to the need of pro-slavery interests to respond to criticisms based on the "universal rights of man," criticisms which mounted as revolutionary agitation developed in the late eighteenth century (Jordan, 1968, chap. 7). This racial ideology did not gain strength until three decades before the Civil War, as criticism of slavery became even more vehement.

In the precarious ideological situation—where the South wanted to defend a political and civic institution of inequality which showed increasingly great prospects for new land exploitation and commercial profit, but where they also wanted to retain the democratic creed of the nation—the race doctrine of biological inequality between whites and Negroes offered the most convenient solution. [Myrdal, 1944, pp. 87–88]

After the war, the ideology survived and was intensified as a means of justifying the continued exploitation of the Black population. Myrdal also argues that the ideology became more prevalent in the North as a way of justifying the national compromise arrived at in the 1870s that allowed the South to continue its oppression of the Blacks (ibid., p. 88).

That, of course, is not the whole story. Racial ideologies become embodied in the thought of future generations who have no conception of the exact context in which they originated, and are thus transformed into broad-based racial prejudice even among people whose interests are not served by it. Oliver Cox described this process several decades ago:

In our description of the uses of race prejudice in this essay we are likely to give the impression that race prejudice was always "manufactured" in full awareness by individuals or groups of entrepreneurs. This, however, is not quite the case. Race prejudice, from its inception, became part of the social heritage, and as such both exploiters and exploited for the most part are born heirs to it. It is possible that most of those who propagate and defend race prejudice are not conscious of its fundamental motivation. To paraphrase Adam Smith: They who teach and finance race prejudice are by no means such fools as the majority of those who believe and practice it. [Cox, 1970, p. 333n.]

Thus race prejudice may be said to take on "a life of its own" with the passage of time, as future generations are socialized to be prejudiced. Still, it is necessary to qualify the qualifier in order not to lose sight of the major point:

> It should be borne in mind that race prejudice is not simply dislike for the physical appearance or the attitudes of one person by another; it rests basically upon a calculated and concerted determination of a white ruling class to keep some people or peoples of color and their resources exploitable. If we think of race prejudice as merely an expression of dislike by whites for some people of color, our conception of the attitude will be voided of its substance. [Ibid., p. 349n.]

In accordance with the internal colonial model, prejudice is manifested in individual acts of discrimination, and serves as a support when aspects of structural discrimination are called into question. The recent controversies about busing and the Bakke decision can serve as cases in point.

Varieties of Internal Colonialism

While there is no clear-cut division of internal colonial theories into different varieties, there is one logical basis for such differentiation that at times emerges in the literature. This has to do with the way in which the interests at stake are depicted. In the United States, for example, it is possible to see all Anglos as benefiting from the system of structural discrimination, as Carmichael and Hamilton charge in their book *Black Power* (1967). On the other hand, one can also argue that only one part of the noncolonized population benefits from internal colonialism. Where the second point of view is accepted, the argument is usually that it is the dominant class among the noncolonized population whose interests are served by this system. Robert Allen analyzes internal colonialism from this standpoint (Allen, 1969). The first type of theory might be called "right" colonial theory and the second "left" colonial theory because of their political implications, but this is only for reference purposes. "Nonclass differentiated" and "class differentiated" colonial theories are more accurate but more cumbersome labels. Some writers are difficult to classify as one or the other. Blauner, for example, is somewhat ambiguous on this question (notwithstanding Prager's "right" interpretation of his writing; see Prager, 1972–73). The implications of the "left" perspective will be dealt with below.

It should also be kept in mind that the practices associated with internal colonialism, as with all types of colonialism, can vary considerably in degree. The degree of inequality associated with colonialism is one of these variable dimensions. A situation such as exists in the Union of South Africa represents a very harsh example of internal colonialism (Wilson, 1973; Adam, 1971; van den Berghe, 1965, 1967). A situation such as the "Celtic fringe" in Britain represents a much milder case (Hechter, 1975). Colonized populations in the United States and Latin America represent a somewhat intermediate position. In the case of Chicanos, it is certainly the case that the existing system is less harsh than it has been at some points in the past. Rather than a sharp distinction between colonized and noncolonized racial/ethnic groups, there is what might be termed a continuum of colonialism.

Evaluation of the Internal Colonial Model

The model of internal colonialism as a theory of racial inequality has several advantages, but also an important limitation. One of the important advantages is its broad scope. It is not limited to the contemporary period, but incorporates a historical dimension that allows us to see more clearly the dynamics of racial inequality as they have developed over time. In this manner we can grasp causal connections that may be obscured in certain historical periods but stand out more strongly in others. One of the more important consequences of this is that the nature of racial prejudice is illuminated, in effect transcending bias theories and incorporating them within a broader framework. Most bias theories do not go into the question of the historical origins of prejudice. Myrdal does, but he is an exception, and in this respect his work converges somewhat with colonial theory. Still, there is an important distinction in that colonial theory stresses the operation of interests in the present and not just in the past, and puts more emphasis on the *structural* aspects of discrimination in the contemporary period.

With respect to deficiency theories, I consider colonial theory to be far more accurate historically and thus more persuasive theoretically as an explanation of racial inequality. In addition, it is more "elegant" in a methodological sense, in that it accounts for a much wider range of phenomena with a relatively small number of variables. Deficiency theories have to come up with different deficiencies for each situation, whereas colonial theories can account for a great deal of racial inequality within the same basic framework. Colonial theories do not completely rule out certain types of "deficiency" explanations of inequality. For example, there is little doubt that an oppressed racial group does not have the same opportunity to acquire education and skills that a dominant group does, and in this sense it could be said to be "deficient." But colonial theories put such factors in a completely different light by tracing their origins to structural discrimination and not to some inherent characteristic of the minority group itself. In addition, such factors are seen as distinctly secondary when compared to the overwhelming direct effects of structural discrimination.

Colonial theories also have the advantage of a broader comparative scope, as well as a broader historical scope, than most other theories. In putting the experience of U.S. racial minorities in a colonial framework, this school of analysis establishes important structural (and historical) similarities with minorities in other countries and with the Third World in general. The perception of these international parallels gives us a better perspective on the local situation and enables us better to evaluate the importance of the various factors involved in perpetuating inequality. It is no coincidence that most comparative analyses of race emphasize structural variables to explain racial stratification and inequality, even if they do not explicitly adopt a colonial perspective (Shibutani and Kwan, 1965; Schermerhorn, 1970; van den Berghe, 1967; Frazier, 1957; Rex, 1970; Wilson, 1973).

The major limitation of colonial theory as it has developed to this point is indicated in a passage of self-criticism from Blauner:

> This suggests a major defect of my study. It lacks a conception of American society as a total structure beyond the central significance that I attribute to racism. Thus my perspective tends to suffer from the fragmented character of the approaches to American race relations that I have just criticized. Conceived to a great extent within the confines of the middle ranges of theory, there is not systematic exposition of Capitalist structure and dynamics; racial oppression and racial conflict are not satisfactorily linked to the dominant economic relations nor to the overall distribution of political power in America. The failure of Marxism to appreciate the significance of racial groups and racial conflict is in part responsible for this vacuum, since no other existing framework is able to relate race to a comprehensive theory of capitalist development. [Blauner, 1972, p. 13]

In order to see in more detail what the Marxist tradition does have to offer for the analysis of racial inequality, it is necessary to review some of these writings. After this I will present a partial synthesis of colonial theory and class analysis.

MARXIST ANALYSIS OF CLASS STRUCTURE IN CONTEMPORARY CAPITALIST SOCIETY

Marxist discussions of the nature of classes in advanced capitalist societies can become very complex, too complex for the purposes of this book. Nicos Poulantzas, for example, goes into considerable theoretical detail on this topic. A more concise and comprehensible alternative is provided in an article by Erik Olin Wright, titled "Class Boundaries in Advanced Capitalist Societies" (Wright, 1976). Wright presents the class structure of such societies as the United States as shown in figure 1.8.

According to Wright's analysis, capitalists, workers, and petty bourgeoisie comprise the three major classes within advanced capitalist society. Capitalists and workers are the classes particular to capitalist society. Petty bourgeoisie, while not without significance, are in a sense holdovers from an earlier, precapitalist mode of production. They are small, independent professionals and businessmen. The three other positions in Wright's diagram are occupied by what he terms "contradictory locations within class relations." Persons who occupy these positions are not clear-cut members of the traditional classes, but occupy locations which are intermediate between two classes, in that they partake of some of the characteristics of both classes. Small capitalists occupy an ambiguous position between large capitalists and petty bourgeoisie. Where the petty bourgeoisie rely entirely on their own labor and that of their families to make a profit, and the large capitalist derives virtually all of his profit from the labor of a large number of employees, the small capitalist relies importantly on his own labor as well as that of a small number of employees.

The semi-autonomous employees include such persons as employed professionals and high-level technical workers such as researchers. They have in common with the workers the fact that they sell their labor and do not own the means of produc-

Figure 1.8. Classes in Advanced Capitalist Society

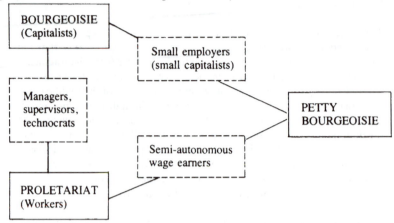

Source: Wright (1976), pp. 27, 37.

tion. At the same time, they have greater autonomy in their work than the prole-tariat, and in this way they resemble the petty bourgeoisie.

The "contradictory location" between capitalists and workers is quite heteroge-neous. At the bottom of this category are the foremen and line supervisors. They are close to the position of workers in that they sell their labor and are close to the pro-duction process, but they function in such a way as to control the labor of others. Above the foremen and line supervisors are the technocrats (technicians) and the middle managers. Above them, and closest to the bourgeoisie in the class structure, are the top managers, who do not own the means of production but who exercise considerable control over the process of production.

A somewhat different analysis is provided by Barbara and John Ehrenreich in their 1977 article, "The Professional-Managerial Class" (Ehrenreich and Ehrenreich, 1977). They do not deal with the existence of contradictory class locations. While re-taining the conventional class divisions of capitalist, worker, and petty bourgeoisie, they argue that a new class has come into existence since the late-nineteenth century, and they propose that this class be called the "professional-managerial class" (PMC). This "new" middle class includes many of the same people that Wright puts in the contradictory location between workers and capitalists, but also most of the semi-autonomous employees. It includes teachers, engineers, scientists, government work-ers, all except the top managers, technicians, culture producers such as writers, and other professionals. They argue that this new class of educated workers has come into existence as a result of developments in the structure of capitalist society, and that it has a common relationship to the system of production and shares a common life style. They state: "We define the Professional-Managerial Class as consisting of salaried mental workers who do not own the means of production and whose major function in the social division of labor may be described broadly as the reproduc-tion of capitalist culture and capitalist class relations" (ibid., p. 13). By this they mean that the class functions in such a manner as to control, shape, and regulate the economic, social, political, and cultural relations that are necessary to perpetuate capitalist society and keep it running as smoothly as possible. Thus the Ehrenreichs propose a four-class framework which is relatively easy to work with, and which I will adopt for constructing the model I describe later in this chapter. For other purposes it may be that Wright's scheme has certain advantages.

Marxist Theories of Racial Inequality

Given the extensive Marxist tradition of social theory, it is disappointing to find how little serious analysis there is of racism and racial inequality. The reason for this undoubtedly traces back to classic Marxist political economy, in which class divisions in capitalist society are heavily emphasized and there is an assumption that they will supersede other kinds of divisions, including those based on race and ethnicity. When Marxist scholar-activists like Lenin were forced to deal with the question of "national minorities," they generally did so in a pragmatic political manner that contributed little to our understanding of the linkage between class and race or ethnicity.

The American Marxist writings that do exist on the subject are marked by considerable heterogeneity, and there is certainly nothing that can be seen as *the* Marxist theory of minority inequality or race relations generally. In addition, these analyses do not seem to flow in any logical or direct manner from basic Marxist theoretical categories, so that it is not unusual for analysts who consider themselves Marxists to come to diametrically opposed conclusions on questions of race. Many leading Marxist scholars barely touch on the subject in their works.

One school of American Marxist thought holds that American capitalism no longer has any compelling need to perpetuate racial divisions. Eugene Genovese is one example. He argues that there is a strong historical connection between the subordination of Blacks and the development of American capitalism, especially during the nineteenth century. But he feels that since the First World War, the relationship between capitalism and racism has become less clear.

> With the decline of sharecropping and tenancy in the South, with urbanization, and with substantial structural changes in the economy, American capitalism no longer needs or generates in the old way racial discrimination as an organized form of class rule. Since the blacks today are prepared to exact a high price for the conditions to which they are subjected, there is good reason to believe that the capitalists as a class and capitalism as a system would purge themselves of racism if they could. Racism, however, is so deeply rooted in American society that it cannot be torn up without fundamental changes in capitalism itself. [Genovese, 1968, pp. 59–60]

Baran and Sweezy likewise believe that the members of the American ruling class see it as in their interest to eliminate racial inequality, but their view is somewhat more complex than that of Genovese. They pose the problem very clearly:

> The conclusion seems inescapable that since moving to the cities, Negroes have been prevented from improving their socio-economic position: they have not been able to follow earlier immigrant groups up the occupational

ladder and out of the ghetto. . . . What social forces and institutional
mechanisms have forced Negroes to play the part of permanent immigrants, entering the urban economy at the bottom and remaining there
decade after decade? [Baran and Sweezy, 1966, p. 263]

Their answer is that three sets of factors are responsible. The first is a number of
private interests, including employers who benefit from divisions among their workers, ghetto landlords, marginal businesses that need cheap labor to survive, and
White workers, who are protected from Black competition for jobs. The second is
race prejudice, which is of historical origin but is reinforced in the contemporary
world by the need of Whites to have a subordinate group on whom they can vent the
frustrations and hostilities generated by class society. The third is the economy's declining need for unskilled and semiskilled labor. The position of the large capitalists
who constitute the ruling class, however, is that any benefits they may derive from
racial subordination are outweighed by the growing revolutionary threat posed by
Blacks in the context of a worldwide anti-imperialist trend. Thus while this class has
endeavored to further racial equality, it has been able to achieve relatively little because of its limited control of the system (ibid., pp. 263–71).

Michael Reich, on the other hand, argues in a widely quoted article that the contemporary capitalist class benefits substantially from the existence of subordinate
racial groups. Reich argues that racial divisions in the society are carried over into
the work force, and that divisions among workers sap their bargaining strength and
thus keep both Black and White wages down, thus widening the gap between workers' and capitalists' income. He attempts to test this proposition by developing a
measure of racism (the ratio of Black median family income to White median family
income) and correlating it at the level of the metropolitan area with measures of inequality among Whites (e.g., the percent share of all White income received by the
top 1 percent of White families). The correlations which result from this procedure
support his argument, even with controls for various other factors (Reich, 1972).

(Of course the limitations of this kind of correlational test should be kept in
mind. In essence all that Reich has shown is that there is a relationship between
Black-White inequality and White-White inequality. Correlations do not show any
direction of causation or even establish causation, since the demonstrated relationship could be a product of another, uncontrolled, factor.)

In general, then, it could be said that there is in fact no *tradition* of Marxist writing in America on race. The scattered Marxist theoretical works on this subject often
seem unaware of other Marxist analyses, so that there is no accumulation of knowledge. In addition, the works frequently contradict each other. Perhaps one reason for
this state of affairs is that many of the writers who have dealt with race have done so
as a sort of sideline, with their main theoretical interests focused elsewhere. The only
really substantial Marxist theoretical work to date on race in the United States is
Oliver Cox's *Caste, Class and Race*, originally published in 1948 (Cox, 1970).

The perspective that Cox presents is in many ways compatible with the present
work, although his data are based on the Black experience and mine on the Chicano.
Cox's framework is essentially that of "left" colonial theory, and while he does not
apply that terminology to the contemporary experience of Blacks, he places American race relations firmly in a colonial context. He develops the theme that modern

race relations had their origins in the colonial systems developed by Europeans after the fifteenth century. He sees racism as an ideology developed to justify those systems, used by the capitalist "to keep his labor and other resources freely exploitable" (ibid., p. 333). He observes that "in the United States the race problem developed out of the need of the planter class, the ruling class, to keep the freed Negro exploitable. To do this, the ruling class had to do what every ruling class must do; that is, develop mass support for its policy. Race prejudice was and is the convenient vehicle" (ibid., p. 475). While the needs of the Southern agricultural capitalist were the most pressing, in Cox's view racial subordination serves the interests of capitalists as a whole in two ways: by providing a sector of workers who are more tractable and manipulable, and by keeping workers as a whole divided among themselves (ibid., p. 487).

While Cox's analysis provides valuable elements for a theory of racial inequality (and I have drawn upon his work to develop my own ideas), it has significant limitations. For a Marxist, his conception of class is certainly anomalous. He discusses the concept of social class in terms of groups of people who share a certain status, and he sees social class systems as peculiar to capitalism (ibid., p. 142). In addition, he distinguishes what he calls "political class" from social class, and characterizes the former concept in terms of organizations (ibid., p. 154). The term "social class," as he uses it, is closer to the non-Marxist conception of class as strata, and neither concept corresponds to what is generally accepted as the Marxist idea of class as defined most fundamentally by the relationship to the means and process of production. Perhaps in part because of this confusion over the notion of class, Cox nowhere works out a systematic relationship between class and racial divisions in American society. While valuable and suggestive, his work is by no means the last word on the subject. Nevertheless, it should have been taken far more seriously by later generations of Marxist writers.

Labor Market Segmentation and Class Fractions

The most valuable contribution of Marxism to the discussion of race is not so much in the explicit analyses of racism as in providing an understanding of the social and economic context in which racism operates. In addition to general class analysis, two lines of thought that have been developed in the last few years appear to be particularly helpful, that of *labor market segmentation* and that of *class fractions*.

The concept of labor market segmentation can be traced to the idea of the dual labor market. Certain researchers, most notably Doeringer and Piore (1971), posited the existence of two labor markets as a means of explaining persistent unemployment among racial minorities. In the primary labor market were found those jobs which offered security and stability, good pay and working conditions, the possibility for advancement, and a stable set of procedures in the administration of work rules. Jobs in the secondary labor market offered the opposite conditions, and were what might be termed dead-end jobs. The concentration of minority workers in the secondary labor market was seen as one reason for their high unemployment rates and other conditions of disadvantage. Most of the growing literature on this topic has dealt with elaborating this basic dichotomy and exploring its ramifications (for a review of this literature, see Torres, 1978).

More recently, other writers have taken up the concept and have attempted to generalize it by speaking of labor market segmentation, and arguing that several dimensions of segmentation exist, including race and sex. They have also introduced a historical perspective and placed the discussion in a Marxist framework (Edwards, Reich, and Gordon, 1975). They present the theme that in the latter part of the nineteenth century there were important trends in the United States that signaled a danger to the hegemony of the capitalist system. The labor force was becoming more homogeneous with the development of the factory system, and the growing proletarianization of the work force was producing labor conflicts that were increasingly taking on a class character and raising broader and more militant demands. Partly as a defense against these trends, capitalists devised an elaborate system of job stratification that involved the proliferation of job categories and the ranking of those jobs in a status hierarchy. The intent was to divide the work force and thus prevent class solidarity from coming about. Associated with this process was the creation of a segmented labor market, in which various segments or submarkets emerged, each with its own set of rules, working conditions, wages, and opportunities. The primary and secondary labor markets were thus created. Minorities and other relatively vulnerable groups (women, youth) were, and are, concentrated in the secondary sector and in less desirable jobs generally. David Gordon develops this theme in greater detail in another work. He feels that employers deliberately filled the worst jobs with people who were the least likely to establish solidarity with better-off workers.

> Gradually, as the composition of the American labor force changed, it became relatively easy for employers to reserve the most "secondary" jobs for teens, women and minority group workers with quite confident expectations that they would not identify with the more advantaged workers and develop a common consciousness about the disadvantages of their jobs. [Gordon, 1972, p. 74]

While these writers mention racial and sexual divisions, most of the work in this vein has continued to stress segmentation based on the structure of occupations. The dimensions of racial and sexual labor market division have largely remained theoretically unintegrated with the rest of their work, although they include descriptive studies of sexual labor segmentation in their collection of essays.

The discussion of class "fractions" in recent years is generally associated with the writings of Nicos Poulantzas, although others have also taken up the concept. Poulantzas argues that there are several types of divisions within classes, of which class fractions are the most important. As he states, "The Marxist theory of social classes further distinguishes *fractions* and *strata* of a class . . . on the basis of differentiations in the economic sphere, and of the role ... of political and ideological relations" (Poulantzas, 1975, p. 23). He describes various fractions, such as the commercial and industrial fractions of the bourgeoisie, and clerks, office workers, and technicians as three fractions within the "new petty bourgeoisie." Fractions, according to Poulantzas, are significant in that they can "take on an important role as social forces, a role relatively distinct from that of other fractions of their class" (Poulantzas, 1973a, p. 28).

Francesca Freedman also discussed class fractions in a recent article, using the concept in a somewhat broader fashion than Poulantzas. She speaks of class fractions as "structural divisions... within a class," and states that such divisions can be based on many factors, including race and sex (Freedman, 1975, p. 43). However, most of her discussion of fractions within the American working class deals with fractions on the basis of the structure of occupations, much as Poulantzas does. Thus she is primarily concerned with distinctions such as skilled versus unskilled workers, industrial versus service workers, and so on. In a footnote at the end of her lengthy article she concludes: "For reasons of lack of space I have omitted the role of minorities and women in the capitalist economy, and therefore in the development of the working class. Many of the fractions we have dealt with here intersect with racial and sexual divisions (ibid., p. 81n.). The tendency to deal with racial and sexual divisions in footnotes and passing references is not unknown in Marxist writings on political economy.

Class Segmentation

The labor market segmentation approach is limited in that racial and sexual divisions in the labor force are relatively neglected. It is also limited in that it concerns itself only with the labor market and not with classes as a whole. Thus this tradition is largely confined to an examination of the working class. The class fraction approach is broader in its conceptualization, in that it is concerned with classes as a whole. However, it shares with the segmentation literature the relative neglect of race and sex, and in addition it does not appear to be as solidly grounded empirically. Both approaches see the divisions with which they are concerned as typically based on the structure of occupations in the economy, although Poulantzas adds political and ideological criteria as secondary factors. The divisions based on the structure of occupations are racially and sexually neutral, and, presumably, they would exist in a capitalist economy even if the work force were entirely homogeneous racially and sexually.

What I am proposing is that there are two major types of intraclass divisions in a capitalist political economy, with each major division having subdivisions. These divisions I propose calling *class segments*. Type 1 consists of divisions based on the structure of occupations. This category can be called *structural class segments*, and can be further broken down as described above by Poulantzas and Freedman. Type-2 divisions are based on the characteristics of the workers themselves, and can be called *ascriptive class segments*, since they are based on ascribed characteristics of persons. Within this broad category are two major subdivisions, one based on race and/or ethnicity, and one based on sex. Racial and ethnic characteristics are, of course, more ambiguous and subject to social definition than sexual characteristics. The formal definition of this Type-2 division is as follows:

An ascriptive class segment is a portion of a class which is set off from the rest of the class by some readily identifiable and relatively stable characteristic of the persons assigned to that segment, such as race, ethnicity, or sex, where the relationship of the members to the means and process of production is affected by that demarcation.

My contention is that Chicanos have been incorporated into the United States' political economy as subordinate ascriptive class segments, and that they have historically been found occupying such a structural position at all class levels. While I have stressed in the definition the relationship to the system of production (i.e., the economic system), a person's class position is typically manifested in all institutions of the society (e.g., the educational system, the political system).

A SYNTHESIS OF INTERNAL COLONIAL
AND CLASS SEGMENTATION APPROACHES

Of the various theoretical models that have been set forth to explain the persistence of racial inequality in the United States, the internal colonial model is the most comprehensive and the one that most accurately reflects empirical reality. The particular variation that I favor is the class differentiated or "left" version of that model. On the one hand, it is consistent with a view of capitalist society as class society, in which the dominant class exercises disproportionate influence on all aspects of the system. Colonialism historically has been established to serve the interests of merchants, industrialists, and would-be landowners, or of the state, which ultimately safeguards the interests of the dominant classes. Internal colonialism is no exception to this rule. In addition, this model is consistent with the role of agricultural and industrial capitalists in the nineteenth-century continental expansion of the United States, and in structuring the subordinate labor force that came into existence in the Southwest on the basis of various racial minorities.

It is sometimes argued that Anglo workers have benefited from internal colonialism, and that their interests are also involved in perpetuating that system. However, this is true in only a very partial sense, and is untrue in a general sense. The argument is often supported by reference to antiminority sentiments and social movements among Anglo workers, based on job competition. However, a careful historical examination reveals that Anglo workers have been reacting to the racially segmented labor system created by employers precisely to undercut the wage standards, organizing efforts, and unity of workers as a whole. To the extent that employers have been successful in these efforts, Anglo workers have seen their enemies as the manipulated minority workers, rather than the manipulators. This misperception, essentially a type of false consciousness, has been encouraged by the racial ideologies developed to support the system, and by the general obscuring of class relations created by the hegemony of capitalist ideology. The impulse of Anglo workers has been to exclude the minority workers from the economy in order to solidify their own position. Only when this effort has been blocked have they gone along with the segmentation of the labor force.

Examination of the objective interests of the Anglo workers leads to the same conclusion. Anglo workers do benefit in a way from being spared the most undesirable work and from being cushioned against the worst dislocations of the economy (via the "buffer" role of the minority workers). However, they lose from the downward pressure exerted on wages by the segmented labor market, and from the use of minority workers as strikebreakers in their reserve role. Most importantly, the divisions created among workers by labor-force segmentation prevent the coming about of class consciousness and the ability of the workers to act in a unified manner to secure their interests. Members of the working class clearly have a much greater interest in uniting politically to change the system as a whole and to abolish classes than in competing with each other for limited gains.

Employers' interests, on the other hand, gain across the board from this system. Dual wage structures lower their labor costs. The buffer role allows the impact of recessions to be concentrated on the most vulnerable and politically least dangerous segment of the workers. The reserve role allows them to expand and reduce their labor force as needed, and to use the reserve labor force as leverage against demands of the employed workers. The most important aspect, however, has to do with the divisions that are created among the workers as a whole, since this allows capitalists to promote what is after all their ultimate interest, the perpetuation of class society itself.

Only two possible disadvantages to employers can be cited. One is the confinement of talented minority workers to jobs where their talents are not fully utilized, but apparently most employers are willing to bear this cost in order to gain the other advantages. In any case, most occupational positions require only that a job be done adequately, not that it be done in a superior manner. In the situation of labor surplus which appears to be a permanent aspect of the American economy, it is not difficult to find workers to perform most jobs adequately. The other disadvantage, which seems to impress some observers, has to do with political unrest among the minority populations, for example, the urban uprisings of the 1960s. From the perspective of the 1970s, it appears that this threat has been satisfactorily blunted through the combined use of selective repression and cooptation (for a good analysis of this process, see Allen, 1969).

Having adopted a class-differentiated colonial perspective, it remains to spell out the nature of structural discrimination in more detail and to relate the model to the American class structure, beyond the specification of class interests outlined above. The relationship is diagrammed in figure 1.9, in which the internal colonial model is reproduced in its "left" variation and in which the class structure is modeled on the Ehrenreich analysis described earlier.

The diagram at the bottom of figure 1.9 represents an elaboration of the box in the top of the diagram labeled "Establishment of a System of Structural Discrimination." Classes are the most general structural elements in a society, and the existence of a system of institutionalized discrimination in the society can be thought of in terms of a set of segmented classes. Segmentation in each class exists to the extent that such institutionalized discriminatory practices exists. If there is none, there is no segmentation. The segmentation line is drawn in a broken manner to indicate that it is not necessarily an impervious line. That is, a member of a racial minority may be in the subordinate segment or in the nonsubordinate segment. Under the latter conditions, he or she would be integrated into the class on the basis of equality with all other nonsubordinate members of that class. All Chicanos are not necessarily in one of the subordinate segments.

The diagram is drawn in a particular manner to illustrate certain points. The class diagram is not drawn in the familiar pyramid fashion because Marxist classes are not strata arranged, one on top of the other, on the basis of income, even though there is a correlation between class and average income. The classes are all drawn the same size because what is portrayed here is the structural relationships, not the relative magnitude of the class memberships. The segmentation line is drawn all the way

Figure 1.9. Internal Colonialism and Class Segmentation

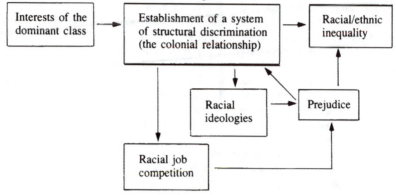

Elaboration of the System of Structural discrimination in Class Terms

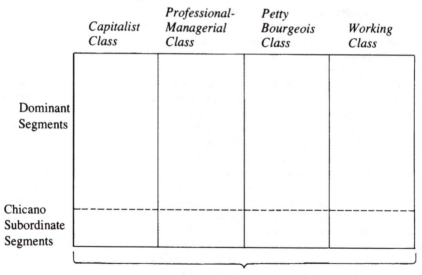

(Chicano subordinate segments together constitute the internal colony)

across the diagram because Chicanos are members of all classes in the United States, but form a subordinate segment within each class.

The central aspect of this diagram is the way in which interests are grouped. A Chicano in the subordinate segment of the working class is still a member of that class, and has interests in common with all members of the working class, for example, in higher wages, better working conditions, the right to bargain collectively, and, ultimately, the establishment of a classless society. These interests are in opposition to those of other classes, particularly the capitalist class. At the same time, Chicano workers have certain interests particular to them, such as the ending of racial discrimination, which, while of benefit to workers generally, would affect them more intensely.

The segmentation line, however, also cuts across class divisions, reflecting the fact that Chicanos in all classes suffer from institutionalized discrimination, even though it takes different forms for each class. This gives Chicanos as a group certain interests in common, based on the common experience of discrimination. Such interests would include equality in economic treatment, the end of housing and educational discrimination, and so on. Thus the various Chicano subordinate segments have certain interests in common, their colonial interests, and certain interests in opposition, their class interests. The different Chicano segments also constitute an internal colony in the sense that they share a common culture, at least in part, and this may be reflected in a shared interest in such things as bilingual-bicultural programs in the schools. Chicanos also constitute a colony with a certain coherence across class lines in the sense that they are liable to be in frequent contact with each other. Thus the bilingual Chicano teacher, a member of the professional-managerial class, comes in contact with Chicano parents from the working class. Chicano social workers are liable to have a largely Chicano clientele, as are other Chicano professionals. Chicano members of the petty bourgeoisie or (small) capitalist class also rely primarily on other Chicanos for their livelihood.

Thus the Chicano situation is complex in terms of interests, and it is not surprising that Chicano political patterns have somewhat of a shifting nature, with, at times, the segmentation division and, at times, the class divisions assuming an overriding importance. While it is not possible in the present work to go into detail on this pattern, it is familiar to most informed observers, and frequently creates political dilemmas. I intend to examine these patterns in more detail in a future work.

To make the system of class segmentation more concrete, it is necessary to spell out the exact nature of the structural discrimination that defines the segmentation line. Here I can do that only for the economic aspects of discrimination, although it should also be done in other areas of social life, such as politics, housing, and education. The five aspects of structural discrimination that affect the working class in the economic sphere should be familiar by now: labor repression, wage differentials, occupational stratification, the reserve role, and the buffer role. The petty bourgeois segment is also subject to certain types of structural discrimination, particularly in being confined to a largely or entirely Chicano clientele in their small businesses or independent professional practices. Few data exist on the Chicano professional-managerial class, but occupational stratification appears to be an important factor for Chicanos who manage to make it into this growing class. From personal observation, it seems that Chicano professionals who work in bureaucracies are often hired only to deal with a Chicano clientele, much as Chicano white-collar workers have historically been employed. Chicano faculty in universities and colleges, for example, are often deemed employable primarily in ethnic studies programs, which are usually run on "soft" money and not considered a permanent aspect of the university. Chicano faculty are overwhelmingly in junior positions, and a kind of informal "revolving door" policy has come into being by which Chicano faculty are terminated when they come up for tenure, and their positions filled with other junior Chicano faculty. At the University of California in Berkeley, for example, the most recent figures indicate that total minority faculty in untenured positions rose from 6.9 percent in 1973 to 13.3 percent in 1976, but minority tenured faculty actually declined from 5.6 to 5.3 percent in the same period. In the latter year, "Hispanic" faculty (a category broader than Chicano) represented only 1.1 percent of the Berkeley faculty ("Fed Report Reveals State of Faculty Affirmative Action," *Daily Californian*, Aug. 8–10, 1977). These patterns reflect, in part, the existence of structural discrimination at lower levels of the public education system, so that few Chicanos reach the university level. But it also reflects certain institutionalized practices at the university level, such as culturally biased standards of evaluation, racially biased patterns of recruiting, and the habit of imposing disproportionate administrative responsibilities on junior Chicano faculty without weighing them seriously in the promotion process.

Class segmentation in the capitalist class must remain largely speculative because of lack of information, although the few data reported earlier on New Mexico tend to bear out the hypothesis. Still, this can be a theoretical advantage in that it allows us to make certain predictions from the model that can be checked empirically. If Chicano capitalists conform to the pattern of the petty bourgeoisie, they will be confined largely to small and perhaps medium-size enterprises, with a principally Chicano clientele. Their position will be maintained through certain institutionalized practices, one of which I predict will be the denial of credit to them by Anglo bankers on the same terms as credit is extended to Anglo businessmen. Other structural mechanisms will probably emerge from empirical studies.

It should be borne in mind that the diagram in figure 1.9 is not intended to depict the situation of all Chicanos. Chicanos in the marginal sector are outside the class system in that they have no organic connection to the system of production. The diagram applies only to Chicanos in the colonized and integrated sectors— which is, however, most of the Chicano population. Also, the emphasis on the existence of segmentation should not obscure the fact that the segmentation line has been weakening at least since the Second World War. Continuation of that trend will mean that class divisions will become more salient as Chicanos become more integrated into the nonsubordinate part of the labor force. A reversal of the trend, or even a situation of stagnation, would undoubtedly lead to greater political mobilization along the colonial axis.

CONCLUSION

Chicano history could be said to start with the Mexican American War, an episode in the territorial expansion of Europe and European-derived societies that began in the fifteenth century. The manner in which the original Chicanos came about links Chicano history firmly with the history of other Third World people who have been subjected to the colonial experience in one or another of its forms. In this case, the imperial expansion of the United States resulted in internal colonialism, a condition which Chicanos have shared with other racial minorities. While the initial conquest affected only certain parts of the Southwest immediately and left others in a more or less peripheral state, the economic penetration which followed in the remainder of the nineteenth century eventually drew all parts of the area within the new order. As the interests of the American dominant class asserted themselves, the lands which remained under Chicano control were expropriated, in some cases rapidly and in others more gradually, and as likely as not under the color of law. It is perhaps in this expropriation that we can most clearly see the role the American state has played in creating and perpetuating the colonial status of Chicanos, although many other examples have been cited.

As part of that process of expropriation, but tied even more strongly to the exploitation of Chicano labor, a system of class segmentation was created in the nineteenth century that bound Chicanos to a structurally subordinate position in the society. With the waves of immigration that swept across the border in the early twentieth century, the numerical presence of Chicanos in the Southwest was greatly expanded. The structure of subordination, however, underwent only minor changes. During the Great Depression, thousands of Chicanos and Mexicanos were expelled from the Southwest as the labor market contracted. At the same time, important changes were made in the political economy of the United States, in particular the growing integration of the state and the economy. This development and others during the 1930s and 1940s set in motion a chain of events which have resulted in significant modifications in the class position of Chicanos in recent decades. Still, while some of these changes have resulted in a lessening of the harshness which has characterized the Chicano situation, the 1970s have brought some ominous trends. These include a new round of hysteria around the issue of undocumented workers, a broad-based backlash against minority demands, and a possible reemergence of marginality, this time on a more permanent basis. And while more Chicanos have become integrated or substantially integrated into the nonsubordinate part of the class structure, the segmentation line remains a major determining factor in most Chicanos' day-to-day reality. For the foreseeable future, the politics of the Chicano community can be expected to revolve around both class and colonial divisions in a complex manner whose outlines we can only dimly perceive in the current period of confusion and redefinition.

REFERENCES

Adam, Heribert. (1971). *Modernizing racial domination: The dynamics of South African politics.* Berkeley: University of California Press.

Allen, Robert. (1969). *Black awakening in capitalist America.* Garden City, NY: Doubleday.

Arrow, Kenneth. (1971). *Some models of racial discrimination in the labor market.* Santa Monica, CA: Rand.

Balandier, G. (1966). The colonial situation: A theoretical approach. In Immanuel Wallerstein, (Ed.), *Social change: The colonial situation* (pp. 34–61). New York: Wiley.

Baran, Paul, & Sweezy, Paul. (1966). *Monopoly capital.* New York: Monthly Review Press.

Barrera, Mario, Munoz, Carlos, & Ornelas, Charles. (1972). The barrio as internal colony. In

Harlan Hahn (Ed.), *People and politics in urban society* (pp. 465–98). Los Angeles: Sage Publications.

Becker, Gary. (1971). *The economics of discrimination*. 2d ed. Chicago: University of Chicago Press.

Benedict, Ruth. (1959). *Race: Science and politics*. New York: Viking Press.

Betts, Raymond. (1968). *Europe overseas: Phases of imperialism*. New York: Basic Books.

Blauner, Robert. (1972). *Racial oppression in America*. New York: Harper and Row.

Block, N.J., & Dworkin, Gerald. (1974). IQ: Heritability and inequality. *Philosophy and Public Affairs*, pt. 1, Summer, 331–409; pt. 2, Fall, 40–99.

Bonacich, Edna. (1972, October). A theory of ethnic antagonism: The split labor market. *American Sociological Review*, 547–59.

Brookshire, Marjorie. (1954). The industrial pattern of Mexican-American employment in Neuces County Texas. Ph.D. dissertation, University of Texas.

Carmichael, Stokely, & Hamilton, Charles. (1967). *Black power*. New York: Random House.

Cartey, Wilfred, & Kilson, Martin. (Eds.). (1970). *The African reader: Colonial Africa*. New York: Vintage.

Clark, Kenneth. (1972). *Dark ghetto*. New York: Harper and Row.

Cox, Oliver. (1970). *Caste, class and race*. New York: Modern Reader (originally published in 1948).

Crowder, Michael. (1964, July). Indirect rule — French and British style." *Africa*, 197–205.

Cruse, Harold. (1968). *Rebellion or revolution*. New York: Morrow.

D'Anotonio, William, & Form, William. (1965). *Influentials in two border cities*. Notre Dame, IN: University of Notre Dame Press.

Davis, Allison, Gardner, Burleigh, & Gardner, Mary. (1941). *Deep south*. Chicago: University of Chicago Press.

Doeringer, Peter, & Piore, Michael. *Internal labor market and manpower analysis*. Lexington, MA: D.C. Heath.

Dollard, John. (1957). *Caste and class in a southern town*. 3d ed. Garden City, NY: Doubleday.

Edwards, Richard, Reich, Michael, & Gordon, David. (Eds.). (1975). *Labor market segmentation*. Lexington, MA: D.C. Heath.

Ehrenerich, Barbara, & Ehrenreich, John. (1977). The professional-managerial class. *Radical America*, pt. 1, March–April, 7–31; pt. 2, May–June, 7–22.

Fanon, Frantz. (1963). *The wretched of the earth*. New York: Grove Press.

Fieldhouse, D.K. (1966). *The colonial empires*. New York: Delta.

Foner, Phillip. (Ed.). (1970). *The black panthers speak*. Philadelphia: Lippincott.

Franklin, Raymond, & Resnik, Solomon. (1973). *The political economy of racism*. New York: Holt, Rinehart and Winston.

Frazier, E. Franklin. (1957). *Race and culture contacts in the modern world*. Boston: Beacon Press.

Freedman, Francesca. (1975, October–December). The internal structure of the American proletariat: A marxist analysis. *Social Revolution*, 41–83.

Furnivall, J.S. (1948). *Colonial policy and practice*. Cambridge, MA: Cambridge University Press.

Gallagher, John, & Robinson, Ronald. (1953, August). The imperialism of free trade. *Economic History Review*, 1–15.

Genovese, Eugene. (1968). Class and nationality in black America. In *Red and Black*. New York: Vintage.

Gonzalez Casanova, Pablo. (1965). Internal colonialism and national development. *Studies in comparative international development*, 1, no. 4: 27–37.

Gordon, David. (1972). *Theories of poverty and underemployment*. Lexington, MA: D.C. Heath.

Gossett, Thomas. (1965). *Race: The history of an idea in America.* New York: Schocken.

Hayden, Tom. (1968, Summer). Colonialism and liberation in America. *Viet-Report,* 32–39.

Hechter, Michael. (1975). *Internal colonialism: The celtic fringe in British national development, 1536–1966.* Berkeley: University of California Press.

Horsman, Reginald. (1973, July–September). Origins of racial anglo-saxonism in Great Britain befor 1850. *Journal of the History of Ideas,* J387–410.

Jensen, Arthur. (1969, Winter). How much can we boost IQ and scholastic achievement? *Harvard Educational Review,* 1–123.

Jensen, Arthur. (1973). *Educability and group differences.* New York: Harper and Row.

Jordan, Winthrop. (1968). *White over black: American attitudes toward the negro, 1550–1812.* Baltimore: Penguin Books.

Kluckholn, Florence, & Strodtbeck, Fred. (1961). *Variations in value orientations.* Evanston, IL: Row, Peterson.

Kohn, Hans. (1958). Reflections on colonialism. In Robert Strausz-Hupe & Henry Hazard, (Eds.), *The idea of colonialism* (pp. 2–16). New York: Praeger

Kuper, Leo, & Smith, M.G. (Eds.). (1971). *Pluralism in Africa.* Berkeley: University of California Press.

Loehlin, John, Lindzey, Gardner, & Spuhler, J.N.. (1975). *Race differences in intelligence.* San Francisco: W.H. Freeman.

Manuel, Herschel. (1965). *Spanish-speaking children of the southwest.* Austin: University of Texas Press.

Memmi, Albert. (1965). *The colonizer and the colonized.* Boston: Beacon Press.

Moynihan, Daniel. (1965, March). *The negro family: The case for national action.* Washington: U.S. Department of Labor.

Myrdal, Gunnar. (1962). *An American dilemma.* New York: Pantheon (originally published in 1944).

Nkrumah, Kwame. (1966). *Neo-colonialism: The last state of imperialism.* New York: International Publishers.

Omvedt, Gail. (1973, Spring). Towards a theory of colonialism. *Insurgent Sociologist,* 1–24.

Poulantzas, Nicos. (1973a, March–April). On social classes. *New Left Review,* 27–54.

Poulantzas, Nicos. (1975). *Classes in contemporary capitalism.* London: New Left Books.

Prager, Jeffrey. (1972–73). White racial privilege and social change: An examination of theories of racism." *Berkeley Journal of Sociology,* 117–50.

Rainwater, Lee, & Yancey, William. (1967). *The Moynihan report and the politics of controversy.* Cambridge, MA: MIT Press.

Reich, Michael. (1972). The economics of racism. In Richard Edwards, Reich, Michael, & Weisskopf, Thomas (Eds.), *The capitalist system* (313–21). Englewood Cliffs, NJ: Prentice-Hall.

Report of the national advisory commission on civil disorders. (1968). New York: Benjamin Books.

Rex, John. (1970). *Race relations in sociological theory.* London: Weidenfeld and Nicolson Press.

Ryan, William. (1971). *Blaming the victim.* New York: Vintage.

Schermerhorn, Richard. (1970). *Comparative ethnic relations.* New York: Random House.

Shibutani, Tamotsu, & Kwan, Kian. (1965). *Ethnic stratification.* New York: Macmillan.

Simpson, George, & Yinger, J. Milton. (1958). *Racial and cultural minorities.* Rev. ed. New York: Harper.

Staples, Robert. (1976, June). Race and colonialism: The domestic case in theory and practice. *Black Scholar,* 37–48.

Stavenhagen, Rodolfo. (1965). Classes, colonialism, and acculturation." *Studies in Comparative International Development,* 1, no. 6: 53–77.

Stein, Stanley, & Stein, Barbara. (1970). *The colonial heritage of Latin America*. New York: Oxford University Press.

Torres, Rudy. (1978, Spring). Political economy of U.S. class structure: Notes on dual labor market theory. Claremont, CA: Claremont Working Papers in Public Policy.

Vaca, Nick. (1970). The Mexican-American in the social sciences: 1912–1970. *El Grito*, pt. 1, Spring, 3–24; pt. 2, Fall, 17–51.

van den Berghe, Pierre. (1965). *South Africa: A study in conflict*. Berkeley: University of California Press.

Warner, W. Lloyd. (1936). American caste and class. *American Journal of Sociology*, September, 234–37.

Wilson, William. (1973). *Power, racism, and privilege*. New York: Macmillan.

Wright, Erik Olin. (1976, July–August). Class boundaries in advanced capitalist societies. *New Left Review*, 3–41.

2

Economic, Labor Force, and Social Implications of Latino Educational and Population Trends

Sonia M. Pérez
Denise De La Rosa Salazar

Demographic data show a dramatic increase in the U.S. Hispanic population over the past decade; early in the next century, Hispanics will become
the nation's largest minority. Gains in educational attainment and economic
stability and mobility have not been proportionate to this growth. By examining recent Census data and other relevant research, this article examines the relationship between Latino population trends and the impact of
this growth on the economy and on education. Data show that Hispanics
represent a significant segment of future workers and taxpayers who will
ensure the solvency of private and public services and benefits, such as Social Security. The analysis suggests that reducing inequality between Hispanics and the rest of society is an economic imperative and that increasing
Hispanic educational attainment and other human capital characteristics
is critical for the full integration of Latinos into the future U.S. work force.
An undereducated, youthful, and growing Hispanic population has implications for labor force participation rates, earnings, socioeconomic stability, and the nation's social welfare. Finally, discrimination, quality of
education, and poverty affect education and labor force status and must
also be addressed.

As underscored by Chapa and Valencia (1993), recent Census data and research
have documented the dramatic growth experienced by the Hispanic population in
the United States over the past decade.[1] With this growth has come some progress.
For example, as the Census Bureau reported in November 1991 (U.S. Department of
Commerce, Bureau of the Census, 1991d), aggregate Hispanic "buying power"—or
after-tax income—increased by 70% between 1982 and 1990, signaling increases in
the Hispanic population as a whole, in their participation in the labor force, and, for
some Hispanics, movement up the economic ladder. But this increase in population
has not been accompanied by a proportionate increase in educational attainment,

economic stability, or political power. Rather, since 1980, there have been slow, modest increases in educational attainment and political representation and—despite high labor force participation rates—a continued concentration of Hispanics in low-wage employment with limited benefits and few opportunities for advancement.

Three facts underscore the need to focus on the growth and socioeconomic status (SES) of Hispanics in the United States. First, Hispanics are a young population (see Chapa & Valencia, 1993). Their median age of 26 is 7 years younger than that of non-Hispanics; they constitute, therefore, a significant portion of this country's future work force. In fact, Bureau of Labor Statistics data show that, by the year 2000, almost one fifth of new entrants into the labor force will be Hispanic (Hudson Institute, 1987). Second, the Hispanic population continues to increase at a rate faster than that of the non-Hispanic population; Chapa and Valencia note that between 1980 and 1990, the Hispanic population grew by 53%—as a result of both natural increase and immigration—and Census projections indicate continued strong growth, with Hispanics expected to become the largest "minority" in the United States early in the twenty-first century. Third, the Hispanic community is undereducated and Hispanics are two-and-one-half times as likely to be poor as non-Hispanics.

The youthfulness of the Hispanic population and its continued growth, as well as its current socioeconomic status (SES), have significant consequences for the U.S. Hispanic community—as well as for the nation in which they will play an increasingly important role. Hispanics represent a growing proportion of both the current and future U.S. labor force; as adults, Hispanics will work in and help manage U.S. businesses, schools, hospitals, and governments. In an aging society, Hispanics represent a significant segment of workers and taxpayers who will ensure the solvency of Social Security, Medicare, public assistance, and other government services.

By examining recent Census data and education and labor market research, this article will examine the relationship between the population trends experienced by the U.S. Hispanic community and the impact of this growth on the U.S. education arena and the economy. Specifically, this article will lay out the connection between education, the labor force, and the SES of Latinos; describe and analyze these issues within the context of the growing Hispanic population; discuss the implications of these changes and trends for the future of different Latino communities and the United States; and offer some policy directions in response to these issues.

OVERVIEW

Hispanics constitute the second largest minority group in the United States, with a mainland population of 22.35 million as of the 1990 Census; currently, about 1 in 11 Americans is Hispanic (9%). Hispanics constitute approximately 36% of the U.S. minority population and, according to Census Bureau projections, are expected to become the largest ethnic minority within the early part of the next century. Moreover, these demographic changes, coupled with the nation's shift from a goods-producing to a service-producing economy, have serious implications for U.S. productivity, competitiveness, and the support and maintenance of government programs and services.

Data from the Office of Civil Rights of the U.S. Department of Education show that, as a proportion of total school enrollment, the Hispanic population increased from about 1 in 16 in 1976 to almost 1 in 10 in 1986, and White student enrollment declined from 76% to 70% of total enrollment during the same period (U.S. Department of Education, Office for Civil Rights, September, 1982 and December, 1987). Further, of the 40.2 million children attending public schools in the fall of 1990, 11% or 4.4 million were Hispanic, up from 8.8% or 3.6 million in the fall of 1984 (U.S. Department of Commerce, Bureau of the Census, 1990a).

Moreover, the proportion of the student population in the elementary grades that is Hispanic has increased whereas the upper grades have experienced a decrease in Hispanic student enrollment, as shown in Table 2.1.

This can be explained by three interrelated factors. First, as discussed above, Hispanics have a lower median age than the rest of the U.S. population. Second, Census Bureau data show that the fertility rate of Hispanic women is higher than that of non-Hispanic women; in 1990, there were 93 births per 1,000 Hispanic women aged 15-44, compared with 64 per 1,000 non-Hispanic women (U.S. Department of Commerce, Bureau of the Census, 1991c). Third, as will be discussed in the next section, Hispanics have a higher dropout rate than any other major population group, which helps to explain their decreased enrollment in the upper-grade levels.

Enrollment figures from the National Education Longitudinal Study of 1988 (National Center for Education Statistics, 1990b) show that Hispanics comprise 10.4% of the approximately 3 million students enrolled in eighth grade in the United States (National Center for Education Statistics, 1990a). About 71.6% of these students are White non-Hispanic, 13.2% Black non-Hispanic, 3.5% Asian or Pacific Islander, and 1.3% American Indian or Alaskan Native. Additionally, 9 out of 10 Hispanic eight graders (90.5%) are enrolled in public schools. Among Hispanic subgroups, 95% of Mexican/Chicano students are enrolled in public schools, compared to 87% of Puerto Ricans, 69.9% of Cubans, and 83.5% of Other Hispanics (De La Rosa & Maw, 1990).

Public school enrollment is projected to rise to almost 44 million in the year 2000, and nearly all the increase will be in minority—especially Hispanic—enrollment (National Center for Education Statistics, 1990a). It is estimated that between 1985 and 2000, there will be an increase of 2.4 million Hispanic children, 1.7 million Black children, and 66,000 White, non-Hispanic children (U.S. Department of Commerce, Bureau of the Census, 1986; also, see Chapa & Valencia, 1993, on Latino youth growth). In some states, Hispanics will constitute the largest single ethnic group within total student enrollment. For example, by 2006, it is estimated that Latino students will make up about 48% of total K-12 student enrollment in California public schools (Macías, 1993). In sum, the impact of Hispanic population growth—of both school-age children and young adults—will immediately be felt by the U.S. school system, but will become equally critical to the labor force as these students make the transition from the classroom to the world of work. Economic growth and development and the quality of the U.S. labor force will, in large part, be contingent on the human capital characteristics of the Hispanic population.

Data from the Census Bureau Current Population Survey (U.S. Department of Commerce, Bureau of the Census, 1991d) show that, in 1991, there were 9.5 million

Table 2.1.   Enrollment in Elementary and High School by Race/Ethnicity, October 1988

	Grades				
	K–4	5–8	9–10	11–12	All
Number (in thousands)					
Total students	14,010	13,803	6,549	5,927	40,289
Hispanic	1,624	1,477	739	578	4,418
White	11,269	11,042	5,259	4,728	32,298
Black	2,114	2,163	1,020	930	6,227
Percentage					
Hispanic	11.6	10.7	11.3	9.6	11.0
White	80.4	80.1	80.1	80.8	80.2
Black	15.1	15.7	15.6	15.7	15.5

SOURCE: U.S. Department of Commerce, Bureau of the Census (1992b).
NOTE: Hispanic students may be of any race. Racial categories include Hispanics, therefore totals may not add up to 100%.

Hispanic workers in the U.S. labor force. By the twenty-first century, as a result of population trends and demographic changes, one third of workers in the U.S. economy will be members of a minority group (Hudson Institute, 1987) and U.S. Latino communities will constitute a significant segment of that proportion. Research and data suggest, however, that although Latinos represent a vibrant and sizable source of workers, their current social, education, and economic status must vastly improve if their demographic power is to be translated into economic strength, both for themselves and for the United States.

A snapshot of the Latino population in the United States indicates that the great majority of Hispanics live in urban areas, have a strong attachment to the labor force, and are disproportionately affected by current social and economic problems. One of the most serious issues facing the Latino community in urban and other areas across the country is that Hispanics remain the most undereducated major segment of the U.S. population. Although educational attainment levels have improved somewhat, Hispanics continue to enter school later, leave school earlier, and receive proportionately fewer high school diplomas and college degrees than other Americans (De La Rosa & Maw, 1990). In 1990, only 51.3% of Hispanics 25 years old and over, compared to 80.5% of non-Hispanics, had completed four years of high school or more.

Trend data show that Hispanics have made only modest gains in educational attainment relative to their population growth during the 1980s; for example, in 1983, less than half of Hispanics had completed four years of high school or more (46.3%); now, slightly more than half are high school graduates (51.3%). Further, almost 10% of Hispanics 25 years old and over had completed four or more years of college as of 1991, compared to only 8.2% in 1983 (U.S. Department of Commerce, Bureau of the Census, 1991d). Despite these increases in levels of educational attainment, Latinos continue to suffer the highest dropout rates of any population group in the country. On average, nearly 2 in 5 Hispanic high school-age students leave school before the 12th grade. As of October 1990, about 37.7% of Hispanics aged 18-24 years were high school dropouts, compared to 15.1% of Blacks and 13.5% of Whites (U.S. Department of Commerce, Bureau of the Census, 1992b). This educational disparity is particularly troubling, not simply for Hispanics and their families but for the nation as a whole. Low educational attainment has two principal effects. First, for Hispanics, it has a significant impact on their position in the labor market and results in their concentration in low-wage, unstable work and in disproportionately high rates of individual and family poverty. Second, because of the size and youthfulness of the Hispanic population, its educational status has long-term social and economic consequences that will affect the development and stability of the U.S. economy.

Data on labor force status show that Hispanic men have the highest labor force participation rate of any major ethnic or racial group in the United States. The data among youth show that even Hispanic young males who are in high school are more likely than their White or Black counterparts to be working or looking for work (Miller, et al., 1988). Hispanic women tend to participate in the labor force at a lower rate than their non-Hispanic counterparts, although data show that the labor force status of Hispanic women is changing. In 1980, less than half of Hispanic women (47.4%) were working or looking for work, compared to slightly over half of both White and Black women (51.2% and 53.1%, respectively); by 1991, more than half of Hispanic women (51.4%) and almost 6 in 10 non-Hispanic women (57.4%) were participating in the paid labor force (U.S. Department of Labor, 1989; U.S. Department of Commerce, Bureau of the Census, 1991d). Labor force data also show that, despite this strong attachment to the labor force, Hispanics, as a group, are concentrated in low-skill, low-wage jobs that tend to be vulnerable to major economic changes.

Table 2.2 below shows the occupational distribution of Hispanic and non-Hispanic workers and illustrates that, partly as a result of low educational attainment levels, Hispanics are underrepresented in jobs for which advanced levels of education or well-developed literacy and numeracy skills are required (e.g., managerial/professional positions). That is, in the managerial/professional specialty area, 26.5% of Whites worked in this area although only 13.2% of Hispanics did. But research shows that low-skill jobs are becoming scarce and that the creation of jobs between now and the beginning of the next century will be in occupations for which most Hispanics will not be eligible—unless their human capital characteristics are enhanced (Hudson Institute, 1987; U.S. Department of Commerce, Bureau of the Census, 1991d). In fact, the U.S. economy is experiencing a transformation from a manufacturing-based to a service-based economy, one in which basic education skills and even a high school diploma are no longer adequate tools for employment. As a result, the growth of the Hispanic population and its potential capacity as future workers to help sustain and develop the U.S. economy is greatly dependent on its improved educational status and its ability to fill available positions in a service-based, educationally competitive economy.

The projected adverse effects of economic restructuring are already being experienced by segments of the U.S. Latino community. Hispanic workers' median earnings were two thirds that of their non-Hispanic counterparts in 1991, $24,240

Table 2.2. Occupational Distribution, Median Weekly Earnings, and Annual Unemployment of Employed Civilians, 1988 (Percentage Distribution)

	Total	White	Black	Hispanic	1988 Median Weekly Earnings by Occupation ($)	1988 Annual Unemployment By Occupation (%)
Total 16 years and over (in thousands)	114,968	99,812	11,658	8,250		
Percentage	100.0	100.0	100.0	100.0		
Occupation						
Managerial/professional specialty	25.4	26.5	15.4	13.2	552	1.9
Executive/administrative/managerial	12.6	13.0	6.8	6.9	547	2.1
Professional specialty	13.0	13.4	8.6	6.3	555	1.7
Technical, sales/administrative support	30.9	31.2	27.8	25.0	347	4.0
Technicians and related support	3.1	3.0	2.8	1.8	448	2.6
Sales occupations	12.0	12.5	7.2	8.8	385	4.5
Administrative support/clerical	15.9	15.7	17.8	14.3	318	3.9
Service occupations	13.3	12.1	23.1	18.9	245	6.9
Private household	0.8	0.7	1.8	1.8		5.7
Protective service	1.7	1.6	2.8	1.5	417	4.0
Service other than private household or protective service	10.9	9.9	18.6	15.6	221	7.4
Precision production, craft/repair	11.9	12.3	8.8	13.5	430	5.4
Operators, fabricators, and laborers	15.5	14.7	22.9	23.9	313	8.3
Machine operators, assemblers	7.1	6.7	10.3	13.1	302	7.7
Transportation, material moving	4.2	4.0	6.2	4.2	389	6.2
Handlers, equipment cleaners, helpers and laborers	4.2	4.0	6.5	6.7	277	11.5
Farming, forestry and fishing[a]	3.0	3.2	1.9	5.4	229	7.0

SOURCE: U.S. Department of Labor, Bureau of Labor Statistics (1989).
a. In 1988, 949,000 individuals were employed as farmworkers. Of this figure, 23.0% were Hispanic, 8.6% were Black, and 23.3% were women.

compared to $34,645. Recent Census Bureau data and other analyses indicate that Hispanic median earnings have declined from 1980 to 1990. Between 1979 and 1988, the gap between Hispanic and White male earnings grew. In 1979, Hispanic male year-round full-time workers earned 72.6% of the annual earnings of comparable White males. By 1988, this figure had fallen to 65.6% (Miranda & Quiroz, 1990). Additionally, research has shown that the gap between Hispanic and non-Hispanic workers in the labor force has widened, not narrowed, in the past decade (Bean & Tienda, 1987; Carnoy, Daley, & Hinojosa Ojeda, 1990; Greenstein, et al., 1988). Finally, an analysis by the Economic Policy Institute (Mishel & Frankell, 1991) released in September 1992 shows that 1990 median family income for Hispanics was 63.5% of White median family income—down from 69.2% in 1973.

Undereducation and a concentration in low-skilled, low-wage work, combined with the recent recession, have also had a major impact on Hispanic unemployment. To illustrate, Figure 2.1 shows that Blacks and Hispanics have had consistently higher unemployment rates than Whites over the past decade. Since the beginning of the economic recession, unemployment has risen steadily, from 5.6% in August 1990 to 7.3% in March 1992. The unemployment rate for Hispanics in July 1992 was 11.9%, compared to 6.7% for Whites and 14.6% for Blacks; Hispanic unemployment levels have been consistently between those of Whites and Blacks.

Finally, the educational status of Latinos and their current position in the U.S. labor market have resulted in disproportionately high poverty rates for Latinos and their families. The most current Census data (U.S. Department of Commerce, Bureau of the Census, 1992a) show that more than one in every four Hispanics (28.7%)—and two in five Hispanic children (40.4%)—are poor. Comparable data show that the poverty rate in 1990 was 11.3% for Whites and 32.7% for Blacks; child poverty rates were 16.8% and 45.9%, respectively. These data indicate that poverty, especially child poverty, among all families is on the rise. Among Hispanics and their families, such poverty brings myriad social problems with costs to the nation. For example, the increase in poverty, especially child poverty, has contributed to record caseload growth in the number of poor Americans—including Hispanics—who have turned to the public "safety net" of unemployment insurance, food stamps, and Aid to Families with Dependent Children (AFDC) (Martínez, 1992).

Existing data indicate that, in addition to facing economic and social challenges, Hispanics are more likely than other Americans to contract certain diseases, receive less preventive care, and have less access to health education or health care—factors that have particularly serious consequences for Hispanic children. Data from the 1990 Current Population Survey (CPS) (U.S. Department of Commerce, Bureau of the Census, 1992a) indicate that almost one in three Hispanics compared to one in eight Whites and one in five Blacks has no health insurance coverage—and these differences hold regardless of whether there is an adult worker in the family (National Council of La Raza [NCLR], 1992a). Finally, Hispanics are more likely than Whites but less likely than Blacks to live in female-headed households. In 1990, almost one-quarter (23.8%) of Hispanic families were maintained by a female householder, with no husband present, compared to about one fifth of White families (19.3%) and more than half of Black families (58.0%) (U.S. Department of Commerce, Bureau of the Census, 1991a, 1991d). The percentage of fe-

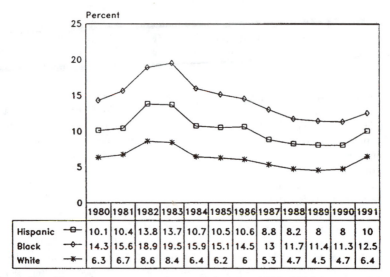

		1980	1981	1982	1983	1984	1985	1986	1987	1988	1989	1990	1991
Hispanic	—B—	10.1	10.4	13.8	13.7	10.7	10.5	10.6	8.8	8.2	8	8	10
Black	—◇—	14.3	15.6	18.9	19.5	15.9	15.1	14.5	13	11.7	11.4	11.3	12.5
White	—*—	6.3	6.7	8.6	8.4	6.4	6.2	6	5.3	4.7	4.5	4.7	6.4

Figure 2.1. Unemployment rates by race/ethnicity: 1980–1991 (persons 16 years and over).
SOURCE: U.S. Department of Commerce, Bureau of the Census (1991a; 1991d; 1991f; unpublished data).

male-maintained families ranges from a low of 19.1% among Mexican Americans and 19.4% among Cubans to 26.1% for Central and South Americans and 43.3% for Puerto Ricans (U.S. Department of Commerce, Bureau of the Census, 1991d). These economic, health, and social issues may well affect the school performance and future of the Hispanic community.

In conclusion, if current trends continue, a large segment of the Hispanic population will have few resources to offer the highly skilled and service-oriented U.S. society. An unskilled, undereducated, and underemployed labor force impedes the economic growth of the nation, increases demand for public assistance and other benefits, and diminishes resources for the support and provision of government services.

HISPANIC EDUCATION: STATUS AND REVIEW[2]

Education is perhaps the most important issue in examining the current SES of the U.S. Hispanic population. In order to respond to the undereducation of Hispanics—from a national policy and a local implementation perspective—it is critical to understand the factors associated with their low educational attainment and limited success in U.S. schools (for a Latino case in point, see Valencia's 1991 analysis of Chicano educational issues). It is also essential to clearly lay out Hispanic educational status within the context of the growing Hispanic population and the changing needs of the U.S. labor force.

This section will provide an overview of the Hispanic educational experience in the United States by specifically examining six principal issues that are inextricably linked with economic opportunities, labor force position, and productivity, and that are affected by the increase in the U.S. Latino population. These are (a) educational attainment levels; (b) dropout rates; (c) test scores; (d) limited-English proficiency; (e) college participation and completion rates; and (f) literacy rates.

Latinos have historically been the most undereducated major population group in the U.S. Data show that, compared to Blacks and Whites, Hispanics have the lowest levels of educational attainment, highest dropout rates, and highest illiteracy rates. These racial/ethnic differences have been highly persistent over time. For example, over a half century ago, in 1940, the median number of years of schooling completed for Chicanos—the majority of U.S. Hispanics—ages 25–64 in California was 7.5 years, compared to 10.5 years completed by Whites (Chapa, 1988; cited in Valencia, 1991). Hispanic educational attainment levels (as indicated by high school and college completion rates) have increased in absolute terms since the 1970s; however, the gap between Latinos and non-Latinos remains wide. Figures 2.2 and 2.3 show that although high school and college completion rates have increased, Latinos continue to lag behind Whites and Blacks. For example, in 1975 (see Figure 2.2), there was a 26.6% difference in the high school completion gap between Whites and Hispanics. In 1989, fourteen years later, the completion gap was 27.5%—virtually unchanged after a decade and a half. The gap for college completion is even worse when the rate difference between Whites and Hispanics is examined (see Figure 2.3). In 1975, the difference was 8.2%; in 1989, the gap grew to 11.9%. Educational attainment levels, as discussed by Chapa and Valencia (1993), also vary among Latino subgroups. Mexican Americans have the lowest levels and Other Hispanics have the highest levels of educational attainment of any subgroup. Finally, more recent data from a 1991 report studying the nation's progress toward meeting the National Education Goals for the year 2000 (adopted by President Bush and state governors in 1989), highlighted similarly discouraging findings; between 1975 and 1990, high school completion rates improved 12% for Black students and 2% for White students, but decreased 3% for Hispanic students (the National Education Goals Report, 1991).

One of the reasons that Latinos have low levels of educational attainment is that they continue to have the highest dropout rates of any major U.S. population group. Dropout data vary from study to study and from state to state, due both to real differences, to the variability in the way dropout data are collected and calculated, and the way in which the term is defined (see Rumberger, 1991). For example, the National Center on Education Statistics (NCES) reports on three types of dropout rates—Event dropout rates, Status dropout rates, and Cohort dropout rates—which generate very different figures.[3]

Regardless of the measure used, Latinos have the highest dropout rates in the country. According to the report by NCES, Hispanics have higher status dropout rates than Blacks and Whites. As indicated in Figure 2.4, 32.4% of Hispanics 16-24 years old were dropouts in 1990, compared to 13.2% of Blacks, and only 9.0% of Whites. Additionally, data released by the Department of Education in September 1992 show that Hispanics 16-24 years old were three times as likely as non-Hispanics to drop out of school (National Center for Education Statistics, August

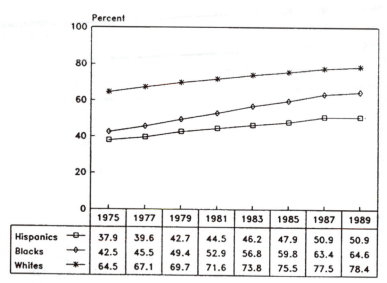

		1975	1977	1979	1981	1983	1985	1987	1989
Hispanics	—▣—	37.9	39.6	42.7	44.5	46.2	47.9	50.9	50.9
Blacks	—◇—	42.5	45.5	49.4	52.9	56.8	59.8	63.4	64.6
Whites	—✳—	64.5	67.1	69.7	71.6	73.8	75.5	77.5	78.4

Figure 2.2. High school completion: Persons 25 years and over by race/ethnicity. *SOURCE:* U.S. Department of Commerce, Bureau of the Census (1991b).

1992). In research on the educational status of Hispanics, the NCLR refers to dropouts as those persons who are not enrolled in school and have no high school diploma. According to Census data analyzed by NCLR, as of October 1988, about 43% of Hispanics aged 19 years old and over were not enrolled in high school and had no high school diploma. This is a decrease from 1986 when the Hispanic dropout was about 50% (Orum, 1986), but is still alarmingly high compared to non-Hispanics. Moreover, Hispanic dropout rates have been reported to range from as low as 7% to as high as 85% depending on the region of the country in question (Orum, 1986).

There are a number of reasons why students drop out of school; however, SES and other aspects of family background are those most consistently linked to dropping out. Research suggests that SES indirectly influences dropout behavior for Hispanics through its influence on other measures of student achievement such as student grades, test scores, and retention (Rumberger, 1991). Students also report school-related or personal reasons for leaving school. In the 1982 follow-up to the High School and Beyond Study, the largest group of Hispanic students (34% of males and 32% of females) reported leaving school because of poor grades (Orum, 1986). But although poor grades are a factor in dropping out, such school performance may be linked to a number of other issues. For example, some students may not have a place to study, if they are living in crowded and economically poor conditions; may be experiencing family problems; or may be in large classes that prevent them from getting the attention and help they need.

Additional data from a 1986 Educational Testing Service study provide further insight into reasons for dropping out of school. The study reported that most Hispanics cited loss of interest in school or boredom, personal reasons, or the need to

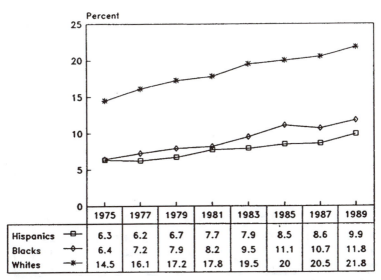

	1975	1977	1979	1981	1983	1985	1987	1989
Hispanics —▭—	6.3	6.2	6.7	7.7	7.9	8.5	8.6	9.9
Blacks —◇—	6.4	7.2	7.9	8.2	9.5	11.1	10.7	11.8
Whites —✳—	14.5	16.1	17.2	17.8	19.5	20	20.5	21.8

Figure 2.3. College completion rates: Persons 25 years and over by race/ethnicity. *SOURCE:* U.S. Department of Commerce, Bureau of the Census (1991b).

work as causes for dropping out (Kirsch & Jungeblut, 1986). Other factors have been suggested as contributors to dropping out, such as marriage, pregnancy, and work; caution should be taken, however, in assessing the relation between student behaviors and choices and the decision to drop out of school. Although a connection is indicated, these factors may not be the cause of students leaving school because there may be other intervening factors, such as family SES and other aspects of family background as mentioned earlier (Orum, 1988).

Another issue that affects the Latino educational experience in the United States is testing (see Valencia & Aburto, 1991a). Academic achievement scores of Hispanics (and Blacks), despite some gains, remain lower than those of White students, and in some cases the gap is widening—such as in conventional educational attainment. As reported by the National Assessment of Educational Progress (NAEP)—a series of tests and surveys given to a sample of 9-, 13-, and 17-year-olds nationwide every two years—minorities appear to be making test score gains in certain subject areas, but not in others. Despite some improvement in Black student reading proficiency scores since 1971, no such gains were made by Hispanics, whose reading achievement scores remain significantly lower than for Whites. Also, the gap in writing performance between minority and White students remains large (De La Rosa & Maw, 1990). Further, as reported by the NCES (1990a), three out of four Hispanic eighth graders cannot pass a test of simple mathematical operations using decimals or fractions. Hispanic eighth graders are far more likely to score below the basic level than at the advanced level in math. The issue of testing is also problematic for many Hispanics who take the national Scholastic Aptitude Test (SAT) for college-bound students (College Entrance Examinations Board, 1985). SAT scores for Latinos increased steadily (but only slightly) during the 1980s; however, Hispanic math and

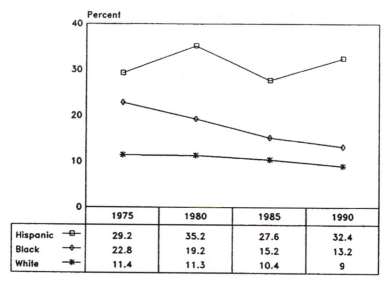

Figure 2.4. High school dropout rates: Percentage of young adults 15–24 without a high school credential (1975–1990).
SOURCE: National Center for Education Statistics (1991).
NOTE: Hispanic rates may vary more than for other groups because of small sample size.

verbal SAT scores continue to lag behind those of their non-Hispanic counterparts. As indicated in Figure 2.5, the gap between the math scores for White and Asian students versus scores for Mexican American, Puerto Rican, and Black students remains large.

Another issue of concern in the educational experience and status of some Hispanic students is limited-English proficiency (LEP) children in the United States—and a significant proportion of those children are Hispanic (De La Rosa, 1991). These numbers are growing in some states; for example, in 1990, California school districts reported that they enrolled 861,531 LEP students, up from 376,794 a decade earlier (De La Rosa, 1991). LEP children present a challenge to policymakers and educators alike; collection of accurate data on English proficiency is crucial. In addition, ensuring that such children receive a quality education that will prepare them for the work force, and that they learn English fluency and maintain their native language, is critical—particularly for the globally competitive work force of the twenty-first century in which a second language will be instrumental to productivity and economic opportunity. Current proposals for increased national standards and testing could have profound implications for the future academic achievement of some Latino students who are limited-English proficient. Those charged with developing a national assessment are considering using an expanded form of NAEP as the model and foundation of this system. However, because a significant proportion of LEP children are omitted from participating in these surveys, the picture that NAEP provides of Latino educational progress is,

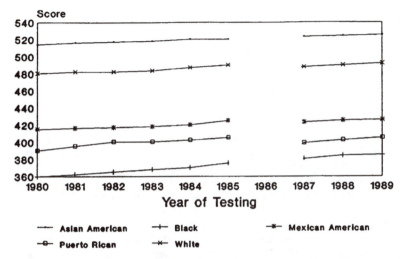

Figure 2.5. Average SAT math scores by race/ethnic group: 1980–1989.[a]
SOURCE: College Entrance Exams Board (1985); De La Rosa & Maw (1990).
a. 1986 data not available.

at best, skewed (De La Rosa, 1991)—thus presenting achievement data that give a more favorable picture than really exists. Without data on LEP students, their educational problems will remain unaddressed and Latino educational status will continue to deteriorate.

Another potential barrier to improved educational status for Latinos involves a recent decision about the use of test scores. Approximately one third of state colleges surveyed expressed their intention to increase testing standards for admissions to technical fields and specialized courses (American Council on Education, 1989, 1990). The raising of standards to levels higher than those achieved by most Hispanic test-takers may further limit Hispanic opportunities for entry into institutions of higher learning.

Latinos also continue to lag behind their non-Latino counterparts in college enrollment and college completion rates. The percentage of Hispanic high school graduates entering college hit a peak in 1976; however, Hispanic enrollment rates have not equaled the 1976 high (over 36%) in any subsequent year (American Council on Education, 1989, 1990). Gains in SAT scores have not been accompanied by gains in college enrollment or in degree attainment. As of October 1988, Hispanic 18- to 19-year-olds comprised only 6.7% of total college enrollment, compared to 9.2% for Blacks and 86.6% for Whites. Hispanic females of the same age cohort enroll in college at higher rates (7.6%) than do Hispanic males of the same age (5.6%). Hispanic females are more likely than males to enroll in college right after high school; however, Hispanic males 20 years old and over have college enrollment rates higher than Hispanic females.

Compared to White high school graduates at all ages, Latino high school graduates continue to have lower rates of college enrollment. Data from the 1988 CPS indicate that 52.9% of Hispanic 18- to 19-year-old high school graduates were enrolled in college, compared to 59.6% of White high school graduates of the same age group. Further, the gap in college enrollment between White and Hispanic students widened between 1976 and 1989. According to the American Council on Education, the enrolled-in-college rate for Hispanic males fell from 39.7% in 1976 to 31.5% in 1988, and plunged further to 27.9% in 1989.[4] The Hispanic female enrolled-in-college rate fell from 33.1% in 1976 to 29.6% in 1989 (American Council on Education, 1989, 1990). In addition, Hispanics who do attend college are heavily concentrated in two-year as opposed to four-year institutions of higher learning. In 1988, the majority (56%) of all Hispanics in higher education were enrolled in two-year institutions, compared with 38% of all students (American Council on Education, 1989, 1990). Hispanic students accounted 7.9% of all students enrolled in two-year colleges, but only 3.6% of those enrolled in four-year institutions.

As noted earlier, as of 1991, college completion for Hispanics remained lower than for Blacks or Whites, with less than 1 in 10 Hispanics over 25 having graduated from college. Only 9.7% of Hispanics 25 years old and over had completed four or more years of college, compared to 22.3% of non-Hispanics. According to the National Education Goals Report (1991), in 1990, only 14% of Hispanic high school graduates ages 25-29 had completed four or more years of college, compared to 16% for Blacks and 27% for Whites (see Figure 2.6). The small proportion of Latino young adults enrolled in institutions of higher learning and completing four years of college is troubling given their growing numbers and their historically undereducated status. It is critical that educational attainment levels of Hispanics—who constitute a significant segment of the population in many cities and states and who will be a major source of workers—increase. Moreover, their participation in rigorous college and university programs will have a direct impact on their ability to assume technical and professional positions in the changing work force of the next century.

Another important issue for the Latino population and the potential competitiveness of the U.S. work force is literacy. An illiterate population can neither work effectively nor participate in a democracy. There is some cause for concern; illiteracy rates for Hispanics are much higher than those for non-Hispanics. By the traditional measure of illiteracy—completion of less than 5 years of schooling—as of 1991, 12.5% of Hispanics 25 years old and over were illiterate, compared to only 1.6% of non-Hispanics. Figures were highest for Mexican Americans, with 15.9% of adults having less than 5 years of education, compared to 8.9% of Central and South Americans, 8.4% of Puerto Ricans, and 7.7% of Cubans. Literacy trend data show that here, too, the gap between Hispanics and non-Hispanics is widening; in 1970, 19.5% of Hispanics, 4.5% of Whites, and 14.6% of Blacks 25 years and over had completed less than 5 years of schooling. In 1989, 12.2% of Hispanics 25 years old and over were illiterate, compared to 2.0% of Whites and 4.8% of Blacks (NCLR, 1992b).

This standard definition of illiteracy does not, however, include the numbers of Hispanics—and other Americans—who have completed higher levels of education but do not have a functional command of literacy and numeracy skills. One survey of functional illiteracy based on tests of reading, writing, and computational skills

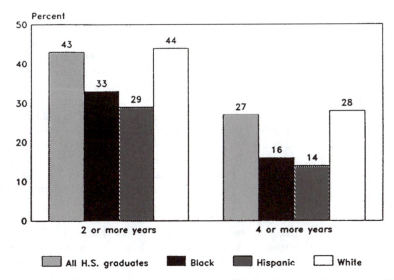

Figure 2.6. College completion: Percentage of high school graduates aged 25–29 who had completed 2 or more years of college (includes junior colleges, community colleges and universities), 1990.
SOURCE: U.S. Department of Commerce, Bureau of the Census (1991b) and National Center for Education Statistics (1991).

found that 56% of Hispanic adults are functionally illiterate in English, compared to 44% for Blacks, and 16% for Whites (Vargas, 1988).

FACTORS AFFECTING THE EDUCATION OF LATINOS

Both the educational status of Latinos and the quality of education they receive are affected by several interrelated factors. These include: poverty; concentration in poor, inner-city, overcrowded, and segregated schools; enrollment below grade level; tracking in nonacademic courses; and limited contact with Hispanic and/or bilingual teachers.

Despite their strong attachment to the paid labor force, Hispanics are two-and-one-half times as likely as non-Hispanics to live in poverty. As a result of their low SES, they tend to live in neighborhoods of concentrated poverty, limited opportunities, and few resources. Moreover, research has shown that children and youth from poor families are more likely than their more advantaged peers to do poorly in school and to be vulnerable to school failure, teenage pregnancy, and other social problems (Children's Defense Fund, 1991; Pérez & Duany, 1992).

Hispanic students are heavily concentrated in urban areas and inner-city schools, which tend to have very limited resources. They are also especially likely to attend overcrowded and segregated schools with few or no Hispanic or bilingual teachers (also, see Chapa & Valencia, 1993; Reyes & Valencia, 1993 for further discussion of Latino school segregation). These urban schools suffer from a limited tax base and must address all the additional problems of the inner city—crime, drugs, a deteriorating infrastructure, and persistent poverty. Further, although school segregation for Blacks has declined during the past decade, increased Latino enrollments and "White flight" from urban school districts have led to the increased segregation of Latino students, and this segregation is the most severe in the largest central-city school districts (Orfield & Monfort, 1988). Moreover findings from a study commissioned by the National School Boards Association indicate that 80% of Hispanic students in the South and Northeast, 71% in the West, and 52% in the Midwest attend schools that are predominantly minority. These findings of de facto segregation, resulting in the isolation of Latinos in low-income areas in major cities, indicate that Hispanics are now far more likely than Blacks to attend segregated schools within big-city school systems.[5]

Attendance in a school with few nonminority students is not the only way that Latino students are segregated. Studies have demonstrated that even within "integrated" schools, Latino students may be segregated by classroom assignment patterns (Orum, 1986; Valencia, 1991; Valencia & Aburto, 1991a). Sometimes special education, English-as-a-second-language (ESL), and bilingual programs are implemented in a way that results in the segregation of Hispanic students even within desegregated schools (see Donato, Menchaca, & Valencia, 1991). Nonacademic tracking also leads to poor educational opportunity for Latino and other minority students. Latinos tend to be disproportionately enrolled in educational "tracks" that prepare students for neither college nor stable employment (NCLR, 1992b). Even among Hispanics who stay in school until their senior year, 75% are enrolled in nonacademic tracks that do not offer the courses, especially in math and science, required to enter college (Orum, 1988).

Enrollment below modal grade also has negative effects on the educational achievement of Latino students. Latino students are more likely than their non-Hispanic counterparts to be held back in school and enrolled below modal grade level (De La Rosa and Maw, 1990). Research indicates that early school failure—or being held back in grade level—is the greatest predictor of later dropping out of school (Orum, 1986). School enrollment data show that at each grade level, a larger percentage of Hispanic children are enrolled below grade level than White or Black children. In 1990, 21.9% of Hispanics 6-8 years old were enrolled below modal grade—and this figure increased to 48.6% for Hispanics aged 15–17 years of age (U.S. Department of Commerce, Bureau of the Census, 1990a). Low Latino participation in Head Start or developmental day care, large classroom sizes with little to no opportunity for individual assistance, and lack of bilingual education and/or language services contribute to this problem.

Finally, there are few bilingual or Hispanic teachers who can act as role models and mentors for Hispanic students (Valencia & Aburto, 1991b; also see Reyes & Valencia, 1993). Although Latino students constituted nearly 10% of the K-12 population, as of 1988, Hispanic teachers were only 2.9% of public- and 2.8% of private-school teachers in U.S. elementary and secondary schools (De La Rosa & Maw, 1990). Studies suggest that because Latinos lack positive role models in their communities, and because so many Hispanic parents have limited education, teachers and other school administrators play a significant role in informing Latino students and their families about educational opportunities and in motivating them to stay in school and pursue a college education. But an analysis of a college board study indicated that Hispanic students receive less career placement assistance than their peers (De La Rosa & Maw, 1990). The paucity of Hispanic educators and school personnel plays a role in the educational experiences of Hispanic students; these findings suggest that an increase in Hispanic school staff would have a positive effect on Hispanic students. However, research points to teacher competency tests as a major obstacle for Latinos attempting to obtain teaching certificates, because of their high failure rates on such tests (Valencia & Aburto, 1991b). Moreover, often Hispanic teachers have fewer credentials than their non-Hispanic counterparts and receive lower salaries. Three out of five (61%) Hispanic public school teachers have only a bachelor's degree, compared to slightly more than half (52%) of non-Hispanic teachers. Further, total earned income and base salaries for Latino teachers are, on average, lower than for non-Latinos (De La Rosa & Maw, 1990).

In sum, several interrelated factors contribute to the poor quality of education that Latinos receive, as well as to the educational crisis within the Latino community. Poverty, low-quality schools, enrollment below grade level, nonacademic tracking, and lack of Hispanic personnel in schools have an impact on the status of Latino education—and play a critical role in the future employability and productivity of the growing Hispanic population. It is important to examine the connection between education and the work force in the context of changing demographics in order to strengthen and expand the opportunities open to Hispanic students and workers. We turn to this subject next.

LABOR FORCE STATUS:
LINKING EDUCATION AND SOCIOECONOMIC STABILITY

Data on the nation's work force are essential to serve the needs of business, labor, Congress, state and local governments, universities, and the general public for research, planning, and economic forecasting. Labor market data are an important indicator of the nation's economic health, and of the economic status of various population groups and specific geographic areas.

The growth rate of the U.S. Hispanic population, like other minority groups, assures that the nation's labor market supply will increasingly be composed of minority workers. But data on the labor market status of Hispanics were not collected regularly by the federal government until 1973 and were not as comprehensive as for other groups until 1977 (Escutia & Prieto, 1987). This data limitation impedes a long-term, comprehensive assessment of the patterns and trends of Hispanics in the labor force; therefore, only data for the past decade will be reviewed. Using these data, this section will examine three variables that help to measure a group's success in the labor market: patterns in employment levels, occupational trends, and earnings levels. These data and analyses reveal that Hispanics have high labor force participation rates, are concentrated in low-wage work vulnerable to labor market changes, have low earnings that are directly related to education levels and occupational status, face high unemployment rates (particularly among certain subgroups), and experience especially high—and disturbing—family and child poverty.

According to the Bureau of Labor Statistics (BLS), there were 9.5 million Hispanics in the labor force in 1991 (U.S. Department of Labor, Bureau of Labor Statistics, 1992). Hispanics accounted for 7.7% of the labor force and are projected to account for 12% of the work force by 2005. In 1991, the proportion of civilians working or looking for work—the labor force participation rate—was about equal among Hispanics and non-Hispanics, 64.7% and 65.3%, respectively (U.S. Department of Commerce, Bureau of the Census, 1991d). Data disaggregated by gender, however, illustrate some differences that have been discussed and analyzed in the literature (Bean & Tienda, 1987). On average, Hispanic men have had consistently higher labor force participation rates than non-Hispanic men. As of 1991, 78.2% of Hispanic men sixteen and older were either working or seeking work, compared to 73.9% of non-Hispanic men. The rate was highest for Central and South American males, at 84.2% and lowest for Puerto Rican males, at 66.4% (see Figure 2.7). By contrast, only about half (52.3%) of Hispanic women were in the labor force in 1991, compared to 57.4% of non-Hispanic women, although, as discussed earlier, this rate is increasing. Among the various Latino subgroups, Central and South American women are the most likely to be employed or actively seeking employment. Puerto Rican women—who have experienced fluctuations in their labor force participation rate over the past decade, as documented in the literature (Bean & Tienda, 1987)—are the least likely to be working or looking for work. Recent Census and demographic data suggest, however, that more women—both Hispanic and non-Hispanic—are entering the U.S. labor force (U.S. Department of Labor, Bureau of Labor Statistics, 1992). Between 1980 and 1991, the number of Hispanic women in the labor force rose by 67% compared with an increase of 23% for non-Hispanic women. Moreover, this increase is due to both a growing Hispanic female population and to an increase in the proportion of Hispanic women entering the labor force (U.S. Department of Labor, Bureau of Labor Statistics, 1992). As later sections will show, these labor force changes have implications for education and training programs, as well as for families, businesses, and public institutions that will have to make accommodations to respond to these changes.

A more accurate measure of the employment status of a group is an examination of employment-population ratios—a factor that is especially important in the context of the growing Hispanic population. This variable measures the proportion of the population that is employed and, over time, indicates the stability of a group's employment. The employment-population ratio is vulnerable to changes in levels of employment and population growth; consequently, employment levels must be maintained at a level comparable to population growth if the employment-population ratio is to remain stable. This ratio is especially critical to measuring the employment level of the Hispanic population, which is experiencing rapid and high rates of growth but, which has not had similar increases in economic and social mobility.

When the increase in numbers of employed Hispanics is less rapid than the pace of their population growth, the employment-population ratio declines. Figure 2.8 illustrates the employment-population ratio for major population groups. With the exception of a slight decrease in the early 1980s, which was most likely a consequence of the recession, the employment-population ratio of Whites has remained relatively stable. This contrasts with the employment-population ratio of both Hispanics and Blacks; it appears that the 1982–1983 recession had a greater impact on both groups

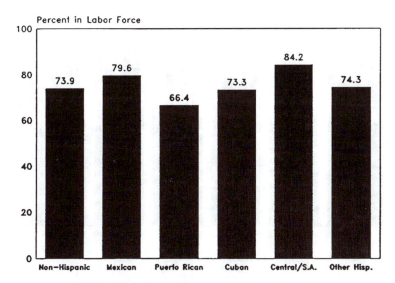

Figure 2.7. Male labor force participation rates 1991.
SOURCE: U.S. Department of Commerce, Bureau of the Census (1991d).

in that they experienced a more marked decline in employment relative to the size of their populations. The strong connection of Hispanics to the labor force has helped their recovery, but the most recent recession, which began in July 1990, has weakened their ability to participate in the work force, relative to their population size and growth.

When employment-population ratios are used, differences in employment status along racial and ethnic lines become clearer. According to the data presented in Figure 2.8, Blacks experience the lowest and Whites the highest levels of employment. The Hispanic employment-population ratio approaches that of Whites, but is lower, even though Hispanics have a higher labor force participation rate than their White counterparts. Whereas Hispanics are more likely to be working or looking for work, Whites are more likely to be employed, relative to their population size.

In examining the link between education and socioeconomic stability and mobility, it is important to review two major issues within labor force status that relate directly to employment. In particular, a closer look at occupational distribution, earnings, and unemployment will give a clearer sense of how labor force status affects poverty and the ability of Hispanics to attain upward mobility and contribute positively to U.S. economic growth.

Despite their high levels of labor force participation, Hispanics continue to be more likely than Whites to be poor and vulnerable to economic instability. Several factors contribute to this depressed SES including employment issues, family structure, discrimination, and reduced commitment and national attention to social and domestic problems. This chapter will examine employment issues in more depth; the following sections will briefly review other factors.

As discussed, Hispanics have made limited gains in economic progress over the

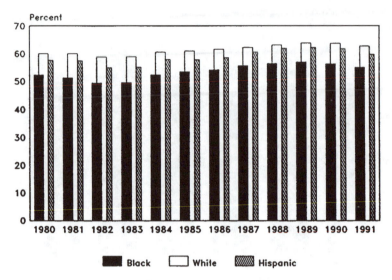

Figure 2.8. Employment-population ratios (1980–1991).
SOURCE: U.S. Dept. of Labor, Bureau of Labor Statistics (1989 and unpublished data).

past decade, but continue to be concentrated in low-skilled, low-wage occupations and experience high rates of unemployment. Table 1.2 in the present article illustrates the occupational distribution of the work force by race/ethnicity and median weekly wages for 1988. The table shows that the Hispanic work force was strikingly underrepresented in managerial/professional occupations; only about one in eight Hispanics (13.2%), compared to slightly more than one in four Whites (26.5%) and more than one in seven Blacks (15.4%) held such jobs in 1988. On the other hand, Hispanics were overrepresented in the occupational category of operators, fabricators, and laborers; almost 23.9% of Hispanics, 14.7% of Whites, and 22.9% of Blacks were employed in these types of jobs that same year. Most Hispanics in this category were employed as machine operators and assemblers. As shown in Table 1.2, Hispanic workers were also more likely than their White counterparts to be employed in the precision production/craft repair industry and less likely than their Black counterparts to work in service occupations.

Data from the March 1991 Current Population Survey (U.S. Department of Commerce, Bureau of the Census, 1991d) also help to illustrate the concentration of Hispanics in low-wage occupations and, in particular, illuminate gender differences. In 1991, slightly more than 1 in 10 Hispanic males (11.4%), compared to more than 1 in 4 non-Hispanic males (27.6%), were employed in managerial and professional jobs, whereas more than 1 in 4 Hispanic men (29.1%), compared to less than 1 in 5 non-Hispanic men (19.1%), worked as operators, fabricators, and laborers. Another 17.1% of Hispanic males worked in service occupations, compared to 9.8% of non-Hispanic males.

Hispanic women are especially concentrated in the lowest-paid jobs. Although the largest proportion of Hispanic women are employed in technical, sales, and administrative support positions (39.8%)—as are women overall—their heavy concentration in service and laborer jobs is markedly larger than that of non-Hispanic women. CPS data show that 15.8% of Hispanic women compared with 28.0% of non-Hispanic women were working in managerial and professional jobs in 1991; 26.2% of Hispanic women compared to 17.0% of non-Hispanic women held service jobs; and 14.0% of Hispanic women compared to 7.6% of non-Hispanic women held jobs as operators, fabricators, and laborers.

As a result of their concentration in low-skill jobs, Hispanic workers earn wages substantially lower than those of non-Hispanics. In 1991, Hispanic men earned a median of $14,141, compared to $22,207 for non-Hispanic men. Mexican American men, among the least-educated of Hispanics overall, had the lowest median earnings ($12,894) whereas Other Hispanic men had the highest median earnings of Hispanic subgroups in 1991 ($18,969) (U.S. Department of Commerce, Bureau of the Census, 1991d). Although Puerto Rican men have a low labor force participation rate, they had relatively high median earnings that year, $18,193. This suggests that their slightly higher levels of education—relative to Mexican men, for example—combined with citizenship status and other factors (e.g., language fluency) affect employment opportunities and earnings.

The median annual earnings of working Hispanic women in 1990 were $10,099, compared to $12,436 for non-Hispanic women. Among subgroups, Mexican American women earned the least ($9,286) and Cuban women the most ($12,904). When earnings of individuals are placed within the context of family income, data continue to show discrepancies. Recent data show that the income gap between Hispanics and Whites is not narrowing. Analyses of Census data indicate that in 1990, White median family income was $38,468, Hispanic family income $24,417, and Black family income $22,325. Moreover, Hispanic median family income, as a proportion of White median family income, has been steadily decreasing since the 1970s (Mishel & Frankell, 1991).

Both educational attainment and occupational distribution affect earning levels and poverty. Workers in jobs that require higher levels of educational attainment, such as professional and managerial positions, enjoy higher earnings than those in unskilled occupations, as previously illustrated in Table 2.2. The table also shows that the 1988 median weekly earnings for occupational categories in which Hispanics were overrepresented, such as operator/fabricator/laborer, were low; they totaled just $313 in 1988. By contrast, the highest-paid occupations—the jobs in which Hispanics were least represented—include managerial and professional specialties with median weekly earnings of $552.

The concentration of Hispanics in low-wage, low-skill work often means that Hispanics face a high risk of unemployment because this work is unstable during times of economic recession. In addition, a lack of skills that are transferable from one industry to another, coupled with low levels of educational attainment, prevent Hispanics from qualifying for work that may be available in other, high-skill industries. This is especially true as the United States experiences rapid economic change.

As a result of education and skill levels, unemployment continues to be a serious problem facing Hispanic workers. Over the past decade, Hispanics faced severe unemployment—with a high of 13.7% at the peak of the recession in 1983 and a similarly high rate currently (see Figure 2.1). Double-digit unemployment rates have

Table 2.3. 1991 Annual Unemployment Rate (in Percentages): 10 States with the Largest Hispanic-Origin Population

	Unemployment Rates	
	Hispanics	Total Population
Arizona	8.0	5.7
California	11.4	7.5
Colorado	6.7	5.0
Florida	9.0	7.3
Illinois	9.9	7.1
Massachusetts	16.5	9.0
New Jersey	9.0	6.6
New Mexico	8.4	6.9
New York	10.4	7.2
Texas	8.6	6.6
United States	11.9	7.7

SOURCE: U.S. Department of Labor, Bureau of Labor Statistics (unpublished data).

been experienced by both the Black and Hispanic communities for the last 10 years. In particular, Hispanic women and Puerto Ricans have had troubling unemployment rates; CPS data show that 9.2% of Hispanic women and 10.3% of Puerto Ricans were unemployed in 1991. Additional data available by state show that 9 of the 10 states with the largest proportion of Hispanics, as a percentage of the state's total population, had Hispanic unemployment rates higher than the 1992 national unemployment rate of 8.2% (see Table 2.3).

There are two additional concerns with unemployment in the Hispanic population. First, official unemployment data do not capture the complete picture as they fail to account for discouraged workers and those working part-time because they cannot find full-time jobs. Second, unemployment insurance—one program of the public safety net available to U.S. workers—does not offer a cushion to Hispanics in the way that it does to non-Hispanic workers. Analyses by the Center on Budget and Policy Priorities (Nichols, Shapiro, & Greenstein, 1991) show that Hispanics are less likely to receive unemployment insurance because of a variety of factors, including employment patterns in seasonal work, and policy and administrative decisions made by state unemployment agencies.

As a result of their low educational attainment levels and tenuous economic and labor market position, Hispanics are more likely than Whites and less likely than Blacks to be poor; although, among Latino subgroups, Puerto Ricans have a poverty rate comparable to, and in some cases exceeding that, of Blacks. As Figure 2.9 shows, between 1980 and 1990, poverty rates have varied among Hispanics, Blacks, and Whites in the United States. Trend data show the sharpest fluctuations occurring among Hispanics and Blacks, whereas the poverty rate for Whites has remained fairly level, at an average of 11%. In the early part of the decade, poverty rates increased slightly for both Whites and Blacks but rose sharply for Hispanics. During

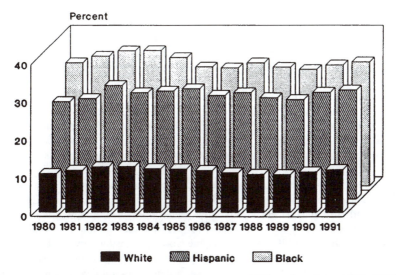

Figure 2.9. Persons below poverty level by race and Hispanic origin: 1980–1991. *SOURCE:* U.S. Department of Commerce, Bureau of the Census (1992a).

the mid-1980s, as the nation began the process of economic recovery from the recession, both Whites and Blacks began to experience decreases in poverty; for Hispanics, however, the poverty rate increased between 1983 and 1985. By 1987, after the rate for Hispanics had fallen slightly, it increased again—as it did for Blacks— although the White poverty rate continued to decrease. The decade ended with all groups experiencing increases in poverty; children were especially likely to be poor among Hispanics, Whites, and Blacks (U.S. Department of Commerce, Bureau of the Census, 1992a).

The growth and persistence of Latino family and child poverty is especially troubling given that Hispanic males have the highest labor force participation rate of any major population group and that the proportion of Hispanic women working or looking for work has been increasing over the past decade. As a result, Latinos are overrepresented among the "working poor," individuals who work but whose earnings are below the official poverty level. Census Bureau data show that one in five Hispanic householders (20.8%) compared to 7.1% of White householders and 14.3% of Black householders in married-couple families with children were poor in 1990. Further, in that same year over half of Hispanics (57.5%) had individual incomes below 200% of the poverty line ($13,600), compared to 55.3% of Blacks and 28.8% of Whites.

ANALYSIS

Education is the most important determinant of any individual's future earnings. As our previous discussion has shown, income and earnings—and economic stability and mobility—vary substantially according to educational attainment. High school graduates have higher incomes and earnings, and are more likely to be employed than those who dropped out of school (also, see Rumberger, 1991, for a discussion of the economic consequences of dropping out of high school). Similarly, income and earnings for persons with college and professional degrees are higher than for those who are high school graduates only. In sum, there is a direct relation between educational attainment and SES. This relation is especially crucial in understanding the current social and economic position of Latinos in the United States. It is also significant within the context of rapid Latino population growth and the deterioration of their labor market position, and critical in formulating appropriate policy responses to address the impact of undereducated and underskilled Hispanics on the economy in the next century.

As the preceding sections have illustrated, Hispanics as a group have lower levels of educational attainment than Whites or Blacks. These attainment differences contribute to Hispanic concentration in low-wage employment and high rates of unemployment and poverty among Hispanic workers and their families. An analysis by Miranda and Quiroz (1990) underscores the close association between low educational attainment, low incomes, and high poverty. In 1988, Hispanic householders with less than four years of high school had a median household income of $14,496, compared to Hispanic householders with four years of high school or some college, whose median income was $25,282. A Hispanic householder who completed four years of college had a median income of $38,140 (see Figure 2.10). Additional data from the Census Bureau show that Hispanic median income in 1988 increased with the number of college years completed, from $17,930 for those completing one to three years of college, to $34,567 for Latinos completing five or more years of college. However, the median income gap between Whites and Hispanics at all levels of educational attainment persists (U.S. Department of Commerce, Bureau of the Census, 1991b). Moreover, the gap is especially marked when family size is considered; because Hispanics, on average, have slightly larger families than non-Hispanics (3.80 versus 3.13 persons, respectively) this income is used to support and maintain more individuals (see Chapa & Valencia, 1993, for within-Latino subgroup differences in family size).

Education is highly regarded as the social and economic equalizer, and as a prerequisite to improving the social and economic status of Latinos. Therefore, the effects of undereducation among Hispanics—and the costs to society as a result—are great. First, Hispanics with low levels of educational attainment face poor economic outcomes. They are limited to low-skilled work in industries that are rapidly declining as the U.S. economy shifts from a manufacturing to a service base. The effects of this mismatch between worker skills and available employment will become more profound as the next century approaches. Moreover, as a result of inadequate human capital characteristics and a lack of skills that are easily transferable from one sector of the economy to another, Hispanics suffer from higher unemployment levels than Whites. As analysis of trend data show, Hispanics' recovery during times of economic recession are slower than that of their non-Hispanic counterparts; in fact, during the mid-1980s Hispanics were the only major racial/ethnic group to experience no improvement in their SES when other groups experienced at least moderate gains (Miranda & Quiroz, 1990).

Second, the economic costs of dropping out of school for Latinos and society as

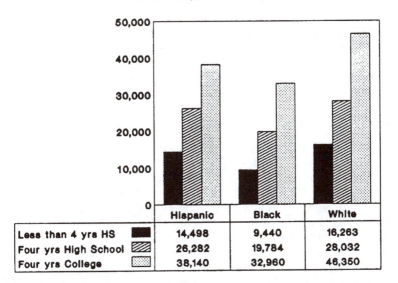

	Hispanic	Black	White
Less than 4 yrs HS ■	14,498	9,440	16,263
Four yrs High School ▨	26,282	19,784	28,032
Four yrs College ▨	38,140	32,960	46,350

Figure 2.10. Median annual income by educational attainment of householder, by race/ethnicity (1988).
SOURCE: U.S. Department of Commerce, Bureau of the Census (1991d).

a whole are immense, due to higher unemployment rates and lower earnings of high school dropouts compared to high school graduates (Rumberger, 1991). For example, as of October 1985, the unemployment rate for 1984-85 high school dropouts was 35.6%, compared to 24.6% for high school graduates not enrolled in college. Further, the median income for male high school dropouts 25 years old and over in 1986 was about 32% lower ($13,401) than for male high school graduates ($19,772) of the same age cohort. That year, female high school dropouts of the same age cohort had a median income of $5,831, compared to $8,366 for female high school graduates. By one recent estimate, the economic costs of persons dropping out of school has been estimated at more than $200,000 per person over a lifetime and more than $200 billion for a one-year cohort of dropouts (Rumberger, 1991). Further, one comprehensive study (Levin, 1972; cited in Rumberger, 1991) identifies seven social consequences of dropping out: forgone national income, forgone tax revenue for the support of government services, increased demand for social services, increased crime, reduced political participation, reduced intergenerational mobility, and poorer levels of health.

But investments in education and increases in educational attainment alone would not proportionately reduce Hispanic poverty or improve Hispanic SES because education is not the only factor that influences and affects the economic position of Latinos in the labor force. In addition to educational attainment and human capital characteristics, several other factors are associated with the poor labor market position of Latino workers: discrimination, quality of education, poverty and its consequences, family structure, and the lack of national response and attention to these issues (see Pearl, 1991, for a discussion of systemic and institutional factors that help shape school failure).

Inequality and lower returns to education due to discrimination in the labor market remain significant obstacles to many Hispanics. Although there continue to be questions about the extent to which discrimination against Hispanics explains earnings and occupational distribution, there is considerable evidence to support the finding that Hispanics suffer from substantial levels of discrimination in education and employment. Recent studies show that Hispanics are now more segregated than Blacks in inner-city schools; the General Accounting Office (GAO) has reported very high rates of employment discrimination associated with the employer sanctions provisions of the Immigration Reform and Control Act (IRCA); and a recent study issued by the U.S. Department of Housing and Urban Development (HUD) found that Hispanic home seekers, both buyers and renters, experienced discriminatory treatment in at least 50% of their encounters with sales and rental agents.[6]

Further research supports these findings. In a study discussed and documented by Reimers (1985), analyses showed that "discrimination in the labor market may be responsible for a wage differential, compared to non-Hispanic white men, of 18% for Puerto Rican men . . . , 12% for Other Hispanic men . . . and 6% for Mexican men" (Reimers, 1985, p. 55). Additional studies examining the disparity in earnings and income among Hispanics and non-Hispanic Whites between 1982 and 1990 reveal that the percentage of the income gap between Hispanic males and non-Hispanic White males that is attributable to employment discrimination falls within a 10%-18% range; moreover, the percentage of the Hispanic female versus the non-Hispanic White male income gap attributable to discrimination falls within a 30%-40% range (Carnoy et al., 1990). Additional research by Torres and de la Torre (1991) discuss the impact of Hispanic employment discrimination on labor force status. Meléndez, Rodríguez, and Barry Figueroa (1991) underscore the role that discrimination plays in accounting for wage discrepancies as well as occupational distribution. Finally, Torres (1992) analyzes discrimination faced by U.S.-born and island-born Puerto Ricans. His findings are striking; the analysis shows that the dollar estimate of discrimination ranges from a low of $1,519 for U.S.-born Puerto Rican males to a high of $8,886 for island-born Puerto Rican females.

The issue of educational quality is another factor that contributes to the labor market position of Latinos in the United States; however, because of an exclusive focus on increasing educational attainment levels as the key to improving Hispanic SES, the issue of quality has been understated and ignored. But it is important and relevant to acknowledge that for many Hispanic students, completion of high school is not sufficient for employment. For others, it may not even be a guarantee of adequate literacy and numeracy skills. Among other factors and issues described above, increasing school segregation and disparities in school financing systems combine to produce a second-class education for some Latinos who complete high school. Research has also shown that segregated schools tend to lack the resources to provide students with a competitive education; that the curriculum in predominantly minority schools tends to be away from advanced-level work and toward low-level work; and that teachers in such schools have less education and experience than their colleagues in predominantly White schools (Donato, Menchaca, & Valencia, 1991; Duany & Pittman, 1990). Moreover, De La Rosa and Maw (1990) documented that Latinos complete fewer "Carnegie units" and fewer advanced math, science, computer, and English courses than White Americans, and are more often "tracked" into nonacademic courses that make access to college difficult. For many Hispanics, the poor quality of education is confirmed by research that shows Hispanics receive the lowest economic return for every year of school completed (Miranda & Quiroz, 1990).

Another issue that is both a consequence of and a contributing factor to the unstable labor market position of Hispanics is poverty. Because of their educational and work force status, Latinos are more likely than non-Latinos to be poor. But, this low SES also translates into limited educational and economic opportunities, poor housing conditions, and concentration in segregated and often unsafe neighborhoods. This leads, in part, to behavior and actions that may perpetuate this poverty. For example, research shows that a Latina adolescent (age 16-19 years), with below-average basic academic skills, and from a poor family is four times as likely to become a teen mother as her counterpart with above-average skills from a family whose income is above the poverty level. It is well documented that teen births, especially among minorities, contribute to mothers' dropping out of school, single-parent families, economic instability, and extremely high poverty rates (Pérez & Duany, 1992).

Family structure and the poverty associated especially with single-parent families also contribute to the overall low SES of the U.S. Latino population. It is also a factor associated with poor educational experiences (De La Rosa & Maw 1990). In 1990, almost one-quarter of Hispanic families were female-headed and these families were especially likely to be poor; children who grow up in female-headed families often face high poverty, myriad social problems, and few educational or other opportunities. Although the great majority of single-parent Hispanic families are headed by women, an increasing number are now maintained by men alone. As the number of single-parent families in all groups continues to rise, the educational and economic arenas will have to respond to help adequately prepare children from such families for future employment.

Finally, immigration is an additional factor that is not principally related to education and labor force, but nevertheless has an impact on both. Recent high levels of immigration contribute to, but are not principally responsible for, Latinos' low educational attainment levels and work force performance. With respect to education, for example, one recent analysis shows that perhaps one third of the differential dropout rate between Hispanics and non-Hispanics between the ages 16 and 24 is attributable to Latino immigrants' relatively higher dropout rate (National Center for Education Statistics, 1992). Put another way, even if Hispanic immigrants were removed from the data entirely, Latino dropout rates would still be twice as high as those of non-Latinos. This finding is consistent with the previous work of Chapa (1988, 1989) and Bean, Chapa, Berg, and Sowards (1991) that demonstrates that by the third generation the educational attainment gap between Mexican Americans and the general population remains essentially constant.

There is some evidence that the large proportion of immigrants in the Latino population has both direct and indirect effects on Hispanic work force performance data. The data demonstrate that recent Latino immigrants, in general, have lower incomes than their native-born Latino counterparts (Borjas, 1987, 1990; NCLR, 1990). Because about one third of all Hispanics are foreign-born, the presence of immigrants has a depressing effect on measurements of Latino poverty. However, as is the case with educational attainment rates, these effects are relatively minor; aggregate Hispanic poverty rates would still be twice as high as those of non-Hispanic Whites even if immigrants were removed from the data entirely (Miranda, 1991; NCLR, 1990).

Moreover, the presence of immigrants may be having some direct, negative effects on the employment and wages of native-born Latinos. Although most credible observers have concluded that immigrants provide net, positive gains for the economy overall (Greenwood, 1983; McCarthy & Burciaga Valdez, 1986; Muller & Espenshade, 1985; Simon, 1989; U.S. Department of Labor, Council of Economic Advisors, 1986) and do not negatively affect groups like African Americans (Borjas, 1987; McCarthy & Burciaga Valdez, 1986; Muller & Espenshade, 1985; Reischauer, 1989), the data with respect to the effects of immigrants on native-born Hispanics is less clear. Theoretically, it is reasonable to expect that recent immigrants would tend to compete in the labor market with first- and second-generation workers of the same ethnicity (Grossman, 1982). Empirically, the data suggest that wage growth in immigrant-dominated industries is lower than in those in which immigrants are not present (McCarthy & Burciaga Valdez, 1986; Muller & Espenshade, 1985). These lower average wages, however, may reflect changes in the work force composition or industrial restructuring unrelated to immigration; in any event, there is no persuasive empirical evidence that immigration is a principal or even major cause of Hispanic poverty or poor labor force performance (NCLR, 1990).

CONCLUSIONS AND POLICY IMPLICATIONS

Developing and implementing effective initiatives to improve the economic status of Hispanics will require action on many fronts. As demonstrated in this article, the undereducation of Latinos is directly and unequivocally linked to this population's subsequent labor force performance and economic status. But as the data cited above also suggest, educational attainment is not the only determinant of the Hispanic community's economic condition. Thus improving the labor force performance and economic status of Latinos will require policy intervention both within and outside the educational sphere.

Establishing the substantive basis for effective education and labor market policy interventions will require a new research and policy analysis agenda. Over the last two decades, most of the Latino-focused research and policy analysis on education and labor force issues has been principally descriptive in nature. At that time, the Census had just begun counting Hispanics as a distinct group and few national, state, and local data bases included Latino subsamples. As a result, the Hispanic population was virtually "invisible" in public policy debates at the time. Thus the first generation of Latino research in the field focused on documenting needs and calling attention to problems; such a focus was clearly appropriate at that time and the need for such efforts continues today.

In the late 1970s and early 1980s, a second generation of research and policy analysis focused on educational segregation and discrimination, bilingual education, and the importance of addressing language issues in order to improve Hispanic labor market performance. This wave of research and policy analysis complemented a Latino-focused "rights" agenda promoted by the principal Hispanic advocacy organizations. As the data cited in this article demonstrate, such issues remain salient at the present time. However, we believe that, in addition to descriptive analyses and the promotion of a "rights" agenda in education and the labor market, future Hispanic research and policy analysis efforts should be simultaneously more focused and more expansive (Valencia, 1991, in his volume *Chicano School Failure and Success: Research and Policy Agendas for the 1990s*, makes a very similar argument). They should be more focused in the sense that descriptive analyses should be accompanied by greater attention to specific policy and program changes (e.g., "what works" analyses) that will directly improve Latinos' educational attainment and labor market performance. They should also be broader in that issues outside the "rights" sphere should also be examined, such as the effects of macroeconomic policy changes on Latinos. Consistent with these themes, we suggest below some general and specific directions for researchers, policy analysts, and advocates.

Educational attainment is the single most important determinant of Hispanics' economic status. Notwithstanding the recognition that educational improvements alone will not result in equal economic status for Latinos, the data reveal that such improvements are an absolute prerequisite for substantial progress in the labor market. Although proscribing specific policy options is outside the scope of this brief analysis, the authors believe that researchers and advocates need to begin to focus more clearly on identifying specific solutions in addition to documenting the scope of the problem. The authors suggest three specific areas of policy focus within the area of education.

First, researchers, policy analysts, and advocates should begin the task of formulating a Hispanic education policy agenda. Most analyses of Hispanic education, including this one, tend to be descriptive rather than prescriptive; that is, they tend to focus on documenting the dimensions of the problem rather than proffering a specific policy agenda for addressing the problem. Even those efforts that address specific programs and policies tend to be limited to single subjects (e.g., bilingual education), or critiquing major proposals offered by others from a Latino perspective. Based on our knowledge, there has been no major, comprehensive effort designed to develop a coherent set of policy proposals from Hispanics and for Hispanics; such an effort is badly needed. This effort should rigorously weigh specific policy options and identify those with the greatest potential for improving Latino educational outcomes. The result should not simply be a "laundry list"; rather, it should lay out a Latino-specific policy agenda based on empirical program evaluation data and pedagogical research.

Second, researchers, policy analysts, and advocates involved in the school reform movement should focus greater attention on "outcome" rather than "process" issues. Much of the school reform debate centers on "process" issues that propose major changes in school financing and placement (e.g., school "choice," structural and organizational changes such as school-based management, and so on). These issues are clearly important and may have significant effect on Hispanic educational attainment (for a critique, however, see Reyes and Valencia, 1993). However, all so-called "process" proposals purport to lead eventually to changes at the classroom level in the way that teachers and students interact; unfortunately, there is a paucity of rigorous research on the specific types of classroom-level changes that would have the greatest beneficial effect on Latino educational outcomes. We believe that the next generation of Hispanic-focused educational research should fill this gap.

Third, policymakers and advocates should work to promote school finance reform. There is a broad emerging consensus that, in order to be effective, pedagogical and structural reforms must be accompanied by increased investments in education. Because Latinos tend to be enrolled in low-income inner-city or rural school districts, Hispanics have much to gain from targeted increases in educational investments at the federal level and/or more equitable school financing formulas at the state level. Although increases in educational resources may not automatically translate into improvements in educational outcomes for Hispanics, improvements in educational attainment and quality for Hispanics do not appear to be achievable in the absence of increased resources. A focus on education will have a direct impact on the human capital characteristics of Latinos and their ability to compete in the changing U.S. economy. Improvements in Hispanic educational outcomes alone, however, cannot fully address Latino labor market problems. Notwithstanding the crucial role played by education as a determinant in Hispanic labor market performance and economic status, at least three other issues need to be addressed.

First, researchers, policy analysts, and advocates should identify and promote specific programs and policies that can reduce labor market discrimination against Latinos. The lower returns to education experienced by Hispanics infers the existence of significant labor market discrimination; this inference has been confirmed both by residual labor market research and empirical "testing" studies. Analyses by NCLR, however, have demonstrated that existing civil rights enforcement programs and policies are remarkably ineffective in protecting Hispanics from discrimination (Gonzales, in press). Moreover, with the exception of some recent work on employment "testing" studies (General Accounting Office, March, 1990), relatively little attention has been paid by Hispanics and others within the mainstream civil rights community to identifying and developing more effective enforcement methods. Latino researchers and policy analysts should help fill this gap.

Second, researchers, policy analysts, and advocates should identify and promote more effective programs and policies to serve Hispanic adults and out-of-school youth. Even if educational outcomes were immediately and substantially improved, the significant number of Latino adults and out-of-school youth who have marginal skills would remain unaffected. In some cases where the state-of-the-art is well developed (e.g., facilitating English speaking and writing skills), increasing human capital skills is principally a question of targeting sufficient resources to the Hispanic population. In other cases, Hispanics are severely and possibly systematically underserved by existing efforts (e.g., job training and Job Corps programs). Improvements will require both greater resource investments and greater equity in resource allocations. In still other cases, integrating certain disadvantaged populations (e.g., welfare recipients, substance abusers, or gang members) into the labor force, effective interventions remain somewhat elusive or unclear. We contend that significant improvements in Latino economic status will require the development and implementation of effective policies and programs to serve these groups.

Third, researchers and policy analysts should begin to assess macroeconomic policy issues from a Hispanic perspective. Every analysis of Hispanic labor market performance, including this one, notes the severe, negative effects that economic restructuring has had on low-wage workers in general and Hispanic workers in particular. Yet, with the notable exception of the current debate over the North American Free Trade Agreement (NAFTA), Latinos are vitually absent from discussion on macroeconomic policy issues (e.g., tax policy or proposals to reduce the federal deficit).[7] Over the next decade, Hispanic researchers and policy analysts should begin to engage these issues.

In conclusion, as the nation enters the twenty-first century, reducing educational and economic inequality between Hispanics and the rest of society has become not just a moral preference but an economic imperative. Latinos will constitute about one fifth of labor force growth between now and the end of the century, as well as a growing proportion of taxpayers supporting Social Security, Medicare, and other transfer payment systems needed to support an aging society. An undereducated, undertrained, and underemployed work force will not only retard the nation's economic output, but will also increase the demand for public assistance and diminish the tax base necessary to support essential government services. Improving the Hispanic community's human capital characteristics—and its economic standing—clearly serves the economic interests of the nation. We believe that Latino researchers and policy analysts can and must play a significant role both in persuading the body politic to act, and in shaping the nation's future education and labor force public policy agenda.

NOTES

1. The terms Hispanic and Latino are used interchangeably throughout this article to refer collectively to Mexican Americans, Puerto Ricans, Cubans, Central Americans, South Americans, and Other Hispanics, those from the Dominican Republic, Spain, or of Spanish-speaking origin. When statistics are cited, there is no difference between the use of the term Latino and the Census's use of the term Hispanic.

2. This section is adapted from chapters 3, 5, and 6 in De La Rosa and Maw (1990).

3. For more details see NCES (1991). The most commonly used measure is the status dropout rate, which "measure(s) the proportion of the population who have not completed high school and are not enrolled at one point in time, regardless of when they dropped out. [Event dropout rates] measure the proportion of students who drop out in a single year without completing high school. [Cohort dropout rates] measure what happens to a single group (or cohort) of students over a period of time" (p. v).

4. "Enrolled in college" is defined as the percentage of high school graduates who are actually enrolled in college in October of a given year.

5. See National Council of La Raza (1992b, p. 27).

6. For more information, see the Civil Rights chapter of National Council of La Raza (1992b).

7. Some Latino organizations have played a role in tax policy debates. For example, NCLR supported the Tax Reform Act of 1986, which removed hundreds of millions of low-income persons from the tax rolls; supported the 1989 expansion of the Earned Income Credit, which provides up to $2,000 to lower-income working families with children; and supported the establishment of a refundable children's tax credit in the 1992 tax bill that was ultimately vetoed and not enacted. Notwithstanding these exceptions, NAFTA is perhaps the only example of a major macroeconomic policy issue in which Hispanics have played a prominent, highly visible role.

REFERENCES

American Council on Education. (1988). *One third of a nation: A report of the commission on minority participation in education and American life.* Washington, DC: American Council on Education.

American Council on Education. (1989). *Minorities in higher education: Eighth annual status report,* 1989 (Office of Minorities in Higher Education [formerly Office of Minority Concerns]). Washington, DC: American Council on Education.

American Council on Education. (1990). *Minorities in higher education: Ninth annual status report 1990* (Office of Minorities in Higher Education [formerly Office of Minority Concerns]). Washington, DC: American Council on Education.

Bean, F., Chapa, J., Berg, R., & Sowards, K. (1991, June). *Educational and sociodemographic incorporation among Hispanic immigrants to the United States.* Paper prepared for a conference on Immigrants in the 1990s. Washington, DC: The Urban Institute.

Bean, F., & Tienda, M. (1987). *The Hispanic population in the United States.* New York: Russell Sage.

Borjas, G. (1987). Immigration, minorities, and labor market competition. *Industrial Labor Relations Review,* 40, 383–392.

Borjas, G. (1990). *Friends or strangers: The impact of immigrants on the U.S. economy.* New York: Basic Books.

Carnoy, M., Daley, H., & Hinojosa Ojeda, R. (1990). *Latinos in a changing U.S. economy: Comparative perspectives on the U.S. labor market since 1939.* New York: Research Foundation of the City University of New York.

Chapa, J. (1988). The question of Mexican American assimilation: Socioeconomic parity or underclass formation? *Public Affairs Comment,* 35, 1–14.

Chapa, J. (1989). The myth of Hispanic progress: Trends in the educational and economic attainment of Mexican Americans. *Journal of Hispanic Policy,* 4, 3–18.

Chapa, J., & Valencia, R. R. (1993). Latino population growth, demographic characteristics, and educational stagnation: An examination of recent trends. *Hispanic Journal of Behavioral Sciences,* 15, 165–187.

Children's Defense Fund. (1991). *The state of America's children.* Washington, DC: Author.

College Entrance Examination Board. (1985). *Profile, college-bound seniors.* Princeton, NJ: Author.

De La Rosa, D. (1991). Education reform is creating a "leper" colony. *Hispanic Link Weekly Report,* 9, 4.

De La Rosa, D., & Maw, C. (1990). *Hispanic education: A statistical portrait 1990.* Washington, DC: National Council of La Raza.

Donato, R., Menchaca, M., & Valencia, R. R. (1991). Segregation, desegregation, and integration of Chicano students: Problems and prospects. In R. R. Valencia (Ed.), *Chicano school failure and success: Research and policy agendas for the 1990s* (The Stanford Series on Education and Public Policy, pp. 27–63). Basingstoke, England: Falmer Press.

Duany, L., & Pittman, K. (1990). *Latino youths at a crossroads.* Washington, DC: Children's Defense Fund.

Escutia, M., & Prieto, M. (1987). *Hispanics in the work force, part 1.* Washington, DC: National Council of La Raza.

General Accounting Office. (1990, March). *Immigration reform, employer sanctions and the question of discrimination.* Washington, DC: U.S. General Accounting Office.

Gonzales, C.(in press). *The empty promise: Civil rights enforcement and Hispanics.* Washington, DC: National Council of La Raza.

Greenstein, R., Porter, K., Shapiro, I., Leonard, P., & Barancik, S. (1988). *Shortchanged: Recent developments in Hispanic poverty, income and employment.* Washington, DC: Center on Budget and Policy Priorities.

Greenwood, M. J. (1983). Regional economic aspects of immigrant location patterns in the United States. In M. M. Kritz (Ed.), *U.S. immigration and refugee policy* (pp. 233–247). Lexington, MA: D.C. Heath.

Grossman, J. B. (1982). The substitutability of natives and immigrants in production. *Review of Economics and Statistics, 64,* 596–603.

Hudson Institute. (1987). *Workforce 2000: Work and workers for the 21st century.* Indianapolis, IN: Author.

Kirsch, I. S., & Jungeblut, A. (1986). *Literacy: Profiles of America's young adults, national assessment of educational progress,* Report 16–Pl-01. Princeton, NJ: Educational Testing Service.

Macías, R. F. (1993). Language and ethnic classification of language minorities: Chicano and Latino students in the 1990s. *Hispanic Journal of Behavioral Sciences, 15,* 230–257.

Martínez, D. (1992). Recession results in welfare and food stamps caseload growth, increases in unemployment. *NCLR Poverty Project Newsletter, 4,* 4.

McCarthy, K. F., & Burciaga Valdez, R. (1986). *Current and future effects of Mexican immigration to California.* Santa Monica, CA: Rand.

Meléndez, E., Rodríguez, C., & Barry Figueroa, J. (Eds.). (1991). *Hispanics in the labor force: issues and policies.* New York: Plenum.

Miller, S. M., Nicolau, S., Orr, M. T., Valdivieso, R., & Walker, G. (1988). *Too late to patch: Reconsidering second-chance opportunities for Hispanic and other dropouts.* New York: Hispanic Policy Development Project.

Miranda, L. (1991). *Latino child poverty in the United States.* Washington, DC: Children's Defense Fund.

Miranda, L., & Quiroz, J. (1990). *The decade of the Hispanic: An economic retrospective.* Washington, DC: National Council of La Raza.

Mishel L, & Frankell, D. (1991). *The state of working America: 1990–1991.* Washington, DC: M. E. Sharpe.

Muller, T., & Espenshade, T. (1985). *The fourth wave, California's newest immigrants.* Washington, DC: National Council of La Raza.

National Center for Education Statistics. (1990a). *The condition of education 1990: Vol. 1. Elementary and secondary education.* Washington, DC: U.S. Department of Education, Office of Educational Research and Improvement.

National Center for Education Statistics. (1990b). *National education longitudinal study, a profile of the American eighth grade: NELS: 88 student descriptive summary, NCES 90–458.* Washington, DC: U.S. Department of Education, Office of Educational Research and Improvement.

National Center for Education Statistics. (1991). *Dropout rates in the United States: 1990, Office of Educational Research and Improvement, NCES 91–053.* Washington, DC: U.S Department of Education.

National Center for Education Statistics. (1992, August). Are Hispanic dropout rates related to migration? *Issue Brief.* Washington, DC: U.S. Department of Education, Office of Educational Research and Improvement.

National Council of La Raza. (1990, April). *Hispanic poverty: How much does immigration explain?* Washington, DC: Author.

National Council of La Raza. (1992a). *Hispanics and health insurance: Vol. I. Status.* Washington, DC: Author.

National Council of La Raza. (1992b). *State of Hispanic America 1991: An overview.* Washington, DC: Author.

The National Education Goals Report. (1991). *Building a nation of learners*. Washington, DC: National Education Goals Panel.

Nichols, M. E., Shapiro, I., & Greenstein, R. (1991). *Unemployment insurance in states with large Hispanic populations*. Washington, DC: Center on Budget and Policy Priorities.

Orfield, G., & Monfort, F. (1988). *Racial change and desegregation in large school districts: Trends through the 1986–87 school year*. Chicago: Council of Urban Boards of Education and the National School Desegregation Project.

Orum. L. S. (1986). *The education of Hispanics: Status and implications*. Washington, DC: National Council of La Raza.

Orum, L. S. (1988). *Making education work for Hispanic Americans: Some promising community-based practices*. Washington, DC: National Council of La Raza.

Pearl, A. (1991). Systemic and institutional factors in Chicano school failure. In R. R. Valencia (Ed.), *Chicano school failure and success: Research and policy agendas for the 1990s* (The Stanford Series on Education and Public policy, pp. 272–320). Basingstoke, England: Falmer Press.

Pérez, S. M., & Duany, L. (1992). *Reducing Hispanic teenage and family poverty: A replication guide*. Washington, DC: National Council of La Raza.

Reimers, C. W. (1985). A comparative analysis of the wages of Hispanics, Blacks, and non-Hispanic Whites. In G. J. Borjas & M. Tienda (Eds.), *Hispanics in the U.S. economy* (pp. 27–75). Orlando, FL: Academic Press.

Reischauer, R. (1989). Immigration and the underclass. *Annals of the American Academy of Political and Social Science, 501*, 120–131.

Reyes, P., & Valencia, R. R. (1993). Educational policy and the growing Latino student population: Problems and prospects. *Hispanic Journal of Behavioral Sciences, 15*, 258–283.

Rumberger, R. W. (1991). Chicano dropouts: A review of research and policy issues. In R. R. Valencia (Ed.), *Chicano school failure and success: Research and policy agendas for the 1990s* (The Stanford Series on Education and Public Policy, pp. 64–89). Basingstoke, England: Falmer Press.

Simon, J. L. (1989). *The economic consequences of immigration*. Cambridge, MA: Basil Blackwell.

Torres, A. (1992). Nativity, gender, and earnings discrimination. *Hispanic Journal of Behavioral Sciences, 14*, 134–142.

Torres, R. D., & de la Torre, A. (1991). Latinos, class, and one U.S. political economy: Income inequality and policy perspectives. In E. Meléndez, C. Rodríguez, & J. Barry Figueroa (Eds.). *Hispanics in the labor force: Issues and policies* (pp. 265–287). New York: Plenum.

U.S. Department of Commerce, Bureau of the Census. (1986). *Projections of the Hispanic population: 1983–2080* (Current Population Reports, Series P-25, No. 995). Washington, DC: U.S. Government Printing Office.

U.S. Department of Commerce, Bureau of the Census. (1990a). *School enrollment—social and economic characteristics of students: October 1989* (Current Population Reports, Series P-20, No. 452). Washington, DC: U.S. Government Printing Office.

U.S. Department of Commerce, Bureau of the Census. (1990b) *What's it worth? Educational background and economic status: Spring 1987* (Current Population Reports, Series P-70, No. 21). Washington, DC: U.S. Government Printing Office.

U.S. Department of Commerce, Bureau of the Census. (1991a). *The Black population in the United States: March 1991* (Current Population Reports Series P-20 464-000, No.). Washington, DC: U.S. Government Printing Office.

U.S. Department of Commerce, Bureau of the Census. (1991b). *Educational attainment in the United States: March 1989 and 1988* (Current Population Reports, Series P-20, No. 451). Washington, DC: U.S. Government Printing Office.

U.S. Department of Commerce, Bureau of the Census. (1991c). *Fertility of American women:*

June 1990 (Current Population Reports, Series P-20, No. 454). Washington, DC: U.S. Government Printing Office.

U.S. Department of Commerce, Bureau of the Census. (1991d). *The Hispanic population in the United States: March 1991* (Current Population Reports, Series P-20, No. 455). Washington, DC: U.S. Government Printing Office.

U.S. Department of Commerce, Bureau of the Census. (1991e). *Money income and poverty status in the United States: 1990.* (Current Population Reports, Series P-60, No. 168). Washington, DC: U.S. Government Printing Office.

U.S. Department of Commerce, Bureau of the Census. (1991f). *Statistical abstract of the United States: 1991* (111th ed.). Washington, DC: U.S. Government Printing Office.

U.S. Department of Commerce, Bureau of the Census. (1992a). *Poverty in the U.S.: 1991* (Current Population Reports, Series P-60, No. 181). Washington, DC: U.S. Government Printing Office.

U.S. Department of Commerce, Bureau of the Census (1992b). *School enrollment—social and economic characteristics of students: October 1990* (Current Population Reports, Series P-20, No. 460). Washington, DC: U.S. Government Printing Office.

U.S. Department of Education, Office for Civil Rights. (1982). *1980 elementary and secondary school civil rights survey.* Washington, DC: Author.

U.S. Department of Education, Office for Civil Rights. (1987). *1986 elementary and secondary school civil rights survey.* Washington, DC: Author.

U.S. Department of Labor. (1989). *The effects of immigration on the U.S. economy and labor market: Immigration and policy research report 1.* Washington, DC: Author.

U.S. Department of Labor, Bureau of Labor Statistics. (1989). *Handbook of labor statistics* (Bulletin 2340). Washington, DC: U.S. Government Printing Office.

U.S. Department of Labor, Bureau of Labor Statistics (1992). *Report 829* (Second Quarter). Washington, DC: U.S. Government Printing Office.

U.S. Department of Labor, Council of Economic Advisors. (1986). *The economic effects of immigration: The economic report of the president.* Washington, DC: U.S. Government Printing Office.

Valencia, R. R. (Ed.). (1991). *Chicano school failure and success: Research and policy agendas for the 1990s* (The Stanford Series on Education and Public Policy). Basingstoke, England: Falmer Press.

Valencia, R. R., & Aburto, S. (1991a). The uses and abuses of educational testing: Chicanos as a case in point. In R. R. Valencia (Ed.), *Chicano school failure and success: Research and policy agendas for the 1990s* (The Stanford Series on Education and Public Policy, pp. 203–251). Basingstoke, England: Falmer Press.

Valencia, R. R., & Aburto, S. (1991b). Competency testing and Latino student access to the teaching profession: An overview of issues. In G. D. Keller, J. Deneen, & R. Magallán (Eds.), *Assessment and access: Hispanics in higher education* (pp. 169–196). Albany: State University of New York Press.

Vargas, A. (1988). *Literacy in the Hispanic community.* Washington, DC: National Council of La Raza.

3

The Structure of Inequality and the Status of Puerto Rican Youth in the United States

Héctor R. Cordero Guzmán

YOUTH OF COLOR IN THE 1990s

In a recent broadcast on ABC News Nightline (May 3, 1993) hosted by Ted Koppel on location from the Woods, a ghettoized housing complex in Jersey City, we learn the story of Hassan. Hassan's tale is similar to that of many young Puerto Ricans, African Americans, and Chicanos in the inner city. The program is filled with the images that have come to acutely characterize the inner city during the Reagan-Bush years: drugs, gangs, and violence on the streets. Hassan's mother is a single woman on public assistance. She is currently going to school. His father is in and out of jail. Hassan's older sister has a nine month old baby. Hassan is fourteen and has two younger brothers, one ten and one seven.

The story weaves together all the images with a single theme: "What will Hassan choose?" He does well in school and has what appears to be a remarkable capacity to repair and re-assemble electronic equipment. He also has a very protective mother. In fact so strong and protective that she assures the camera, without hesitation, that if any drug dealer ever approaches Hassan she will personally kill the pusher. She, like the vast majority of parents, wants Hassan to do well but is aware of what surrounds him. "What will Hassan choose?" This is the world of fast money, fast sneakers, fast clothing, and fast drugs: "What will Hassan choose?"

While watching the program, I could not keep myself from thinking about all of the statistics and probabilities that capture the factors that directly affect the type of life that Hassan will lead but none of which he selected. The point, I thought, is not so much what Hassan will choose but, rather, what kinds of choices will we, as a society, allow Hassan to make. I asked myself: will we, as a society, learn from his experience? Will we, as a society, appreciate his skill and develop his talent? Or will we, as a society, condemn Hassan for the collective crime of systematic prejudice? For being on the "wrong side" of a structure of inequality that systematically denies Hassan, and many other African-American, Chicano and Puerto Rican youth, equal access to opportunity in education and in the labor market?

This essay is an attempt to search for some of those answers. In order to do that I will discuss, and illustrate with relevant statistics, some of the systemic obstacles that our youth, particularly African Americans and Latinos, confront throughout their life course and that hinder their capacity to realize their full human potential. My goal is to have the reader ask him or herself, critically, whether a society that systematically limits the opportunities it makes available for youth on the basis of color, gender, and class can demand that those who are being excluded "choose to do for themselves" what in fact only a privileged few have the resources and the opportunity to do.

PUERTO RICAN YOUTH IN PERSPECTIVE

The last two decades have seen the continuation and, in important respects, the accentuation of troublesome trends in the socio-economic status of Latino and African-American youth. The available data show that over time the proportion of youth of color who have attended high school and received a high school diploma increased and the differences between them and whites decreased. At the same time differences in rates of participation in the labor market and unemployment between whites and other youth showed an increase. For example, the proportion of white, African-American, and Puerto Rican males 23 to 25 years of age who had completed high school or more was, respectively, 67.5%, 36.3% and 24.1%, in 1960; 80.4%, 58.8%, and 38.8% in 1970; and 86.7%, 73.3%, and 57.8% in 1980. This suggests that there still are significant differences in the levels of completed education but that these have stabilized for whites and have converged over time with those of African Americans and Puerto Ricans. In contrast, the unemployment figures show a fluctuating trend towards racial divergence. If we consider again young men 23 to 25 years of age we find that the unemployment rates for whites, African-Americans, and Puerto Ricans, respectively, were 5.7%, 11.2%, and 8.8% in 1960; 4.6%, 8.2%, and 6.0% in 1970; and 9.1%, 16.4%, and 12.3% in 1980.

The troubling nature of these trends led to a proliferation of research on the patterns, causes, and consequences of youth employment, in general, and African-American and Latino youth un- and under-employment in particular. In their path-breaking work in *The Black Youth Employment Crisis*, Freeman and Holzer summarize the major findings of the National Bureau of Economic Research conference as follows:

> A variety of social and economic factors have contributed to the crisis. On the demand side of the market, we find evidence of several determinants, including local labor market conditions and demographics, discriminatory employer behavior, and the unattractive characteristics of the job held. On the supply side of the market, we find aspirations and churchgoing, opportunities for crime, the family's employment and welfare status, education, and the willingness to accept low wage jobs all to be important factors.

The findings from these studies, prepared by a prestigious group of economic researchers, though important for certain specialized audiences, mainly served to corroborate what thousands of members of the African-American, Chicano, and Puerto Rican communities already knew. In our community, it has been well known that throughout their lives youth of color confront different sets of resources and socially constructed circumstances. This means that we face a different mode of integration into the school system, into institutions of higher education, and into the primary sector of the labor market.

Today, it is quite clear to researchers, policy makers, community activists, and parents, though admittedly in different ways, that any effort launched at integrating youth of color into the educational system, into the labor market, and into other social institutions must be predicated on a methodical analysis of the individual, structural, and institutional features that characterize the current forms of socioeconomic inclusion and exclusion. These processes must be analyzed and understood as experienced and felt by *all* social actors rather than as rudimentary features in simplistic and de-contextualized abstractions of an idealized social formation. In other words, individual outcomes can not and will not change without concurrent changes in the institutional forces that propel youth of color in one direction by blocking systematic access to others. This means, fundamentally, that the prevailing assumption that opportunities are widely and uniformly available for all youth and that youth of color, in particular, would succeed only if they developed the right attitude, imitated the correct role models, persevered in whatever type of school they are placed, and availed themselves of the necessary connections that lead one to "make it" in the world of work must be challenged. However, we must make clear that we are not arguing that our youth do not have any choices, but rather that they are embedded within a system of social production that places systematic, concrete, and cumulative limits on the types of opportunities and on the level and quality of resources that are vested in them and thus on the choices that they can and do make.

THE DEMOGRAPHICS OF YOUTH AND FAMILY POVERTY

One of the main problems in determining the socio-economic status of Puerto Rican youth is that statistics are often not gathered by group, or that when they are gathered they are usually not broken down by national origin but are presented in combination with those of the total Hispanic population. Recent efforts, like the Resource Guide prepared by Angela L. Carrasquillo, provide important discussions of key debates on the status of Latino youth, and present statistics that are helpful to researchers, policy makers, and members of the community. In this article I have drawn, among others, from Carrasquillo's work, the Children's Defense Fund report (Miranda) on Latino youth, and our work at the Centro in order to provide an alternative interpretation of the causes and consequences of the current socio-economic trends among Puerto Rican youth.

The Latino population is relatively young. In 1988 almost one out of every three Latinos in the country was under 15 years of age. The median age for Latinos of Puerto Rican origin in 1990 was 27.0 years of age whereas for Mexican-Americans it was 24.1 compared to 33.5 years for the rest of the population. The proportion of Puerto Ricans below 18 years of age was 36.7%, while it was 37.4% among Mexican-Americans and 26.2% for the rest of the population.

In terms of household income and poverty there has been a well documented change in composition and a decline in the socio-economic status of Puerto Rican families relative to other families. This means that Puerto Rican youth are being reared in families that have different resources with which to support and supply their multiple needs. The economic figures for 1991 show that median household income was $16,169 for Puerto Ricans, $22,439 for Mexican Americans and $29,943 for the rest of the population. Simply put, Puerto Rican households in 1991 averaged a little more that half the income of that of the total population.

The poverty rate for children shows similar trends. A recent report by the Children's Defense Fund provides concrete population figures. In 1989, there were 2.603 million poor Latino children in the U.S. out of a population of 7.186 million Latino children or 36.2 percent. The bulk of Latino children in the U.S., 5.028 million, are Mexican-American and 1.867 million of them are poor (37.1%). Puerto Rican children totaled 750,000 with 48.4% or 364,000 living below the poverty line. If one adds the number of children slightly (between 100% and 200%) above the poverty line, the number for Puerto Ricans slightly above or below poverty climbs to 73.1%. Similarly, the proportion of children who live below half the poverty line is 22.2%. Essentially, these numbers mean that out of every four Puerto Rican children one lives well below the poverty line, one lives below the

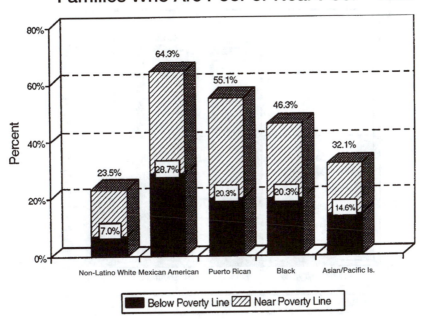

Percent of Children In Married-Couple Families Who Are Poor or Near Poor - 1989

Figure 3.1.
Source: Miranda 1991, Graphs 16 and 19, pp. 23, 24.

line, one lives slightly above, and the fourth one lives clearly above the poverty threshold.

Family structure is consistently correlated to poverty rates. Gary Sandefur and Marta Tienda find that 43.9% of Puerto Rican households were headed by females. This proportion is almost identical to that of African Americans (43.7%) and substantially higher than that of whites (12%). This difference is important because female-headed households have much higher poverty rates than married-couple families. For Puerto Rican female-headed households the poverty rate was 74.4% while the poverty rate for similar white households was 36.2%, or almost half that of Puerto Ricans. However, one still finds that Latino children are quite likely to be poor in married-couple households. One out of every five Puerto Rican children (20.3%) living in a married-couple family was poor. This figure is higher than the 7.0% figure for the white population but lower than the 28.7% level for Mexican Americans. In other words, Puerto Rican children in married-couple families are three times more likely to be poor than white children in similarly structured families, while children in single headed families have a poverty rate that is two times higher (see Tables).

The socio-economic status of families and individuals in the Island of Puerto

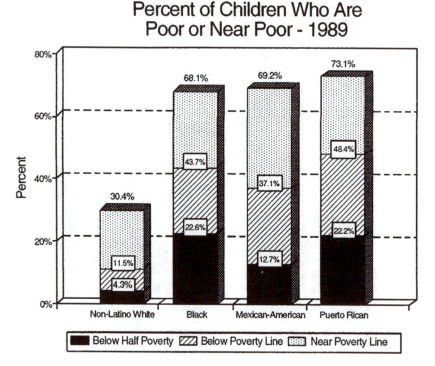

Percent of Children Who Are Poor or Near Poor - 1989

Figure 3.2.

Source: Miranda 1991, Graphs 18 and 20, pp. 24, 26.

Rico is connected to that of Puerto Rican families in the United States through migration, trade, and the operation of labor markets. In a recent report using figures from the 1990 Census, the National Council of La Raza reported that 58% of the population residing in Puerto Rico lived below the poverty line. The numbers also showed that the poverty rate for youth in Puerto Rico was 66.7%. The report added that 22.3% of youth aged 16 to 19 had dropped out of high school meaning, presumably, that they were not enrolled in school at the time of the census. Of this group 87.2% were either unemployed or out of the labor force. In other words, about 20% of Puerto Rican youth 16 to 19 years of age were neither in school or at work.

A brief overview of the statistics on Puerto Rican families and youth shows that they are relatively young and much poorer than the rest of the population which means that, clearly, these families have fewer material resources at their disposal. This is true for families located either in Puerto Rico or in the United States.

HOUSING CONDITIONS AND
THE HEALTH STATUS OF PUERTO RICAN YOUTH

Housing and health issues are intimately related to the educational and economic outcomes for youth. In a paper prepared in 1988, Dolbeare and Canales found that in 1983 Latinos had the highest incidence of housing problems. For Puerto Ricans the problems were especially acute. Puerto Ricans were the least likely to own their own dwellings, 21.5% compared to 50% for other Latinos. Housing costs for Puerto Ricans were the highest when compared to other Latino groups, and the conditions of the dwellings were the worst. Let me illustrate this with some figures from the study. Roughly 5% of Puerto Rican dwellings did not have adequate plumbing. In addition, 18% of the dwellings had rodent infestation; 12% had open cracks or holes; 10% had broken plaster, had the paint peeling, or had at least one room without electricity; while 10% of the houses had roof leaks. Fully 17% of all Mexican and 23% of all Puerto Rican households did not have a telephone.

The material conditions of the dwellings reflects the economic conditions of the community and are centrally related to both the physical and mental health status of the population. Puerto Ricans have the highest rates of infant mortality and the highest incidence of low birth weight among Latinos. In addition, the cumulative incidence of AIDS is 2.7 times higher among hispanics than among non-hispanic white youth. Another epidemic that has received less academic attention is the question of homicides among Puerto Rican youth both in the Island and in the mainland. A recent paper by Donna Shai (1992) from Villanova found that in the 1989–1990 period the homicide rate for Puerto Rican, white, and African-American males 15–19 years of age in New York City was, respectively, 84.71, 25.02 and 208.67 per 100,000. The comparable figures for males and females in the country in 1985, respectively, were 7.3 and 2.7 for whites, 46.4 and 10.3 for African Americans, and 32.4 and 3.0 in the Island of Puerto Rico. Essentially, the figures show that Puerto Rican and African-American youth, particularly young males, are much more likely to die violently than white youth. The issue, of course, is not just that youth of color are more likely to be murdered than white youth, but that in absolute

Poverty Rates of Children In Female-Headed Families - 1989

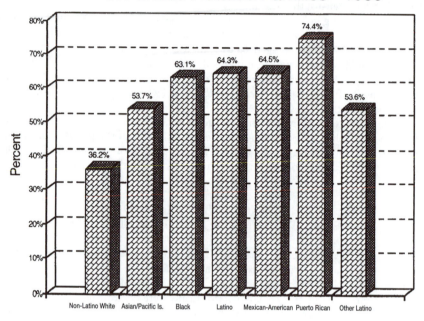

Figure 3.3.
Source: Miranda 1991, Graph 21, p. 27.

terms the quality of life has deteriorated to the point that they are dying violent deaths in high numbers at very young ages.

THE SCHOOL SYSTEM AND PUERTO RICAN YOUTH

According to the *Atlas of the 1990 Census,* the two largest school districts in the country are the New York City school system with 930,440 students and the Puerto Rico Department of Education with 650,720 students. The third and fourth largest districts are in Los Angeles with 609,746 and in Chicago with 408,201 students. This means that most Puerto Rican youth are being educated in systems that are quite large and that have extensive bureaucracies.

The main issues in the debates over elementary and secondary education evolve around two seemingly contradictory issues: a) theories that put emphasis on the functional role of the educational system either in perpetuating social inequalities or in democratizing opportunities for social mobility; and, b) research and advocacy around the question of whether the school system is properly addressing the multiple needs of students from diverse backgrounds and whether it is properly preparing them for higher education and for integration into the formal labor market. In their book on schooling and work, Carnoy and Levin argue that as "a product and shaper of social discord, the school is necessarily caught up in the larger conflicts inherent in a capitalist economy and a liberal capitalist state." For them, then, schools are arenas in which the narrow needs of employers for a qualified workforce and conflicts over redistribution and democratization are played out.

Let me elaborate briefly on some of the contemporary debates on the school system. The first key issue is access to quality schools. Gary Orfield has shown that Latino children are increasingly attending schools that are mostly segregated. Segregation is an important factor because, as Massey and Denton have illustrated, it is also related, among other things, to the quality of schools. In commenting on the educational process of Latino youth, Angela Carrasquillo from Fordham University says:

> Unfortunately, too many low-income Hispanic families are not becoming productive contributing members of society due to disproportionately high academic failure. One of the reasons for this failure is that Hispanic students are not attending the most successful schools. They are often in segregated schools, made up of mostly Hispanic and African American students, in which educational resources and physical facilities are mediocre. At times Hispanic students are placed in programs not suited for their needs. Equality becomes a responsibility of the school rather that the student. Quality programs as well as financial programs are not offered in most of the schools that Hispanic children and youth attend.

Despite the reservations one might have over defining the process of educational attainment mainly in terms of "success" or "failure," the central point is that students of color are attending institutions that seem, clearly, not to be responding to their needs. The question in this sense is not so much whether students as individuals "fail" or "succeed" but rather whether the structure of the school, the community, and the society in which schools are embedded is adequately addressing and fulfilling the needs of students of color. Arguably, if only a few students were not completing their high school education and going on to college one might want to focus primarily on the individual factors that determine the specific outcome. However, when between one third and one half of the population is not completing their high school education, particularly in the inner cities, this seems to be evidence that there are more systematic exclusionary forces at work. In this sense "push-out" is a more accurate concept than "drop-out" to describe the totality of the process.

Access to quality schools is intimately tied to retention. Measures of retention are inherently difficult to compute but there is consensus that the drop-out, or more accurately, the push-out rate for Latino youth is the highest in the country. Carrasquillo, for example, cites a study by The National Commission on Secondary Schooling for Hispanics that found that 45% of Mexican American and Puerto Rican students who enter high school never finish. This compares to a figure of 17% for white youth. According to Carrasquillo, some of the factors that have been identified as affecting Latino retention in school are: "(a) Poorly equipped and overcrowded schools; (b) Lower per pupil expenditures;(c) Segregated schools; (d) Schools at times understaffed and with limited basic resources; (e) High rate of grade repetition; (f) Lower expectations by the school system; (g) High enrollment in vocational and general education programs."

These factors operate in conjunction with other school characteristics to disproportionately exclude Latino youth. In his research on schools, Orum identified features such as attendance, discipline and promotion policies, language used for instruction, availability of special instruction to meet special needs, and provisions to ensure parental involvement as critical school-level variables influencing Latino retention. As Carrasquillo notes, Latino children are at a disadvantage from the earliest of grades and these disadvantages increase over the life course as more and more obstacles are placed in the students' path.

Tracking, special education, language, and curriculum development are other central components that need to be carefully analyzed in order to understand the position of Puerto Rican youth in the school system. The evidence shows that Puerto Rican children are more likely to be placed in the low ability groups and more likely to be assigned to special education programs. These programs were not originally developed to address the specific needs of the students that they currently serve, and their stigmatizing role has repercussions throughout the students' academic life. Placement in low ability tracks and in special education programs is intimately tied to bilingual education and to curriculum development. Most Puerto Rican educators agree that Puerto Rican pupils need not only instruction in their native language (Spanish or English) and a mechanism that allows them to become literate and proficient in both Spanish and English, but also that the curriculum, or what is actually taught in the schools, needs to be tied to the students' life experiences and to the broader experience of other marginalized and non-marginalized groups in society.

PUERTO RICAN YOUTH AND THE LABOR MARKET

In recent years there has been an increasing amount of research on the labor market status of Latinos. In their recent book, *Latinos in a Changing Economy*, Rebecca Morales, Frank Bonilla, and their collaborators show how, particularly after 1970, the process of industrial restructuring and a change to a services dominant economy, in conjunction with a re-organization in the international division of labor and increases in migration, have led to increases in social stratification and inequality. It is within this macro-economic context, combined with the changing dynamics of racial and ethnic discrimination and segregation, that we must place the changing status of youth of color.

The figures that I will discuss in this section pertain mainly to young males. Unfortunately, the research literature has not focused on the status of young Puerto Rican women in the labor market. What we know about the labor market status of Puerto Rican women, in general, in that over the last three decades there has been a precipitous decline in their participation in the formal paid labor market. In 1950, Puerto Rican women had among the highest rates of labor force participation at 38.9%. By 1970 these rates had declined around 10% in absolute terms and had also declined relative to the rates of white and Other Hispanic women.

The proportion of young Puerto Rican males enrolled in school in 1980 continued its secular increase from the 1960 and 1970 level, but still there continued to be a large gap between Puerto Ricans and whites with a 10 to 15 percentage point difference for those between 17 and 22 years of age. It is important to note that the gap between Puerto Ricans and whites in the proportion of young males enrolled in school showed a substantial decrease between 1960 and 1980. For those between the ages of 20 and 22 years, 34.0% of whites were enrolled in school but only 18.9% of Puerto Ricans. The rates of participation in the labor force, however, decreased in absolute terms from their 1970 level for most age groups. The gap between Puerto Rican and white youth in labor force participation rates decreases with age to about a 14 percentage point difference between ages 20 to 25. Essentially, young Puerto Ricans males are going to school at a higher rate but participating less in the formal labor market.

In 1980 about 80% of whites were in the labor force while the comparable figure for Puerto Ricans was 67%. Between 1970 and 1980 there were also increases in Puerto Rican youth unemployment particularly at ages 17 to 19, and the difference in level between them and whites aged 20 to 25 continued to be about 1.33 times higher. For those enrolled in school, Puerto Rican rates of labor force participation were almost half what they were for whites at the younger ages, and they decreased with age while unemployment was almost double particularly for the group 17 to 22 years of age. For those not enrolled in school, the gap in participation rates was largest at the earliest ages (about 22 percentage points) and so was the gap in unemployment. The unemployment rate for Puerto Rican young males not enrolled in school was around 16% while it was around 11% for whites. In essence, gaps in participation and employment between Puerto Rican and white youth remain large across the range of ages from 17 to 25 years old and are somewhat independent of whether the person is enrolled in school or not.

In sum, the pattern that emerges when we look at labor force participation and unemployment clearly shows changes over time characterized by marked increases in non-participation and unemployment among young Puerto Rican males relative to whites. Trends in school enrollment show a modest increase for those 17 to 19 between 1960 and 1970 and larger increases between 1970 and 1980 for all age groups. However, the relative gap between Puerto Ricans and whites 20 to 22 years of age continues to be large, indicating that a smaller share of the Puerto Rican youth population is going on to college.

An analysis of demographic, educational, and labor force data clearly shows that gaps in Puerto Rican young male employment relative to those of whites have changed from slightly higher levels of Puerto Rican participation in the formal labor market in 1960 to relatively low levels in 1980. These trends coincide with a narrowing of the gap between whites and Puerto Ricans in levels of school enrollment; the number of years of completed education; and a reduction in the proportion of the young Puerto Rican male population that is Island born, resident in a central-city location, and concentrated in New York state.

Quite clearly the role of youth in the labor market must be tied to an analysis of the institutional changes that have occurred in the U.S. economy during the last three decades. In their introduction to the special issue of the *Hispanic Journal of Be-*

havioral Sciences on Puerto Rican poverty and labor markets Clara Rodríguez and Edwin Meléndez suggest that,

> Among the most important factors [explaining Puerto Rican poverty] are: the concentration of Puerto Ricans in cities and regions (e.g. New York and Chicago) that have undergone a rapid transition from a goods-producing economy to a service-oriented one; limited opportunities in housing markets that, in turn, limit the kinds and numbers of job opportunities that are available, quality of schools, and the quality of public services; and the persistence of racial and gender discrimination.

The role of discrimination in the labor market has been debated and contested both inside and outside of academia. A recent Urban Institute/GAO hiring audit can be a useful instrument in making some preliminary assertions about the extent and nature of discrimination against Latino youth in the labor market. The audit was conducted as follows: eight Latino men between 19 and 24 years of age were paired with eight Anglo men of the same age. Resumes were prepared and standardized so as not to reflect any significant differences in prior training or experience among the candidates. Every Sunday, a sample of jobs was selected from the newspaper and the applicants were made to follow the instructions in the ad. The beginning of the audits was alternated so that Anglos and Latinos within each of the eight pairs got to start the same number of audits (that is Anglos would go first in audit one and Latinos would go first in audit two and so on). The jobs selected were mostly entry level positions. There were 360 audits completed in Chicago and San Diego and, of these, 302 went all the way to the job offer stage. The outcomes were divided into three stages: application, interview, and job offer.

The results were quite revealing. Looking at the total number of times that testers reached each stage, we notice that 95% of Anglos got to fill out applications whereas 91% of Latinos did likewise. This indicates that during the initial contact Latino testers were less favored than Anglo testers, due either to heavier screening or just to a refusal to deal on the part of the employers. The biggest difference occurred between the application and the interview stages. The study found that 64% of Anglos were invited for an interview while only 48% of Latinos were. Essentially, 31% of Anglos and 43% of Latinos were eliminated even before the employer got a chance to interview them in person, and either test or otherwise asses their qualifications. After the interview the rejection rate for Anglos and Latinos was the same, 21% for Anglos and 20% for Latinos. All in all, 43% of Anglos and 28% of Latinos got job offers.

The Urban Institute Report also offers examples of qualitative differences in treatment between similarly qualified job seekers. These were instances in which both Anglo and Latino testers filled the application, but the Anglo got the job offer and the Latino did not. At face value this might seem random, but a closer examination of the context might reveal otherwise:

> The setting is a restaurant and the position advertised entailed greeting customers, sitting them at the tables and giving them the menus. The Latino went in, filled the application and received a five minute interview. He was then told that they were going to look into other candidates and that he would be notified once they

Figure 3.4.
Sergio Arau, *La Netafísica*. Editorial Planets Mexicana S.A. de C. V.

made the decision. The Anglo partner went in about ten minutes after that. He emerged thirty minutes later and notified the Latino that he had gotten the job. That evening the Anglo called the place to turn the job down which meant that the position was open again. The Latino called the next morning to inquire about the status of his application and was told that the position had been filled.

On several occasions both the Anglo and the Latino filled the application, got the interview and the job offer, but were directed to different jobs within the firm. This instance is quoted in the GAO report: "The Latino tester filled out an application for a busboy job and had a short interview. The interviewer described the basics of the job and the pay. The Anglo tester filled out the application and had a longer interview during which he was told that he could soon move up to a higher paying bartender position or even a position as a host if he worked well." At another job, both the Anglo and the Latino got the offer, but the Anglo was told by the interviewer: "the minute you walked in the door I could see that you were of management quality." He was provided an explanation of how he could make it up the firm's occupational ladder.

In some cases, there was not even an effort made to screen the Latino tester over the phone. This example is also quoted in the GAO report:

A pair of testers applied for a position with a manufacturer that was listed under "shipping" in the Sunday *Chicago Tribune*. The advertisement specified that the company wanted a "dependable, hardworking person" and that the applicants should contact "Bill." The Latino tester called the specified number and, after inquiring about the job, was told by Bill that the position was filled. The Anglo tester called in 15 minutes later and "Bill" invited him for an interview later that day. After a 15 minute interview, the Anglo tester was offered the position.

The authors of the Urban Institute Report (Cross et al., 1989) argue that the figures from the audit are an underestimate of discrimination. This is due, they suggest, to the fact that employers who advertise in newspapers are less likely to discriminate than employers who hire by word-of-mouth or other informal methods. However, the fact remains that overall Latinos received unfavorable treatment in 31% of the audits.

CONCLUSION

In a recent report by state senator Franz S. Leichter of New York entitled "Access, Excellence and the Economic Future of New York: The Forgotten Promise," the Senator makes a case for linking the substantial decline in the state's higher education budget with the increases in funding for correctional facilities. This is a point that has been made before most visibly by the Reverend Jesse Jackson in his speech to the 1992 democratic convention. The report shows that in 1982 New York spent $330 million managing a prison population of 28,000. A decade after the figures changed to $1.3 billion to manage 69,763 inmates. State spending in education has been declining drastically since 1986–1987 to a level of $2.7 billion in 1992–1993. Commenting on these trends, Senator Leichter says: "Just last month, SUNY Chancellor D. Bruce Johnstone warned that SUNY may be forced to start closing campuses if state budget cuts persist, because it cannot accommodate the number of students it currently has. And what about the nearly 60,000 more who will be applying by 1996? Perhaps they should apply to the prison system, where, no doubt, their incarceration would be lavishly funded."

The question, of course, is not just rhetorical given the available evidence showing that entry into higher education is intimately related to youth's access not only to further education but to a position in the labor market that would ensure a modicum of economic mobility and independence.

Researchers, policy analysts, community groups, and families all need to insist that definitions of the problem, and thus the search for solutions, reflect the lived experiences of youth. This lived experience must be tied, both theoretically and practically, to the systematic development of programs aimed at incorporating African-American, Puerto Rican, Chicano, and other youth of color into the fabric of society. But in order for this to occur we must demand that the current fabric of society also change. Our communities cannot pretend to find answers from those who neither understand the problem (because they can, are, and want to be distanced from its manifestations) nor seek to transform the ways in which the social structures operate to produce and reproduce systematic inequality in this society.

While it is true, in principle, that youth have choices, it is also true that these choices are more restricted for African-American and Latino youth. Once some access is obtained, this does not mean that institutions work in the same way and invest the same resources in majority and minority youth. In other words, not only is the range of choices for our youth restricted, but their systematic under-valuation affects their capacity and propensity to choose among the alternatives they do have and to succeed in gaining entry to key social institutions. This is a point that must not be set aside, for it permeates the way in which researchers, policy makers and advocates ask questions, and it clearly affects the ways and places in which they seek answers to the plight of our youth. Again, I ask, what will we, as a society, allow and encourage Hassan, María, and many other of our youth to choose?

REFERENCES

Bean, Frank D. and Marta Tienda. *The Hispanic Population of the United States.* (New York: Russell Sage, 1987).

Bonilla, Frank and Rebecca Morales. "National and Regional Policy Agendas in an Era of Ethnic Diversity and Growing Inequality," in Rebecca Morales and Frank Bonilla (eds.) *Latinos in a Changing U.S. Economy.* (Newburry Park, CA: Sage Series on Race and Ethnic Relations, 1993).

Bowles, S. and H. Gintis. *Schooling in Capitalist America.* (New York: Basic Books, 1976).

Carnoy, Martin and Henry M. Levin. *Schooling and the Democratic State.* (Palo Alto: Stanford University Press, 1985).

Carrasquillo, Angela L. *Hispanic Children and Youth in the United States.* (New York: Garland Publishing, Inc., 1985).

Cordero Guzmán, Héctor R. "The Socio-Economic and Demographic Determinants of Differences in the Wages of Puerto Rican and White Youth: 1959–1980." Paper presented at the Social Science Research Council's Workshop on the Causes and Consequences of Puerto Rican Poverty. (New York: Centro de Estudios Puertorriqueños, Hunter College/CUNY, 1993).

Cross, Harry, et. al. *Employer Hiring Policies: Differential Treatment of Hispanic and Anglo Job Seekers.* (Washington, D.C.: The Urban Institute, 1990).

De Freitas, Gregory. *Inequality at Work: Hispanics in the U.S. Labor Force.* (Oxford: Oxford University Press, 1991).

Dolbeare, C. N. and J. A. Canales. *Hispanic Housing Crisis.* (Washington, D.C.: National Council for La Raza, 1988).

Fernández, Roberto. "Structural Factors in Hispanic Youth Achievement." Unpublished Manuscript, Center for Urban Affairs and Policy Research, Northwestern University, 1992.

Freeman, Richard B. and Harry Holzer. "The Black Youth Employment Crisis: Summary of Findings" in Richard B. Freeman and Harry Holzer (eds.), *The Black Youth Employment Crisis.* (Chicago: The University of Chicago Press, 1986).

General Accounting Office (GAO). *Report to Congress: Immigration Reform, Employer Sanctions and the Question of Discrimination.* (Washington, D.C.: General Accounting Office, 1990).

Hernández, José. *Puerto Rican Youth Employment.* (Maplewood, N.J.: Waterfront Press, 1983).

Hinojosa-Ojeda, Raul, Martin Carnoy, and Hugh Daley. "An Even Greater 'U-Turn': Latinos and the New Inequality," in Edwin Meléndez, Clara Rodríguez, and Janis Barry Figueroa (eds.) *Hispanics in the Labor Force: Issues and Policies.* (New York: Plenum Press, 1991).

Kirschenman, Joleen and Kathryn Neckerman. "'We'd Love to Hire Them, But . . .': The

Meaning of Race for Employers," in Christopher Jenks and Paul Peterson (eds.) *The Urban Underclass*. (Washington, D.C.: The Brookings Institution, 1991).

Leichter, Franz, S. "Access, Excellence and the Economic Future of New York: The Forgotten Promise." Unpublished Report, 1993.

Massey, Douglas S. and Nancy Denton. *American Apartheid: Segregation and the Making of the Underclass*. (Cambridge: Harvard University Press, 1993).

Mattson, Mark T. *Atlas of the 1990 Census*. (New York: Macmillan, 1992).

Miranda, Leticia C. *Latino Child Poverty in the United States*. (Washington, D.C.: Children's Defense Fund, 1991).

National Council of La Raza. *Poverty Project Newsletter*. Vol. 4 no 2. (Washington, D.C.: NCLR, 1992).

National Council of La Raza. *Poverty Project Newsletter*. Vol. 4 no 4. (Washington, D.C.: NCLR, 1993).

Orfield, Gary. *Public School Desegregation in the United States*. (Washington, D.C.: Center for Political Studies, 1983).

Orum, L. *Making Education Work for Hispanic Americans: Some Promising Community-Based Practices*. (Washington, D.C.: National Council of La Raza, 1986).

Rodríguez, Clara and Edwin Meléndez. "Puerto Rican Poverty and Labor Markets: An Introduction." *Hispanic Journal of Behavioral Sciences*. 14, 1 (1992):52–75.

Rosenbaum, James E. et. al. "Market and Network Theories of the Transition from High School to Work: Their Application to Industrialized Societies" *Annual Review of Sociology*. 16 (1990):263–99.

Sandefur, Gary and Marta Tienda. "Introduction: Social Policy and the Minority Experience," in Gary Sandefur and Marta Tienda (eds.) *Divided Opportunities: Minorities, Poverty, and Social Policy*. (New York: Plenum Press, 1988).

Shai, Donna. "Child Mortality and Poverty among Puerto Ricans in New York City and in Puerto Rico, 1980-1990." Paper presented at the Social Science Research Council's Workshop on the Causes and Consequences of Puerto Rican Poverty. (New York: Centro de Estudios Puertorriqueños, Hunter College/CUNY, 1992).

Tienda, Marta, Katharine Donato and Héctor Cordero Guzmán. "Schooling, Color, and the Labor Force Activity of Women," *Social Forces*. 71, 2 (1992):365–395.

Tienda, Marta and Leif Jensen. "Poverty and Minorities: A Quarter-Century Profile of Color and Socioeconomic Disadvantage." in Gary Sandefur and Marta Tienda (eds.) *Divided Opportunities: Minorities, Poverty, and Social Policy*. (New York: Plenum Press, 1988).

Torres, Andrés and Clara E. Rodríguez. "Latino Research and Policy: The Puerto Rican Case." in Edwin Meléndez, Clara Rodríguez, and Janis Barry Figueroa (eds.) *Hispanics in the Labor Force: Issues and Policies*. (New York: Plenum Press, 1991).

Torres, Andrés and Frank Bonilla. "Decline Within Decline: The New York Perspective," in Rebecca Morales and Frank Bonilla (eds.) *Latinos in a Changing U.S. Economy*. (Newbury Park, CA: Sage Series on Race and Ethnic Relations, 1993).

Wilson, W. J. *The Truly Disadvantaged*. (Chicago: University of Chicago Press, 1987).

4

Latinos, Class, and the U.S. Political Economy
Income Inequality and Policy Alternatives

Rodolfo D. Torres and Adela de la Torre

INTRODUCTION

Few studies analyze the mechanisms that cause inequality in earnings, employment, and occupational achievement between Latino and non-Latino populations. Compared to analyses of income for blacks, relatively little attention has been devoted to the study of income determination among Latino populations. Previous studies consider income inequalities from the perspective of human capital theory. In this chapter, we will consider two dominant theoretical perspectives for explaining income inequality: the human capital model and the class/structural model. Then we will review related empirical studies of Latino populations. After critiquing the human capital and class/structural perspectives, we will discuss policy initiatives emerging from these two competing models on income inequality. Lastly, we will consider future research directions for the analysis of income determination and employment among Latinos in the United States and conclude with some thoughts on the challenges we face in the post-Reagan era in constructing policy alternatives and initiating a movement that secures economic and political justice.

Dramatic changes are expected in the racial and ethnic composition of new entrants into the labor force in southern California. Between 1980 and 1990, non-Latino whites are projected to compose only one out of five new workers; blacks will make up one out of six, and other non-Latino groups one in nine. About one-half of the expected expansion of the labor force will come from Latino residents, and most of these will be of Mexican origin (Muller & Espenshade, 1985, p. 166). Ethnic changes in southern California's labor force in the 1990s will be even greater. The number of non-Latino whites (female and male) will decline, and new workers of Mexican origin will account for three out of four new workers in the region. According to a recent study sponsored by the Urban Institute (Muller & Espenshade, 1985), even without further immigration or internal migration, the majority of workers added to the labor force in southern California over the next twenty years would be Latino, primarily of Mexican origin.

So, there is little doubt that Latinos compose one of the fastest growing groups in the labor market and will soon become the largest minority in the United States. However, little is known about the process by which Latinos enter and participate in the labor market, which is particularly troubling because of the continuing serious inequalities in income, wages, and occupational achievement compared to white non-Latino workers. Little research of a longitudinal nature has been completed, partly because of the difficulty, until recently, of identifying Latino national-origin groups in census information. Changes in census categories identifying Latinos have created problems of compatibility between 1950 and 1970. With the inclusion of Latino identifiers in the Census Bureau's annual Current Population survey since the 1970s, and with the release of the 1976 Survey of Income and Education (SIE) microdata file, empirical work has become more feasible. Now it is possible to distinguish considerable socioeconomic variation within national-origin groups, allowing for separate analysis of populations with origins in Mexico, Cuba, Puerto Rico, Central and South America, and a residual "other-Hispanic" grouping.

Theory determines to a considerable extent what we observe. Theory also determines what we do not observe. Theoretical perspectives facilitate our asking certain questions. Consequently, it is important to consider the theoretical perspectives shaping the empirical investigations discussed in this chapter.

INCOME INEQUALITY AND DISCRIMINATION: THE ROLE OF HUMAN CAPITAL MODELS

There have been several major attempts to understand the persistence of discrimination in the market place. Clearly, this interest has stemmed from the empirical observations that show not only significant income differentials between black and white workers, at any given point in time, but continuing through many decades, and also the low occupational employment status for these workers (Bergmann, 1971; Brown, 1977; Reich, 1981). In addition to this concern for the plight of the black worker, recent empirical evidence on the Hispanic worker shows similar labor market trends and experiences (Rochin 1988).

Although several demand-side models have been developed to explain theoretically labor market discrimination—such as the Becker (1957) model, the Bergmann (1971) crowding model, and the Spence (1973) signaling model—the supply-side human capital models have been the major focus of several studies in economics and in sociology.

Supply-side models, such as the human capital model, shift the focus from employer tastes and informational problems within the labor market that result in discriminatory hiring/training policies, to those factors that affect workers' productivity before they enter the market place. Here, human capital theory is used in order to understand the investment decisions in general training by non-white workers and white workers. The implicit assumption in this model is that non-white workers and women are treated fairly in the labor market even though their opportunity sets may have been constrained prior to entering the market place; that is, from such institutional barriers as unequal access to quality schools, limited access to social services, and the like.

Given that market forces are independent of institutional constraints, the low wages received by non-white workers and/or their occupational segregation is a result of their choice not to invest in training or education that would improve their social and economic status. Thus, the responsibility of low wages and low occupational status is a result of choices made by these workers not to obtain the work credentials necessary for employment in high-wage sectors. What appears as labor market discrimination, therefore, merely reflects non-optimal decision-making practices by non-white workers.

These non-optimal decisions that are made by non-white workers benefit some sectors of the economy, even though there is an overall misallocation of resources. In this model, those who gain from this misallocation are those who employ unskilled workers, which occurs because there is an artificially high supply of unskilled, potentially high-productivity workers.

The human capital model, unlike the demand-side models, suggests that there are no distortions in the labor market, and that both employer and workers operate rationally in the labor market. The employer pays the workers the value of their marginal product and the workers rationally weigh the returns they will receive from investments in human capital. Thus,

> racism is embedded in political and social institutions . . . markets are affected only to the extent that they register the effects of racism while performing their technical task of guiding resources to their most efficient use. (Weaver, 1978, p. 306)

Other critics of the human capital model are concerned with the exclusion of class and class conflict as important factors in explaining labor market phenomena. Bowles and Gintis (1975) argued that an adequate theory of human resource utilization must include theories of production and of social reproduction. They claimed that human capital theory offered no theories of production and of social reproduction. Class issues influence the demand for labor. Ownership of capital and control structures in capitalist enterprises significantly influence the incentive of workers. Although the human capital perspective focuses on workers' individual characteristics and attributes, this perspective seems to limit itself to consideration of their technical skills as related to productive capacity. The human capital perspective ignores labor history, wherein management has used race, sex, age, ethnicity, and formal educational degrees to fragment the labor force. Issues of power and class are fundamentally involved in accounting for labor demand in allocating workers to positions, structuring jobs, and defining the productivity of workers. The complexity of the labor market is not expressed by a human capital perspective that considers as free market matching of technically defined skills with technically defined production requirements.

For the past twenty years, human capital explanations have provided explanations of income differences for black and white populations. Historically, throughout the twentieth century, measured skill disparities between blacks and whites have narrowed. However, income inequality between the two populations did not begin to narrow until the 1960s. Using 1940 census data, Zeman focused on years of schooling and on-the-job training, two of the most important determinants of income according to the human capital model. Incomes of both races increased with schooling and age, but the rate of increase in income was much higher for white men. Zeman's study suggested that giving blacks the same amount of education as whites would accomplish little to reduce income inequality. Further research in the 1950s tended to confirm Zeman's findings (Smith, 1984, p. 685). Even the early work of Thurow (1969), based on the microlevel 1960 census tapes, continued to show low returns in schooling for blacks in addition to dramatic declines in their relative earning potential throughout their careers. Economists focused on market discrimination against black skilled labor and government discrimination, which contributed to lower quality education in black schools, to explain declining black-white income ratios with schooling. Theories of discrimination accounted for differences in job investment: either blacks were seen as being denied jobs with human capital growth, or they were confined to secondary labor markets.

In the late 1960s and early 1970s, two factors contributed greater credibility to human capital analysis (Smith, 1984, p. 686). First, there was a continued substantial rise in black-white income ratios. Second, analysis based on micro-data tapes from the 1967 Survey of Economic Opportunity and the 1970 census suggested that rates of return to education appeared as high for blacks as for whites, the latter being especially true for higher education. Nevertheless, the historical validity of the human capital perspective continued to be questioned (Ashenfelter, 1977; Darity, 1982; Levin, 1978). The significant rise in relative black income that began during the mid-1960s coincided with the enactment of the 1965 Civil Rights Act. Some critics of the human capital model attribute considerable importance to antidiscrimination legislation as the explanation for this rise in black income (Freeman, 1973). The long historical record continued to show that although there had been a steady convergence in human capital characteristics between blacks and whites, income inequality for blacks had not changed much until the late 1960s.

A more recent, careful analysis of the historical trends in schooling, income, and labor market participation for blacks and whites indicates a stronger case for human capital explanations of these trends. Smith (1984, p. 695) found that generations of blacks who were born between 1886 and 1905 had an impact on the interpretations of time-series changes in their relative income that lasted for forty years. As long as they remained a large part of the total labor force, there was no reason to expect much convergence in income ratios based on human capital elements alone. Once these cohorts left the labor market in the 1960s and 1970s, improvements in economic conditions of black men became evident. Smith and others now argue that black men of recent cohorts do not encounter career prospects that differ from those of white men. They see the fundamental problems as the wide inequalities that exist when labor market competition begins. Smith (1984) concluded that the large income gap between white and black men that exists when careers begin may be due substantially to racial discrimination. However, this perspective now places more confidence in the human capital model, asserting that as the human capital of blacks increases relative to whites, black wages will also increase accordingly.

Empirical studies based on the extended human capital model vary considerably owing to differences in the variables that are included, definitions and ways of operationalizing the same variables, data sets applied, and measurement. However, these models do conform in certain general ways. Most studies find that, in contrast to studies of blacks, educational attainment is the most important income differential between the Latino and non-Latino white population. The low wages of Latinos in the labor market are not strongly accounted for by wage discrimination as occurs with black-white wage comparisons. Instead, wage differences between Latino and white workers are caused by the lower levels of human capital characteristics (e.g., education and job skills) found among the Latino population.

The research of Reimers (1985, p. 55) showed, for comparative purposes, a 23% wage-offer gap between black and white men. Less than one half of this gap can be explained by different individual characteristics. Educational differences account for only 10% of the inequality. As much as 14% of the wage-offer difference may be due to discrimination. The Reimers study identified a significant wage difference between Latinos and non-Latino white men. Educational differences accounted for about one half of the wage difference. Statistically controlling for differences in socioeconomic characteristics of the two groups, the wage gap was substantially reduced, to 6%. This residual, unexplained gap in income was attributed to discrimination.

In analyzing the differences in unemployment rates between Latino and non-Latino white populations, DeFreitas (1985) found that individual characteristics accounted for most of the gap. However, the residual or unexplained difference suggested that discrimination also played a role in creating the higher unemployment rates for Latinos compared to the white population.

The effects of education on income vary significantly across Hispanic-American groups. Generally, these studies indicate that income returns to education for Latinos are lower than they are for whites, but it varies by nationality. Using 1975 data, Reimers (1985) found that Hispanic-Anglo wage ratios for men ranged from low of seventy-two cents for Mexicans to a high of eighty-nine cents for Cubans.

Since a substantial number of Latinos are foreign-born, other variables enter the human capital equation, including nativity, English-language proficiency, length of time in the United States, and nationality. In particular, the impact of English-language proficiency has been the focus of several empirical studies. A study by Grenier (1984) concluded that language attributes play a significant role in wage levels of Hispanic male workers. In addition, he found that Hispanic workers whose mother tongue was Spanish had lower returns to education relative to those whose mother tongue was English. In a later study, McManus (1985) estimated the costs of language disparity for Hispanics and the impact of English-language proficiency on wages of Hispanics. He estimated the aggregate cost of language disparity for three Hispanic male groups who had varying levels of English proficiency (i.e., those designated as "very well," "well," and "not well"). For his sample, he estimated an aggregate cost of language disparity of $45 million, which he suggested reflected an underestimate of the true cost of language disparity as Spanish-speakers account for approximately one-half of the English-deficient speakers. A final study focusing on the impact of English language ability on labor market opportunities of Hispanics and East Asian immigrant men is by Kossoudji (1988) who also concluded that it was costly to lack English proficiency; however, this cost is not shared equally by all ethnic groups. Instead, at every skill level, Hispanics appear to bear a higher cost for their language deficiency relative to Asians owing to reduced observed earnings and fewer occupational opportunities. A critical assumption of many of these empirical studies is that the marginal value product of the individual worker is adversely affected by lack of English proficiency. If this assumption is valid and if the lower observed wages of Hispanics is explained primarily by the lack of English proficiency, then the obvious policy implication would be to increase the level of English proficiency for this group to enhance their wage level and occupational choice. At the same time, underlying this policy recommendation is the subtle suggestion that affirmative-action programs are not the best policy alternatives for increasing the income levels of Hispanics.

Similar policy implications can be gleaned from the Reimers (1985) study. She concluded that race had no significant impact on the wages of Latino men, and that discrimination in the labor market may be responsible for wage differences of 18% for Puerto Ricans, but only 6% for Mexican men compared to non-Latino white men (p. 55).

All Latino groups (except Mexican Americans born in the United States) had lower returns to education than Anglo men (Reimers, 1985, p. 41). Compared to the earning increases of 6.1% per grade of additional schooling that was completed by Anglo men, other-Hispanics earned 3.4% and Mexicans 5.4%. Except for Cubans and other-Hispanics, foreign-born Latinos had lower returns from their education in the United States than native-born men of their ethnic group (Reimers, 1985, p. 44).

Studies show that returns to foreign work experience are much smaller than returns to work experience in the United States (Reimers, 1985, p. 45). Immigrants from Mexico, Puerto Rico, and Central and South America gain little in earnings based on their prior work experience outside of the United States. In terms of earnings, these immigrants are viewed the same as new entrants into the labor market. There are also differences in returns between immigrants to the United States and Americans with regard to their work experience. Mexican, other-Hispanic, and black male immigrants have higher initial returns to work experience in this country than their native-born counterparts. However, their experience also peaks more quickly. Puerto Rican, Cuban, and Central or South American immigrant men have lower initial returns to work experience than do the native-born (Reimers, 1985, p. 45). Reimers also found that in states where Latinos constituted a larger proportion of the population, white and Cuban men earned at least as much as they earned elsewhere (p. 49). However, Mexican, Puerto Rican, and other-Hispanic men received lower wages than elsewhere, which may be evidence of discrimination affecting Latinos when they represent a larger proportion of the population. These conditions could also result from Mexicans and other-Hispanics choosing to work where there are many other Latinos, regardless of the lower wage rates in these regions.

Studies of the determinants of Latinas' wages show some differences from men. Reimers (1985) reported that Mexican women's average wage offers are 20% lower than white non-Hispanic women (p. 70). After compensating for regional cost-of-living differences, the gap narrowed to 16%. Years of schooling was found to account for 93% of the real wage offer gap. Puerto Rican and Cuban women's wages are about the same as that of white non-Hispanic women. The most likely explanation offered is that white non-Latin American women tend to be employed in white-collar jobs, whereas minority women with comparable education are more often employed in blue-collar jobs that provide higher wages. Again, just as for Latinos, Reimers (1985) argued that race is not an important factor in explaining the lower wages of Latin American women (p. 72). Immigrant status accounts for small differences in the wage gap for women, from 0.2% for Mexican women to 8% for Central and South American women. English language problems cause wage differences ranging from none for Puerto Rican women to 8% for Cuban women. The larger families of Mexican women are considered a factor in explaining the 3% wage gap when compared to their Anglo counterparts, but represent minimal differences for other groups of Latinas.

A study by Carlson and Swartz (1988), which examined wage disparities across racial and ethnic groups, found that women's earnings for all groups were less sensitive to human capital characteristics than those of white men. If Mexican and Puerto Rican women were paid, using the same white male earnings function, given their productive characteristics, less than one half of the observed earning gap between the two groups would have remained. From their empirical study, it was suggested that all groups of women experience a greater influence from discrimination than do men; however, much of the disparity in women's earnings can be attributed to productive characteristics and hours worked.

Generally, the human capital studies suggest that ethnic discrimination is not a major determinant in the earnings of Mexican, Puerto Rican, and Cuban women, although it is more of a barrier to Central and South American and other-Hispanic women. On the whole, all Latin American women receive lower returns for their work than do white non-Hispanic women (Reimers, 1985, p. 74). The reason for this is because Latin American women have less access to jobs with training and promotion opportunities, and often have more children than do white non-Hispanic women, which is another factor that lowers their wages.

THE CLASS/STRUCTURAL MODEL

Prior to the development of an articulated class/structural model of income determination by such labor economists as Reich, Gordon, and Edwards (1973), alternative explanations of wage and occupational determination were developed by institutional economists such as Fisher (1953), Kerr (1954), and Doeringer and Piore (1971) that challenged the accuracy of the human capital approach. In particular, the Doeringer and Piore (1971) dual labor market model provided critical contributions in understanding the role of nonmarket forces in labor market allocations.

The concept of the dual labor market was developed in response to the observation that no single labor market exists (Kerr, 1954). In fact, in certain sectors of the economy, the allocations of labor and the determination of wages appears to be insulated from market forces. Doeringer and Piore (1971) attempted to explain the mechanisms and institutions that allocated labor under these conditions. In order to deal with the problem theoretically, their suggestion was to develop the concept to the internal labor market and the theory of the dual labor market. An internal labor market is defined as an "administrative unit within which pricing and allocation of labor is governed by a set of administrative rules and procedures" (Doeringer & Piore, 1971, p. 1). They attributed the emergence of this market to the rise of skill specificity, increased on-the-job training, and custom. According to them, it also evolved to give the worker and the employer more security in the work place. However, at the same time that the internal labor market stabilized the relationship between the worker and the employer, it also institutionalized discriminatory labor market practices.

The three major categories of instruments that can result in these discriminatory practices are: (1) entry, (2) job allocation, and (3) wage. Non-market entry requirements, such as union membership, by definition are discriminatory because they segregate a group of workers from the labor market as qualified only for certain jobs. Both job allocation and wages that are non-market determined (e.g., based on a seniority system), also promote differentiation within the work force that may have no relationship to productivity. Thus, with this system a more productive non-white or white worker may not receive a fair return on his or her skill level.

The persistence of low wages and low job status, however, must be analyzed within the broader framework of the dual labor market. The dual labor market consists of a primary and a secondary labor market. Generally, the primary labor market has the following features: high wages, good working conditions, employment stability, chances of advancement, equity, and due process in the administration of work rules. (Doeringer & Piore, 1971) Given these characteristics, the development of an internal labor market follows within this sector as nonwage aspects of employment increase in importance. In contrast, jobs in the secondary labor market generally do not have internal labor markets and possess many of the following features:

low wages and fringe benefits, poor working conditions, high labor turnover, little chance of advancement, and often arbitrary and capricious supervision. (Doeringer & Piore, 1971, p. 165)

The dual labor market analysis specifically arose as an attempt to understand the labor force problems of the disadvantaged, particularly non-white workers in urban areas, whose problems had previously been attributed to unemployment. A major conclusion drawn from the model was that non-white workers were confined to jobs in the secondary labor market, and that high unemployment rates were a characteristic of jobs in that sector. Thus, policy should be aimed at minimizing the entry barriers (e.g., via manpower training programs) into the primary labor market, or creating conditions so that jobs in the secondary sector can acquire some of the characteristics of the primary labor market in order to develop more stable work relationships.

The major problems that Doeringer and Piore attempted to approach with the dual labor market analysis were in explaining the persistence of non-white workers in jobs that were characterized as secondary labor market occupations. They attempted to explain this persistence by examining lower income life-styles and the characteristics of secondary jobs, such as lack of stability and low skill requirements. Thus, these workers have neither the incentive nor the model to acquire the necessary skills to enter the primary labor market. Furthermore, employers have no incentive to invest in training their workers, given their behavioral characteristics, nor do they have the incentive to stabilize the work relationship. The net effect is that non-white workers are caught in dead-end, low-paying jobs with slim chances of entering the primary labor market.

Although discrimination against non-white workers does and can occur in the primary labor market, this problem is of lesser importance than the problem of concentration of non-white workers in the secondary labor market—a problem deeply rooted in the subculture of non-white workers and the structure and nature of the secondary labor market. Discrimination against non-white workers, therefore, is a product of these two factors and can only be eliminated by breaking the links that attach the non-white workers to the secondary labor market.

The major weakness in the institutional models is that discrimination appears to be exogenously determined; that is, we are left with the question: How did discriminatory treatment of non-white workers arise in their model? Not attempting to explain the origins of discrimination results in a circular argument. For example: Why are non-whites overrepresented in the secondary labor market? Is this because they are discriminated against and less productive? But why are they less productive and discriminated against? Is this because they are in the secondary labor market where the proper skills and behavioral traits needed for the primary labor market are unattainable? And so the vicious circle continues.

Unlike the dual labor market analysis, which limits its discussion to the narrow confines of the labor market, a class/structural perspective considers three basic units of analysis: macrosocial structures, classes, and individuals. This perspective argues that social structures and classes are equally significant in determining individual income. In addition, the structuralist perspective considers these three units as interdependent. A fully developed theory of income inequality must recognize the characteristics of the social structures within which income is determined.

With an analysis of the social basis of the income determination process, specific analysis of income determination at the class level can take place. Income determination at the class level can be considered by two factors: the analysis of income determination within classes, and the analysis of the ways in which the entire income determination process is shaped by class conflict. Class relations are believed to influence income determination of individuals. Classes are organized social forces that enter into conflict and change social structures. According to Wright (1979), class conflict influences the income determination process in two basic ways: first, through union struggles over wages, unemployment insurance, and other social welfare benefits, and second, by transforming the social structures within which income determination occurs.

From the structural perspective, the analysis of individual-level income determination involves two dimensions: first, the way in which individual choices and actions can change a person's position within class relations through inter- or intraclass mobility, and second, the various processes which affect those specific individual choices influencing the individual's income within a certain class location. Certainly, the individual's education, for example, has a bigger impact on the income of a manager than of a worker. This perspective considers class and social structural relationships which influence individual consciousness.

Human capital research does not focus on wage discrimination as the most important form of discrimination occurring within the labor market. A class/structural perspective regards wage differences as the result of the location of workers within the labor market, in terms of industrial sector and occupation. Here we consider three major noncompetitive labor market structures: dual labor markets, occupational segmentation, and ethnic enclaves.

Industrial dualism argues that the organization of the product markets (as monopolistic or competitive) determines the relative bargaining of firms and workers (Gordon, 1972). Firms belong either in the core sector or the periphery. Higher earnings are realized in the core sector while lower wages are earned in the peripheral sector.

Occupational segmentation considers the degree of control an individual has in the work environment. Edwards (1979) identified three occupational segments. Secondary jobs are those requiring little formal training and are characterized by low pay, no career mobility, and high turnover. A subordinate primary segment are those jobs attached to the top segment requiring some formal training, and are characterized by limited career mobility, and moderate pay and benefits. The independent primary jobs, those requiring considerable training, are characterized by real career mobility opportunities, high pay, good benefits, and low turnover. About two thirds of the Latino labor force is located in the peripheral industries and more than 60% is concentrated in the low-wage occupational segment (Melendez, 1988, p. 1).

Empirical studies have found significant differences in earnings in core and peripheral industrial sectors after taking into account workers' characteristics. Workers in core industries earn 30% to 40% higher wages and experience lower turnover (Bibb & Form, 1977; Kallenberg & Althauser, 1981). Studies of occupational segmentation indicate that workers in secondary jobs do, in fact, experience less upward mobility and have lower wages, whereas those in primary sector jobs experience higher salaries and more job mobility (Gordon, 1972). The labor market segmentation models view the evolution of the labor market as a function of the level of the development of the productive forces. By examining the historical development of capitalism in the United States, it is possible to trace the corresponding changes in the labor market, that is, at each stage (competitive, monopoly, and advanced monopoly) the labor market must adapt in order to reproduce the social relations of production. However, in the latter two stages of capital accumulation, capital becomes concentrated at an uneven rate; thus, the production process itself becomes segmented into competitive and monopolistic sectors and the dual labor market that develops reflects this uneven sectoral growth.

In the segmentation model, racist labor practices are viewed as tools to aid in further dividing and conquering the working class. Any divisions within the working class are played upon in order to break down worker solidarity. Divisions that are due to both race and sex are a given in this model, resulting in a glossing over of the origins and processes by which a certain group is selected for discriminatory practice. Most empirical studies have focused on the black experience, with little research considering the Latino labor market experience.

A recent study by Melendez (1988) has examined the effects of labor market structure on Latino labor markets in New York City. Melendez considered several categories of Latinos: Mexicans, Puerto Ricans, Cubans, and other-Hispanics using the 1980 census data. The findings from his study indicate that labor market structures (in this case, industrial sectors and occupational segmentation) are important determinants of Hispanic, non-Hispanic, black, and white hourly wages in New York City. In fact, labor market structure explains a substantial proportion of Latino wage differences from non-Latino white populations. About 16% to 19% of the difference is explained by primary-segment location for Hispanic men and 36% to 58% for Hispanic women. Working within core industries can explain about 7% to 14% of the Latino wage gap for men and about 4% to 7% for women. Melendez found that discrimination is still an important factor in accounting for the wage gap for Latin Americans. Discrimination was responsible for about one third of the wage gap for Mexican, Puerto Rican, and Cuban men. Although the wage gap was much smaller for women than men, discrimination accounted for one fifth to one half of the gap. This study of the New York City labor force determined that whites have higher returns to education and job experience than do blacks and Latinos. Finally, Melendez found that education was the single most important factor for all Latino groups in explaining the earnings gap between them and the white population. However, the proportion of the wage gap explained by differences in education varies greatly among the different Latino groups. Human capital characteristics account for 25% to 50% of the ethnic wage differences, and reduces by more than 50% women's wage differences.

Previous studies of structural theories of labor market segmentation have barely touched upon the interaction of class and ethnicity, and not much attention has been paid to ethnically organized economic activities. Recently, Portes and Bach (1985) integrated the concept of ethnic enclaves with analysis of segmented labor market theory. Their analysis involved a six-year period. Contrary to the human capital model, immigrants do not arrive as isolated individuals, but rather have access to the resources of the larger groups to which they belong. Portes and Bach argued that an immigrant's ability to utilize individual human capital is influenced by class position, social networks, and state policies. State policies may work to direct immigrant groups into secondary markets. Ethnicity, rather than individual skills, may combine with an immigrant's working-class background to link secondary labor employers to new workers. For some immigrant groups, however, another structure operates within the labor market: the ethnic enclave.

Ethnic enclaves are distinct economic formations characterized by spatial concentrations of immigrants who organize a variety of enterprises to serve their own market and the general population (Portes & Bach, 1985, p. 203). Ethnic enterprises possess two essential traits: the presence of immigrants with sufficient capital to create new opportunities for economic growth and an extensive division of labor within the enclave. The enclaves develop as the first wave of immigrants send over an entrepreneurial class. The growth and diversification of this class offer subsequent immigrants from the same ethnic group employment opportunities unavailable to immigrants entering regular labor market sectors. Studies show that these entrepreneurial activities can expand because they are able to reproduce (on a local scale) some of the characteristics of monopolistic control that account for the success of firms in the larger economy. Ethnic entrepreneurs use new immigrant workers to suppress unionization and to capitalize through pooled savings and rotating credit systems (Cheng & Bonacich, 1984; Light, 1972). The labor organization of immigrant enclave economies requires recent arrivals to take the worst jobs first. Immigrants are willing to stay in these secondary-type jobs because they open paths of upward mobility that are unavailable outside the immigrant enclave. Expanding enclave firms are expected to create managerial-level openings or self-employment for members of the same minority.

Ethnic enclaves differ from the secondary sector: ethnic ties permeate the class relationship with a sense of collective purpose and solidarity forces discipline on the part of the workers; however, it also demands obligations from the managers to provide training and skill upgrading for the workers.

Portes and Bach (1985) showed how Cuban entrepreneurs in Miami merged into the local economy through the growth of a small-scale entrepreneurial class, which was assisted by the established social network within the Cuban community. However, it is also important to recognize that the majority of the sample had entered the outside economy, moving into the segmented primary and secondary sectors. They found that ethnicity in the secondary sector was associated with lower rewards and subordinate social and economic positions than those generally found among the immigrant minorities. Their study concluded that individual skills operated differently depending on where immigrants worked. In the enclave, Cuban education contributed to occupational gain early in the resettlement experience and over time. Also, workers benefited from work experience in Cuba and from the additional experience they gained in the United States. Outside the enclave in the secondary sector, there were few benefits or rewards for individual skills. Previous education in Cuba penalized occupational workers. Workers in the secondary sector moved upward by accumulating economic resources transferred from Cuba or acquired over time in the United States.

In all, Portes and Bach (1980, 1985) found that the process of occupational and income attainment among Cuban immigrants was significantly influenced by the availability of ethnically organized enclaves. Self-employment and economic returns on human capital, made possible through the operation of enclaves, had little to do with the individual abilities of immigrants. Instead, their upward economic achievements depended on the enclave social structures that received and supported them. In contrast, although many Mexicans had greater education and occupational training than did Cuban immigrants, few Mexican immigrants in the Portes study became small businessmen within six years of their arrival in the United States. Portes and Bach claimed that Mexican immigrants do not have an enclave option but, instead, are entrenched in a long historical working-class migrant flow.

Beginning with the works of Simmel, sociologists have been interested in how group size influences social behavior and social structure. Recently, labor market analysts have investigated how the relative size of minority populations in the labor market influences minority wages relative to the white majority. Studies have reached different conclusions, in part, because they use different dependent variables (income and occupational status) to demonstrate increasing or decreasing inequality. Also, most studies treat minority populations as homogeneous, with no attempt to account for the increasing heterogeneity found within minority groups today.

There are two general explanations for the widening disparity of income between the white majority and the minority populations. One argument is that discrimination increases as minority workers compete for scarce resources, thereby threatening the majority economically and politically. This results in discrimination against minorities both in access to educational institutions and to good jobs in the work place. A second explanation is that when threatened by growth of the minority population, the majority will use its control of capital to subordinate minority workers, using them as sources of cheap labor and for driving down wages

(Bonacich & Modell, 1980). Consistent with other studies, Borjas (1985) and Tienda and Lii (1987) found that Latinos working in labor markets with larger shares of minorities earned less than Latinos working in areas with smaller minority concentrations. The losses of earnings of black, Latino, and Asian men associated with residence in areas with high minority concentrations were greatest among the college educated and lowest among those who had not completed high school. College educated whites gained most from these minority concentrations. Whites with less education did not gain from increased minority density. Tienda and Lii suggested that Asians and Latinos appear to compete more with each other than with whites in the markets where they are disproportionately represented (p. 160). Significant disparities in earnings between highly educated men from minority groups and whites suggest that schooling, by itself, is not sufficient to narrow the earnings gap (p. 162). These findings coincide with other studies showing that socioeconomic inequalities between majority and minority income increase as the proportion of minorities in the labor market grows. Reich (1971) argued that racial/ethnic inequality increased owing to the suppression of labor union growth or labor militancy as well as the reduction in minority access to educations that are needed to make gains in the labor market.

Another perspective suggests a more positive relationship between increases in minority populations and minority income. Frisbie and Neidart (1977) found that in terms of occupational status, both majority and minority workers benefited from labor market concentration of minority workers, but that only white workers gained financially. They argued that discrimination might be lessened in areas of minority concentration if racial and ethnic minorities were successful in creating and developing economic enclaves that insulate minority workers from competition with the white majority. Once a minority population reaches a certain size, it develops internal high-status jobs and income generation through minority enterprises. Another explanation supporting this positive relationship is that as the minority population grows, so will its political power and its strength in economic bargaining (Reich, 1981). Increased political power will then lead to the enactment of legislation supporting equal opportunities or equal pay for equal work in the labor force for minority workers (Bonacich & Modell, 1980).

INDUSTRIAL POLICY

Conventional policy recommendations for reducing income inequality focus on conclusions drawn from the human capital model. Proposals typically suggest increasing formal schooling, providing job training for minorities, and improving English-language fluency for immigrant groups. To the extent that differences in individual characteristics like education and job training explain differences in income, policies should emphasize education and job training. However, the human capital approach translates into a myopic view of policy changes that might contribute to a change in income disparities for the Latino population. It provides a narrow view of production and an even more limited understanding of social reproduction in the economy.

The human capital model, interpreted at face value, can be used to support a victim-blaming explanation of inequalities in income. The intense focus on individual characteristics suggests that the individuals are responsible for inadequate schooling, weak job skills, and a poor command of the English language.

Policy recommendations based on the class/structuralist model offer different solutions for rectifying the disparity of income for minorities. From this perspective, income inequalities result from the normal operation of the labor market. That is to say, income inequality is a structural aspect of the capitalist economy and does not derive entirely from individual differences in skills and competencies. More importantly, this model posits that class, which is defined as position within the social relations of production, plays a central role in mediating income inequality in a capitalist society.

Since the middle 1970s, restructuring has radically influenced American corporations. Increasingly, foreign economic and political conditions are influencing domestic labor and welfare policies. During the 1970s, the economy in the United States moved rapidly from a goods-producing to a service-producing economy. Since the 1982 recession, most new jobs have been created in the service sector, and service-sector workers are worse off economically than their counterparts in the manufacturing sector.

These international economic and political changes have contributed to sharp declines in profits for corporations, which have responded by restructuring in ways that significantly affect labor and minority incomes. Some of the changes in corporate structure have had a clear impact on depressing labor conditions. Interregional and international shifts of capital have contributed to the highly visible cycles of plant closures in the United States. The plant closures that have received the widest attention occurred in such areas of the economy as the automobile, tire, and steel industries.

With introduction of new technologies, jobs in electronics and telecommunications face de-skilling. Wage cuts accompany the process of de-skilling occupations. Highly centralized companies with well-defined internal career paths are being replaced by smaller operations with fewer long-term career opportunities—even occupations are being "downsized." Management practices in the 1980s regularly demanded wage freezes, staff reductions, and two-tiered pay systems.

The impact of the tremendous growth in part-time employment or contingency work by Latinos in the labor force must be considered. In order to increase flexibility in organizations, a new emphasis has been placed on converting full-time jobs into part-time jobs, contracting jobs to non-union firms, and increasing numbers of new homeworkers, as a special labor version of "outsourcing." Informal estimates of part-time or contingent labor suggest an increase from eight million part-time workers in 1980 to 18 million today. Increasing the size of the contingent work force allows management to reduce the firm's benefit expenses. The Employee Benefits Research Institute in Washington, D.C., reported that, in 1986, 70% of all part-time employees had no company-provided retirement plan and 42% had no company-provided health insurance. Contingency workers also received a lower hourly wage compared to full-time employees. A recent study of forty-four different service and manufacturing industries found that part-time workers were paid lower hourly wages than were full-time workers, and they were less likely to be covered by health insurance and pension plans, even after statistically controlling for differences in workers' characteristics (Ehrenberg, Rosenberg, & Li, 1991). These changes will heavily impact Latinos in the part-time labor force.

Current debates center on whether low-wage jobs are growing at the expense of high-wage jobs and whether the middle class is disappearing. In a recent study completed for the U.S. Congressional Joint Economic Commission, two economists, Bluestone and Harrison, were asked to address these issues (Harrison, 1987; Bluestone & Harrison, 1988). They found that average hourly, weekly, and annual wages and salary incomes of individual workers peaked in the early-to-mid 1970s. Since that time, incomes have either stagnated or fallen. Median weekly earnings have yet to reach their 1973 peak. Presently, real working-class incomes stand at about the same level as in 1960. Bluestone and Harrison also found that between 1973 and 1979, about one fifth of all net new employment created in the United States paid annual wages and salaries lower than the 1973 median wages (about $7,400 in 1986 prices). The trend subsequently worsened. Between 1979 and 1985, over 40% of all net new employment paid these low wages. Indeed, these changes strongly suggest a proliferation of low wages in our newly restructured economy.

All sectors of the economy have experienced increases in part-time labor, wage freezes, and union bashing. However, Bluestone and Harrison concluded that the growth of the service sector is particularly responsible for these dismal trends. They found that, between 1979 and 1985, only 6% of net new jobs in manufacturing paid yearly wages below $7,400. Forty percent of the jobs being created in the service sector were paying $7,400 or less. In their study, they determined that service sector workers were seven times more likely to earn wages below the poverty line than were manufacturing workers (Harrison, 1987, p. 10). Policy-makers need to consider reorganizing the performance and remuneration of service-sector jobs instead of denying their growth.

FUTURE RESEARCH

Certainly, the 1990 census should provide major new data for the exploration of income determination among minority populations. A methodological problem with human capital studies is that cross-sectional data are used to impute causal forces. Better longitudinal studies or time-series analyses are needed to explain more accurately gender differences in the determination of income. Far more research is needed on the ethnic enclave economies that are developing in Los Angeles, San Diego, San Francisco-San Jose silicon valley, Houston, San Antonio, and other urban areas in the Southwest. Los Angeles will provide the opportunity for researchers to explore relationships among several ethnic enclaves within the city, including Korean, Chinese, Vietnamese, Mexican, and perhaps Central American entrepreneurs who establish themselves along with their labor forces. To what extent are these minority groups competing among themselves?

More research is needed on the impact of corporate restructuring of Latinos in the labor market. How are Latinos doing as contingent or part-time workers? How are they doing in the middle-class professions? In general, more research is needed on Latinos within specific labor markets.

Now that it is possible to differentiate among Latino groups in the measurement of factors determining their income, policy analysts should begin to consider the differential impact their policy recommendations will have on these groups. The human resource analysts have shown that Latinos are a heterogeneous group, and that their different locations within the work force must be taken into consideration when formulating labor and educational policies. Research that does not differentiate the Hispanic populations according to class and national origins will indubitably lead to misguided policy.

What effects will the 1986 immigration law have on native-born Latino employment and income? Research is needed to better understand the impact of urban undocumented workers on the incomes of other minority groups. Further research is also needed to examine the relationship between local economic development and the growth of the marginal sectors of the labor market. Are we seeing the exacerbation of the problems of their sector and a formation of Chicano/Latino underclass in the urban political economy and social structure? How to create a substantial number of quality jobs for this group is of crucial importance to a comprehensive research agenda.

Last and most important, future empirical research on the Chicano/Latino economic condition must be recast in a more rigorous analytical and theoretical framework. A critical analysis of the capitalist state and class structure is conspicuously absent in studies of the Latino population. In particular, what is missing, in the growing body of quantitative approaches to the study of Chicano/Latino inequality, is a conceptualization of the centrality of class, both background and position, and the relationship of such positions in determining earnings, employment, and unemployment. The absence of an analysis of the capitalist wage-labor system and class relations with its structural inequalities of income and power is a serious shortcoming. Future investigation of income inequality must include class position within the social relations of production as an independent variable. For example, a landmark work—*Race and Class in the Southwest* by Mario Barrera (1979)—can serve as a guide for future research on Latinos in a changing political economy. His theoretical contribution, which lay in defining, locating, and connecting the subordinate class position of Chicanos with the institutionalized patterns of discrimination and the interests of capital, remains critical. However, his focus on structural relations needs to be integrated into a broader theoretical framework that allows for ideological, political, and cultural forms of resistance to capitalist hegemony. Recent work in state theory posits that the state rather than production is the site of conflict and counter-hegemonic struggles. To what extent are racial/ethnic relations a sphere of action autonomous from economic relations? In what ways do race, gender, and class structure each other? What is the role of the state in this process? Research on the accumulation and legitimation needs of the state can provide needed theoretical clarity to an understanding of Chicano inequality, and what public policies are needed to address it, in a liberal capitalist democracy. Thus, the theoretical imperative of doing research should become the moral imperative of policy and social reconstruction.

Full employment and increased affirmative action should be two inseparable demands of a progressive program for economic democracy and Chicano/Latino equality in the post-Reagan era. A third demand should address both overall economic inequality and racial inequality in a programmatic manner (e.g., a national policy that would raise the wages of low-wage workers more rapidly than those of high-wage workers)—a solidarity wage. For a fuller discussion of a solidarity wage, see

Bowles, Gordon, and Weisskopf (1983, pp. 283–284). This demand, in conjunction with the demands for full employment and affirmative action, represent what French sociologist Andre Gorz (1968, pp. 7–8) termed "non-reformist reforms"—that is, policy changes which bestow greater power and democratic rights to the "average" citizens in their daily lives as workers and consumers.

As indicated in this chapter, conventional policy recommendations for addressing income disparities among groups have indeed been based on human capital models. At the same time, there *are* a set of initiatives that have attempted to deal with a different category of problems. That is, we have seen special unemployment payments given to steel workers in the early 1980s to protect them from the effects of "unfair foreign competition," a lengthening of workers' compensation periods to handle the same problem, and the bailout of several large industrial and financial firms (such as Lockheed, Chrysler, First Republic Bank of Texas, and the Continental Bank of Illinois). The rationale for these government ventures into the marketplace was not based on a human capital model. Instead, they were "structural" in the sense that a situation was defined as being abnormal or outside the acceptable limits of the "structure of economic relations." Once trade, banking, and bankruptcy crises of these corporate giants were defined in this way, exceptions were made, and they could be administered to without disturbing the underlying corporate ideology.

Industrial policy is fundamentally structural, too. Its difference is that the above interventions have been crisis-oriented exceptions, whereas industrial policy implies the adoption of an ongoing explicit commitment to channel developments for the industrial structure as a whole. The question, then, is how should this be done? A democratic approach to industrial policy might insist on (1) equal representation of workers on supra-organizational boards; (2) initiatives that not only protect the established position of privileged workers, but also raise the access of unprivileged Chicano/Latino workers to better and more stable jobs; and (3) geographic preference that channels quality jobs into Chicano communities, which are supported by local control and democratic participation.

In effect, what we are positing is that policy makers have already quietly recognized the need to correct economic outcomes when they are the result of warped or unacceptable structural disturbances. Perhaps a point of departure relevant to Latino workers and communities would be to say, Why not define instances of structural inequality and resource deprivation as unacceptable, too? This could serve as the rationale for government interventions, just as the government has resolved to help big corporations who are in need.

Future policy research on contemporary Latino issues should be conducted within a framework of politics of social change. Advanced intellectual groundwork, though essential, cannot substitute for political practice. In these post-Reagan years, the struggle for economic and social justice will require the development of organizations and the marshaling of new social forces and movements that are committed to structural economic reforms. Also necessary is the advancement of a compelling vision of equity and grassroots participation upon which forms of economic democracy could be articulated and practiced in the electoral arena. The policy and political initiatives that are outlined in this chapter will only come at considerable cost, but the benefits could be enormous—a more democratic economy.

REFERENCES

Ashenfelter, O. (1977). Comments on Smith-Welsh's black-white male earnings and employment: 1960-1970. In T. Juster, Ed., *The distribution of economic well-being*. National Bureau of Economic Research Studies in Income and Wealth, No. 41. Cambridge, England: Bollinger.

Barrera, M. (1979). *Race and class in the southwest*. Notre Dame: University of Notre Dame Press.

Becker, G. S. (1957). *The economics of discrimination*. Chicago: University of Chicago Press.

Bergmann, B. (1971). The effects of white incomes of discrimination in employment. *Journal of Political Economy, 79*(2), 294–313.

Bibb, R., & W. Form. (1977). The effects of industrial occupational and sex stratification on wages in blue-collar markets. *Social Forces* (June), 974–996.

Bluestone, B., & B. Harrison. (1988). *The great U-turn: Corporate restructuring and the polarizing of America*. New York: Basic Books.

Bonacich, E., & J. Modell. (1980). *The economic basis of ethnic solidarity: A study of Japanese Americans*. Berkeley: University of California Press.

Borjas, G. (1985). Jobs and employment for Hispanics. In P. San Juan Cafferty & W. C. McCready, Eds., *Hispanics in the United States: A new social agenda*. New Brunswick, NJ: Transaction Books.

Bowels, S., & H. Gintis. (1975). The problem with human capital theory—A Marxian critique. *American Economic Review, 65*(2), 74–82.

Bowles, S., D. Gordon, & T. Weisskopf. (1983). *Beyond the waste land*. Garden City: Doubleday-Anchor Press.

Brown, P. (1977). *The inequality of pay*. Berkeley: University of California Press.

Carlson, L. A., & C. Swartz. (1988). The earnings of women and ethnic minorities, 1959–1979. *Industrial and Labor Relations Review, 41*(4), 530–545.

Cheng, L., & E. Bonacich. (1984). *Labor immigration under capitalism*. Berkeley: University of California Press.

Darity, W. A. (1982). The human capital approach to black-white earnings inequality: Some unsettled questions. *Journal of Human Resources*, 18, 72–93.

DeFreitas, G. (1985). Ethnic differentials in unemployment among Hispanic-Americans. In G. Borjas & M. Tienda, Eds., *Hispanics in the U. S. Economy*. New York: Academic Press.

Doeringer, P., & M. Piore. (1971). *Internal labor markets and manpower analysis*. Lexington, MA: Health-Lexington Books.

Edwards, R. (1979). *Contested terrain*. New York: Basic Books.

Ehrenberg, R., P. Rosenberg, & J. Li. (1991). Part-time employment in the United States. In R. Hart, Ed., *Employment, unemployment and hours of work*. London: Allen & Unwin.

Fisher, L. (1953). *The harvest labor market in California*. Cambridge: Harvard University Press.

Freeman, R. (1973). Changes in the labor market for black Americans, 1948–1972. *Brookings Papers on Economic Activity*, 1, 67–120.

Frisbie, W. P., & L. Neidart. (1977). Inequality and the relative size of minority populations: A comparative analysis. *American Journal of Sociology*, 82, 1007–1030.

Gordon, D. M. (1972). *Theories of poverty and underemployment: Orthodox, radical and dual labor market perspectives*. Lexington, MA: D. C. Heath.

Gordon, D. M., R. Edwards, & M. Reich. (1982). *Segmented work, divided workers*. Cambridge, England: Cambridge University Press.

Gorz, A. (1968). *Strategy for labor*. Boston: Beacon Press.

Grenier, G. (1984). The effects of language characteristics on the wages of Hispanic-American males. *Journal of Human Resources*, 19(1), 35–52.

Harrison, B. (1987). The impact of corporate restructuring on labor income. *Social Policy*, 18(2), 6–11.

Kalleberg, A., W. Michael, & R. P. Althauser. (1981). Economic segmentation, worker power and income inequality. *American Journal of Sociology*, 87(3), 651–683.

Kerr, C. (1954). *Balkanization of the labor markets*. Berkeley, CA: Institute of Industrial Relations, Reprint No. 59.

Kossoudji, S. A. (1988). English language ability and the labor market opportunities of Hispanic and East Asian immigrant men. *Journal of Labor Economics*, 6(2), 205–228.

Levin, H. M. (1978). *Education and earnings of blacks and the "Brown" decision*. Unpublished manuscript.

Light, I. (1972). *Ethnic enterprises in America: Business and welfare among Chinese, Japanese, and blacks*. Berkeley: University of California Press.

McManus, W. S. (1985). Labor market cost of language disparity: An interpretation of Hispanic earnings differences. *American Economic Review*, 75(4), 818–827.

Melendez, E. (1988). *Labor market structure and wage inequality in New York City: A comparative analysis of Hispanic and non-Hispanic blacks and whites*. Unpublished manuscript, MIT, Department of Urban Studies and Planning, Cambridge.

Muller, T., & T. Espenshade. (1985). *The fourth wave: California's newest immigrants*. Washington, DC: Urban Institute.

Portes, A., & R. L. Bach. (1980). Immigrant earnings: Cuban and Mexican immigration in the United States. *International Migration Review*, 14, 315–341.

Portes, A., & R. L. Bach. (1985). *Latin journey: Cuban and Mexican immigrants in the United States*. Berkeley: University of California Press.

Reich, M. (1971). The economics of racism. In D. M. Gordon, Ed., *Problems in political economy: An urban perspective*. Lexington, MA: D. C. Heath.

Reich, M. (1981). *Racial inequality*. Princeton: Princeton University Press.

Reich, M., D. Gordon, & R. Edwards. (1973). A theory of labor market segmentation. *American Economic Review*, 63, 359–365.

Reimers, C. (1985). A comparative analysis of the wages of Hispanics, blacks and non-Hispanic whites. In G. Borjas & M. Tienda, Eds., *Hispanics in the U. S. Economy*. New York: Academic Press.

Rochin, R. I. (1988). *Economic perspective of the Hispanic community*. Unpublished manuscript, The Tomas Rivera Center, San Antonio, Texas.

Smith, J. (1984). Race and human capital. *American Economic Review*, 74(3), 685–698.

Spence, M. (1973). Job market signaling. *Quarterly Journal of Economics*, 87(3), 355–374.

Thurow, L. C. (1969). *Poverty and discrimination*. Washington, DC: Brookings Institution.

Thurow, L. C. (1975). *Generating inequality*. New York: Basic Books.

Tienda, M., & D. Li. (1987). Minority concentration and earnings inequality: Blacks, Hispanics and Asians compared. *American Journal of Sociology*, 93(2), 141–166.

Weaver, F. S. (1978). Cui Bono and the economic function of racism. *Review of Black Political Economy*, 8(3), 302–313.

Wright, E. O. (1979). *Class structure and income determination*. New York: Academic Press.

II
HISTORICAL VIEWS OF LATINOS AND SCHOOLING

5

History, Culture, and Education

George I. Sánchez

There are nearly four million persons with Spanish-Mexican antecedents in five southwestern states: Arizona, California, Colorado, New Mexico, and Texas. Most of them speak Spanish and, considering the circumstances, remarkably good Spanish. Although most of them speak English also, it is quite surprising that there are many present-day Spanish-Americans whose families have been exposed to the English language since the American occupation about one hundred thirty years ago, and yet they speak only Spanish. When one compares this situation with that of European immigrants who came to this country much later—Italians, Germans, Poles, and so on—many of whom have lost their original vernaculars, it would seem to indicate an unprecedented cultural tenacity (except for some Indian tribes, the Eskimos, and the Aleuts).

Why have these Americans of Spanish-Mexican backgrounds been so stubborn in relinquishing *their* vernacular? What institutions and forces made this possible? One would expect to find some concerted effort of these people to retain their language, some source of cultural pride. Or, one would expect that the English-speaking dominant group had recognized the values inherent in preserving the Spanish language and had instituted programs to that end. That is, one would expect some positive reason—some wise head, institution, or policy that has conserved this cultural resource. Sad to say, the major factor is none of these but a complex of factors that are much more negative than positive. The conservation of the heritage of the Spanish language is an eloquent illustration that it is, indeed, an ill wind that does not blow someone some good! But let us approach the matter with circumspection.

We must understand both the positive factors in the development of the Spanish language, its introduction and perpetuation in this area, and the negative forces that have resulted in the failure to make this population monolingual and English-speaking. The former is, essentially, a matter of tracing historical antecedents; the latter is one of evaluating the failure of the schools in their obstinate persistence to make English the only language of this group. This failure, more than anything else, has preserved Spanish in a bilingualism of a wide qualitative range, although among the disadvantaged classes the Spanish is superior to the English, and there is also a large group of persons of Spanish-Mexican descent whose English is excellent and whose Spanish is very limited or nonexistent.

This dualism suggests that this chapter be presented in three parts: first, a historical perspective of the positive features of the process; second, an attempt to evaluate, with historical and other evidence, why the schools have not succeeded in obliterating Spanish as the mother tongue of most Americans of Mexican descent in the Southwest; and third, a brief attempt to blend these two, seemingly disparate parts into a constructive summary. Each part will have a separate bibliography, and except where specific data from a source are quoted or paraphased, there will be no footnotes.

I   SPANISH IN SPAIN, NEW SPAIN, AND THE AMERICAN SOUTHWEST

The Spanish language heritage of Americans of Spanish-Mexican descent has many historical, geographic, and ethnic facets, which we will try to present in logical separation in this part of the chapter.

Spain and Spanish

We usually think of Spanish as a Latin language, *romance*. It is that, of course, but in some important ways it is not Latin, not even European. Spain has been a cultural crossroads from the earliest days of recorded history. Prehistoric man, Phoenician, early Greek, Carthaginian, and other early peoples blended their genes and cultures to form the Spaniard that later the Romans and then their conquerors ruled. The languages of the people of Spain received infusions from all of these cultural contacts, especially from the Latin of the Romans. Then came the greatest invasion of all, that of the Arabic-speaking Moslems in 711 A.D.

The "Moors" were in Spain for almost eight hundred years, ruling virtually all of the Iberian Peninsula for a time, until they were slowly pushed southward by the Christian armies. During this long period a remarkable process of acculturation took place. Although at times the conflict was bitter and bloody, there were long periods when Christians, Sephardic Jews, and Moslems lived in comparative peace and tolerance. Cities controlled by the Moslems tolerated the subordinate Christian people; those controlled by the Christians, in turn, tolerated the subordinate Arabic-speaking minority. In both, the Jews played a leading role as businessmen, brokers, financial counselors. The effect of this strange coexistence on the Spaniard—and on the Spanish language—is incalculable. The Sephardic Jews and the Moslems brought to Europe the wisdom of the Middle East, of Egypt, of North Africa. They brought institutions, technologies, value systems, instruments, and formal learning that, blended with what they found on the peninsula, produced the Golden Age of Spain in the fifteenth and sixteenth centuries.

Although the effects of this acculturation are evident in many fields—architecture, religion, agriculture, educational institutions, political science, folklore, value systems, and so on—nowhere is it so clearly revealed as in the Spanish language. Today there are at least four thousand words in Spanish that are not Latin but Arabic. Many of the words for luxuries little known to the Iberian Christians before the coming of the Moslems are Arabic. The finest jewels are *alajas*, pillows are *almohadas*, fine carpets are *alfombras*. Although the Christian could say "Que Dios nos . . ." when he expressed a devout hope, he quickly adopted the Moslem prayer to Allah to the same effect that has become the Spanish word *ojalá* ("would that . . ."); this expressing condition contrary to fact, necessarily requires the subjunctive mode. Then there are the words that refer to a process, such as *adobar* ("to conserve"). The word adobe, now a good English word, comes from this verb; and one may have, in Spanish, an *adobe* of meat or of vegetables just as one may have an *adobe* of clay and straw.

There are many other Spanish words that are written and pronounced virtually the same way in Arabic and in Spanish. The words for shoes, for trousers, for neckties, for socks, for shirts, and for many other articles are essentially the same in Arabic as in Spanish. It is not within the scope of this chapter to point out the contributions of Visigoths and Greeks, and others, in the formulation of Spanish. Suffice it to note that although the foundations of Spanish are Latin, *romance*, the structure is a variegated one to which many tongues contributed.

Spanish and New Spain

When Spain, in the phenomenally expansive mood of its Golden Age, came to what today is Mexico, it did not come to a wilderness nor to a cultural vacuum. There were millions of people in the area that came to be known as New Spain, people who presented a kaleidoscope of cultures, of languages, and of degrees of civilization. Conservative estimates place their number at ten million, although there are authoritative sources that go far beyond this estimate. The bibliography to this chapter lists sources that elaborate upon the indigenous peoples of New Spain at the time of the Conquest, and reveal the wide scope of the cultural attributes of these peoples. More particularly, these sources reveal a great linguistic variety. The Mayan language, the language of the Aztecs, the languages of the Pueblos, the language of the Otomíes— these and many others differed from each other as much as Chinese differs from English. Peoples living in close proximity spoke vastly different languages. Some, like the Navajos, had linguistic relatives very far away—the closest relatives of the Navajos (and their customs, the Apaches) were in the interior of Alaska. These variegated tongues have had a tremendous influence in the development of Spanish in this part of the New World. In the three colonial centuries, less than one million Spaniards came to New Spain—one million Spanish-speaking people among ten or more million native peoples who spoke diverse languages.

Also, in New Spain the Spaniard came upon flora and fauna, processes, and customs, for which he had no terminology and so had to accept native designations. Although that strange, wonderful new bird, the turkey, could be described as *gallina de la tierra* (as people in New Mexico still call it), or the Spanish word *pavo* could be used (as it is in some places), it was very easy to fall into calling it a *guajolote*, or a *cócono*, or some other Indian name. In many instances there were alternatives, but what to call a "ring-tail cat"? It had to be *cacomistle* (which now is the proper English word for that beautiful creature). In the nomenclature of birds and animals, regionalism and a great deal of confusion prevail because of the variety of native languages and the application of Spanish names to creatures that were unknown in Spain. So the raccoon is a *tejón* (Spanish for badger) to some, *mapache* to many others, whereas *tejón* is still a badger in places like New Mexico. In many instances, however, alternatives were virtually impossible. A *quetzal* could hardly be called by any other name, nor could a mocking bird (*sinsontle*), although one can stretch things a little and call him a *burlón* (which really means "mocker" and has an unkindly connotation). The names of plants (*mesquite*, for a simple illustration), the names of foods (*nixtamal, tamales, chile,* etc.), and the names of many objects in Mexican Spanish are Indian. The centuries of contact between the invaders from the Iberian peninsula and the peoples they conquered gave a wondrous flavor to the language of New Spain. It is this well-seasoned Spanish that is the heritage of the Americans of Mexican descent in the Southwest.

The Spanish-Speaking in the Southwest

Spanish-speaking people have been settled in the Southwest for more than 350 years. The villages north of Santa Fe, New Mexico, founded in 1598, are second only to St. Augustine, Florida, settled in 1565, as the oldest settlements of Europeans on the mainland of the United States. The New Mexico settlements, followed a century later by those in Texas and later by those in California, represent a Spanish colonial effort that left an indelible imprint upon the history and culture of the Southwest and the United States. More importantly, that colonial endeavor left people from California to Texas whose descendants constitute a part of the group we now refer to, very loosely, as Spanish-speaking.

The colonial Hispanos were not culturally homogeneous. The Nuevo Mexicanos, settled in the region as early as 1598, were different from their cousins, the Californios and the Texanos, who arrived much later. The date of migration and settlement, the attendant cultural concomitants, geographic isolation, natural resources, the number and kind of Indians among whom they settled, and many other factors resulted in not one Spanish-speaking people but several, each with distinctive cultures. The outlook on life and the values, the allegiances, the biology, the very speech of these colonial settlers varied greatly; and though all were Spanish-speaking, they can be thought of as different peoples.

Until about the mid-nineteenth century, the Californios, the Nuevo Mexicanos, and the Texanos went their separate cultural ways, held together only lightly by, first, the slender threads of Spain and, later, for a brief time, the uncertain bonds of independent Mexico. The annexation of Texas and the occupation of the rest of the Southwest by the United States changed the course of human affairs in the region, but the change was a slow one, unplanned and haphazard. The United States had not developed the social and cultural institutions to carry out an effective program of acculturation among her new citizens. The new states and territories were left to shift for themselves, with an understandable lack of success. The Spanish-speaking peoples of the Southwest remained Spanish-speaking and culturally isolated unassimilated citizens, subject to the ever increasing dominance of a foreign culture.

Other things being equal, time alone would have had its influence, and the Hispanos would have become full-fledged English-speaking Americans. However, not only were the social institutions inadequate, but also changing conditions made it impossible for time alone to bring about their assimilation. After 1870 the southwestern scene changed rapidly. The coming of the railroad brought new economic opportunities and made old ones more attractive. The region ceased to be the "Wild West." It became instead a land where minerals and lumber, cotton and corn, cattle and sheep, fruits and vegetables gave rise to new economic empires.

These developments in themselves were not hindrances to acculturation. On the contrary, they should have done much to aid it, just as economic expansion in the East accelerated the Americanization of the heterogeneous masses from Europe. However, in addition to the fact that southwestern developments were based largely in rural life and on the production of raw material in the East, this area was sparsely populated and, insofar as the "American Way" was concerned, culturally immature and insecure. Worse still, since labor for the new enterprises was not available from the East, the Southwest had to turn to Mexico and the Orient. As a consequence, the region, already suffering from cultural indigestion, added to its troubles by importing thousands of Mexican families, again postponing the day for the incorporation of its Spanish-speaking population.

Even thus enlarged by immigrants from Mexico, the Indo-Hispanic group could have been assimilated had the United States taken time to assess the cultural issues and the increasingly complex socioeconomic problems—particularly those of this ethnic minority. But before 1910 almost no one seemed aware that there were far-reaching issues and problems. Virtually no thought was given to the educational, health, economic, or political rehabilitation of the Hispanos. And after 1910 the opportunity had passed. Until then the issues and problems were still of manageable proportions. They were soon to grow beyond all hope of quick solution.

The Mexican Revolution of 1910-1920 and World War I combined to bring many thousands of Mexicans to the Southwest. Large numbers came as displaced persons, driven across the border by a chaotic civil war. Even larger numbers came as contract laborers, recruited by the trainload to work the beet fields of Colorado, the gardens and groves of California, the railroads of the entire West, the copper mines of Arizona, the cotton fields of Texas, even the iron works of Chicago and the coal mines of West Virginia.

The consequences of this free and easy dipping into the cheap labor reservoir of Mexico are not difficult to observe. What for brevity I choose to call "cultural indigestion" can be documented by health and educational statistics, by pictures of the slums of San Antonio, and by depressing socioeconomic data from all over the Southwest. Suffice it to say that once again the Southwest pyramided problem upon problem, burdening itself with a situation for which sooner or later there would be a costly reckoning.

In a way, World War I served a good purpose. Full employment, good wages, and the educative results of military service stimulated acculturation in the Southwest. However, the issues were much too large and complex to be met adequately by the by-products of war. More research, more planning, and more well thought-out action programs were needed.

The "boom and bust" days of the twenties and the slow recovery during the thirties saw a little alleviation of the socioeconomic difficulties confronting the

Southwest. Thousands of Mexican nationals were repatriated through the joint efforts of the United States and Mexico. However, natural increase soon more than made up for their loss. The depression years bred more misery, more problems. During these critical times there was a growing interest in the plight of the unemployed, of out-of-school youth, and of common people in general. This interest was first expressed by state and national surveys: President Hoover's Committee on Social Trends, California Governor Young's Committee on Labor, and the Texas Educational Survey are examples. The "New Deal" reforms helped to relieve some of the most acute problems and stimulated the nation to a greater consciousness of its socioeconomic defects. In particular, more attention was given to studies of underprivileged groups and of cultural and "racial" minorities.

The condition of the Spanish-speaking people in the Southwest was not completely overlooked. Taylor's studies in California and Texas called attention to the plight of the agricultural worker, particularly the migrant Mexican. Manuel, at the University of Texas, was inaugurating educational studies of the Spanish-speaking group. Sánchez was working in the fields of bilingualism and of school finance and administration in New Mexico. Tireman, also in New Mexico, was addressing himself to the teaching problems presented by the bicultural situation. Other researchers concerned themselves with a variety of spot studies.

Some reform measures looking toward the effective accumulation of its population (50 percent Spanish-speaking) were undertaken by New Mexico in the thirties. These involved far-reaching changes in the sources and distribution of school funds, improvement of public health services, more scientific land use, increased and more effective political action by Spanish-speaking voters. As a result, by 1940 the Spanish-speaking people of New Mexico were more nearly assimilated than those of any other southwestern state.

There were similar improvements during the same period in parts of Colorado, Arizona, and California. Texas, on the other hand, lagged far behind. The educational and health levels of the Texas-Mexican were the worst in the region. There fundamental civil rights were most flagrantly violated. Effective Spanish-speaking leadership was lacking. Conditions of employment and standards of living were woefully low. In a manner of speaking, Texas had become the "horrible example" in the acculturation of Spanish-speaking people. However, there was a growing realization there as elsewhere that none of these states could attain its potential cultural stature until the maladjustments were overcome, and in the last few years Texas has begun to buckle down to the long-postponed task of incorporating the Spanish-speaking one-sixth of its population.

World War II had its good effects also. As in World War I, military service and improved economic conditions gave a great boost to the assimilation of Spanish-speaking people. In addition, largely in response to pressure from Spanish-speaking groups, the federal government began to sponsor programs designed to improve the bicultural situation in the Southwest. More importantly, Mexico and the United States agreed to regulate the flow of Mexican labor northward across the border.

Whether the two governments realized it or not, this struck at one of the roots of the overall problem. As noted, time and again, just as we have been on the verge of cutting our bicultural problems to manageable proportions, uncontrolled mass migrations from Mexico have erased the gains and accentuated the cultural indigestion. Now, when the entire Southwest is inaugurating large-scale programs of acculturation, the control of Mexican immigration is most necessary. It would be short-sighted and tragic indeed if the two governments were to deviate from this sound path toward acculturation.

The most serious threats to an effective program of acculturation in the Southwest have been the population movements from Mexico: first, by illegal aliens, the so-called "wetbacks," then by the *bracero* program, and finally by the commuters. Unless we can end the legal or illegal entry of large numbers of Mexican aliens, much of the good work that state and federal agencies are doing will go for naught; much more time and effort and many more millions of dollars will be required to bring Texas and her sister states to a desirable cultural level.

II   BILINGUALISM IN THE SOUTHWEST: A TRAGI-COMEDY

In trying to assess both the teaching of English in the Southwest to children whose mother tongue is Spanish, and the persistence of Spanish, we are torn between two ways of getting across a basic point: current practice doesn't make sense. One could use the "academic" approach, muster an unassailable array of evidence—historical, experimental, comparative, and the like—and, by prolific footnoting of authoritative sources, make a case for the thesis implied in the heading above. This thesis, that we have been foolish in dealing with the English-Spanish dichotomy of the southwestern cultural reality, can be documented easily. One could with equal confidence appeal to common sense and simple logic, and in plain English, to puncture the balloon that has been blown up with the hot air of "language handicap," the perils of bilingualism, and all the other clichés with which educators cover their lack of preparation and understanding. I will use both approaches, emphasizing the former at first and the latter subsequently.

Historical Perspective

The place of vernacular languages in education has been a concern for many centuries. The influence of language development upon personality, the function of language in our thinking process, and the implications of bilingualism have occupied thinking people profoundly. The subject is a vast one in which distinguished contributions have been made over a long time.

It is not the shrinking world that justifies the study of foreign languages and demands the conservation of the foreign home-language resources of our peoples; the wisdom of the ages dictates it. The recorded history of foreign home-language in education goes back four thousand years to the time when the Semitic Akkadians conquered Sumer and gradually imposed their tongue, Hebrew, upon the Sumerians.[1] In turn, Aramaic supplanted the old Hebrew language, and just as Sumerian had become a "sacred language" when Hebrew became the vernacular, so Hebrew became the "sacred language" and Aramaic the vernacular. Time after time through the ages a foreign home-language has become the medium of religious instruction as a new language became the vernacular: for Hebrew, Greek, Latin, Arabic; in India, China,

Europe, Russia, in our hemisphere; in the spread of Buddhism, Christianity, Judaism; in the Hellenization of Rome, the Latinization of Europe, the Westernization of the Americas; in the rise and fall of imperialistic colonialism. In each of these we find bilingualism in education.

These examples point to the unquestionable value of the vernacular in education, particularly when the mother tongue is not the language of instruction. For further support for our conclusion we can turn to the great thinkers of modern history who have expressed their views on this topic: Juan Luis Vives, Pedro de Gante, John Amos Comenius, John Locke, Johan Heinrich Herbart, John Dewey; and to contemporary psychologists, linguists, and philosophers such as Frank Laubach, who have concerned themselves with the place of foreign languages in education. It is a shock, then, to observe in the schools of the Southwest how violence has been done to the lessons of history and the views of great thinkers.

It is very clear that in teaching native and foreign languages, we are dealing with more than a twenty-minute period in the daily schedule, with more than superficial sophistication, with more than vocational advantage and financial profit. The works of Vives, Herbart, and Dewey (particularly *How We Think*) show the vital role of language in intellectual development, the overwhelming significance of a child's mother tongue in the process of education in a second language. These factors have been completely ignored in the teaching of Spanish-speaking children in the schools of the Southwest. Herein lies part of the explanation why many of these schools, particularly those in Texas, find teaching English to Spanish-speaking children an almost overwhelming task, and why their failure is excused by assigning to the child's home-language a deleterious influence upon his educational development.

A quotation from the careful historical study of vernacular languages in education mentioned earlier applies here.

From time to time in education the question has arisen whether a child should be taught in some language other than his native language. In those cases where some language other than the native language has been used as the vehicle of instruction, usually the results, if objectively viewed, were convincing enough from an empirical basis to bring about a change in policy. The effectiveness of using the native language is tied in with the interpretration of emotion and language. For the preponderent group of children, emotional satisfaction and release accompany the use of the vernacular; while frustration accompanies the use of some other language. Neglect of the native language or, worse still, its suppression is damaging to the morale of the student, and results in rebellion against, or apathy toward the educational process. Especially in the beginning years of school, but later as well, facility in using verbal symbols is essential for facility of thinking. The processes of thought seem to be blocked by the awkward use of the language.

This in no way means that the introduction of a second language, with the goal of developing bilingualism, blocks the processes of thought. Where a second language is introduced at the proper time with sufficient motivation for the student, it might be considered distinctly a potential aid to thinking. The Iliolo experiment has given objectively derived information on the use of the vernacular and the introduction of a second language. The vernacular was shown clearly to have advantages as the language of instruction, and the students, with whom it had been so used, were able in six months of studying a second language, to catch up with a matched control group which had been studying the second language for two years, and using it as the language of learning for all school subjects.[2]

There is much evidence to support the conclusions reached in this historical research. Of telling significance also are the experiments and conclusions of modern psychologists and sociologists.[3] For instance, Maier relates an experiment in which a rat was rewarded with food when it jumped for a certain card and was not rewarded when it jumped for another card.[4] Then the cards and consequences were interchanged, with a resulting sense of failure and frustration for the rat. Maier says, "He soon restrains his tendency to jump, holding himself in a crouching position on the platform in a hopeless or defiant attitude." How many times have I seen this repeated by children with a foreign home-language. How many times have I seen a child cringe and crouch, physically and emotionally, because the language of the home was taboo at school and the language of the school was nonfunctional at home. Here is the genesis of the *pachuco*, the delinquent.

Social psychologists recognize the fundamental importance of esteem in personality formation and motivation. For example, Maslow, in a report on "A Theory of Human Motivation," emphasizes that "Satisfaction of the self-esteem need leads to feelings of self-confidence, worth, strength, capacity, and adequacy of being useful and necessary in the world."[5] What can contribute more to self-esteem than the recognition and appreciation of one's vernacular? We all love to be addressed, even if brokenly, *en la lengua que mamamos* ("in the language we suckled," in our mother tongue). So in filling the esteem need, as well as in avoiding psychological confusion, the home-language of the child is a highly potent educational instrument. Cheavens, again summarizing, says:

Use of the vernacular languages of minority groups living among people of another language has usually sped up the process of acculturation and made easier the learning of a second language for communication with the majority group. Where this policy has not been followed and the vernacular language has been neglected or suppressed, the result has been a continued cleavage between the minority group and the majority groups.[6]

A study at McGill University also supported the idea that bilingualism is highly desirable.[7]

The Southwestern Reality

As stated earlier, this matter of a foreign mother tongue can be approached in various ways. For us in the Southwest it is a matter for simple language and simple logic. Instead of operating in the abstract, we can use our everyday circumstances as a basis for our convictions about the place of a foreign home-language in our culture and the value of that language in learning English. We do not have to defend the merits of acculturation and bilingualism. We derive much of our cultural substance from Spanish, a native "foreign" language, a language bequeathed by Cabeza de Vaca, de Niza, Serra, Zavala, and a host of others. It takes only very elementary research to see how the Spanish-Mexican contribution undergirds the culture of the Southwest.

Limiting our remarks to Texas, one cannot help seeing how Texans identify with Spanish-speaking people. The terminology of the cattle country (rodeo, lariat, ranch, remuda) the place names, the names of people, the every day words (adobe, amigo, patio), and the customs of daily living all evidence this accumulation. And all of this is capped by the satisfaction of those Anglos who are bilingual and those Latins who know English as well as they know Spanish. The Alamo is as much a symbol of biculturalism as it is of political freedom. After all, it was a Mexican flag flying at the staff that the heroes of the Alamo defended. So we in Texas do not consider the problem of foreign home-language as remote, or of narrow significance in educational psychology, in curriculum, and in the teaching process. Foreign home-language is real to us, and the prospects are just as real.

Contradictorily, because of unfortunate incidents in our past, a tradition of disparagement developed here toward "that Mexican" and all that the term stood for, including language. Along with that, the immature psychology of "speak American" and the defensive provincialism of "despise that furriner" have led to the downgrading of the Spanish language and of those who speak it. Otherwise competent scholars speak of the language of the people of the Southwest as "border Spanish," as a dialect to be avoided. Some, in their ignorance, even refer to it as "Mexican," distinguishing it from Spanish to avoid dignifying it (and ignoring the fact that the Mexican language is *Náhuatl*).

We extol the virtues of foreign languages in the development and the achievements of the educated man; we decry their decline in public education; we view with alarm our backwardness when we compare ourselves with the Russians and others, we subsidize the teaching of foreign languages. Yet in the Southwest, one of the world's great languages is suppressed. It does not make sense.

In Texas there are about 300,000 Spanish-speaking children in the public elementary schools, and more than 35,000 in the secondary schools. For only a negligible few of them is Spanish being used as an educational device; and, if they succeed (and many do not) in retaining and developing their home-language, it is not because the public schools have planned it so. What a waste of the assets of the vernacular in education.

Education and Reality

An annotated bibliography on the education of Spanish-speaking people in the United States,[8] although not all-inclusive, lists almost nine hundred items: books, articles, bulletins, and theses. I have been working professionally in this field for more than forty years, and I have been highly critical of our schools' efforts for at least three-fourths of those years; still I was amazed at the persistence of the assertion that bilingualism is bad, that a foreign home-language is a handicap, that, somehow, children with Spanish as a mother tongue were doomed to failure—in fact, that they were ipso facto less than normally intelligent.

This sounds like an exaggeration, but these views can easily be documented. For example, in the first draft of a recent handbook for teachers of preschool-age, non-English-speaking children, the Texas Education Agency says, in the second sentence of the introduction, "Solely because of the language barrier, approximately 80 percent of the non-English-speaking children have had to spend two years in the first grade before advancing to the second."[9] The devastating fact is that Spanish-speaking children in Texas schools *do* spend two or more years in the first grade and then, frequently, more than one year in succeeding grades until in sheer frustration they drop out of school. But to attribute this educational tragedy to the fact that they begin school speaking only Spanish is a gratuitous conclusion not borne out by the history of education in this country or elsewhere. One of the most important facets of the genius of the American school has been that—without distinction as to caste, class, home-language, national origin, and the like—it has been able to process children from all over the world in its normal operations as they become, for the most part, averagely well-educated English-speaking citizens. To excuse the failure of the Texas schools to do the usual job by accusing the Spanish-speaking children of virtually inherent fault reveals a professional blindspot so elementary that it is difficult not to question the professional competence and integrity of the educators responsible. As a result of my protest, the draft of the handbook was changed to read in the published version, "Through no fault of their own, many non-English-speaking children have had to spend two years in the first grade before advancing to the second."[10] I protested that too, of course, for the implication is that the fault lies in the fact that they were born into Spanish-speaking families; this is certainly no admission that the fault lies in the schools. This is pathetically demonstrated in the "migrant bulletin," suggesting that one way of determining who is eligible for preschool instruction can be discovered by "Noting all eligible children whose names indicate that they are of foreign extraction."

In Texas, much more than in the rest of the Southwest (though the rest is not entirely blameless), Jim Crowism has extended into the educational system.[11] As late as the 1940's, some school systems segregated "Mexican" children throughout the twelve grades of the public school. This extension has served to blind school people, from those of the highest authority to those at the classroom level, to the fact that they have used "language handicap" and "bilingualism" to justify "racial" discrimination and their failure to do the kind of teaching job with these children that the American school has done with hundreds of thousands of other children who were similarly situated. Somehow, too, the political effectiveness of the Mexican-American has been spotty, so that the educational policy in New Mexico (where the Spanish-American has carried political weight for generations) and that in Texas (where political awakening of the Latin-American is just now taking place) have stood out as contrasts. The other southwestern states fall between these extremes, with educational effort reflecting the Mexican-Americans' political effectiveness.

What should be emphasized is that factors other than professional considerations have determined what should be done in the education of spanish-speaking children. In the process, language and language-teaching have been so distorted that only a resort to common sense and the fundamental principles of the teaching profession can shock us back to the conclusions that the pages of history and the research literature underline.

Much is being made in Texas of the efficacy of summer sessions for non-English-speaking children who will enroll in the first grade in September.[12] It is widely implied that these summer sessions constitute the solution to the perennial and frustrating problem of the child with a "language handicap," and statistics are offered to prove that the majority of the children who attend these summer programs do not have to spend two or more years in the first grade but make the grade in one year (many do not). It is abundantly self-evident that the extension of good education downward is good for all children and that one should expect children who are fortunate enough to get a preschool preparation for the first grade to make better progress, at least during the first few years, than their less fortunate fellows. It stretches credulity, however, when it is alleged that a few weeks of vocabulary building during the summer can substitute for the extra one, two, or more years that (by implication) a Spanish-speaking child otherwise would have to spend in the first grade.

What is being argued is, in effect, that a forty- to sixty-day summer session program for Spanish-speaking children is the equivalent of the extra nine months (or more) that the children would have to spend in the regular school in the first grade if they did not have the summer program. There must be something radically wrong with the regular first grade operation if the schools can do in eight weeks (summer) plus nine months (regular year) what, otherwise, takes eighteen or more months of regular school instruction. Why not do the equivalent of the eight-week summer program at the beginning of the regular year? Then, even at worst, one could expect logically that at the end of the first grade the children would be no less than eight weeks short of competence for second grade work—and, of course, hardly proper subjects for the repetition (one, two, or more times) of the entire first grade work.

This illogic is repeated in the "Texas Project for Migrant Children."[13] So-called pilot schools have been established, in South Texas, where children of agricultural migrants are arbitrarily segregated from the other children. All of the migrants there are of Mexican descent. There is great pride that the migrant children achieve as much in vocabularly and reading comprehension tests as the children in the regular schools. The fact is that the regular children, on the average, made only .58 of a grade progress per school year in comprehension.[14] Also, in the migrant schools 38 to 45 percent (or more) of the time is allotted to "English, Language Arts," a much higher percentage than in the regular schools.[15] This kind of statistical legerdemain by a state education agency is wondrous to behold.

Although Texas is probably the "horrible example," the other states are not thereby exonerated. One more illustration from the "migrant bulletin": the statement is made that "Most of the migrant children are educationally retarded from one to three years." Maybe this is true, but no proof is offered. However, a table accompanying the article shows that, on the average, on the comprehension pretest, the migrants were only .10 of a grade behind the regulars in the second grade; only .05 of a grade in the third grade; .17 of a grade in the fourth; .16 in the fifth; and .43 of a grade in the sixth. Adding the statement above and these figures gives a resounding condemnation of the regular program.

In the only official statistical report of its kind for that state, the Texas Education Agency in 1957 revealed that there were 61,584 Spanish-surname children in the first grade in the public schools of the state, that only 15,490 reached the eighth grade, and that there were only 5,261 in the twelfth grade.[16] Add to this the previously quoted (under-) statement that "Solely because of the language barrier, approximately 80 percent of the non-English-speaking children have had to spend two years in the first grade before advancing to the second." The statistical evidence is an eloquent indictment of the educational program, which goes far beyond the condemnation of errors that a forty-to-sixty-day summer session program in vocabulary building will eliminate or even make much of a dent. No complacency is warranted, and little satisfaction can be derived from the unquestionable good that the summer schools do. Unless drastic reforms are instituted in the programs of the regular schools, the pupil statistics of a few years hence will not be much different from those of 1957—even if, in the meantime, every child were to go to a summer school. The 1960 U. S. Census of Population bears this out.

As has been implied, indictments such as these are not as applicable to the schools for the rest of the Southwest as they are in Texas, but it is not difficult to find illustrations of the same faults in other states. Numerous practices would be funny if they were not so tragic. One school system, by regulation of its school board, required that all children with a Spanish surname spend three years in the first grade. A federal court changed that. A doctoral dissertation proved that Spanish-speaking children who had preschool instruction in English did better in school than those who did not have that advantage. There have been various "experiments" wherein the intelligence of Spanish-speaking children has been "measured" by partially or completely translated tests. One test publisher reports that the company's intelligence test (standardized in English) was administered in Spanish to Spanish-speaking children—without even token recognition of the fact that translation does irreparable damage to the test norms and that the Spanish of the children was untutored (unlike the situation of the English-speaking norm children). Other investigators, proud of their recognition of the "language handicap" of Spanish-speaking children, have chosen to test the intelligence of these children with "nonverbal" tests, overlooking completely that the nonverbal tests are as culturally based as the verbal tests and that neither can test what is not there.

Then there are the teachers who are so impressed with the "inherent" talent of the "Mexicans" in music and art that they believe this supposed talent explains (and justifies) inferior achievement in less exotic fields—an inferior achievement that is a product not of the "artistic temperament" of the child but of the inadequacy of the educational program. One could mention the remarkably consistent positive correlation between "racial" prejudice and discriminatory practices that have used the excuse that the children had a "language handicap." Again, the federal court cases reveal some of the tragi-comedy of the situation. In one case, the parents of a Spanish-name child were very happy that the little girl had to be sent to the segregated "Mexican" school because there she could learn Spanish.

One could go into a lengthy recital of the varied irrationalities that have characterized the "teaching of English" to Spanish-speaking children in the Southwest, irrationalities that have vitiated the thinking of both top-level experts and less "authoritative" workers. Such a recital would serve only a negative purpose. One can do better (with the negative features in mind) by trying to find out ways of doing a better job.

The Ways Out

The lessons of history, the experience of other countries, the dictates of ordinary judgment suggest various ways for the school to approach the education of children with a mother tongue other than which is the language of the school. A number of these approaches will be summarized.

1. It is virtually impossible to avoid the conclusion that children should be started off in their formal education in the mother tongue. There can be an argument as to when the second language should be introduced and to what extent it should supplant the mother tongue, but the evidence is overwhelming that the home-language should be the springboard for the proper development of the second language. This procedure, followed in some countries now and in the past, has demonstrated its merit. However, it has some serious disadvantages in our society. For instance, it would involve the "segregation" of the foreign home-language child, a practice with many features that are not only objectionable but intolerable under our philosophy of the "unitary" school and our denial of the "separate but equal" doctrine. This incompatibility of our way of life with what might be pedagogically ideal leads us to the contemplation of possible compromises or alternatives.

2. The first compromise would be that the mother tongue be used partially in the instruction program. This partial use of the child's vernacular could vary from the teaching of one or more subjects of the curriculum to an occasional and informal use in the everyday relationships between the teacher and the pupil. The advantages to the child with English as a mother tongue are obvious. This would call for teachers who are bilingual and so is not feasible, at the moment, in many schools of the Southwest. However, the talent potential for large numbers of bilingual teachers is here, and it would require no great effort to recruit Spanish-speaking high school graduates to enter teacher education programs if there were reasonable assurance of employment.

With notable exceptions (New Mexico is probably tops in this regard), the teacher of Spanish-Mexican descent is seldom found in schools where the enrollment is predominantly of the dominant (Anglo) group. Further, that teacher (who is woefully in the minority even in schools where most of the children are Latins) usually is admonished that she must not use Spanish in dealing with Spanish-speaking children. Incidentally, Spanish-speaking children generally are forbidden to use their mother tongue, and it is not unusual for severe punishment to be meted out, even in high schools, if pupils resort to Spanish in their conversation. In a climate of this sort, language teaching and language development go out the window, and the teaching of English becomes bewildering, frustrating, and oppressive to the child, who sometimes rebels violently.

3. There is, as a natural consequence of the above rationale, the possibility that the schools, even without bilingual teachers, could give status to the vernacular of the Spanish-speaking child and employ teachers who would give him a sense of satisfaction and belonging in his accomplishment in the Spanish language and the culture it represents. In another publication I offer rules that will help non-Spanish-speaking

persons to pronounce Spanish names, words, and phrases correctly.[17] This compromise fits in with everything the authorities in intercultural education advocate. Under this plan, the dominant group child benefits as much or more as does the child in the subordinate group. The procedure would involve only more professional sophistication and could be attained easily if the educators would concede that the schools are dismal failures in the education of Spanish-speaking children.

I am reminded here of the findings of Ginzberg and Bray.[18] They have shown that southern Texas, where the Spanish-speaking people are concentrated, had an almost unbelievable rejection rate for "educational reasons" during the draft of World War II—a rejection rate that was, in terms of area and population, the worst in the nation, not counting the statistics on Negroes but including those on Indians. If these schools are doing such a poor job for the Spanish-speaking child, they cannot be doing justice even to the English-speaking youngster.

4. There can be no argument that, speaking generally, the Spanish-speaking child in the Southwest is socially and economically disadvantaged. In health, wealth, and welfare he is at or near the bottom of the scale when compared with his fellow Americans.[19] This offers special challenges to the school, in the teaching of English as in all parts of the curriculum, for any child, regardless of mother tongue. The fact that his state of socioeconomic disadvantage is usually accompanied by a lack of knowledge of the English language is nearly always interpreted as "language handicap," or "bilingualism." As a consequence of this confusion, the school addresses itself to a fruitless hunt into the mysteries of the deleterious effects of being unable to speak English, instead of adapting its program to the requirements of children who are disadvantaged socioeconomically. An ordinarily good school, confronted with the challenge of handicapped children, would give special care to the selection of teaching personnel, would keep class size to a minimum, and would channel more of its special aids and services to them than elsewhere.

There are various legitimate questions that can be asked about teaching English to Spanish-speaking children. To qualify, should the teacher know Spanish? The answer is, "To qualify, the teacher of Spanish-speaking children should be an unquestionably good teacher." It would help for such a good teacher to know Spanish (to have casual conversation with the child, to talk with the parents, to appreciate the problems and virtues of bilingualism), but the important thing is that she be a good teacher and that she be given an opportunity to do her job (reasonable class size, at least average help from her superiors, and the like). If the teacher does not know Spanish, she should at least understand why some of her Spanish-speaking pupils have particular difficulties.

5. The importance of a reading readiness program for children in the first grade is hardly a subject of debate, though one might debate the duration of such a program. For English-speaking children such programs should extend beyond the middle of the first year; this may be a radical position, but let us agree that the English-speaking child should undergo a reading readiness program of six weeks at the beginning of the first grade.

If the English-speaking child, who has been acquiring facility in oral English for six years before enrollment in school, needs a six-week readiness program before starting to read, shouldn't the readiness program of the non-English-speaking child take longer? Should the Spanish-speaking child be expected to be as ready to read with six weeks of "readiness" as the child with six years and six weeks? This is not an argument for having the Spanish-speaking child spend more than one year in the first grade, for his language development is essentially the same as that of his English-speaking fellow student. But he does need extra time, before beginning to read, to acquire facility in the recognition and use of the new linguistic labels. This is not an argument, either, for separating the two groups of children in the first grade. It will not hurt the English-speaking child to extend his readiness program to eight or twelve weeks or more. In the process, the Spanish-speaking child will have a chance to get a good start in the catching up process that should be virtually complete by the end of the third grade. Criteria for judging progress and grade placement should be modified accordingly; for it is with the development and progress of the child that the school is concerned, not with seeing to it that predetermined standards are rigorously met. The assumptions upon which those standards are based are usually grossly inapplicable. Failure to take such matters into account is behind the failure of many schools to do an adequate job for the non-English-speaking child.

The "Teaching of English"

Stated or implied throughout this chapter is the conviction that the schools of the Southwest are not faced really with a problem of language handicap, in the fact that large numbers of the pupils come to school speaking little or no English. The issues are not truly linguistic, but rather lie in the areas of social policy, of school organization and administration, of educational philosophy, and of pedagogical competence. There are many thousands of persons in the Southwest whose mother tongue was Spanish, who were socially and economically disadvantaged (that is, who were in the same environmental situation as that of the Spanish-speaking children who fail miserably in many public schools today), and who did "make the grade." To attribute this to the suggestion that "they were different" does not accord with statistics on the distribution of intelligence. The fundamental difference between them and their unfortunate fellows was the quality of the school. Good schools—and by this we do not mean anything extraordinary, just good schools as judged the country over-take the "problem" of the Spanish-speaking child in stride. In the others we are confronted not with handicapped children but with handicapped schools.

III   CONSERVATION OF SPANISH IN THE SOUTHWEST

It should be clear that the retention of the Spanish language by Americans of Spanish-Mexican descent in the Southwest has been the function of default, rather than of any concerted popular or institutionalized effort. The Spanish-speaking whom the United States acquired through the American occupation of the nineteenth century were almost totally illiterate. As noted in *Forgotten People*[20] and in the works of numerous other students, little was done for the Americanization of this population group in the nineteenth century or in the twentieth, for that matter, in some of the areas where the Spanish-speaking population existed in large concentrations.[21]

   The educational level of this group is extremely low, as reference to the latest figures of the United States Bureau of the Census will show. One would expect a fairly low level of linguistic proficiency among this population. Oddly enough, but not inexplicably so, their Spanish is of good quality. This is a result in large part of their isolation from the dominant, English-speaking group. In part, too, it is a result of the strange phenomenom that has made Mexico, as Don Federico de Onís once said, the country where, on the whole, the best Spanish is spoken. The Mexicano, whether in Mexico or in the United States Southwest, has had a flair for the Spanish language, whether he were literature or not. Of course, many in the Southwest fall into barbarisms that are the result of a meager vocabulary, of English-named articles and practices for which there are no Spanish equivalents, and of the almost total lack of formal tutoring in the language. In some parts of the Southwest, as in the mountains of Kentucky and Tennessee, many archaic expressions are still common for the same reasons in both places: isolation and lack of education.

One could point to the feeble efforts of the Spanish-language press, or to those of organizations of Spanish-speaking people, or to the fact that Spanish is an official language in New Mexico and was widely used in politics and in the Legislature until recent years. Credit is due these, of course, but the fact remains that, in the Southwest, Spanish has been retained as a major language primarily by the default of the institutions of social incorporation. This default, although producing unfortunate results in other spheres, could be turned to tremendous advantage. Some suggestions are made in this paper. Others will occur to those who recognize bilingualism and multilingualism as of great value not only in our relations with the rest of the world, but also in the enhancement of the human spirit, in the development of the highest order of humanism.

REFERENCES

Gilberto Cerda, Berta Babaza y Julieta Farías, *Vocabulario Español de Texas*, University of Texas Hispanic Studies, Vol. V (Austin: The University of Texas Press, 1953).

Ernesto Galarza, *Strangers in Our Fields* (Washington, D.C.: Joint United States-Mexico Trade Union Committee, 1956).

Galarza, *Merchants of Labor* (Private publication: 1031 Franquette Street, San José, California, 1965).

Charles F. Marden and Gladys Meyer, *Minorities in American Society*, 2nd ed. (New York: American Book Company, 1962); see especially ch. 6.

George I. Sánchez, *Mexico—A Revolution By Education* (New York: Viking Press, 1936).

George I. Sánchez, *Forgotten People* (Albuquerque: The University of New Mexico Press, 1940).

Carey McWilliams, *North from Mexico* (Philadelphia: Lippincott, 1943).

NOTES

1. Sam Frank Cheavens, "Vernacular Languages in Education" (Unpublished doctoral dissertation, University of Texas, 1957).

2. *Ibid.*, pp. 50–51.

3. Bruce S. Meador, "Minority Groups and Their Education in Hays County, Texas" (Unpublished doctoral dissertation, University of Texas, 1959).

4. Norman R. F. Maier, *Frustration: The Study of Behavior without a Goal* (New York: McGraw-Hill Book Company, 1949).

5. A. H. Maslow, *Motivation and Personality* (New York: Harper and Brothers, 1954).

6. Cheavens, "Vernacular Languages," pp. 516–517.

7. W. E. Lambert and Elizabeth Peal, "The Relation of Bilingualism to Intelligence," *Psychological Monographs: General and Applied*, No. 546, 76, 27 (1962).

8. George I. Sánchez and Howard Putnam, *Materials Relating to the Education of Spanish-Speaking People in the United States —An Annotated Bibliography* (Austin: The Institute of Latin American Studies, The University of Texas, 1959).

9. Texas Education Agency, "Handbook for the Instructional Program for Preschool-Age Non-English-Speaking Children" (First Draft, 1960).

10. Texas Education Agency, *Preschool Instructional Program for Non-English-Speaking Children* (1960).

11. George I. Sánchez, "Concerning Segregation of Spanish-Speaking Children in the Public Schools, "Inter-American Educational Occasional Papers, IX, University of Texas, December, 1951.

12. Louis Alexander, "Texas Helps Her Little Latins." *The Saturday Evening Post*, August 5, 1961, pp. 30–31, 54–55.

13. Texas Education Agency, *The Texas Project for Migrant Children* (1964).

14. *Ibid.*, p. 11.

15. *Ibid.*, p. 4.

16. Texas Education Agency, *Report of Pupils in Texas Public Schools Having Spanish Surnames, 1955–56* (August, 1957).

17. George I. Sánchez and Charles L. Eastlack, *Say It the Spanish Way* (Austin: The Good Neighbor Commission of Texas, 1960).

18. Eli Ginzberg and Douglas W. Bray, *The Uneducated* (New York: Columbia University Press, 1953).

19. United States Bureau of the Census, *U.S. Census of Population: 1950*, Vol. 4, Special Reports, Part 3, Chapter 6, "Persons of Spanish Surname" (1953); United States Bureau of the Census, *United States Census of Population: 1960*, "Persons of Spanish Surname," Final Report PC(2)-1B (Washington, D.C.: U. S. Government Printing Office, 1963); Robert H. Talbert, *Spanish-Name People in the West and Southwest* (Fort Worth: Leo Potishman Foundation, Texas Christian University, 1955).

20. George I. Sánchez, *Forgotten People* (Albuquerque: University of New Mexico Press, 1940).

21. George I. Sánchez, "The American of Mexican Descent," *The Chicago Jewish Forum*, 20, 2 (Winter, 1961–62).

6

Roused from Our Slumbers

Guadalupe San Miguel, Jr.

"We were wholly unprepared politically, educationally, socially when the avalanche of Americans fell upon us. . . . And it is our place and our duty now to learn American ways, to send our children to American schools, to learn the English language, not that we are ashamed of our Mexican descent, but because these things will enable us to demand our rights and to improve ourselves."

—Graduate of a Mexican private school, quoted in J. González,
"Social Life in Cameron, Starr, and Zapata Counties"

"We have been roused from our slumbers, and may we never sink into repose until we have conveyed a clear and undisputed inheritance to posterity, to the end that a backward race, in this age of civilization may tread hand in hand in all the various walks of life amongst the enlightened races of today."

—Constitution of LULAC

In the 1920s several studies found that Texas Mexicans, especially those residing in the rural areas of Karnes, Dimmit, and Nueces counties, were indifferent toward public education or else were unaware of its advantages.[1] Since approximately 75 percent of all Mexicans in the state lived in rural communities, this was a significant finding.[2] Paul Taylor, in his studies of Dimmit and Nueces counties, argued that this attitude was the result of a multitude of contemporary and historical circumstances. Poverty, discrimination, and lack of school facilities helped explain the apparent lack of interest in education. "Historically," he noted, "the heritage of the Mexican laborers in the county is one of but very slight formal education, and among a large proportion, none at all, either in Mexico or Texas."[3]

The Texas Mexican population he interviewed substantiated his argument. For instance, one person at Catarina (Dimmit County) stated that many of the Mexicans there had large families and needed the children to work. "It is good for the parent, but not for the children," he noted. "The parents who are indifferent to school for their children," he added, "are those who have had no school themselves [and] who neither read nor write." Another individual from Nueces County stated that "a lot of non-attendance is due to the parents." "They are uneducated," he continued, "and don't realize what their children are deprived of."[4] An old vaquero from Nueces County blamed the "Spanish" leaders for keeping "our eyes closed" but then stated that the Mexicans did not like school because "they like to dance and drink." Finally, one person from Dimmit County explained how poverty and the need to work had kept him and his family from going to school:

> My father was poco pobre and there were twelve children, so we had to work and could not go to school. . . . My son, born in Mexico, did not go to school in Asherton. We are poor and he had to work.[5]

While the majority of Texas Mexicans were indifferent toward education Taylor found that a select few were beginning to express an intense interest in public schools. For instance, a poor, illiterate tenant farmer growing cotton and corn and living in a mesquite, mud-plastered jacal told Taylor, "I don't want my boy to work. I want him in school." "If I die and the children have no education," he continued, "it will be muy duro for them." Another young Texas Mexican cotton picker who had been to school one year exclaimed:

> Now I cry with both eyes because I have not better education. If I had education I could have a position and work with my head. Now I work hard and only with my hands.[6]

This changing attitude toward education was most apparent in the small towns, especially among the better-educated individuals such as clerks, steadily employed laborers, and small merchants.[7] These individuals—most of whom had not had to overcome the overt hostility of rural educators, extreme poverty, or lack of educational facilities—showed a great interest in public schools. Their desire for education was expressed in the comments and complaints they made about discriminatory treatment in the schools. One urban Texas Mexican complained: "They don't give us an equal chance. We just want a chance." Another complained that the superintendents in the county did not want to educate Texas Mexicans. "It is hard to convince the farmers," he continued, "that you should educate the Mexicans, that the country would be better with good and loyal citizens."[8]

Others complained against inadequate instruction and untrained, insensitive teachers. One Texas Mexican said: "In the Mexican schools they have young, inexperienced teachers who are sometimes uninterested." "They have inadequate equipment," he added. According to him, local school officials "are just taking the money received for the Mexicans and spending it for the American school." A leading Texas Mexican made the following observations:

> They [parents] say, what is the use of sending children to school. We sent them four or five years and they can't get out of the first or second [grade] readers. The trouble may be with the teachers . . . [they] don't know how

to teach the children English, and the children and parents don't take an interest until it is too late, and then the children have to go to work.[9]

One person, born and raised in Texas, complained that the Mexican schools were no good, the "girl teachers" were inexperienced high school graduates, and the school superintendent was uncaring. Even a Texas Mexican from the rural parts of Nueces County agreed that "the teachers don't put no attention on the Mexican school." "The children just sit there all day long," he stated. "It is hard to send children five or six miles in winter," he added, "and they don't pay no attention."[10]

Several individuals complained against the nonenforcement of the compulsory school law. One of them from Nueces County wished that "they could put in jail all who don't go to school." Another said that the attendance law should be enforced. "They are not so poor," he argued, "but that they could send their children to school."[11]

Besides expressing dissatisfaction with the lack of educational opportunities, there was some evidence of individual communities taking the initiative to develop their own schools. For instance, Texas Mexican communities in at least three towns in Dimmit County established private schools or after school classes for their children. Established largely as a result of their dissatisfaction with the public schools and partly to retain their native language and culture, these private schools usually had small classes, irregular attendance, and inadequate instruction. But they revealed a strong concern for community-controlled education.[12]

One of these private schools was located in Big Wells, Dimmit County. Although no name was provided, one of the persons associated with the school described it to Taylor. According to this person, the Mexican school was started in November 1928. School was held for five days a week from 4:00 to 8:00 p.m. It had three grades and the pupils were from six to eighteen years of age. The cost for attending was five cents per day per child, however, additional children from the same family would not be charged extra. The school taught the following courses: hygiene, gymnastics, manual training, drawing, Spanish, grammar, arithmetic, geometry, diet, clothing, and the cause of high infant mortality. The children, both Mexican nationals and Texas Mexicans, were taught in their own language. The teacher was a Texas Mexican female who was provided with furnished quarters by the parents. According to Taylor, she "eked out a livelihood by supplementing her tuition fees with commissions from peddling medicines, toilet articles, Mexican periodicals, etc."[13]

In addition to establishing their own schools, several communities raised money to purchase playground equipment for their children in the segregated public schools.[14] They also pressured local school districts to provide better educational facilities and opportunities for their children. In some cases, parents kept their children away from school as a way of applying pressure on local school districts. One such effort to boycott the schools occurred in 1928 in Dimmit County.[15] According to one of the participants, the teachers did not speak any Spanish and did not understand the Mexican children. Anglo students called the Mexican children greasers and other pejorative names. Mexican parents were so upset with the lack of adequate instruction and discriminatory treatment that they asked for a separate school under their control. When the board denied their request, they took their children out of school until they got a teacher with "a better disposition toward the Mexicans."[16]

The greater interest in and desire for public education was a reflection of the profound social and cultural changes taking place within the Texas Mexican community. These changes were in no small part due to the tremendous work of a new statewide organization of American citizens of Mexican descent—the League of United Latin American Citizens or LULAC.

LULAC AND ATTITUDES
TOWARD PUBLIC EDUCATION

LULAC was the organizational response of a conscientious group of Americans of Mexican descent to the deteriorating socioeconomic conditions which the entire community faced in the first three decades of the twentieth century. During the period from 1900 to 1930 the Mexican population, especially the well-to-do and the least-educated, experienced a tremendous amount of economic deprivation, political manipulation, and loss of social status.[17] Texas Mexicans were increasingly accused of being disloyal to the United States and of being unworthy of admission to this country. They also were blamed for the growing rates of juvenile delinquency, illiteracy, and crime.[18] Unwanted except as a source of cheap labor, Texas Mexicans were discouraged or prohibited from participating in politics, denied their civil rights, and discriminated against in all spheres of life.[19]

Of particular importance was the increasing violence against persons of Mexican descent, their continual denial of justice in the courts, and the heightened contempt shown toward them by Anglos. In South Texas, for instance, Mexicans were brutally murdered and lynched by vigilante groups or by law enforcement agencies themselves.[20] In Central Texas signs such as "No lots sold to Mexicans" and "No Mexicans admitted" were prominently displayed. The contempt toward Mexicans was so great that at a 1910 session of the legislature State Rep. J. T. Canales, the only Texas Mexican legislator, was referred to as the "greaser from Brownsville." Several years later, Canales' outspoken defense of Texas Mexicans was reason enough for a member of the much-despised Texas Rangers to threaten his life.[21]

Although despised by the larger society and politically powerless, individuals of Mexican descent attempted to better their own working and living conditions. They conducted isolated legal challenges or journalistic exposés of discriminatory practices by judicial, administrative, and educational agencies.[22] In some cases, they engaged in school boycotts or in strikes against unfair labor practices.[23] Most important, the Mexican community throughout the state organized social and civic organizations to defend themselves against increasing acts of physical and cultural violence by Anglos.

In 1910, for instance, several prominent residents of Mexican descent along the border held a conference to organize an association to protect the rights and interests of all Mexicans in the state.[24] Although unsuccessful in establishing a permanent statewide organization, this conference laid the basis for future attempts. Organizing efforts continued into the 1920s, but it was not until 1929 that a permanent, unified statewide organization was finally founded. This organization was the League of United Latin American Citizens.[25]

LULAC was different in many ways from traditional organizations such as the mutual aid societies found in the Mexican communities.[26] First and foremost was the socioeconomic and citizenship status of the founders of this organization. All of the individuals involved in LULAC either were born in the United States or were naturalized citizens. They were the first generation of Americans of Mexican descent. They were also part of an extremely small but vocal middle-class element within the Mexican American community.[27] Despite great obstacles, these individuals managed to achieve a modicum of social and economic success. Printers, lawyers, businesspersons, and college-trained individuals formed the core of LULAC's leadership.[28]

An example of the type of men who founded LULAC is Ben Garza, first president general of LULAC.[29] Garza's story is that "of a poor boy who rose from a humble home to the position of leadership and stability which he held during his last years."[30] At fifteen, Garza's father died, leaving him as the head of a household of eight. In order to help support his mother and his six brothers, he quit school. Three years later he moved to Corpus Christi to take a job as a waiter in a local café. With his earnings he helped his younger brother Joe finish high school and then two years of college. During the war he moved to Rockport, about thirty miles north of Corpus Christi, to work in the government shipyards. In 1919 he and three other business associates purchased the Metropolitan Café in Corpus Christi. Several years later, he bought a 50 percent share of the restaurant, and with his one remaining partner he also bought the building in which it was located. One month before he died, Garza made the final payment on the building.

Besides being a prominent Corpus Christi businessman, Garza was also a civic leader. He dedicated his efforts to bettering the conditions of the Mexican population in the state. At one point he accompanied a delegation to Washington to protest a proposed bill which would have reduced Latin American immigration to the states.[31] In 1929 he became one of the founders of LULAC and its first general president. M. Machado, another founder, attributed the success of LULAC to Garza's excellent organizational skills, fine common sense, and strong grasp of fundamental principles.[32] Garza was also a member of several other civic organizations, including the Knights of Columbus and Woodmen of the World. At the age of forty-four he died of poor health in Kerrville.

The purposes and aims of LULAC were another way in which the organization was significantly different from the existing groups within the community. Unlike the existing groups which provided primarily social services to the Mexican population, LULAC proposed to integrate the community into the political and social institutions of American life. The constitution of LULAC illustrates this fundamental transformation from self-help and protective to assimilative activities. According to the constitution, one of the central aims of the organization was to "develop within the members of our race, the best, purest, and more perfect type of true and loyal citizen of the United States of America."[33]

The making of citizens itself was not a major concern of LULAC, since over half of all the Mexicans living in South Texas were already citizens.[34] Rather, they were more concerned with the making of active citizens who would practice their citizenship by participating in the dominant political, economic, and social institutions of the land.

"This organization is not a political club," stated the LULAC constitution, "but as citizens we shall participate in all local, state and national political contests." "However," it continued, "in doing so we shall ever bear in mind the general welfare of our people, and we disregard and abjure once and for all any personal obligation which is not in harmony with these principles."[35]

In pledging allegiance to the United States government, LULAC members also de-emphasized dependence on Mexico for moral sustenance. Instead of looking to Mexico for guidance, advice, and intellectual nourishment, the new generation of Americans of Mexican descent now looked to the political institutions of the United States for solutions to their problems. As the LULAC constitution stated, the organization was formed to "define with absolute and unmistakeable clearness our unquestionable loyalty to the ideals, principles, and citizenship of the United States of America."[36]

The first generation of Mexican Americans looked toward their own united political and social efforts for solutions to their problems. "We should endeavor to develop aggressiveness of the right sort and be able to pursue our own initiative instead of waiting for someone else to do the things we have thought of doing but never put into execution," noted an editorial in the *LULAC News*, the organization's newspaper. This sentiment was best expressed by one of LULAC's members in 1934 in *La Prensa*, a San Antonio newspaper. According to this LULAC member, "The Latin American people, and only they can solve the educational problems that confront us. . . . Only the Latin American people can do this—a united people, firmly resolute, true to the principles of progress and to the betterment of our brothers."[37]

While desirous of the support of all Mexicans residing in Texas, including those who were not citizens, LULAC understood that it would have to fight its battles alone. Emphasis thus was placed on selecting "as our leaders those among us who demonstrate, by their integrity and culture, that they are capable of guiding and directing us properly." Since their unity was essential for advancing their cause, LULAC also proposed to "resist and attack energetically all machinations tending to prevent our social and political unification."[38]

Conscious of themselves as an emerging middle class, LULAC members assumed the responsibility of educating and protecting the Mexican American population and incorporating it into the dominant institutions of their country. But their integration was not to be achieved at the expense of their cultural background.

This group of individuals was not calling for the total assimilation of the Mexican American population into Anglo cultural society as has been suggested by some authors.[39] Integration into Anglo American political and social life was to be a selective process. "Undoubtedly," noted Alonso Perales in 1929, "the two greatest obstacles for the Americanization of the Mexican in Texas are the racial prejudice which the Anglo-Saxon harbors against us and certain customs which are repugnant to ours, but the Mexican American has adjusted himself to the latter, adopting only what there is of good in them." In order not to be misunderstood, LULAC encoded this strong belief into the organization's constitution. Accordingly the constitution declared that one of LULAC's aims was "to assume complete responsibility for the education of our children as to their rights and duties and the language and customs of this country; the latter insofar as they may be good customs."[40]

Cultural pride was not to be neglected either. "We solemnly declare once and for all to maintain a sincere and respectful reverence of our racial origin of which we are proud." In 1929 *El Paladín*, the organization's newspaper, emphasized that the above declaration "ought to be proof that our efforts to be rightfully recognized as citizens of this country do not imply that we wish to become scattered nor much less abominate our Latin heritage, but rather on the contrary, we will always feel for it the most tender love and the most respectful veneration."[41] The English language and Anglo American social customs were to be learned, but not at the expense of the Texas Mexicans' own language and traditions. Cultural pride, retention of the Spanish language, and the physical and cultural defense of the Mexican heritage were as much goals of the new organizations as were the acquisition of English, the training for citizenship, and the struggle for equality for the residents of Mexican ancestry.

An integral part of the LULAC campaign to incorporate Texas Mexicans into the political institutions of the society was the eradication of discriminatory treatment based on national origin—or "race" as it was then known.[42] The LULAC constitution reflected this sentiment. According to one of its bylaws, the organization proposed to "eradicate from our body politic all intents and tendencies to establish discriminations among our fellow citizens on account of race, religion, or social position as being contrary to the true spirit of Democracy, our Constitution and Laws." The organization also proposed to "destroy any attempt to create racial prejudices against our people, and any infamous stigma which may be cast upon them, and we shall demand for them the respect and prerogatives which the Constitution grants to us all."[43]

J. Luz Saenz, one of the founders of LULAC, summarized the organization's position with respect to the elimination of discrimination against Mexicans in the following way:

As long as they do not educate us with all the guarantees and opportunities for free participation in all the activities which constitute the fountains of national life; as long as they wish to raise up on high the standard of SUPREMACY OF RACES ON ACCOUNT OF COLOR . . . , as long as they continue to stir up the fire of historical prejudices, past or racial, so much more they will put off our conversion [into Americans] and the total carrying out of our obligations as full citizens.[44]

A third way in which this new organization represented a significant departure from past groups concerned the manner in which it planned to accomplish its purposes. LULAC proposed to involve only those who met its restrictive criteria for membership. Unlike the mutualista organizations which welcomed both Mexican immigrants and Mexican American citizens, LULAC limited its membership to those who were U.S. citizens of Latin ancestry, eighteen years or over, male, and, to a large extent, registered voters.[45]

Alonso Perales, one of the founders of LULAC, stated that only by using the rights they had as citizens could they help to solve the socioeconomic problems of all the Mexicans living north of the border. "The day the Mexican American betters his own conditions and finds himself in a position to make full use of his rights of citizenship," he stated in 1929, "that day he will be able to aid the Mexican citizen in securing what is due him and to help him assure himself of his own welfare and happiness."[46]

LULAC proposed to use all the political means available to accomplish their goals. Not only would they participate in the local, state, and national elections, but "with our vote and influence [we will] place in public office men who show by their deeds, respect and consideration for our people." In addition to participating in elections, LULAC would seek "to secure equal representation of our people on juries and in the administration of Governmental affairs."[47]

Legal methods for accomplishing their goals were also considered. Generally, LULAC would "use all the legal means at our command to the end that all citizens in our country may enjoy equal rights, the equal protection of the laws of the land and equal opportunities and privileges." "Secretly and openly," the LULAC constitution stated, "by all lawful means at our command, we shall assist in the education and guidance of Latin Americans and we shall protect and defend their lives and interests whenever necessary." In addition to legal recourse, LULAC proposed to "create a fund for our mutual protection, for the defense of those of us who may be unjustly prosecuted and for the education and culture of our people."[48]

All means, with the exception of one, were used in their struggle for equality. This one exception was violence. "We shall oppose any radical and violent demonstrations," LULAC proposed, "which may tend to create conflicts and disturb the peace and tranquility of our country."[49]

Education in the eyes of many was to play an important role in the general strategy of incorporating Mexicans into the dominant institutions of the land and for elevating their general socioeconomic and political status.[50] But in order to obtain more schooling, it was necessary to struggle against obstacles impeding the educational progress of all Mexicans. For this reason, the struggle became twofold. On the one hand, LULAC members had to modify existing discriminatory educational policies and practices in order to improve the accessibility and quality of public schooling for Mexican American children. On the other hand, they had to go among their own people and disseminate their faith in public education.

LULAC believed that, while Mexican Americans as a group were not provided with adequate public services, they likewise were to blame for not taking advantage of those that were provided for them.[51] As a prominent LULAC member from Nueces County stated, "if you have not been treated like you should or have not the standard of living [you should have] it is your own fault." According to this LULAC member, if Mexican Americans suffered humiliation or discrimination at the hands of Anglos they had no one but themselves to blame.[52]

With respect to public education, LULAC members also believed that Mexican Americans were to blame for their discriminatory treatment at the hands of Anglo school officials.[53] According to one of its members, "All the problems in the education [of Mexicans] have two basic considerations: Anglo actions, in many cases, and the lack of Mexican activity in the others." According to this individual, much of the racial discrimination seen in the public schools is due "to the Anglos who do not understand or do not desire to understand our people's psychology." "At that same time," he argued, "this is the result of the Latin American, who does not demand his rights nor does he try to find solutions to these problems which serve as obstacles for his children."[54]

Two important cultural characteristics of the Mexican American population were identified as detrimental to school progress: language and attitudes. According to a LULAC member, for example, about 90 percent of the problem was that Mexican Americans did not talk English at home or teach English to their children. "If you talk English," he noted, "you will think and act like Americans." LULAC members in general firmly believed that English was "necessary for the enjoyment of our rights and privileges" and thus declared it to be the official language of the organization. Members of the organization also pledged to speak and teach English to their children.[55] In addition to the language problem, LULAC also believed that Mexican Americans did not have a strong desire to attend public schools. Paul Taylor in his studies of Dimmit and Nueces counties found that this was the case with those who lived in rural areas, but less so with those residing in small towns and among the better-educated Mexicans similar to LULAC members.[56]

As a way of remedying this problem, LULAC began to promote the adoption of American behavior, cultural values, and communication patterns. "We try to impress upon them first, the importance of the English language," stated a LULAC member, and "second, the importance of educating their children even if it is too late for them."[57] They also began to promote increased access to more and better education. "Without doubt, to the end that we make ourselves valued and respected," stated Perales, "we shall have to effect our own intellectual redemption." "If we, the Mexican American and the Mexican citizens raised in the United States, are to occupy the honorable place that we merit," he added, "it is indispensable to educate ourselves."[58]

Besides promoting education among their own group, LULAC members believed that the organization should strive for better and more formal schooling for all Mexicans.[59] More education, according to this view, would increase earning power and indirectly improve the living standards of all Mexicans. This, in turn, would elevate the social status of the Mexican community. An editorial in the *LULAC News* provided this educational perspective in 1931. It said:

> Again and again at different times our orators of the League have expressed their belief that the fundamental and basic problem of our race in Texas and the United States was education. Educate the children of Mexican extraction and we will measure up to the requirement of American standards.[60]

LULAC AND THE CAMPAIGN
FOR EDUCATIONAL EQUALITY

Popularizing the benefits of education among their own group was not as difficult as was the campaign to improve the accessibility and quality of public schooling for Mexican American children. Lacking sufficient resources to bring about significant reform in education, LULAC focused largely on challenging the local practice of establishing segregated schools for these children.

Segregation on the basis of ancestry was perceived by the new generation of Mexican Americans as the major obstacle to educational progress and to the learning of English. Local school officials argued that segregation was necessary for instructing non-English-speaking youngsters and for shielding them against the social ostracism they encountered in Anglo schools. But for the Mexican American population in general and LULAC in particular, segregation was an attempt to deny them equal educational opportunities. One Texas Mexican farmer in Nueces County, for example, noted that "the teachers don't put no attention on the [segregated] Mexican school." He continued:

> Having children all together is better. Then the teachers who teach the white boys have to do the same for the Mexicans. They know there is a separate school, and don't pay attention to the Mexicans. If I pay a poll tax and send my children to school it [segregation] is not right.[61]

A rural Mexican agreed that when their children attended school with whites they "learn to speak English better." One high school student stated, "Separate, you never learn to talk English well," while another said, "Together . . . we would learn faster."[62]

Segregation also was not conducive to making better Americans. "As long as we segregate," stated a Corpus Christi resident, "we can't make good citizens." He added, "Mexicans will think they are inferior."[63]

While a handful of Mexican Americans argued on behalf of school segregation, many opposed it by the late 1920s. One Anglo teacher in Corpus Christi noticed this change in attitude toward segregation among Mexican Americans. "The Mexican parents used to prefer their children to be Mexicans first, and Americans afterwards," she stated. "Now, the Mexicans are gradually coming to resent the separate schools."[64]

Illustrative of the new attitude toward segregation was the comment made by a Mexican American in Robstown, near Corpus Christi. He said:

> They used to keep the Mexicans separate to the fourth grade. They were slow to learn, and claimed they did not have the right kind of teacher. Now they have built a modern Mexican school. There is separation for three grades. It may be all right, on account of language. But the Bohemian and German and other non-English speaking children go to the American school, and some Mexicans want their children to go there.[65]

LULAC members had a similar view toward segregation. This view was best expressed by R. de la Garza in the *LULAC News* of 1931. He stated:

> Why do they discriminate on our children? They [school officials] claim that a majority of our children are ill-fed and unclean! Are they? I leave your own hearts to answer that. They state that our speaking a different language requires segregation. Let them segregate our children in the first grades until they have learned enough English to hold their own with other whites. If some of them are unclean, let them be placed in different schools until they have learned to be clean. BUT WE MUST BATTLE SEGREGATION BECAUSE OF RACE PREJUDICES![66]

La Liga Pro-Defensa Escolar (League for the Defense of Our Schools), a coalition of over fifty social, civic, labor, and religious organizations in San Antonio, also reflected this sentiment when it emphatically stated that "segregation based on race, whether it be in the elementary or secondary schools, is absolutely intolerable.[67] Besides being perceived as the major obstacle to educational progress, segregation was also considered the most visible manifestation of discriminatory treatment in the public schools.[68]

The first challenge to the practice of placing Mexican American and Anglo schoolchildren in separate classes occurred in 1928 before LULAC had become a statewide organization.[69] In that year Felipe Vela filed a complaint with the state superintendent of public instruction against the Charlotte Independent School District located in Atascosa County, south of San Antonio. The child in the case was represented by Hon. Earl D. Scott, judge of Atascosa.[70]

The Charlotte Independent School District, with fewer than five hundred school-age children, maintained a segregated public school system. "It has been the custom for many years," noted the summary statement of this decision, "for the children of Mexican nationality to attend school at one building and the white children of all other nationalities at the other building."

Felipe Vela had an adopted child, Amada Vela, whose "race" was of unknown origin. The child's parents sought to enroll her in the building occupied by the other white children, but the board of trustees instead assigned her to the Mexican school. Vela argued that the child was not Mexican and should have the same privilege of instruction that was accorded the other American children. Having been denied the right to enroll his child in the non-Mexican school, he appealed directly to the state superintendent of public instruction for a decision. "The question is before the State Superintendent," the summary declared, "to determine whether or not Amada Vela should be required to attend the Mexican school."

Several issues related to the central question were summarily dismissed by both sides before the case reached the state superintendent's office. First, both sides agreed that the board of trustees did not have the legal authority to segregate Mexican children in one school on a racial basis. Thus, "with this admission, the question is eliminated from consideration as to whether or not the child, Amada Vela, is of Mexican parentage." Second, it was understood that Amada Vela did not live within the ward designated for the Mexican school but because her adoptive parents were Mexican she had been assigned to this school. The school officials defended the assignment of Mexican children to one separate school as necessary for instructional reasons. "It is well understood that non-English-speaking children should be given special instruction," they argued, "and it is probably to the best interests of such children that they be placed in one room or in one school in order that the character of instruction given will be different from that given to English-speaking children."

The superintendent of public instruction, S. M. N. Marrs, agreed with them that if instructional reasons accounted for the separate Mexican school, the local school officials would be within their legal rights to do so. "It would follow, however," Superintendent Marrs continued, "if there are Mexican children who speak English fluently and understand its meaning that they should be classified with the American children." Upon examination, Superintendent Marrs found that Amada Vela was intelligent, spoke English fluently, and was able to translate Spanish into English and English into Spanish. He argued that her assignment to the American school would certainly not "interfere with the progress of the American children with whom she might be classed." In addition, Marrs argued that placement in the Mexican school was not in the best interest of the child. "The fact that the large majority of the Mexican children do not speak English, and when they do so it is with reluctance," he further noted, "places this child at a disadvantage should she be assigned to the Mexican school." Unsatisfied with this decision, the board of trustees made a vigorous appeal to the State Board of Education to reverse the superintendent's formal response. The State Board declined to reverse it.

Although successful, this particular case had little significant impact on the community, since it only applied to one individual. Two years later, LULAC made its initial legal challenge to segregation in *Independent School District v. Salvatierra*. Unlike the Vela complaint, this segregation case was a class action suit against the school officials of Del Rio—a small rural border town located in Val Verde County in South Texas.[71] This suit is of historical importance for several reasons. It was the first case in which the courts were asked to exercise their power of judicial review to determine the constitutionality of the actions of a local school district with respect to the education of Mexican Americans. The court pointed out this problem in the following manner:

> It is a matter of pride and gratification in our great public educational system and its administration that the question of race segregation, as between Mexicans and other white races, has not heretofore found its way into the courts of the state, and therefore the decision of no Texas court is available in the disposition of the precise question present here.[72]

Second, the findings of the court of civil appeals of Texas reaffirmed existing legal principles and laid the basis for the determination of future challenges to segregation.

In this particular court case several Mexican American parents alleged that their children were being denied the equal protection of law under the Constitution because a separate school was maintained for them by the Del Rio Independent School District. The Del Rio school system was comprised of four school buildings and a school athletic field, all located on the same piece of land. The high school and two elementary schools designated for Anglos were at one end, the athletic field was in the middle of the property, and the Mexican or West End school, a two-room building, was at the other end.[73]

On January 7, 1930, the board of trustees ordered an election to be held the following month to determine if they should issue and sell bonds in the sum of $185,000 "for the purpose of constructing and equipping public free school buildings of material other than wood and the purchase of the necessary sites therefore in said school district." The election also authorized the levy and collection of taxes to pay off the bonds. The bond election passed and in due course the bonds were issued and sold. The local school trustees determined that they would use the bond monies to construct a new senior high school building and to remodel and enlarge the elementary schools. The two-room Mexican school, "constructed of brick and tile, was to be enlarged by adding five rooms, including an auditorium of the same material."

The Mexican American parents alleged "that unless prevented by this litigation, the school authorities will continue this segregation in the West End building as now constructed and extend it to the proposed enlarged structure when it shall be completed and equipped." More specifically, they contended that the acts and conduct of appellants are designed to affect, and do actually accomplish, the complete segregation of the school children of Mexican and Spanish descent [in certain elementary grades] from the school children of all other white races in the same grades, thereby excluding the one from the classrooms of the other, and denying to them the right and privilege of mingling with those of the other races in the common enjoyment of identical school facilities, instruction, associations, and environment.[74]

The Mexican American parents were not questioning the quality of the facilities nor the content of the instruction provided to these children. Their complaint centered rather on the placement of Mexican American children in facilities separate from the Anglo children in the school district.

According to the court, the local school district had not gone beyond the administrative powers delegated to it by constitutional and statutory provisions. Although it agreed in principle that "the school authorities have no power to arbitrarily segregate Mexican children, assign them to separate schools, and exclude them from schools maintained for children of other white races, merely or solely because they are Mexicans," it found that in this particular case they were not engaging in such activities. The court declared that since school officials were not "at this time enforcing unlawful segregation," the Mexican American parents had no legal course of action open to them.[75]

The court also found that the school district's method of classifying Mexican students as non-English speakers for placement purposes was not arbitrary or unconstitutional. The Mexican American parents alleged that local school officials unlawfully discriminated against their children by placing them in separate facilities on the basis of ancestry. The local superintendent replied that Mexican students were not assigned to the separate facilities merely because they were Mexicans. Their classification, grading, and assignment to the West End school were based on instructional reasons. "I was not actuated by any motive of segregation by reason of race or color in doing what I said I did," he declared. "The whole proposition," he added, "was from a standpoint of instruction and a fair opportunity of all children alike. That was the only consideration I had in the matter."

More specifically, the local school superintendent gave two major reasons for placing all these children in the Mexican school. The first reason had to do with their late enrollment and irregular attendance. "Well, we had a peculiar situation as regards people of Spanish or Mexican extraction here," testified the local superintendent. He added:

We found a great percentage of these people are at work in cotton fields and on ranches, and some of them go entirely out of the district in the fall season, that is, return in the fall and enter school late and in considerable numbers, and where you have already organized your classes on a basis of a certain size which represents the most efficient instruction possible you are greatly hampered if a great number of people continue to drop in.

The second major reason used by the superintendent was related to the language problem. According to his testimony, the Mexican student's language needs were different from the Anglo child's. Most of these students when placed in a classroom with English-speaking children, he stated, "are handicapped because they are slow in reading English and read it with difficulty, and as a consequence, fail in considerable numbers in English and history." Although they were more apt in mathematics, he added that the "decided peculiarities" of the Mexican students "can be better taken care of in those elementary grades by their being placed separately from the children of Anglo-Saxon parentage."[76]

Finally, in assessing the constitutionality of the local school officials' actions the court failed to find any evidence indicating intent to discriminate on the part of the local school officials or evidence of discriminatory action against Mexican American children. It concluded that the placement policies and practices were not "unlawful or violative even of the spirit of the Constitution."[77] Thus, in this first important legal challenge to racial discrimination in the public schools, the court stipulated that it was unconstitutional to segregate Mexican students based on national origin grounds, but it did allow segregation on educational grounds.

LULAC members were greatly disheartened by this decision.[78] At a special convention called on November 29, 1931, LULAC discussed what course of action to pursue. Since segregation had to be based on other grounds besides race, a resolution was adopted urging all LULAC members to encourage scientific studies to determine "what constitutes justifiable segregation for purposes of instruction . . . and how long it should continue."[79]

Lacking financial resources, an adequate professional staff, and an atmosphere conducive to legal change, LULAC lessened its stress on legal challenges to segregation and instead emphasized other measures.[80] The issue of school segregation, LULAC members decided, should be resolved without resorting to the courts if possible.[81] Informal consultations and persuasion were strongly emphasized as a more viable strategy for changing conditions in the public schools. "We would get acquainted with superintendents, principals and teachers," stated Louis Wilmot, one of the founding members of LULAC, "and we tried to persuade them to do away with segregation and with discriminatory educational practices." According to Wilmot, "We gained more by getting acquainted with administrators and elected officials than by demonstrations."[82]

The politics of persuasion was successful in some cases. Take the case of Seguin, located some forty miles southeast of San Antonio. On September 7, 1932, all its schools were opened except for the "Mexican school." LULAC formed a small committee to find out why it remained closed and was told that Mexican parents did not send their children to school until after the cotton-picking season ended. After several negotiating sessions school officials agreed to open the Mexican school if LULAC assured them that students would enroll. LULAC members agreed and within several days approximately ninety Mexican American children of both sexes enrolled in the elementary school.[83]

In other cases, LULAC members sent letters to their state legislators in support of bills having an impact on the education of Mexican Americans. One such incident occurred in February 1937 when the San Antonio LULACs encouraged all other chapters to write their local legislators in support of an educational finance bill. They urged that state legislators attach a rider to the next appropriation bill authorizing the state superintendent of public instruction to withhold the state per capita allotment of educational funds from any school district that failed to provide equal educational facilities to all school-age children residing in the district. "Heretofore," argued the San Antonio council, "these allotments have been notoriously diverted to satisfy political pressure needs while the real need has gone begging." "Our children have been the victims of these injustices. We do not ask for any special privileges. All we ask is equal educational facilities to all children irrespective of racial extraction," it added.[84]

LULAC also continued to speak out against unfair treatment and discrimination in the schools. In 1939 Ezequiel Salinas, state president of LULAC, took several steps to improve the deplorable condition of Mexican American children in the public schools. He encouraged the state superintendent of public instruction, L. A. Woods, to reprimand several local school districts for discriminating against Mexican American children.[85] He also appeared before an education conference attended by one hundred Texas school superintendents and spoke in favor of eliminating racism and distortions of Mexican Americans in history textbooks. Before his term expired, Salinas worked for and supported a Works Progress Administration school construction project in Hondo aimed at solving overcrowded conditions in the public schools.[86]

In addition to fighting discriminatory school policies and practices, LULAC members promoted education among their own community in various ways. They spoke to individual parents and appeared before parent groups. At these meetings they encouraged the parents to send their children to school and to make demands upon local school officials.[87]

To promote public school attendance LULAC established a scholarship fund. The purpose of this fund was to assist "meritorious" and "zealous" students in the community in acquiring a college education. "The rise and fall of power in a nation is through its citizenry, and history has clearly shown that internal needs, regardless of the nature or size, may be cured by education. Why not then, fight the many hazards that the Latin faces in this country by assisting in our humble way, the coming generation?" Ruben R. Lozano, the chairperson of the first Educational Committee of LULAC argued. "Let us provide them with the necessary and many times tested weapon of thinking in a higher sphere," he added. In November of 1932 LULAC, for the first time in its history, awarded three scholarships.[88]

Complementing LULAC's scholarship activities were its efforts to organize local chapters of Parent-Teacher Association (PTA). In places large and small where a significant percentage of Mexican American children predominated, LULAC chapters encouraged and assisted parents in organizing local PTAs. At Dilley, Cotulla, San Antonio, Kingsville, and other cities parents organized and began to seek better facilities and an improved education for their children.[89] Slowly, the faith LULAC had in public education was being disseminated among the Mexican American community. To a large extent LULAC was instilling hope for the future and incorporating the parents into the cultural world of Anglo America.

In addition to these activities, LULAC became involved in improving the public schools provided for their children in key local communities, focusing especially on overcrowded conditions. San Antonio was one such community where LULAC members engaged in this improvement campaign. During the early 1930s LULAC organized a school committee to investigate the nature of the schools provided to Mexican American children, especially those residing in the West Side barrio. In

1934 they issued a status report on these schools. The report issued by the LULAC Committee on Public School Buildings and Recreational Facilities found that only 12,334 Mexican American school-age children—or 56.5 percent—were enrolled in the public schools. Anglo enrollment stood at 12,224. Although the difference in enrollment between Anglos and Mexican Americans was minuscule, the nature of the facilities provided for them was not. For instance, there were twenty-eight schools with 368 rooms in the Anglo communities but only eleven schools with 269 rooms for the Mexican American students. The LULAC school committee argued that the law allowed no more than thirty-five children per classroom, yet there were forty-eight children per room in the Mexican American schools and thirty-three per room in the Anglo schools. In order to meet the requirements of the law, it was necessary to add eighty-four classrooms to the Mexican American schools.

The Anglo schools had a total of eighty-two acres of land for recreational purposes but there were only twenty-three acres for the Mexican American schools. The school district spent a total of $439,636 or $35.96 per Anglo child, but only $302,224 or $24.50 per Mexican American child. Finally, the Anglo neighborhoods had air-conditioned "palaces" while the Mexican American community only had deteriorating wooden frame buildings.[90]

The only response received from the San Antonio Board of Education was that it did not have any funds nor did it expect to have any in the near future. LULAC viewed this response to its demands for better school facilities as "inconsiderate." According to its data the board of education had in the last several months appropriated $200,000 for one of the junior high schools and $750,000 for the South Side high school. Furthermore, the board had bought parade grounds for the Brackenridge High School for the sum of $19,500. It had then spent a large sum of money to build a roof garden and dance hall for the school. None of these schools were located in the Mexican American community.

At the end of the 1933-1934 school year, the board of education also voted over $500,000 to raise teachers' salaries. While LULAC agreed with the necessity of the raise, it argued that "in view of the existing emergency the School Board should have set aside a reasonable sum of money to relieve the congested condition of the western schools." In an effort to appease LULAC the board of education bought about fifteen frame rooms which had been abandoned by the Peacock Military Academy, an old private school. These were moved to the West Side to relieve the congestion in the schools. Afterward the board held a press conference asserting that they had just built a new school for the western part of the city. "The said frame dwellings," argued LULAC, "are inadequate and unsafe."[91]

Despite the placement of annexes and other temporary school improvements, LULAC argued that there was still need for five large elementary schools with a total number of ninety-four rooms to accommodate 3,269 pupils in the overcrowded schools. School records revealed that over 1,300 fifth-grade pupils, including those who had graduated in May 1934, were planning on entering junior high school during the 1934-1935 school year. "It is imperative that another junior high school be provided to accommodate them," stated LULAC. Under these crowded conditions all schoolchildren were deprived "of receiving a proper education from a moral, physical, social, and intellectual standpoint." "So long as these conditions are permitted to continue and so long as the San Antonio Board of Education continues to neglect to remedy the situation," it added, "just so long will the advancement of all school children of the said eleven western elementary schools be retarded."[92]

In response to these deplorable conditions, LULAC called for a public meeting at Sidney Lanier Junior-Senior High School to discuss this report. The meeting was held on October 2, 1934, and was attended by L. A. Woods, state superintendent of public instruction. At this meeting, information was passed out and discussed on the conditions of the Mexican schools on the West Side. At a later date, Woods wrote to LULAC acknowledging the accuracy of conditions it reported. According to him, the president of the school board and the school superintendent were aware of these conditions and had expressed a desire to better them.

Unlike the state superintendent, LULAC members did not believe that the local officials were concerned about the West Side schools. Based on their information, the local officials were planning on spending approximately $900,000 on a new school for the Anglo side of town and nothing on the West Side schools. LULAC members expressed their frustrations to Woods and argued that they should receive part of the funds. He agreed with them and recommended that if no funds were made available to improve the conditions in the West Side schools the organization should seek legal redress. However, he did not feel this step would be needed. "Frankly," he told LULAC, "I am of the opinion that the first step the School Board should take is to remedy the dismal conditions of the west side schools of the city, and I believe if you continue working as you have been up until now, the Board will accede to your just demands."[93]

After receiving Woods' encouraging letter, LULAC sent out 162 letters to prominent Anglos from San Antonio explaining to them the conditions of the schools and asking for their support. Many of them responded favorably. Franklin J. Spears, a prominent lawyer, wrote a letter to the president of the school board and to the board members asking them to meet with LULAC to discuss this situation. The chairperson of the LULAC school committee also wrote a letter requesting a meeting with the board. Both of the letters were ignored.[94] On November 22, 1934, the school board was reported to have said:

> We do not see the necessity for meeting with LULAC. Since January I called to the Board's attention the conditions [with regard to the West Side schools] and since then we have tried everything possible to provide these people more facilities. We have constructed a new school with 16 rooms. . . . If we were free from outside interference, the Board could go about its business in a much better way.[95]

In response to this rejection and accusation of outside interference, LULAC called for a large meeting of all those organizations interested in bettering the schools in the West Side. Over seventy-two social, civic, labor, and religious organizations responded to this call. Two days later, on November 30, 1934, representatives from these seventy-two organizations presented a petition to the school board and requested a meeting with it. The board refused to honor the petition and ignored their request. Eleuterio Escobar, chairperson of the LULAC school committee, offered to resign his position if it would encourage the board to meet with selected representatives of the Mexican American community, but he received no answer.[96]

Having been rejected and ignored several times, the LULAC school committee decided to form a coalition of all the organizations interested in promoting better schools on the West Side. On December 18, 1934, a new independent organization—Liga de Defensa Escolar (League for the Defense of Our Schools)—was founded.[97] The Liga was comprised of thirty-seven social, civic, commercial, and religious organizations.[98] It sought to present a "united front, under a perfect and harmonious union, to obtain for school children and for the youth and especially for those that reside in the west side of the city, more advantages and better school facilities."[99]

For over fourteen years this organization held conferences in the community on the lack of educational opportunities and sought to persuade local school board members to promote changes in the schools. Despite the Liga's work and the dedication of community members to the educational cause, conditions on the West Side changed little over the years.[100]

NOTES

1. Davis and Gray, *Rural Schools*; Taylor, *Mexican Labor*; Taylor, *American-Mexican Frontier*.

2. Manuel, *Education of Spanish-speaking Children*, pp. 45–46.

3. Taylor, *American-Mexican Frontier*, p. 204.

4. Taylor, *Mexican Labor*, p. 303; Taylor, *American-Mexican Frontier*, p. 204.

5. Taylor, *American-Mexican Frontier*, p. 204; Taylor, *Mexican Labor*, p. 383.

6. Taylor, *Mexican Labor*, p. 383; Taylor, *American-Mexican Frontier*, p. 205.

7. Taylor argued that for the most part rural Mexicans encountered too many obstacles to their education. "These rural Mexicans," he stated, "are poor, lack transportation facilities, rely on the labor of their children and often move from place to place; they have no great urge to educate their children, and are of the type which in California resists compulsory attendance when work is available, because they want the earnings of their children's labor" [*American-Mexican Frontier*, p. 206].

8. Ibid., p. 207.

9. Taylor, *Mexican Labor*, pp. 383–384; Taylor, *American-Mexican Frontier*, p. 204.

10. Taylor, *Mexican Labor*, p. 384; Taylor, *American-Mexican Frontier*, p. 205.

11. Taylor, *American-Mexican Frontier*, p. 206.

12. Taylor, *Mexican Labor*, p. 385.

13. Ibid.

14. Taylor, *American-Mexican Frontier*, p. 207.

15. For an example of an earlier boycott, in San Angelo in 1910, see De Leon, "Blowout."

16. Taylor, *Mexican Labor*, p. 375.

17. A small group of individuals was experiencing limited social and economic mobility at this same time. For instance, Mexicans began to buy property, graduate from high school, and move to more skilled jobs within certain occupations. See Taylor, *American-Mexican Frontier*, pp. 176–190, for additional information on this middle-class group in Nueces County.

18. Slayden, statement, pp. 4846–4849; Davis, *Illiteracy*; Max S. Handman, "Preliminary Report on Nationality and Delinquency: The Mexican in Texas."

19. Alonso S. Perales, *El méxico-americano y la política del sur de Tejas*; "Mexican Rights in the U.S."; Weeks, "The Texas-Mexican."

20. Violence against Mexicans, especially by law enforcement agencies, led to a two-

month investigation of the Texas Rangers by the state legislature in January 1919. This investigation was triggered by J. T. Canales' effort to reorganize the Ranger force. At the investigation individuals testified that the Rangers, local peace officers, and citizens had killed approximately two hundred Mexicans from 1916 to 1919. Others accused the Rangers of killing from five hundred to five thousand Mexicans during the decade. As a result of this investigation, a bill was enacted reducing the Texas Rangers to a total of only seventy-six men [Texas, *General Laws*, 1919, pp. 263–266]. For an overview of this investigation as well as general accounts of widespread conflict along the border during the early decades of the twentieth century, see Pierce, *Rio Grande Valley*, pp. 93–111, and Stambaugh and Stambaugh, *Rio Grande Valley*, especially pp. 204–230.

21. *La Crónica*, March 2, 1911, cited by José E. Limón, "Primer Congreso," p. 89. See Stambaugh and Stambaugh, *Rio Grande Valley*, pp. 228–230, for a brief discussion of Canales' response to the threat on his life by the Texas Rangers.

22. Meyer Weinberg, *A Chance to Learn: The History of Race and Education in the United States*, p. 164. On the journalistic exposés of school discrimination, see, for instance, the series of articles published by *La Crónica*. See especially "La exclusion de los niños mejicanos en la mayor parte de las escuelas oficiales de Tejas es positiva," December 17, 1910, p. 1; "Tanto los niños mexicanos como los mexico-americanos son excluidos de las escuelas oficiales—¿Ya se olvidaron los tratados de Guadalupe?" December 24, 1910, p. 1; "La exclusion de los niños mejicanos de las escuelas americanas en algunas partes de Tejas," January 26, 1911, p. 3; "La exclusion en las escuelas de los condados de Frio, Bee, Hays, Bastrop, Comal, Caldwell, Blanco, etc.," February 9, 1911, p. 1.

23. De Leon, "Blowout"; Zamora, "Labor Activity," pp. 221–238; Cisneros, "La clase trabajadora."

24. For an analysis of this conference see Limón, "Primer Congreso," pp. 85–117.

25. For an incomplete history of LULAC see Garza, "League of United Latin American Citizens," and Robert A. Cuellar, "A Social and Political History of the Mexican American Population of Texas, 1929–1963," pp. 11–29 (both master's theses). Moises Sandoval (*Our Legacy: The First Fifty Years*) provides an in-house look at LULAC and its development over the last fifty years. For a fascinating narrative of the issues, speeches, and dynamics of establishing LULAC in 1929 see various typewritten documents which were published in the organization's unofficial newspaper, *El Paladin*, especially the issues dated February 22 and May 24, 1929.

26. See Kaye Lynn Brigel, "Alianza Hispano-Americana, 1894–1965: A Mexican American Fraternal Insurance Society" (Ph.D. diss.), for a history of one of the largest and most enduring mutual aid societies in the Southwest, and Julie Leininger Pycior, "La Raza Organizes: Mexican American Life in San Antonio, 1915–1930, as Reflected in Mutalista Activities" (Ph.D. diss.), for a history of mutualista activities in San Antonio from 1915 to 1930. For an overview of mutualist organizations and their activities in the United States during this general period see Hernández, *Mutual Aid*.

27. This was also the case with LULAC's predecessor, La Orden Hijos de America (the Order Sons of America). For instance, out of the original seven men who founded the Order Sons of America in 1921, there were two printers, one professional boxer and his trainer, one coffee salesman, one baker, and one warehouse packer (Sandoval, *Our Legacy* p. 7).

28. Ibid., pp. 12–13; Garza, "League."

29. A more prominent founder of LULAC was M. C. González, an attorney from San Antonio. For clips of his life history, see M. C. González Papers, folder I.

30. *LULAC News*, March 1937.

31. He also became intimate friends with Vice President John N. Garner, who was Speaker of the House when Garza accompanied the delegation (*LULAC News*, March 1937).

32. Mauro M. Machado, "The Word 'United'," *LULAC News*, February 1938, pp. 15–16.

33. The earliest copy of the Constitution of the League of United Latin American Citizens that I have been able to locate was published in 1931. The aims and purposes of the organization, which later became article II of the constitution, can be found in Perales, "Unification," pt. 1, pp. 1–2.

34. H. T. Manuel estimated that nearly 52 percent of the total number of Mexicans in Texas were citizens (*Education of Spanish-speaking Children*, p. 5).

35. Constitution of LULAC, art. II, sec. 12.

36. Ibid., art. II, sec. 5.

37. "Why an Education?" *LULAC News*, February 1937, p. 3; Gus C. García, "La educación de los latinoamericanos en el estado de Texas," *La Prensa*, December 6, 1934, p. 4 (author's translation).

38. Perales, "Unification," pt. 3, pp. 8–9; Constitution of LULAC, art. II, secs. 14, 23.

39. See, for instance, Miguel David Tirado, "Mexican American Community Political Organizations: The Key to Chicano Political Power." Tirado argued that LULAC committed its members and their families to "total assimilation" into American society.

40. Perales, "Unification," pt. 3, p. 5; Constitution of LULAC, art. II sec. 7; "Our Attitude before History," *El Paladín*, June 14, 1929, p. 3.

41. Constitution of LULAC, art. II, sec. 7; "Our Attitude," *El Paladín*, June 14, 1929, p. 3.

42. M. C. González, "What is LULAC?" *Alma Latina*, March 1932, p. 1.

43. Constitution of LULAC, art. II, secs. 2, 9, 22.

44. J. Luz Saenz, "Our Attitude with Respect to Public Schools," *El Paladín*, May 18, 1929, pp. 13–14.

45. There were two types of members—active and passive. Only registered voters could become active members and hold office. See Constitution of LULAC, art. III, secs. 1, 3.

46. Perales, "Unification," pt. 3, pp. 8–9; see also Perales, *El méxico-americano*.

47. Constitution of LULAC, art. II, secs. 11, 12, 13.

48. Constitution of LULAC, art. II, secs. 3, 8, 11.

49. Constitution of LULAC, art. II, sec. 18.

50. The Constitution of LULAC states: "We shall encourage the creation of educational institutions for Latin Americans and we shall lend our support to those already in existence" (art. II, sec. 20).

51. O. D. Weeks aptly stated this sentiment in the following manner: "The problem with which they and their racial brothers are faced in Texas and the United States have been created quite as much by their own deficiencies as by the deficiencies of the Anglo American in his dealings with them" ("The League of United Latin American Citizens: A Texas-Mexican Civic Organization," pp. 277–278).

52. Taylor, *American-Mexican Frontier*, p. 315. See also Perales, "Unification," pt. 5, for similar views regarding Mexican Americans and their political status.

53. Rodolfo A. de la Garza argued that educational discrimination existed against Mexican Americans because "we have brought [it] upon ourselves by our own carelessness" ("Our School Children," *LULAC News*, November 1932, p. 9).

54. Gus C. García, "La educación," *La Prensa*, December 4, 1934, p. 4 (author's translation).

55. Taylor, *American-Mexican Frontier*, p. 316; Constitution of LULAC, art. II, sec. 4.

56. Taylor, *American-Mexican Frontier*, pp. 204–206, 375, 383–385.

57. Ibid., p. 268.

58. Perales, "Unification," pt. 4. See also Perales, "My Message to the League of United Latin American Citizens," *El Paladín*, July 5, 1929, pp. 1–2.

59. Although they supported education for the masses, some LULAC members believed that only the exceptionally endowed should receive a higher education—that is, only those who showed promise should receive a college education. See, for instance, Perales, "Unification,"

pt. 4. Not all members agreed with Perales. For instance, Taylor quotes one member who stated, "We urge the Mexicans to sacrifice for more school and college training" (*American-Mexican Frontier* p. 316).

60. *LULAC News*, August 1931, pp. 12–13. See M. C. González, "The Aim of LULAC," *LULAC News*, March 1932, for a similar view.

61. Taylor, *American-Mexican Frontier*, p. 223.

62. Ibid.

63. Ibid., p. 224.

64. Ibid.

65. Ibid.

66. De la Garza, "Our School Children," *LULAC News*, November 1932, p. 9.

67. García, "La educación," *La Prensa*, December 6, 1934 (author's translation).

68. Most Mexican Americans, regardless of their social standing in the community or length of residence in Texas, attended segregated schools and experienced some form of discrimination. For the impact of public school attendance on Mexican Americans in one high school in Corpus Christi, see Guadalupe San Miguel, Jr., "Endless Pursuits: The Chicano Educational Experience in Corpus Christi, Texas" (Ph.D. diss.), pp. 184–223.

69. The names of the organizations which emerged to form LULAC were La Orden Hijos de América (the Order Sons of America), the Knights of America, and the Latin American Citizens League. For a list of the individuals representing each of these organizations, see *El Paladín*, February 22, 1929, pp. 1–2.

70. S. M. N. Marrs, *Decision in "Vela vs. Charlotte Independent School District."* The decision was handed down November 28, 1928. The entire decision is reprinted in Manuel, *Education of Spanish-speaking Children*, pp. 82–84.

71. *Independent School District vs. Salvatierra*. The appeal was filed on October 29, 1930.

72. Ibid., p. 794.

73. Ibid., p. 791.

74. Ibid., p. 794.

75. Ibid., p. 796.

76. Ibid., p. 792.

77. Ibid., p. 795.

78. The Supreme Court refused to hear LULAC's appeal in November 1931.

79. F. Valencia, editorial, *LULAC News*, November 1931, p. 3.

80. Carl Allsup, "Education is Our Freedom: The American G.I. Forum and the Mexican American School Segregation in Texas, 1948–1957," p. 31; Rangel and Alcala, "Project Report," p. 335; Clinchy, "Equality," p. 184. According to all of these writers, any opportunity to continue litigating this issue and to exert any further leverage on American institutions was made difficult by the Depression. The lack of funds and professionals also inhibited the filing of additional court challenges to school segregation.

81. Valencia, editorial, *LULAC News*, November 1931, p. 3.

82. Louis A. Wilmot, interview with author, May 3, 1977.

83. *LULAC News*, November 1932, p. 19.

84. *LULAC News*, February 1937, p. 4.

85. Superintendent Woods threatened to cut off state aid from the Ozona School District in South Texas for segregating Mexican children (editorial, *LULAC News*, January 1940, quoted in Garza, "League," p. 30). See Sandoval, *Our Legacy*, pp. 33–40, for more information concerning LULAC's educational activities during this period.

86. Editorial, *LULAC News*, January 1940, quoted in Garza, "League," p. 30.

87. See for instance, R. de la Garza, "Reorganization of Latin-American Rural Education," *LULAC News*, March 1933; see also *LULAC News*, February 1932, pp. 6, 19.

88. Ruben R. Lozano, "An Appeal," *LULAC News*, November 1932, p. 5. LULAC initially passed a resolution on November 29, 1931, to establish a scholarship fund (*Alma Latina*, March 1932, p. 9). The awarding of scholarships was one of the most enduring programs of LULAC. For a brief overview of the new scholarship programs established by LULAC during the 1970s, see Sandoval, *Our Legacy*, pp. 44–51.

89. *LULAC News*, April 1932, pp. 5, 6, 11; October 1932, p. 4; November 1932, p. 13; January 1933, p. 5. Also see *Alma Latina*, March 1932, p. 10.

90. Committee on Public School Buildings and Recreational Facilities, *More and Better Schools for the Western Section*, p. 2; García, "Education," p. 4.

91. Committee on Public School Buildings, *Better Schools*, pp. 4–5.

92. Ibid., pp. 5–6.

93. Eleuterio Escobar, "Respetable auditores," pp. 1–2 (author's translation).

94. Ibid., pp. 5–6.

95. Ibid., pp. 6–7.

96. Ibid., pp. 7–8.

97. Liga Pro-Defensa Escolar, *Acta primordial*. The Liga was an independent organization, but LULAC members were invited to participate. Escobar was unanimously chosen by its members to become president of the Liga.

98. See Constitución general de la Liga Pro-Defensa Escolar, p. 4, for a list of these organizations. The Liga's constitution was in Spanish.

99. Constitución general de la Liga, p. 3 (author's translation).

100. Although the Liga failed to significantly improve the West Side schools, its efforts did bring about some changes. Evidence of the limited impact it had on the school board can be gleaned from a letter Franklin Spears, state representative, wrote to E. Escobar. In it he stated: "I was talking with the president of the school board the other night, and he advises me that an elementary school is going to be built on the West Side costing not less than one hundred twenty thousand dollars ($120,000). This is not what I feel that the people on the West Side are entitled to, but it is at least a beginning" (J. Franklin Spears to E. Escobar, letter, February 16, 1937, E. Escobar Papers, box 2, folder 1).

REFERENCES

Allsup, Carl. (1977). Education is our freedom: The American G.I. forum and the Mexican American school segregation in Texas, 1948–1957. *Aztlan* 8 (Spring), 27–50.

Cisneros, Victor B. (1975). La clase trabajadora en tejas, 1900–1920. *Aztlan* 6 (Summer), 239–268.

Cuellar, Alfredo. (1970). Perspective on politics. In Joan Moore & Alfredo Cuellar (Eds.), *Mexican Americans* (pp. 137–168). Englewood Cliffs, NJ: Prentice-Hall.

Davis, E.E. (1923). *A report on illiteracy in Texas*. Bulletin no. 2328. Austin: Bureau of Extension, University of Texas, July 22.

Davis, E.E., & Gray, C.T. (1922). *A study of rural schools in Karnes county*. Bulletin no. 2246. Austin: University of Texas.

DeLeon, Arnoldo. (1974). Blowout 1910 style: A chicano school boycott in west Texas. *Texana* 12, 124–140.

Handman, M.S. (1926). The Mexican immigrant in Texas. *Southwestern Political and Social Sciences Quarterly* 7 (December), 33–41.

Hernandez, Jose Amaro. (1983). *Mutual aid for survival: The case of the Mexican American*. Malabar, FL: Robert E. Krieger Publishing Co.

Límón, Joe E. (1974). El primer congreso Mexicanista de 1911: A precursor to contemporary chicanismo. *Aztlan* 5 (Spring), 85–117.

Manuel, H.T. (1930). *The education of Spanish-speaking children in Texas.* Austin: University of Texas Press.

——. (1944). Education of the Spanish-speaking child. In *Proceedings of an inter-American conference*, April 14–15 (pp. 17–35), Waco, Texas.

Perales, Alonso S. (1931). *El mexico-americano y la politica del sur de Texas.* San Antonio, TX: by the author, Paul S. Taylor Collection.

Pierce, Frank Cushman. (1917). *A brief history of the lower Rio Grande valley.* Menasha, WS: George Banta Publishing Co.

Rangel, Jorge C., & Alcala, Carlos M. (1972). Project report: De jure segregation of chicanos in Texas schools. *Harvard Civil Rights-Civil Liberties Law Review* 7 (March), 307–391.

Sandoval, Moises. (1979). *Our legacy: The first fifty years.* Washington, DC: League of United Latin American Citizens.

Stambaugh, J. Lee, & Stambaugh, Lillian J. (1954). *The lower Rio Grande valley of Texas.* San Antonio: Naylor Co.

Taylor, Paul S. (1971). *An American-Mexican frontier: Nueces County, Texas.* Reprint. New York: Russell. (originally published in 1934, Chapel Hill: University of North Carolina Press.)

——. (1930). *Mexican labor in the United States: Dimmit County, Winter-Garden district, south Texas.* University of California Publications in Economics, vol. 6, no. 5. Los Angeles: University of California Press.

Weinberg, Meyer. (1977). *A chance to learn: The history of race and education in the United States.* New York: Cambridge University Press.

7

Culture, Language, and the Americanization of Mexican Children

Gilbert G. Gonzalez

During the segregation period, Americanization was the prime objective of the education of Mexican children. Authorities reorganized schooling administration and practices whenever the Mexican population rose to significant numbers in a community and whenever Mexican children because increasingly visible on the school registers. This reorganization established special programs, including Americanization classes, and applied to both children and adults in urban and rural schools and communities. The desired effect was the political socialization and acculturation of the Mexican community, as well as, ironically, the maintenance of those social and economic relations existing between Anglos and Mexicans. Indeed, more than anything else, Americanization tended to preserve the political and economic subordination of the Mexican community. Moreover, Americanization merged smoothly with the general educational methodology developed to solve the "Mexican educational problem," as it went hand in hand with testing, tracking, and the emphasis upon vocational education.

SOCIAL THEORY AND AMERICANIZATION

Americanization was the practical form of the general sociological theory of assimilation, and assimilation was the specific application of the general theory of the organic society to the problem of immigrants and ethnicity in modern industrialized societies.[1] Consequently, Americanization corresponded in most respects with the dominant social theory at the turn of the century. Organic theory arose as a response to emerging social conditions of advanced capitalist countries in the late nineteenth century and focused upon problems of social order in a complex, urban industrial environment. It offered a critique of Social Darwinism and subsequently replaced it with a view of society as governed primarily by social, not uncontrollable natural or biological, forces. Society was perceived as a single entity, organic, that is, without critical internal contradictions, with a life of its own, composed of interrelated and interdependent parts, each functioning as part of a single whole. An early proponent of organic theory and a pioneer in American sociology, Charles H. Cooley defined society as "a complex of forms and processes each of which is living and growing by interaction with the others, the whole being so unified that what takes place in one part affects all the rest. It is a vast tissue of reciprocal activity."[2]

The forerunner of modern functionalism, the theory of the organic society, conformed to the ideological and institutional foundations of the existing social order. Consequently, the theory of assimilation that provided the practical basis for Americanization programs was designed to solve in "in-house" needs of a society governed by a dynamic capitalist system of production and characterized by a particular form of division of labor.

According to the organic theory of society, the maintenance of the modern social order is based upon a common "apperception mass" (experiential heritage) that subsequently forges a unified organization of individuals, although separated and differentiated by the economic roles corresponding to the complexity of a modern industrial society. The division of labor is highly complex; individuals are objectively interdependent, and individual roles cannot be separated from the whole.[3] However, individuals must have a subjective consciousness of interdependence and a commitment to engage cooperatively in the productive process, and if not, the unity of society is seriously weakened. The absence of common norms undermines the social order; consequently, its survival is only as secure as the norms binding individuals together. The sociologist Florian Znaniecki, addressing the question of social order, summarized the prevailing views on the role of culture and social relations in society.

> . . . uniformities of social systems, like those of cultural systems, are chiefly the result of a reflective or unreflective use of the same cultural patterns in many particular cases. There is obviously a fundamental and universal, though unreflective, cultural pattern in accordance with which all kinds of lasting relationships between individuals and their social milieu are normatively organized and which we denote by the term "social role.[4]

W. I. Thomas and Robert E. Park, major figures and collaborators in race relations and assimilation theory, strongly advocated the organic view of society. Fred Wacker writes that Park's race relations theory "emphasized organic solidarity of societies."[5] Consequently, the Thomas-Park conception of the integration of immigrants into society first and foremost concerned the functioning of the whole of society. The purpose of society, wrote Park, "is to organize, integrate, and direct the energies resident in the individuals of which it is composed."[6] Consequently, Morris Janowitz describes Thomas as a "'functionalist' in the sense that he believed that hypothetical and value-oriented questions should be raised about the conditions under which optimum social relations would occur."[7] Above all else, it was the "effort to establish and maintain a political order in a community that has no common culture."[8]

ASSIMILATION THEORY AND FOLK
VERSUS MODERN SOCIETIES

The theory of assimilation derived directly from the very process of modernization that resulted in that sharp historical break distinguishing feudal, agrarian societies from capitalist-industrial, urban societies. In the late nineteenth century, European capitalist development wrought massive changes that accounted for the merging and eventual disappearance of small ethnic and linguistically diverse communities, initially scattered and separate, into a single dominant national institutional structure and culture.[9] Thus, according to European sociologists who initially analyzed this process and consequently constructed theories, the trend toward cultural amalgamation was not merely an American phenomenon, but the universal fate of all folk or peasant societies wherever they confronted an industrial bureaucratic social order. Moreover, they argued that the cultural composition of folk societies directly contradicted the culture of modern societies, thereby making traditional societies incompatible with industrial societies and a threat to their maintenance and development. Although social scientists espoused a deterministic view of the assimilation process—that is, that the peasant societies and their traditions will inevitably slip into worldwide oblivion—they also held the belief that an applied state-run program of assimilation can guide this evolutionary process. In the United States, this deliberate government-sponsored assimilation process was called simply, "Americanization."

Ethnic culture allegedly corresponded to a traditional society, justifiable and even necessary in a premodern context, but incompatible with the modern industrial setting.[10] Traditional societies manifested a spontaneous, but isolated, culture springing from a simple division of labor and, in turn, reinforcing that simple division of labor. Moreover, assimilation theory contended that traditional ethnic culture rejected external governmental methods to achieve normal social relations characteristic of modern societies. Social relations within folk societies sprang spontaneously from the very nature of the society. Thus, villages comprised self-contained social units having no need to relate in significant ways outside of their society. Theoretically, the ethnic village achieved a social harmony from its simple productive organization. In the modern context, the spontaneous and self-directed society characteristic of the traditional village conflicted with the need for the centralized state to intervene in the complex social process to create a consciousness that conformed to national policies and therefore impersonal exigencies. Theoretically, the traditional mind tended to respond to personalistic, familial, and communal ties and distrusted the impersonal, nonfamilial, and distant bureaucratic forces characteristic of modern societies.

Given that an evolutionary process was eliminating diverse ethnic cultures whose distinctiveness was that they were preindustrial or peasant societies, the majority culture that corresponded to the most modern stage of human societies inevitably became the embracing and dominant culture.[11] When ethnic diversity in a single society entailed peasant (or ethnic) cultures surrounded by an industrial culture, it constituted a formidable obstacle to modernization and posed serious threats to the exigencies of modern political life.

Within the assimilation process, language formed the core of transformation.

The lack of a common language makes social cohesion impossible. In support of this view, Park and E. W. Burgess wrote that a common language becomes "indispensable" to the welfare of society and that "its absence is an insurmountable barrier to assimilation." On the basis of a common form of communication, "a gradual and unconscious modification of the attitudes and sentiments" occurs. Once a common language is established a "unity of experience and of orientation" takes hold; a community with a unified sense of "purpose and action" develops.[12] Thus, from smaller social units a single large social unit emerges, but it can do so only upon the foundation of a common language.

Other issues remain, however. When coupled with class consciousness and political action, ethnicity poses even further problems for the realization of an organic society. Such occurred when the presence of large numbers of working people who descended from first- and second-generation immigrants from traditional societies and who formed the backbone of the union movement threatened the political and economic stability in the United States at the end of the nineteenth century. This was especially true in the industrial Northeast where first- or second-generation ethnics comprised 75 percent of the population.[13] The assimilative process consequently emphasized the ideological integration of these cultures into the dominant political ideology, entailing citizenship, patriotism, and allegiance to traditional American values and symbols. The integration of all social elements into a single unified and cohesive social order involved this process.

APPROACHES TO ASSIMILATION

At least three schools of thought engaged in the debate over assimilation. The first, the Neo-Lamarckian school, best exemplified in the sociology of E. A. Ross and the historiography of John R. Commons, rejects the possibility and desirability of assimilation on the ground that the "new" immigrants were biologically and culturally inferior to native American stock and therefore unassimilable.[14] This anti-immigrant wing of organic theory opted instead for severe immigration restriction as the key to social integration. In so doing it helped to shape negative stereotypes and whip up anti-immigrant sentiment that undoubtedly found its way into the Americanization practice.

The approach taken by Thomas and Park essentially argued that the dominant culture would eventually replace the immigrants' Old World consciousness through a process of a "natural" assimilation combined with Americanization classes. However, effective assimilation required immigrants to be allowed to fashion their own structures, organization, and nationalistic consciousness.[15] Following the corporate notions of Emile Durkheim, they contended that internally integrated immigrant structures were indispensable for the organic solidarity of society. As Joseph Hraba explains, eventually immigrant structures would disappear:

> The new order of Park is that of Durkheim. As individuals in industrial cities are freed from the bonds of the folk past and are diffused throughout a complex division of labor, vocational interests and the economic interdependence of vocational groups replace folk identity as the expression of solidarity in modern society. . . .[16]

Americanization must and would take place, but it could do so on the foundation of the language, heritage, "memories," and organization of the immigrant communities. Any other approach, argued Thomas and Park, would prove counterproductive. Yet, Thomas found serious faults with the heritage of some nationalities and races and, in so doing, undoubtedly contributed to the restrictionists' arguments.

> Every country has a certain amount of culturally undeveloped material. We have it, for instance, in the Negroes and Indians, the Southern mountaineers, the Mexicans and Spanish Americans, and the slums. There is a limit, however, to the amount of material of this kind that a country can incorporate without losing the character of its culture.[17]

Staunchly opposed by Thomas and Park, the third approach involves essentially the actual practice of Americanization programs. While they did agree that immigrant folk values could not permanently adapt to the American system, they opposed any form of Americanization that did not allow for the expression of ethnic consciousness and heritage as part of the Americanization process. The practice of Americanization by and large demanded the immediate and total cultural transformation of the immigrant community. Thomas quoted a statement made in 1918 by the superintendent of New York schools as an example of the approach undergirding Americanization programs across the United States. "Broadly speaking, we mean [by Americanization] an appreciation of the institutions of this country, absolute forgetfulness of all obligations or connections with other countries because of descent or birth."[18] Americanization early appeared as an "ordering and forbidding" exercise—intolerant and more negative than positive in its methods and objectives toward the communities being introduced into the "welcoming" society.

Americanization teachers viewed immigrant communities as threats to the well-being of society. The immigrants and their cultures became the locus of destabilizing influences in society for supporters of Americanization. With such a negative frame of mind toward the immigrant community, these practitioners launched Americanization programs throughout the Southwest.

The historians Maxine Sellers,[19] Ricardo Romo,[20] and Mario Garcia[21] have linked the Mexican Americanization experience with the national Americanization effort, but our analysis stipulates that we highlight the significant differences between European and Mexican experiences. First, the Americanization of the Mexican community occurred in a legally segregated system. Secondly, it was both rural and urban, as contrasted with the European experience, which was overwhelmingly urban. Thirdly, it was heavily influenced by the regional agricultural economy, which retarded a "natural" assimilation process. Finally, immigrants from Mexico could not escape the effects of the economic and political relationship between an advanced capitalist nation, the United States, and a semicapitalist, semifeudal nation, Mexico, the latter increasingly under the political and economic sway of the United States. None of the contributory European nations had such a relationship with the United States, and thus, their national cultures tended to be judged more on an equal footing with that of the United States. The Mexican case has historically been one of a nation struggling to realize its national interests against the nationalism of a rising world power. This factor alone would have made for a significant modification in the objectives and manner in which Americanization was applied to the Mexican community.

THE AMERICANIZATION OF MEXICAN CHILDREN
IN THE SCHOOL

In the first half of the twentieth century, when the Mexican community was more rural, separate, and identifiable than it is today, the schooling system constructed a cultural demarcation between a superior and an inferior culture. Assimilation, then, involved not just the elimination of linguistic and cultural differences, but of an entire culture that assimilation advocates deemed undesirable. Americanization programs assumed a single homogeneous ethnic culture in contact with a single homogeneous modern one, and the relationship between the two was not that of equals. Cultural differences explained in part the socioeconomic differences between the populations that bore these cultures. The dominant community, enjoying greater wealth and privileges, claimed its position by virtue of alleged cultural superiority. In one way or another, nearly every Mexican child, whether born in the United States or in Mexico, was treated as a "foreigner," as an alien, and as an intruder. The Los Angeles school superintendent voiced a common complaint in a 1923 address to district principals. "We have these [Mexican] immigrants to live with, and if we Americanize them, we can live with them. . . ."[22] The objective was to transform the Mexican community into an English-speaking and American-thinking community.

In addition, Americanization, wrote the superintendent of a southern California school district, "sets up those activities that will bring about the acceptance of aliens of American ideals, customs, methods of living, skills, and knowledge that will make them Americans in fact."[23] The Americanization program of a La Habra, California, labor camp (a project funded by a public school) entirely operated upon the assumption that Mexican "behavior patterns, the beliefs, the convictions . . . have . . . to be transformed in conformity with the new environment."[24] Americanization programs based upon academic and popular literature tended to reinforce the stereotypes of Mexicans as dirty, shiftless, lazy, irresponsible, unambitious, thriftless, fatalistic, selfish, promiscuous, and prone to drinking, violence, and criminal behavior.[25] The La Habra Americanization teacher, Jessie Hayden, saw "Mexican apathy, . . . an infirmity of the will, forever the promise of manana" as dragging "upon the wheels of such progress as might exist" in the Mexican community,[26] but felt that the "Mexican people are slowly struggling toward light," the light of American culture that allows the Mexican community to "realize the darkness with which they are surrounded."[27]

Sixteen years later, a Phoenix, Arizona, principal also offered his diagnosis and prescription for the cultural illumination of the Mexican community:

Much more classroom time should be spent teaching the [Mexican] children clean habits and positive attitudes towards others, public property, and their community in general. . . . [The Mexican child] can be taught to repeat the Constitution forward and backward and still he will steal cars, break windows, wreck public recreational centers, etc., if he doesn't catch the idea of respect for human values and personalities.[28]

A statement concerning the sexual habits of Mexican children by the assistant supervisor of the Compulsory Education Department of the Los Angeles city schools typified both the method of cultural analysis and the fairly widespread stereotype of alleged Mexican promiscuity. He wrote:

> Authorities on the Mexican mind agree that after the age of 12–14 educational and higher ambitions turn to inclinations of sex impulse . . . the average [Mexican] boy and girl revert to the native instinct and throw up the sponge, where the more fortunate are anxious to emulate their American classmates in an effort at resistance.[29]

Similarly, Professor E. E. Davis of the University of Texas, asserted in a 1923 publication:

> The American children and those of the Mexican children who are clean and high-minded do not like to go to school with the dirty "greaser" type of Mexican child. It is not right that they should have to. There is but one choice in the matter of educating these unfortunate children and that is to put the "dirty" ones into separate schools till they learn how to "clean-up" and become eligible to better society.[30]

These assertions, we presume, had some relation to classroom practice. Americanization, then, was an oppressive curriculum and objective enforced to acculturate the Mexican community. Educators may or may not have recognized the oppressive nature of school policies inasmuch as they were frequently rationalized in terms of the needs, interests, and welfare of the Mexican people. The Anglo image of the culture in Mexican communities appears to have instilled in educators an exaggerated sense of guardianship of the American way of life.

The Americanization literature, however, was not uniformly negative in intent. The intent seemed more often patronizing than negative, more insensitive than malicious. Administrators asked teachers to be "genuinely" interested in teaching the Mexican child. A principal of a San Antonio Mexican school suggested that teachers acquire a "knowledge of the characteristics of the Mexican children" and that it was "of first importance" for effective instruction to take place. To this end, special lessons were developed by the school district for the training of teachers in Mexican schools.[31] The supervisor of the K–8 schools in El Paso urged teachers in Mexican schools to "have a knowledge of Mexican history, and of the racial and cultural background of the Mexican people."[32] A common approach to the "Mexican educational problem" involved employing teachers who knew "something of the psychology of the Mexican." Consequently, many teaching colleges and universities created special courses for the effective instruction of Mexican children. The University of Southern California, the University of California, the University of Texas, and the Texas College of Arts and Industries, among others, offered courses for the preparation of teachers planning to work in areas with high Mexican enrollment.

These institutions gave teachers ample opportunity to learn about current theories of Mexican culture and to translate them into classroom practice. School districts commonly adapted their Americanization methods to the presumed intelligence, personality, culture, and environment of the Mexican child.[33] Those teachers who became familiar with the social science literature concerning Mexicans were considered better able "to cope with the problems presented by their little Mexican pupils."[34]

Many school districts instituted in-service training for the teaching of Spanish-speaking children. Large districts with high Mexican enrollment, such as Los Angeles and San Antonio, organized courses to help their teachers understand the objectives of, and learn the methods for, the effective Americanization of Mexican children. Smaller districts at the time, such as Phoenix, El Paso, Santa Ana, Fresno, and San Diego, did likewise. California led the southwestern states in Americanization by establishing, in 1916, a Division of Immigrant Education within the Department of Education for the promotion, development, and improvement of Americanization programs. Out of this larger effort, many districts, such as Los Angeles, Long Beach, Santa Ana, and Oakland, established special Departments of Americanization (or sometimes Departments of Immigrant Education) and placed a supervisor in charge of these programs within the schools. When programs such as these were in operation, officials expected a much more effective Americanization curriculum. In Texas and Arizona, school administrators placed special emphasis upon the publication of bulletins and guidelines for the instruction of Spanish-speaking children.

Nothing short of total cultural transformation would satisfy many leaders in education. Vera A. Chase, an instructor in education at the Arizona State Teachers College (which later became known as Arizona State University), argued that the educational problems of Mexican children, in large part, grew out of the "cultural heritage" of the "non-English speaking child."[35] Furthermore, she stated:

> The immigrant child is different to the extent that he lives in a world of different standards and traditions. He comes more nearly to resemble the American group in his needs, interests, and achievements as his home environment becomes more like that of the American child. At some point in his advance he merges into the group for whom the other curriculum bulletins have been prepared.[36]

Chase did not offer her recommendations without acknowledging that Americanization had national political ramifications. She, like many educators, felt that for the benefit both of the larger society and of the immigrant, the immigrant child "must learn to live as nearly as possible in the way American people live [and] drop traditions and customs that conflict with American culture."[37] If the Mexican failed to assimilate, he remained "an isolated and ineffective element" and his relations with Americans were necessarily "distant and unsatisfactory, if not tinged with hostility."[38]

One researcher synthesized the teaching methods of thirty southern California schoolteachers working with Mexican children. The classroom served as a center where desirable traits slowly replaced "undesirable traits." Teachers urged Mexican children to "make fun of the lazy ones" in the classroom; to overcome uncleanliness by making a dirty child feel uncomfortable; to compare Mexican and American homes for the sake of imitation; and to overcome the "racial" desire to show off by ridicule.[39] One of the main weapons utilized by teachers in this process was imitation. "Since imitation is so dominant in the Mexican nature," she wrote, "opportunity should be provided for the Mexican to mingle with Americans worthy of imitation."[40] The state superintendent's office required California teachers to base Americanization upon this tendency to imitate. Since the homes of Mexican children were "so meager and simple," they hardly knew "what is normally done in a kitchen or a bedroom." Consequently, the state Department of Education recommended that course work include class visits to "an American home of four or five rooms" or examination of "carefully selected pictures."[41]

Even though teachers generally felt that Mexicans were endowed with a deficient or inferior cultural heritage, many held that this culture had some virtues that might perhaps be preserved. These virtuous traits, however, were but the flip side of the coin, for they placed the Mexican child in an inferior and paternalistic context. Observers often described Mexican culture as "gay, light-hearted," unaffected by the fast-paced materialistic American society, and passionately devoted to "color, music and dancing."[42] In essence, these paternalists credited Mexican children with having special talent in art and crafts. Annie S. Reynolds wrote, in her federally sponsored study, that "every opportunity to develop" artwork should be assigned to the Mexican child. "Here is a phase of education," she concluded, "in which Spanish-speaking pupils are certainly not handicapped." She added that "emphasis on book study is entirely inadequate to their needs."[43]

Very often teachers made attempts to stress Mexican traditions in the curriculum, for example, in music, dance, art, architecture, patriotic celebrations, history, and current events. While it may have seemed to some that the classroom actually preserved Mexican culture by displaying a Mexican flag on Cinco de Mayo (Mexico's second Independence Day, celebrating the expulsion of French forces in 1864) or a Diego Rivera reproduction, the purpose of these displays was to get the child to feel more secure.[44] Gradually, however, class practice separated the child entirely from these symbolic representations. The practitioners would determine which Mexican virtues were proper for integration and which were to be eliminated. The cultural model, with its superior-to-inferior continuum, mirrored the political and economic relations between the Mexican and Anglo communities. Even in the attempt to assimilate, theory and practice at once reflected and strengthened the social relations of the community.

LANGUAGE AND ASSIMILATION

The essence of Americanization programs across the Southwest was language instruction. In fact, most of the literature on the education of Mexican children focused on language. This might be expected since English was the medium of instruction. Here again, theory also combined with practical questions since many southwestern school districts had large Spanish-speaking populations. In 1936 Los Angeles, for example, had forty-four thousand such children enrolled in its schools.[45] In San Antonio half of the school population was non-English-speaking, the vast majority Spanish-speaking. Moreover, 1930 estimates indicated that 90 percent of the Mexican children enrolled for the first time in Texas public schools could not speak or understand English.[46]

The language conflict, of course, presented a very real educational barrier. However, rather than addressing the problem as a practical one of overcoming the language gap in order to facilitate instruction, the school officials directed their energy to solving the larger problem, the Americanization of non-English-speaking children. The theoretical foundation for the emphasis on language came directly from contemporary interpretations of assimilation. This explains why the director of elementary education of the San Antonio public schools stated in the introduction to an article on the curriculum for Mexican children, that the "first step in making a unified nation is to teach English to the non-English speaking portion of the population."[47] Similar views appeared frequently in the literature on the education of Mexican children. For example, the assistant superintendent for Immigrant Education and Elementary Evening Schools in Los Angeles, bluntly stated that as to "the need of a common national language, there can be no debate," thus asserting that this task was as significant as any other in the public school system.[48] Thus, educators expected Americanization instruction to result in the termination of Spanish language usage in the community. A Grandfalls, Texas, schoolteacher wrote that in that system's Americanization program, "first place has been given to the substitution of English for Spanish in school life."[49]

Most educators who commented on the topic firmly believed that Spanish failed as a medium through which learning takes place. For example, in an educational manual published by the Arizona Department of Education, the author warned the teachers of Mexican children that language and culture were nearly identical. The failure of Mexican children "to learn English in their daily life" implied a retention of the "customs and traditions of their native land," which had a negative effect upon the educational problems of bilingual children.[50] "Bad habits," customs, and attitudes retarded learning; therefore, assimilation could not be realized until Spanish was eliminated.

The superintendent of Eagle Pass, Texas, schools followed conventional wisdom when he wrote that a Mexican child "is foreign in his thinking and attitudes" until he learns to "think and talk in English."[51] "The first great problem in Americanizing these children," he warned, was the teaching of English "to children whose vernacular is a foreign language." When the child has acquired English he has "already acquired much of the culture and outlook of the American." Presumably, the English-speaking child became an equal and full member of society, whereas the child who failed to learn English retained "the culture, ideals, customs, thought, and attitudes of another race and another people."[52]

School districts that segregated via spatial boundaries, followed the same language policies as districts that segregated on the basis of nationality or language. The Los Angeles School District utilized the former method when it created "neighborhood" schools or schools largely attended by first- and second-generation Mexican children. By the early 1920s, neighborhood schools functioned in the immigrant quarters and operated in much the same fashion as segregated or Mexican schools. The principal objective of the neighborhood school involved Americanizing Mexican children and educating them vocationally to the "level" of their abilities.[53] So-called foreign opportunity rooms also existed in schools whose student bodies were of mixed nationality. In 1924, Los Angeles operated forty-five such classes for non-English-speaking children as part of the overall Americanization effort. In the junior high schools, officials made provisions for the teaching of "American ideals of conduct, of education, and of home life" for non-English-speaking students. Lessons emphasized learning "the English language and the elements of American citizenship."[54]

A related and common assumption held that a diversity of languages in a single society predisposed that society to political antagonisms between language groups. Junius L. Meriam, a professor of education at the University of California, Los Angeles, engaged in pedagogical research on Mexican school children, warned that whenever distinct language-groups exist in a society, conflict is inevitable:

> Bilingualism becomes an acute problem when two languages spoken are of different families. . . . Here exists a situation, due to speech conflict, that usually cloaks, if it does not only express, a conflict of races. If those dwelling in the same land . . . can by sincere instruction in a second language, meet on common ground and . . . develop common interests, then springs into life the possibility of mental, spiritual, and artistic progress for all concerned.[55]

The Departments of Education of the southwestern states periodically published guidelines for the instruction of bilingual children. Their prescriptions generally followed a pattern of methodology and theory. While department officials permitted only English as the language for communication and instruction, Spanish was often allowed for the translation and definition of words. In general, as in Grandfalls, Texas, "All children were requested to speak English" in the classroom. In the early stages of the Grandfalls program, instructors followed a liberal policy; later on, they applied more stringent codes of conduct. For example, teachers forbade a child to leave the school grounds at noon "unless he asked permission in English."[56] The system of punishment seemed to work, as evidenced by this report on the Grandfalls Americanization classes: "Now in the third year of this effort in Americanization even the teachers are beginning to see some worth—with results. English is spoken in the [school] house and on the playground during school hours: nine until four."[57] In the Harlingen, Texas, Mexican schools, the principal instituted an English Club comprised of children who had not spoken Spanish in the previous six weeks. Membership fluctuated, and only members could participate in the quarterly picnics and other club activities held on a regular basis. Those who spoke Spanish during any of the activities were required "to remain in the room and study."[58] The English Club used the "honor system" to some extent, and according to the principal, teachers "checked each day by roll call, as to whether or not they [the children] have spoken English." Instead of answering "present," children responded with "English" or "Spanish." Students caught in a lie were "suspended from the club for the first offense" and expelled for the second. If their only transgression was to have spoken Spanish, they were allowed back in the club after a week of "nothing but English."[59]

The Arizona state superintendent's office advised teachers that "every phase of school life" of the Mexican child "should take part in promoting the meaningful use of English."[60] Without the English language, warned the superintendent, Mexican people would not realize "effective citizenship."[61] Indeed, in the schooling atmosphere based upon the forcible elimination of one language, by another, school authorities organized the system of rewards and punishments accordingly. The child achieved "success" when he learned English and became Americanized; a child "failed" when he remained a non-English speaker. The Arizona State Course of Study for Bilingual Children arrived at a standard for successful behavior and learning on the part of the Mexican child when it posed the following questions: "Does he try to accommodate himself to American culture as represented by the school setting; does he try to learn to speak English?" If the child made an "honest effort" and if he "responded with genuine interest to the school situation," then the Course of Study concluded that the child had met minimal standards for Americanization. "He should feel pride," continued the Course of Study, "in making progress in the accepted task of learning a new language."[62]

Rural Americanization proceeded as facilities and curriculum developed. The goal, however, varied little from the pattern established in the Southwest. The 1945 logbook of a Ventura County, California, first-grade schoolteacher recorded a popular method of teaching English—peer pressure. The logbook read: "On Tuesday we reviewed our rules for walks and went to town to buy pumpkins for our jack-o-lanterns. The slogan shouted by the children as they started off was 'Talk in English.' And they did."[63]

School officials often combined English instruction with direct attempts to manipulate the "aliens'" cultural standards. For example, many segregated schools in the Southwest contained showering facilities where children were obliged, after a morning inspection, to shower. In the East Donna, Texas, Mexican school, a twelve-room building served five hundred students in which "morning inspections in each classroom [were] regularly conducted," and children who failed to pass inspection were "required to wash before they [were] permitted to begin the day's activities." If their clothes were dirty, they were required to change into clean clothes loaned by the school "in emergency cases."[64]

As illustrated by a teacher's guide issued by the state of California, English instruction complemented the cleanliness program. The method of instruction recommended must have been humiliating for the children. In one particular model classroom vignette, the teacher helps a child wash his hands and face and comb his hair. Upon completion of the assignment, the teacher brings "him before class and [comments] favorably upon his accomplishment and looks, as [in] 'Look at José. He is clean.'"[65]

The objective of the English instruction program for non-English-speaking children included creating a way of life characterized by initiative, cooperation, courtesy, cleanliness, and a desirable home life. "Help them to want to be clean," urged the California *Guide for Teaching Non-English-Speaking Children*, "and provide opportunities for making cleanliness possible."[66] The *Guide* also suggested a method of teaching "habits and attitudes that make home life clean, comfortable and happy."[67] Consequently, English drills incorporated practice in setting the dinner table and arranging bedrooms and living rooms. Such instruction also included "constant and careful work . . . to promote correct enunciation and pronunciation." Through the

program, which combined language and culture, the state expected a cultural transformation:

> Constant contact with an environment that ministers to the love of the
> beautiful and orderly creates an abhorrence of anything that is not well-
> ordered and clean. Through this subtle, indirect influence the standards of
> foreign homes may be raised, for when these children grow up they will not
> be happy in an environment widely different from that to which they have
> been habituated.[68]

Through the program of Americanization, the Mexican child was taught that
his family, community, and culture were obstacles to schooling success. The assumption that Mexican culture was meager and deficient implied that the child came into
the classroom with meager and deficient tools with which to learn. This implication
was quite consciously woven into the methodology and content of instruction.

Americanization, as a curricular activity, endured well into the late thirties, and
even then, educators did not abandon the objective of assimilating Mexicans into the
dominant culture; they merely changed the appearance of the program. Proponents
of "Americanization" ceased referring to it as such, but the essential features of the
program remained. Language and culture continued to be major educational concerns, and the identification of the Spanish language and Mexican culture as contradictory to educational success lost no ground in conventional theory and practice.
Throughout the first half of the century, school policies treated the culture of the
Mexican child as unworthy of equality with the dominant culture.

The segregated rural and urban Mexican communities contrasted markedly
with the communities of the dominant society. Proponents of assimilation applied
their policies to Mexicans with little effort because of the size, geographic isolation,
cultural cohesion, and occupational homogeneity of Mexican communities. Consequently, educators generally approached the assimilation issue with single-minded-
ness. While integration was not quite the objective, eliminating the core of Mexican
"folk culture" (i.e., replacing Spanish with English), certainly took precedence as an
educational goal of assimilationists. To be sure, introducing new norms of health,
nutrition, and child rearing were secondary to the education process.

In the educational decision-making process of the first half of the century, the
Mexican community offered little political input. Moreover, few social scientists or
educators found this lack of political involvement to be of major consequence. No
lasting and significant changes could be realized, many thought, until Mexicans were
Americanized.

NOTES

1. Joseph Hraba, *American Ethnicity* (Ithaca, NY: F. E. Peacock Publishers, Inc., 1979),
pp. 32–33.
2. Charles H. Cooley, *Social Process* (New York: Scribner, 1926), p. 26.
3. Hraba, *American Ethnicity*, pp. 76–83.

4. Florian Znaniecki, "On Social Roles and Social Circles," in Marcello Truzzi, *Sociology: The Classic Statements* (New York: Random, 1971), p. 113.

5. Fred Wacker, *Ethnicity, Pluralism, and Race* (Westport, Conn.: Greenwood, 1983), p. 44.

6. Ralph H. Turner, Introduction to *Robert E. Park on Social Control and Collective Behavior,* edited by Ralph H. Turner (Chicago: University of Chicago Press, 1967), p. xi.

7. Morris Janowitz, *W. I. Thomas on Social Organization and Social Personality* (Chicago: University of Chicago Press, 1966), p. xlvii.

8. R. E. Park and E. W. Burgess, "Competition, Conflict, Accommodation, and Assimilation," in Truzzi, *Sociology,* p. 126.

9. Hraba, *American Ethnicity,* pp. 31–33.

10. See Mario Garcia, "The Americanization of the Mexican Immigrant," *Journal of Ethnic Studies* 6, no. 2 (1978).

11. Park and Burgess, *Introduction to the Science of Sociology* (Chicago: University of Chicago Press, 1969), p. 757.

12. Ibid., p. 128.

13. David Ward, *Cities and Immigrants: A Geography of Change in Nineteenth Century America* (New York: Oxford University Press, 1971), p. 51.

14. See Wacker, *Ethnicity, Pluralism, and Race,* pp. 16–17.

15. Ibid.

16. Hraba, *American Ethnicity,* p. 36.

17. W. I. Thomas, "Assimilation and Old World Traits Transplanted," in Janowitz, *W.I. Thomas,* p. 198.

18. Quoted by Thomas, "Assimilation and Old World Traits Transplanted," p. 204.

19. Maxine Sellers, "The Education of the Immigrant Woman 1900–1915," *Journal of Urban History* 6, no. 3 (1978).

20. Ricardo Romo, *History of a Barrio in East Los Angeles* (Austin: University of Texas Press, 1984).

21. Garcia, "Americanization of the Mexican Immigrant."

22. Susan B. Dorsey, "Mrs. Pierce and Mrs. Dorsey Discuss Matters Before the Principal's Club," *Los Angeles School Journal* 6, no. 25 (5 March 1923): 59.

23. Merton E. Hill, *The Development of an Americanization Program* (Ontario, Calif.: Board of Trustees, Chaffey Union High School and Chaffey Junior College, 1928), p. 5.

24. Jessie Hayden, "The La Habra Experiment in Mexican Social Education" (Master's thesis, Claremont Colleges, Claremont, California, 1934), p. 191.

25. See Charles Clifford Carpenter, "A Study of Segregation versus Non-Segregation of Mexican Children" (Master's thesis, University of Southern California, 1935), p. 152.

26. Hayden, "The Habra Experiment," p. 27.

27. Ibid.

28. H. F. Bradford, "The Mexican Child in Our American Schools," *Arizona Teacher Parent* 27 (March 1939): 199.

29. Leonard John Vandenbergh, "The Mexican Problem in the Schools," *Los Angeles School Publications* 11, no. 34 (14 May 1928).

30. E. E. Davis, *A Report on Illiteracy in Texas,* University of Texas Bulletin no. 2328 (Austin: University of Texas Press, 1923), p. 30.

31. James Kilbourne Harris, "A Sociological Study of a Mexican School in San Antonio, Texas" (Master's thesis, University of Texas, Austin, 1927), p. 13.

32. Lucy Claire Hoard, *Teaching English to the Spanish-Speaking Child in the Primary Grades* (El Paso: El Paso Public Schools, 1936), p. 9.

33. Simon Ludwig Treff, "The Education of Mexican Children in Orange County" (Master's thesis, University of Southern California, p. 1.

34. Katherine Hollier Meguire, "Educating the Mexican Child in the Elementary School" (Master's thesis, University of Southern California, 1938), p. 8.

35. Vera A. Chase, *Course of Study for Elementary Schools of Arizona.* State Department of Education Bulletin no. 13 (Phoenix: State Department of Education, 1939), p. 9.

36. Ibid., p. 10.

37. Ibid., p. 12.

38. Ibid., p. 13.

39. Betty Gould, "Methods of Teaching Mexicans" (Master's thesis, Los Angeles: University of Southern California, 1932), pp. 79–86.

40. Ibid., p. 57

41. California Department of Education, *A Guide for Teachers of Beginning Non-English Speaking Children,* Bulletin no. 8 (1932), p. 29.

42. Ibid.

43. Annie S. Reynolds, *The Education of Spanish-Speaking Children in Five South-western States* (Washington, D.C.: U.S. Department of the Interior, Office of Education), p. 22.

44. See, for example, Gould, "Methods of Teaching Mexicans," pp. 93–96.

45. "Education of Foreign Language Groups," *California Journal of Elementary Education* 5, no. 2 (November 1936): 67.

46. Herschel T. Manuel, *The Education of Mexican and Spanish Speaking Children in Texas* (Austin: University of Texas, 1930), p. 150.

47. Elma A. Neal, "Adapting the Curriculum to Non-English Speaking Children," *Elementary English Review* 8 (September 1929): 183.

48. Ruby Baughman, "Elementary Education for Adults," *The Annals of the American Academy* (1920): 161.

49. Laura Frances Murphy, "An Experiment in Americanization," *Texas Outlook* 23, no. 11 (November 1939): 23.

50. Chase, in *Course of Study for Elementary Schools of Arizona,* states, "If immigrant parents make no decided effort to learn and use English in their daily life, it is probably that they cling to the customs and traditions of their native land. Whenever this is true it has a deep significance in all education problems concerning their children."

51. Manuel, *Education of Mexican and Spanish-Speaking Children in Texas,* pp. 126–27.

52. Ibid., p. 127.

53. "Neighborhood Schools," *Los Angeles School Journal* 10 no. 28 (21 March 1927): 14; also see Vandenbergh, "Mexican Problem in the Schools," p. 15.

54. Edith M. Bates, "The Non-Curricular Child in the Junior High School, *Los Angeles School Journal* 11, no. 3 (26 September 1927): 23; also, Harry M. Shafer, "Americanization in the Los Angeles Schools, "*Los Angeles School Journal* 7, no. 34 (12 May 1924): 31; and Mary Cunliffe Trautwein, "A History of the Development of Schools of Foreign-Born Adults in Los Angeles" (Master's thesis, Los Angeles: University of Southern California, 1928), p. 98

55. Junius Meriam, *Learning English Incidentally: A Study of Bilingual Children.* Project in Research in Universities Bulletin, no. 15 (Washington, D.C.: Government Printing Office, 1938), pp. 14–15.

56. Laura Frances Murphy, "An Experiment in Americanization": 23.

57. Ibid.

58. J. T. Taylor, "The Americanization of Harlingen's Mexican School Population," *The Texas Outlook* 28 (September 1934): 38.

59. Ibid.

60. Arizona State Board of Education. *Course of Study for Elementary Schools for Arizona: Instruction of Bilingual Children,* Bulletin no. 13 (1939), p. 26.

61. Ibid.

62. Ibid., p. 42.

63. Pauline Jeidy, "First Grade Mexican-American Children in Ventura County," *California Journal of Elementary Education,* 15, nos. 3–4 (February–May 1947), pp. 200–201.

64. Gladine Bowers, "Mexican Education in East Donna," *Texas Outlook* 15, no. 3 (1931): 29.

65. California Department of Education, *Guide for Teachers,* p. 24.

66. Ibid., p. 2.

67. Ibid. See also "A Course in English for Non-English-Speaking Pupils," *State Department of Education Bulletin* 7, no. 3 (March 1932): 24.

68. Ibid.

8

Living Borders/ *Buscando América*
Languages of Latino Self-Formation

Juan Flores and George Yudice

LATINOS AS A SOCIAL MOVEMENT

"My grandparents didn't get special language instruction in school. In fact, they never finished high school because they had to work for a living." Latinos hear this and similar statements every time the question of bilingual education comes up. Such statements highlight an important difference—the maintenance of another language and the development of interlingual forms—between this "new" immigrant group and the "older," "ethnic" immigrants. The fact is that Latinos, that very heterogeneous medley of races and nationalities,[1] are different from both the "older" and the "new" ethnics.[2] To begin with, Latinos do not comprise even a relatively homogeneous "ethnicity." Latinos include native-born U.S. citizens (predominantly Chicanos—Mexican-Americans—and Nuyoricans—"mainland" Puerto Ricans) and Latin American immigrants of all racial and national combinations: white—including a range of different European nationalities—Native-American, Black, Arabic and Asian. It is thus a mistake to lump them all under the category "racial minority," although historically the U.S. experiences of large numbers of Mexican-Americans and Puerto Ricans are adequately described by this concept.[4] Moreover, both of these groups—unlike any of the European immigrant groups—constitute, with Native-Americans, "conquered minorities."[5]

If not outright conquered peoples, other Latin American immigrants heretofore inhabitants of the "back yard" over which the United States claims the right of manifest destiny, have migrated here for both political and economic reasons, in part because of U.S. intervention in their homelands. From the time of José Martí, who lived in New York for over one third of his life during the 1880s and 1890s, slowly establishing the foundations for the Cuban independence movement, to the 1980s sanctuary movement for Central American refugees, U.S. actions (military incursions as well as economic sanctions) in Latin America have always generated Latin American migrations. The policies of U.S. finance institutions (supported by the U.S. government and, at times, by its military), moreover, have brought enormous foreign debt to Latin America and with it intolerable austerity programs that have induced many to seek a living in the United States.[6]

The result is a U.S. Latino population projected to be over 30 million in 1990, a minority population unprecedented in the history of the United States. Sheer numbers are in themselves influential, but the way in which the numbers increase is more important. As a result of continuous immigration over the last 30 years, as well as the historical back-and-forth migration of Mexican-Americans and Puerto Ricans and more recently of other national groups, Latinos have held on to Spanish over more generations than any other group in history. Ninety percent of U.S. Latinos speak Spanish.[7] In contrast, speakers of Italian dwindled by ninety-four percent from the second to the third generation.[8]

The civil rights movement spurred new forms of consciousness and political action among Chicanos and Nuyoricans. They and other Latinos have been able to use the language issue as a means to mediate diverse types of political enfranchisement and social empowerment: voting reform, bilingual education, employment opportunities, and so on.

In fact, the conditions for identity-formation, in all its dimensions (social, political and especially aesthetic), have been largely provided by the struggle over how to interpret language needs and the adjudication and legislation, on that basis, of civil rights directed primarily (but not exclusively) to Latinos.

In recognition of these conditions, which were not in place when the two major trends in ethnicity theory (the "melting pot" of the early twentieth century and the "new ethnicity" of the '50s and '60s) emerged, we feel that there is greater explanatory power in "new social movement's approach to Latino identity. By "new social movements" we refer to those struggles around questions of race, gender, environment, religion and so on, which cannot be fully encompassed under the rubric of class struggle and which play out their demands on the terrains of the body, sexuality, language, etc., that is, those areas which are socially constituted as comprising the "private" sphere. This is not to say that the inequalities (and causes rooted in relations of production) referred to by class analysis have disappeared. On the contrary, from the perspective we adopt, such inequalities (and their causes) can be seen to multiply into all spheres of life. Capitalist society does not cause racism any more than it does linguistic stratification; it does, however, make all these differences functional for the benefit of hegemonic groups. A social movement approach does not so much disregard class exploitation as analyze how racism, sexism, linguistic stratification, etc. are mobilized through "both discursive positions and control of the means of production and coercion."[9] Under these circumstances, political agency is, according to Stanley Aronowitz,

> constituted in the gap between the promises of modern democratic society and its subversion by the various right-wing states. politics renews itself primarily in extra-parliamentary forms which, given the still potent effectivity of the modern state form, if not its particular manifestations of governance, draws social movements into its orbit. Some call this cooptation, but it is more accurate to understand it as a process related to the economic and cultural hegemony of late capitalism, which draws the excluded not only by its dream work, but by the political imaginary that still occupies its own subjects.[10]

What is particularly different about the new social movements is that they enter the political arena by "address[ing] *power itself* as an antagonist," such that they must deploy their practices in the cultural as well as economic spheres. To understand Latinos, then, we must understand the conditions under which they enter the political arena. Among these conditions, which were not in place when the "ethnic" (European) immigrants negotiated their enfranchisement in the U.S., are the welfare state (which in part brought to the fore the terrains of struggle and which neo-conservatives are currently attempting to dismantle) and the permeation of representation by the consumer market and the media.

In what follows, we explore how Latino identity is mediated and constructed through the struggle over language under such "post-modern" conditions.

THE STRUGGLE OVER LANGUAGE

First of all, the name, "America." Extrapolating from Edmundo O'Gorman's meditation on the "invention of America,"[11] we might say that "America" has been conceived over and over again throughout history. The name "remains the same," but it has had successive reconceptualizations (it is rewritten in the Borgesian sense that Pierre Menard rewrote *Don Quixote)* and with each one the terrain changes. The current mass migration of Latinos to the United States engenders such a process of reconceptualization, bringing to mind F. J. Turner's notion of America as a moving frontier and giving it another twist so as to invent a new trope: America as a "living border." If the "discovery" of "America" transformed the ocean into a frontier on whose other side lay a "new" world, and if that new world was subsequently defined by the westward movement and capitalization of the margin, under-*writing* "the record of social evolution"[12] or modernity and providing a "'safety valve' for the discontent of a new industrial proletariat"[13] largely comprised of European immigrants, then the latest reconceptualization of America by Latinos is a cultural map which is all border, like the inter-lingual speech (or Spanglish) of Chicanos and Nuyoricans.

> I[. . .] opt for "borderness" and assume my role: My generation, the *chilangos* [slang term for a Mexico City native], who came to "el norte" fleeing the imminent ecological and social catastrophe of Mexico City, gradually integrated itself into otherness, in search of that other Mexico grafted onto the entrails of the et cetera . . . became Chicano-ized. We de-Mexicanized ourselves to Mexi-understand ourselves, some without wanting to, others on purpose. And one day, the border became our house, laboratory, and ministry of culture.[14]

Contemporary Latino artists and writers throw back the anxiety of ambivalence cast upon them as an irresolvable perplexity of naming and placing. Gómez-Peña talks of "this troubled continent accidentally called America" and "this troubled country mistakenly called America."[15] "AmeRícan," announces Tato Laviera in the title poem of his third book of Nuyorican poetry, "defining myself my own way many ways Am-e-Rícan, with the big R and the accent on the í."[16] The hallowed misnomer unleashes the art of brazen neologism. The arrogance of political geography backfires in the boundless defiance of cultural remapping. The imposed border emerges as the locus of re-definition and re-signification. The cover illustration of *AmeRícan* boasts a day-glo Statue of Liberty holding aloft a huge *pilón* of liberty, the majestic torch of *comida criolla, ajo y plátano*. Latino taste buds water with *mofongo* and *mole*. "English only Jamás!," "Sólo inglés, no way!"

Latino affirmation is first of all a fending off of schizophrenia, of that pathological duality born of contending cultural worlds and, perhaps more significantly, of the conflicting pressures toward both exclusion and forced incorporation. Another Nuyorican poet, Sandra María Esteves, thematizes this existential split in much of her work: "I am two parts / a person boricua / spic past and present alive and oppressed."[17] Esteves enacts the bewilderment, darting back and forth between unreal options and stammering tongues, "Being Puertorriqueña Americana Born in the Bronx, not really jíbara Not really hablando bien But yet, not gringa either, Pero ni portorra pero sí portorra too Pero ni que what am I?"[18] She cannot "really" be both, she realizes, but she senses a unique beauty in her straddling position, and is confident in the assertion, which is the title of her poem, that she is "Not Neither."

Contrary to the monocultural dictates of the official public sphere, the border claims that it is "not nowhere." This first gestus of Latino cultural practice thus involves an emphatic self-legitimation, a negation of hegemonic denial articulated as the rejection of anonymity. Though no appropriate name is available in the standard language repertoires, whether English or Spanish, namelessness is decidedly not an option. Whatever the shortcomings and misconceptions of bureaucratic bilingualism, alinguality is neither the practiced reality nor a potential outcome of Latino expressive life. The interlingual, border voice characteristically summons the tonality of the relegated "private" sphere to counter the muzzling pressure of official public legitimation.

The trope of a border culture is thus not simply another expression of postmodern aesthetic indeterminacy, along the lines of Derrida's decontextualized frame or *parergon*, "the incomprehensibility of the border at the border,[19] or a Baudrillardian simulacrum (*neither* copy *nor* original).[20] The trope emerges, rather, from the ways in which Latinos *deploy* their language in everyday life. It corresponds to an ethos under formation; it is *practice* rather than *representation* of Latino identity. And it is on this terrain that Latinos wage their cultural politics as a "social movement." As such, Latino aesthetics do not pretend to be separate from everyday practices but rather an integral part of an ethos that seeks to be politicized as a means to validation and self-determination. And it is precisely the projection of this ethos into the culture at large and into the political arena that threatens the dominant "Anglo" culture with loss of control of its physical and metaphorical borders. As the shrillest voices of the English Only movement have put it, such Latino language and cultural practices threaten national unity and security.[21] Latino disregard for "our borders" may result in the transformation of the United States into a "mongrel nation."[22]

There are misguided persons, specifically Hispanic immigrants, who have chosen to come here to enjoy our freedoms, who would legislate another language, Spanish, as co-equal and co-legal with English. . . . If Hispanics

get their way, perhaps someday Spanish could replace English entirely . . .
we ought to remind them, and better still educate them to the fact that the
United States is not a mongrel nation.

Language has been accurately characterized as "an automatic signaling system,
second only to race in identifying targets for possible privilege or discrimination."[23]
Unpack the discourse against the language of Latinos and you've got a panoply of
racist and classist repudiations:

> These children of illegal aliens will remain part of that population which
> never learns English, and threatens to make America a bilingual country
> costing the American taxpayer billions of dollars.
>   Token citizenship will not help poor, unskilled Hispanics when they
> find themselves in a permanent underclass, isolated by a language barrier.
> The hopes that brought them here in the first place will turn to despair as
> they become dependent upon government handouts . . .
>   Congress has presented the indigenous population of Mexico with an
> open invitation to walk across our Southern Border.[24]

Language, then, is the necessary terrain on which Latinos negotiate value and
attempt to reshape the institutions through which it is distributed. This is not to say
that Latino identity is reduced to its linguistic dimensions. Rather, in the current
socio-political structure of the United States, such matters rooted in the "private
sphere," like language (for Latinos and other minorities), sexuality, body and family
definition (for women and gays and lesbians), etc., become the semiotic material
around which identity is deployed in the "public sphere." The purpose always seems
to be to maintain hegemony or to negotiate empowerment of those groups that have
been discriminated against on such bases.

The attack on the perceived linguistic practices of Latinos is a vehicle for attacks
on immigration, bilingual education, inclusion of Latinos in the services of the welfare state and, above all, a repudiation of the effect that Latinos are having in reshaping U.S. culture. Furthermore, such attacks highlight the influence that the
dominant groups in the U.S. expect Latinos to have on foreign policy. Their rhetoric
harbors the fear that U.S. imperialism in Latin American countries is boomeranging
and eroding U.S. hegemony.

The language question then is a smoke screen for the scapegoating of Latinos
on account of recent economic, social and political setbacks for the United States.
"Anglo insecurity" looks to the claims of Latinos and other minority constituencies for the erosion of the United States' position in world leadership, the down-
turn in the economy and the bleak prospects for social mobility for the next
generation.[25] In fact, now that dominant U.S. national rhetoric seems no longer
able to project a global communist bogey, due to political changes in the Soviet
Union and Eastern Europe, this rhetoric will increasingly consolidate its weapons
against Latinos as the drug-disseminating enemy within. The War on Drugs will increasingly become a War on Latinos and Latin Americans, as the recent brutal U.S.
invasion of Panama has demonstrated. Furthermore, U.S. intervention in Latin

America will increase as "the Pentagon searches for new ways to help justify its spending plans."[26]

TOWARD A MULTICULTURAL PUBLIC SPHERE
(VERSUS HEGEMONIC PLURALISM)

The effect of dominant U.S. reaction to the special language needs that Latinos project and the rights that they claim on that basis has been to strengthen the moves toward unity on the part of diverse Latino communities. Otherwise divided by such identity factors as race, class and national origin, there are economic, social and political reasons in post-civil-rights U.S. why Latinos can constitute a broadly defined national and trans-national federation which aspires to reconceptualize "America" in multicultural and multicentric terms that refuse the relativist fiction of cultural pluralism. It is for this reason that we have proposed to look at Latino negotiation of identity from a social movement perspective rather than a (liberal-sociological) ethnicity paradigm.

It is a commonplace among contemporary theorists of ethnicity in the U.S. that the assimilationalist or "melting pot" paradigm of the first half of the century "failed to explain what it most needed and wanted to explain—the persistence of racial stratification . . ."[27] The "new ethnicity" paradigm, which emerged to remedy the failure of assimilation theory and, as we stated above, to counter the gains made by blacks and other "racial minorities" in the wake of civil rights activism, makes the basic claim that ethnicity becomes the category around which interests are negotiated when class loses its moorings in post-industrial society. The "new ethnicity" can be understood to form part of what Habermas has posited as a "neo-conservative post-modernism," that is, the rejection of "cultural modernism," because it has eroded traditional moral values and the continued espousal of infrastructural modernity or capitalism cum technical progress and rational administration.[28] The false premise of this argument, of course, is that the economy can be independent of culture; this theory thus serves the purpose of providing a cultural (or ethnic) politics in post-industrial society with no need to resort to economically based categories such as class: "In trying to account for the upsurge of ethnicity today, one can see this ethnicity as the emergent expression of primordial feelings [or "reenchantment," G. Y. and J. F.], long suppressed but now reawakened, or as a 'strategic site' chosen by disadvantaged persons as a new mode of seeking political redress in the society."[29] The falsity of the model, of course, is that blacks and other "racial minorities" can be equated with white "ethnic" groups.[30] The result is reinforcement of existing class inequalities expressed in ethnic/racial terms.[31]

"Racial" movements could be understood to be the first of the "new social movements" or "new antagonisms" that call into question forms of subordination (bureaucratization and consumer commodification of "private" life) in the post-World War II U.S. They do not, however, retreat from "cultural modernism"[32] (the erosion of traditional moral values undergirded by class, race and gender discriminations) but rather extend it to the point of questioning "infrastructural modernism." Among the challenges is the push to legitimize the adjudication and legislation of rights on the basis of group need rather than the possessive individuals terms that traditionally define rights discourse.[33] "New ethnicity" theory is only one of a panoply of strategies by which neo-conservatives have sought to contest the extension of rights on the basis of group criteria (affirmative action, headstart programs, anti-discrimination statutes and so on). The result has been the acknowledged loss of foundations for rights and the shift to a paradigm of interpretability. Group rights must take place, then, in a surrogate terrain, like language or the family. According to Minow,

> One predictable kind of struggle in the United States arises among religious and ethnic groups. Here, the dominant legal framework of rights rhetoric is problematic, for it does not easily accommodate groups. Religious freedom, for example, typically protects individual freedom from state authority or from oppression by private groups. Ethnic groups lack even that entry point into constitutional protection, except insofar as individuals may make choices to speak or assemble in relation to a chosen group identity.[34]

If the framework of rights is an impoverished one for the struggles of the new social movements, then what has been the means to greater political participation? One alternative has been to engage in the struggle of needs interpretations. According to Nancy Fraser, "political issues concerning the interpretation of people's needs [are translated] into legal, administrative and/or therapeutic matters,"[35] *differentially* according to the identificatory features (race, class, gender, religion and so on) of the group.

Fraser goes on to argue that in each branch (juridical, administrative, therapeutic) of the late capitalist welfare state, there are gender and racially defined subsystems such that certain genders and races are positioned differently as regards possession of rights or eligibility for benefits and services.[36] The struggle around needs, then, is more typical of those groups that are socially "marked."[37]

Such "markedness" is at work in the struggle over Latino *language needs*; it was only by arguing for the legitimacy of the need for special language education that the Bilingual Education Act of 1968 was legislated as a civil right.[38] And it is around this "need" that dominant groups have launched their counter-attack. Some of the arguments for bilingual education posit a need for a positive self-image premised on the validation of the mother language and the culture of the minority student. However, based on instrumental rationality, dominant groups insist that the need of immigrant groups is to assimilate into mainstream society and thus the only special educational benefit that need be provided is special English instruction.

During the Carter administration, bilingualism and biculturalism were weakened by a new bilingual education (1978) that limited access to bilingual programs and required teachers to know English as well as Spanish. A 1979 study "exposed" bilingual programs to be "a strategy for realizing the social, political and economic aspirations of the Hispanic peoples."[39] Carter himself said: "I want language taught—not 'ethnic' culture, etc."[40]

Arguments for and against bilingual education aside, our point is that the struggle over needs interpretations—in this case around the need for special language education—is what in the present historical conjuncture in the U.S. mediates accumulation of value politically, economically and socially. Latinos, after all, have made significant gains (they have professionalized) in the educational system because they can more easily qualify for the job requirements (Spanish language literacy) of bilingual education. Language, as we shall demonstrate below, is also the terrain on which Latino "aesthetics of existence" or affirmative self-formative practices operate.

According to Habermas, oppositional, resisting discourses emerge when the validity of legal norms is questioned from the perspective of an everyday practice that refuses to be depoliticized by the "steering mechanisms" of law, bureaucracy and consumerism.[41] Through such resistant everyday practices, Latinos have contributed to reshaping the public sphere of American society. Or perhaps it would be more exact to say they have contributed to the emergence of a contestatory "social sphere" which blurs the public/private dichotomy because needs "have broken out of the domestic and/or official economic spheres that earlier contained them as 'private matters.'"[42] Another way of conceiving this contestation is to imagine social space as networks of conflicting and allied public spheres. What is defined as "private" from the purview of one, is "public" or political from the purview of another.

The relevance of casting Latino negotiation of identity as a contribution to the creation of an alternative public sphere can be brought out by situating it within Oskar Negt and Alexander Kluge's expanded understanding of the concept. They do not limit it to 1) the institutional settings of public opinion (media, parliaments, etc.) but extend it to 2) "the ideational substance that is processed and produced within these sites," and 3) "a general horizon of social experience,"[43] or "drive toward self-formation and self-reconstruction" (in the collective sense of "self") which is limited or crippled by the first sense.[44] An alternative model can be culled from Bakhtin's writings on "behavioral ideology" and the constitution of identity through the reaccentuation of speech-genres. Ideological or discursive production is institutionally bound but is generally (except in cases of outright force) open to modulation whereby persons "author themselves" or make discourse "one's own" in the media of speech and behavioral genres.[45] Our utterances are necessarily enunciated and organized within such genres, which bear institutional marks. Self-formation is simultaneously personal and social (or private and public) because the utterances and acts through which we *experience* or gain our self-images are reaccentuated in relation to how genes have institutionally been made sensitive or responsive to identity factors such as race, gender, class, religion and so on.

In post-modernity, "private" identity factors or subject positions may become unmoored from institutionally bound generic structures, turning "intimacy [. . .] the practical touchstone for the substance of the public sphere."[46] Experience, situated thus, is what fuels the utopian and contestatory potential of self-formation:

> What is even more significant is that subjective or psychological phenomena are now increasingly seen as having epistemological and even practical functions. Fantasy is no longer felt to be a private and compensatory reaction against public situations, but rather a way of reading those situations, of thinking and mapping them, of intervening in them, albeit in a very different form from the abstract reflections of traditional philosophy or politics.[47]

Alternative public spheres, with their different, situated knowledges, are for Negt and Kluge, constituted by the conflictual back and forth *crossover* of everyday experience and fantasy over the boundaries of the hegemonic public sphere.[48]

On the other hand, the hegemonic public sphere itself "tries to develop techniques to reincorporate fantasy in domesticated form."[49] This is precisely the function of "new ethnicity" theory: to co-opt the alternative public sphere of a multicultural society in such a way that ethnic difference is reduced to its superficial signs, or from Negt and Kluge's perspective, a sublimation of the "unconscious practical criticism of alienation."[50]

BOWING TO PROSPERO: RICHARD RODRIGUEZ' REPRIVATIZATION OF CROSSOVER EXPERIENCES

There is no better example of the attempt to channel the "crossover" toward an ersatz pluralism than Richard Rodriguez' "middle-class pastoral": *Hunger of Memory: The Education of Richard Rodriguez.*[51] It is the story of a now influential "public" man who traded his former identity (as oppressed working class Chicano), his former symbolic authorities (his parents), his former language (Spanish) by assimilating to the *gringo* middle class under the tutelage of new symbolic authorities (his teachers and intellectual mentors, especially Richard Hoggatt). His life reads like an advertisement against bilingual education; Spanish is the "private" language of the ethnic, English the "public" language of empowerment:

> Supporters of bilingual education today imply that students like me miss a great deal by not being taught in their family's language. What they seem not to recognize is that, as a socially disadvantaged child, I considered Spanish to be a private language. What I needed to learn in school was that I had the right—and the obligation—to speak the public language of *los gringos*. The odd truth is that my first-grade classmates could have become bilingual, in the conventional sense of that word, more easily than I. Had they been taught (as upper-middle-class children are often taught early) a second language like Spanish or French, they could have regarded it simply as that: another public language. In my case such bilingualism could not have been so quickly achieved. What I did not believe was that I could speak a single public language . . .
>
> Fortunately, my teachers were unsentimental about their responsibility. What they understood was that I needed to speak a public language . . .[52]

This passage conceals a romanticized projection concerning the "privacy" of Spanish, for Rodriguez clearly recognizes that Spanish could also be a "public" language. He makes this recognition only to discard it on the basis that his disadvantaged status could not let him aspire to an alternative publicity in Spanish. It is his own rejected sentimentalism towards Spanish, then, which lies at the root of the bad faith that he attributes to bilingual educators and others who seek to keep, cultivate or invert Latino culture and language as a competing, alternative public discourse. Instead, Rodriguez draws a tighter and tighter net around that which he (and the dominant culture) has defined as private until it is strangled out of existence and he emerges as his own abstracted interlocutor: "I hear an echoing voice—my own resembling another's. Silent! The reader's voice silently trails every word I put down. I reread my words, and again it is the reader's voice I hear in my mind, sounding my prose.[53] Who is this interlocutor but the symbolic Other (the law of the Anglo father or teacher) with whom he has identified after his linguistic and cultural "castration":

> I write today for a reader who exists in my mind only phantasmagorically. Someone with a face erased: someone of no particular race or sex or age or weather. A gray presence. Unknown, unfamiliar. All that I know is that he has had a long education and that his society, like mine, is often public (*un gringo*).[54]

Regarding the "castration" metaphor (which marks the moment of entry into the "public" realm of the symbolic), it should be remembered that Rodriguez has symbolically renounced his Chicanoness by attempting to shave off the darkness of his skin:

> I took my father's straight razor out of the medicine cabinet. Slowly, with steady deliberateness, I put the blade against my flesh, pressed it as close as I could without cutting, and moved it up and down across my skin to see if I could get out, somehow lessen, the dark.[55]

At the end of this same chapter ("Complexion"), his public identity has made his skin color meaningless. It is the value that he has gained as a public individual (*un gringo*) which contextualizes his complexion's meaning:

> The registration clerk in London wonders if I have just been to Switzerland. And the man who carries my luggage in New York guesses the Caribbean. My complexion becomes a mark of my leisure. Yet no one would regard my complexion the same way if I entered such hotels through the service entrance. That is only to say that my complexion assumes its significance from the context of my life. My skin, in itself, means nothing.[56]

After this thought, Rodriguez returns to consider *los pobres mexicanos* with whom he has worked during the summer. Their skin color signifies disadvantage, it speaks their "private" silence to him: "Their silence is more telling. They lack a public identity. They remain profoundly alien."

This is surely a comforting thought for conservatives who would like to see all entitlements for Latinos removed. They need not fear the blurring of boundaries between public and private. Rodriguez charges that it is the advocates of bilingual education and minority compensation who have sold their identity to bureaucratic policy makers:

> The policy of affirmative action, however, was never able to distinguish someone like me (a graduate student of English, ambitious for a college teaching career) from a slightly educated Mexican-American who lived in a

barrio and worked as a menial laborer, never expecting a future improved. Worse, affirmative action made me the beneficiary of his condition. Such was the foolish logic of this program of social reform.[57]

Yet it is he who has cashed in on his legitimation of middle-class privilege. The irony is that despite his disavowal of Chicano or minority status, he is read and his book is assigned in numerous college English courses precisely because he reassures "anguished Anglos" that the "latinization of America will, in time, lead to Hispanic integration."[58] He has spoken against bilingual education and affirmative action from Reagan's White House and has done quite well on the college lecture circuit as Prospero's tamed servant (a nifty turn of events for a book that begins thus: "I have taken Caliban's advice. I have stolen their books. I will have the run of this isle.").[59]

It is no mere coincidence that Rodriguez is one of only two Latino writers (the other is Luis Valdez) cited by Werner Sollors in *Beyond Ethnicity: Consent and Descent in American Culture*,[60] for he fits the refurbished rhetoric endemic to the "ethnicity paradigm": viz. the negotiation of assimilation and cultural pluralism. "The language of consent and descent has been flexibly adapted to create a sense of Americanness among the heterogeneous inhabitants of this country."[61] Both Sollors and Rodriguez coincide in deriving this dynamic of consent and descent from the Puritans to the most recent immigrants. Sollors quotes Timothy Smith to the effect that the process of immigration (uprooting, migration, resettlement, community-building) constituted for the Puritans a transcendent experience that laid the basis of American ethnicization. This process, according to Smith and Sollors, even includes Afro-American *immigrants*![62] and the literature that it, the ethnicization process, provides, functions as a "handbook" or a "grammar" for "socialization into the codes of Americanness."[63]

Rodriguez, in a recent *New York Times* supplement, *A World of Difference*, appeals first to the grammar school and then to consumerism for the "handbook" that can harmonize the diversity that constitutes the United States:

Language is the lesson of the *grammar* school. And from the schoolmarm's achievement came the possibility of a shared history and a shared future. . . . At the bank or behind the counter at McDonald's, or in the switch room of the telephone company, people from different parts of town and different parts of the country, and different countries of the world learn that they have one thing or another in common. Initially, a punch clock. A supervisor. A paycheck. A shared irony. A takeout lunch. Some nachos, some bagels, a pizza. And here's a fortune cookie for you: Two in their meeting are changed.[64]

CROSSING OVER THE CONTRADICTIONS OF LATINO MARKET AND MEDIA

Rodriguez is not entirely correct, however, about the integrative force of consumerism for producing assimilated "Americans." Diverse Latino communities are also partially united by market and media courting of the 100+ billions of dollars that the 30+ millions of Latinos offer. One advertising agency's pitch to businesses reads: "[O]ur market is very young and very very sensitive. You don't have the clutter of the Anglo market."[65]

Language, again, is the terrain on which the heterogeneous constituencies of Latinos are rallied not only as consumers but also as cultural subjects. This is certainly a major factor that was not in place when theories of ethnicity were devised to account for the incorporation of the "older" immigrants into U.S. society. Language is the major cultural glue provided by Spanish Television. Two of the major networks, Univisión and Telemundo, highlight the transnational and unifying character of their programming. Indeed, Telemundo's slogan is: "*Telemundo: uniendo a los hispanos.*"

Strategies of marketing and the commercial media have not joined the English Only movement, nor do they seem to share the anxieties over cultural balkanization or contamination which propel it. Rather, the corporate "publicity sphere" has availed itself of the multicultural reality as a way of targeting consumer markets and taste cultures. Although for their own interested motives, advertisers reach out to the "Hispanic" market with campaigns custom-made for the culture, with special attention to holidays, family and religious life, and to the up-beat, success-story side of Latino experience. Citibank, for example, makes an effort to salute prominent Hispanic businessmen, especially those who "got help along the way from Citibank. One owns a chain of travel agencies; another runs six McDonald's franchises." They claim with pride that, worldwide, Citibank "employs more Hispanics and does more business with Hispanics than any other bank."[66] Pan Am has even adapted its jingles— "it is a very musical market"—to appeal to its "Hispanic" customers, "so we retained the theme but added a Latin feel with percussion and woodwind instruments."[67]

The Spanish language, of course, figures prominently in this ethnically tailored publicity. While many campaigns are rendered simultaneously in Spanish, advertisers recognize that translation is not enough. Here again the "Latin feel" plays a key role. Pepsi Cola, for instance, took pains, and advice from their "Hispanic" marketing agency, to adapt their slogan "Catch that Pepsi spirit":

> If we had put that straight away into Spanish, viewers would have considered it voodoo, something about a spirit flying through the air. So we changed it to read, "Vive el sentir de Pepsi." That means, "Live that Pepsi feeling." That's what the English slogan intends to say, but you have to known the idiosyncrasies of the market to put it across.[68]

Citibank goes even further; beyond capturing in Spanish the spirit of the English copy, they resort to the bilingual pun to catch the sympathetic giggle of potential customers and make them feel included. "We're going to play on the language here," their spokesman at Castor Spanish International says, "telling them that 'We always say sí at Citibank' (pronounced see-tee-bank in Spanish)."[69]

Ironically, this practice of linguistic and cultural adaptation on the part of commercial publicity is more suggestive than the traditional public sphere of Latino expression, especially those dimensions of it that go beyond mere responses to hegemonic negation. As publicity agents suggest, "When translation isn't enough, try 'trans-creation.' " The idea of "trans-creation," for the advertisers, a

gimmicky term aimed at maximizing specificity in targeting differentiated consumer publics, is appealing and apt as a characterization of border culture expression and self-definition. As one "Hispanic" media executive puts it, the "proper
execution" calls for a sense of "the familiar Spanish patois of the community, reflecting not only different words and meanings, but also differences of rhythm of
speech and inflection." Latino artists and poets also need to "trans-create" in this
sense, at least at a tactical level, as does the wider Chicano and Nuyorican community in its everyday speech and expressive practices. In order to vocalize the
border, traversing it is not enough; we must be positioned there, with ready and simultaneous access to both sides.

Perhaps the commonality between these two otherwise divergent worlds is the
issue of needs. The advertiser bent on "reaching" and "selling" the Hispanic market, and the Latino cultural agent who would voice and envision the people's lifeworld, both inhabit a public sphere conceived of as the arena for the articulation
and satisfaction of collective needs. Beyond the contention over rights and policies,
the force of consumption, understood in its broadest sense, holds sway in the culture of experience. Here the private sphere, rather than being categorically autono-
mized, informs the public and even fuels the drive for social legitimation.
"Trans-creation," whether from commercial or expressive and representational motives, serves to counteract the reduction of social experience to the dominion of laws
and consensual ethical norms.

Such "crossovers" are a reality today, rooted in the bilingualism and biculturalism of Latinos. Many critics have correctly pointed to the erosion and misrepre-
sentation by the mass media of traditional cultural forms and experience. But the
market and the media are not the only forces in society and their interaction with
other factors such as state bureaucratic apparatuses, law and social institutions,
can have consequences that go beyond the simplistic "colonization" of the Latino
lifeworld. For example, the contradiction created in the dominant classes by divergent treatment of Latino language practices (opposition in the "social" sphere
and enthusiastic acceptance and application in the commercial sphere) has opened
up a space in which Latinos negotiate new cultural forms that impact upon the culture at large.

Compromised as it is, even Coors turns to Spanish-language advertising to undo
the negative effects of its hiring policies with regard to Latinos;[70] this demonstrates
the extent to which consumerism blurs the cultural boundaries that so threaten dominant non-Latino groups. Those dominant groups that fear the "threat" of Latinization of U.S. culture, if also owners of businesses or directors of social and political
institutions that could profit from Latino patronage, often find themselves having to
cater to the needs interpretations of Latinos. The hysterical objections made against
the public reach of Latino ethos through market and media, objections similar to
those against bilingual education, only testify to the pervasiveness of Latino
influence:

> Freedom of speech is not unlimited. As Justice Brandeis has pointed out, no
> one is free to shout "fire" in a crowded theater. Speech and information are
> often curtailed in matters relating to national security, for example. Cutting
> off American citizens from sources of information in the language of their

country, fostering language segregation via the airwaves, these are major problems that warrant the steps we propose [i.e., limiting the growth of Spanish-language radio stations].[71]

Latino experience in the U.S. has been a continual crossover, not only across geo-political borders but across all kinds of cultural and political boundaries. Political organization, for example, is necessarily coalitional; in order to have an impact Latinos have formed alliances to elect officials who will represent their interests. Throughout the sixties and seventies, Latinos formed or reformed dozens of national lobbying organizations. Uppermost in their lobbying efforts are counterarguments against discriminatory practices in immigration, hiring and educational policies, opposition to government intervention in Latin America, especially Central America and, of course, promotion of language issues. It should be added that Latinos of all backgrounds (with only the partial exception of Cuban Americans) are assiduous supporters and participants in the solidarity and sanctuary movements. These forums are very important because they exert a progressive influence, especially as regards women's issues like abortion, on groups that have a conservative cultural heritage. Furthermore, the political and cultural crossover involved in these activities contributes to the creation of alternative public spheres in the United States.

Crossover does not mean that Latinos seek willy nilly to "make it" in the political and commercial spheres of the general culture. These spheres are vehicles which Latinos use to create new cultural forms that cross over in both directions. The music of Willie Colón, Rubén Blades, and other U.S.-based Latino and Latin American musicians is a new pan-Latino fusion of Latin-American forms (Cuban *guaguancós*, Puerto Rican *plenas*, Dominican *merengues*, Mexican *rancheras*, Argentine *tangos*, Colombian *cumbias*, barrio drumming) and U.S. pop, jazz, rock, even do-wop, around a salsa base of Caribbean rhythms, particularly Cuban *son*. Salsa cuts across all social classes and Latino groups who reside in New York, home ground of this fusion music. Originating in the barrios, it made its way to "downtown" clubs and across borders to the diverse audience of the Latin American subcontinent. The crossovers have resulted in a convergence phenomenon that does not represent anything other than its malleability and openness to incorporation.[72]

Salsa, perhaps better than any other cultural form, expresses the Latino ethos of multiculturalism and crossing borders. Willy Colón, for example, became a *salsero* precisely to forge a new "American" identity:

Now look at my case; I'm Puerto Rican and I consider myself Puerto Rican. But when I go to the island I'm something else to them. And in New York, when I had to get documents, I was always asked: "Where are you from?" "I'm American." "Yeah, but from where?" They led me to believe that I wasn't from America, even though I have an American birth certificate and citizenship. . . . I live between both worlds but I also had to find my roots and that's why I got into salsa.[73]

Finding one's "roots" in salsa means creating them more from the heterogeneous sounds that traverse the barrio than going back to some place that guarantees authenticity. Salsa is the *salsero's* homeland and the means to self-validation.[74]

Despite its popularity and certain minor breakthroughs, salsa has not (yet?) "made it" in mainstream U.S. culture. Latino artists and entrepreneurs have had to form their own labels, an alternative recording industry. Only in recent years, especially with the impetus of Rubén Blades's thematization of "crossing over" in the film "Crossover Dreams," has the dominant recording industry not only taken on *salseros* on national labels (Blades's *Agua de Luna*, based on the stories of García Márquez, is on Elektra) but also marketed them nationally. Furthermore, the alternative public spheres of contemporary rock, such as "Rock Against Racism," have been opened up by the collaborations of such "mainstream" musicians as the Rolling Stones, David Byrne and Paul Simon with *salseros*, Chicano rockers such as Los Lobos and Latin American stars such as Milton Nascimento and Caetano Veloso.[75] Hip Hop has also brought together Afro-Americans, Latinos and Afro-Latin Americans.[76]

TRANS-CREATING A MULTICULTURAL AMERICA

Rubén Blades has insisted that a culturally effective crossover, which he prefers to call "convergence," is not about "abandonment or sneaking into someone else's territory. I propose, rather, convergence. Let's meet half way, and then we can walk either way together."[77] At the end of the interview he adds that he does "not need a visa" for the musical fusion that he seeks. He does not want "to be in America" but rather participate in the creation of a new America.

Latinos, then, do not aspire to enter an already given America but to participate in the construction of a new hegemony dependent upon their cultural practices and discourses. As argued above, the struggle over language signals this desire and the opposition to it by dominant groups. This view of language, and its strategic operationality in achieving a sense of self-worth, is the organizing focus of Gloria Anzaldúa's *Borderlands/La Frontera: The New Mestiza*.[78] "Ethnic identity is twin skin to linguistic identity—I am my language. Until I take pride in my language, I cannot take pride in myself."[79] Like Rondón's arguments about salsa,[80] the language of the new mestiza is the migratory homeland in which "continual creative motion [. . .] keeps breaking down the unitary aspect of each new paradigm."[81] Anzaldúa acknowledges that her projection of a "new mestiza consciousness" may seem cultureless from the perspective of "male-derived beliefs of Indo-Hispanics and Anglos;" for her, on the contrary, she is

> participating in the creation of yet another culture, a new story to explain the world and our participation in it, a new value system with images and symbols that connect us to each other and to the planet.[82]

Another way of constructing Anzaldúa's mestiza poetics is as an articulation of the premise that all cultural groups need a sense of worth in order to survive. Self-determination, which in this case focuses on linguistic self-determination, is the category around which such a need should be adjudicated and/or legislated as a civil right. In order for this right to be effective, however, it would have to alter the nature (or, to be more exact, the social relations) of civil society.

Such a claim, constructed in this way, only makes sense in a social structure that has shifted the grounds for enfranchisement from one of rights discourse to the interpretations that underpin such discourse. What is the justification, however, for needs interpretation? Our claim is that group ethos, the very stuff (or the "ethical substance," in Foucault's terminology)[83] of self-formation, is what contingently grounds the interpretation of a need as legitimate so that it can be adjudicated or legislated as a right. Another claim is that group ethos is constituted by everyday aesthetic practices such as the creative linguistic practices of Latinos that in the current historical conjuncture do not amount to subalternity, but rather to a way of prying open the larger culture, by making its physical, institutional and metaphorical borders indeterminate, precisely what we have seen that the dominant culture fears.

Latino self-formation as trans-creation—to "trans-create" the term beyond its strictly commercialist coinage—is more than a culture of resistance, or it is "resistance" in more than the sense of standing up against concerted hegemonic domination. It confronts the prevailing ethos by congregating an ethos of its own, not necessarily an outright adversarial but certainly an alternative ethos. The Latino border trans-creates the impinging dominant cultures by constituting the space for their free intermingling—free because it is dependent on neither, nor on the reaction of one to the other, for its own legitimacy. Dialogue and confrontation with the "monocultural other" persists, but on the basis of what Foucault has called "the idea of governmentality," "the totality of practices, by which one can constitute, define, organize, instrumentalize the strategies which individuals in their liberty can have in regard to each other."[84]

It is in these terms that the positing of a relatively self-referential cultural ethos for oppressed groups can evade the attendant essentialist or exceptionalist pitfalls. For this ethos is eminently practical, not an alternative to resistance but an alternative form of resistance, not a deliberate ignorance of multicultural realities but a different and potentially more democratic way of apprehending them. The strategic value of this "relationship of self to self" is of utmost importance, since it defines the position from which to negotiate the existing relations of power as domination. For rather than aiming at some maximally transparent communication among hierarchically divergent subject positions, in Habermas's sense, the goal of this cultural-ethical self-formation is the adequate constitution and definition of the subject position itself. As Foucault explains in his critique of Habermas:

I don't believe there can be a society without relations of power, if you understand them as means by which individuals try to conduct, to determine the behavior of others. The problem is not of trying to dissolve them in the utopia of a perfectly transparent communication, but to give one's self the rules of law, the techniques of management, and also the ethics, the ethos, the practice of self, which would allow these games of power to be played with a minimum of domination.[85]

"Practice of self" is understood here to refer to individuals, but is readily transferable to collective self-conducts; the relations of power are called strategic "games," but the re-writing of the rules, or the playing out of other games with other rules, clearly interfaces with the dynamics of political and cultural struggle. And the utopian horizon, which Foucault discards in its Habermasian version, is still present in this strategy of minimizing domination, especially when the view is toward the process of collective self-formation among oppressed and "other" groups. Gómez-Peña, that reliable voice of the border perspective, addresses this futuristic dimension in terms that also suggest the content and tactics of the new ethos, the alternative, multicultural "practice of self":

> The U.S. suffers from a severe case of amnesia. In its obsessive quest to 'construct the future,' it tends to forget or erase the past. Fortunately, the so-called disenfrachised groups who don't feel part of this national project have been meticulously documenting their histories. Latinos, blacks, Asians, women, gays, experimental artists and non-aligned intellectuals have used inventive languages to record the other history from a multicentric perspective. Our art functions both as collective memory and alternative chronicle, says Amalia Mesa-Bains. In this sense, multicultural art, if nurtured, can become a powerful tool to recapture the desired historical self. The great paradox is the fact that without this historical self, no meaningful future can ever be constructed.[86]

Ethnicity-as-practice is primordially genealogical, intent as it invariably is on a recapturing and re-constituting of the past. It relies, as Michael M. J. Fischer terms it, on the "post-modern arts of memory," the collective power of recall that is only a power if it functions actively and constitutively. This retrospective, testimonial search is for Fischer "a (re)invention and discovery of a vision, both ethical and future-oriented. Whereas the search for coherence is grounded in a connection to the past, the meaning abstracted from that past, an important criterion of coherence, is an ethic workable for the future."[87] The "alternative chronicle" is more than merely re-cuperative: it is eminently functional in present self-formative practice and anticipatory of potential historical self-hood. Sandra María Esteves, in a poem cited earlier ("I am two parts / a person boricua / spic"), bemoans the forcible, physical loss of her antecedence: "I may never overcome the theft of my isla heritage . . . I can only imagine and remember how it was." But that imagination and remembrance enliven her dream-work, which in turn "realizes" that lost reality in a way that leads to eventual and profound self-realization. Her poem ends, "But that reality now a dream teaches me to see, and will bring me back to me."[88]

In the post-modern context, the mnemonic "arts" of border expression are conducted in "inventive languages," a key phrase of Gómez-Peña signaling the characteristic expressive tactic of this process. Language itself, of course, is the most obvious site of Latino inventiveness. Whether the wildest extravagance of the bilingual poet or the most mundane comment of everyday life, Latino usage tends necessarily toward interlingual innovation. The interfacing of multiple codes serves to de-canonize all of them, at least in their presumed discrete authority, thus allowing ample space for spontaneous experimentation and punning. Even for the most monolingual of Latinos, the "other" language looms constantly as a potential resource, and the option to vary according to different speech contexts is used far more often than not. "Trans-creation," understood in this sense of intercultural variability and transferability, is the hallmark of border language practice. The irreverence implicit in trans-creative expression need not be deliberately defiant in motive; it reflects rather a largely unspoken disregard for conventionally bounded usage insofar as such circumscription obstructs the need for optimal specificity of communicative and cultural context. The guiding impulse, articulated or not, is one of play, freedom and even empowerment in the sense that access to individual and collective referentiality cannot ultimately be blocked. Interlingual puns, multi-directional mixing and switching and the seemingly limitless stock of borrowings and adaptations attest to a delight not only in excluding and eluding the dominant and exclusionary, but in the very act of inclusion within a newly constituted expressive terrain. Rather than rejecting a language because of its association with a repressive other, or adopting it wholesale in order to facilitate passage, Latino expression typically "uses" official discourse by adapting it and thereby showing up its practical malleability.

Nuyorican vernacular includes the verb "gufear," from which has derived the noun "el gufeo." The colloquial American word "goof" is clearly visible and audible, and certainly the "Spanglish" usage has its closest equivalent in the phrase "goofing on" someone or something. But as a cultural practice, "el gufeo" clearly harkens to "el vacilón," that longstanding Puerto Rican tradition of funning and funning on, fun-making and making fun. Popular culture and everyday life among Puerto Ricans abound in the spirit of "el vacilón," that enjoyment in ribbing at someone's or one's own expense, for which a wider though overlapping term is "el relajo." We might even speak, in fact, of a Puerto Rican ethos of "el relajo" which, in its interplay with "el respeto," serves to mark off consensual guidelines for interpersonal behavior.[89] Setting limits of "respectability" and testing them, "relaxing" them, conditions the dynamic of Puerto Rican culture at the level of behavioral expression. The role of "el relajo," often practiced of course by the subaltern classes in their interaction with their masters, is not derivative of or conditioned by "el respeto"; rather, the delineation of individual and group dignity draws its power from the ability to "relax (on)" the prevalent codes of "respect."

Terms and practices like "el vacilón and "el relajo" are the Puerto Rican version of the Cuban "choteo," perhaps the most widely understood usage among the Latino nationalities and having its particular variants in the diverse national cultures. In all cases, "el choteo" involves irony, parody and many of those elements which Henry Louis Gates, Jr. has identified as constitutive of "signifyin(g)" in the African-American tradition: repetition, double-talk and semantic reversals and, most generally, gestural imitation for the sake of refiguring.[90] Colonial and elite cultures in Latin America have been constant prey to "el choteo," which also operates within and among the group to bolster or deflate spirits, whichever seems appropriate. The "signifying monkey" might instead be a dog, or a mule or a pig, or even "un bobo," a town fool or simpleton. But like "signifyin(g)," "el choteo" does have its agent, some unsuspected, improbable master of the trope who embodies the arts of memory and (re-)invention.

"El gufeo" takes the process even one step further: Latino "signifyin(g)" in the multicultural U.S. context adds to the fascination of its home-country or African-American counterparts because of its interlinguality. Double-talk in this case is sustained not merely by the interplay of "standard" and vernacular significations but by the crossing of entire language repertoires. Border vernacular in fact harbors a plurality of vernaculars comprised of their multiple interminglings and possible permutations. The result is not simply an extended range of choices and juxtapositions, the kind of "splitting of tongues" exemplified by border poet Gina Valdés at the end of her poem "Where You From?":

> soy de aquí
> y soy de allá
> I didn't build
>   this border
> that halts me
> the word fron
> tera splits
> on my tongue.[91]

The real "signifyin(g)" potential of this discourse resides in the actual interpenetration of semantic and syntactic fields, when meanings and structures become destabilized and their referential uniformity discarded. The poetry of bilingual practitioners like Alurista and Tato Laviera abounds in this kind of doubling, another striking example being the play on the words "sunrise"- "sonrisa" (smile) that occurs in the writings of both Victor Hernández Cruz and Louis Reyes Rivera. Hernández Cruz ends his often cited poem "You gotta have your tips on fire" with the lines,

> You never will be in the wrong place
> For the universe will feel your heat
> And arrange its dance on your head
> There will be a Sun/Risa
> on your lips
> But
> You gotta have your tips on fire
> Carnal[92]

In "Problems in Translation" Reyes Rivera takes up the same interlingual pun to dramatize his "discovery" of a connotative richness in his effort to adopt a new-found Spanish vocabulary:

> Esa sonrisa
> is not just a smile
> but a brilliance you lend
> from the life in your eyes
> the width of your mouth
> as they both
> give rise to the meaning of sunfilled
>   spread
> across
>   your

> boned
gentle
> > face.[93]

Poetic and colloquial language use is of course only the most obvious and readily illustrated case of re-figuration in Latino cultural expression. Examples are multiplied when account is taken of the traditions of musical "signifyin(g)" in salsa, Latin jazz, *Tejano* and Latin rock, or the characteristic interplay of Caribbean or Mexican visual worlds with North American settings among Nuyorican and Chicano artists. One thinks of Jorge Soto and his "signifyin(g)" on that classical work of a Puerto Rican painting, Francisco Oller's "El Velorio" (1893). Soto reenacts and transfigures the *jibaro* wake of the original by populating the scene with the trappings of New York tenement life. A particularly suggestive example from recent years is provided by the "casitas," the small wooden houses which have proliferated in the vacant lots of the South Bronx, El Barrio and other Puerto Rican neighborhoods. Though modeled after working-class dwellings on the Island of earlier decades, before the industrialization process overran the neighborhoods with concrete boxes, the "casitas" are typically decorated and furnished with objects pertinent to the immediate New York setting: billboards, shopping cans, plastic milk canons and the like. The effect is a remarkable pastische in which otherwise disparate visual and sculptural worlds cohabit and collapse into one another in accordance with the intergenerational historical experience of the Puerto Rican migrant community. Perhaps most impressive cultural "signifyin(g)" occurs as the contrasting of urban spatial languages, as the tropical "casita" with its strong rural reminiscences in the form of open porches, truck gardens and domestic animals jars with and yet strangely complements the surrounding scene of strewn lots and gutted buildings. Nostalgia and immediacy parody each other in the "invention" of a tradition that captures, in striking and cogent ways, the texture of "multiculturalism" in contemporary "America."[94]

For, as Gómez-Peña suggests, in order for the "multicultural paradigm" to amount to more than another warmed-over version of cultural pluralism, the entire culture and national project need to be conceived from a "multicentric perspective." It is at the border, where diversity is concentrated, that diversity as a fact of cultural life may be most readily and profoundly perceived and expressed. It is there, as Gloria Anzaldúa describes it in her work *Borderlands/La Frontera*, that the mestiza "learns to juggle cultures. She has a plural personality, she operates in a pluralistic mode. . . . Not only does she sustain contradictions, she turns the ambivalence into something else."[95] Renato Rosaldo sees in Anzaldúa's Chicana lesbian vision a celebration of "the potential of borders in opening new forms of human understanding": "She argues that because Chicanos have long practiced the art of cultural blending, 'we' now stand in a position to become leaders in developing new forms of polyglot cultural creativity. In her view, the rear guard will become the vanguard."[96]

Understood in this sense, multiculturalism signals a paradigmatic shift in ethnicity theory, a radically changed optic concerning center and margins of cultural possibility. The presumed "subcultural" tributaries feel emboldened to lay claim to the "mainstream," that tired metaphor now assuming a totally new interpretation. Tato Laviera once again is playing a pioneering role in this act of resignifying; in his new book, entitled *Mainstream Ethics*, Laviera demonstrates that it is the very concurrence of multiple and diverse voices, tones and linguistic resources that impels the flow of the whole culture of "America." The challenge is obviously aesthetic and political in intent, but it is also, as the title indicates, an eminently ethical one. "It is not our role," the book's introduction announces, "to follow the dictates of a shadowy norm, an illusive *main*stream, but to remain faithful to our collective and individual personalities. Our ethic is and shall always be current." Appropriately, the Spanish subtitle of the volume, "*ética corriente*,"[97] is more than a translation; it is a "transcreation" in the full sense, since "current" or "common," with its rootedness in the cultural ethos of everyday life, stands in blatant contrast to the fabricated, apologetic implications of "mainstream" in its conventional usage.

The Chicano poet Juan Felipe Herrera has an intriguing *gufeo* fantasy. "What if suddenly the continent turned upside-down?" he muses:

> What if the U.S. was Mexico?
> What if 200,000 Anglosaxicans
> were to cross the border each month
> to work as gardeners, waiters,
> 3rd chair musicians, movie extras,
> bouncers, babysitters, chauffeurs,
> syndicated cartoons, feather-weight
> boxers, fruit-pickers & anonymous poets?
> What if they were called waspanos,
> waspitos, wasperos or wasbacks?
> What if we were the top dogs?
> What if literature was life eh?[98]

The border houses the power of the outrageous, the imagination needed to turn the historical and cultural tables. The view from the border enables us to apprehend the ultimate arbitrariness of the border itself, of forced separations and inferiorizations. Latino expression forces the issue, which tops the agenda of American culture, the issue of geography and nomenclature:

> Let's get it straight: America is a continent not a country. Latin America encompasses more than half of America. Quechuas, Mixtecos and Iroquois are American (not U.S. citizens). Chicano, Nuyorrican, Cajun, Afro-Caribbean and Quebequois cultures are American as well. Mexicans and Canadians are also North Americans. Newly arrived Vietnamese and Laotians will soon become Americans. U.S. Anglo-European culture is but a mere component of a much larger cultural complex in constant metamorphosis.[99]

For the search for "America," the inclusive, multicultural society of the continent has to do with nothing less than an imaginative ethos of re-mapping and re-naming in the service not only of Latinos but all claimants.

NOTES

1. We agree with Guillermo Gómez-Peña that "[t]erms like 'Hispanic,' 'Latino,' 'Ethnic,' 'minority,' 'marginal,' 'alternative' and 'Third World,' among others, are inaccurate and loaded with ideological implications . . . In the absence of a more enlightened terminology, we have no choice but to utilize them with extreme care." "The Multicultural Paradigm. An Open Letter to the National Arts community," *High Performance* (Fall 1989): 20.

2. We have decided to emphasize "Latino" for, unlike "Hispanic," it is not an identity label imposed by the politicized statistics of the Census Bureau and the market who seek to target particular constituencies for political and economic manipulation. As for the shortcomings of "Latino," we hope that this article contributes to their critique. In a nutshell, the term "older immigrants" refers to the way in which assimilationist or "melting pot" sociologists (from Robert Park to Milton Gordon) constructed the experiences of late nineteenth and early twentieth-century immigrants according to a dynamic of contact, accommodation and assimilation that eventually amalgamated them into the dominant culture. The term "new ethnics" refers to the period of (white) ethnic revival, largely coinciding with civil rights struggles and their aftermath, in which "racial minorities and white ethnics became polarized on a series of issues relating to schools, housing, local government and control over federal programs." This revival has also been understood as the dying flash of white ethnicity in a longer historical process of acculturation. Cf. Stephen Steinberg, *The Ethnic Myth. Race, Ethnicity, and Class in America* (Boston: Beacon Press, 1982), pp. 48–51.

See also Richard H. Thompson, *Theories of Ethnicity. A critical Appraisal* (Westport, CT: Greenwood Press, 1989), for whom the "rediscovery of ethnicity [by its American observers] is largely a response to the black protest movement of the 1960s, the state's subsequent definition and legitimation of that movement as an ethnic (but not primarily a class) movement, and the resulting increase in the United States of other ethnically defined movements by Hispanics, Asian-Americans and "white ethnics," who, observing the 'success' of black organization and the state's receptivity to it, have quite unmysteriously followed a similar track" (93).

3. "Racial minority" is a term used to distinguish the historical experiences (enslavement and/or institutional exclusion from political economic and especially social enfranchisement) of certain groups (viz. African-American, Latinos, Asian-Americans and Native-Americans) from those of European immigrant groups for whom the dynamics described by ethnicity theories made possible the enfranchisements denied to the former. Cf. Michael Omi and Howard Winant, *Racial Formation in the United States. From the 1960s to the 1980s* (New York: Routledge & Kegan Paul, 1986.

4. The historical discrimination against Mexican-Americans and Puerto Ricans is an experience which cannot be permitted to disappear by projecting Latinos as an overarching group. Such discrimination involves a complex of racial, class and "otherness" factors which often make middle-class sectors of other Latino groups anxious and seek to dissociate themselves. On the other hand, the fact that discrimination has been directed to all Latino groups contributes to a pan-Latino rejection of discrimination aimed at any particular group.

5. Cf. Steinberg, pp. 24, 40 *et passim.*

6. The increase in the Latin American population in the United States can be more accurately compared with the *overall* European influx rather than with the numbers of any one particular group. If Latin American immigration, in conjunction with the high birth rate of U.S. Latinos, continues into the next century (which is likely), then proportionately the number of Latinos will rival or supersede that of the European immigrants since the turn of the nineteenth century. From 1820 to 1930, the estimated "net immigration of various European nationalities" is as follows: Germans, 5,900,000; Italians, 4,600,000; Irish, 4,500,000; Poles, 3,000,000; Canadians, 2,800,000; Jews, 2,500,000; English, 2,500,000; Swedes, 1,200,000; Scots and Scots-Irish, 1,000,000. Cf. Steinberg, ibid., p. 41.

7. Cf. Michael Lev, "Tracking the Hispanic TV Audience," *The New York Times* (December 13, 1989): D 17. Lev's figures are taken from a Nielsen Hispanic Television survey funded by two of the largest Spanish TV networks, Univisión and Telemundo Group, Inc.

8. Such decreases are comparable for other European immigrant populations in the United States. Cf. Joshua Fishman, et al., *Language Loyalty in the United States* (The Hague: Mouton, 1966), pp. 42–44.

9. Stanley Aronowitz, "Post-modernism and Politics," *Social Text*, 18 (Winter 1987/88): 108. Reprinted in Andrew Ross, ed., *Universal Abandon? The Politics of Post-modernism* (Minneapolis: University of Minnesota Press, 1988), pp. 46–62.

10. Ibid.

11. Edumndo O'Gorman, *The Invention of America. An Inquiry into the historical nature of the New World and the meaning of its history* (Bloomington: Indiana University Press, 1961).

12. Frederick Jackson Turner, "The Significance of the Frontier in American History," *The Frontier in American History* (New York: Holt, 1920), p. 11.

13. Richard Slotkin, *The Fatal Environment. the Myth of the Frontier in the Age of Industrialization, 1800–1890* (New York: Atheneum, 1985), p. 40.

14. Guillermo Gómez-Peña, "Documented/Undocumented," in *Multi-Cultural Literacy. Opening the American Mind*, eds. Rick Simonson and Scott Walker (Saint Paul, MN: Graywolf Press, 1988), p. 127 challenges.

15. "The Multicultural Paradigm," p. 20.

16. Tato Laviera, *AmeRícan* (Houston: Arte Público, 1984), p. 95.

17. Sandra María Esteves, *Tropical Rains* (New York: African Caribbean Poetry Theater, 1984).

19. Jacques Derridá, "The Parergon," *October*, 9(Summer 1979): 20.

20. Cf. Jean Baudrillard, *De la Séduction* (Paris: Galilée, 1979). Apropos of the simulacrum, Latin Americans have dealt with problems of cultural identity in terms of the "neither-nor" since the conquest. The difference between "neither-not" (or "not nowhere") is that the former is usually expressed by elites who feel in an ambivalent position vis-à-vis metropolitan cultural valuation while the latter is situated in the struggles of subordinated groups against a cultural "nonexistence" which elites are too often willing to exploit.

Enrique Lihn has parodied the *ninguneísta* discourse in *El arte de la palabra* (Barcelona: Pomaire, 1979). "We are nothing: imitations, copies, phantoms: repeaters of what we understand badly, that is, hardly at all: dead organ grinders: the animated fossils of a prehistory what we have lived *neither here nor there*, consequently, anywhere, for we are aboriginal foreigners, transplanted from birth in our respective countries of origin" (p. 82; our emphasis). This is a parody of the anxious discourse of those elites who seek to define the nation. Roberto Schwarz has written an in-depth critique of this kind of "national problem." "Brazilian Culture: Nationalism by Elimination," *New Left Review*, 167 (January/February 1988): 77–90.

21. Cf. R. Butler, "On Creating a Hispanic America: A Nation within a Nation?" quoted in Antonio J. Califa, "Declaring English the Official Language: Prejudice Spoken Here," *Harvard Civil Rights-Civil Liberties Law Review*, 24 (1989): 321.

22. Terry Robbins, Presentation at Florida International University (October 8, 1987), quoted in Califa, p. 321. Terry Robbins is a former head of U.S. English operations in Florida.

23. Deutsch, "The Political Significance of Linguistic Conflicts," in *Les Etats Multilingues* (1975).

24. An English First analysis of Immigration Reform and Control Act of 1986, Pub. Law No. 99–603, 1986 U.S. Cong. Code & Admin. News (100 Stat.) 3359, quoted in Califa, p. 313. Calif, "Declaring English the Official Language: Prejudice Spoken Here," *harvard Civil Rights-Civil Liberties Law Review*, 24, (1989): 328.

25. Cf. Joshua Fishman, "'English Only': Its Ghosts, Myths and Dangers," *International Journal of the Sociology of Language*, 125, 132 (1988), quoted in Califa, p. 329.

26. "Government and private experts agree that the threat of war with the Soviet Union is diminishing. As a result, the nation's military services argue that a portion of the Pentagon budget in the 1990's must be devoted to combating drugs and being prepared to bring American military power to bear in the third world." Stephen Engelberg, "In Search of Missions to Justify Outlays," *The New York Times* (January 9, 1990): A14.

27. Thompson, p. 90.

28. Cf. Jurgen Habermas, "Modernity—An Incomplete Project," in *The Anti-Aesthetic. Essays on Post-Modern Culture*. ed. Hal Foster (Port Townsend, WA: Bay Press, 1983), p. 14.

29. Daniel Bell "Ethnicity and Social Change," in Nathan Glazer and Daniel P. Moynihan, eds., *Ethnicity: Theory and Experience* (Cambridge: Harvard University Press, 1975), p. 169, as quoted in Thompson, op. cit., p. 99.

30. According to Michael Omi and Howard Winant, the formation of the concept of ethnicity in the United States is rooted in a different historical conjuncture than ours and, thus, occludes this difference if invoked to account for the negotiation of value by non-European immigrants: "But both assimilationist and cultural pluralism had largely emphasized European, white immigrants, what Kallen called 'the Atlantic migration.' The origins of the concepts of 'ethnicity' and 'ethnic group' in the U.S., then, lay outside the experience of those identified (not only today but already in Park's and Kallen's time), as *racial* minorities: Afro-Americans, Latin Americans, Native Americans and Asian Americans (blacks, browns, reds and yellows). The continuity of experience embodied in the application of the terms of ethnicity theory to both groups—to European immigrants and racial minorities—was not established; indeed it tended to rest on what we have labelled the *immigrant analogy.*" *Racial Formation in the United States*, pp. 16–17.

31. As Stephen Steinberg argues, "Kallen's model of a 'democracy of nationalities' is workable only in a society where there is a basic parity among constituent ethnic groups. Only then would ethnic boundaries be secure from encroachments, and only then would pluralism be innocent of class bias and consistent with democratic principles." *The Ethic Myth*, pp. 260–261. The reference is to Horace Kallen, "Democracy Versus the Melting Pot," in *Culture and Democracy in the United States* (New York: Boni and Liveright, 1924). This critique extends to later studies like Nathan Glazer, *Affirmative Discrimination* (New York: Basic Books, 1975).

32. "[N]umerous new struggles have expressed resistance.

33. Laclau and Mouffe, p. 184. See also Martha Minow, "We, the Family: Constitutional Right and American Families," in *The Constitution and American Life*, ed. David Thelen (Ithaca: Cornell University Press, 1988), p. 319. "Against the new forms of subordination, and this from the very heart of the new society. Thus it is that the waste of natural resources, the pollution and destruction of the environment, the consequences of productivism have given birth to the ecology movement. Other struggles, which Manuel Castells terms 'urban,' express diverse forms of resistance to the capitalist occupation of social space. The general urbanization which has accompanied economic growth, the transfer of the popular classes to the urban periphery or their relegation to the decaying inner cities, and the general lack of collective goods and services have caused a series of new problems which affect the organization of the whole of social life outside work. Hence the multiplicity of social relations [not subordinatable to "class"] from which antagonisms and struggles may originate: habitat, consumption, various services, can all constitute terrains for the struggle against inequalities and the claiming of new rights." Ernesto Laclau and Chantal Mouffe, *Hegemony and Socialist Strategy. Towards a Radical Democratic Politics* (London: Verso, 1985), p. 161.

Given that these new forms of subordination and terrains of struggle were not in place before World War II, the conditions of possibility for group self-understanding are no longer those which made prior theories of ethnicity socially and politically operational.

34. "We, the Family," p. 322.

35. Nancy Fraser, "Women, Welfare, and Politics," in *Unruly Practices. Power, Discourse and Gender in Contemporary Social Theory* (Minneapolis: University of Minnesota Press, 1989), p. 154.

36. For example, "[I]n the 'masculine' subsystem . . . claimants must rove their 'cases' meet administratively defined criteria of entitlement; in the 'feminine' syb-system, on the other hand, claimants must prove conformity to administratively defined criteria of need." Ibid.

37. "[I]n a given context the presence of a particular unit is in contrast with its absence. When this situation holds it is usually the case that the unmarked form is more general in sense or has a wider distribution than the marked form." John Lyons, *Introduction to Theoretical Linguistics* (Cambridge: Cambridge University Press, 1969), p. 79. The example chosen by Lyons demonstrates that markedness is directly related to socially instituted norms of "generality." One can say "Is the dog a he or a she?" but one would not ask the same if referring to a "bitch," whose gender is necessarily female. Markedness relies on already instituted norms of generality; the theory, however, does not question the grounds on which such a generality is instituted. As regards ethnicity, "WASP"s are taken to be the unmarked form, while other groups are understood as "unmarked." And yet, nearly 90% of U.S. citizens are not WASPs.

38. In an April 1988 study—"New Voices: Immigrant Students in the U.S. Public Schools," financed by the Ford Foundation, it was argued that "schools were doing a poor job of meeting the immigrant students' *needs* (our emphasis). Cf. Associated Press, "Study Finds Obstacles Exist for Immigrant Schoolchildren," *The New York Times* (May 10, 1988). Both this and another study advocated increasing the number of Hispanic teachers to meet the cultural needs of students and thus ease the increasing dropout rate and other apparent education dysfunctionalities. Cf. Peter Applebome, "Educators Alarmed by Growing Rate of Dropouts Among Hispanic Youth," *The New York Times* (March 15, 1987): 22.

39. Quoted in Thomas Weyr, *Hispanic U.S.A. Breaking the Melting Pot* (New York: Harper & Row, 1988), pp. 62–63.

40. Ibid.

41. Jürgen Habermas, *The Theory of Communicative Action. Vol. II. Lifeworld and System: A Critique of Functionalist Reason*, trans. Thomas McCarthy (Boston: Beacon Press, 1987), p. 365.

42. Fraser, p. 156.

43. Oskar Negt and Alexander Kluge, "The Public Sphere and experience: Selections," trans. Peter Labanyi, *October*, 46 (Fall 1988), p. 60, translator's note.

44. Fredric Jameson, "On Negt and Kluge," *October*, 46 (Fall 1988): 159.

45. Cf. V. N. Voloshinov, *Marxism and the Philosophy of Language*, trans. Ladislav Matejka and I. R. Titunik (New York: Seminar Press, 1973), pp. 91–97 and M. M. Bakhtin, "The Problem of Speech Genres," in *Speech Genres and Other Late Essays*, trans. Vern. W. McGee (Austin: University of Texas Press, 1986), pp. 61–102.

46. Oskar Negt and Alexander Kluge, *Geschichte und Eigensinn* (Frankfurt; Zweitausendeins, 1981), p. 944, quoted in Jameson, p. 172.

47. James, p. 171.

48. Ibid., p. 78.

49. Ibid., p. 79.

50. Ibid., p. 76.

51. (Boston: David R. Godine, 1982).

52. Ibid., p. 19.

53. Ibid., p. 187.

54. Ibid., p. 182.

55. Ibid., p. 124.

56. Ibid., p. 137.

58. Thomas B. Morgan, "The Latinization of America," *Esquire* (May 1983): 56.

59. Ibid., p. 3.

60. (New York: Oxford University Press, 1986), pp. 46, 153, and 241.

61. Ibid., p. 259.

62. Ibid., p. 54–55.

63. Ibid., p. 7.

64. (April 18, 1989), p. 16.

65. Patrick Barry, "When translation isn't enough, try 'trans-creation'," Special supplement on "The Hispanic Market," *Advertising Age* (February 14, 1983): M–21.

66. Ibid., p. M 26.

67. Ibid.

68. Susan Dentzer, "Learning the Hispanic Hustle," *Newsweek* (May 17, 1982): 84.

69. Barry, p. M 26.

70. "[A] show of disregard can cost a firm heavily in lost sales, as the Adolph Coors Co. discovered several years ago. Charged by Hispanic groups with discriminatory hiring practices that led to a boycott of its products, the brewer has fought to rebuild its image, in part by making donations to Hispanic causes." Dentzer, p. 86.

71. Letter from Gerda Bikales, executive director of U.S. English, to the Secretary of the Federal Communications Commission (September 26, 1985), quoted in Califa, pp. 319–20. Cf. also Associated Press, "Group Wants to Stop Ads in Spanish," *San Jose Mercury News* (December 23, 1985).

72. "[E]l barrio es el hilo conductor"; "[la salsa] representa plenamente la convergencia del barrio urbano de hoy [porque asume] la totalidad de ritmos que acuden a esa convergencia"; "La sala no es un ritmo, y tampoco es un simple estilo para enfrentar un ritmo definido. La salsa es una forma abierta capaz de representar la totalidad de tendencias que se reúnen en la circunstancia del Caribe urbano [incluyendo Nueva York] de hoy; el barrio sigue siendo la única marca definitiva." Cf. César Miguel Rondón, *El libro de la salsa. Crónica de la música del caribe urbano* (Caracas: Editorial Arte, 1980), pp. 32–64 *et passim*. "We object to Philip Morris or any other companies who are advertising in languages other than English," said Stanley Diamond, head of the California chapter of U.S. English, an advocacy group. "What they are doing tends to separate out citizens and our people by language." ". . . This fall Diamond . . . chapter launched a coupon mail-in protest against a Spanish-language Yellow Pages . . ." "We certainly would feel that the corporations, the telephone company with the Spanish Yellow Pages should change . . . We will do everything we can to put this advertising in English only . . . and in no other language," said Diamond. In Florida, U.S. English spokeswoman Terry Robbins . . . has written as a private citizen to McDonald's and Burger King protesting Spanish in fast-food menus. "Why does poor Juan or Maria have a problem ordering a Whopper?" she asked. "It isn't that they aren't able to, they don't want to."

73. Humberto Márquez, "Willie Colón inventa cosas para que la vida no duela," *El Diario de Caracas* (February 23, 1982): 14–15.

74. Ibid.

75. Cf. Jon Pareles, "Dancing Along with David Byrne," *The New York Times* (November 1, 1989): C 1. George Lipsitz makes a similar argument about Los Lobos' networking with other groups to create a new mass audience, a new public sphere: "For [drummer] Pérez, the world of rock-and-roll music is not a place that obliterates local cultures by rendering them invisible; rather it is an arena where divers groups find common ground while still acknowledging important differences. The prefigurative counter-hegemony fashioned by Los Lobos has indeed won the allegiance of musicians from other marginalized cultures. Their songs have been recorded by country and western star Waylon Jennings as well as by polka artist Frankie Yankovic. The Cajun accordion player and singer Jo-El Sonnier views Los Lobos as artists

whose cultural struggles parallel his own." "Cruising Around the Historical Block—Post-modernism and Popular music in East Los Angeles," *Cultural Critique*, 5 (Winter 1986–87), p. 175.

76. Cf. Juan Flores, "Rappin', Writin', and Breakin': Black and Puerto Rican Culture in New York, *Dissent* (Fall 1987): 580–84.

77. *Chicago Sunday Times* (January 26, 1987).

78. (San Francisco: Spinsters/Aunt Lute, 1987).

79. Ibid., p. 59.

80. See note 71.

81. Ibid., p. 80.

82. Ibid., p. 81.

83. The "ethical substance" is one of the four dimensions that comprise "ethics." It delimits what moral action will apply to: for example, the pleasures among the Greeks, the flesh among the early Christians, sexuality in Western modernity, and, we argue, group ethos—ethnic, feminist, gay, lesbian, etc. - in multi-cultural societies. Cf. Michel Foucault, *The Use of Pleasure* (New York: Vintage, 1986), pp. 26–28.

84. Michel Foucault, "The Ethic of Care for the Self as a Practice of Freedom," in *The Final Foucault*, eds. James Bernauer and David Rasmussen (Cambridge: MIT Press, 1988), p. 19.

85. Ibid., p. 18.

86. Gómez-Peña, "The Multicultural Paradigm," p. 22.

87. Michael J. Fischer, "Ethnicity and the Post-Modern Arts of Memory," in James Clifford and George E. Marcus, eds. *Writing Culture: The Poetics and Politics of Ethnography* (Berkeley: University of California Press, 1986), p. 196.

88. Esteves, *Yerba Buena*.

89. Cf. Antonio Lauria, "'Respeto,' 'relajo' and Interpersonal Relations in Puerto Rico," *Anthropological Quarterly*, 37, 2 (1964): 53–67.

90. Henry Louis Gates, Jr., *The Signifying Monkey: A Theory of Afro-American Literary Criticism* (New York: Oxford University Press, 1988).

91. Gina Valdés, "Where You From?" *The Broken Line/La Línea Quebrada*, 1, 1 (May 1986).

92. Victor Hernández Cruz, *Snaps*.

93. Louis Reyes Rivera, *This One For You* (New York: Shamal, 1983).

94. For discussions of *casitas* see the planned volume sponsored by the Bronx Council on the Arts, especially Luis Aponte, "*Casitas* as Place and Metaphor" and Joseph Sciorra, "'We're not just here to plant. We have culture': A Case Study of the South Bronx *Casita, Rincón Criollo*." Cf. the discussion of Sciorra's work in Dinita Smith, "Secret Lives of New York: Exploring the City's Unexamined Worlds," *New York* (December 11, 1989): 34–41.

95. Anzaldúa, p. 79.

96. Renato Rosaldo, *Truth in Culture: The Remaking of Social Analysis* (Boston: Beacon, 1989), p. 216.

97. Tato Laviera, *Mainstream Ethics* (Houston: Arte Público Press, 1988).

98. Juan Felipe Herrera, "Border Drunkie at 'Cabaret Babylon-Aztlán,'" *The Broken Line/La Línea Quebrada*.

99. Gómez-Peña, "The Multicultural Paradigm," p. 20.

III

CONSTRUCTING LATINO(A) IDENTITIES

9

¿Somos RUNAFRIBES?
The Future of Latino Ethnicity
in the Americas

Gonzalo Santos

> *"Debemos dejar de ser todo eso que nunca hemos*
> *sido y que no seremos nunca."*
>
> —Aníbal Quijano (1988)

> *"I am not his-panic, her-panic, or anybody's-panic!"*
>
> —Alurista (circa 1982)

I LO QUE HAY DETRÁS DE LA ETNICIDAD MODERNA

Ethnicity, understood broadly as peoplehood, is as old as history. Ethnicity is different than mere social bonding. As gregarious beings, we know humans have always bonded to lead a social existence, beginning with kinship relations. But conceivably, in the span of human history, the kin-clusters of humans could have simply kept bonding socially into larger and larger socio-cultural units until the entire species became a single socio-cultural configuration, just as, say, other species exist as a single herd or colony. But humans have never gone that far, even under conditions of close proximity. Instead, for reasons of ecological and social adaptation in ancient times, and increasingly in the past few thousand years for reasons of political and economic power, humans have consistently *bounded* their socio-cultural life as "peoples," aggregating in a myriad of socio-cultural units much smaller than the species, "granulating" as distinct "peoples" even within large state formations (e.g., empires) or vast civilizations.

Humans have endlessly conceptualized a we-ness in relation to themselves as the insiders' criteria for "belonging" to a people, while simultaneously ascribing (and frequently imposing) a complementary other-ness to their perceived outsiders. That is, ethnicity is historically constructed by collectivities always in relation to other collectivities, a dual social process that, as circumstances change, fastens or shifts the boundaries of peoplehood from the inside out and from the outside in, through consensual or conflictive processes.

Not all relations between peoples have been hierarchical, antagonistic, or competitive. There have been many instances in which relations between peoples were egalitarian, harmonious, and symbiotic.[1] But in the 500-year lifespan of the modern capitalist world-economy, almost all the non-European peoples incorporated into its expansionist social system were forced to interact with the Europeans along various patterns of super-subordination, and, as a result, were dramatically remolded. The bitterly contested, constantly evolving, hierarchical patterns of ethnic relations have reflected and partially embodied the natural history of this most peculiar social system, defined and driven by the endless accumulation of capital and the self-regulated market (Wallerstein, 1983; Polanyi, 1957).

Modern ethnicity has served both as a stratifying medium for the accumulators of capital and as an indispensable element in the ideology of resistance by those who have suffered the exploitation and oppression that has accompanied the capitalist process of production, exchange, and accumulation. Modern ethnicities have not only been invented and imposed from the *top down* by some dominant groups (mostly European elites) on others (mostly non-Europeans)—the former redefining themselves in the process—but they have also been reshaped and reclaimed from the *ground up* by the latter against the former. In the course of these struggles both the incorporated non-European peoples and the incorporating Europeans metamorphosed dramatically into new ethnic entities, bounded communities of consciousness. These new ethnicities of "race" and "nation," both of which are purely modern socio-political constructs, have overlapped and competed with the older ethnicities based on religion, kinship, language, etc. . . .[2]

Why were the incorporated peoples outside Europe not Europeanized and simply subordinated by force as exploited workers (wage, slave, etc.)? Why has ethnicity, in all its modern manifestations, been such a central feature of the capitalist world-system?

First, let us look at it from the top down. Marx pointed out long ago (Marx, 1967) that the capitalists could not accumulate capital without somehow tying up production relations with an unequal distribution of the social product, something which in turn would reproduce a system of social stratification. He revealed how the capital-wage relation served precisely as a medium of surplus value creation, social stratification, and capital accumulation. But Marx was wrong in thinking that this relation, in and of itself, was enough of a profit-making dynamo to make capitalism self-sustainable; that so-called "primitive accumulation" was only needed to jump-start the capitalist engine; and that once it got going, the capitalist world-system would self-propel purely on the fuel provided by the surplus produced through the capital-wage relation. Historically, the capital-wage relation was limited mostly to some regions of Europe and North America until fairly recently. It was never on a global scale the main, let alone the sole, medium of capital accumulation. The people-to-people relations of domination have yielded much more surplus to the accumulators, through colonial conquest, slavery, peonage, contract labor, etc. Ethnic stratification has historically been one of the most essential and flexible forms of social stratification (perhaps *the* main form) for the world-system as a whole, without which capitalist accumulation would have been a much slower and delimited historical phenomenon.

The actual structures of social stratification outside Europe in historical capitalism were based on the imposition of productive activities on various non-European direct producers, adopting forms of coerced labor that were designed to coincide with hierarchical ethnic social orders defined and imposed by the European accumulators and their politico-military entrepreneurs. These coerced-labor processes and ethnicities were imposed simultaneously, usually with extreme levels of violence and calculated to maximize profits.[3] The incorporated non-European direct producers of the plantations, mines, and haciendas experienced the crushing of their previous ethnic identities and watched themselves being crudely re-cast to fit the European specifications of "who they were." As Eric Wolf (1982) puts it, the non-European peoples have been treated by the Europeans (and their ethnocentric social sciences) as "peoples without history" or "peoples outside history."

But the indigenous (or transplanted) direct producers, initially subjected brutally to a totally artificial and dehumanizing process of re-ethnicization, at first resisted being stripped of their prior ethnicity and rejected adopting a new one. Eventually, however, they adopted their imposed ethnicity and used it to fight back, to resist their economic exploiters and ethnic oppressors. In time, they redefined themselves with altogether new ethnic identities, now defined on their own terms, abandoning those imposed from above for ethnicities proclaimed from the bottom.[4]

Crucial as ethnicity has been in the life of the modern world-system, anti-systemic social science has never succeeded in explaining it other than in a class-reductionist way.[5] Ethnic consciousness has been treated traditionally by the Marxist literature the *ne plus ultra* of "false consciousness," destined to weaken in the heat of class struggle or as capitalism itself develops (not to mention its extinction in the era of socialism). The vibrant, enduring, manifold manifestations of contemporary ethnicity (mostly from the bottom up) under "late capitalism"—*and* "really-existing socialism,"—bedevils the anti-systemic social sciences. Ethnicity, clearly, is not withering away, nor is it just an epiphenomenon of the capitalist class struggle What *has* declined is the relative vitality of all top-down ethnicities vis-à-vis the emerging bottom-up ones.

Anderson (1983: 12), for example, described the appropriation of nationalism by the anti-systemic movements in this way:

[S]ince World War II every successful revolution has defined itself in *national* terms . . . and many "old nations" once thought fully consolidated, find themselves challenged by "sub"-nationalisms within their borders— nationalisms which, naturally, dream of shedding their sub-ness one happy day. The reality is quite plain: the "end of the era of nationalism," so long prophesied, is not remotely in sight. Indeed, nation-ness is the most universal legitimate value in the political life of our time.

The post-colonial and post-revolutionary "new nations" have also found themselves increasingly challenged by "sub"-nationalisms.[6] But besides these national and subnational anti-systemic ethnicities, "transnational" (continental or regional) ethnicities have played an ever-increasing important role. Examples of the latter are the pan-African movement (worldwide and in Africa), the pan-Islamic movement (and its pan-Arab subset), third-worldism, *latinoamericanismo*, and *indigenismo*.

Furthermore, in this era of global eco-crises (produced by the flawed developmentalism of both East and West), purely interhuman communication is giving way to a new discourse between humans and their world; and that, in turn, is helping millions of people to redefine themselves and to challenge the underlying assumptions behind their historically exhausted ethnicities, especially those generated and imposed from above. For the first time since European modernity "disenchanted the world" (Todorov, 1985), there is a growing, world-wide, environmentally-centered, "one-world" sense of peoplehood. The 1989 Minamata Declaration,[7] to give but the most recent example, calls upon all anti-systemic peoples' movements to set out to achieve in the twenty-first century the historic construction of a global "transborder people." This new conception envisions combining the rich diversity of peoples with a global eco-centered peoplehood. It summons us to abandon the deep anthropocentric perspective embedded in all modern ideologies, right and left, and to value equally all life forms and life processes on Earth (Schell, 1982).

What do all these ethnicities have in common? They have all sprung from the bottom up in the last half-century or so, initiated by the anti-systemic peoples' movements of the world-system. A credible social science must account for their existence in its theory as well as explain their historic specificities and potentialities. Neither pro- nor anti-systemic social science are anywhere close to reaching this point, the former enchained by Eurocentrism and structural functionalism, the latter crushed under the weight of decades of dogmatic thinking.

What is happening to the people's sense of peoplehood? On the positive side, perhaps what Chicano poet Aberlardo Delgado (1978: 3) calls the "*yo sí, tú no-ism*," of the hierarchical ethnic, class, and gender orderings of the modern world-system is slowly giving way to a newly-found "*yo sí, tú también-ism*" of a new world-system, currently in gestation and yet to be established. There is much evidence that suggests that the world-system and the eco-system are evermore dangerously at odds in their fundamental logics. No historical social system can long last that way. The new tolerance for thriving ethnic diversity is tied in the end to a new tolerance for ecological diversity.

We are witnessing, in sum, the simultaneous historic recovery (re-invention?) of the harmonious, symbiotic, and egalitarian relations some of our indigenous ancestors held among themselves, and between themselves and their world. *¿No será que nos estamos re-indigenizando, a pesar de que creimos que eso era irreversible?*

II LO QUE PASÓ Y DEBE PASAR EN LATINOAMÉRICA

From the sixteenth century to the end of World War II, the interstate system[8] facilitated the evolution of various continental patterns of ethnic stratification, through the wholesale conquest, colonization, and domination of the indigenous inhabitants of vast territories of the planet. Enormous colonial caste societies developed, all ideologically based on the newly invented, top-down *racial* ethnicities—such as the historical invention of the "Indians" (or "Reds"), the "Africans" (or "Blacks"), the "Asians" (or "Yellows"), and the "Europeans" (or "Whites"). The "races," initially mere absurd European constructs, evolved into social phenomena, historical entities. Degrading labels were indeed adopted to condemn to the same subordinated status millions of non-Europeans.[9] The Europeans changed, too: from being Christian vassals of this or that lord, they *became* "Europeans," and "Whites."

Consider the case of colonial Spanish America. As Spain conquered the New World, the ethnic transformation of conqueror and conquered was dramatic. The Spaniards imposed on the New World peoples a simplistic but overarching racial ethnicity to distinguish them as *the conquered* from themselves as *the conquerors*. Those they conquered were now supposed to be *"indios."*[10] They themselves became *gente de razón*. The category of *"indio"* artificially lumped together an estimated 90 to 112 million people who belonged to hundreds of completely different social systems and cultures, ranging from "Stone Age" band societies to "High Civilizational Systems." Nevertheless, their universal subjugation to the same Spanish-identified "people," and their transformation into a single gigantic class of disposable slaves and servants, had nothing artificial about it.[11] Nor was there anything artificial in the sudden transformation of the commoner Spaniards arriving in the New World as *de facto* masters over any indigenous person or collectivity they encountered. The Spaniard was automatically admitted into a privileged, ethnic, group.

Indian consciousness, a new Indian identity, emerged as the colonial social order of *castas* was put in place. The indigenous peoples of Spanish America *began to act as modern Indians*, both in their acts of submission and accommodation and in their acts of resistance. Wherever large concentrations of Africans developed in the New World the same phenomenon occurred,[12] even though Africans *in* Africa, then constituting a rich civilizational mosaic (Wolf, 1982: 195–231), would not develop an "African" consciousness until after the 1880s, *after* Africa was almost completely carved out into European colonies.[13]

The *casta* structures of racial stratification that paralleled the sharp class stratification of the colonial agrarian and extractive societies outlived the nineteenth-century republican period (the glory days of the *Criollo* export-oriented land oligarchy). They continued throughout Latin America, overlapping nation-building efforts, well into the twentieth century.[14] The vast *mestizaje* helped to sublimate racial into national identity, a metamorphosis that truly began to take place with the advent of the Mexican Revolution, but it eroded racial stratification slowly and only partially.

Today, 500 years after the conquest, no people or ethnic group in Latin America is the same. The Indians went from the condition of original peoples, with their own singular cultural attributes, to that of anodyne Indians, ever more detached from their original culture and forced to assimilate to the general population of the country where they live. Nonetheless, they continue being Indians, given their self-identification and their resistance to full assimilation, and because the people who mistreat them considers them Indians.[15]

Ribeiro (1982: 9) distinguishes between two main categories of Indians today: the myriad of tiny, isolated, and endangered indigenous villages, or *microctnias*, clinging to life by adhering to communitarian traditions, and the still great demographic blocks of Indians from areas of high pre-Colombian civilization, the *macroctnias*. Seen until recently only as *campesinos*, the *macroetnias* increasingly see themselves as oppressed peoples with aspirations for full autonomy, quite outside of, or even against, the assimilationist schemes for "developing" the nation-states in which they are embedded. Given the extreme oppression these groups still endure, Ribeiro sees a latent tendency toward "veritable inter-ethnic wars." To avoid them, he calls for the establishment of a "Latin American Federation" in which the indigenous peoples can "reconstruct themselves as authentic cultures so they may flourish again as autonomous civilizations." This programme can easily be expanded to include Latin America's groups of African ancestry.

But the opposite has been happening. Between 1900 and 1950 a period of transition to U.S. sponsored "modernization" and the beginnings of industrialization occurred, stimulated by U.S. direct investments and state policies of "economic growth towards the inside." An optimist *desarrollistat* nationalism from above emerged which sought state-sponsored capitalist economic development.[16] All aspects of "traditional society" were looked upon as retrograde, including indigenous culture and social organization. Vast urbanization and massive migration flows to the United States accompanied the rapid economic growth. Modernization brought spectacular wealth to a few, heightened living standards to the new de-ethnicized, Americanized, urban middle classes, while it brought "modern poverty" and "modern repression" to the majority.[17] After a failed experiment with import substitution in the 1960s, Latin America's economies became internationalized and ever-more subordinated to the core of the world economy. When the world economy entered into a deep contraction period in the mid-seventies, Latin America's economics began to collapse. The developmentalist illusion crashed in the 1980s. In its wake, the colossal disparities of income and living standards between different classes and ethnic groups stand as a grotesque monument to modernization.

Politically, after the Cuban Revolution stood up to the then world-begemonic U.S. state, Latin America experienced a wave of fascist regimes and U.S.-sponsored wars of counterinsurgency. In the 1980s the large-scale repression has continued, but it has been surgically applied (e.g., Central America, Grenada).[18] The upshot of the large-scale intra-national and international migratory flows produced by the macro-economic dislocations and the political upheavals of the 1960s, 1970s, and 1980s, has been the radical transformation of the ethnic identities of large numbers of Latin Americans, who resurrected an anti-systemic, anti-imperialist *latinoamericanismo* not seen since the days of Bolivar.

Unfortunately, the *latinoamericanismo* of the last few decades has not gone far enough, despite its great contributions to the world's anti-systemic movements. It has not yet gone deep enough into the historic consciousness of the continent, an identity glossed over by the wild rush to a "modernity" instrumentalized by both the capitalist accumulators and their anti-systemic opponents into *una modernidad que negaba y niega lo indio y lo africano.* For true equality, a new framing ethnic identity must emerge, one that casts aside the old obsession with perpetuating European ideological roots for all our thoughts, or with defining them in relation to the latest European intellectual trends. And it must break with the "modernization" visions imported from the United States that are counterfeit and inimical to our social health. Now that Latin Americans know their political size, they must discover their ethnic depths. The project is nothing less than to meld the still-strong Latin American transborder ethnicity with the visions of the indigenous peoples of the New World and Africa, and to metamorphose the blend into a new sense of modernity: *una nueva visión de lo que somos, o debemos ser, para dejar de ser lo que nunca fuimos y no vamos a ser jamds.*

But we must be clear on the dual nature of ethnicity. Today, the anti-systemic movements and the ruling classes use and dispute among themselves the nature and political direction of Latin American ethnicity. These two opposing poles of *latinoamericanismo* contend in a continent where the vast majority of modern-day Indians and Blacks, and to a lesser extent Mestizos and Mulattos, have never ceased to be acutely impoverished and denied true social, economic, and political equality with the descendants of the various Euro-Americans that have settled in Latin America. The elites of the latter continue to dominate, successfully hidden behind the national identities and the half-hearted *latinoamericanismo* they constructed from the top down in the last century-and-a-half. The fraud of "racial democracy" has been sustained up to the present and needs to be exposed. Recovering *lo indio y lo africano* will therefore involve a fight along ethnic and class lines.

That being said, the new anti-systemic movements of Latin America ought to reconsider the names that imprison our peoples more than describe them. Insofar as the terms "*indio*," and "*negro*" are erroneous, fraudulent European labels that hide the dehumanization of people, they ought to be discarded for others. They don't describe people as much as they describe the *peoplelessness of people*. "*América Latina*," on the other hand, is a purely *Criollol* oligarchic term that sustains a Europeanized, colonized vision of us manufactured in the core of the world-system. The name "Latin American" denies our Indian and African roots and glosses over their tragic history. The recovery of Latin America's historic time and vision necessarily will involve constructing socially a new social conception of ourselves, inventing a new name to reflect our indigenous roots, and envisioning the liberation of hundreds of millions of dispossessed and exploited peoples of the continent. To remain a misnamed people is a sure sign of being a lost, disempowered, and defrauded one.

We will continue to have a transborder ethnic identity in Latin America, but the question is which one it will be, the one endlessly promoted from the top down, hegemonic today, or the one constantly struggling to emerge from the bottom up? To denote the latter, I propose the adoption of the term *RUNAFRIBE*. *RUNA* strands for the indigenous peoples of the continent, for it means "people" in Quechua, the still living but ancient *lingua franca* of the Andean civilizational system.[19] *AFRI* stands for Africa, signifying the African presence and impact on the hemisphere. *RIBE* stands for the Caribbean. *IBE* stands for Iberia, and finally, *E* stands for Europe as a whole. More important than the name of a new ethnicity from the ground up, of course, are the social movements that can make their goal the implementation of a new vision of continental liberation. A new sense of peoplehood must accompany those movements, if and when they arise again.[20]

III LO QUE HAY DETRÉS DE LO "HISPANIC" Y LO "LATINO" EN LOS ESTADOS UNIDOS

In the United States, as elsewhere, ethnic groups are studied ontologically, as objects essentially immutable in historic time, provoking endless discussions on whether they "are" something or the other, instead of looking at what they are becoming.

Currently, some assert that Chicanos and Puerto Ricans in the mainland United States are "Hispanics" or "Latinos," while others argue that they are two distinct "minorities" who just happen to speak the same "foreign" language. A better approach is historical sociology, which asks process-centered questions. How, why, and in what context, for instance, were these and the other U.S. ethnicities historically produced and reproduced? How and why have these ethnicities changed in time? What informs and contributes to their evolving sense of peoplehood, and how do their current experiences of oppression and their visions of liberation effect it? Are they converging into broader ethnicities and who supports and who resists this convergence, and why? I attempt a preliminary exploration of these questions below.

Long before the convergence of Chicanos and Puerto Ricans as Latinos, Euro-Americans, Indians, and Blacks converged separately but simultaneously as racial ethnicities. They were constituent parts of a brutal racial order disguised under the facade of a rational, modern society. In the United States, from the earliest colonial period, the northwestern Europeans erected a structure of ethnic stratification based on the same invented racial ethnicities-from-above that their Iberian cousins to the south used. But the U.S. social structure was much more rigid because it did not recognize the intermixing of the Europeans with the other "races," not even as *castas*—processes that, although unacknowledged, continued anyway on a fairly large scale. The Euro-Americans in the U.S. forged instead a "dual society" (Ringer, 1983) consisting, on the one hand, of a "People's Domain" under the full protection of the law and open to all European immigrants and their presumed "untainted" offspring, a democratic domain that functioned as the proverbial melting pot of "White Americans," and, on the other hand, of the extra-legal, socially-isolated domain of the "tainted others," the "inferior races."

In the mid-nineteenth century, inspired by the rapid ethnic amalgamation of a large number and variety of European workers in the United States, Marx and Engels wrote in their *Communist Manifesto* (1975: 56–57),

> The working men have no country. . . . National differences and antagonisms between peoples are daily more and more vanishing, owing to the development of the bourgeoisie, to freedom of commerce, to the world market, to uniformity in the mode of production and in the conditions of life corresponding thereto. The supremacy of the proletariat will cause them to vanish still faster.

A rosy internationalist prophesy, but, as they missed the whole picture, flawed: the voluntary Euro-American amalgamation process they observed in the U.S. corresponded to the coerced amalgamation of the vast diversity of non-Europeans cast as "inferior races." This dual process represented an immense social leap upwards for the huddled masses of peasants and workers initially brought to the New Republic from Europe as cheap labor pools. Once they shed their older ethnicities, the immigrants could henceforth claim White-skin privileges and superior status over all the *other*, non-White peoples, and even claim *their lands* if found within the expanding state boundaries of their newly adopted "nation-state."

Initially, the abolition of European indentured servitude corresponded to the establishment of African chattel slavery. Afterwards, the "only" adoption fee the European immigrants had to pay was that, before they were unleashed on the so-called "frontier" as settlers, they had to go through the proletarianization stage of working for wages in the East-coast manufacturing centers.[21] Given that the political economy of the new country was (outside the slave-master relation) based on the cash nexus, wage work was the only way the peasants from Europe could raise the needed cash to pay for transportation to the ever-receding Western frontier. They also had to pay for the militarily "cleared" homestead land, the high land taxes, food and supplies, etc. . . . Most Euro-American immigrants proved more than willing to gamble with wage labor for a while—they had little choice. Many did make it to the frontier to become farmers on lands still soaking with Indian blood, but many stayed entrapped in the East, adding sediment upon sediment of "free" labor to the burgeoning manufacturing urban centers. A few even made it as entrepreneurs, quickly learning to exploit the labor of subsequent immigrants.[22]

The trajectory of the "non-Europeans" was quite different. Chicanos and Puerto Ricans came into being as "U.S. oppressed nationalities" in 1836–1848 and 1898, respectively. Their processes of national and state formation were interrupted when they were territorially annexed as a result of predatory wars launched by the same expansionist core state.[23] Far from amalgamating with the Euro-Americans, they were considered "non-Europeans" in partial fallacy and, until recently, were excluded from the "American Creed" as were all other "mixed breeds."[24] The national and the racial elements thus coexisted from the very beginning in the social construction of these ethnicities. To complicate matters more, both peoples continued to be affected dramatically by immigration flows to and from their respective "homelands," something which resulted in being stereotyped and mistreated as purely "immigrants," despite many generations of U.S. residency. That is, the experience of xenophobia has also forged these ethnicities.

In the 1970s, as a result of this complicated history, Chicanos were said by some to constitute an "oppressed (or submerged) nation,"[25] or an "internal colony."[26] The Chicano people were deemed, from this point of view, to possess the right of national self determination, the right to scale from the current Anglo-dominated state and establish an independent new state.[27] Chicanos (and the Southwest) were seen by others as the "occupied portion" of a "divided nation" that ought to be re-united to Mexico.[28] Still others insisted that Chicanos merely "belonged" to the most oppressed stratum of the multinational U.S. working class, and whose main struggle, therefore, should be the class struggle, either in its reformist[29] or in its revolutionary variants.[30] Others, finally, maintained that Chicanos were an assimilating U.S. "ethnic minority," whose main struggles should center on their democratic civil rights as "American citizens;" it followed that their struggles should be channeled through the electoral process, and that their goal should be cultural self-determination—bilingualism, biculturalism—and socioeconomic opportunity. Equivalent positions existed for the Puerto Ricans.[31]

But these heated debates of the 1970s have been increasingly preempted in the 1980s by the widespread labeling of both groups as "Hispanic," and by treating them, as well as all other Spanish speakers in the U.S., as generic constituents of a single "ethnic minority." Besides being a complete falsification of history, the really important questions are: Is this current "Hispanization" of Chicanos and Puerto Ricans also a falsification of their present ethnic dynamics? If so, how long will it take this "falsification" to become a historical reality?

The Puerto Ricans began their great migration to New York after World War

II, only to be entrapped there as a cheap labor pool[32] at the same time that U.S. capital expanded to "offshore" facilities (including Puerto Rico itself). The War on Poverty, Great Society programs, affirmative action, and the civil rights legislation of the 1960s passed them by because they were recent arrivals and had no political clout.[33] Almost half of the Puerto Rican people left the island in the last four decades, and although they initially concentrated in New York, they eventually began to move to other states. By 1980, half of the two million Puerto Ricans in the mainland had dispersed to other states, away from New York (Moore and Pachon, 1985: 56–58). But their condition did not improve, and actually deteriorated from the bottom levels of the previous three decades. With the exception of the Native Americans, they are now the worst-off ethnic group in the U.S.[34] They have been hit hard by the macro-structural shifts of the economy, by the shrinking and segmented labor markets, and by other social structures of ethnic stratification. The contraction of the world economy of the 1970s and 1980s has prolonged the half-century baptism of fire the Puerto Ricans have endured in the mainland.

If Puerto Rico was one of the first offshore production sites for U.S. capital, northern Mexico became the close second. Since the 1960s, millions of Mexicanos have gone to work in the U.S.-owned border *maquiladoras* for ten times less than comparable Anglos working on the other side of the border, while millions of other Mexicanos keep working at worse wages for U.S. agrobusinesses, producing winter vegetables and canned foods for the U.S. market.[35] As Mexico began to feel the dislocations produced by a contracted world economy in the mid-1970s, yearly two-directional flows of millions of Mexicano undocumented workers across the border became commonplace, far exceeding the legal Mexicano immigration numbers (Sassen, 1988: 63). Over a million are deported every year,[36] so that the new long-term Mexican residents in the U.S. live, as Cockroft (1986) puts it, as "outlaws in the promised land."[37]

Given the still prevalent structural exclusion of most Chicanos from the primary sector of the economy, the large immigration waves, and the pattern of segregated barrios, the level of ethnic identification between Chicanos and Mexicanos continues to be extremely high in the border region, and only less as you move away from the border. Chicano-Mexicano identity and ethnicity is strong and dynamic, and because it is historically grounded, it will not disappear soon.[38] It will merely adapt, as it has for half a millennia, to the dehumanizing, uprooting, stratifying processes of the capitalist world-system.[39]

Just as with the Puerto Ricans, significant diffusion of Mexicanos and Chicanos extends throughout the United States. As both groups have migrated, they and other Spanish-speaking peoples have met and begun to live, work, and struggle together. Their common oppression is the historico-material basis for the militant *Latinismo* that has reappeared in the U.S. after a prolonged half-century dormancy.[40] The various groups developed an awareness from their grassroots political action of being *a Latin American people* equally but separately subjected to brutal national dismemberment, severe social dislocations, unrelenting racial discrimination, continuous cultural oppression, and widespread poverty and economic exploitation. They have begun to adopt an umbrella ethnicity, calling themselves *Latinos*, in Chicago, in San Francisco, in New York, in Washington, D.C., and elsewhere. This is a new ethnicity emerging from the bottom up.

Felix M. Padilla, the foremost student of Latino ethnicity in Chicago, reports

(1985) that Latino ethnicity is situational, mostly at the city level of politics; that it happily and easily coexists with the much more core national-origin ethnicities of the Puerto Ricans and the Chicanos; and that it springs from the leadership of the community organizations and anti-systemic movements of these peoples. This is a clear example of an emerging anti-systemic pan-ethnicity constructed from the bottom up by the locked-out peoples Anderson alluded to. And it is happening in the U.S. wherever Central Americans, Dominicans, Puerto Ricans, and other Latin American groups are suffering from the same persistent, structural conditions, discrimination, exploitation, and prejudice.

This new ethnicity is not merely reactive, it is creating an affirmative culture of great beauty and vision. Totti (1987), describes the accelerated rise of Latino culture in New York City (the music of Rubén Blades, the poetry of Laviera [1984]). Totti also notes the accelerated rate of Latino intermarriage, the stronger commitment to Spanish as the *lingua franca* of Latinismo (retaining English for "external" communication), and, most importantly, the increasingly stronger political alliance between Puerto Ricans and Dominicans. Padilla (n.d.) has demonstrated how Salsa music is clearly developing as a cultural expression of Latino cooperation and reality, and how the lyrical content of Salsa music is fostering and spreading the idea of Latino consciousness and unity. Politically, De la Garza (1988) reports the increasingly stronger electoral muscle of Latinos, citing 2,950 currently elected Latino officials in six selected states, including one governor, four state executives and 117 state legislators, half of whom are Chicanos. All of them meet regularly to hammer out the "Latino agenda."

What explains these phenomena in a larger context? What is happening to the United States as we approach the end of the century is that the "non-Europeans," the non-peoples of "American History," until recently denied by law—and still denied *de facto*—full and equal access to all the spheres of the "People's Domain," are turning around the old tactic of the melting pot, previously used by the Euro-Americans, and using it in their own way: they are voluntarily engaging in a partial amalgamation, one that does not "melt" or erase their historical diversity, but one more akin to a big *canasta de fruta*, full of many flavors and healthy to the body and soul, evoking Delgado's "yo sí tú también-ism." The Latin Americans in the United States are creating their *Latino* pan-ethnicity that way. But this is by no means an original invention. It is merely traversing the same path already traversed by the African-Americans, the Native-Americans, and the Asian-Americans. These are all equivalent pan-ethnicities.

In the last few years, the processes of the world economy have become so integrated that state boundaries have begun to dissolve. The "nation-states" are becoming more and more irrelevant and unable to cope with the globalization of everything, including productive activities, markets, environmental and economic crises, communications, culture, etc. The previous functions of the interstate system are being rapidly transferred to a vastly transnationalized and oligopolized inter-enterprise system.[41] As Polanyi (1957) prophesied, the institutions of the self-regulated market are imposing on society the commodification, bureaucratization, and depolitization of all aspect of social life, endangering in the process "human life and its surroundings." The market mentality is supplanting the highly imperfect ideologies of popular democracy and state sovereignty with the new emphasis on efficiency, unlimited consumption, and absolute managerial power. The private is swallowing the public in front of our very eyes and on a global scale. It is, therefore, not strange that ethnicities begin to be conceived, prefabricated, and marketed in federal bureaus and ad agencies.

In the core of the world-system, ethnicity is becoming internationalized as well. The European Common Market countries will practically fuse, finally, in 1992. The Pacific Rim region, the new axis of the world economy, is generating an extra-national entity encompassing China, Japan, Korea, and others. An "identity" is bound to follow. The United States is beginning to promote the idea of a North American Common Market made up of itself, Canada, and Mexico. The Canadians have already become, for all practical purposes, fully incorporated, preempting the divisive English-French internal tensions. The Mexican economy has become incorporated for the most part already, but Mexicano immigrants have not yet gained free access to the U.S. labor market, quite the contrary, nor has the Mexican Government dared to publicly endorse the U.S. plan. But a merger is not even necessary for Latino ethnicity to spread. According to Sassen (1989), New York City and Los Angeles have become "world cities." They are "nodes of control and management of the global economic system." Latinos make up vast pools of cheap labor there, locked in a downward spiral as the two cities prosper. Who can still argue that the deteriorating condition of Latinos in the U.S. is a purely domestic issue, with purely domestic causes and effects?

Where is this leading? Will it dissolve in time? Will the "dual society" persist along its traditional European/non-European line of cleavage? Assuming sharp ethnic stratification continues in the U.S., will Latinos seek broader alliances with Indians and African-Americans to effectively defend themselves from their common, persistent oppression? And in doing so, will Latinos recover their own true ancestral roots, Chicanos recover their Indian roots and Caribeños their African roots? Is it hard to imagine Latino ethnicity eventually linking up with the other non-European ethnicities in the U.S., giving rise to a *People of Color pan-ethnicity*? Can the hierarchical structures of ethnic stratification in the United States only be metamorphosed in *this* way and by *these* peoples? Isn't this the *real* class struggle, at the broadest level, in the United States? What about the Latinos in Latin America? Indeed, they nurture the U.S. Latinos with immigrants and with their deepening *latinoamericanismo*. Could it be that, eventually, the U.S. Latinos and the Latin Americans will meet on a new plane, the plane of a new historic vision? Will it prove necessary to have unity of consciousness and of action in this entire hemisphere, as well as in the other continents, to finally overcome the immanent class and ethnic stratifications of the modern world-system?

Such metamorphoses will only happen as a result of struggle with power, ideological and physical, as Frederick Douglass foresaw. The infant ground-up pan-ethnicities are *already* engaged in a deep struggle for life against the ideologies promoted from above by the media outlets, state bureaucracies, and other elites of all types and colors. Witness the hemispheric resurgence of the most fanatic Christian obscurantism (the fundamentalist evangelicals), the resurgence in national chauvinism (*patrioterismo*), reckless militarism, hedonism, and consumerism. On top of all that, the anti-systemic pan-ethnicities have to contend as well with the parallel, *pro systemic* ethnicities manufactured from the top down to *define* us ahistorically, to *channel* us back to our place, to *co-opt* us. In the case of the Chicanos, Puerto Ricans, and other U.S. Latinos, I am referring, of course, to the pre-fabricated pan-ethnicity of the *Hispanic*.

Martha Giménez (1989) has exposed what is behind this state-sponsored label for our peoples: it originated as a statistical construct hatched in the federal bureaucracy for the initial specific purpose of using it in the 1980 U.S. census, but with profound long-term political implications.[42] Among other things, the Hispanic label includes all Spaniards—never oppressed in the New World—as well as all members of the (mostly Euro-American) elites of Latin America that happen to migrate to the U.S. every time there has been the slightest popular unrest among "their" historically dispossessed masses (i.e., their vast "minorities," in the North American sense).[43] Now these elites are welcomed to the U.S. as a "protected class," eligible to receive affirmative action benefits. And all this generosity towards the privileged occurred at the same time that the U.S. systematically denied entry to masses of Central American refugees victimized by the U.S. war of counterinsurgency there, the very people who ought to qualify for U.S. aid.

As Margarita Melville (1988: 78–79) put it, referring to the "Hispanics" that have come to the U.S. from Batista's Cuba and Somoza's Nicaragua:

> The people who have *remained* in Cuba and Nicaragua have *more in common* with Mexican Americans and Puerto Ricans than with other Latin Americans, in terms of their ethnicity and self-perception vis-à-vis Anglo Americans. . . . Exiles from Cuba and Nicaragua and upper-class Central Americans tend to participate in competitive ethnicity in the United States. On the other hand, refugees from El Salvador and Guatemala are escaping persecution of landed elites, and their ethnic interface is one of colonial ethnicity [my emphasis].

These Latin American elites *have never ceased to be*, for the most part, ethnically and politically indistinguishable from their Euro-American relatives in the United States. Furthermore, as Giménez (1989) points out, Hispanic ethnicity covers up (and promotes) the long-standing Latin American "brain drain" of qualified Latin American professionals, whose employment is routinely used to pad affirmative action figures in the U.S. at the expense of the historically oppressed U.S. ethnic groups. Add the bonus of getting "instant" professionals and other highly educated adults paid for by their country of origin. This practice resembles the old colonial racket of Indian land "traded" with the European immigrants for their wage labor without informing the Indians. Except this time, both the Euro-American workers and the real "minorities" are left out of the deal. That is not customary in the U.S. racial order, and the Euro-Americans are bound to react strongly against the whole theory and practice of "race-specific" programs and entitlements, non-European immigration, affirmative action, etc.[44] The White backlash has begun, and racial tensions are bound to increase.

Finally, of course, the label hispanic is meant to gloss over, dilute, and suppress the much stronger national ethnicities of Chicanos and Puerto Ricans. It obfuscates the historic roots of their condition as oppressed people, and it conflates the cultural diversity of these groups into an amorphous mass. Hispanicization reduces the sense of heritage to only the Spanish in our cultures at the expense of the other roots, thereby promoting a brittle, shallow, commercialized, malleable identity.

We will not remain the same. Either we *re-make ourselves or we will be re-made by others*. Ethnicity is not a static attribute; it is a contending arena of dynamic social relations that "crystallize" in an identity, a sense of peoplehood. The "internal" battle is not between the Latino, Chicano, and Puerto Rican ethnicities, for they are essentially anti-systemic, complementary, mutually-reinforcing ethnicities *a la Lalo Delgado*. At most they merely manifest dynamic tension. The fight to the death is between the "Hispanic" ethnicity from the top down, on the one side, and Latino, Chicano, and Puerto Rican ethnicities from the bottom up, on the other. Our sense of peoplehood is at stake.

The class and ethnic struggles of these decades have been, in part, a struggle between names and their sponsors. The names contain either the seeds of liberation or the seeds of alienation. Which side our intellectuals take now on this question will be crucial to the next stage mobilization. *¿Como nos vamos a mover?* The Latino artists already took sides, precursors of social change as artists usually are, and much more so than our social scientists. They are not waiting for others but are helping to forge the new Latino culture, with their ear close to the people. The community leaders tend to be divided on this question depending how close to the ground and how far away from Washington they are. The academic intellectuals, including the students, have shown to be more confused, more vulnerable to the siren song of "Hispanic opportunity" or, in the opposite direction, to the attractive myths of immutable ethnicity (ultra-recontra-super-Chicanismo); but they are also much more exposed to "Latinization" as they combat racism in higher education, as they protest U.S. policy in Latin America, as they meet the refugees.

Who we are and what we become is, in fact, a central issue of not only our peoples, but of all humanity. It is an issue intimately tied to the nature and dynamics of the five-century-old social system that has engulfed us all. Ultimately, the commodification of everything has to stop somewhere and the socialization of everything begin anew. The resurgence of all forms of ethnicity in the world economy is just one more self-protecting mechanism of societies stripped much too much of their social purposes, which is life itself, not profit. Ultimately, the endless accumulation of capital is not life-sustaining. One or the other will have to go. In that struggle, we will have to re-invent ourselves over and over again. Today Latino, tomorrow RUNAFRIBES, perhaps in time *comunidad mundial*.

NOTES

1. Roughly five hundred indigenous environmentally specialized, actively trading, differentiated peoples ("tribes") apparently coexisted in this way in California in the last one thousand years before the European expansion into the New World, (Coe, 1986: 79–81). Many more examples from ancient history can be found in Wenke (1984).

2. Modern nationalism, the most "modern" of ethnicities, has its genesis in *intra*-European rivalries, but the inventing (and imposing) of modern racial ethnicities occurred mostly outside Europe, usually initiated by the European upper classes, but not always. Bonacich (1972) convincingly argues that in the case of non-European immigrants to the U.S.,

the subordinated European classes and their descendants initiated antagonistic ethnic stratification processes against the non-European, *against* the wishes of "their" capitalists who were always hungry for cheap labor. The faith line between "top" and "down" groups, therefore, shifts in historic time and space, but has generally tended to be defined, until very recently, on a world-system scale, by the dichotomy "European/Non-European" much more than by social class. The same may be said of the United States, although not of Europe, where the reverse is true. See Wilson (1980) for the classic argument of "the declining significance of race" in the recent period of U.S. history.

3. Wallerstein (1974: 38, 87) asserts that the specific mode of labor control called wage-work, per se, is not what defines capitalism, but production for the endless accumulation of capital, and that historical capitalism required the simultaneous "development of variegated methods of labor control for different products and different zones of the world-economy. [e.g., slavery, serfdom, tenancy, peonage, yeoman farming, wage-work, etc.] . . . A moment's thought will reveal that these occupational categories were *not randomly* distributed either geographically or *ethnically* within the burgeoning world-economy" [my emphasis].

The opposite point of view (the so-called "mode-of-production" school) reduces the domain of capitalism to the areas where the capital-wage relation predominates, and hence, locates its historical origins in late-eighteenth-/early-nineteenth-century class-stratified Northwestern Europe. It therefore cannot avoid completely missing from its field of vision the large-scale, well-articulated structures of *capitalist* ethnic stratification the *same* European elites built outside the region for centuries as part of the division of Labor of a single world-economy. This is, in my opinion, the cardinal error that accounts for the many flawed Marxist analyses of nation, race, and ethnicity.

4. Noel (1968: 170), quoting Shibutani and Kwan (1965: 202, 212), describes the process of consciousness-formation among newly created subordinated ethnic groups: "Consciousness of shared fate is essential to effective unified action but it generally develops only gradually as the members of a particular social category realize that they are being treated alike despite their differences. 'People who find themselves set apart eventually come to recognize their common interests,' but for those who share a subordinate position common identification usually emerges only after 'repeated experiences of denial and humiliation.'"

5. The pro-systemic social sciences tend to treat all non-dominant ethnicities as "aberrant," "irrational" phenomena, or as stubborn remnants of "traditional society" doomed to disappear as capitalism breaks down all barriers. Dominant ethnicities (e.g., "Anglo-Saxon Culture"), on the other hand, are idealized as virtuous and modern, glorified as the true standard of peoplehood under "enlightened capitalism." Other scholars examine ethnicity completely abstracted from the historical social system it is embedded in, focusing instead on the individual, on genetics, or on "human nature." For a thorough critique see Geschwender (1978) and Santos (1989).

6. Eric Hobshawn (1977: 13) noted over a decade ago that the "Marxist movements and states have tended to become national not only in form but in substance." The post-Marxist democratic movements and states that burst on the world stage in 1989 have the same ethnic character, but, as Helene D'encausse (1988) predicted long ago, with a vengeance: old fending sub-nationalisms have resurfaced and are now rampant in Eastern Europe and the U.S.S.R. Today the partydocratic socialist societies are caught by surprise by the resilience and double-blade nature of ethnicity. Tomorrow it will be globalizing capitalism's turn.

7. In the Summer of 1989, 120,000 Japanese and 290 representatives from grass-roots movements from 33 countries met in Japan in a series of 16 international conferences and festivals, all under the theme of "People's Plan for the 21st Century" [PP-21]. At the end of it, participants met, drafted, and approved the Minimata Declaration. See PP-21 (1989).

8. The modern states did not appear or develop in isolation from each other, but, from the beginning of their territorial and political incorporation to the modern world-system, have

belonged to a geo-political system that is itself vertically stratified, namely, the interstate system of core, semi-peripheral, and peripheral states. For how the "cycles" of the interstate system relate to the "cycles" of the interenterprise system, see Arrighi (1986), Bousquet (1980), and Bergesen (1980).

9. For an in depth study of these structures in the colonial New World, and an explanation of the remarkable differences in the treatment of the indigenous peoples of North America and Spanish America, see Santos (1988a).

10. The Portuguese denoted the wide variety of indigenous peoples they found (and sought to enslave) in Brazil as *Negro du terra*, to distinguish them from the other (African) enslaved peoples brought to the *same* sugar plantations in Brazil. See Lockhart and Schwartz (1983: 198).

11. In the course of less than a century of Spanish rule, an estimated ninety-five percent of the indigenous population in the conquered areas disappeared, through slaughter, slave labor, or epidemics (Sánchez-Albornoz, 1974, 32–37).

12. See Thompson (1987) for the entire New World, and Beltrín (1972, 1985) for colonial and contemporary Mexico.

13. See Rodney (1974), Murphy (1972), and Babu (1981).

14. For an in-depth critique of the myth of Brazilian "racial democracy," see Fernandes (1969). See Mörner (1967, 1979) and Harris (1964) for Latin America as a whole. For the genocide of the Amazonian peoples see Bodard (1971), and for the ethnic conflict in contemporary Peru see Quijano (1980).

15. Just as with Indian-ness, African-ness and White-ness are much more a socio-cultural phenomenon than a racial one in Latin America, with dramatic shifts in the "boundaries" from place to place. Be that as it may, Martner et. al. (1986: 141) project that by the year 2000, the total anticipated population of 535 million Latin Americans will be made up of 28 million Indians, 64 million Blacks, 176 million Whites, and 267 million Mestizos. But Tannenbaum (1947: 8) noted long ago: "The identification of the mulatto as white, and the tendency to speak of the Negro as being whitened out in Brazil, make most contemporary statements misleading." In the same vein Ribeiro (1982: 10) states: "[T]hose of us considered 'White' Latin Americans are actually *Mestizos* with more indigenous blood than European." This means that a significant fraction of the 176 million "Whites" are "whitened" Mestizos and Mullatos.

16. Cardoso & Faletto (1972) and Jenkins (1987).

17. Not to mention "modern ecocide." See Evans (1979) for the disastrous impact the alliance of the multinational corporations, the repressive state, and local oligarchy have had on Brazil.

18. For a poignant exposé of sham democracy in Latin America in the 1980's, see Petras et al. (1986).

19. There are a number of reasons why I chose this particular indigenous word: the Andean world produced, perhaps, the most advanced civilizational system in the Pre-Colombian New World (Keatinge, 1988), certainly the largest, geographically. Quechua was then and is now the *lingua franca* of that region. Perhaps the Andean world produced, as Quijano (1988) claims, not just a profoundly appealing way of life in the past, but still contains a vital but unrecovered vision of the future as well, with its large-scale reciprocity, its sense of time, and its sense of joy in collective solidarity. The world is the indigenous Andean peoples' word for collective self-identification *still* used today, a self-name untouched by any European influence. Furthermore, the fully-deserved, notorious reputation of chauvinism we Mexicanos have in Latin America convinced me to look outside Mesoamerica for a word to substitute for "Indian." Finally, the word *RUNA* happily ends with an "a," allowing me to place the African root next, leaving the European root appropriately, to the end.

20. This emphasis on names is hardly irrelevant or frivolous. It may be instructive to follow the phonological and orthographic battles the Chinese waged along with their other bat-

tles. In the mid-nineteenth century, the opening of China to the Western World led to the *brazen corruption* of Chinese names and sounds to fit *European* tastes, in tandem with the total subjugation and practical dismemberment of the country itself by European imperialism. In the early 1970s and in a matter of months after the Chinese, now a world power, re-opened their country to the West, they demanded the Western would to adopt *their* orthography and phonology for all Chinese names. "Peking," for example, was to be spelled "Beijing" thereafter. The Western countries quickly complied, despite longstanding usage of the previous terms. Perhaps the difference in treatment was due to the fact that by the second time around China had recovered its sovereignty and had accumulated 30 years of national construction and ethnic self-respect. Notice how now that the Chinese are having serious internal problems, "Peking" has begun to reappear in the Western print media.

21. The Euro-American capitalists learned to use the frontier as a "carrot" to attract labor, as an essential two-stage mechanism in the corification of the United States. Artificial barriers were erected to force the poor immigrants to work for a wage for a medium term period in the east coast productive sites. Without these barriers the capitalists would not have been able to exploit immigrants in the factories and plantations for long, defeating the whole idea of using immigration as a source of labor. See Marx (1967: 766) for the famous example of the Australian planter who "lost" all "his" workers to the frontier for lack of such barriers.

22. Some immigrants, like the Swedish, had the resources to "skip" the first stage and go directly to the West. Others, like the Irish, were deliberately sent to the frontier to serve as a buffer between the Indians and the English settlements. See Ringer (1983), Nash (1982), Morgan (1975), Pearce (1988), Jennings (1976), Axtell (1985), Jordan (1968), Berkhofer (1978), and Santos (1988a).

23. For the study of Chicano and Latino ethnicities, see Padilla (1985), Keefe and Padilla (1987), and Mirandé (1985). For Puerto Ricans in the mainland U.S., see Rodriguez (1989). The Cuban and Central American cases are not discussed in this paper. See Santos (1986) for an explanation of what made the new North American republic succeed in attaining core status, while the other new republics of the rest of the hemisphere were increasingly peripheralized.

24. When half of Mexico's territory was forcibly annexed by the U.S. in 1836–1848, and Puerto Rico was swallowed in 1898, the rigid structures of ethnic stratification enforced by the Euro-Americans in the United States were as rigid as ever. The flood of the mid-century gold rush precipitated the last great westward expansion of the "frontier." The U.S. had gained core status and was now deeply contending for hegemony with Britain in the Pacific and in the New World. But the New Republic was a cauldron of racial antagonisms, leading to the Civil War, and, as the frontier vanished, to violent class-struggles between the increasingly proletarianized Euro-Americans and their Euro-American capitalists. The two processes were not unrelated. See Bonacich (1972) and Wilson (1980).

25. See League of Revolutionary Struggle (1979), and its predecessor, August Twenty-Ninth Movement (1976).

26. See Almaguér (1971; 1975), Barrera (1972; 1979), and Flores (1973). For a good critique of Chicano internal colonialism, see Almaguér himself (1976).

27. A variant is to claim Chicanos should struggle for "regional autonomy" in a socialist United States. See October League (1975).

28. For a working-class version of the divided-nation thesis, see C.A.S.A. (1976).

29. This has been a consistent position of the Communist Party (USA). See their pamphlet, (circa early 1970s).

30. A good example, which although focused on the African-American case is meant to include all other nationalities in the U.S., is in Revolutionary Communist Party (1977).

31. Cf. Puerto Rican Socialist Party (1975). Resistencia Puertorriqueña (1973). Corretjer (1977). Committee in Solidarity with Puerto Rican Independence et al. (1979). Taller de Formación Politica (1982).

32. See Bonilla and Campos (1982), Campos and Bonilla (1982), and Bonilla (1985).

33. Arrighi (1984) claims that during the New Deal Era the workers employed in the primary sector of the economy acquired immense "workplace bargaining power," or WBP, due to the generalization of "Fordism." This power consisted mainly of the ability to sabotage the expensive and complex machinery and to drastically reduce the "throughput production quotas" of the modern production processes without having to resort to class organization. The Euro-American male workers, who traditionally held the primary-sector jobs, used their power to secure high wages and benefits and to exclude women and non-Euro-American workers from this sector. This reinforced the pronounced ethnic and gender stratification in the United States. After World War Two, to counteract the workers' WBP, the U.S. capitalists began to transnationalize their investments and production activities "offshore" on a global scale. They also coopted the unions by using union contracts to contain wildcat activity and guarantee stability. The result was that in the last two decades, as millions of jobs were exported abroad to cheap Third World labor markets, the situation of the Euro-American workers deteriorated. Nevertheless, a disproportionate amount of the women and people of color in the U.S. have remained in the lower lungs of the segmented labor market, unorganized or locked-out of employment altogether. The now-defunct New Deal "social contract" never uplifted them.

34. Median family income in 1986 for Puerto Ricans was $14,584, as compared to $19,995 for Chicanos and $30,231 for "non-Hispanics" (Schwartz, 1988). See also Moore and Pachon (1985), and Borjas and Tienda (1985).

35. See Fernández (1977) and Burbach and Flynn (1980).

36. Moore and Pachon (1985: 55) report 4.5 million Mexicanos were deported in the five-year period 1976–1980, and in the eighties the yearly rate of deportation has stayed over a million every year.

37. The population of Chicanos and Mexicanos in the United States doubled in the 1970s and by 1987 there were 12 million more in the United States (from just 3.5 million in 1960) (Schwartz, 1988).

38. Arce (1981: 188) states: "Chicano identity continues to be predominantly Mexican, in spite of national government, media, and academic infatuations with labels such as 'Chicano,' 'Hispanic,' and 'Spanish-speaker.'"

39. See Santos (1988b).

40. Exactly 51 years ago, the Guatemalan revolutionary and labor organizer Luisa Moreno, led the Puertorriqueñíos from Harlem, the Cubanos from Tampa, the Mexicanos from the Southwest, and many others, into forming a class-conscious, militant, *Congreso de los Pueblos de Hablo Español,* the precursor of today's national latino organizations and coalitions. See Camarillo (1987) and Acuña (1988: 235–239).

41. These world enterprises are evermore immune to the dictates of any single state, they internalize ever larger commodity, financial, and labor markets previously open to competition, and they are aggressively pursuing the further internationalization of all production processes.

42. See Choldin (1986), for a revealing account of the actual process of re-designing the Latino count for 1980. In it, Choldin proudly acknowledges the "co-optation" goal that the federal agencies sought to achieve by involving the militant Latino organizations in the design process, conceding the political nature of the enterprise.

43. The term "minority," as used in the United States, makes "minorities" of the Black South Africans, or Black Brazilians, or Indian Bolivians, or Indian Guatemalans, all vast numerical majorities in their countries. It is another sham promoted by the real minority of the world-system: the European rulers and accumulators.

44. For a racist call for the large-scale importation of trained European "instant adults" and the closing of Asian and Latino immigration, see Wattenberg (1989).

REFERENCES

Acuña, Rodolfo. 1988. *Occupied America, A History of Chicanos*, 3rd ed., Cambridge: Harper & Row.

Aguirre Beltrín, Gonzalo. 1972. *La Población Negre de México: México* Fondo de Cultura Económica. 1985. *Cuijla*. México: Fondo de Cultura Económica, Cultura sep.

Almaguér, Tom's. 1971. "Toward the Study of Chicano Colonialism," *Aztldn* II, 1, Spr. 1971, 7–21.

———. 1975, "Class, Race, and Chicano Oppression," *Socialist Revolution*, V 25, July–Sept. 1975, 71–99.

———. 1976. "Beyond Internal Colonialism: Some Theoretical and Political Queries," paper read at the Fourth Annual Meeting of the National Association of Chicano Social Scientists, El Paso, Texas, Apr. 1976.

Anderson, Benedict, 1983. *Imagined Communities, Reflections on the Origin and Spread of Nationalism*. New York: Verso.

Arce, Carlos H., 1981. "A Reconsideration of Chicano Culture and Identity," in *Daedalus*, Spring 1981: 177–191.

Arrighi, Giovanni, 1986. "Custom, Innovation and Competition: Long Waves and Stages of Capitalist Development." Paper presented at the international workshop "Technological and Social Factors in Long Term Fluctuations," Certosa di Pontignano, Siena, Italy, Dec. 15–17, 1986.

Arrighi, Giovanni and Beverly J. Silver, 1984. "Labor Movements and Capital Migration: The United States and Western Europe in World-historical Perspective," in Charles Bergquist, ed., *Labor in the Capitalist World Economy*. Beverly Hills: Sage.

August Twenty-Ninth Movement (Marxist-Leninist), 1976. *Fan the Flames, A Revolutionary Position on the Chicano National Question*. Pamphlet, Los Angeles.

Axtell, James, 1985. *The Invasion Within, The Conquest of Cultures in Colonial North America*. New York: Oxford University Press.

Babu, A.M., 1981. *African Socialism and Socialist Africa*. London: Zed Press.

Barrera, Mario, 1979. *Race and Class in the Southwest, A Theory of Racial Inequality*. Notre Dame: University of Notre Dame Press.

Barrera, Mario, Carlos Muñoz, & Carlos Ornelas, 1972. "The Barrio as Internal Colony," in Harlan Hahn, ed., *Urban Affairs Annual Review IV: Urban Politics and People*. 1972, 465–498.

Bergesen, Albert, 1980. "Cycles of Formal Colonial Rule," in Hopkins, T. K. & Wallerstein, I., eds., *Processes of the World System*. Beverly Hills: Sage.

Berkhofer, Robert F., Jr., 1978. *The White Man's Indian, Images of the American Indian from Columbus to the Present*. New York: Alfred A. Knopf.

Bonacich, Edna, 1972. "A Theory of Ethnic Antagonism: The Split Labor Market," *American Sociological Review*, 37 (October): 547–559.

Bonilla, Frank, 1985. "Ethnic Orbits: The Circulation of Capitals and Peoples," in *Contemporary Marxism*, 10. 1985: 148–165.

Bonilla, Frank and Ricardo Campos, 1982. "Imperialist Initiatives and the Puerto Rican Worker: From Foraker to Reagan," in *Contemporary Marxism*, 3. 1982: 5–17.

Borjas, George J., and Marta Tienda, eds. 1985. *Hispanics in the U.S. Economy*. Orlando: Academic Press, Inc.

Bousquet, Nicole, 1980. "From Hegemony to Competition: Cycles of the Core?", in Hopkins, T. K. & Wallerstein, I., eds., *Processes of the World System*. Beverly Hills: Sage.

Burbach, Roger and Patricia Flynn, 1980. *Agribusiness in the Americas*. New York: Monthly Review Press & NACLA.

Camarillo, Albert, 1987. "Mexicans in American Cities: The Social and Political Adaptation of Mexican Americans, 1900–1940." Paper presented at the annual meeting of the Organization of American Historians, April 1987.

Campos, Ricardo and Frank Bonilla, 1982. "Bootstraps and Enterprise Zones: The Underside of Late Capitalism in Puerto Rico and the United States," in *Review*, V, 4, Spring 1982: 556–590.

Cardoso, Fernando H. and Enzo Faletto, 1972. *Dependencia y Desarrollo en América Latina*. México: Siglo XXI Editores.

C.A.S.A., General Brotherhood of Workers, 1976. *Salute to the National Chicano Forum*. Pamphlet distributed at the National Chicano Forum, Salt Lake City, Utah, May 27–30, 1976.

Choldin, Harvey M. 1986. "Statistics and Politics: The 'Hispanic Issue' in the 1980 Census," in *Demography*, 23, 3, August 1986: 403–418.

Cockroft, James D. 1986. *Outlaws in the Promised Land, Mexican Immigrant Workers and America's Future*. New York: Grove Press, Inc.

Coe, Michael, Dean Snow and Elizabeth Benson, 1986. *Atlas of Ancient America*. New York: Facts on File Publications.

Committee in Solidarity with Puerto Rican Independence, et al. 1979. *Toward People's War for Independence and Socialism in Puerto Rico: In Defense of Armed Struggle*. Pamphlet.

Communist Party (USA), circa early 1970s. *Toward Chicano Liberation*.

Corretjer, Juan Antonio, 1977. *La Lucha Por La Independencia De Puerto Rico*, quinta ed. Guaynabo, Puerto Rico: no pub.

D'encausse, Helene Carrere, 1988. *Islam and the Russian Empire: Reform and Revolution in Central Asia*. Berkeley: University of California Press. [Originally *L'Empire Eclaté: La révolte des nations en U.R.S.S.*, 1978.]

De la Garza, Rodolfo O., 1988. "Latinos and State Government: Toward a Shared Agenda," in *Journal of State Government*, 61, March-April 1988: 77–80.

Delgado, Abelardo, 1978. *Under the Skirt of Lady Justice*. Denver: Barrio Publications.

Evans, Peter, 1979. *Dependent Development. The Alliance of Multinational, State and Local Capital in Brazil*. Princeton: Princeton University Press.

Fernandes, Florestan, 1969. *The Negro in Brazilian Society*. New York: Columbia University Press.

Fernández, Raúl A. 1977. *The United States-Mexico Border, A Politico-Economic Profile*. Notre Dame: University of Notre Dame Press.

Flores, Guillermo, 1973. "Race and Culture in the Internal Colony: Keeping the Chicano in His Place", in Frank Bonilla and Robert Girling, eds., *Structures of Dependency*. Palo Alto: Nairobi Press, 1973, 189–223.

Geschwender, James A. 1978. *Racial Stratification in America*. Dubuque, Iowa: Wm. C. Brown Co. Publishers.

Giménez, Martha E. 1989. "The Political Construction of 'Hispanics,' Statistical Politics in the 1980s," in Mary Romero and Cordelia Candelaria, eds. - *Estudios Chicanos and the Politics of Community*. Colorado Springs: National Association of Chicano Studies, 66–85.

Harris, Marvin, 1964. *Pattern of Race in the Americas*. New York: Walker & Co.

Hobshawn, Eric, 1977. "Some Reflections on 'The Breakup of Britain,'" *New Left Review*, 105 (September-October 1977) 13.

Jenkins, Rhys, 1987. "The Internationalization of Capital," in Eduardo P. Archetti, Paul Cammack and Bryan Roberts, eds., *Latin America, The Sociology of Developing Societies*. New York: Monthly Review Press.

Jennings, Francis, 1976. *The Invasion of America: Indians, Colonialism, and the Cant of Conquest*. New York: W. W. Norton.

Jordan, Winthrop D. 1968. *White Over Black, American Attitudes Toward the Negro, 1550–1812*. Chapel Hill: The University of North Carolina Press.

Keefe, Susan E., and Amado M. Padilla, 1987. *Chicano Ethnicity*. Albuquerque: University of New Mexico Press.

Laviera, Tato, 1984. *American Folklore*. n.p.: Arte Público.

League of Revolutionary Struggle (M-L), 1979. "The Struggle for Chicano Liberation," in *Forward*, No. 2, August 1979.

Lockhart, James and Stuart B. Schwartz, 1983. *Early Latin America: A History of Colonial Spanish America and Brazil*. Cambridge: Cambridge University Press.

Martner, Gonzalo, et. al. 1986. *América Latina Hacia el 2000. Opciones y Estrategias*. Caracas: Editorial Nueva Sociedad.

Marx, Karl, 1967. *Capital*, 3 vols., New York: International Publishers.

Marx, Karl and Frederick Engels, 1975. *Manifesto of the Communist Party*. Peking: Foreign Language Press.

Melville, Margarita B., 1988. "Hispanics: Race, Class, or Ethnicity?", in *The Journal of Ethnic Studies*, 16, 1, Spring 1988: 67–83.

Mirandé, Alfredo, 1985. *The Chicano Experience. An Alternative Perspective*. Notre Dame: University of Notre Dame Press.

Moore, Joan and Harry Pachon, 1985. *Hispanics in the United States*. Englewood Cliffs: Prentice-Hall.

Morgan, Edmund S., 1975. *America Slavery, American Freedom: The Ordeal of Colonial Virginia*. New York: W. W. Norton.

Mörner, Magnus, 1967. *Race Mixture in the History of Latin America*. Boston: Little, Brown & Co. 1970. *Race and Class in Latin America*. New York: Columbia University

Murphy, E. F. Jefferson, 1972. *History of African Civilization*.

Noel, Donald, 1968. "A Theory of the Origin of Ethnic Stratification," *Social Problems*, 16, Fall 1968, pp. 157–172.

October League (Marxist-Leninist), 1975. "Chicano Liberation, Resolution of OL's Third Congress," in *Class Struggle*, No. 2, Summer, 1975.

Padilla, Felix M. 1985. *Latino Ethnic Consciousness, The Case of Mexican Americans and Puerto Ricans in Chicago*. Notre Dame: University of Notre Dame Press.

———. n.d. "Salsa Music as a Cultural Expression of Latino Consciousness and Unity." Unpublished manuscript.

Pearce, Roy Harvey, 1988. *Savagism and Civilization: A Study of the Indian and the American Mind*. Berkeley: University of California Press.

Petras, James F., et al. 1986. *Latin America: Bankers, Generals, and the Struggle for Social Justice*. Totowa, N.J.: Rowman & Littlefield.

Polanyi, Karl, 1957. *The Great Transformation*. Beacon Hill: Beacon Press.

PP-21, 1989. "The Minamata Declaration." *AMPO, Japan-Asia Quarterly Review*, Vol. 21, Nos. 2–3, 1989: 6–9.

Puerto Rican Socialist Party, 1975. *Political Thesis of the Puerto Rican Socialist Party, The Socialist Alternative*. New York: North American Congress on Latin America.

Quijano, Aníbal, 1980. *Dominación y Cultura: Lo Cholo y el Conflicto Cultural en el Perú*. Lima: Mosca Azul Editores.

———. 1988. *Modernidad, Identidad y Utopía en América Latina*. Lima: Mosca Azul Editores.

Resistencia Puertorriqueña, 1973. *The Puerto Rican National Question*. Pamphlet.

Revolutionary Communist Party, USA. 1977. "Living Socialism and Dead Dogmatism, The Proletarian Line and the Struggle Against Opportunism on the National Question in the U.S.," in *The Communist*, Vol. 1, No. 2, May 1, 1977: 110–166.

Ribeiro, Darcy, 1982. "La Nación Latinoamericana." *Nueva Sociedad*, Septiembre/Octobre 1982: 5–23.

Ringer, Benjamin B. 1983. "*We the People*" *and Others: Duality and America's Treatment of Its Racial Minorities*. New York: Tavistock Publications.

Rodney, Walter, 1974. *How Europe Underdeveloped Africa*. Washington, D.C.: Howard University Press.

Rodríguez, Clara E. 1989. *Puerto Ricans Born in the U.S.A.*. Boston: Unwin Hyman.

Sánchez-Albornoz, Nicolís, 1974. *The Population of Latin America: A History*. Berkeley: University of California Press.

Santos, Gonzalo F. 1986. "The Early Foundations of the U.S. Model of Accumulation." Unpublished manuscript.

———. 1988a. "Why were the North American Indians not Enslaved? Ethnoracial Stratification and Coerced Labor Forms in the Colonial New World." Paper presented at the XIV International Congress of the Latin American Studies Association, March 17–19, 1988, New Orleans.

———. 1988b. "The Historic Roots of the Chicano People: The Southwest Before the Anglo-American Onslaught." Unpublished Manuscript.

———. 1989. "Ethnicity and the World-System. The Historical Construction of Peoplehood." Unpublished Manuscript.

Sassen, Saskia. 1988. *The Mobility of Labor and Capital*. Cambridge: Cambridge University Press.

Schell, Jonathan. 1982. *The Fate of the Earth*. New York: Avon Books.

Schwartz, Joe. 1988. "Hispanics in the Eighties," in *American Demographics*, January 1988: 43–45.

Shibutani, Tamostu and Kian Kwan. 1965. *Ethnic Stratification: A Comparative Approach*, New York: Macmillan.

Taller de Formación Politica. 1982. *La Cuestión Nacional, El Partido Nacionalista y el movimento obrero puertorriqueño. Río Piedras, Puerto Rico: Ediciones Huracán*.

Tannenbaum, Frank, 1947. *Slave and Citizen: The Negro in the Americas*. New York: Vintage Books.

Thompson, Vincent Bakpetu. 1987. *The Making of the African Diaspora in the Americas 1441–1900*. New York: Longman.

Todorov, Tzvetan. 1985. *The Conquest of America, The Question of the Other*. New York: Harper & Row.

Totti, Xavier. 1987. "The Making of a Latino Ethnic Identity," in *Dissent*. Fall 1987: 537–542.

Wallerstein, Immanuel. 1974. *The Modern World-System I, Capitalist Agriculture and the Origins of the European World-Economy in the Sixteenth Century*. New York: Harcourt Brace-Jovanovich.

———. 1983. *Historical Capitalism*. London: Verso.

Wattenberg, Ben J. 1989. "The Case for More Immigrants," in *U.S. News and World Report*, Feb. 13, 1989.

Wenke, Robert J. 1984. *Patterns in Prehistory, Humankind's First Three Million Years*, 2nd ed. New York: Oxford University Press.

Wilson, William Julius. 1980. *The Declining Significance of Race, Blacks and Changing American Institutions*, 2nd. ed. Chicago: The University of Chicago Press.

Wolf, Eric. 1982. *Europe and the People Without History*. Berkeley: University of California Press.

10

Latino/"Hispanic"–Who Needs a Name?[1]
The Case Against a Standardized Terminology

Martha E. Gimenez

INTRODUCTION

In 1985 I found out that the affirmative action office of the university where I work was counting me as a "minority faculty," member of the so-called "Hispanic ethnic group." It was then that I became interested in the label and its implications for the people it identifies. I found its political construction and usage particularly worthy of examination because it abolishes, for all practical purposes, the qualitative historical differences between the experiences and life chances of U.S. minority groups of Mexican and Puerto Rican origin, and those of Latin American and Spanish peoples. The label imputes to Latin Americans a contrived "Hispanic ethnicity" while minoritizing them in the process (i.e., defining them as members of a minority group even though they have never been historically oppressed as such in the United States.)[2] Because the label is used in the context of affirmative action, it places professional and skilled immigrants in objective competition with members of the U.S. minority groups and forces them to pass, statistically, as members of an oppressed group.

Although the political and ideological unintended functions of this label are numerous and complex, in this article I will examine primarily the adequacy of the theoretical and methodological grounds presented in its defense. I will argue that, far from being useful for social science research and effective policy making and implementation, the "Hispanic" label fulfills primarily ideological and political functions. It cannot replace preexisting theoretical (*social class* and *minority group*) and descriptive (*natural origin* and *socioeconomic status*) categories of analysis; its presence in scientific and popular discourse adds nothing to knowledge while it strengthens racist stereotypes.

The Terms of the Debate

As I began to examine the theoretical and political significance of this label, a colleague told me about several relevant articles published in the *American Journal of*

Public Health which proved to be very interesting and useful; to my knowledge, they form the only scholarly debate on this important issue (1–5).

In these articles, both the defender and the critics of the "Hispanic" label agree on the need for a "standardized terminology"; i.e., an all-encompassing "umbrella" term useful to identify all the population it labels. The critics make a persuasive case for using the term "Latino," rather than "Hispanic," exposing the racist implications of the latter (1, p. 355; 5, p. 15), pointing out the problems it creates for implementing Civil Rights legislation (1; see also 6), and its roots in the history of U.S. economic and political domination over Latin America since the days of the Monroe doctrine (3). Acknowledging that Latino, like Hispanic, is a generic term to ensure comparability of samples and research findings they suggest that social scientists, in their work, should identify also national origin (e.g., Mexican, Puerto Rican, etc.), nativity (U.S. or foreign born), and/or generation. Since people living in the Southwest identify themselves in a variety of ways (e.g., Hispano, Mexicano, Manito, Chicano, Raza, etc.), regional variations ought to be taken into account as well.

The defender (4) considers Hispanic a better term on scientific, political, and pragmatic grounds. *Pragmatically*, because the statistics compiled by the federal government and government agencies use the Hispanic label, and social scientists and policy makers should avoid using a different term. This would create confusion, establishing social scientists in the role of relabeling millions of people who self-identified as such in the 1980 Census. Also, inhabitants of the Southwest who identify themselves with a regional label find Latino unacceptable, while readily agreeing to the Hispanic identifier. Unlike Latino, therefore, the Hispanic label ensures greater population coverage. *Scientifically*, it is important to have comparable data.[3] The use of the label in data gathering ensures coverage and consistency; the fact that it is used in the collection of vital and health statistics creates the possibility for trend analysis (4, p. 70). Consistent use of the label is also important from the standpoint of policy making and implementation, because the goal of public health specialists is "to make progress in standardizing . . . ethnic and social classification systems so that we may move forward in our understanding of the health needs of all our populations" (4, p. 69). *Politically*, the label identifies a minority group subject to severe discrimination. Defending the minority status of Hispanics, Treviño argues that "despite the fact that Hispanics had lived in the U.S. for more than 400 years [they] were still less educated than Blacks, about as poor, had no more luck in getting good jobs, received less health care" (4, p. 71). To replace Hispanic with Latino would undermine, in Treviño's opinion, new affirmative action protection for Hispanics because, academically defined, Latino designates "the peoples, nationalities or countries such as the French, Italian, Spanish, etc. whose languages and culture are descended from the Latin"; this would make eligible under affirmative action people whom the term Hispanic currently excludes (4, p. 70).

Regardless of their differences about the relative merits of Latino versus Hispanic as umbrella terms, critics and defender agree about the need to have, in addition to a standardized terminology, as much information as possible about the populations under study, to identify needs, factors affecting health, access to health services, and so forth. In spite of the arguments advanced in its support, however, the label does not help either social scientists or policy makers because it only creates an artificial population; i.e., a statistical construct formed by aggregates of people who differ greatly in terms of national origin, language, race, time of arrival in the United

States, culture, minority status (see, for example, 3; 5; 9, pp. 9–10; 10), social class, and socioeconomic status. The empirical referent of "Hispanic" fully justifies these assessments: "[T]his statistical construct has hardly any relation to the real world" (10); "[it] vastly oversimplifies the situation. The heterogeneity of the Hispanic population reduces the term to a merely heuristic device" (9, p. 9). It is here that the main theoretical and methodological problems are located. Succinctly stated: What can this, or any other "umbrella" term, identify? Is it a minority group? Is it an "ethnic" group? What is the meaning of the data gathered about this population?

THE PROBLEM OF INTERPRETATION: WHAT DO DATA AND RESEARCH FINDINGS ABOUT "HISPANICS" ACTUALLY MEAN?

It is fascinating to observe how those writing about "Hispanics" (discussing public policy issues, or reporting research findings and vital statistics) do so while fully cognizant (with exceptions) of intrapopulation variations of such magnitude as to render statements about "Hispanics" in general either meaningless or suspect. These are some representative statements: The birth rates for 1983 and 1984 for the "Hispanic" population "were about 50 percent higher than those for the non-Hispanic population. . . . [T]he fertility rate for all Hispanic women was 42 percent above the rate for non-Hispanic women" (11, p. 2). "[T]he median age of the Hispanic population is 6-7 years below that of the non-Hispanic population . . . almost 8 years below that of the White population, and almost 2 years below that of the Black population" (9, p. 21). "Hispanic population increases at 5 times rate of rest of U.S." (12). These are descriptive statements, useful (it may seem) for comparing "Hispanics" with whites, blacks, and Asians. What is the *meaning* and *purpose* of such comparisons? Is it possible to account for those patterns, or to make such comparisons, without creating stereotypes? The demographic characteristics (age and sex structure) and composition (income, education, and occupational distribution) of the "Hispanic" population can be described. Any attempt to account for those characteristics, or for differences in fertility (or anything else) must rest, however, either upon well-established empirical generalizations (e.g., the inverse relationship between income, education, and fertility), which do not necessitate the racial/ethnic classification of the population, or upon stereotypical generalizations about "Hispanic" culture.

The mass media and politicians exploit data about the youth, higher fertility, and growth rate of the "Hispanic" population in ways that, ultimately, intensify racist fears among those worried about low white fertility, increase the likelihood of conflict with blacks (who see their communities competing for scarce resources with an evergrowing "minority" group), and strengthen stereotypes about "Hispanic" cultural traits and the perception that their presence will contribute to increased social problems and tax payers' burdens: e.g., growth of the "Hispanic" population will make it more difficult to eradicate poverty, will increase welfare expenditures, will increase the demands for health care and other social services, and, given their high fertility, they will be the largest minority group by the year 2060 (13).

Poverty, however, is not something inherent in people's genes or culture; it depends on class location and individual resources. Furthermore, if immigration from

Mexico and Central America continues to be composed mainly of poorly educated, low-skilled workers and displaced peasants, the percentage of "Hispanics" below or close to the poverty level will remain high and might even increase. This kind of inference, however, is precluded by generalizations stressing the "Hispanicity" of the population that, regardless of their authors' motives, have inherently misleading latent or unanticipated ideological effects. In the popular consciousness, as well as among social scientists, "Hispanicity" seems to be equivalent, at best, to "traditional culture" and, at worst, to the culture of poverty. A statement taken from research on young mothers illustrates this point (14, p. 11):

> [T]he findings for Hispanic mothers, who report generally higher fertility expectations and lower educational expectations than do other mothers, suggest that these women represent a relatively unacculturated subgroup, with more traditional attitudes toward motherhood and higher education for women.

The overgeneralization about "traditional" culture cited above is quite typical of the mass media and the "modernization" school of U.S. social scientists, still caught in the simplistic understanding of historical change as a process of modernization; i.e., change from traditional (e.g., "Hispanic") to modern (e.g., U.S.) culture. In fact, the assumption of the "traditional" nature of "Hispanic" culture or "ethnicity" is built in research that compares "Hispanic" (or Puerto Rican, Mexican, Cuban, or Central and South American) fertility (or any other demographic or social pattern) with white and black patterns. Typical of this kind of reasoning is the following (15, p. 376):

> Hispanic origin is now an important control variable in the analysis of religious [fertility] differentials. Hispanics are a growing proportion of the U.S. population, they have high fertility, and about three-fourths of them are Catholic. Whether or not Hispanics were included had a dramatic effect on the size of the religious differential. . . . As the size of the Hispanic population grows, and more are foreign born and from high-fertility societies, we can expect this effect to become more pronounced.

Within the parameters of this discourse, high fertility reflects religion and the culture of "high fertility societies." A more sophisticated theoretical analysis of fertility as a rational household survival strategy within given structural conditions of existence (see, for example, 16), would focus researchers' attention on the social class, socioeconomic strata, and actual opportunity structure confronting some "Hispanic" women in this country. What appears as an effect of religion and/or the culture of high fertility or "traditional" societies might be the outcome of conditions of existence similar, in their demographic effects, to those conducive to high fertility in the lower strata of the working class, and in rural and urban subsistence sectors everywhere (17). Everyone writing about "Hispanics," especially social scientists and policy makers, ought to pay attention to Cafferty and McCready's warning about the dangers entailed in assuming "certain behavioral characteristics based on group identity. [T]he serious thinker expresses legitimate concern when he worries that any examination of Hispanics in the United States may result in negative stereotyping" (18, p. 5).

If general statements about "Hispanics" are problematic, are statements about national origin aggregates (e.g., Mexican, Puerto Rican, Cuban, Central and South American) any better? Most social scientists supplement general statements with observations and data about the different aggregates included under the umbrella term. For example, the report about births of "Hispanic" parentage also indicates that, although "Hispanic" women begin child-bearing at young ages, the percentage of live births to teenagers was higher among Puerto Rican (21.3 percent) and Mexican (18.0 percent) mothers than among Cuban (8.2 percent) and Central and South American (8.1 percent) mothers. Mothers' educational attainment also varied according to national origin, with the highest level found among Cuban and Central and South American mothers, and the lowest among Mexican mothers (11, pp. 2-3). Those populations also differ in their age structure: Puerto Ricans are the youngest group (median age, 20.7) and Cubans the oldest (median age, 33) (9, p. 22).

To the extent that researchers use national origin not simply descriptively, but as a proxy for culture as the main independent variable, there is a real danger of developing stereotypes about each of those populations. For example, why are teenage births so few among Cuban and Central and South American mothers? Would a purely demographic explanation (e.g., age structure) suffice? Why is educational attainment greater in these groups? Census data show substantial differences in levels of income and educational attainment among the national origin groups in which data about "Hispanics" are usually classified. Data about the foreign born are limited, but what are available show striking differences between them (Table 10.1) and indicate that a great deal of important information is lost in the construction of "Hispanics" and national origin groups. Each national origin aggregate is different from the others in terms of historical origins, minority status, problems with language, class structure, socioeconomic stratification, and, last but not least, reception by the "host" country. (Compare the reception given to the Cuban bourgeoisie and middle class who fled to Miami after Castro took power with the treatment given to the people living in Mexican and Puerto Rican territories after the annexation, or to Mexican and Puerto Rican manual workers migrating to the United States throughout the 20th century.) This means that it is as misleading to make general statements about "Hispanics" as it is to make them about, for example, Puerto Ricans, Argentines, Cubans, and so forth. To avoid the possibility of constructing stereotypes in the process of interpreting data, social scientists need to go beyond cultural explanations to examine class and socioeconomic status differences within each aggregate. Were they to do so, they would most likely find greater behavioral similarities between "Hispanics" and non-"Hispanics" of the same social class than between "Hispanics" of different social classes and/or national origin. On the other hand, similarities between "Hispanics" and non-"Hispanics" of similar class and socioeconomic status should not be reduced to the result of "acculturation"; they are, after all, something to be expected given the relationship between class location and people's life chances. Excessive reliance on culture as the major explanatory variable limits researchers' ability to make sense of information already available. For example, critical of the widely held belief that culture is the main barrier between "Hispanics" and success-

Table 10.1 Selected characteristics of the population by selected country of birth: 1980[a]

Nationality and selected country of birth	Total persons, thousands	High school grad.	College grad.	Prof. specialty	Service occup.	Median household income, 1970 dollars
Native	212,466	67.7%	16.3%	12.3%	12.7%	$17,010
Foreign born						
Mexico	2,199	21.3%	3.0%	2.5%	16.6%	$12,747
Colombia	144	62.8%	14.6%	8.1%	15.8%	$15,883
Dominican Republic	169	30.1%	4.3%	3.1%	18.5%	$10,130
El Salvador	94	41.4%	6.5%	2.6%	31.7%	$12,261
Ecuador	86	56.0%	9.3%	5.3%	14.7%	$15,402
Guatemala	63	42.7%	6.9%	3.9%	27.9%	$13,385
Cuba	608	54.9%	16.1%	9.2%	12.2%	$16,326
Argentina	69	70.9%	24.2%	16.3%	13.1%	$18,892

Source: U.S. Bureau of the Census. *Statistical Abstracts of the United States: 1987*, Ed. 107, p. 30. Washington, D.C., 1986.

[a]

ful "Americanization," Cafferty states: "The economic success of Cuban immigrants in Miami and of some Dominican immigrants in New York suggest that Hispanic culture, as such, is no obstacle to achievement" (19, p. 41). This statement fails seriously to challenge cultural explanation for "Hispanics'" relatively low socioeconomic standing; what had to be indicated also is the fact that some immigrant populations are more successful not in spite of their culture, but because of the resources (economic and/or human capital) they bring with them. Generalizations about national origin groups, e.g., "Mexican immigrants earn less and achieve lower occupational levels than others" (19, p. 41), if isolated from additional data, cannot but unwittingly create stereotypes about those groups.

To sum up: *the problem facing social scientists and public health specialists in trying to make sense of the data collected by federal, state, and other agencies is a problem not only of comparability but of meaning.* The avowed aim of using a standardized terminology is improvement in the identification of an ethnic group that is also, presumably, a minority group (an issue to be examined in the next section). However, the heterogeneity of the population included under the umbrella term undermines the validity of defining it, for social research and policy purposes, as an "ethnic group" (i.e., a group with *common* cultural characteristics).

To speak about "Hispanic" fertility, child-rearing habits, health subculture, migration patterns, etc., is to engage in empty talk, at best, or in stereotyping. The heterogeneity of national origin groups, in turn, undermines generalizations about the entire group. It seems that social scientists doing research about "Hispanics" are beginning to recognize the problems inherent in relying on ethnicity as the main independent variable, and the advantages in studying social class variations in behavior, attitudes, etc. As one social scientist acknowledges, "[T]he problem with ethnicity is that it has been overused as the sole explanation for all types of behavior among Hispanics" (20, p. 180). To state, for example, that "Hispanic men do not readily accept the notion that they are ill and, therefore, will not visit the physician in the same proportions" (20, p. 161) (as whites, presumably) is as stereotypical as saying, for example, that Mexican men distrust modern medicine. It is important, on the other hand, to learn that "Mexican-American men with low education [have] high levels of distrust of modern medicine and doctors; and that age, sex, education, and income [are] powerful factors in explaining utilization of health services" (20, p. 161).

What is needed to make sense of the data collected under national origin categories is a breakdown of the information on the basis of not only nativity and length of stay in the United States, but social class and socioeconomic status as well. In the United States there is a great deal of overlap between race, ethnicity, and class, so that a large proportion of "Hispanics" are located in the lower strata of the working class. This situation leads to the masking of the effects of social class and socioeconomic status under the cover of "ethnicity" (a code word primarily used to refer to the culture of those considered "nonwhites"), to the point that researchers—normally trained in viewing class and culture only as analytically different things—feel that it is very difficult to separate the effects of each (see, for example, 20, pp. 179–183). Dialectically, however, culture is not a thing one learns or unlearns (thus becoming "acculturated"): it is the lived experience of people shaped by their location in the class and socioeconomic stratification systems. Therefore, research should be aimed not at the assessment of the amount of variance to be explained by class or by culture, but to establish the complex connections between culture, behavior, and their objective basis in people's class location. But this approach, which would result in better social research and more effective policies, cannot be pursued because researchers are trained, to some extent, to consider social class superficially (i.e., reducing it to socioeconomic status), mechanically "controlling" for education, income, and/or occupation whenever possible. Furthermore, even if concerned with social class and socioeconomic status differences, social scientists are constrained by having to use data specifically designed to construct "ethnicities" while providing scant information about class and socioeconomic status indicators. As long as social scientists and policy makers spend time and resources in the construction of standardized terminologies for the identification of politically constructed "ethnicities" (e.g., whites, blacks, "Hispanics," Asians) through the racialization and ethnicization of national origin, improvements in data collection are not likely to contribute to credible, nonstereotypical research findings and effective policy making and implementation. In fact, standardized terminologies pose problems for dealing with data about *all* the "racial" and "ethnic" categories currently in vogue. The problems inherent in lumping together populations heterogeneous in terms of class, socioeconomic status, culture and national origin obtain also for the white, black, and Asian populations.

THE COERCIVE NATURE OF SELF-IDENTIFICATION: DOES IT CONFIRM THE EXISTENCE OF A SINGLE MINORITY GROUP?

Forty percent of those whom demographers (21) analyzing Census responses classify as "Hispanics" using secondary identifiers gave a negative answer to the Spanish/Hispanic origin Census question;[4] instead, they wrote their country of origin in the space left for "other" in the question designed to establish race.[5] Those who exhibited the greatest "consistency," self-identifying as "Spanish/Hispanic" in addition to secondary "Hispanic" identifiers (place of birth, ancestry, Spanish "race," surname, and language) (21, p. 8), were primarily of Mexican and Puerto Rican origins and had considerably lower socioeconomic status (in terms of income, occupation, and education) than the "inconsistent" 40 percent mentioned above. "Inconsistent" respondents were primarily Central and South Americans; a small percentage were Puerto Ricans and Cubans, and a higher percentage, Mexicans (21, pp. 9–17).

These facts, from my standpoint as a sociologist who is also Latin American (specifically, Argentine), indicate that a large percentage of Latin Americans not only know precisely who they are but prefer their historical identities (e.g., Mexican, Colombian, Argentine, etc.) to a label devised by some government officials, conservative politicians, and academics. (I am indebted to Rodolfo Alvarez [Department of Sociology, University of California, Los Angeles] for calling my attention to the relationship between the invention of "Hispanics" and the "Nixon Southern Strategy.")* Those respondents are telling U.S. social scientists and politicians who presume to know better—e.g., "[A]fter more than thirty years of experimentation with enumeration strategies, we should by now know what a Hispanic is" (4, p. 71)—that they are, in fact, wrong. That, however, is not the way U.S. social scientists interpret their response. In their eyes, it is a case of response error (9, p. 10) or worse. According to Treviño, this means that they (the "inconsistent" respondents) "perceive Hispanic ethnicity to constitute a race," and "use of interviewer-observed race would result in most of this 40 percent being reclassified as White. . . . [M]ost of these Hispanics are White Hispanics who do not believe or understand they are White" (4, p. 70). In fact, as a casual reading shows, the question intended to elicit "race" is poorly constructed; it cues people for racial categories *and* national origin (21, p. 5). Treviño's interpretation is exceedingly problematic in its implications, and as patronizing as that offered by Tienda and Ortiz (21, pp. 11–15):

> [T]hese individuals were likely to be Hispanics with ambivalent ethnic identities who misreported their origin either because they objected to the lack of response choices on the full-enumeration item (e.g., no Venezuelan, Argentine, etc. choices), or who deliberately denied their Hispanic origins. . . . [I]nconsistent "Hispanic" [*sic*] respondents . . . appear to exhibit ambiguity about their "Hispanicity" [*sic*].

Using the status inconsistency perspective, they suggest that it is desire to assimilate and upward mobility that presumably lead people to hide their ethnic identity: "Ambiguity in their social identity derives from their desire to be recognized by the majority group (non-Hispanics) based on their socioeconomic credentials". (21, p. 15). This interpretation overlooks the politically constructed nature of the label (22, 23), which makes it unrealistic to expect a universally favorable reception. That many respondents chose to write their national origin where they did, while declining to accept a "Spanish/Hispanic origin," reveals, in all likelihood, neither error, ignorance, or an effort to hide an embarrassing "ethnic" identity, but rejection of the coercive nature of the self-identification question. The question forces respondents to agree to having "Spanish/Hispanic" origin, something which for a substantial number of people makes no sense, both in terms of their actual ancestry and/or in terms of their historical sense of who they are and/or (in the case of Latin Americans) their nationalist allegiance to their country of origin. The status inconsistency perspective is a subtle exercise in "majority" power. It "scientifically" neutralizes the assertion of an alternative identity (or the scholarly critique of the label, as the case may be), ignoring its historical structural determinants and reducing it to the effect of psychological states: i.e., suppression of, or ambivalence about, "real" ethnic identity, an identity that exists mainly in the eyes of the "majority" beholder.

   On the other hand, the relatively low socioeconomic status of those who "agreed" to being labeled "Hispanics" and the fact that 74.2 percent of them were of Mexican American (59.8 percent) and Puerto Rican (14.4 percent) origin (21, p, 13)—two historically evolved U.S. minority groups with origins in colonial conquest—suggest that the ideological construction of reality to which people are exposed through the mass media and state power (via the Census itself) might be more effective among those politically less powerful because of their minority status within the U.S. ethnic stratification system.

   The preceding discussion highlights some of the problems entailed by the use of a self-identification question to enumerate an ethnic group that, in this case, is presumably a minority group. The Civil Rights approach to the amelioration of problems created not only by discrimination but by the normal functioning of the capitalist economy, generates self-interest in agreeing to being identified as a member of a minority group; under such conditions, "consistent responses" are far from yielding scientifically useful information (21, p. 20; 23).

Given the characteristics of the population included under the umbrella term, the "Hispanic" label does not identify a minority group; it only adds together a variety of peoples, 25 percent of whom (Cubans, other Latin Americans, and a proportion of "Other Spanish") "have not lived in the U.S. for more than 400 years," and cannot claim to have been *historically* subject to racial discrimination and economic operation in the United States. Like the Cuban bourgeoisie, or the small number of Argentine immigrants whose median household income in 1980 was higher than that of the native-born population (Table 10.1), some are, in fact, quite privileged. This situation has not remained unnoticed (9, p. 10; 1, p. 355):

> [N]ot all Hispanics agree that they themselves are part of a minority group, and some who claim minority status for themselves would reject it for certain others (for example, they might reject it for well-educated professionals who immigrate from South American countries).[6]
>
> Continued use of the term "Hispanic" [*sic*] or "Spanish Origin" [*sic*] denies the very basis upon which discrimination has been based, and confuses the basis for civil rights and affirmative action efforts.

This situation is politically counterproductive: it sets the basis for political opportunism, it strengthens the perception of people in racial terms, and because it minoritizes foreign technical workers, scientists, and professionals, it creates a misleading appearance of minority advancement (6, pp. 46–52). Treviño dismisses this issue too lightly (4, p. 70): not only can foreigners legally seek minority status protection under affirmative action (though they are protected against discrimination in employment by the Civil Rights Act of 1866), but also minority status is routinely imposed upon them by employers, whether employees agree to being thus labeled and counted or not. As Lowry points out, "[T]ypically, an ethnic identity is assigned to each employee by his employer, based on whatever clues can be found in physiognomy, speech patterns, name, and place of birth. Employees rarely know how they have been classified" (23, pp. 61–62). Third-party identification is another important source of data unreliability whose effects in the construction of "ethnicity" are, for all practical purposes, impossible to assess or eradicate. In vital statistics, both in birth and death certificates, third-party identification creates populations different from those identified by Census data. To make matters worse in terms of comparability and quality of data, there are three different methods to assign race/ethnicity to the newborn: the National Center for Health Statistics instructions, "Hispanic" parentage, and the race/ethnicity of the mother and father. Depending on the method, the "ethnicity" of the infant will vary; comparisons between "Hispanics" and non-"Hispanics" will yield different results (25, 26). Insistence on considering "Hispanic" anyone who has at least one "Hispanic" parent or ancestor betrays a remarkable obsessions with racial purity and racial classification that should not remain unnoticed or escape criticism at a time when racism is, presumably, under attack. It also indicates allegiance to a reified concept of culture, as if it were genetically inherited. In the light of the problems examined here and in the preceding section, continued use of this label can only have political motivations; e.g., the cultural or racial legitimation of economic success of failure, or the belief—among some minority leaders—that greater numbers mean, necessarily, greater power. As the example of Africa indicates, numbers and political strength are not necessarily equivalent. The differences among "Hispanics" are greater than their imputed commonalities: it is unlikely that they may become united as a single political force, although they may form local alliances around single-issue objectives (for an assessment of the political potential of the label, see 27).

CONCLUSION

The "Hispanic" label is eminently political: it identifies neither an ethnic group nor a minority group. It is the temporary outcome of political struggles between the major parties to win elections, particularly in the Southwest, and will serve its role as long as political alignments, the terms of acceptable political discourse, and the definition of legitimate channels of access to social and health services, education, and the road to upward mobility for minority groups remain unchanged. Central to the dominant political discourse is the notion that the "majority" has access to health, social services, education, and employment opportunities through the impersonal mechanism of market allocation. Minorities, on the other hand, are disproportionately poor, are less educated, earn lower incomes, and are relatively excluded from the better-paying jobs not because they are also disproportionately working class (where they occupy the lower strata), unemployed, or underemployed, but because of their culture and nonmarket processes such as, for example, racial discrimination and segregation. *Their problems, it follows, require nonmarket solutions* (e.g., affirmative action and development of policies designed to maximize their access to needed social and health services, education, etc.) *contingent upon the identification of the population whose needs have to be served*. Individuals and groups, therefore, have to accept whatever legal identity and social status they are given to qualify for benefits and have access to legal protection; at this time, that means accepting the "Hispanic" label. Public health officials, policy makers, and social scientists, on the other hand, are concerned with the quality and comparability of the data. However, as I have argued in this article, the label is far from being appropriate for social research, and for policy making and implementation; on the contrary, it has created an irresolvable tension between political and research needs that, in the long run, will result in ineffective policies and the accumulation of data of doubtful significance. Cafferty and McCready's assessment of the label is correct (28, p. 254):

> [P]olicies are created for Hispanics which help some and harm others because there are . . . no "generic" Hispanics. . . . "Hispanics" [sic] is much too generic a term for policy makers and . . . much greater information and insight must be generated in order to enable our contemporary system to make intelligent and productive responses to the needs of these citizens and newcomers to the country.

The real issue, in the last instance, is not whether Latino or "Hispanic" is a better umbrella term, but whether it is wise to have an umbrella term at all. In my view, the answer is self-evident. Regardless of politicians' concerns for numbers, social scientists and policy makers must seriously confront the problems attached to this and any other umbrella term: the stereotyping and minoritization of foreigners; the transformation of minority groups into mere statistical categories, thus subverting the historical reasons for their situation and their claims upon the resources of the state; the creation of a synthetic or artificial "ethnicity"; the production of data difficult to interpret in nonracist or stereotypical fashion; and so on.

There is a simple alternative to the umbrella term: to acknowledge the existence of qualitative differences in the history, culture, class and social stratification, and racial/ethnic composition of populations that ought to be publicly named by their real historical names, and understood (through social research) and treated (through social and health policies) in their own right. These populations are the following:

- Two minority groups: people of Mexican and Puerto Rican descent who, because of the historical conditions surrounding their entry into the United States, the integration of the U.S. economy with that of Mexico and Puerto Rico, and the presence of migration flows and counterflows, constitute two special populations with features and problems of their own. Because of the heritage of economic exclusion and racial discrimination, it is in their context that affirmative action makes sense.
- Four additional aggregates: Cuban immigrants, Central American refugees, Central American immigrants, and South American immigrants. Privileged classes within these immigrant populations do very well; those who do not, do poorly because of lack of human capital. The determinants of the social stratification and the needs of these populations are different from those subject to generations of racial/ethnic discrimination. Policies designed to serve their needs should, therefore, differ from those designed to ameliorate the historical effects of discrimination (29).

These six populations are themselves stratified on the basis of class and socioeconomic status: this ought to warn social researchers and policy makers against making generalizations, assuming a common culture or "ethnicity" as the major explanatory variable. To identify these populations in terms of national origin is easy (except in the case of undocumented workers and refugees) and, politically, less laden with racist innuendos than the effort to minimize their differences by placing them all under a common label. The need to identify Spanish-speaking populations to provide better health care and other social services does not justify the use of a label that, because it racializes national origin and triggers the perception of recipients in terms of stereotyped "Hispanic" traits, may generate a "blaming the victim" understanding of their problems and the provision of low quality services. In the last instance, access to good health care is not a function of race, ethnicity, or language skills; it is a function of social class and location in the socioeconomic stratification system; a social science truism that bears repeating over and over in a social, academic, and policy-making context that downplays the existence of class differences and their impact upon people's life chances. Advocates of a standardized terminology should assess its short-term benefits for gathering data of doubtful quality in the light of its long-term political, ideological, and scientific costs, and give it up.

NOTES

I would like to thank Estevan T. Flores, Benjamin F. Hadis, and Richard Rogers for their helpful suggestions.

1. I use quotation marks around "Hispanic" to indicate my critical stance toward the label. In the article, whenever the label is mentioned in the context of someone else's discourse, it will be written without quotation marks.

2. Working-class, unskilled Latin Americans, particularly undocumented workers, are economically exploited and disproportionately found in the worst jobs and in the poverty population, not because of their "Hispanicity" and "minority group status," but because of their lack of language skills and "human capital." On the other hand, middle-class, upper-middle-class, and petty bourgeois Latin Americans do very well, not in spite of their "ethnicity" (i.e., they are not examples of "minority success" or "assimilation" to "minority" values), but because their social class entails ownership of economic and/or human capital.

3. Federal, state, and private agencies, on the other hand, often do not use the same codes for race, thus making it difficult to compare data from different sources. See, in this respect, references 7 and 8.

4. The Census self-identification question is as follows:
   Is this person of Spanish/Hispanic origin?
   No (not Spanish/Hispanic).
   Yes, Mexican, Mexican American, Chicano.
   Yes, Puerto Rican.
   Yes, Cuban.
   Yes, other Spanish/Hispanic.

5. The Census question is as follows:
   Is this person

White	Asian Indian
Black or Negro	Hawaiian
Japanese	Guamanian
Chinese	Samoan
Filipino	Eskimo
Korean	Aleut
Vietnamese	Other _____ Specify _____
Indian (Amer.)	
Print Tribe: _____	

6. An interesting illustration of the effects of including well-educated South American professionals in the "Hispanic minority group" is the recent award of a minority fellowship, by Boulder's local newspaper, to a high school senior "minority" student, the talented and multilingual (speaking English, Spanish, French, and German) Argentine-born son of two Argentine university professors (24). This example clearly shows how the statistical definition of minorities makes a travesty of the concept and subverts the goals of policies devised to do away with discrimination.

REFERENCES

Beck, J. Hispanic immigration tests U.S. *Daily Camera* (Boulder), September 11, 1987, p. 4A.

Borjas, G. J. Jobs and employment for Hispanics. In *Hispanics in the United States*, edited by P. S. J. Cafferty and W. C. McCready, pp. 146–157. Transaction Books: New Brunswick, N.J., 1988.

Cafferty, P. S. J., and McCready, W. C. Introduction. In *Hispanics in the United States*, edited by P. S. J. Cafferty and W. C. McCready, pp. 1–6. Transaction Books: New Brunswick, N.J., 1988.

Choldin, H. M. Statistics and politics: The "Hispanic" issue in the 1980 Census. *Demography* 23: 403–418, 1986.

Daily Camera (Boulder), April 1988.

Giachello, A. I. Hispanics and health care. In *Hispanics in the United States*, edited by P. S. J. Cafferty and W. C. McCready, pp. 159–194. Transaction Books: New Brunswick, N.J., 1988.

Gimenez, M. E. Minorities and the world-system: Theoretical and political implications of the internationalization of minorities. In *Racism, Sexism, and the World-System*, edited by J. Smith et. al., pp. 39–56. Greenwood Press: Westport, Conn., 1988.

Hayes-Bautista, D. E. Identifying "Hispanic" population: The influence of research methodology on public policy. *Am. J. Public Health* 70: 353–356, 1980.

Hayes-Bautista, D. E., and Chapa, J. Latino terminology: Conceptual basis for standardized terminology: Conceptual basis for standardized terminology. *Am. J. Public Health* 77: 61–68, 1987.

Hayes-Bautista, D. E. On comparing studies of different raza populations. *Am. J. Public Health* 73: 274–276, 1983.

Lowry, I. S. The science and politics of ethnic enumeration. In *Ethnicity and Public Policy*, edited by W. A. Van Horne, pp. 42–62. University of Wisconsin System: Milwaukee, Wis., 1984.

Mamdani, M. *The Myth of Population Control.* Monthly Review Press: New York, 1972.

Mamdani, M. The ideology of population control. In *And The Poor Get Children*, edited by K. L. Michaelson, pp. 39–49. Monthly Review Press: New York, 1984.

Mosher, W. D., et al. Religion and fertility in the United States: The importance of marriage patterns and Hispanic origin. *Demography* 23: 367–379, 1986.

Mott, F. L. The pace of repeated childbearing among young American mothers. *Fam. Plann. Perspect.* 18: 5–12, 1986.

Muñoz, C. Chicano politics: The current conjuncture. In *The Year Left 2*, An American Socialist Yearbook, pp. 35–52. Verso: New York, 1987.

National Center for Health Statistics. Births of Hispanic parentage, 1983 and 1984. *Monthly Vital Statistics Report.* NCHS: Washington, D.C., 1987.

Petersen, W. Who's what? 1790-1980. *Wilson Q.* 9: 110, 1985.

Rogers, R. G. Ethnic Differences in Infant Mortality: Fact or Artifact? Unpublished manuscript, 1988.

Sullivan, T. A., et al. Alternative estimates of Mexican American mortality in Texas. *Soc. Sci. Q.* 65: 609–617, 1980.

Sullivan, T. A. A demographic portrait. In *Hispanics in the United States*, edited by P. S. J. Cafferty and W. C. McCready, pp. 7–32. Transaction Books: New Brunswick, N.J., 1988.

Tienda, M., and V. Ortiz. "Hispanicity" and the 1980 Census. *Soc. Sci. Q.* 67: 3–20, 1986.

Treviño, F. M. Standardized terminology for standardized populations. *Am. J. Public Health* 77: 69–72, 1987.

Treviño, F. M. Uniform minimum data sets: In search of demographic compatibility. *Am. J. Public Health* 78: 126–127, 1988.

Westermeyer, J. Problems with surveillance methods for alcoholism: Differences in coding systems among federal, state, and private agencies. *Am. J. Public Health* 78: 130–133, 1988.

Yankauer, A. Hispanic/Latino—What's in a name? *Am. J. Public Health* 77: 15–17, 1987.

11

Nomads and Migrants
Negotiating a Multicultural Postmodernism

Rafael Peréz-Torres

This is the place where everyone takes command
No man's land

—Latin Alliance

Postmodernism and multiculturalism, seldom discussed as if they belong together, might remind us of bickering partners. Each of these contested terms serves as a center of attraction, collects friends, makes enemies, coordinates allies, sets up networks of information. These networks seldom cross. The camps that identify themselves with these positions offer each other only the most cursory nod of recognition. This despite the fact that postmodernism and the multicultural share many affinities: a valuation of marginality, a suspicion of master discourses, a resistance to empty conventions.

Maybe part of the problem is that these polysyllabic terms—postmodernism and multiculturalism—seem to engender more questions and tensions than answers and resolutions.

Is postmodernism primarily an aesthetic or historical condition? Does it describe the site of elite cultural interests or define a more general system of production and consumption? Does postmodernism really exist at all as a significant epistemological break from modernism? A schematic breakdown of postmodern theorists might run something like this: Ihab Hassan and Brian McHale (aesthetic postmodernism), Jean-François Lyotard (positively decentering postmodernism), Jean Baudrillard (nihilistically decentering postmodernism), Hal Foster (critical postmodernism), Andreas Huyssen (culturalist postmodernism), Fredric Jameson (repressive postmodernism), Jürgen Habermas (modernist postmodernism). This list, however, does little to resolve the question: what do we enact when we utter the word "postmodern"?

By contrast (but no less problematically), notions of the multicultural seem so clear that there debate rages about its definition. While a stormy debate still continues about what to do with the multicultural, the term itself within both academic and popular discourses generally invokes notions of "diversity." Multiculturalism implies a recognition that North American societies have become more culturally, racially, and ethnically diverse. Our curriculum therefore needs to address this reality. Perhaps, if one were seeking an even more adventurous version of academic multiculturalism, one might acknowledge not just a present demographic diversity but a historical re-examination in which past contributions to American culture by non-white, non-European peoples are acknowledged. What controversy exists over the term arises out of the way the academy is to treat multiculturalism: does its incorporation into the curriculum corrupt or challenge or enhance institutional knowledge?

At the root of these controversies, obviously, lie the issues of cultural power and the politics of signification. These issues circle back to postmodernism.

While they should be viewed as sympathetic conditions—postmodernism and multiculturalism are not coterminous—neither should they be understood as synonymous with poststructuralism. The point to make here is that a discussion of multiculturalism and postmodernism should help clarify how these terms can be used productively to construct an inclusive discourse about cultural empowerment.

Rather than view the crossing of the multicultural with the postmodern as a "grafting" of one interest onto another (or subordinating one under another), the concerns associated with the multicultural and the postmodern interpenetrate and traverse. They come finally to shape one another. Multiculturalism must refuse the position of civilizational Other in relation to the dominant cultural field. It cannot be used, as Susan Suleiman suggests, simply as a "political guarantee postmodernism needs in order to feel respectable as an avant-garde practice" (116).[1] People of color cannot be required to act as the conscience of contemporary cultural discourse.

Simultaneously, the postmodern valuation of difference—informed by poststructuralist thought—must come under scrutiny by "minority" discourses. This is true if the "margin" is to claim any constructive and empowering space within academic and cultural institutions. It is also true if postmodernism is to do something more than resurrect a hollow monument to abstract difference and a reified margin. In their introduction to the volume of *Cultural Studies* devoted to Chicano cultural production, Rosa Linda Fregoso and Angie Chabram argue that the invocation of difference within poststructuralist discourses should come under sharp scrutiny:

> poststructuralism's concept of "difference" as a category imposed on and used to describe the cultural identities of people of color . . . subsumes ethnic identity into a universal category of difference without attention to our specific historical internal differences. Furthermore, this notion of difference is predicated on a singularity which takes as its center the Western speaking subject and which posits that all people of color are different to this subject yet transparent among themselves. (207)

Difference, as Fregoso and Chabram (and Spivak and hooks and West and others) argue, becomes within some poststructuralist discourses a reified category. This does nothing more than to reinscribe the centrality of those who define difference. More damaging, as George Yúdice argues, is that the deployment of marginality by poststructuralism becomes "the condition of possibility of all social, scientific, and cultural entities . . . that constitutes the basis for a new, neo-Nietzschean 'freedom' from moral injunctions" (214). Under the poststructural, everything is marginal, so the margin can no longer serve a critical function. Everybody dances across a Brownian cultural universe, fragmentary and decentered.

Some critics refuse this diffusion of the margin. Speaking from a self-defined radical marginality, bell hooks seeks to distinguish qualities of marginalization: "Postmodernist discourses are often exclusionary even as they call attention to, appropriate even, the experience of 'difference' and 'otherness' to provide oppositional political meaning, legitimacy, and immediacy when they are accused of lacking concrete relevance" (23). The postmodern looks to the historically marginal in order to supply a political consciousness and relevant dimension. The position hooks takes regarding the postmodern conflates the postmodern with the poststructural, a move of which one must remain suspicious. Bracketing for the moment a discussion that distinguishes postmodernism from poststructuralism, hooks's observation about the abstraction of difference by contemporary cultural discourse is well taken. This stand cannot, however, serve as an excuse to cast off the postmodern as a problem that does not involve the historically marginal. Indeed, hooks refuses disengagement. She seeks instead to recuperate the critical potentiality of postmodernism for constituencies positioned by dominant discourse as "different" and "other." These constituencies, hooks argues, engaging with the postmodern condition of decentered subjectivity, can take advantage of ruptures and gaps that make space for oppositional practices. The discontinuous terrain of the postmodern can allow Others to stake a claim in a new cultural order.

I would like to discuss, in the pages that follow, how and why that stake should be claimed.

1. IT'S A SCHIZO WORLD

From a strategic standpoint, the postmodern infatuation with alterity clears ground by which the multicultural can articulate the highly textured and multiplicitous condition of marginality. For example, Guillermo Gómez-Peña—a Mexican-born performance artist and MacArhur Fellowship winner—treats in his work the transnational and transitional identities to be found in the borderlands. As a Mexican who identifies with Chicano issues, Gómez-Peña resists any easy categorization of identity: "I believe in multiple identities. Depending on the context I am Chicano, Mexican, Latin American, or American in the wider sense of the term. The Mexican Other and the Chicano Other are constantly fighting to appropriate me or reject me. But I think my work might be useful to both sides because I'm an interpreter. An intercultural interpreter" (Carr 43). This vision of the multicultural self as translator suggests that the subject of the borderlands crosses numerous cultural and historical configurations. Rather than underscore place, this view foregrounds the movement inherent in a constructively decentered subjectivity.

The vision of multiple identities articulated by Gómez-Peña clearly resonates with the issues of schizophrenia that characterize postmodern discourse. Viewing postmodern schizophrenia critically, Fredric Jameson sees schizoid disconnection as the near triumph of late capitalist hegemony. Jameson argues that in modernism, reification "liberated" the Sign from its referent. So modernist culture could play with systems of meaning separate from connections to an "outside world." In postmodernism, reification liberates the Signifier from the Signified. The systems of meaning themselves break down. Postmodernism thus begins "to project the mirage of some ultimate language of pure signifiers which is also frequently associated with schizophrenic discourse" ("Periodizing" 200). Language becomes a language disorder. Syntactical time breaks down, leaving behind a succession of empty signifiers, absolute moments of a perpetual present. The links of the signifying chain snap, leaving behind nothing but the rubble of distinct and unrelated signifiers:

> The connection between this kind of linguistic malfunction and the psyche of the schizophrenic may then be grasped by way of a two-fold proposition: first, that personal identity is itself the effect of a certain temporal unification of past and future with the present before me; and second, that such active temporal unification is itself a function of language, or better still of the sentence, as it moves along its hermeneutic circle through time. If we are unable to unify the past, present and future of the sentence, then we are similarly unable to unify the past, present and future of our own biographical experience or psychic life. (*Postmodernism* 26–27)

The rupture within the linguistic realm finds its homology in all epistemological realms. The rubble of language functions in the same way that the rubble of history or the rubble of identity function: sites of postmodern dissolution in which all things, now detached and free-floating, collapse into—within Jameson's conceptualization—the marketplace.

Simply put, Jameson overstates the case. The equation of schizophrenia with postmodernity neutralizes any historical memory. This process of historical amnesia may be at work within the general discourses of mass cultural hypnotism. (Media representations of the noxious presidential "elections" serve as good an example as any. Where in the mass media are stored memories of the war with Iraq, the savings and loan bailouts, the upward redistribution of wealth?) As the 1992 insurrection in Los Angeles should serve to show, historical memory cannot be erased with the punch of a button. This is particularly true among those communities and constituencies who have borne the brunt of history. Another example lies in the construction of the AIDS quilt—memory serves to inform acts of defiance and rage.

Gilles Deleuze and Félix Guattari give schizophrenia a more positive spin than Jameson. Schizophrenia characterizes a revolutionary tendency of desire that produces liberating movements against the structures of systemic order. Modern societies are caught "between the Urstaat that they would like to resuscitate as an overcoding and reterritorializing unity" and the schizophrenic "unfettered flows that carry them toward an absolute threshold." Our societies organize themselves around systems that can move either toward a regime of stratified order or dissolve into fluid movement toward a joyful chaos. Societies thus "recode with all their might, with world-wide dictatorship, local dictators, and an all-powerful police, while decoding—or allowing the decoding of—the fluent quantities of their capital and their populations. They are torn in two directions: archaism and futurism, neoarchaism and ex-futurism, paranoia and schizophrenia" (260). Deleuze and Guattari speak more persuasively to the potentially empowering movements a dissolution of systems—deterritorialization—can entail. However, the fact that these deterritorializations also resonate with dispossession and displacement grounds the "lines of flight" along which desire moves. The anti-oedipal model—strung between paranoia and schizophrenia—does little to ground the historical effects of capitalism. The driving forces of capitalism and its reterritorializing processes always haunt migrations, invasions, enslavements, and other multicultural deterritorializations. It is very easy to value schizophrenia when it doesn't drive you crazy.

Neither the conceptualization by Jameson nor that by Deleuze and Guattari adequately addresses the multiple subjectivities—constrained by historical conditions but constructively empowering nonetheless—suggested by Gómez-Peña. His description of a multiple subject-position is not simply a dissolution of self or anarchically transgressive—it is a position of translation, of interpellation, of liberation, of confinement. As a historically inscribed position, it manifests the numerous discontinuities and disruptions inherent to its various localities.

2. MAPPING BORDERLANDS

Overlapping the grids of postmodernism and multiculturalism changes their configurations. It brings each discourse into sharper focus so that the diversity and multiplicity of each terrain becomes clearer. For example, Hal Foster, Jürgen Habermas, and Andreas Huyssen have noted—each in their own way and for different ends— that there are at least two discernible strains of postmodernism: the culturally resistant and the neoconservative.[2] The neoconservative postmodern rejects modernism, reduces it to a style, and elides the pre- and postmodern in "a resurrection of lost traditions set against modernism, a master plan imposed on a heterogeneous present" (Foster xii). The nostalgia for tradition—rather than the critical examination of what tradition means—marks a neoconservative agenda that seeks to impose social control based on words like "morality" and "justice" and "quality." Empty convention returns in force (anti-choice arguments, the idea of reverse discrimination, p.c. bashing).

To counteract this neoconservative construction of the post/anti-modern, the critic must articulate what comprises a resistant rather than a reactionary postmodernism. Foster provides an incisive sketch of this critical cultural practice:

> A postmodernism of resistance, then, arises as a counter-practice not only to the official culture of modernism but also to the "false normativity" of a reactionary postmodernism. In opposition (but not *only* in opposition), a resistant postmodernism is concerned with a critical deconstruction of tradition, not an instrumental pastiche of pop- or pseudo-historical forms, with a critique of origins, not a return to them. In short, it seeks to question rather than exploit cultural codes, to explore rather than conceal social and political affiliations. (xii)

In a move sympathetic with multicultural concerns, resistant postmodernism seeks to problematize the bases— "morality" and "justice" and "quality"—upon which exclusivity rests. "Justice" within a suburban courtroom infused by a dominant social discourse might very well mean something quite different than it does on a street corner in South-Central Los Angeles infused with social discontent. Multicultural concerns and a resistant postmodernism seek to scrutinize the political and cultural affiliations terms like "justice" and "quality" enact.

The attention to detail and locality implicit to Foster's concept of resistant postmodernism resonates with the demand for specificity and historical acuity voiced by multicultural critics. Wahneema Lubiano, for one, argues that the general celebration of the multicultural by postmodern critics serves to collapse a highly textured space. She argues against a blind affirmation of African American cultural products that ostensibly give voice to demands for justice and mortality: "morality for whom, when, and under what circumstances? It seems to me more useful to think of African American postmodernism as a way to negotiate particular material circumstances in order to attempt some constructions of justice" (157). The discourse of African American (and may I add multicultural) postmodernism serves to work toward the construction of justice, not the proclamation of some originary source of justice.

Yet, while roughly outlining the shape of a resistant postmodernism, pointing toward issues of multiplicity and locality as possible sites of postmodern and multicultural confluence, I have avoided a singularly thorny issue: what do I mean by "multicultural"? Where the term "postmodern" has stimulated an academic critical industry, "multicultural" has not. What it has done, of course, is create a pedagogical industry in which it seems every anthology or panel discussion strives to be multicultural. The voice of the Other in the academy is a big-ticket item.

The ideological category "diversity" collapses into notions of the multicultural and brings home—in these post-1960s, post-civil rights, postmodern times—in a new guise the dream of *e pluribus unum*. Reed Way Dasenbrock, for example, defines multicultural literature as "both works that are explicitly about multicultural societies and those that are implicitly multicultural in the sense of inscribing readers from other cultures inside their own textual dynamics" (10). The multicultural serves an educational purpose. It makes manifest the dream of a benign liberal plurality and draws diverse constituencies together through greater understanding. This blithe use of the term "multicultural" ultimately leads to an evacuation of any critical potential. Multicultural texts in Dasenbrock's argument manifest little more than a "respect for difference." The counterdiscursivity of multicultural texts—their refusal to engage in a dominant system of symbolic exchange—is reduced in Dasenbrock's argument to a heuristic element, "teaching" readers about multicultural difference and making them "literate" in the multilingual "world" of the characters. All differences can be understood; all differences can be overcome.

The introduction to one of the many multicultural anthologies published in the last few years similarly typifies the pluralistic bent behind much academic use of the term "multicultural." This particular collection, *Braided Lives*, emerges from a collaboration between the Minnesota Council of Teachers of English and the Minnesota Humanities Commission:

> Both organizations share a mission of promoting the study of literature as part of the humanities and of contributing to quality education for all Minnesotans. Both also agree that the multiplicity of American views, beliefs,

and histories is a story that always must be heard. . . . We dreamed of a strikingly beautiful collection of stories and poems that would reveal the abundance and diversity of American writing. (Minnesota Council 9)

Here again, hollow diversity. Everyone is different, and let us celebrate that difference. Within the body of the collection, however, something else occurs. The stories collected in *Braided Lives* are divided into four sections: Native American, Hispanic American, African American, and Asian American. The representative stories reprinted in the collection undercut the empty pluralism promised by the introduction. Each of these multicultural groups is marked racially, economically, and ethnically as contemporary "others" in the United States. Each presents devalued cultures that historically have been silenced or marginalized in the rush to develop and expand Euro-American capital interests.

The incorporation of historically silenced voices into this collection (which it must be said is an excellent anthology, obviously thoughtfully collected, full of fine literary texts) indicates that the power behind the term "multicultural" is not its reliance on simplistic notions of plurality and diversity. This forms a neoconservative position in which the multicultural can be appropriated as the logical extension of the Melting Pot. All Americans are different equally. Hence the clichéd move taken by a number of conservatives like Dinesh D'Souza and Lynne Cheney who bemoan the ostensible "fact" that the rush to political correctness limits personal freedoms and makes p.c. a new McCarthyism. Real "diversity," they argue, means that everybody—from WASPs on down—should function on a level playing field. This vision of a colorless, classless, sexless world represents the type of ahistoricity and easy revisionary politics for which postmodernism—a reactionary postmodernism—is rightly attacked.

"Multicultural," when used to designate devalued cultures, inserts a historical consciousness into discussions about cultural representation. It serves to reconnect the present to the past, but in a critical way that highlights absence and dispossession. These absences and dispossessions are replicated in the institution of culture according to master narratives invoking "great traditions" and "universality." In this respect, the multicultural engages with postmodernism in ways that challenge institutionalized notions of culture, knowledge, and tradition. Houston Baker has observed: "Fixity is a function of power. Those who maintain place, who decide what takes place and dictate what has taken place, are power brokers of the traditional. The 'placeless,' by contrast, are translators of the non-traditional. . . . Their lineage is fluid, nomadic, transitional" (202). Baker makes an exceedingly important observation. Simultaneously, we want to keep in mind that the "placeless" multicultural are "non-traditional" only from a central hegemonic perspective. Multiculturalism negotiates with other traditions; it employs and deploys discredited traditions as part of a strategy of survival and resistance. Multiculturalism does not simply involve the recuperation of "lost" traditions in order to prove the richness and diversity of "America," as the framers of the introduction of *Braided Lives* suggest. Rather, multiculturalism interrogates which traditions are valorized and by whom, which are devalued and by whom, which serve to empower marginalized peoples, which serve even further to disempower, which traditions provide strength, how traditions provide agency, when traditions provide knowledge. Thus, when one engages with issues of cultural power and the politics of signification and scrutinizes the ideas of history and tradition, the constellations of multiculturalism and postmodernism inevitably intersect and overlap.

3. TRAVELING JONES

Historically, the two-way dispersal of information and knowledge in a post-WWII context marks the double emergence of multiculturalism and postmodernism. This double emergence became most apparent in the realm of the university. It was in the university of the 1960s where knowledge produced both by the colonized (national-ist agendas, civil rights reform, third world marxist praxis) and the colonizers (universal humanism, individualism, military-industrial technology) converged. Moreover, it was in the university that trenchant social and political demands—the Civil Rights Movement, postcolonial national liberations, internal nationalisms claimed by various racial and ethnic groups—found their most powerful voices and greatest legitimation in the United States.[3] The university structures responded to stu-dent and faculty demands that discredited forms of "other" knowledge must be in-corporated into educational institutions. Hence the establishment of "special" programs: Women's studies, Afro-American programs, Chicano studies, Native American studies, Asian American studies.

The same historical conditions that impelled universities toward inclusion de-fined the larger cultural terrain—of which the university is but one manifestation—called the postmodern. Andreas Huyssen suggests that the postmodern forms a critically pluralistic cultural site:

> It was especially the art, writing, film making and criticism of women and minority artists with their recuperation of buried and mutilated traditions, their emphasis on exploring forms of gender- and race-based subjectivity in aesthetic productions and experiences, and their refusal to be limited to standard canonizations, which added a whole new dimension to the cri-tique of high modernism and to the emergence of alternative forms of cul-ture.(27)

This fragmentation of the cultural scene beginning in the 1960s allowed Picasso's African masks to no longer stand as silent witnesses to the master's craft. They could now speak. One might argue that Huyssen too easily elides demographic diversity with genuine institutionalized cultural transformation. However, his argument is compelling. In the construction of postmodernism, the colonized, refusing silence, gave voice to the knowledge and experience not only long absent from the halls of museums and universities but which, quite literally, built those halls. From this per-spective, it is impossible to talk about either postmodernism or multiculturalism as if their rejections of institutional culture were entirely discrete events.

However, it is equally impossible to talk about either as if they were perfectly harmonious. Theorizing about multiculturalism leads inevitably to problems of domination and hermeticism. Multiculturalism tends to be forged outside the ivy walls of academe. Theory tends within those walls to turn in on itself. Edward Said is correct to note: "Left to its own specialists and acolytes, so to speak, theory tends to have walls erected around itself . . ." ("Traveling" 247). There is no getting around the fact that most critical theory is an elitist and exclusive project meant to address, as Said notes, the three thousand academic workers harvesting in ever smaller fields of intellectual engagement.[4] This does not preclude the potential uses of theory, however:

> To measure the distance between theory then and now, there and here, to record the encounter of theory with resistances to it, to move skeptically in the broader political world where such things as the humanities or the great classics ought to be seen as small provinces of the human venture, to map the territory covered by all the techniques of dissemination, communication, and interpretation, to preserve some modest (perhaps shrinking) belief in noncoercive human community: if these are not imperatives, they do at least seem to be attractive alternatives. And what is critical consciousness at bottom if not an unstoppable predilection for alternatives? ("Traveling")

Toward this end, theories of postmodernity and the multicultural provide powerful tools by which to explore the expanding limits of each other. Each project ultimately seeks to walk skeptically in the broader political world of contemporary American culture. The goal, then, in crossing postmodernism and multiculturalism is to employ theory as a generalizing practice, "'to make us see' connections, homologies, similarities, and isomorphisms among disconnected and disparate realities. . . . In this sense, then the capacity of theory to generalize and travel among constituencies can have a positive and progressive impact on the constituencies themselves, each of which is enabled to look beyond its immediate area or zone" (Radhakrishnan, "Culture" 17). Theory constructs bridges (problematic, "abstract," elite, "intellectual") across which cultural critics move as they articulate a critical vocabulary by which to understand the expanded field of "the Americas."

In this regard, I propose a migratory sensibility. What proves to be a metaphorical notion in the poststructural (a Deleuze-Guattarian "deterritorialization") can be used to trace the relationships between postmodernism (a cultural condition connected to, though not identifiable with, poststructuralism) and the multicultural (a cultural identity premised upon a history of voluntary or enforced migrations). Rather than allow the term "migration" to remain metaphorical, therefore, an astute critic would insist upon the fact of deterritorialization as a historically grounded, painful, and often coerced dislocation. This dislocation can enact another form of deterritorialization—the dissolution of ordering systems valued by Deleuze and Guattari. These dislocations result from political and economic disruptions solicited and supported by the very centers of empire—Europe and the United States—in which the turmoil over multiculturalism erupts. The term "migration," therefore, marks the nexus where economic, social, linguistic, political, theoretical, discursive fractures converge.

A migratory reading, in order to move across this treacherous terrain of literal rupture, suggests a strategy of continual negotiation. The landscape permits only tentative articulations. No firm foothold ensues. Lisa Lowe, in articulating the discursive field of Asian American identity, notes that Peter Wang's film *A Great Wall* performs a filmic "migration" by "shuttling between the various cultural spaces; we are left, by the end of the movie, with a sense of culture as dynamic and open, the result of a continual process of visiting and revisiting a plurality of cultural sites" (39). The term "migration" here—while evoking a history of actual displacement and economic exploitation—again becomes a metaphor characterizing the movement between fixed cultural sites. The different cultural spaces among which Wang's film moves seem—by Lowe's description—to exist as static sites. The description does not high-light the interpenetrability of these different cultural sites, an interpenetrability that forms the openness and dynamism of culture. (Only the film and Lowe's discussion of the film as cultural objects convey a sense of that dynamism). Despite these minor limitations, Lowe's use of "migration" does help articulate a cultural identity—in this case Chinese American—that moves in ways elsewhere called postmodern: "we might consider as a possible model for the ongoing construction of ethnic identity the migratory process suggested by Wang's filming technique and emplotment: we might conceive of the making and practice of Asian American culture as nomadic, unsettled, taking place in the travel between cultural sites and in the multivocality of heterogeneous and conflicting positions" (39). This heterogeneity arises not merely from undifferentiated "difference." The multivocality that marks a migratory process arises from conflicting systems of signification. These significations emerge from the crossing of contestatory discourses, contradictory positions. What can a Chicano do when the forms of knowledge passed along at home—folklore, legend, ballad, spirituality—are discredited from a socially dominant perspective? Yet that dominant social perspective forms one which informs identity construction as well. One reaction is to deny the discredited knowledge—as Richard Rodriguez does in his much-publicized *Hunger of Memory*. Another reaction is to embrace all that is nondominant, a move that sometimes results in an unexamined nativism. The multicultural, as I propose it, resides in the tension between these two poles. The result is a multiplicity of identities, a perpetual movement among numerous subject positions. None forms a fully privileged realm.

4. SETTLEMENTS

As I previously suggested, multiculturalism has been an academic player primarily in the already very tired game of curricular reform. Insert this topic not simply as an example of equine flagellation. Rather, debates over the curriculum are always about power. They revolve around the control of cultural reproduction: who is to be the gatekeeper of knowledge, who to determine what concerns characterize that national body? One element of resistance among the various decentered subjectivities of our postmodern and multicultural worlds centers on the re-examination of the idea of tradition. Unlike the impression left by the media and the hype surrounding curricular reform, it is not proponents of multiculturalism who clamor for the destruction of the canon. The perceived threat to academic rigor, the much publicized loss of "tradition" and "reason" wrongly and even purposely associated with multiculturalism, proves little more than a smoke screen. This screen covers an anxiety over a perceived loss of cultural control.

Multiculturalism cannot seek to negate "tradition" or "the canon" since it cannot deny—on the contrary, tries to fore-ground—preconstituted social contradictions. Rather than decry canonical literary forms—a move, one might note, associated with the now canonized historical avant-grade—multicultural artists often embrace and transform and intervene in the canon. In addition—as evidenced by the constant return to forms of folk knowledge, oral literature, legend, and myth as literary precursor and inspiration—multicultural artists bring to the cultural field other traditions and canons heretofore absent from institutional study.

All this is not to say that multiculturalism does not question (the metaphor is often "explode") the canon. It does so, however, only as it lives at the rupture—of histories, of cultures, of social and aesthetic practices—with which it cannot do away. Rather than bury, exile, or fire the canon, the multicultural critic seeks out the discontinuities made evident through its deployment within institutionalized academic spaces. Rather than deny the centrality of Shakespeare, Chaucer, Milton (or Eliot, Pound, Stein)—those great figures in the pantheon of "English" literature that burn brightest in the constellation of Anglo-American literary tradition—the multicultural critic scrutinizes their prominence. Why are they prominent? How does this preclude multicultural literature from gaining a foothold in the canon? What type of dialogue is being created between canonical and multicultural literatures?

Curricular controversy is just one site where issues of the postmodern and the multicultural clearly converge. Postmodern suspicion of master narratives and empty tradition provides the multicultural with ammunition as it seeks out the discontinuities—historical, aesthetic, linguistic, institutional—inherent in the controversy.

From the other side, the multicultural provides an insight into the critical potential of postmodernism. Postmodernism, several critics note, is plagued by its seeming inability to offer a position beyond the diffused and defused webs of social organization. In the slippery ground of the postmodern, no Archimedean point exists from which to construct an effective critical discourse. While multiculturalism does not offer a purely Other space, its compromised and interpenetrated position does allow for a historically inscribed space which is not like this one. The multicultural explores ways that enable forms of agency and identity within a decentered world. It points toward a resistant postmodernism already at hand.

The dissolution of self from Self marked within the postmodern as the "death of the subject" stands within the multicultural as a (always-already present) form of alienation. The decentralized subject finds its perfect and painful analogue in the decentered migrant displaced by economic and/or political violence. Alienation is not a condition unique to multicultural subjects, as the Chicano critic and poet Rafael Jesús González observes: "The question of identity, the desire for integration of the self, the preoccupation with recovering a sense of ontological potency is a theme that runs through all 20th century [modernist] Western poetry" (130). The Chicano as multicultural member of contemporary society stands at the alienating but familiar rupture between industrialization and human value. The Chicano as an example of the multicultural stands in this alienated landscape with a difference: "What is interesting about Chicano poetry is not its preoccupation with alienation as such, but that it is so conscious of it, that it so clearly links alienation with cultural dislocation" (130). The migratory experience—the negotiated journey of agency, the quest for justice, the reconfiguration of community and family—reveals strategies for empowerment with which the rest of the postmodern socius might do well to catch up. The troubled histories of economic displacement and political persecution that haunt

the migrations of Mexicans and others to this country provide a glimpse into strategies of survival in which decentered subjectivity is not replaced with a simplistic paradigm of origin or tradition. Rather, a highly dynamic and fluid form of social
organization, cultural affirmation, and personal identification emerges.[5]

Those critics interested in multicultural issues who dismiss postmodernism as a
"white problem" err in one of two ways. By refusing to theorize multicultural issues
within the postmodern space of the university, they deny their own assigned position
in the institution—their "unavoidable starting point," as Gayatri Spivak articulates
in "Theory in the Margin." Thus they wield power blindly. Or, conversely, they posit
their position as beyond the institution—banishing themselves to a margin that "as
such is wholly other"—and so deny academic power altogether.

Either position prevents them from capitalizing on Lyotard's observation: "To
the obsolescence of the metanarrative apparatus of legitimation corresponds the crisis of metaphysical philosophy and of the university institution which in the past relied on it" (xxiv). The conditions of postmodernity and the exigencies of the
multicultural can function symbiotically if the concerns of those historically config-
ured as Other, alien, marginal are inserted into this ruptured cultural space. The
power of this relationship is readily evident in the unease demonstrated by the Hilton
Kramers, the Allan Blooms, the Roger Kimballs of academia. It is no wonder they
feel under siege. Needless to say, these defenders of culture seem to invest their energies so fully in keeping the hordes at bay that they (willfully?) forget some important truths. Their treasured "culture" has only ascended its privileged throne thanks
to a very dirty history of armed confrontation, warfare, economic imperialism, and
colonial exploitation. Their defense rests on the separation of the best that is thought
and known from the rest of the dirty world. This rationale masks what Walter Benjamin's theses on history reveal so brilliantly: "There is no document of civilization
which is not at the same time a document of barbarism" (256). The canon debate
comes down to this: who serves a political master more—those who assert Benjamin's observation or those who deny it?

The multicultural within the institutional space of the academy seeks to reveal
the barbarity implicit in the cultural documents encased and replicated by the university. More importantly, scholars working within multicultural fields help to reveal
not just the discontinuities present in the institutional creation and preservation of
culture. They present configurations of power and knowledge based in marginal
communities and histories. They explore realms of justice and morality constructed
locally, specifically, often in opposition to master narratives. They work within the
larger cultural movement that rejects master narratives of Western Culture in order
to give voice to (among others) the illegitimate knowledges of the multicultural. Here
the trajectories of postmodernism and multiculturalism most clearly converge.

5. DISPERSAL

Yet no sooner do they meet than they again seem to diverge. For the postmodern
dissolution of the subject—a fact viewed as either inevitable (à la Jameson) or desirable (à la Baudrillard)—runs counter to the desires expressed by the multicul-

tural. In the margin, subjectivity is a condition still staunchly to be sought.[6] Post-modernism, if it is understood as a poststructural position, fails to allow for the construction of self-identity. In his discussion of the postmodern condition, Lyotard claims, for example: "The narrative function is losing its functors, its great hero, its great dangers, its great voyages, its great goal" (xxiv). He slides from the dismissal of *grand récits* (a useful move for advocating the multicultural) to a questioning of agency *in toto* (a move not so useful). His conflation of postmodernism and poststructuralism marks the weakness of his definition. As Radhakrishnan underscores:

> Post-structuralist thought perpetuates itself on the guarantee that no "break" (Althusser) is possible with the past even though its initial intentional trajectory was precisely to make visible this very "break," valorize it *qua* "break," and then proceed towards a different and differential creation. Post-structuralist intentionality thus desiccates itself, allegorizes this desiccation, and offers this allegorically perennial revolution as the most appropriate defense against the reproduction of such categories and structures as Self, Subject, Identity, etc. ("Feminist")

Radhakrishnan's critique of poststructuralism underscores Huyssen's observation that "French theory provides us primarily with an archeology of modernity, a theory of modernism at the stage of its exhaustion" (40). The endless subversion of meta-narratives within certain forms of poststructuralism has led—as critics from Seyla Ben-Habib to Christopher Norris have noted—to an endless playfulness, a polysemic perversity in which agency and empowerment can only be judged by their performative power. Lyotard's devaluation of all narrative functions *en masse*—his refusal of a break that would allow for a privileged social/political/cultural creation—represents an allegorization of his refusal of grand narratives. Multicultural texts are the products of a discontinuous history marked by an asymmetrical relationship to power. Exploited and dispossessed, the multicultural within history reveals the breaks—the contradictions, the limitations, the barbarity—of master narratives, and this in order to "proceed towards a different and differential creation."

Lyotard's work exemplifies the most pernicious poststructuralist traits—ahistoricity and decontextualization. On the one hand, the grand narratives he is so quick to dismiss still stimulate the cultural, social, political systems which define and regulate our lives at almost every level. On the other, these master narratives do not represent *all* narratives. Micronarratives, migratory readings, articulations of the local perpetually divide and reproduce themselves. These narratives must, if postmodernism is to save itself, be given privilege. While "justice" and "liberation" may be terms linked to metanarratives, the construction of these terms within particular localities and among people who have not received justice or achieved liberation is a process that will continue.

The narratives that seek to enact justice proceed, fully aware of, but not hamstrung by, the knowledge that the Enlightenment project may at times manifest itself in cancerous eruptions of blind inhumanity, violent upheaval, and spiritual desecration. Nations and cultures still struggle for freedom from colonial and neocolonial denigration and exploitation; the disempowered still try to articulate an affirmative identity of the self and of agency; the dispossessed still hope for a more equitable distribution of food and funds.

Postmodernism—in order to be resistant, critical, and finally, compatible with multicultural issues—cannot dismiss notions of narration, subjectivity, agency. These subjects must be subject to scrutiny, contextualization, and reconceptualization within a postmodern multicultural space. The problem for the postmodern critic, as Huyssen argues, is "to redefine the possibilities of critique in postmodern terms rather than relegating them to oblivion" (9). However, what we understand the Self to be cannot be dismissed as a nostalgic ideological construction employed to perpetuate capitalism.

One critical trajectory Huyssen traces, intersecting both postmodern and multicultural terrains, follows the construction of subjectivity, especially in terms of cultural formation. The self-assertion of minority cultures and their emergence into public consciousness, for example, have helped collapse the strict modernist separation of high and low culture: "such rigorous segregation simply does not make much sense within a given minority culture which has always existed outside in the shadow of the dominant culture" (23). In the 1960s, "minorities" and "marginals" finally entered into the consciousness of the university and other cultural institutions. The repercussions of this entrance are still with us.

We see, for instance, the emergency of nationalisms among both the inner and outer colonized—minority groups in the United States and nationalist movement groups throughout the world—in the postmodern 1960s. We see the formation of academic fields created within and against academic and other institutions in the 1970s. We see an increase in the numbers of professionals and intellectuals of color in the 1980s. None of these phenomena is without its contradictions, dislocations, and ruptures: genealogies which are as conflicted and potentially violent as any other. We can agree with Huyssen, however, that "to reject the validity of the question Who is writing? or Who is speaking? is simply no longer a radical position in 1984 [let alone now]. It merely duplicates on the level of aesthetics and theory what capitalism as a system of exchange relations produces tendentially in everyday life: the denial of subjectivity in the very process of its construction" (44).

To reposition subjectivity within theoretical discourses—especially those focusing on the postmodern—remains an obviously complex matter. At one extreme, we find a Jamesonian postmodernity populated by subjects in a corporate, collectivized, post-individualistic age. This conceptualization leaves slight room for those constituencies which, like multicultural groups, have historically led collectivized (and marginalized) lives. At another extreme stands the poststructural position that subjectivity represents a constructed, ideologically infused text. This offers little to the historically disempowered who posit a sense of agency as an empowering rather than a repressive act. When performed by those (inner and outer) colonized or postcolonized groups who have been denied individuality, representation, subjectivity, and agency, the reclamation of a self proves a resistant act. The emancipatory potential of that perpetual demystification machine—poststructuralism—as well as liberal humanism's empowering notion of individuality and agency, changes when applied to those who have suffered the greatest violence spawned by the expansionist policies of European Enlightenment.

6. LOCALITY

One area in which issues of agency and empowerment play themselves out resides in the field of politics. Given the decentralization and fragmentation of the postmodern condition, how can political agency prove effective? On what principles does a political movement base itself? Having given up on master narratives like "revolution," "liberation", "Marxism", how can political action occur?

Jameson argues that the type of local politics available within the postmodern precludes any real political engagement. From Jameson's Marxist position, politics can work only when coordinating local and global struggles for a transfiguration of the here-and-now. The purely local cannot successfully challenge that which forms the global dimension—economics. By focusing on the micropolitics of the local—the politics of postmodernity—we are left with a politics marked by a willed euphoria of some metaphysical permanent revolution. This euphoria, from Jameson's view, is a compensation formation for our times when genuine or "totalizing" politics are no longer possible.

Jameson does offer some slight consolation. It will be "politically productive" and "a modest form of genuine politics" to attend to such things as the waning of a visible global dimension, the ideological resistance to the concept of totality, the shearing away of such apparent abstractions as the economic system and social totality (*Postmodernism* 330).

This sort of "secondary" or "minority" politics may indeed prove to be the political legacy of postmodernism, but not exactly as Jameson envisions it. The challenge posed by the postmodern is to employ the legitimate concerns of the local in reshaping the global without reproducing forms of discursive violence. How to move from local concern to global change without, for instance, reinscribing the marginal? Boaventura de Sousa Santos observes that postmodern knowledge "favors the near to the detriment of the real. To be pragmatic is to approach reality from [William] James's 'last things,' that is, from consequences, and the shorter the distance between acts and consequences, the greater the accuracy of the judgment on validity" (100). In other words, the total can be at hand. The ethics of a self practiced in solidarity with others lends a legitimacy to immediate political struggle and action. In this sense (among others) postmodern knowledge can be understood as "local." Modernist foundationalist epistemologies, to borrow Rorty's term, cease to function.

Postmodern knowledge—local, proximate—while not totalizing, is, Santos argues, total: "The localism involved is the localism of context, not the localism of static spaces and immemorial traditions. It is an internationalist localism, without a solid genius loci . . ." (100). Postmodern knowledge works at the interstices of paradigms, negotiates through (historical, cultural, economic) contexts. The specificity of the local does not preclude connections to larger systems of social organization. The local and its politics need not remain superficially "local." Not a politics of populism, politics of the local represents a politics of rhizomic resistance.

Thus Wahneema Lubiano scrutinizes David Harvey's invocation of the 1960s "revolutionary" slogan—"Think globally. Act locally." This scrutiny emerges from the concern over what precisely a politics of rhizomic resistance may signify. A multicultural postmodern political practice of the local, Lubiano finally admonishes, "in cultural resistance terms, might require some lack of sureness, confidence, some awareness of what Spivak [in *The Post-Colonial Critic*] calls 'vulnerability' (18), or, to paraphrase

Foster [in *The Anti-Aesthetic*] a willingness to recognize that a representation may 'mean' differently in place, in moment, and in particular minds" (159). A multicultural postmodernism foregrounds the localism of context, the specificity of devalued knowledges and histories repressed by the hegemonic "political unconscious," and the potential for the local to achieve some significant and lasting social change.

From Jameson's view, however, there is no escaping the need for a global (class-bound) vision of politics. To describe the longing for class politics of some older type as simply some "nostalgia," he notes, "is about as adequate as to characterize the body's hunger, before dinner, as a 'nostalgia for food'" (*Postmodernism* 331). We might admire the metaphor but remain suspicious of its point.

Jameson incessantly privileges class over race as a site upon which to contest discourses of oppression. In "Periodizing the 60s," he argues that the merger of the AFL and CIO in 1955 formed

> a fundamental "condition of possibility" for the unleashing of the new social and political dynamics of the 60s by forcing the demands made by blacks, women and other minorities out of the classical institutions of an older working-class politics. Thus "liberated" from social class and released to find new modes of social and political expression, their concerns could only focus on the local rather than global.(181)

Kicked out of the global political arena, the marginal are left to squabble among local issues that preclude any genuine systemic transformation.

Boaventura de Sousa Santos allows us a somewhat different view of this historical development. He argues that "the relative weakening of class practices and of class politics has been compensated for by the emergence of new agonistic spaces that propose new social postmaterialist and political agendas (peace, ecology, sexual and racial equality) to be acted out by new insurgent groups and social movements" (97). He goes on to note that the discovery that capitalism produces classes, and "that classes are the organizing matrix of social transformation" was a nineteenth-century discovery: "The twentieth century enters the historical scene only when it discovers that capitalism also produces racial and sexual differences and that these can also be nodal points for social struggles" (97). The multicultural provides critical insight into the processes by which racial and ethnic others can form and have formed "nodal points for social struggle." Santos's position offers a vision of politics beyond class, one which moves away from a showdown between a powerful master discourse (Marxism) and a contradictory or negating discourse (radical locality). Politics of locality do not seek to overthrow a Marxist revolutionary project with another master narrative. Rather, the narrative of locality functions to supplement other narratives, other political configurations.

7. MIGRATION

Multiculturalism can form a discourse which, as it critiques violence, precludes the violence of replication. To be an effective discourse, it cannot propose the substitution of one master discourse for another. Homi Bhabha, therefore, argues for a supplementary minority position. Bhabha seeks to articulate agency and empowerment for the marginal couched not in terms of overthrowing (and so replicating) or capturing (and therefore employing) the powers of the state: "Insinuating itself into the terms of reference of the dominant discourse, the supplementary antagonizes the implicit power to generalize, to produce the sociological solidity" (306). The multicultural critic must be aware of avoiding the processes that replicate, reflect, reproduce the tyranny of globalizing discourses even as they are combated.

Hence the significance of negotiation as a technique associated with the migratory. The point becomes not to deny the potentiality of postmodern thought for multicultural issues, nor to erase one's position as a compromised critic of dominant culture, nor to negate multiculturalism's ability to speak to and with and through postmodernism. Rather—caught between the rock of practice and the hard place of theory—one might want to attempt a series of negotiations that wed a contractual sense of power and a navigational sense of journey. A migratory reading wends between the Scylla of the local and the Charybdis of the total, between the devil that historical and cultural specificity can be and the deep murky seas of essentialization and homogeneity. This rough passage, Linda Hutcheon suggests, is "inside yet outside, inscribing yet contesting, complicitous yet critical" (158). A complicitous critique, the migratory represents a model by which difficult cultural and political terrain can be successfully traversed. More to the point, the migratory also evokes within its discursive strategies the same process of negotiation undertaken by migrant groups caught between poverty and repression in their homelands and cultural dislocation and oppressive marginalization in the centers of power to which they flee.

A practice already implicit in the multicultural condition becomes the necessary element for deploying multicultural issues within a postmodern cultural space: continuous critical negotiation, an endless engagement with contradictory positions. These engagements seek neither to refute nor overthrow particular historically inscribed concepts. Instead, they attempt "to engage with the 'anterior' space of the sign that structures the symbolic language of alternative, antagonistic cultural practices" (Bhabha 313). This engagement takes the form of a type of genealogy, the tracing of the discontinuous region of multicultural subjectivity, the retelling of stories otherwise forgotten. To form a resistant practice across the fields of the multicultural and the postmodern involves a process that discovers or recovers the discredited histories of groups circumscribed by regimes of repressive discursive practices.

This proposal does not posit a clear field of cultural play. It is more like a heavily guarded borderland, a potential threat at every step. There stands at one point the poststructuralist valuing of difference as a dissociated and ahistorical quality bearing no relevance to the actual histories of those constructed as racially or sexually different. At another point, there stands the suspicion of postmodernity as a new, subsuming, and repressive master narrative, sacrificing historical and cultural specificity for a project of elite self-interest. Again at another position, one finds those who would privilege class at every turn over race as a compelling catalyst for social and political change. Compound these issues with the postcolonial valuation of such modern notions as "nation" and "agency"; add a fear of the homogenization of difference; join this to the problematic dismissal of narrative as a compelling and powerful force. We are left with a terrain scarred by discursive and political rupture.

Yet this should not deter us from explaining and exploiting the potentialities inherent in a crossing of sympathetic—though not synonymous—intellectual projects. Theories of the postmodern form an academic discourse by which to interject multicultural issues into the boardrooms and backrooms (let alone classrooms) of institutionalized educational systems. George Yúdice, in his essay "Marginality and the Ethics of Survival," persuasively concludes that intellectuals "need not speak for others, but we are responsible for a 'self-forming activity' that can in no way be ethical if we do not act against the 'disappearance' of oppressed subjects" (230). Though academics cannot always speak to economically, racially, politically oppressed peoples at home and abroad, we can speak about and against their dangerous and denigrated positions. An engagement of the multicultural with the postmodern acts, finally, as a self-conscious and self-critical move against disappearance.

NOTES

I wish to acknowledge the University of Wisconsin System Institute on Race and Ethnicity, which provided funding for the period in which I wrote this essay. I am indebted as well to Gordon Hunter and Larry Scanlon for their keen readings and helpful suggestions.
   1. Suleiman refers to the crossing of feminism with postmodernism in this quote. She herself notes that the same argument can be made "for the alliance between postmodernism and the Third World minorities or Afro-American writers, male and female" (127).
   2. Foster's introduction to The Anti-Aesthetic argues for a critical postmodernism that stands in contradistinction to a neoconservative antimodernism. Habermas in his well-known "Modernity—An Incomplete Project" like Foster argues that postmodernism represents a neoconservative reaction against modernism, but implies that any critical postmodernism is really another turn in the modernist project. Huyssen in "Mapping the Postmodern" seeks to articulate those modalities where postmodernism finds its most powerful critical focus—among green, women, and minority movements.
   3. "The 60s was, then, the period in which all these 'natives' [minorities, women, etc.] became human beings, and this internally as well as externally: those inner colonized of the first world—'minorities,' marginals, and women—fully as much as its external subjects and official 'natives.' All these 'natives' of gender, race, etc.—new social and political categories—are related to a crisis in the more universal category of social class, the institutions through which a real class politics expressed itself" (Jameson, "Periodizing" 181). As a descriptive statement, Jameson is correct. However, later in this essay I will critique his all too easy conflation of race and class politics.
   4. In "Opponents, Audiences, Constituencies, and Community," Said suggests that academic publishers function upon the same market principles as publishers of cookbooks, exercise manuals, and others in "a very long series of unnecessary books" (3). He goes on to argue for interference across academic and other disciplines as a means of intervening in the safe reproduction of specialized knowledge. I would argue that this is an articulation of a resistant postmodern and multicultural strategy.
   5. For a fascinating discussion of an example of this dynamic process of identity construction, see Roger Rouse's "Mexican Migration and the Social Space of Postmodernism." His article studies the migration patterns of residents from Aguililla, Mexico, who take up simultaneous residence in Redwood City, California: "the resulting contradictions have not come simply from persistence of past forms and contemporary adjustments or from involvement in district lifeworlds within the United States. Rather, they reflect the fact that Aguilillans see their current lives and future possibilities as involving simultaneous engagements in places associated with markedly different forms of experience" (14).

6. Here Elizabeth Fox-Genovese's much cited observation proves apt: "From the perspective of those previously excluded from the cultural elite, the death of the subject or the death of the author seems somewhat premature. Surely it is no coincidence that the Western white male elite proclaimed the death of the subject at precisely the moment at which it might have had to share that status with women and peoples of other races and classes who were beginning to challenge its supremacy" (134).

REFERENCES

Baker, Houston. *Blues, Ideology, and Afro-American Literature.* Chicago: University of Chicago Press, 1984.

Benjamin, Walter. "Theses on the Philosophy of History." *Illuminations: Essays and Reflections.* Trans. Harry Zohn. Ed. Hannah Arendt. New York: Schocken, 1969. 253–64.

Bhabha, Homi K. "DissemiNation: Time, Narrative, and the Margins of the Modern Nation." *Nation and Narration.* Ed. Homi K. Bhabha. New York: Routledge, 1990. 291–322.

Carr, C. "Columbus at the Checkpoint: Guillermo Gómez-Peña Rediscovers 'America.' " *Village Voice* (22 October 1991): 43–44.

Dasenbrock, Reed Way. "Intelligibility and Meaningfulness in Multicultural Literature in English." *PMLA* 102 (1987): 10–19.

Deleuze, Gilles, and Félix Guattari. *Anti-Oedipus: Capitalism and Schizophrenia.* Trans. Robert Hurley, Mark See, and Helen R. Lane. Minneapolis: University of Minnesota Press, 1983.

Foster, Hal, ed. "Postmodernism: A Preface." *The Anti-Aesthetic: Essays on Postmodern Culture.* Port Townsend, WA: Bay Press, 1983. ix–xvi.

Fox-Genovese, Elizabeth. "The Claims of a Common Culture: Gender, Race, Class, and the Canon." *Salmagundi* 72 (Fall 1986): 131–43.

Fregoso, Rosa Linda, and Angie Chabram. "Chicana/o Cultural Representations: Reframing Alternative Critical Discourses." *Cultural Studies* 4.3 (1990): 203–12.

González, Rafael Jesús. "Chicano Poetry/Smoking Mirror." *New Scholar* 6 (1977): 127–37.

Habermas, Jürgen. "Modernity—An Incomplete Project." *The Anti-Aesthetic: Essays on Postmodern Culture.* Ed. Hal Foster. Port Townsend, WA: Bay Press, 1983. 3–15.

hooks, bell. "Postmodern Blackness." *Yearning: Race, Gender, and Cultural Politics.* Boston: South End Press, 1990. 23–31.

Hutcheon, Linda. "The Post-modern Ex-centric: The Center That Will Not Hold." *Feminism and Institutions: Dialogues on Feminist Theory.* Ed. Linda S. Kauffman. Cambridge: Basil Blackwell, 1989. 141–65.

Huyssen, Andreas. "Mapping the Postmodern." *New German Critique* 33 (1984): 5–52.

Jameson, Fredric. "Periodizing the 60s." *The 60s Without Apology.* Ed. Sohnya Sayres, Anders Stephanson, Stanley Aronowitz, and Fredric Jameson. Minneapolis: University of Minnesota Press, 1984. 178–209.

———. *Postmodernism, or, The Cultural Logic of Late Capitalism.* Durham: Duke UP, 1991.

Lowe, Lisa. "Heterogeneity, Hybridity, Multiplicity: Marking Asian American Differences." *Diaspora* 1 (1990): 24–44.

Lubiano, Wahneema. "Shuckin' Off the African-American Native Other: What's 'Po-Mo' Got to Do with it?" *Cultural Critique* 18 (1991): 149–86.

Lyotard, Jean-François. *The Postmodern Condition: A Report on Knowledge.* Trans. Geoff Bennington and Brian Massumi. Minneapolis: University of Minnesota Press, 1984.

Minnesota Council of Teachers of English and Minnesota Humanities Commission. *Braided Lives: An Anthology of Multicultural American Writing.* St. Paul: Minnesota Humanities Commission, 1991.

Radhakrishnan, R. "Culture as Common Ground: Ethnicity and Beyond." *MELUS* 14 (1987): 5–19.

———. "Feminist Historiography and Post-Structuralist Thought: Intersections and Departures." *The Difference Within: Feminism and Critical Theory*. Ed. Elizabeth Meese and Alice Parker. Philadelphia: John Benjamins, 1989. 189–205.

Rodriguez, Richard. *Hunger of Memory: The Education of Richard Rodriguez*. New York: Bantam, 1982.

Rorty, Richard. *Philosophy and the Mirror of Nature*. Princeton: Princeton UP, 1980.

Rouse, Roger. "Mexican Migration and the Social Space of Postmodernism." *Diaspora* 1.1 (1991): 8–23.

Said, Edward. "Opponents, Audiences, Constituencies and Community." *Critical Inquiry* 9 (1982): 1–26.

———. "Traveling Theory." *The World, the Text, and the Critic*. Cambridge: Harvard UP, 1983. 226–47.

Santos, Boaventura de Sousa. "The Postmodern Transition: Law and Politics." *The Fate of Law*. Ed. Austin Sarat and Thomas R. Kearns. Ann Arbor: U of Michigan P, 1991. 79–118.

Spivak, Gayatri Chakravorty. *The Post-Colonial Critic: Interviews, Strategies, Dialogues*. Ed. Sarah Harysm. New York: Routledge, 1990.

———. "Theory in the Margin." *Consequences of Theory*. Ed. Jonathan Arac and Barbara Johnson. Baltimore: Johns Hopkins UP, 1991. 122–44.

Suleiman, Susan Rubin. "Feminism and Postmodernism: A Question of Politics." Ed. Ingeborg Hoesterey. Indianapolis: Indiana UP, 1991. 111–30.

West, Cornel. "Black Culture and Postmodernism." *Remaking History*. Ed. Barbara Kruger and Phil Mariani. Seattle: Bay Press, 1989. 87–96.

Yúdice, George. "Marginality and the Ethics of Survival." *Social Text* 21 (1989): 214–36.

12

Movimientos de Rebeldía
y las Culturas que Traicionan

Gloria Anzaldúa

Esos movimientos de rebeldía que tenemos en la sangre nosotros los mexicanos surgen como ríos desbocanados en mis venas. Y como mi raza que cada en cuando deja caer esa esclavitud de obedecer, de callarse y aceptar, en mi está la rebeldía encimita de mi carne. Debajo de mi humillada mirada está una cara insolente lista para explotar. Me costó muy caro mi rebeldía—acalambrada condevselos y dudas, sintiendome inútil, estúpida, e impotente.

Me entra una rabia cuando alguien—sea mi mamá, la Iglesia, la cultura de los anglos—me dice haz esto, haz eso sin considerar mis deseos.

Repele. Hable pa' 'tras. Fuí muy hocicona. Era indiferente a muchos valores de mi cultura. No me deje de los hombres. No fuí buena ni obediente.

Pero he crecido. Ya no soló paso toda mi vida botando las costumbres y los valores de mi cultura que me traicionan. También recojo las costumbres que por el tiempo se han provado y las costumbres de respeto a las mujeres. *But despite my growing tolerance, for this Chicana* la guerra de independencia *is a constant.*

THE STRENGTH OF MY REBELLION

I have a vivid memory of an old photograph: I am six years old. I stand between my father and mother, head cocked to the right, the toes of my flat feet gripping the ground. I hold my mother's hand.

To this day I'm not sure where I found the strength to leave the source, the mother, disengage from my family, *mi tierra, mi gente,* and all that picture stood for.

I had to leave home so I could find myself, find my own intrinsic nature buried under the personality that had been imposed on me.

I was the first in six generations to leave the Valley, the only one in my family to ever leave home. But I didn't leave all the parts of me: I kept the ground of my own being. On it I walked away, taking with me the land, the Valley, Texas. *Gané mi camino y me largué. Muy andariega mi hija.* Because I left of my own accord *me dicen, "¿Cómo te gusta la mala vida?"*

At a very early age I had a strong sense of who I was and what I was about and what was fair. I had a stubborn will. It tried constantly to mobilize my soul under my own regime, to live life on my own terms no matter how unsuitable to others they were. *Terca.* Even as a child I would not obey. I was "lazy." Instead of ironing my younger brothers' shirts or cleaning the cupboards, I would pass many hours studying, reading, painting, writing. Every bit of self-faith I'd painstakingly gathered took a beating daily. Nothing in my culture approved of me. *Había agarrado malos pasos.* Something was "wrong" with me. *Estabá más allá de la tradición.*

There is a rebel in me—the Shadow-Beast. It is a part of me that refuses to take orders from outside authorities. It refuses to take orders from my conscious will, it threatens the sovereignty of my rulership. It is that part of me that hates constraints of any kind, even those self-imposed. At the least hint of limitations on my time or space by others, it kicks out with both feet. Bolts.

CULTURAL TYRANNY

Culture forms our beliefs. We perceive the version of reality that it communicates. Dominant paradigms, predefined concepts that exist as unquestionable, unchallengeable, are transmitted to us through the culture. Culture is made by those in power—men. Males make the rules and laws; women transmit them. How many times have I heard mothers and mothers-in-law tell their sons to beat their wives for not obeying them, for being *hociconas* (big mouths), for being *callajeras* (going to visit and gossip with neighbors), for expecting their husbands to help with the rearing of children and the housework, for wanting to be something other than housewives?

The culture expects women to show greater acceptance of, and commitment to, the value system than men. The culture and the Church insist that women are subservient to males. If a woman rebels she is a *mujer mala.* If a woman doesn't renounce herself in favor of the male, she is selfish. If a woman remains a *virgen* until she marries, she is a good woman. For a woman of my culture there used to be only three directions she could turn: to the Church as a nun, to the streets as a prostitute, or to the home as a mother. Today some of us have a fourth choice: entering the world by way of education and career and becoming self-autonomous persons. A very few of us. As a working class people our chief activity is to put food in our mouths, a roof over our heads and clothes on our backs. Educating our children is out of reach for most of us. Educated or not, the onus is still on woman to be a wife/mother—only the nun can escape mother-hood. Women are made to feel total failures if they don't marry and have children. "*¿Y cuándo te casas, Gloria? Se te va a pasar el tren.*" Y yo les digo, "*Pos si me caso, no va ser con un hombre.*" Se *quedan calladitas. Sí, soy hija de la Chingada.* I've always been her daughter. *No 'tés chingando.* Humans fear the supernatural, both the undivine (the animal impulses such as sexuality, the unconscious, the unknown, the alien) and the divine (the superhuman, the god in us). Culture and religion seek to protect us from these two forces. The female, by virtue of creating entities of flesh and blood in her stomach (she bleeds every month but does not die), by virtue of being in tune with nature's cycles, is feared. Because, according to Christianity and most other major religions, woman is carnal, animal, and closer to the undivine, she must be protected. Protected from herself. Woman is the stranger, the other. She is man's recognized nightmarish pieces, his Shadow-Beast. The sight of her sends him into a frenzy of anger and fear.

La gorra, el rebozo, la mantilla are symbols of my culture's "protection" of women. Culture (read males) professes to protect women. Actually it keeps women in rigidly defined roles. It keeps the girlchild from other men—don't poach on my preserves, only I can touch my child's body. Our mothers taught us well, "*Los hombres nomás quieren una cosa*"; men aren't to be trusted, they are selfish and are like children. Mothers made sure we didn't walk into a room of brothers or fathers or uncles in nightgowns or shorts. We were never alone with men, not even those of our own family.

Through our mothers, the culture gave us mixed messages: *No voy a dejar que ningún pelado desgraciado maltrate a mis hijos.* And in the next breath it would say, *La mujer tiene que hacer lo que le diga el hombre.* Which was it to be—strong, or submissive, rebellious or conforming?

Tribal rights over those of the individual insured the survival of the tribe and were necessary then, and, as in the case of all indigenous peoples in the world who are still fighting off intentional, premeditated murder (genocide), they are still necessary.

Much of what the culture condemns focuses on kinship relationships. The welfare of the family, the community, and the tribe is more important than the welfare of the individual. The individual exists first as kin—as sister, as father, as *padrino*—and last as self.

In my culture, selfishness is condemned, especially in women; humility and self-lessness, the absence of selfishness, are considered virtues. In the past, acting humble with members outside the family ensured that you would make no one *envidioso* (envious); therefore he or she would not use witchcraft against you. If you get above yourself, you're an *envidiosa*. If you don't behave like everyone else, *la gente* will say that you think you're better than others, *que te crees grande.* With ambition (condemned in the Mexican culture and valued in the Anglo) comes envy. *Respeto* carries with it a set of rules so that social categories and hierarchies will be kept in order: respect is reserved for *la abuela, papá, el patrón*, those with power in the community. Women are at the bottom of the ladder one rung above the deviants. The Chicano, *mexicano*, and some Indian cultures have no tolerance for deviance. Deviance is whatever is condemned by the community. Most societies try to get rid of their deviants. Most cultures have burned and beaten their homosexuals and others who deviate from the sexual common. The queer are the mirror reflecting the heterosexual tribe's fear: being different, being other and therefore lesser, therefore sub-human, inhuman, non-human.

HALF AND HALF

There was a *muchacha* who lived near my house. *La gente del pueblo* talked about her being *una de las otras*, "of the Others." They said that for six months she was a woman who had a vagina that bled once a month, and that for the other six months she was a man, had a penis and she peed standing up. They called her half and half, *mita' y mita'*, neither one nor the other but a strange doubling, a deviation of nature that horrified, a work of nature inverted. But there is a magic aspect in abnormality and so-called deformity. Maimed, mad, and sexually different people were believed to possess supernatural powers by primal cultures' magico-religious thinking. For them, abnormality was the price a person had to pay for her or his inborn extraordinary gift.

There is something compelling about being both male and female, about having an entry into both worlds. Contrary to some psychiatric tenets, half and halfs are not suffering from a confusion of sexual identity, or even from a confusion of gender. What we are suffering from is an absolute despot duality that says we are able to be only one or the other. It claims that human nature is limited and cannot evolve into something better. But I, like other queer people, am two in one body, both male and female. I am the embodiment of the *hieros gamos*: the coming together of opposite qualities within.

FEAR OF GOING HOME: HOMOPHOBIA

For the lesbian of color, the ultimate rebellion she can make against her native culture is through her sexual behavior. She goes against two moral prohibitions: sexuality and homosexuality. Being lesbian and raised Catholic, indoctrinated as straight, I *made the choice to be queer* (for some it is genetically inherent). It's an interesting path, one that continually slips in and out of the white, the Catholic, the Mexican, the indigenous, the instincts. In and out of my head. It makes for *loquería*, the crazies. It is a path of knowledge—one of knowing (and of learning) the history of oppression of our *raza*. It is a way of balancing, of mitigating duality.

In a New England college where I taught, the presence of a few lesbians threw the more conservative heterosexual students and faculty into a panic. The two lesbian students and we two lesbian instructors met with them to discuss their fears. One of the students said, "I thought homophobia meant fear of going home after a residency."

And I thought, how apt. Fear of going home. And of not being taken in. We're afraid of being abandoned by the mother, the culture, *la Raza*, for being unacceptable, faulty, damaged. Most of us unconsciously believe that if we reveal this unacceptable aspect of the self our mother/culture/race will totally reject us. To avoid rejection, some of us conform to the values of the culture, push the unacceptable parts into the shadows. Which leaves only one fear—that we will be found out and that the Shadow-Beast will break out of its cage. Some of us take another route. We try to make ourselves conscious of the Shadow-Beast, stare at the sexual lust and lust for power and destruction we see on its face, discern among its features the under-shadow that the reigning order of heterosexual males project on our Beast. Yet still others of us take it another step: we try to waken the Shadow-Beast inside us. Not many jump at the chance to confront the Shadow-Beast in the mirror without flinching at her lidless serpent eyes, her cold clammy moist hand dragging us underground, fangs barred and hissing. How does one put feathers on this particular serpent? But a few of us have been lucky—on the face of the Shadow-Beast we have seen not lust but tenderness; on its face we have uncovered the lie.

INTIMATE TERRORISM: LIFE IN THE BORDERLANDS

The world is not a safe place to live in. We shiver in separate cells in enclosed cities, shoulders hunched, barely keeping the panic below the surface of the skin, daily drinking shock along with our morning coffee, fearing the torches being set to our buildings, the attacks in the streets. Shutting down. Woman does not feel safe when her own culture, and white culture, are critical of her; when the males of all races hunt her as prey.

Alienated from her mother culture, "alien" in the dominant culture, the woman of color does not feel safe within the inner life of her Self. Petrified, she can't respond, her face caught between *los intersticios*, the spaces between the different worlds she inhabits.

The ability to respond is what is meant by responsibility, yet our cultures take away our ability to act—shackle us in the name of protection. Blocked, immobilized, we can't move forward, can't move backwards. That writhing serpent movement, the very movement of life, swifter than lightning, frozen.

We do not engage fully. We do not make full use of our faculties. We abnegate. And there in front of us are the crossroads and choice: to feel a victim where someone else is in control and therefore responsible and to blame (being a victim and transferring the blame on culture, mother, father, ex-lover, friend, absolves me of responsibility), or to feel strong, and, for the most part, in control.

My Chicana identity is grounded in the Indian woman's history of resistance. The Aztec female rites of mourning were rites of defiance protesting the cultural changes which disrupted the equality and balance between female and male, and protesting their demotion to a lesser status, their denigration. Like *la Llorona*, the Indian woman's only means of protest was wailing.

So *mamá, Raza*, how wonderful, *no tener que rendir cuentas a nadie*. I feel perfectly free to rebel and to rail against my culture. I fear no betrayal on my part because, unlike Chicanas and other women of color who grew up white or who have only recently returned to their native cultural roots, I was totally immersed in mine. It wasn't until I went to high school that I "saw" whites. Until I worked on my master's degree I had not gotten within an arm's distance of them. I was totally immersed *en lo mexicano*, a rural, peasant, isolated, *mexicanismo*. To separate from my culture (as from my family) I had to feel competent enough on the outside and secure enough inside to live life on my own. Yet in leaving home I did not lose touch with my origins because *lo mexicano* is in my system. I am a turtle, wherever I go I carry "home" on my back.

Not me sold out my people but they me. So yes, though "home" permeates every sinew and cartilage in my body, I too am afraid of going home. Though I'll defend my race and culture when they are attacked by non-*mexicanos, conosco el malestar de mi cultura*. I abhor some of my culture's ways, how it cripples its women, *como burras*, our strengths used against us, lowly *burras* bearing humility with dignity. The ability to serve, claim the males, is our highest virtue. I abhor how my culture makes *macho* caricatures of its men. No, I do not buy all the myths of the tribe into which I was born. I can understand why the more tinged with Anglo blood, the more adamantly my colored and colorless sisters glorify their colored culture's values—to offset the extreme devaluation of it by the white culture. It's a legitimate reaction. But I will not glorify those aspects of my culture which have injured me and which have injured me in the name of protecting me.

So, don't give me your tenets and your laws. Don't give me your lukewarm gods. What I want is an accounting with all three cultures—white, Mexican, Indian. I want the freedom to carve and chisel my own face, to staunch the bleeding with ashes, to fashion my own gods out of my entrails. And if going home is denied me then I will have to stand and claim my space, making a new culture—*una cultura mestiza*—with my own lumber, my own bricks and mortar, and my own feminist architecture.

THE WOUNDING OF THE INDIA-MESTIZA

Estas carnes indias que despreciamos nosotros los mexicanos asi como despreciamos y condenamos a nustra madre, Malinali. Nos condenamos a nosotros mismos. Esta raza vencida, enemigo cuerpo.

Not me sold out my people but they me. *Malinali Tenepat*, or *Malintzin*, has become known as *la Chingada*—the fucked one. She has become the bad word that passes a dozen times a day from the lips of Chicanos. Whore, prostitute, the woman who sold out her people to the Spaniards are epithets Chicanos spit out with contempt.

The worst kind of betrayal lies in making us believe that the Indian woman in us is the betrayer. We, *indias y mestizas*, police the Indian in us, brutalize and condemn her. Male culture has done a good job on us. *Son los costumbres que traicionan. La india en mí es la sombra: La Chingada, Tlazolteotl, Coatlicue. Son ellas que oyemos lamentando a sus hijas perdidas.*

Not me sold out my people but they me. Because of the color of my skin they betrayed me. The dark-skinned woman has been silenced, gagged, caged, bound into servitude with marriage, bludgeoned for 300 years, sterilized and castrated in the twentieth century. For 300 years she has been a slave, a force of cheap labor, colonized by the Spaniard, the Anglo, by her own people (and in Mesoamerica her lot under the Indian patriarchs was not free of wounding). For 300 years she was invisible, she was not heard. Many times she wished to speak, to act, to protest, to challenge. The odds were heavily against her. She hid her feelings; she hid her truths; she concealed her fire; but she kept stoking the inner flame. She remained faceless and voiceless, but a light shone through her veil of silence. And though she was unable to spread her limbs and though for her right now the sun has sunk under the earth and there is no moon, she continues to tend the flame. The spirit of the fire spurs her to fight for her own skin and a piece of ground to stand on, a ground from which to view the world—a perspective, a homeground where she can plumb the rich ancestral roots into her own ample *mestiza* heart. She waits till the waters are not so turbulent and the mountains not so slippery with sleet. Battered and bruised she waits, her bruises throwing her back upon herself and the rhythmic pulse of the feminine. *Coatlaopeuh* waits with her.

> *Aquí en la soledad prospera su rebeldía.*
> *En la soledad Ella prospera.*

IV
THE POLITICS OF LANGUAGE

13

English Only
The Tongue-tying of America

Donaldo Macedo

During the past decade conservative educators such as ex-Secretary of Education William Bennett and Diane Ravitch have mounted an unrelenting attack on bilingual and multicultural education. These conservative educators tend to recycle old assumptions about the "melting pot theory" and our "common culture," assumptions designed primarily to maintain the status quo. Maintained is a status quo that functions as a cultural reproduction mechanism which systematically does not allow other cultural subjects, who are considered outside of the mainstream, to be present in history. These cultural subjects who are profiled as the "other" are but palely represented in history within our purportedly democratic society in the form of Black History Month, Puerto Rican Day, and so forth. This historical constriction was elegantly captured by an 11th-grade Vietnamese student in California:

> I was so excited when my history teacher talked about the Vietnam War. Now at last, I thought, now we will study about my country. We didn't really study it. Just for one day, though, my country was real again. (Olsen, 1988, p. 68)

The incessant attack on bilingual education, which claims that it serves to tongue-tie students in their native language, not only negates the multilingual and multicultural nature of U.S. society, but blindly ignores the empirical evidence that has been amply documented in support of bilingual education. An example of a truly tongue-tied America materialized when the ex-foreign minister of the Soviet Union, Mr. Eduard Shevardnadze, began to deliver a speech in Russian during a recent commencement ceremony at Boston University. The silence that ensued was so overwhelming that one could hear a pin drop. Over 99% of the audience was saved from their monolingualism thanks to the intervention of an interpreter. In fact, the present overdose of monolingualism and Anglocentrism that dominates the current educational debate not only contributes to a type of mind-tied America, but also is incapable of producing educators and leaders who can rethink what it means to prepare students to enter the ever-changing, multilingual, and multicultural world of the 21st century.

It is both academically dishonest and misleading to simply point to some failures of bilingual education without examining the lack of success of linguistic minority students within a larger context of a general failure of public education in major urban centers. Furthermore, the English Only position points to a pedagogy of exclusion that views the learning of English as education itself. English Only advocates fail to question under what conditions English will be taught and by whom. For example, immersing non-English-speaking students in English as a Second Language (ESL) programs taught by untrained music, art, and social science teachers (as is the case in Massachusetts with the grandfather clause in ESL Certification) will hardly accomplish the avowed goals of the English Only movement. The proponents of English Only also fail to raise two other fundamental questions. First, if English is the most effective educational language, how can we explain that over 60 million Americans are illiterate or functionally illiterate (Kozol, 1985, p. 4)? Second, if education solely in English can guarantee linguistic minorities a better future, as educators like William Bennett promise, why do the majority of Black Americans, whose ancestors have been speaking English for over 200 years, find themselves still relegated to ghettos?

I want to argue in this paper that the answer lies not in technical questions of whether English is a more viable language of instruction or the repetitive promise that it offers non-English-speaking students "full participation first in their school and later in American society" (Silber, 1991, p. 7). This position assumes that English is in fact a superior language and that we live in a classless, race-blind society. I want to propose that decisions about how to educate non-English-speaking students cannot be reduced to issues of language, but rest in a full understanding of the ideological elements that generate and sustain linguistic, racial, and sex discrimination. That is, educators need to develop, as Henry Giroux has suggested, "a politics and pedagogy around a new language capable of acknowledging the multiple, contradictory, and complex subject positions people occupy within different social, cultural, and economic locations" (1991, p. 27). By shifting the linguistic issue to an ideological terrain we will challenge conservative educators to confront the Berlin Wall of racism, classism, and economic deprivation which characterizes the lived experiences of minorities in U.S. public schools. For example, J. Anthony Lukas succinctly captures the ideological elements that promote racism and segregation in schools in his analysis of desegregation in the Boston Public Schools. Lukas cites a trip to Charlestown High School, where a group of Black parents experienced firsthand the stark reality their children were destined to endure. Although the headmaster assured them that "violence, intimidation, or racial slurs would not be tolerated," they could not avoid the racial epithets on the walls: "Welcome Niggers," "Niggers Suck," "White Power," "KKK," "Bus is for Zulu," and "Be illiterate, fight busing." As those parents were boarding the bus, "they were met with jeers and catcalls 'go home niggers. Keep going all the way to Africa!'" This racial intolerance led one parent to reflect, "My god, what kind of hell am I sending my children into?" (Lukas, 1985, p. 282). What could her children learn at a school like that except to hate? Even though forced integration of schools in Boston exacerbated the racial tensions in the Boston Public Schools, one should not overlook the deep-seated racism that permeates all levels of the school structure. According to Lukas:

Even after Elvira "Pixie" Paladino's election to The Boston School Committee [in 1975] she was heard muttering about "jungle bunnies" and "pickaninnies." And John "Bigga" Kerrigan [head of the School Committee] prided himself on the unrestrained invective ("I may be a prick, but at least I'm a consistent prick"), particularly directed at Blacks ("savages") and the liberal media ("mother-fucking maggots") and Lem Tucker, a Black correspondent for ABC News, whom Kerrigan described as "one generation away from swinging in the trees," a remark he illustrated by assuming his hands upwards, and scratching his armpits. (Lukas, 1985, p.282)

Against this landscape of violent racism perpetrated against racial minorities, and also against linguistic minorities, one can understand the reasons for the high dropout rate in the Boston public schools (approximately 50%). Perhaps racism and other ideological elements are part of a school reality which forces a high percentage of students to leave school, only later to be profiled by the very system as dropouts or "poor and unmotivated students." One could argue that the above incidents occurred during a tumultuous time of racial division in Boston's history, but I do not believe that we have learned a great deal from historically dangerous memories to the degree that our leaders continue to invite racial tensions, as evidenced in the Willie Horton presidential campaign issue and the present quota for jobs as an invitation once again to racial divisiveness.

It is very curious that this new-found concern of English Only advocates for limited English proficiency students does not interrogate those very ideological elements that psychologically and emotionally harm these students far more than the mere fact that English may present itself as a temporary barrier to an effective education. It would be more socially constructive and beneficial if the zeal that propels the English Only movement were diverted toward social struggles designed to end violent racism and structures of poverty, homelessness, and family breakdown, among other social ills that characterize the lived experiences of minorities in the United States. If these social issues are not dealt with appropriately, it is naive to think that the acquisition of the English language alone will, somehow, magically eclipse the raw and cruel injustices and oppression perpetrated against the dispossessed class of minorities in the United States. According to Peter McLaren, these dispossessed minority students who

populate urban settings in places such as Howard Beach, Ozone Park, El Barrio, are more likely to be forced to learn about Eastern Europe in ways set forth by neo-conservative multiculturists than they are to learn about the Harlem Renaissance, Mexico, Africa, the Caribbean, or Aztec or Zulu culture. (McLaren, 1991, p. 7)

While arguing for the use of the students' native language in their educational development, I would like to make it very clear that the bilingual education goal should never be to restrict students to their own vernacular. This linguistic constriction inevitably leads to a linguistic ghetto. Educators must understand fully the broader meaning of the use of students' language as a requisite for their empowerment. That is, empowerment should never be limited to what Stanley Aronowitz describes as "the process of appreciating and loving oneself" (1985). In addition to this process, empowerment should also be a means that enables students "to interrogate and selectively appropriate those aspects of the dominant culture that will provide them with the basis for defining and transforming, rather than merely serving, the wider social order" (Giroux & McLaren, 1986, p. 17). This means that educators should understand the value of mastering the standard English language of the wider society. It is through the full appropriation of the standard English language that linguistic minority students find themselves linguistically empowered to engage in dialogue with various sectors of the wider society. What I must reiterate is that educators should never allow the limited proficient students' native language to be silenced by a distorted legitimation of the standard English language. Linguistic minority students' language should never be sacrificed, since it is the only means through which they make sense of their own experience in the world.

Given the importance of the standard English language in the education of linguistic minority students, I must agree with the members of the Institute for Research in English Acquisition and Development when they quote Antonio Gramsci in their brochure:

Without the mastery of the common standard version of the national language, one is inevitably destined to function only at the periphery of national life and, especially, outside the national and political mainstream. (READ, 1990)

But these English Only advocates fail to tell the other side of Antonio Gramsci's argument, which warns us:

Each time that in one way or another, the question of language comes to the fore, that signifies that a series of other problems is about to emerge, the formation and enlarging of the ruling class, the necessity to establish more "intimate" and sure relations between the ruling groups and the popular masses, that is, the reorganization of cultural hegemony. (Gramsci, 1971, p. 16)

This selective selection of Gramsci's position on language points to the hidden curriculum with which the English Only movement seeks to promote a monolithic ideology. It is also part and parcel of an ongoing attempt at "reorganization of cultural hegemony" as evidenced by the unrelenting attack by conservative educators on multicultural education and curriculum diversity. The ideological force behind the call for a common culture can be measured by the words of syndicated columnist Pat Buchanan, who urged his fellow conservatives "to wage a cultural revolution in the 90's as sweeping as the political revolution of the 80's" (Giroux, 1991, p. 15). In other words, as Henry Giroux has shown, the conservative cultural revolution's

more specific expressions have been manifest on a number of cultural fronts including schools, the art world, and the more blatant attacks aimed at rolling back the benefits constructed of civil rights and social welfare reforms constructed over the last three decades. What is being valorized in the dominant language of the culture industry is an undemocratic approach to social authority and a politically regressive move to reconstruct American life within the script of Eurocentrism, racism, and patriarchy. (Giroux, 1991, p. 15)

Derrick Z. Jackson, in his brilliant article "The End of the Second Reconstruction," lays bare the dominant conservative ideology that informs the present cultural hegemony when he argues that "From 1884 to 1914, more than 3,600 African-Americans were lynched. Lynching is passé today. AIDS, infant mortality, violence out of despair, and gutted public education do the same trick in inner cities neatly redlined by banks" (1991, p. 27). In contrast to the zeal for a common culture and English only, these conservative educators have remained ominously silent about forms of racism, inequality, subjugation, and exploitation that daily serve to wage symbolic and real violence against those children who by virtue of their language, race, ethnicity, class, or gender are not treated in schools with the dignity and respect all children warrant in a democracy. Instead of reconstituting education around an urban and cultural studies approach which takes the social, cultural, political, and economic divisions of education and everyday life as the primary categories for understanding contemporary schooling, conservative educators have recoiled in an attempt to salvage the status quo. That is, they try to keep the present unchanged even though, as Renato Constantino points out:

Within the living present there are imperceptible changes which make the status quo a moving reality. . . . Thus a new policy based on the present as past and not on the present as future is backward for it is premised not on evolving conditions but on conditions that are already dying away. (1978, p. 201)

One such not so imperceptible change is the rapid growth of minority representation in the labor force. As such, the conservative leaders and educators are digging this country's economic grave by their continued failure to educate minorities. As Lew Ferlerger and Jay Mandle convincingly argue, "Unless the educational attainment of minority populations in the United States improves, the country's hopes for resuming high rates of growth and an increasing standard of living look increasingly dubious" (1991, p. 12).

In addition to the real threat to the economic fabric of the United States, the persistent call for English language only in education smacks of backwardness in the present conjuncture of our ever-changing multicultural and multilingual society. Furthermore, these conservative educators base their language policy argument on the premise that English education in this country is highly effective. On the contrary. As Patrick Courts clearly argues in his book *Literacy for Empowerment* (1991), English education is failing even middle-class and upper-class students. He argues that English reading and writing classes are mostly based on workbooks and grammar lessons, lessons which force students to "bark at print" or fill in the blanks. Students engage in grudgingly banal exercises such as practicing correct punctuation and writing sample business letters. Books used in their classes are, Courts points out, too often in the service of commercially prepared ditto sheets and workbooks. Courts's account suggests that most school programs do not take advantage of the language experiences that the majority of students have had before they reach school. These teachers become the victims of their own professional ideology when they delegitimize the language experiences that students bring with them into the classroom.

Courts's study is basically concerned with middle-class and upper-middle-class students unburdened by racial discrimination and poverty, students who have done well in elementary and high school settings and are now populating the university lecture halls and seminar rooms. If schools are failing these students, the situation does not bode well for those students less economically, socially, and politically advantaged. It is toward the linguistic minority students that I would like to turn my discussion now.

THE ROLE OF LANGUAGE IN THE EDUCATION
OF LINGUISTIC MINORITY STUDENTS

Within the last two decades, the issue of bilingual education has taken on a heated importance among educators. Unfortunately, the debate that has emerged tends to recycle old assumptions and values regarding the meaning and usefulness of the students' native language in education. The notion that education of linguistic minority students is a matter of learning the standard English language still informs the vast majority of bilingual programs and manifests its logic in the renewed emphasis on technical reading and writing skills.

I want to reiterate in this paper that the education of linguistic minority students cannot be viewed as simply the development of skills aimed at acquiring the standard English language. English Only proponents seldom discuss the pedagogical structures that will enable these students to access other bodies of knowledge. Nor do they interrogate the quality of ESL instruction provided to the linguistic minority students and the adverse material conditions under which these students learn English. The view that teaching English constitutes education sustains a notion of ideology that systematically negates rather than makes meaningful the cultural experiences of the subordinate linguistic groups who are, by and large, the objects of its policies. For the education of linguistic minority students to become meaningful it has to be situated within a theory of cultural production and viewed as an integral part of the way in which people produce, transform, and reproduce meaning. Bilingual education, in this sense, must be seen as a medium that constitutes and affirms the historical and existential moments of lived culture. Hence, it is an eminently political phenomenon, and it must be analyzed within the context of a theory of power relations and an understanding of social and cultural reproduction and production. By "cultural reproduction" I refer to collective experiences that function in the interest of the dominant groups rather than in the interest of the oppressed groups that are objects of its policies. Bilingual education programs in the United States have been developed and implemented under the cultural reproduction model leading to a de facto neocolonial educational model. I use "cultural production" to refer to specific groups of people producing, mediating, and confirming the mutual ideological elements that merge from and reaffirm their daily lived experiences. In this case, such experiences are rooted in the interest of individual and collective self-determination. It is only through a cultural production model that we can achieve a truly democratic and liberatory educational experience. I will return to this issue later.

While the various debates in the past two decades may differ in their basic assumptions about the education of linguistic minority students, they all share one common feature: they all ignore the role of language as a major force in the construction of human subjectivities. That is, they ignore the way language may either confirm or deny the life histories and experiences of the people who use it.

The pedagogical and political implications in education programs for linguistic minority students are far-reaching and yet largely ignored. These programs, for example, often contradict a fundamental principle of reading, namely that students learn to read faster and with better comprehension when taught in their native tongue. The immediate recognition of familiar words and experiences enhances the development of a positive self-concept in children who are somewhat insecure about the status of their language and culture. For this reason, and to be consistent with the plan to construct a democratic society free from vestiges of oppression, a minority literacy program must be rooted in the cultural capital of subordinate groups and have as its point of departure their own language.

Educators must develop radical pedagogical structures which provide students with the opportunity to use their own reality as a basis of literacy. This includes, obviously, the language they bring to the classroom. To do otherwise is to deny minority students the rights that lie at the core of a democratic education. The failure to base a literacy program on the minority students' language means that oppositional forces can neutralize the efforts of educators and political leaders to achieve decolonization of schooling. It is of tantamount importance that the incorporation of the minority language as the primary language of instruction in education of linguistic minority students be given top priority. It is through their own language that linguistic minority students will be able to reconstruct their history and their culture.

I want to argue that the minority language has to be understood within the theoretical framework that generates it. Put another way, the ultimate meaning and value of the minority language is not to be found by determining how systematic and rule-governed it is. We know that already. Its real meaning has to be understood through the assumptions that govern it, and it has to be understood via the social, political, and ideological relations to which it points. Generally speaking, this issue of effectiveness and validity often hides the true role of language in the maintenance of the values and interests of the dominant class. In other words, the issue of effectiveness and validity becomes a mask that obfuscates questions about the social, political, and ideological order within which the minority language exists.

If an emancipatory and critical education program is to be developed in the United States for linguistic minority students in which they become "subjects" rather than "objects," educators must understand the productive quality of language. James Donald puts it this way:

> I take language to be productive rather than reflective of social reality. This means calling into question the assumption that we, as speaking subjects, simply use language to organize and express our ideas and experiences. On the contrary, language is one of the most important social practices through which we come to experience ourselves as subjects. . . . My point here is

that once we get beyond the idea of language as no more than a medium of communication, as a tool equally and neutrally available to all parties in cultural exchanges, then we can begin to examine language both as a practice of signification and also as a site for culture struggle and as a mechanism which produces antagonistic relations between different social groups. (1982, p. 44)

It is to the antagonistic relationship between the minority and dominant speakers that I want to turn now. The antagonistic nature of the minority language has never been fully explored. In order to more clearly discuss this issue of antagonism, I will use Donald's distinction between oppressed language and repressed language. Using Donald's categories, the "negative" way of posing the minority language question is to view it in terms of oppression—that is, seeing the minority language as "lacking" the dominant standard features which usually serve as a point of reference for the minority language. By far the most common questions concerning the minority language in the United States are posed from the oppression perspective. The alternative view of the minority language is that it is repressed in the standard dominant language. In this view, minority language as a repressed language could, if spoken, challenge the privileged standard linguistic dominance. Educators have failed to recognize the "positive" promise and antagonistic nature of the minority language. It is precisely on these dimensions that educators must demystify the standard dominant language and the old assumptions about its inherent superiority. Educators must develop liberatory and critical bilingual programs informed by a radical pedagogy so that the minority language will cease to provide its speakers with the experience of subordination and, moreover, may be brandished as a weapon of resistance to the dominant standard language of the curriculum.

In this sense, the students' language is the only means by which they can develop their own voice, a prerequisite to the development of a positive sense of self-worth. As Giroux elegantly states, the students' voice "is the discursive means to make themselves 'heard' and to define themselves as active authors of their worlds" (Giroux & McLaren, 1986, p. 235). The authorship of one's own world also implies the use of one's own language, and relates to what Mikhail Bakhtin describes as "retelling a story in one's own words" (Giroux & McLaren, 1986, p. 235).

A DEMOCRATIC AND LIBERATORY EDUCATION FOR LINGUISTIC MINORITY STUDENTS

In maintaining a certain coherence with the educational plan to reconstruct new and more democratic educational programs for linguistic minority students, educators and political leaders need to create a new school grounded in a new educational praxis, expressing different concepts of education consonant with the principles of a democratic, multicultural, and multilingual society. In order for this to happen, the first step is to identify the objectives of the inherently colonial education that informs the majority of bilingual programs in the United States. Next, it is necessary to analyze how colonialist methods used by the dominant schools function, legitimize the Anglocentric values and meaning, and at the same time negate the history, culture, and language practices of the majority of linguistic minority students. The new school, so it is argued, must also be informed by a radical bilingual pedagogy, which would make concrete such values as solidarity, social responsibility, and creativity. In the democratic development of bilingual programs rooted in a liberatory ideology, linguistic minority students become "subjects" rather than more "objects" to be assimilated blindly into an often hostile dominant "common" culture. A democratic and liberatory education needs to move away from traditional approaches, which emphasize the acquisition of mechanical basic skills while divorcing education from its ideological and historical contexts. In attempting to meet this goal, it purposely must reject the conservative principles embedded in the English Only movement I have discussed earlier. Unfortunately, many bilingual programs sometimes unknowingly reproduce one common feature of traditional approaches to education by ignoring the important relationship between language and the cultural capital of the students at whom bilingual education is aimed. The result is the development of bilingual programs whose basic assumptions are at odds with the democratic spirit that launched them.

Bilingual program development must be largely based on the notion of a democratic and liberatory education, in which education is viewed "as one of the major vehicles by which 'oppressed' people are able to participate in the sociohistorical transformation of their society" (Walmsley, 1981, p. 74). Bilingual education, in this sense, is grounded in a critical reflection of the cultural capital of the oppressed. It becomes a vehicle by which linguistic minority students are equipped with the necessary tools to reappropriate their history, culture, and language practices. It is, thus, a way to enable the linguistic minority students to reclaim "those historical and existential experiences that are devalued in everyday life by the dominant culture in order to be both validated and critically understood" (Giroux, 1983, p. 226). To do otherwise is to deny these students their very democratic rights. In fact, the criticism that bilingual and multicultural education unwisely question the traditions and values of our so-called "common culture" as suggested by Kenneth T. Jackson (1991) is both antidemocratic and academically dishonest. Multicultural education and curriculum diversity did not create the S & L scandal, the Iran-Contra debacle, or the extortion of minority properties by banks, the stewards of the "common culture," who charged minorities exorbitant loan-sharking interest rates. Multicultural education and curriculum diversity did not force Joachim Maitre, Dean of the College of Communication at Boston University, to choose the hypocritical moral high ground to excoriate the popular culture's "bleak moral content," all the while plagiarizing fifteen paragraphs of a conservative comrade's text.

The learning of English language skills alone will not enable linguistic minority students to acquire the critical tools "to awaken and liberate them from their mystified and distorted views of themselves and their world" (Giroux, 1983, p. 226). For example, speaking English has not enabled African Americans to change this society's practice of jailing more Blacks than even South Africa, and this society spending over 7 billion dollars to keep African-American men in jail while spending only 1 billion dollars educating Black males (Black, 1991).

Educators must understand the all-encompassing role the dominant ideology has played in this mystification and distortion of our so-called "common culture" and our "common language." They must also recognize the antagonistic relationship between the "common culture" and those who, by virtue of their race, language, ethnicity, and gender, have been relegated to the margins. Finally, educators must develop bilingual programs based on the theory of cultural production. In other words, linguistic minority students must be provided the opportunity to become actors in the reconstruction of a more democratic and just society. In short, education conducted in English only is alienating to linguistic minority students, since it denies them the fundamental tools for reflection, critical thinking, and social interaction. Without the cultivation of their native language, and robbed of the opportunity for reflection and critical thinking, linguistic minority students find themselves unable to re-create their culture and history. Without the reappropriation of their culture, the valorization of their lived experiences, English Only supporters' vacuous promise that the English language will guarantee students "full participation first in their school and later in American society" (Silber, 1991, p. 7) can hardly be a reality.

REFERENCES

Aronowitz, S. (1985, May). Why should Johnny read. *Village Voice Literary Supplement*, 13.
Black, C. (1991, January 13). Paying the high price for being the world's no. 1 jailor. *Boston Sunday Globe*, 67.
Constantino, R. (1928). *Neocolonial identity and counter consciousness*. London: Merlin Press.
Courts, P. (1991). *Literacy for empowerment*. South Hadley, MA: Bergin & Garvey.
Donald, J. (1982). Language, literacy, and schooling. In *The State and popular culture*. Milton Keynes: Open University Culture Unit.
Ferlerger, L., & Mandle, J. (1991). *African-Americans and the future of the U.S. economy*. Unpublished manuscript.
Giroux, H. A. (1983). *Theory and resistance: A pedagogy for the opposition*. South Hadley, MA: Bergin & Garvey.
———. (1991). *Border crossings: Cultural workers and the politics of education*. New York: Routledge.
Giroux, H. A. & McLaren, P. (1986). Teacher education and the politics of engagement: The case for democratic schooling. *Harvard Educational Review*, 56(3), 213–238.
Gramsci, A. (1971). *Selections from Prison Notebooks*, (Ed. and Trans. Quinten Hoare & Geoffrey Smith). New York: International Publishers.
Jackson, D. (1991, December 8). The end of the second reconstruction. *Boston Globe*, 27.
Jackson, K. T. (1991, July 7). Cited in a *Boston Sunday Globe* editorial.
Kozol, J. (1985). *Illiterate America*. New York: Doubleday Anchor.
Lukas, J. A. (1985). *Common ground*. New York: Alfred A. Knopf.
McLaren, P. (1991). Critical pedagogy: Constructing an arch of social dreaming and a doorway to hope. *Journal of Education*, 173(1), 9–34.
Olsen, L. (1988). *Crossing the schoolhouse border: Immigrant students and the California public schools*. San Francisco: California Tomorrow.
Silber, J. (1991, May). *Boston University Commencement Catalogue*.
Walmsley, S. (1981). On the purpose and content of secondary reading programs: Educational and ideological perspectives. *Curriculum Inquiry*, 11, 73–79.

14

Racism, Language Variety, and Urban Minorities
Issues in Bilingualism and Bidialectalism

John J. Attinasi

Divergence from "standard" English is easily perceived. Dialect differences are frequently the instrument or excuse for discrimination along racial, ethnic, geographic, and educational lines. For two U.S. populations in particular, African Americans and Latinos, physical differences and socioeconomic indicators reinforce linguistic stigma, and all three are used to rationalize separation, prejudice, inequality, and more blatant forms of racism that are expressed in or linked to language. Among African Americans, dialect differences in English speech, writing conventions, and communication styles are used both to explain away differential treatment by outsiders, and to strengthen the group's cohesion in the face of devaluation and separatism. Similar language-based stigma and resistance are found among Latinos through Spanish and Latino varieties of English. In this essay I explore several aspects of language discrimination, especially its educational dimensions, and offer perspectives on the dynamics of clashes between vernacular and standard language forms in relation to Latino and African-American groups. Balanced against the external discredit of linguistic varieties, subordinate group resistance and self-respect help maintain ethnolinguistic vitality.

Verbal expressions accompany oppressive policy and acts. Persons are dehumanized when referred to as "those people," "males," or "females." Terms such as *underprivileged* and *non-English proficient* perpetuate a deficit theory regarding cultural diversity. The insistent anglicization of unusual names and the corrective repronunciation of accented speech send messages of devaluation regarding vernacular and non-native speech varieties.

In education, neglect and illegality are linked to race when funding for desegregation efforts is misdirected to receiving schools in "white" neighborhoods, leaving overcrowded and inner-city schools with Latino and African-American majorities underfunded and unchanged (Hess and Warden 1988). Using compensatory monies to bolster a bureaucracy rather than to teach children is more easily tolerated in a school system that is mostly nonwhite (Hess 1991: 25–26). "Special education" disproportionately enrolls urban minority children. Unfortunately, those who need the most receive the least. Special programs suffer first in budget crises; unsettled urban school strikes disrupt the year for inner-city children. High teacher turnovers, the placement of inexperienced teachers in urban schools, and the continuation of non-certified persons in bilingual and special education are common practices, but over-looked. Racial correlates cannot be discounted in such educational situations. Multicultural subordinate populations (Latinos, African Americans, Native American Indians, and many Asian groups) are further victimized educationally by low expectations. The student is undereducated because the group is assumed to be incapable of more than past low-achievement average scores. Students and teachers then enter a conspiracy of silence in which neither bothers to exert effort, and neither disturbs the other's very different school (and after-school) subcultures. The gap continues and widens. The prophecy fulfills itself, and a language is created to rationalize or mitigate the situation.

Beyond the classroom, other forms of institutional and personal linguistic discrimination need exploration. In schools, universities, and in the streets of cities, recent signs of bigotry and racist verbal assault have been, sadly, more open and injurious than ever. Police brutality erupted into a destructive aftermath in Los Angeles in 1992; it was clearly racial. Unfortunately, such violence continues, in Detroit and elsewhere. Polarizations beyond black and white to anti-Asian, anti-Latino sentiments, and tensions across groups compound longstanding patterns of white-to-black discrimination.

Also in 1992, Native Americans reminded others that ethnic oppression and racism in the Americas is five hundred years old. Being treated as less than human, less than "*cristiano*" or "*castellano*," Native-American Indian people have fathomed the links between language, group identity, and human dignity. The treatment of Latinos, who share a Native-American heritage, and African Americans, who were transported throughout the Americas as an alternative to the failed enslavement of indigenous peoples, are two more facets of one problem—racism. Today, racism is "dysconscious," embedded in the status quo (King 1991). It underlies fatalism in the face of hierarchy and paternalism that erupts into machismo and self-righteousness. Depending on its variety, racism perpetuates, or neglects, or quietly laments persisting inequality.

Several analyses of the linkages among language and discourse, discrimination, and racism have been undertaken. In the formative period of studying the sociolinguistics of Black English, sensitive white researchers explored the structural integrity and logic of this vernacular variety (Kochman 1972; Labov 1972a, b). More recently, African-American authors have collaborated with committed social scientists from other backgrounds to investigate the cultural dimensions of African-American discourse, and the sociolinguistic politics of exclusion (Gay and Baber 1987; Smitherman-Donaldson and van Dijk 1988).

> Language and discourse are vital in reproducing racial oppression and control of Blacks and other minorities. Whether in informational or institutional contexts, whether among the elite or the public at large, racial oppression becomes structural, rather than individual or incidental, when its conditions are shared by the dominant group. Reasons, motivations, goals and interests must be communicated. They are linked with opinion

and attitudes, and [receive] expression, verbalization and persuasive formulation in various types of talk and text. (Smitherman-Donaldson and van Dijk 1988: 17)

The difference between prejudice and racism is the power to enforce sentiments of bigotry. Therefore, discriminatory language used by minorities is inherently weaker than similar language directed by members of more powerful groups at subordinated people. If X hates Y but has little economic or political clout to affect the life of Y, he or she cannot do anything about it. X can lash out with an insult or a brick, but the effect is temporary and local. It is much different if Y can impede X's employment, deny a home, or prevent him or her from enjoying an acceptable quality of life. In a classroom confrontation, a racial epithet against a white can be diffused by the prevailing relations of power and social climate; whereas the verbal devaluation of a minority person is reinforced by disparities in neighborhoods, housing, employment, mean test scores, school tracking, and treatment in public places. An educational system that excludes, discourages, or "can't find" certain groups of people participates in a web of racism, ranging from "color-blind" social invisibility and condescending smiles to epithets, vandalism, and violence.

The forms of inequality, from neglect to ugly racism, are structured and implemented through language. In linguistic interaction, issues of control over people and resources may surface overtly and undermine interaction covertly. The linguistics of racism extends beyond the legal squabble over "fighting words," that is, whether racist language should be protected as free speech unless it is directed at a specific person in a hostile way.

At elementary and secondary educational levels, children are frequently victimized with racial dimensions at both the core and surface of undereducation. Terms of reference, manner of address, inattention, low expectations, and lack of equity need to be explored and catalogued for their ethnic and racial dimensions. Thus, language manifests the unfinished business of emancipation from inequality and of completing the civil rights agenda is a multitude of social contexts, nearly all of which have verbal expression or communicative interaction attached.

Focusing directly on language, there are three levels of current social practice in which racism is expressed by, or related to, language: overt racism, covert racism, and suppression of linguistic varieties. The rise of campus racism and the proliferation of skinheads, "Aryan" groups, and political catalysts such as David Duke have been seen by some as symptoms of something new, perhaps because many young people support such overt racism. Hate speech and nativist rallies, both in the United States and Europe, openly express superiority and inferiority based on race and ethnicity. The racial label or slur on a college campus, the stereotype, racist graffiti, and fighting words are erroneously considered new. Such expressions are simply old-fashioned hate: persistent bigotries from the Jim Crow and Nazi eras that have not died. Inaction to oppose such racism either is permitted because these expression are thought to be too new and different for anyone to know how to combat them or is the result of a legal paralysis by which conservative libertarians invoke First Amendment rights of free speech. Less sophisticated people know that, despite legal injunctions and civil rights legislation, prejudice has continued unbroken throughout U.S. history in negative images and practices that suppress those outside the culture of power.

Covert racism flows as a softer current that exists in attitudes, in social interaction, and in the workplace. Privatized lives, personal defenses, and conservative enterprises result in an insidious disconnection from a diverse society. People seemingly cannot take the time, risk the investment— or jeopardize the deal—to work with people who are "other." Moreover, a refined "racism without racists" exists in many institutions, especially schools (Massey et al. 1975). It is characterized not so much by overt or covert acts as by quiet desperation. Nonracists perpetuate racism by being unaware or by simply giving up and retreating from the challenge to maintain, and follow through on, high expectations for children whose talents are clouded by societal circumstances. Combating such tendencies requires vigilance against longstanding stigmas, and the courage to challenge the racial stratification we all inherit as part of institutional cultural climates. But denial has its consequences. Acting "color-blind" in a color-conscious world results in a vicious ignorance of the social antecedents to, and present implications of, race and ethnicity. The invisibility of persons of color progresses from "We are all the same" to "They just stopped participating."

Third, and related to overt and covert racism, is the muzzle. Dialogue is silenced through power relations that delegitimize arguments and ideas that are not articulated in acceptable discourse or fashionable jargon (Delpit 1986, 1988). The English-only movement attempts to degrade and repress the validity of ideas (and speakers) of over a hundred languages existing in the United States. Silence itself is also a powerful from of linguistic discrimination, especially when lack of response or long delays may repress or abort communication. If verbal communication does occur between powerful and subordinate groups, it can be interrupted by insistence on standard form and official languages that tend to diminish the message of the powerless by setting the rules of interchange in favor of the powerful.

"White-only" country clubs, blatant campus graffiti, racist jokes, blaming the victim, acting color-blind, and listening more to form than content are examples of the continuum from overt to covert sociolinguistic discrimination. As it becomes more indirect, racism does not become less devastating, only less tangible.

OVERT LINGUISTIC RACISM

The significance of prejudice conveyed through speech merits careful analysis because language is socially pervasive and pointedly visible. Language variety acts as a "badge of ethnicity and symbol of social interaction," as sociolinguist Joshua Fishman has phrased it. Words are an ingredient of discrimination, not just its instrument. Overt racism in language is clearest in racial slurs—here language is a weapon. Epithets are hurled. Taunts constitute aggression. Words can be the bullets of political suicide. Racially hostile speech may have the force of assault, despite any freedom-of-speech protections.

Beyond prohibited threat and libel, a legal controversy rages concerning whether psychological injury through racist language passes beyond the protection of "free speech," or whether only direct inciting of violence may be punished (Cole 1991). An extreme civil liberties argument contends that offensive expression is constitutionally protected. The battle continues in local, state, and federal courts over the legality of expressions that stimulate anger or resentment related to race, and even the Supreme Court has considered the right of universities to censure racist expression (Ferrell 1992). A fear expressed by First Amendment absolutists is that speech control may be enforced more severely against minorities than against their oppressors. "The same first amendment that protects the right of a David Duke to speak freely on racial issues protects the same right for a Louis Farrakhan," according to a litigation counsel in a sexism case at George Mason University (Glasberg 1991). Another argument emphasizes the responsibility of educational institutions to set standards for an intellectual, civilized society and to promote learning by all groups. In that view, campus racism should not be allowed on the grounds that expressions of racist hate create a hostile environment. Even when they are indirect, slurs and racial devaluations are socially injurious and may threaten persons from groups underrepresented in higher education. Thus minority students sense discomfort and find it impossible to pursue an education in environments where bigotry is allowed. Educational institutions, as inclusive communities, have the right to set policy regarding acceptable intellectual dialogue, and to punish persons, fraternities, or other groups for speech that has racist, sexist, or other innuendos. (Swift and severe penalties in politics and sports are frequent.) The central issue in several university cases is the role of language in the responsibility of schools to balance constitutionality and free expression and to eliminate bigotry in order to promote equal educational opportunity and an ethical intellectual and social climate.

Explicit bigotry in language may be seen in its most blatant form in overt slurs, offensive jokes, and names. Derogatory ethnic labels abound, and at least eight types may be identified (Allen 1990). One type is based in shortened names: *Mex* for Mexican; *Spic*, from a mispronunciation of "speak," or from the attempt to pronounce the abbreviation *Hspc* for Hispanic; *Flip* for Filipino; and *Hunkie* (Honkie) for immigrants from the Austro-Hungarian empire. A second type derives from negative stereotypes: *swamp rat* for Acadian or 'Cajun; *pigsticker* for eastern Europeans who often worked in the packing industries of the Midwest; *wetback* for Mexicans who may have crossed the Rio Grande (or other land or water borders); *spear-chucker* for African Americans, based on ignorance promoted by Tarzan-type movies about African nations; *spaghetti-bender, beaner, or greaser* because of foods and the appearance of southern Europeans and Latin Americans. (I am kept from mentioning even worse epithets based on stereotypes only by the limits of bad taste.) A third type includes derogatory ethnic labels based in metaphor: *chocolate* and *white-bread* for dark and light skin color; *redskin, kike, coffee,* and others based on appearance. A fourth type is derisive ethnic nuances present in verbs: to *gyp* (Gypsy), to *jap* (Japanese), to *jew* (Jewish), to *welsh* (Welsh). A fifth type comprises the many stereotypical nicknames: *Jan Kees* (Dutch version of John Doe) became *Yankee*; *Mick* (Irish); *Tony* (Italian); *Sapphire* (African American); *Hiawatha* (Native American). A sixth type includes limited-use slurs based on military experience or in-group beliefs in items, such as *Charlie* (Vietnamese, in addition to the African-American generic for white men, *Mr. Charlie); Sally* or *Miss Ann* (generic name for white women); and *Kunta Kinte* (African person in the United States). A seventh type is made-up numbskull jokes based on ethnic slurs and stereotypes of the ignorant minority; for example, substitute an ethnic slur for "numbskull" in, "How many numbskulls does it take to change a light bulb?"

Finally, whereas it is clear that putting down another group attempts to reinforce or assert the superiority of those issuing the put-down, a more sensitive situation is found in the eighth type, the self-ascribed epithet. In-group self-ridicule, with varying degrees of humor and malice, is documented in epithets, jokes, and other overt language usage—for example, Italians who refer to themselves as *dagos*, or Black Americans who call each other *nigger*. Dick Gregory used the "n-word" as a book title in the 1970s but probably would not do so today. Numerous African-American comedians play fast and loose with the term, and poets are sensitive to the baggage that it carries in various pronunciations and contexts. Rappers find shock value without resorting to four-letter profanity in the frequent use of the word. When African-American entertainers use "niggah" in public, they create a double standard: black use of the term is not derogatory, but white usage is racist. There are two dangers in such an in-group/out-group dual standard: first, that permission for others to use the term is implied; and second, that the group tacitly accepts the stereotypes about itself through the facile use of the derogatory ethnic label.

Euphemistic terms abound that still seem racially loaded—*urban poor, culturally deprived, culture of poverty, underclass, disadvantaged, underprivileged, minority,* and *GI* (a person from Gary, Indiana, which is over 90 percent African American) have all been used to refer to nonwhite minority groups. Their offensiveness varies. So does the reception of supposedly neutral social science labeling. In *Drylongo: a Self Portrait of Black America,* an old-timer's skepticism spoke volumes: "Sometimes I think all this anthropology is just another way of calling me a *n——*" (Gwaltney 1980: xix).

Others have gone to greater lengths than I have reflected here to develop an appropriate analysis of overt linguistic racism (Allen 1983, 1990; Allport 1954; Greenberg et. al. 1988). Lists of such terms are simply descriptive, and perhaps trivial, but the cumulative cultural and psychological effects of blatant, "humorous," and stereotyped racial language are not. We next turn to more subtle forms of linguistic discrimination.

COVERT RACISM

Today's climate of public concern with being politically correct channels most of the expression of discrimination to covert and symbolic levels, avoiding the blatant derogatory ethnic label. Instead, ethnic distinction and discrimination are reflected indirectly, in behavior, attitudes, reactions to speech and speakers, and "nonoffensive" linguistic expressions that may be voiced in polite company. Several areas of analysis can help clarify contemporary linguistic discrimination, including verbal codes, nonverbal communication, and language attitudes.

Overt racists are blunt and intolerable, but others who allow themselves to discriminate in order to maintain a quality of life that is insulated from racial intrusions, and undisturbed economically or visually, embody more antiseptic and socially acceptable racism. "Communicative apartheid" might serve as a label for this stance. A few examples may illustrate the phenomenon. Many professions and professional meetings remain mostly white; nonwhites are absent in "good neighborhoods" in the suburbs and from most of the managerial levels of business. People in the corporate world (and elsewhere) prefer to work with people they know and trust. The infamous old boys' network lingers, despite affirmative action and set-asides for women and minorities. This segregated world can be rationalized by its participants, especially when money is involved. Trust is built by interaction and destroyed by breakdowns in communication. Delays, "dropping the ball," lack of performance without satisfactory explanation or petition for extension—in other words, the hard core of business negotiations—are more difficult when neither party can be sure of what the other is saying at verbal and nonverbal levels. People who speak the same language are able to establish trust and satisfactorily negotiate proposed tasks and their modification when things do not go as planned. If people cannot speak to and read each other, they are less confident in the business transaction.

This situation is interpretable in terms of the psycholinguistic concept of synchronicity, or "communicative mirroring." When people are having a rewarding conversation, verbal and nonverbal interaction synchronizes ("That was a great meeting. We had a good talk. I think we got somewhere. We really speak the same language"). Linguistic analysts note congruent body position among interlocutors. Eye-contact conventions, utterance length, nods, facial gestures, turn-taking cues, and intonation patterns further signal mirrored interaction.

Moreover, it is now clear from child development research that speech intonation is conditioned by dialect and family communicative patterns perceived even before birth. Speech patterns that are comfortable for acquiring information, negotiating, or socializing are learned and practiced. Socialization during youth reinforces linguistically separated subcultures, whether ethnically white, Latino, or African-American, based on geographic region, religion, or social class. By adulthood, we have all come to feel comfortable with certain discourse conventions about the form of a discussion, the use of examples, or valid appeals to authority. Familiar vocabulary items may be repeated and have power. (Each microculture has its buzz words.) Question and request structures are internalized, and, in the end, one knows how a decision has been reached or if a conversation has finished. (For some Native-American cultures, no conversation is finished, no decision is final.)

In brief, people often want to hear and be with their own, and they suspect the other. Formal sociolinguistic conventions are reinforced by cultural content. The message of the other is best delivered by in-group brokers of the "other" microculture. This is why men learn about feminism from enlightened men and why white performers like Mick Jagger, the Beatles, Elvis, and Vanilla Ice made millions off Black music, selling it to general (white) markets. African Americans and Latinos may prefer to listen to Black or Latin singers and enjoy Black movie actors or Spanish television. Minority clients may more easily respond to and understand a salesperson or teacher from their respective group. A group is moved by preaching in Black American churches, or by the pageantry of the Roman Catholic religion. After five days of working for "the (white) man," an African American might be heard to say: *"I don't want to hear no white people today."* Spanish speakers may react similarly, as did the Cuban mother on the Upper West Side of New York City, in the movie *El Super*. One morning, her daughter was listening to the radio in English, and the mother said: *"Apaga ese radio. Hoy no quiero escuchar el inglés."* (Turn off that radio; I don't want to hear English today.) White Americans frequently react in the same way to Spanish and Black English on television, radio, or in public places: they don't want to hear it. (These are my own sociolinguistic observations, based on many years of observation of intergroup communication and interaction across languages, dialects, and settings.)

Such examples help us to identify the most subtle and unconscious forms of contemporary covert linguistic racism. A failure of mirroring between whites, Blacks, and Latinos results in linguistic mismatch, devaluation of ability and character, and a presentation of self across group borders that results in the reinforcement of the stratified status quo. This often occurs in educational and employment settings, even where liberal attitudes and affirmative action plans seek out racial equity. After a nonwhite person interviews before a mostly white panel, the following may be heard: *"The resumé was good, but they interviewed poorly." "The committee did not feel confident." "There's something that bothers me." "I feel the other candidate could become a team player more successfully." "I just don't think this will work."*

The larger issue is that, together, communicative apartheid, linguistic conventions, privacy based in linguistic varieties, and mirrored synchronicity add up to a dysconscious climate of prejudice that is made concrete in interaction, conflict, or avoidance. Keeping marginalized people at the periphery is the essence of racism, and language often facilitates it.

The problem is two-sided. We value and respond to our own group, and our own dialect or language variety. Hence the value of role-model teachers, and the economic advantage of a diverse sales force and advertising campaign. On the other side, racial separation appears almost natural. Resistance among minority groups provides a safety zone against the climate of xenophobia. Separation is rooted in the deepest origins of our socialization, perhaps even in our speech perceptions before birth. Infant response to tone of voice and pitch contours emerges very early (Pérez and Porres-Guzmán 1992: 29). Weir (1966) has reported that five-to-eight-month-old babies of Chinese and American English-speaking parents had different intonation patterns in their babbling. Heath's study of language socialization in three U.S. sociolinguistic groups found clear differences in verbal inputs to, and interpretations of, infant vocalization (1983: 75–76, 344–354).

Our challenge is to overcome encapsulation within single language varieties (from which both the ghettoized purist and the isolated minority suffer) by expanding dialect-specific patterns to proficiency along a continuum of linguistic varieties. This amplification of repertoire would at once empower the marginalized, encourage multidialectal understanding, and promote communicative acceptance to enable communication between groups. Knowledge can change attitudes and influence behavior. We therefore need an understanding of the sociolinguistic dimensions of attitudes, based on the theoretical and empirical study of status differences among language varieties.

Covert racial discrimination patterns based on linguistic features such as accent and intonation have been classified through investigation of the persistence and status of language varieties by sociolinguists and social psychologists. This research enables us to raise the focus of discussion from explicit linguistic usage to implied metalinguistic levels (Gere and Smith 1979; Hecht and Ribeau 1988; Obudho 1976). In everyday interaction among ordinary people distinctions are not usually made among the content of speech, the manner of speaking, and the speakers themselves. Nonstandard features of speech stand out, seem to be intolerable, insupportable, or just plain wrong, and are invoked to justify avoidance and exclusion. In effect, persons and their group, not just their speech, are excluded. The public imagines itself to be reacting to speech (with the rationale that it "sounds bad," is inaccurate, or unintelligible), but the net result is opposition to the speaker, discrimination against the group, and resistance to supposed infringement on the language and culture of power.

Discrimination may occur in tone of voice, choice of vocabulary, facial expression, gesture, and posture that encode attitude and engender reaction. Mutual linguistic antagonism may yield a mockery of dialect varieties and languages, or an exaggeration of dialect. In response, resistance culture develops, and vernacular forms persist and may seem overemphasized (*"loud jive talk"*). Non-English languages may be flaunted (*"They speak Spanish in front of you and make you wait"*). Aversion may originate from either the powerful or the powerless, since languages exhibit several dimensions of "prestige."

How do we order and compare linguistic varieties? Social psychology has the dubious honor of probing and analyzing commonly held conceptions, which are often stereotypes. In operationalizing the relationships among varieties, sociolinguistic power has been plotted along two dimensions: standardization and vitality (fig. 14.1). Standardization is the degree to which one variety of a language has been refined to become "standard," "a prestige variety used as an institutionalized norm in a community" (Crystal 1987: 430). The development of a single spoken variety into a standard gives prestige to the source variety but actually involves differences from all spoken varieties. Possible opposite terms, *nonstandard or substandard*, seem negative, even pejorative, and imply grammatical elitism. *Vernacular*, as an objective term for the pole opposite the standard, places no judgment on the value of coexistent varieties. Rather, the term *vernacular* refers to "the indigenous language or dialect of a community" (Crystal 1987: 35).

In figure 14.1, boldface type indicates the varieties under discussion in this essay. Varieties are plotted on the chart with respect to their standardization and vitality. English as a worldwide linguistic phenomenon has great currency as both a first and second language. Media standards and major literary vehicles, such as Received Pronunciation of English, Parisian French, and Castillian Spanish, are important standardized varieties. Second-tier varieties, both standardized and vital through official (though nonprimary) language status, include Guaraní, Catalán, Flemish and Québecois. Black English vernaculars are strong in vitality, though not standardized. Spanish in the United States is standardized through its hemispheric and global connections. Its vitality is undeniable, yet limited by controversy and unofficial status. Bilingual education, media, and public services, as well as demographic strength, nonetheless place it in the upper right quadrant. Similar situations may apply to Welsh and Irish, with less vitality. Colonial languages are becoming less vital, but neither extinct nor fossilized, as are standardized classical Latin and Greek. Regional dialects have limited vitality and nearly no standardization; immigrant varieties participate in the standard. Language mixtures (code switching, pidgins) and working-class urban dialects are vernaculars with little standardization, and varying elements of vitality. Plotting standardization and vitality of varieties in particular speech communities should be a determination based on empirical research and documentation.

Literary, political, and institutional support have enabled dialects to become standardized through acceptance over time. In fact, there are several standards in operation for any language, despite royal academies and purist thinking that there is

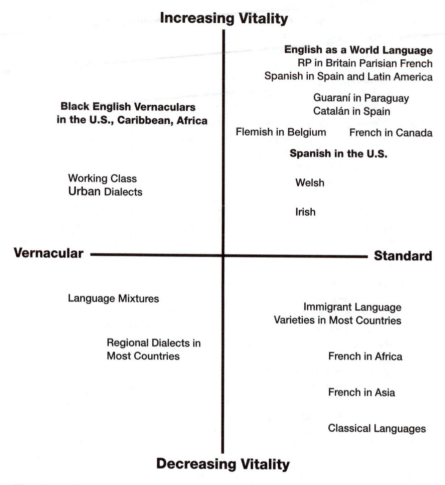

Fig. 14.1. Two primary sociocultural factors affecting language attitudes (adapted from Ryan, Giles, and Sebastian 1982: 6).

but one English, one Spanish, or one French. The operational habits of work, electronic media, and printed information enable several accepted conventions to coexist—societal (regional, class, occupational) standards, literary standards within genres, even publication-specific standards and broadcast standards—each appropriate to varying contexts.

The vitality dimension is dynamically interwoven with that of standardization. Originally conceived as a sociopsychological composite factor, vitality accounts for the sense within an ethnolinguistic group of being "a distinctive and active collective entity in intergroup situations" (Giles, Bourhis, and Taylor 1977: 308). The components of ethnolinguistic vitality help analyze various social aspects of intergroup strength in relation to the structure and usage of language varieties. Language vitality may be determined by analyzing sociolinguistic status, demography, and institutional support (fig. 14.2). Status factors reflect the group's economic and political power, its social and historical standing, and the international prestige of the language. Demographic factors relate to the size and dynamics of the linguistic community. Institutional support refers to the use of the variety in a wide range of social institutions, both formal and informal, including mass media (especially written forms), the home, houses of worship, social settings, and schools (Haners and Blanc 1989: 162–166).

These two dimensions, standardization and vitality, are useful in understanding the various types of prestige, loyalty, and devaluation that language varieties attract. Standardization is a relatively clear dimension related to written language norms, conventional spelling, and formal rules of grammar. Spanish has a standardized form that gives economic and literature status to the language of Latinos, even the non-standard varieties, which may be developed into standard forms. On the other hand, Ebonic varieties (language usages derived from the African diaspora) are vernacular and are written only as approximations of speech (Gay 1987: 66). Nonetheless, vernacular varieties of English and other languages, urban and rural regional dialects, and sociolects based in class, economic, and educational status are dynamic and should be described for their vitality and validity without prejudgment. Many types of code switching and English varieties spoken by Latinos, in addition to regional spoken dialects of Spanish, might also be seen as "working-class vernaculars" (Flores, Attinasi, and Pedraza 1981).

The vitality of vernaculars has increased in status as a result of institutional support from the electronic media, which allow spoken varieties to be broadcast widely, and through the eloquent verbal language of orators who speak compellingly without compromising dialect features. For instance, the status of Ebonic speech has been increased by the language of the Black-American clergy and public figures such as Rev. Jesse Jackson, the Chicago alderman Danny Davis, or the late mayor of Chicago Harold Washington. César Chávez and Russell Means speak in ways that evoke the voices of Latino and Native-American struggles. The population increases among Latinos in the United States and of African Americans strengthens the demographic support of vernacular varieties of Spanish and English. Institutions and media as diverse as churches, desktop publishing, salsa music, rap recordings, radio and television, and literary works of African-American, Latin American, and U.S. Latino writers have enhanced the institutional vitality of non-mainstream cultures and their accompanying language varieties.

No one denies the power of standard forms, especially in writing, as a means of access to a wider audience (Edwards 1982; Greene 1981: 66). This essay is written in standard English, not in Spanish, and with few strictly oral colloquialisms. Its purpose is to reach a wider audience who may only read English, or who use it as a second language. But spoken strategies beyond the controlled use of standard written English may be necessary for discussion, understanding, analysis, and application of this condensed written format. (Conversations about the ideas presented here, their application to practice for teachers, and discussions with students may necessitate a wider use of spoken language in varieties of Spanish, English, and other languages). It is neither logical nor legitimate to assume that all discourse in standard literate form is intelligent, or to insist that clarity or brilliance may be expressed only in standard form.

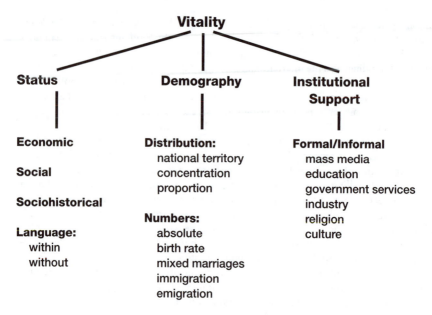

Fig. 14.2. Taxonomy of structural variables affecting sociolinguistic vitality (from Giles, Bourhis, and Taylor 1977: 509).

For most African-American Ebonic linguistic varieties, cultural conventions exist, but formal textual standardization does not, although Kréol in Haiti and Papiamentu in Curaçao do have standardized written forms. Vitality, on the other hand, seems to be increasing for African-American varieties, and aspects of vernacular are amplifying the standard through the fiction and poetry of African-American authors, from the classics of Langston Hughes and Paul Laurence Dunbar to the contemporary works of writers like Toni Morrison, Ishmael Reed, and Terry McMillan. Legal rulings (Smitherman 1981) and the development of cultural identity in language use (Gay and Baber 1987) have increased the status of and support for vernaculars, thus enhancing their vitality. To the chagrin of purists who claim to speak only what is in the dictionary, many topical phrases from wide sources, including Spanish and Black English colloquialisms, are becoming current in standard English as that language expands (and its dictionaries continuously incorporate new words and expressions).

Against this sociolinguistic backdrop, the evaluation of language varieties unfolds and evolves. Attitudes toward language varieties frequently express covert racial attitudes. Evaluations of dialects and accents do not reflect simply linguistic or aesthetic elements but rather couch expressions of the status and prestige accorded the speakers of these varieties. Social psychologists have explored how listeners rate speakers on scales of competence (e.g., job status, intelligence) and liability (e.g., friendliness, trust). The overall conclusion is that standard speech is preferred. Kalin (1982: 155), for example, reported that standard accent was rated higher on competence and likability scales by both in-group and out-group members; Hopper

(1977) found a positive reaction to Black speakers who spoke standard English. On the other hand, a minimum nonstandardness was sufficient to elicit the stereotype of African-American speech. Progressive increases in Ebonic nonstandard features of speech samples had little effect on raters' negative reactions. This is the language-variety correlate of the old race-conscious "one-drop rule"; one grain of Black speech and the person is categorically devalued.

In several attitudinal experiments regarding Mexican-American speech, the situation of esteem is similar: as accent increased, the value rating by Anglos descended (Carranza 1982). When looking at Latino raters, however, studies suggest that for-eign-born Mexican Americans ascribe more prestige to accented speech than do U.S.-born Mexican Americans (Baird 1969; Brennan, Ryan, and Dawson 1975). This implies that foreign-born Mexicans in the United States have a more positive self-im-age than do U.S.-born Mexican Americans. The hegemony of Anglo culture is re-flected in the finding that self-concept among Mexican Americans became more negative as time in the United States increased. The implication from this work is that the U.S. experience engenders and reinforces biracially divided language atti-tudes (standard vs. all others), as pointed out by Rodriguez (1989: 50–51). Puerto Ricans and other Latinos in the United States who experience a multidimensional stratification in Latin America (based on economic status, partially on color, and with linguistic dimensions involving sociolects of Spanish) are pressed into a per-plexing two-dimensional world where the educated professional, the nonliterate worker, and even indigenous Native Americans who speak Spanish as a second lan-guage are considered "Hispanics," with no distinction made among them.

The discrimination against speakers of vernaculars and those who speak stan-dard varieties of languages other than English seems to be the result of a monolingual view of prestige, at least in the Anglophone world. British "received pronunciation" seems to be at the top of the scale, confounding whites who speak U.S. dialects when they encounter black West Indians or Africans who speak prestige-attracting British varieties. The phenomena reviewed here, whether discrimination against vernaculars or devaluation of accentedness, are part of a covert scale that places a single group (and supposedly a single language variety) in a position of honor, at the expense of all others in a sort of pecking order. But the monolithic prestige scale has its contra-dictions, and nowhere are they more visible than in English-only nativism.

SUPPRESSION OF LINGUISTIC VARIETIES AND THE ENGLISH-ONLY MOVEMENT

Silencing, or linguistic suppression, is the ultimate dehumanization through lan-guage. Both dialect suppression and language prohibition exclude speakers from di-alogue with the culture of power. In this respect, discrimination against speakers of Black English vernaculars and exclusion of speakers of languages other than Eng-lish have the same social effect. Vernacular speakers are disenfranchised or dis-missed for not speaking standard English. This is taken to the extreme when English receives exclusive rights. Standard English elitism and English-only movements dis-criminate against bilingual persons for both of their languages, especially if they speak English with an accent or working-class vernacular English. The prestige of

English does not need legal support, given the English origins of U.S. history and the currents of isolationism and nativism that have periodically arisen in the United States (Crawford 1992). Recognizing the danger of linguistic chauvinism, the National Council of Black Studies recognized that English-only policies could have a negative impact on black students, although it is evident that most African Americans are unaware of the personal or wider impact of the English-only movement (Smitherman 1992).

The legal, practical, and ideological consequences of English exclusiveness in the United States have been vigorously debated over the past decade, as nineteen states passed provisions giving official status to English (Platt 1990). The ideological effect of such laws is to reinforce the mistrust of non-English languages, speakers, and cultures. In California's 1986 referendum on English (Proposition O), the English press implied that language minority groups were being manipulated by local politicians. Much of the rhetoric assumed that inability to speak English (not even thought of as "knowing other languages") could be equated with the inability to speak and even the inability to think (Woolard 1989: 277). The ideology was that non-English languages were cultural prisons and that English would liberate minorities and protect their rights; but the practical effect was to deprive language minorities of many avenues of social access, including access to learning English through bilingual methods. Such laws seem to impact most severely on the elderly and women, sectors that are the least bilingual among language minority groups. Continued divisiveness, not unity, has been the effect of English-only. Those who support language diversity are thought to be un-American, and those who speak other languages are seen as deviant and dependent, rather than as bearers of a precious human resource. Zentella (1988) offers an impassioned explanation of that ideology and defends multilingualism: "Language is not the real issue; it is a smokescreen. The browning of America is under way, and as the face of America changes, so must our definition of 'American.' The United States is not home only to English-speakers; the American dream is not dreamt in English only."

Whereas the suppression of languages other than English is a clear case of linguistic discrimination, the censure of dialects and what Delpit (1988) has called "the silenced dialogue" are more subtle. The silencing of linguistic variety frequently occurs in professional settings dominated by white males, and in discourse that frequently uses military and sports metaphors. Women's ways of knowing, Ebonic rhetorical styles, the accent of the English-as-a-second-language speaker, and the hesitance of disabled persons tend to be neglected and disempowered. It is doubly devastating when the speaker is both from a minority group and a woman. The setting might be a staff meeting. An issue is on the table. Various persons are giving presentations or opinions. When an African American, Hispanic, or Asian takes the floor and begins to speak, the focus of attention is broken. People refer to papers, move in their seats, get a coffee, begin a side conversation. Afterwards, they say that the person had a point but that it wasn't clear, couldn't be followed, was off the mark.

In schools and universities, the subtler forms of discrimination in the situations just described are compounded. Schools are stratified by a student-teacher-administrator hierarchy. In urban schools, the higher the stratum, the fewer the minorities (in suburban schools, minority representation is less overall). Even in integrated schools, more elite and higher-track programs contain fewer minorities. Schools are thus environments for covert racism, even if blatant derogatory ethnic labels are controlled. Speakers of languages other than standard English and of vernacular dialects suffer devaluation and negative language attitudes and their social-psychological consequences. These consequences, broadly, are societal and personal: the inequities of institutional racism without overt racists, and the silencing of inchoate ideas if they are not framed in accepted linguistic form. In the educational arena, this often results in polarization or communication breakdown, to the great detriment of the most innocent victims of all, schoolchildren.

In educational circles, despite years of analysis, the verbal-deprivation myth persists regarding both non-English speakers (chiefly Mexicans and Puerto Ricans, but others as well) and vernacular speakers of English (certainly African Americans, but others depending on geographic region). In all cases, the myth is accompanied by tenacious errors regarding cognitive deficiency or social deficit. First, the language system or psychophysical reasons are blamed for any inability to perform on standardized measures, and for the lack of achievement in the economic marketplace. Second, social environment and verbal interaction are blamed for lack of access to standard forms. These mind-sets persist today, even through Labov noted over two decades ago that "the myth of verbal deprivation is particularly dangerous because it diverts attention from the real defects of our educational system to imaginary defects of the child" (1972a: 202). In the 1990s, issues of Afrocentric curriculum, biliteracy, and language development have sparked a new debate, with emphasis on the cultural resources, funds of knowledge, and linguistic abilities that children bring to school. These resources may be seen as starting points for acquiring standard forms and succeeding in general academic subjects.

In the 1980s, moves to institutionalize Black English through pre-school primers were correctly viewed as patronizing, a liberal idea that furthered the ghettoization of and discrimination against African Americans. Modeled on the bilingual education notion of home-language literacy first and transfer of skills later, the inept analogy fortunately did not gain wide adoption. No one has successfully reduced Black English to a definitive written form, primarily because of its verbal roots and wide variation (Goodwin 1990; Hewitt 1986; Smitherman 1977: 70). Still, denial persists regarding the existence and sociolinguistic vitality of Ebonic language varieties, usually among standard-English purists with normative—not descriptive—frames of reference. The speech of African Americans cannot (and should not) be taught in a standard formulaic manner. Nonetheless, awareness of the vitality of vernaculars and a transformation back and forth between vernacular and standard English varieties provide essential strategies for valid and successful pedagogy. The same arguments have been advanced regarding other languages as the foundation of bilingual and bicultural education: analogical processes promote divergent thinking, respect for communicative skill builds self-esteem, and the transfer of ideas from vernacular variety to standard English strengthens both grammar and content.

Dialect awareness for teachers has been mandated by courts (*King v. Ann Arbor* 1979; Simpkins and Simpkins 1981; Smitherman 1981), and sociolinguistic concepts are emphasized in training sessions for teachers (Gere and Smith 1979). The challenge in such cases is clear: if workshops are provided by academic linguists, they may bore the audience with descriptive facts, antagonize practitioners who are purists, and ultimately neglect to provide concrete strategies for academic improvement. Such inservice sessions will not reduce language-based racial discrimination. The recommendations may remain mild and unsatisfying: know that these structural and discourse differences exist and have their own logic; respect your students and their family speech patterns; but you still have to—somehow—get them to speak and write in the standard form. Such admonishments are inadequate to overcome overt, covert, or suppressive linguistic racism.

One study of African-American linguistic patterns in mathematical problem solving concluded only that educators should "seek out the knowledge of linguists" and "declare Black education a national emergency" (Orr 1987: 215). Intriguingly titling her study *Twice As Less*, the author noted confusion and multiple paraphrases as children verbalized mathematical relationships. Beyond analyzing dialect structure and its lack of mathematical precision, however, Orr neglected to probe other connections between mathematical conceptualization and verbal expression. An Afrocentric educator might take a different approach, emphasizing first the accomplishments of African engineering (ancient Egypt, Zimbabwe), the prowess of African-American mathematicians (Benjamin Banneker's work with Pierre l'Enfant in the design of Washington, D.C.), the accomplishments of local scientists and teachers, and the mathematical relationships in everyday occurrences, from skip rope to household budgets. Next, mathematical understandings expressed in vernacular paraphrases could be matched to standard forms of mathematical statement through dialect translation. This is the frequent practice in tutorial and group study sessions among foreign students, and even among standard-English speakers. Linguistic flexibility coupled with mathematical knowledge could allow additional minority group students to find their voice in technical subjects.

Beyond the academic agenda of applied linguistics, James Baldwin offered an op-ed opinion in the July 29, 1979, *New York Times* on the Ann Arbor decision regarding Black English vernacular speakers and public school teaching. "If Black English Isn't a Language, Then Tell Me, What Is?" challenged educators to recognize that deeper issues confront all groups who do not share the language of power:

> The brutal truth is that the bulk of White people in America never had any interest in educating Black people, except as this could serve White purposes. It is not the Black child's language that is in question, it is not his language that is despised: it is his experience. A child cannot be taught by anyone who despises him, and a child cannot afford to be fooled. A child cannot be taught by anyone whose demand essentially is that the child repudiate his experience, and all that gives him sustenance, and enter a limbo in which he will no longer be Black, and in which he knows he can never become White. Black people have lost too many children that way.

The consequences of these wider societal problems return us to the very real problems of implementation and application, the follow-up necessary once linguistic consciousness is raised. Teachers are not entirely to blame, since they are too often asked to change their attitudes and approaches after only brief exposure to sociolinguistics and social psychology. The ability to move beyond liberal cheerleading is lacking in much of professional development, and teachers need concrete ways to adjust the patterns of their own interaction and practice.

DEMOCRATIZING LANGUAGE VARIETY

A radical alternative to the teaching of Black dialect provides potential answers to the dilemma faced by educators of children from diverse linguistic and dialect backgrounds. This alternative derives from "whole-language" proponents in the United States (Goodman 1965), literacy movements based in the theories of Paulo Freire of Brazil (1970, 1971), and the pedagogical implications of the Freirean method elaborated by Emilia Ferreiro of Argentina (1971, 1977). Whole language emphasizes speaking, listening, reading, and writing as components of literacy that follow natural language development; it deemphasizes spelling and grammar and concentrates on authentic uses of language. Freire recognizes the cultural basis of all learning and the need for critical consciousness-raising to create a motivating personal connection to the quest for literacy.

Ferreiro, who spent most of her professional life on reading methods for Latin American children, presents a simple proposal that could be adopted at nearly no cost for both dialect speakers of English and speakers of other languages, such as Hispanics. It is simply this: have children read standard texts aloud and then translate what they read into their home dialect. The concept of dialect translation gives legitimacy to spoken varieties without artificially creating divisive dialect reading materials. The key to the method lies in the question: which spoken language does the written language transcribe? (Ferreiro and Teberosky 1982: 259). The answer proposed by dialect translation respects the linguistic notion of language variety and presents an antiracist stance regarding vernaculars.

Language in its written form is basically a representation of deeper lexical and syntactic structures that can be rendered by various verbal forms. (The example of *photography, photographic,* and *photo* illustrates how phonetic rendering of stress and vowel allophones are surface phenomena of deeper psycholinguistic regularities.) Since speech never mirrors writing exactly (and does not need to), writing should not necessarily be understood as the phonetic transcription of speech. Although elementary stages of language-experience writing emphasize the transcription of speech, in finished writing editing enables the writer both to condense, and to elaborate upon, spoken communication. The argument by Ferreiro is that no single spoken dialect need be exclusively represented in writing, but that writing functions as a supraordinate variety, capable of encoding many pronunciations. In most languages, a wide variety of syntactic alternatives also may be accommodated within the conventions of grammaticality: "The written signs may correspond to phonic forms that do not coincide exactly with the actual sounds, but if the semantic similarities linking forms of the same lexeme are reflected in writing, then the writing system lends itself easily to dialect variations of pronunciation. Consequently, none of these dialect variations enjoys the status of correct pronunciation for learning to read" (Ferreiro and Teberosky 1982: 260).

Thus we should allow children to learn to read the way they speak. This does not require a change in materials but rather in the way the literacy process is conceived. It demands that we agree that there are no bad dialects. It demands a change in the phonic teaching approach—with its emphasis on spelling, grammar, and decoding. In the same way, Spanish speakers may learn to read Spanish in their spoken dialect—but it is still Spanish. The next step is retranslation from the vernacular—

now made legitimate—to the standard. The value of the standard derives not from elite prestige, but from wider access. Vernacular speakers of English may read in dialect forms and interpret dialect syntax from standard form (as happens in paraphrase). In the process, recognition of standard form is achieved, again with the all-important acknowledgment of sociolinguistic appropriateness and vitality based in the pragmatic relativity of each variety. Ferreiro and Teberosky cite cases where "Black preschool children learn to read by themselves, and read, in Black English, texts written not in White English but simply in English" (1982: 261, quoting Smith 1973). In both the multidialectal and multilingual cases, nonthreatening speechwriting comparisons and cross-comparison of vernacular language and dialect varieties allow access to the standard and simultaneously clarify the position of the standard in the sociolinguistic compass.

Dialect variation should not be confused with pronunciation defects or disability. The misdiagnosis of a dialect speaker or non-English speaker as a person with communication disorders is all too frequent, and the high incidence of minority children in special education should be carefully examined. On the other hand, there are numerous instances of legitimate language disabilities and communication disorders not being assessed and treated, especially among non-English speakers, because no one in the school team knew how to evaluate in the native language, diagnose the problem, separate it from linguistic conventions in Spanish or English, and prescribe an intervention. Special education travesties present further examples of subtle linguistic racism without racists, which allows the machinery of the educational establishment little access to the linguistic culture of power.

Barriers contain subordinated groups when these groups are silenced. Whether we consider African Americans and Latinos in the United States or the undereducated working class in developing nations, discrimination against subordinated people is facilitated by their inability to speak in the dominant variety, or to control literate standards. (Literacy was denied African Americans prior to Emancipation; contemporary reading scores show a sad continuation of the pattern.) Ferreiro and Teberosky (1982) assert that whether it is justifiable ideologically or not, linguistic accommodation—meaning mastery of the standard—must precede the eradication of discrimination and will require that the powerless learn another form of discourse, in literate form as well as in spoken. Freire (1970) goes further and links learning standard forms to conceptual development and liberation. Gay and Baber (1987) and Smitherman (1977), with a different approach, argue that expressive nonstandard communications are essential acts of assertion and self-description that can lead to self-esteem, identity development, and the communicative foundations for social change. Both views have validity: "Forms of speaking are learned, especially by children, in speaking contexts, in communicative situations. Let us teach people, if judged necessary, how to speak other dialects. But we must not demand this as a prerequisite to learning to read, because it would establish an invalid causal relationship" (Ferreiro and Teberosky 1982: 262).

The normative insistence on standard speech for access to reading is compounded in the United States by a longstanding two-category (white- black) racial ideology (Rodriguez 1989: 50). This thinking is indicative of a binary attitude in which the culture of power is considered a one, and all others are zero. With the surge in Asian and Latino populations, and the five-hundred-year reminder of Native

Americans, the terms of the dichotomy might more properly be white versus non-white. Nevertheless, this racial binary feeds a mindset that remains far too simplistic—we-they, good-bad, valuable-dispensable. Linguistic correlates of the dichotomy include standard versus nonstandard, and English versus non-English. The term *limited English* makes no reference to a speaker's prior linguistic resources and fuels the devaluation that reduces the language, culture, ability to think, and thus the humanity of vernacular and ethnolinguistic groups to zero. Not only does such a conceptual reduction condone a have versus have-not society, but it promotes the neglect of diverse cultural resources and contributions and closes avenues of access to them. The dichotomy pressures students either to try to change who they are or to negate themselves culturally, resulting in low self-esteem or self-rejection. This double bind pressures most nonwhite groups to revere and accept the dominant culture wholly and uncritically, only to enjoy partial access to its benefits. This is the classical pattern of cultural hegemony: fascination with the attainable world of the oppressor and uncritical acceptance of pressures to assimilate. The negative views of self and of one's vernacular speech and home culture place both bilinguals and English-dialect speakers in a dilemma regarding education and access to the wider society. First is the negative prestige of hating school and not succeeding; second is the contradiction of trying to excel in spite of oneself. Low self-esteem is counterproductive to acquiring new information; effective learning requires critical thinking, selective synthesis, and the active personal application of knowledge. Ferreiro's suggestion, as an alternative, retains the rootedness in cultural consciousness that Freire considers essential and at the same time provides flexible and natural linguistic experiences that lead to standard literacy.

Four solutions may be advanced to answer the ever-widening dichotomy that places both non-English and vernacular speakers in situations of linguistic inequality. These are: change speech, change attitudes, retain high standards, and allow diversity to flourish within the form and content of clear and creative linguistic expression.

There are two sides to speech modification. First, in the interest of access to the language of power, multicultural speakers need to learn standard varieties. This does not imply removal or suppression of vernacular home languages and local dialects. Rather, the example of dialect translation and the life experiences of successful role models who have developed bidialectalism and biliteracy should be guideposts. Second, all speakers have to excoriate racism from language. Words can be weapons, and slurs are assaults. Both verbal and nonverbal communication has to be sensitive to pervasive tendencies toward discriminatory discourse and must remove prejudice and hostility from speech, reference, and innuendo.

In terms of changing attitudes, it should be recognized that *everyone* speaks a dialect, and that each language variety has its own appropriateness and validity. Validity is more than standardization; it includes vitality. This helps us understand the attraction and endurance of vernacular forms. It is also necessary for teachers, employers, and supervisors to remove low expectations in interaction with non-English and vernacular English speakers, and to be sensitive to the erroneous association of standard expression with logic and cognitive skill. Teachers should remove rote activity from their teaching of the standard form and engage students in creative, accelerated learning where the development of standard expression is a by-product, not a prerequisite, for literate activity. Furthermore, pedagogy needs to revise its approach to standard and canonical works. Teaching based in biculturalism and bilingualism connects learning to family and promotes multicultural communication. Afro- and Latinocentric education may be seen as an early apprenticeship for global learning, which it also enriches. As a response to the dismissal of nonprestigious cultures, dialect differences and language minority communities should be seen in their role of affirming culture as self-worth and as survival, through traditions rich in verbal and emotional treasures. Once they are valued by formal educators, such reservoirs of culture become funds of knowledge in the service of education, rather than discarded markers in the increasing gulf between human cultures.

Next, acceptance of language variety does not require the absence of norms or standards. The opposite is true: successful persons from minority groups have had to be doubly competent to survive, let alone excel, in a discriminatory environment. The role-model writers, verbal artists, and teachers from multicultural groups attest to both the rigorous paths to excellence, and the humbling fulfillment when their achievement retains its connection to culture. An education that does not provide access to the widest cultural achievement does a disservice to all students. Majority-group monolinguals need also to understand the limits of their own socialization in the United States, with its isolationist tendencies, and, through multicultural contact and learning other languages, strive to overcome prejudgments and narrowness.

Finally, allowing diversity to flourish encapsulates the entire issue: it would

1. Recognize the valid contribution of speakers, whatever their speech;
2. Enable access to norms, literacy, standard communication, and the informational marketplace, without requiring the negation or eradication of varieties as the cost of admission;
3. Invigorate and enlighten the repertoire of all participants by infusing variety into the standard, promoting the notion of language expansion rather than purism;
4. Understand that literacy focuses on shared communication through the content of messages, not on accent or dialect phonology.

Since language is visible, ubiquitous, and both individual and societal, linguistic racism and discourse discrimination remain insurmountable barriers to completing the unfinished business of the civil rights agenda. Concerted effort and shared work to eradicate hostile, negligent, and suppressive sociolinguistic environments may constitute a primary instrument to close the gap between the principles of equal justice and educational opportunity and the fact of social inequality.

REFERENCES

Allen, Irving L. 1983. *The Language of Ethnic Conflict: Social Organization and Lexical Culture.* New York: Columbia University Press.

———. 1990. *Unkind Words: Ethnic Labeling from Redskin to WASP.* New York: Bergin and Garvey.

Allport, G. W. 1954. *The Nature of Prejudice.* Cambridge, Mass: Addison-Wesley.

Baird, Susan J. 1969. *Employment Interview Speech: A Social Dialect Study in Austin, Texas.* Ph.D. diss., University of Texas, Austin.

Baldwin, James. 1979 July 29. "If Black English Isn't a Language, Then Tell Me, What Is?" *New York Times.*

Brennan, E. M., E. B. Ryan, and W. E. Dawson. 1975. Scaling of Apparent Accentedness by Magnitude Estimation and Sensory Modality Matching. *Journal of Psycholinguistic Research* 4: 27–36.

Carranza, Miguel A. 1982. Attitudinal Research on Hispanic Language Varieties. In *Attitudes toward Language Variation,* ed. Ellen Bouchard Ryan and Howard Giles, 63–83. City: Press

Cole, Elsa K. 1991. Equality of Access and the Problem of Hate Speech. Paper presented at the 4th Annual Conference on Racial and Ethnic Relations in American Higher Education, San Antonio. Ann Arbor: University of Michigan Office of the General Counsel.

Crawford, James. 1992. *Hold Your Tongue: Bilingualism and the Politics of "English Only."* Reading, Mass: Addison-Wesley.

Crystal, David. 1987. *The Cambridge Encyclopedia of Language.* New York: Cambridge University Press.

Delpit, Lisa. 1986. Skills and Other Dilemmas of a Progressive Black Educator. *Harvard Educational Review* 56:379–385.

———. 1988. The Silenced Dialogue: Power and Pedagogy in Educating Other People's Children. *Harvard Educational Review* 58:280–298.

Edwards, John R. 1982. Language Attitudes and Their Implications among English Speakers. In *Attitudes toward Language Variation,* ed. Ellen Bouchard Ryan and Howard Giles, 20–33. City: Press

Ferreiro, Emilia. 1971. *Les Relations Temporelles dans le Langage de l'Enfant.* Geneva: Droz.

———. 1977. *Problemas de la Psicología Educational.* Buenos Aires: Producciones Editorials IPSE.

Ferreiro, Emilia, and Ana Teberosky. 1982. *Literacy before Schooling.* Boston: Heineman.

Ferrell, C. S. 1992. Hate Crimes Ruling Puts Campuses on Guard. *Black Issues in Higher Education* 9 (10): 1, 50–51.

Fishman, Joshua.

Flores, Juan, John Attinasi, and Pedro Pedraza. 1981. La Carreta Made a U-Turn: Puerto Rican Language and Culture in the United States. *Daedalus* 110:193–217.

Freire, Paulo. 1970. *Pedagogy of the Oppressed.* New York: Seabury.

———. 1971. *Education for Critical Consciousness.* New York: Seabury.

Gay, Geneva. 1987. Ethnic Identity Development and Black Expressiveness. In *Expressively Black,* ed. Geneva Gay and Willie Baber, 35–76. New York: Praeger.

Gay, Geneva, and Willie Baber, eds. 1987. *Expressively Black.* New York: Praeger.

Gere, Anne Ruggles, and Eugene Smith. 1979. *Attitudes, Language, and Change.* Urbana, Ill.: National Council of Teachers of English.

Giles, H., R. Y. Bourhis, and D. M. Taylor. 1977. Towards a Theory of Language in Ethnic Group Relations, In *Language, Ethnicity, and Intergroup Relations,* ed. full name Giles, 307–348. New York: Academic Press.

Glasberg, V. M. 1991. Offensive Expression, Free Speech, and Campus Civility. *Black Issues in Higher Education* 8 (14):21.

Goodman, K. 1965. Dialect Barriers to Reading Comprehension. *Elementary English* 42(8): 639–643.

Goodwin, Marjorie Harness. 1990. *He-Said-She-Said: Talk as Social Organization among Black Children.* Bloomington: Indiana University Press.

Greenberg, Jeff, S. L. Kirkland, and Tom Pysnczyaski. 1988. Some Theoretical Notions and Preliminary Research Concerning Derogatory Ethnic Labels. In *Discourse and Discrimination,* ed. Geneva Smitherman-Donaldson and Teun A. van Dijk, 46–72. City: Press

Greene, Marvin. 1981. Implications of the King Case. In *Black English and the Education of Black Children and Youth*, ed. Geneva Smitherman, 62–70. City: Press

Gwaltney, John Langston. 1980. *Drylongo: A Self Portrait of Black America*. New York: Random House.

Haners, Josiane, and Michel Blanc. 1989. *Bilinguality and Bilingualism*. New York: Cambridge University Press.

Heath, Shirley Brice. 1983. *Ways with Words: Language, Life, and Work in Communities and Classrooms*. New York: Cambridge University Press.

Hecht, Michael, and Sidney Ribeau. 1988. Afro-American Identity Labels and Communication Effectiveness. In *Language and Ethnic Identity*, ed. William B. Gudykunst, 163–170. Philadelphia: Multilingual Matters.

Hess, G. A., Jr. 1991. *School Restructuring, Chicago Style*. Newbury Park, Calif.: Corwin.

Hess, G. A., Jr., and C. A. Warden. 1988. Who Benefits from Desegregation Now? *Journal of Negro Education* 57:536–551.

Hewitt, Roger. 1986. *White Talk, Black Talk: Interracial Friendship and Communication amongst Adolescents*. New York: Cambridge University Press.

Hopper, R. 1977. Language Attitudes and the Job Interview. *Communication Monographs* 40:296–302.

Kalin, Rudolf. 1982. The Social Significance of Speech in Medical, Legal, and Occupational Settings. In *Attitudes toward Language Variation*, ed. Ellen Bouchard Ryan and Howard Giles, 148–163. City: Press

King, Joyce E. 1991. Dysconscious Racism: Ideology, Identity, and the Miseducation of Teachers. *Journal of Negro Education* 60:133–146.

King v. Ann Arbor Schools. 1979. Memorandum Opinion and Order in the case of *Martin Luther King Junior Elementary School v. Ann Arbor School District Board*, by Judge Charles W. Joiner, In *Black English and the Education of Black Children and Youth*, ed. Geneva Smitherman, 356–358. Detroit: Wayne State University Press.

Kochman, Thomas, ed. 1972. *Rappin' and Stylin' Out*. Champaign: University of Illinois Press.

Labov, William. 1972a. *Language in the inner City*. Philadelphia: University of Pennsylvania Press.

———. 1972b. *Sociolinguistic Patterns*. Philadelphia: University of Pennsylvania Press.

Massey, Grace C., Mona V. Scott, and Sanford Dornbusch, 1975. Racism without Racists: Institutional Racism in Urban Schools, *Black Scholar* 7 (November): 10–19.

Obudho, Constance E. 1976. *Black-White Racial Attitudes: An Annotated Bibliography*. Westport, Conn.: Greenwood.

Orr, Eleanor. 1987. *Twice As Less: Black English in the Performance of Black Students in Mathematics and Science*. New York: Norton.

Pérez, Bertha, and María Torres-Guzmán. 1992. *Learning in Two Worlds: An integrated Spanish/English Approach to Biliteracy*. New York: Longman.

Platt, Bill. 1990. *Only English? Law and Language Policy in the United States*. Albuquerque: University of New Mexico Press.

Rodriguez, Clara E. 1989. *Puerto Ricans: Born in the USA*. Boston: Unwin Hyman.

Ryan, Ellen Bouchard, and Howard Giles, eds. 1982. *Attitudes towards Language Variation: Social and Applied Contexts*. London: Arnold.

Ryan, Ellen B., Howard Giles, and Richard Sebastian. 1982. An Integrative Perspective for the Study of Attitudes toward Language Variation. *Attitude toward Language Variation*, ed. Ryan and Giles, 1–19. City: Press

Simpkins, Gary, and Charlesetta Simpkins. 1981. Cross Cultural Approach to Curriculum Development. In *Black English and the Education of Black Children and Youth*, ed. Geneva Smitherman, 212–240.

Smith, F., ed. 1973. *Psycholinguistics and Reading.* New York: Holt, Rinehart and Winston. Quoted in Emilia Ferreiro, *Problems de la psicología educational*, 261.

Smitherman, Geneva. 1977. *Talkin and Testifyin: The Language of Black America.* Boston: Houghton Mifflin.

———. 1992. African Americans and "English Only." *Language Problems and Language Planning* 16:235–248.

———, ed. 1981. *Black English and the Education of Black Children and Youth.* Detroit: Center for Black Studies and Wayne State University Press.

Smitherman-Donaldson, Geneva, and Teun A. van Dijk, eds. 1988. *Discourse and Discrimination.* Detroit: Wayne State University Press.

Weir, R. 1966. Some Question on the Child's Learning of Phonology. In *The Genesis of Language: A Psycholinguistic Approach*, ed. F. Smith and G. E. Miller. Cambridge, Mass.: MIT Press.

Woolard, Kathryn A. 1989. Sentences in the Language Prison: The Rhetorical Structuring of an American Language Policy Debate. *American Ethnologist* 16: 268–278.

Zentella, Ann Celia. 1988. English Only Laws Will Foster Divisiveness, Not Unity; They Are Anti-Hispanic, Anti-Elderly, and Anti-Female. *Chronicle of Higher Education*, November 23.

15

Returned Migration, Language, and Identity
Puerto Rican Bilinguals in Dos Worlds/Two Mundos[1]

Ana Celia Zentella

The poem "Dos Worlds/Two Mundos" was written by a Rochesterican, Henry Padrón, in 1982 (an excerpt is given in the Appendix). It portrays a bilingual's struggle with the two worlds represented by the two languages he/she knows, a struggle which can cause cultural conflict and "un tremendo strain en tu brain." In this regard, the Puerto Rican experience is no different from that of every other poor immigrant with a foreign-language background. The linguistic literature is full of examples of the we-they dichotomy experienced by members of language minorities when they attempt to participate in the dominant society (Gumperz 1964, 1976; Fishman 1966). The "we" language, that spoken at home, the mother tongue, is endowed with many positive affective variables such as intimacy and solidarity, but it is considered low in prestige. The "they" language, in contrast, enjoys high status because it is linked with the outside world of power and money (Lambert 1972). In some communities, the high and low linguistic codes are kept strictly apart (Ferguson 1964; Fishman 1967), but in others, such as the Chicano and Puerto Rican communities in the United States, the pervasiveness of the close cultural contact and the resulting lack of functional differentiation are reflected in code switching, as in Padrón's poem. Often, code switching is misinterpreted as evidence only of lack of linguistic knowledge. But a spate of recent research has proved that switching serves many significant social and discourse functions beyond that of filling in forgotten phrases or word (Gumperz 1976; McClure 1977; Valdés 1981; LPTF 1980; Zentella 1985). Nor does code switching signal the deterioration of one or both of the languages involved; in fact, switchers display formidable syntactic knowledge by switching at points that maintain the grammatical integrity of both languages at the same time (Poplack 1979; Sankoff and Poplack 1980). Thus code switching allows us to make a graphic statement about the way we live with a foot in each of "dos worlds/two mundos."

In the United States, code switching helps us to hold onto some of our Spanish, in the face of ever-mounting pressures to become English monolinguals. Strong community support for bilingual education reflects our commitment to retain Spanish while learning English. But even with, and mostly without, bilingual education, our children do become English-dominant as they go through the educational process. If they remain in the community as adults, however, increased contact with recent immigrants and the assumption of adult roles renew their fluency in Spanish (Flores et al. 1981: Zentella 1987).

This is the scenario which seems to be challenging the traditional pattern of immigrant language loss by the third generation in the United States (Pedraza et al. 1980). For many Puerto Ricans, however, there is an added wrinkle, and that is that the polarity that constitutes the two worlds of the community can suddenly reverse itself, and people who were once struggling to hold onto their Puerto Ricanness and Spanish in the United States can suddenly find themselves struggling to hold onto their "Nuyoricanoness" or "Rochestericanness" and English in Puerto Rico.

The Puerto Rican experience is unique because the United States has controlled both homeland and new-land political, economic, and educational systems since 1898, when Puerto Rico became a colony of the United States, and it continues to play a key role in the push-pull of the migration flow (Bonilla 1983). The revolving-door migration of Puerto Ricans, which represents a distinct departure from the usual immigrant pattern, challenges the prevalent model of assimilation and demands a reevaluation of the objectives and impact of many governmental policies, such as the proposed English language amendment, and of some educational approaches, particularly transitional bilingual education.

RETURNED MIGRANTS

Just as the earlier waves of Puerto Rican immigration to the United States had repercussions for the educational system and all the social services here, the return of approximately 35,000 people per year to Puerto Rico since 1973 has caused widespread reaction there (Underhill 1981). Almost 20 percent of Puerto Rico's entire population of nearly three million are Puerto Ricans who have returned to the island after living in the United States, and their offspring. They amount to approximately 10 percent of the total public-school enrollment, or close to 70,000 pupils. Approximately two-thirds of the children of returnees in the school system were born in the United States and spent more than five years here before going to the island. Many of them learned to function primarily or only in English, whether they were born in Puerto Rico or not, and could not adjust to monolingual Spanish classes in Puerto Rico. Some 14,000 attend remedial classes in basic skills as part of the Migrant Child Education Program (Freidman 1982). Another 45,000 are enrolled in bilingual education programs in 17 municipalities across the island, predominately concentrated in the metropolitan area (Junta de Planificación 1980).

The introduction of bilingual instruction in Puerto Rico for the children of returnees, who had initially been pushed out of the island because of economic problems and now were not welcomed back because of the same worsening problems, fanned the flames of the language debate. This debate has polarized the island's political and intellectual leadership ever since the U.S. troops landed in 1898 and imposed "English-only," i.e., as the medium of instruction and in all legal proceedings, leading to educational failure for thousands and resulting in great socio-political unrest (Zentella 1981).

As a result, the language behavior, attitudes, and even dress of these youngsters are topics of island-wide concern. A government publication devoted to the Immigrant Population of Puerto Rico reflects this concern forthrightly:

> Por otro lado la immigración tiene otras implicaciones a nivel social. Los puertorriqueños que regresan y sus descendientes, los cuales estuvieron exuestos a una cultura y modo de vida completamente distintos al nuestro, traen consigo una serie de patrones de vida, valores morales y actitudes hacia la autoridad que peuden entrar en conflictos con los de la población no migrante (Junta de Planificación 1980: 45).

> [On the other hand the immigration has other implications at the social level. The Puerto Ricans who return and their descendants, who were exposed to a culture and a life style completely different from ours, bring with them a series of behaviors, moral values, and attitudes toward authority which can come into conflict with those of the nonmigrant population.]

This quote should have a familiar ring for anyone acquainted with the literature on immigrants to the United States; with the elimination of the words "Puerto Ricans who return," the statement is a classic warning about the cultural conflict caused by foreigners, reappearing today in the propaganda of the proponents of the English language amendment, especially English First and U.S. English (Zentella 1988).

The Planning Board clearly assumes that Puerto Ricans in the United States are exposed to a culture with which island Puerto Ricans have no contact, and that the differences between them may cause conflict. My interest in the cultural and linguistic issues raised by these assumption, and in the returnees' perceptions of their experience, led me to undertake this research with teenagers in Puerto Rico.[2]

This paper presents the results of observations of, and individually taped interviews with, 4.3 junior and senior high school students (23 females, 20 males) in bilingual programs in Bayamon and Levittown, conducted in 1983.[3] The students ranged in ages from 12-20, with 81 percent (35) in the 16-18-year-old bracket. Sixteen percent were born in Puerto Rico and 26 percent had lived there before their most recent migration, but most had never lived in Puerto Rico before moving there from one to three years previously. They came from working-class backgrounds in New York, Chicago, Philadelphia, and Hartford and were living in lower-middle-class urbanizations just outside the capital in Puerto Rico. Nearly the entire group were English-dominant bilinguals (41/43). They were interviewed in both English and Spanish, except for two newcomers who were unable to speak or understand Spanish, and they were observed during their free periods on the school grounds.

We shall report on three aspects of the study here:

1. the link between Puerto Rican cultural identity and language;
2. attitudes toward bilingualism and biculturalism;
3. the future of Spanish and English in Puerto Rico.

PUERTO RICAN CULTURAL IDENTITY AND LANGUAGE

The language debate in Puerto Rico is not an intellectual exercise in the pros and cons of linguistic purity. It brings Puerto Ricans face to face with a basic cultural issue which has significant political ramifications. That issue is, does language change/loss necessarily spell cultural loss? More pointedly, are returnees who cannot speak Spanish Puerto Ricans? Given the influence of 400 years of Spanish rule, the history of struggle against the United States's imposition of English, and the lack of other national identifiers, the survival of Spanish has become inextricably linked for many with the survival of Puerto Rican identity and that of the Puerto Rican nation itself. The depth of feeling for Spanish is frequently communicated in emotional newspaper articles, such as "En la escencia del ser puertorriqueño nuestro idioma español posee una fuerza singular de identidad irrefutable" [In the essence of the Puerto Rican being, our Spanish language possesses a singular strength of irrefutable identity] (Casillas Alvarez 1983). Even when some scholars attempt to broaden the definition of Puerto Rican to include features other than language, they do not dispense with language. When philologist Rubén del Rosario maintains that "Es evidente que lo que hace al puertorriqueño no es sólo la lengua (su entonación, sus palabras, su frascologia particular)" [It is evident that what makes a Puerto Rican is not only the language (its intonation, its words, its particular phraseology)] (Rosario 1983), he nevertheless starts from the premise that "el ser puertorriqueño envuelve el consevar vivo el idioma corriente de nuestra pueblo" [being Puerto Rican entails the live conservation of the common language of our people]. Then, in what I interpret as a veiled reference to the returnees, he advises, "Mientras Ud. esté en Puerto Rico y se considere boricua, hablará igual que nosotros y preferriá el español para expresarse por escrito" [While you are in Puerto Rico and consider yourself Puerto Rican, you will speak like us and prefer Spanish when expressing yourself in writing] (Rosario, 1983: 16). United States Puerto Rican scholars generally heed this advice, and they pass it on to their students because they fear the negative reactions that can be stirred up if it is ignored. On a visit to the island, one United States Puerto Rican sociologist was quoted in a newspaper as saying, "To be Puerto Rican is to be inseparable from your language, so it is particularly offensive to any Puerto Rican to listen to anyone who claims to be Puerto Rican and does not know the language" (Betances, quoted in Ghigliotty 1983).

Parallel with the consistent identification of Puerto Rican identity with the Spanish language is a concern for the repercussions of extended contact with English. Many of the island's intellectuals and others believe that English has had a continuously deteriorating effect on the Spanish of Puerto Rico and that, as a result, Puerto Rico's national identity itself is being threatened. Well-known writers are reluctant, however, to link publicly their constant railing against the mutilation of Spanish and "la crisis cada vez má acentuada que vive el español en Puerto Rico" [the ever more accentuated crisis of Spanish in Puerto Rico] (González 1982) to the presence of the returnees. Consider the following newspaper article by the well-known writer, Salvador Tió, whom claims to have coined the terms "Spanglish" decades ago, in which he catalogs the deterioration of Spanish and English and predicts that both will be buried in Puerto Rico:

La confusión del sentido de las palabras; los calcos que llegan hasta la cal-
comania; los préstamos tan crecidos que exponen a muchos individuos a la
quiebra total de la expresión, están contribuyendo a desfigurar la lengua
propra. Pero si es grave lo que le está sucediendo al español, mucho más
grave es lo que le está sucediendo al inglés. A este paso la isla de Puerto
Rico puede llegar a ser, en pocas generaciones, el cementerio de las dos
grandes lenguas de América (Tió 1982: 24).

[The confusion in the meaning of words, calques to the extreme of calco-
mania, borrowings so numerous that they make many individuals suscepti-
ble to a total breakdown in communication, are contributing to a
disfiguring of the language itself. But if what is happening to Spanish is serious, what is happening to English is much more serious. At this rate, the
island of Puerto Rico may come to be, in a few generations, the cemetery of
the two great languages of America.]

Although Tió lays the blame for this situation at the door of U.S. experimentation
with school language policy during the first half of this century, many of his readers
may understandably conclude that the largest group of bilinguals in their midst, the
return migrants, share some of the blame.

Although most intellectuals are loath to attack the returnees directly, at least one
prominent anthropologist, Eduardo Seda Bonilla, has openly questioned the right of
a group that does not speak Spanish to consider itself Puerto Rican, labelling it
"pseudo-ethnicity" (Seda Bonilla 1975). The writer of a letter to the editor of a major Spanish daily expressed herself much more categorically:

. . . ni los 500,000 nacidos, criados y educados en Nueva York son puertorriqueños aunque vayan a cien mil desfiles puertorriqueños, vivan 100
anos en Puerto Rico o sus padres hayan tenido la dicha de haber nacido en
esta encantadora isla. Accepte la realidad: si usted nació, se crió y educó en
Estados Unidos, es americano y no puertorriqueño. Es tambien neoy-
orquino (Vélez 1983).

[. . . nor are the 500,000 born, raised, and educated in New York, Puerto
Ricans even if they go to 100,000 Puerto Rican parades, live 100 years in
Puerto Rico, or if their parents were lucky enough to have been born on
this enchanted island. Accept reality: if you were born, raised, and educated
in the United States, you are American and not Puerto Rican. You are also
a New Yorker.]

Support for the Nuyoricans against charges such as these comes from unexpected
quarters, the pen of Puerto Rico's renowned literary figure and *independentista* independence supporter in exile, José Luis González. González is one of the most vo-
ciferous critics of the effect of English on Spanish; he believes it is replacing Spanish
vocabulary and syntax (1982). One would expect him to be equally critical of the
group that has these language characteristics, but, when he is confronted with the reality that some who identify as Puerto Ricans cannot speak Spanish well or at all, he
prefers to attack those who dare to judge them:

¿Tienen derecho a sentirse y declarse puertorriqueños los "niuyoricans" cuya lengua materna es el inglés o en muchos casos el todavía poco analizado "espanglish?" De entrada hago constar que la pregunta misma me parece ociosa, porque los unicos que tienen derecho histórico y moral al responder a ella son los proprios "niuyoricans" cuya lengua materna no es el español que se habla en Puerto Rico. Si ellos se consideran puertorriqueños y como tales exigen que se les reconozca, ¿quién es el juez llamado a dictaminar sobre la legitimidad de su pretensión? Alguien, acaso, cuyos antepasados no fueron obligados por la necesidad de abondonar la isla? Me consta que esos jueces autodesignados abundan en la isla, pero lo cierto es que su autoridad moral no me convence del todo (González 1983: 8).

[Do "nuyoricans" whose mother tongue is English or in many cases the still little analyzed "Spanglish" have a right to feel and declare themselves Puerto Rican? From the outset I want to make clear that the question itself seems idle, because the only ones who have the historic and moral right to answer it are the "nuyoricans" themselves whose mother tongue is not the Spanish of Puerto Rico. If they consider themselves Puerto Ricans and ask to be recognized as such, who is the judge called upon to decide on the legitimacy of their claim? Someone, perhaps, whose forbears were not obliged by necessity to leave the island? I am aware that self-appointed judges abound on the island, but the truth is that their moral authority does not completely convince me.]

González's backhanded defense of the returnees is not totally convincing either, particularly since comments about the differences between the returnees and the rest of Puerto Rico's population are not limited to a few critics with questionable motives. That these differences are frequently commented on in their schools and communities is attested to by the students themselves, and it is to their own experience and attitudes, rarely reported on in the press, that we must turn for a more accurate and complete picture of these issues.

The widespread interest in the returned-migrant "problem" and the increased intensity of the attacks on Spanish and English do not appear to be disconnected, and this is not lost on the returnees. They too have strong views on the matter. For one, they definitely do not believe that they are deteriorating the island's Spanish: 87 percent rejected this, and 76 percent of them said they were not damaging the English language. Those who agree that they were having a deleterious effect on the languages could mention only slang words as evidence. Most important is their position on the link between language and culture.

We asked the bilingual teens in Puerto Rico whether it is possible for someone who speaks only English to be Puerto Rican. There was more agreement among them on this issue than on any other: 91 percent of the students believe that it is possible for someone who speaks only English to be Puerto Rican. This attitude had been probed earlier in the New York Puerto Rican community by Joshua Fishman's groundbreaking study (Fishman et al. 1971) and more recently by John Attinasi and members of the Language Policy Task Force of the Centro de Estudios Puertorriqueños (Attinasi 1979; LPTF 1980). The Centro found that 100 percent of the 91

East Harlem residents, mainly adults, and all 62 bilingual teachers they interviewed in New York agreed that "you can speak English and be part of Puerto Rican culture." In our study, we referred only to English monolinguals, specifically excluding people who know English in addition to Spanish, and this may account for the 9 percent difference in our results.

In both the Puerto Rico and New York studies, there was less agreement about the inverse situation, that is, whether Spanish speakers could be part of North American culture. In Puerto Rico, where I limited the example to Spanish monolinguals, only 63 percent of the students believed that Spanish monolinguals could be part of North American culture, whereas 94 percent of the East Harlem sample agreed with the Centro's less limiting question that "people who spoke Spanish could be Americans." For both groups, Puerto Rican national identity apparently allows for more flexibility in terms of language than does North American identity, an attitude which directly reflects their experiences in Puerto Rican and North American communities.

When the question was put more directly, "Is Spanish necessary for Puerto Rican identity?" (Centro research in New York) and "Is Spanish indispensable for Puerto Rican identity" (my research in Puerto Rico), the results were less overwhelming, particularly in the Puerto Rico sample, but they still included the majority of both groups: 83 percent of the East Harlem residents and 61 percent of the bilingual students in Puerto Rico thought that Spanish was not necessary/indispensable for Puerto Rican identity. The response of the bilingual teens on the island fell between that of the East Harlem residents and the New York bilingual teachers; 62.5 percent of the teachers judged Spanish as necessary to Puerto Rican cultural identity, and 37.5 percent found it unnecessary.

The teens in Puerto Rico were asked the same question in still another way, in terms of their response to the widely advertised slogan of Puerto Rico's English language daily, the *San Juan Star*. Hourly on the radio in Puerto Rico, the *Star* announced, "Porque ser puertorriqueño no es una (sic) cuestión de idioma" [Because being Puerto Rican is not a question of language]. The teens clearly aligned themselves with the newspaper's position, which had been widely repudiated in the local press: 81 percent of them agreed with the slogan, reaffirming that these youngsters feel quite comfortable with the notion of Puerto Rican identity without a language requirement. Needless to say, this attitude does not endear them to the island's intellectuals.

But comments about the differences between the returnees and the rest of Puerto Rico's population are more widespread than those of a few writers or academics. Evidence that it is a more generalized phenomenon is found in the terms of address that their neighbors and family used with them: 74 percent have been called "gringo," 58 percent "nuyorican," and 51 percent "americano." Of these, "nuyorican" is the one they are most likely to use among themselves.[4] The "americano" and "gringo" labels are of particular interest because they indicate that native islanders are incorporating the returnees into national groupings formerly limited to Anglos. Some returnees have been quite hurt by these labels, others say they are used in jest, and still others react defensively. Seventeen-year-old Harry's response to them is typical of those who accept the fact that their bicultural identity exposes them to attack in both of their worlds:

H: A mi me llega to' igual. Soy "bilingue," "gringo," "blanco," "white boy."
ACZ: Cuando lo dicen, ¿qué quieren decir con eso? ¿Es un insulto?
H: If they say it *insulto*, they say "dirty gringo" and all this bull crap, pero que a mí—I was in New York and I was called SPIC about one hundred fifty times. I didn't do nothin to them in New York, why am I going to say something here just because they call me a gringo. In New York, you defend yourself because they call you a Puerto Rican; here you defend yourself because they call you a gringo.
[H: I take it all the same. I am "bilingual," "gringo," "white," "white boy."
ACZ: When they say it, what do they mean by it? Is it an insult?
H: If they say it *as an insult*, they say "dirty gringo" and all this bull crap, but to me . . .]

Whatever their reaction to the terms, one result is that these youngsters are being defined as distinct from the native population. They, in turn, participate in this redefinition of their identity by referring to themselves as "we/us, the bilinguals" or "nosotros, los bilingües," and to their fellow students who are native-born Puerto Ricans as "they/them, the regulars," "ellos, los regulares." These terms mimic the school's division into *programma regular* with all classes in Spanish and *programma bilingüe* with math, social studies, and science in English, but that does not explain the more telling distinction they make between "us, the bilinguals" or "nuyoricans," and "them, the Puerto Ricans." When challenged with, "What do you mean? Aren't you Puerto Rican?" their response is "Yeah, but you know, the *real* Puerto Ricans, from here." This is, of course, the other side of the "americano/gringo" coin; both groups have adopted labels for the differences they perceive between them.

ATTITUDES TOWARDS BILINGUALISM
AND BICULTURALISM

Before we arrive at the conclusion that these differences represent irreparable cleavages in the Puerto Rican fabric, it is important to consider other data and to look beyond answers to questions, or poems, at actual behavior. It is not hard to find evidence of the Nuyoricans' positive attitudes toward Spanish and Puerto Rico. We found that all of them speak Spanish or are trying to learn it; they are all committed to raising their children bilingually; and nearly one-half of the group plans to remain in Puerto Rico when they are on their own. They like the climate, the beaches, the relative calm, and the hospitality of Puerto Rico, and they do not have fond memories of the dirt, the crime, and the danger that they left behind in the working-class ghettoes of the United States. These attitudes are as characteristic of them as their longing for the transportation, activities, and jobs of the States and their acceptance of an English-speaking Puerto Rican identity.

    There is less conflict in these behaviors and attitudes than some might think. Bilinguals in Puerto Rico seem to be saying that they want to be counted as Puerto Ricans and want the same for their children but they do not want it to depend on their knowledge of Spanish. This is a realistic response to their go-come relationship with the island. Less than a year after this study, five of the group had moved back to the States. We must also consider the effect of the criticisms made against their Spanish in view of a study by Ramos Perea (1972) which found that fluency in Spanish was crucial in the successful adjustment of junior-high-school returnees. In the group I studied, everyone had less confidence in their Spanish ability than in their English ability; most rated it as fair.[5] Many had been told by teachers, family, and neighbors that they talked "*mata*" or "killed" or "Spanglish." Nuyorican Spanish is generally stigmatized on the island. In a study which asked Puerto Rican college students to judge various speech styles, a bilingual Nuyorican speaking Spanish was judged most negatively on all scales. Island born/raised and U.S. born/raised students alike evaluated the Nuyorican speaker as the most unfriendly, the most passive, and the laziest of all (Irizarry 1981). These results are similar to those of the matched guise experiments made famous by Lambert et al. (1960) where the standard dialect or high language is consistently rated superior to the nonstandard or low code.

When the returnees speak the language they know best, they sometimes encounter ridicule and hostility from working-class island teens. They attribute the negative reaction to their speaking English to envy; that is, they believe they are resented because they can speak it and the "Puerto Ricans cannot, but would love to." This is probably an accurate estimation of the well-documented power of the metropolis's language in every colonial setting.[6] In Puerto Rico it is certainly true that in the competition for scarce jobs, the applicant who knows English has an advantage. The returnees and their children also have an educational edge of two and four years respectively over the permanent residents, which helped them fare better in the 1975 crisis (Junta de Planificación 1980). The harsh economic realities of an island plagued by a 50 percent unemployment rate, with 70 percent of its population on food stamps, in no small measure contribute to the islander vs. migrant misunderstandings.

Any analysis of the returnee vs. islander conflict must be viewed in the context of the political and economic forces that have resulted in the massive displacement and replacement of Puerto Rican people from their island. A people's language attitudes and behavior are shaped by the nature of their experiences with the social structure around them. Adolescents caught in the middle of the transfer of people and payments can be expected to reflect this conflict in their notions of identity and language.

They attempt to resolve the conflict via their commitment to bilingualism and biculturalism, only to encounter hostility to this solution in the United States and Puerto Rico. Nor are they without concern about the repercussions of biculturalism. Although 81 percent asserted that it was possible to be bicultural, 50 percent doubted that it was healthy, citing confusion as a problem. Given their situation, caught between the idealized dreams of their parents and the worsening economic crisis in Puerto Rico, we cannot expect these youngsters to be free of conflict or to refrain from transforming traditional values.

On the other hand, many of these same youngsters, particularly the *salseros*, as lovers of latin dance music—mainly from the lower class—are called, were surprised to find the accelerated pace of Americanization on the island; in some ways they feel that they are more Puerto Rican than their *roquero*, that is, rock-music-loving, more middle-class cousins who never left. Their experience belies the island government's claim cited above, that "The Puerto Ricans who return and their descendants . . .

were exposed to a culture and life style completely different from ours" (Junta de Planificación 1980). *Salseros* often complain that it is easier to find rock-music radio stations and discotheques in Puerto Rico than any that feature latin *salsa*. It seems easier for the government to blame the island's cultural upheaval on the returnees than on the unfettered U.S. penetration of island media and markets. The adolescents make a convenient scapegoat, and they suffer for it. In Tato La Viera's play *Am-e-Rican* (1985), his poem 'Nuyorican' accurately captures their feelings:

. . .	. . .
ahora regreso, con un corazón	[now I return, with a Puerto
boricua, y tú, me desprecias,	Rican heart, and you reject
me miras mal,	me, you look at me funny,
me atacas mi hablar,	you attack the way I talk,
mientras comes mcdonalds en	while you eat McDonalds in
discotecas americanas,	american discotheques,
y no pude bailar la salsa	and I couldn't dance salsa
en san juan, la que yo	in San Juan, the one that I
bailo en mis barrios	dance in my ghettoes
lleno de tus costumbres,	full of your customs,
así que, si tú no me quieres,	so, if you don't want me,
pues yo tengo un puerto rico	well I have a super delicious
sabrosisímo para buscar	Puerto Rico to find
refugio en Nueva York,	refuge in New York,
y en muchos otros callejones	and in many other alleyways
que honran tu presencia,	that honor your presence,
preservando todas tus	preserving all your
costumbres, así que,	customs, so,
por favor, no me hagas	please, don't make me
sufrir, sabes.	suffer, you know.]

THE FUTURE OF SPANISH AND ENGLISH IN PUERTO RICO

Nothing represents the transformation that the migrants represent better than the teens' opinions about the future of Spanish in Puerto Rico. A commentator's prediction that Spanish will not be spoken on the island in 50 years found support among the bilinguals in Puerto Rico; approximately 40 percent either agreed with the prediction, thought it possible, or did not know. Even though most of the group were of the opinion that Spanish *will* be spoken in Puerto Rico in 50 years, it is more significant that the majority were not distressed by the prospect of a non-Spanish-speaking Puerto-Rico in the future: 56 percent stated that it would not bother them if the prediction were to come true. This differs radically from the response of the East Harlem residents, 96 percent of whom believed "Spanish should be maintained in Puerto Rico." The difference between the "should" and "will" wordings may account for most of the 50 percent difference, but there is the possibility that the young bilinguals in Puerto Rico have extended their acceptance of a Puerto Rican identity without Spanish to include a Puerto Rico without Spanish.

Why should this occur in Puerto Rico and not New York? Undoubtedly the differences in the groups offer a partial explanation; for example, only English-dominant teenagers constituted the Puerto Rican sample, whereas the East Harlem residents covered a wide range of age groups, mainly Spanish-dominant. Furthermore, it is not difficult to understand why cultural issues tend to be idealized in New York's alienating ghettos. This phenomenon has been noted often in Nuyorican poetry which abounds in lush, warm images of a "tropical paradise" Puerto Rico (Algarín and Piñero 1975). Perhaps the teens we interviewed in Puerto Rico believed that Puerto Rico should remain Spanish-speaking before they migrated to the island; they may have changed their opinion after confronting the reality of the impressive economic power of English on the island.

Since almost half of the Puerto Rico sample *did* care if Spanish were not spoken in Puerto Rico, we were intrigued by the variables that might account for the intragroup difference in attitude. Despite the fact that the most opposing attitudes toward Puerto Rico vs. the United States and Spanish vs. English were held by two females (that is, one female was the most pro-United States and English but another was the most pro–Puerto Rico and Spanish), gender is the variable that promises to provide the most rewarding explanations of the difference within a group. Although the majority of the males and females agreed on most questions, there were several indicators of greater female conservatism in matters of language loyalty. For example, the only students who stated that English monolinguals could *not* be considered Puerto Rican were women. Also, females supported the notion that Spanish is indispensable to Puerto Rican identity 18 percent more than the males (48 percent vs. 30 percent). In addition, whereas the women were equally divided as to whether or not they would care if Spanish were spoken in Puerto Rico in 50 years, the men showed less ambivalence: 67 percent of them would not care. Although our sample was too limited to allow us to assert that language loyalty is stronger among Puerto Rican bilingual females than males, there is enough sociolinguistic evidence of female concern for maintaining appropriate linguistic norms in this and other communities to suggest that further investigation will corroborate our initial findings (Labov 1972; Trudgill 1974; Zentella 1987). The appropriate norms may be the most conservative in the community, or they may be the ones on the cutting edge of change. In either case, women seem to take the language pulse of the community, perhaps to guide their children accordingly.

In our study of growing up bilingual in New York City (Zentella 1981), we found that older migrant women were the most likely to speak Spanish in their social networks and the least likely to be bilingual. In contrast, although younger women tended to become English-dominant as rapidly as their brothers, their passive knowledge of Spanish surpassed that of their male siblings, as did their code-switching skill. The language proficiency and attitudes of each age- and gender-related network reflected the totality of their cultural experience in the United States. Males, who were more likely to go beyond the confines of their buildings and blocks, acquired the English fluency and skills, particularly in Black English vernacular, necessary for their participation in other networks. Older women and their female charges were more limited to house and childcare responsibilities and were responsible for contacts with the family in Puerto Rico; these activities maintained their links to Spanish. In addition to being socialized in the norms for appropriate Spanish usage, the younger women became keenly aware of the survival value of English in the world of education, housing, social services, and employment. They demonstrated and reflected their ability to manoeuver in public and private domains, both of which required Spanish and English, by becoming fluent bilinguals and excellent code switchers. When they move to Puerto Rico, the latter style is still their badge of ingroup membership with other Nuyoricans, but, in addition, they adopt the norms that stress the link between Puerto Rican identity and fluent Spanish for communication in the wider community. Undoubtedly, other factors, particularly age of arrival in Puerto Rico, combine with gender (those who arrive during their preteens or pre-'hang-out' years generally seem to experience less conflict with the language and customs than those who arrive between 15 and 18 years old) to provide a better picture of the differences among the returnees. Most important, until longitudinal studies are conducted, we do not know if these students, male and female alike, will change their minds about the role of Spanish in Puerto Rican culture in a few years, after they try to enter the work force in Puerto Rico and take on other adult roles.[7]

LANGUAGE-POLICY ISSUES

As the data stand now, we can imagine the reaction to what we have presented of those whose every fiber cries out against the vision of a non-Spanish-speaking Puerto Rico. Those in Puerto Rico who can exert some influence on policy must be able to move beyond the initial reaction of shock without rushing to support policies that represent the values of a well-educated and prosperous class who may posture about the inviolability of Puerto Rico's Spanish identity while they cultivate and cherish their own bilinguality. The clash between what some preach and what they practice came to the public's attention during the March 1982 polemic over Senator Peña Clos's legislation in favor of outlawing instruction carried out in English in all the public and private schools in Puerto Rico (Morales 1982). Although many applauded the Senator's efforts to bring the private schools back into the Spanish fold, others questioned his sincerity when they learned that he and his children were educated in English in Puerto Rico. The legislation was doomed from the beginning because most leaders of all political persuasions send their children to private schools where instruction is in English. Furthermore, the last 45 years of educational policy in Puerto Rico prove that the elimination of teaching in English does not necessarily bring about an improvement in the teaching of Spanish.

The truth is that Puerto Rican youngsters on both sides of the ocean are trapped in educational systems that produce failure (Santiago 1984). The bilingual programs that only some of them get to attend are, on the whole, neither well funded nor well supported and are linked to a deficit model, although many are successful despite these limitations. If the returnees I met in Puerto Rico had been able to learn to read and write in Spanish in the United States, they would not have needed bilingual education in Puerto Rico. If Puerto Ricans on the island learned English in the English classes that are required of all students in every grade, they would not have to fall behind when they transfer to the mainland. Students in the United States and Puerto Rico want to learn English as well as Spanish, and too many feel that they are not learning either well enough.

CONCLUSION: TOWARDS AN ADEQUATE POLICY

What, then, is a viable language for Puerto Ricans? I have tried to convey some of the unique features of the situation which force us to discard traditional models and to question vested ideologies. Instead, we start from the premise that the Puerto Rican community differs from the more stable European immigrant communities of the late-nineteenth and early-twentieth centuries. In addition, there are different classes in the Puerto Rican community and different social realities for each class, not to mention for each racial and gender grouping within each class, both here and in Puerto Rico. Up to now the positions that have enjoyed the most favor have been articulated by the most organized and powerful group, but we have not heard from the majority. For that majority of Puerto Ricans—who are lower working class—migration and reverse migration in response to the vagaries of a fluctuating interlocking economy are a fact of life and a matter of survival. Their pursuit of English, Spanish, and a dual cultural identity may be anathema to secure professional politicos, but it is essential to their survival and should not be judged apart from that sobering truth. Educational policy makers in particular must grapple with this complexity and reject inadequate objectives and methodologies, including that of limiting bilingual education to a transitional model. As much as it hurts their vision of what they wish were true, they must acknowledge the impact of repeated migration. This requires acceptance of a dual U.S.—Puerto Rican identity and of what Attinasi has called "interpenetrating bilingualism":

> The fluid and creative use of all the environmental language resources at hand without purist separation of languages and without wholesale condemnation of the varieties spoken either by uneducated Spanish speakers or English speakers, including Black English vernacular (Attinasi 1983: 10).

That is what some support in the United States as the only successful avenue to oral and literate proficiency in Standard Spanish as well as Standard English, but can we expect Puerto Rico to embrace it? The political stakes in Puerto Rico are so high that that which unaffected linguists can view dispassionately, that is, language change, shift, even extinction, cannot be divorced from the historical struggle against colonial domination. Given the highly charged status issue and the assumption that bilingualism paves the road for statehood, it should not surprise us to find fervent supporters of bilingual education in the United States who question the concept in Puerto Rico. Leading members of the recently (1985) organized 'Comité pro Defensa del Vernáculo [Committee for the Defense of the Vernacular] have published numerous articles and sponsored various conferences in which they rail against cultural schizophrenia, impoverishment of the language, and what they view as the dangerous repercussions of biculturalism. Among their solution is, on the one hand, strong support for maintenance bilingual education for all Puerto Ricans in the United States, but on the other hand, a limited transitional approach in Puerto Rico that emphasizes Spanish in bilingual programs for migrants. Is this a hypocritical stance, or one that accurately reflects the different realities? An adequate answer must be based on future comparative ethnographic and attitudinal studies, now sorely lacking.

APPENDIX: EXCERPT FROM "DOS WORLDS—TWO MUNDOS," BY HENRY I. PADRON

Cuántos tendrán que pasar
until we realize
lo que está pasando
people moving
to and fro
todos siempre
llamándonos 'bro'
  qué pasa
    raza
  Qué pasa
con mi raza
lots of party
lots of laughter

Always somethin
  hapnin
  Porqué será
que nuestro futuro
ya preparado está
without us having a say
on what affects
us from day to day

Quizás you don't
understand lo que
está pasando
  porqué es que nuestra
lengua
is slowly disappearing

Es la programación
que le han dado
a nuestra nación

Nuestra juventud en tremendo lio estan
they don't know from
where they vienen
y no saben to where they van

Aunque muchos
listos y muy bien preparados están

Trying to understand this system

[How many will have to pass by
until we realize
what is happening
people moving
to and fro
everybody always
calling us 'bro'.
  what's happening
    race
What's going on
with my race
lots of party
lots of laughter

Always somethin
  hapnin
Why is it
that our future
is prepared already
without us having a say
on what affects
us from day to day

Maybe you don't
understand what
is happening
why is it that our
language
is slowly disappearing

It's the programming
that they have done
to our nation

Our youth are in a big mess
they don't know from
where they come
and they don't know where they're going

Although many are ready
and very well prepared

Trying to understand this system

mejor dicho cistern	better yet cistern
can cause you mucho pain	can cause you a lot of pain.
Puede causar un tremendo	It can cause a tremendous
strain en tu brain. . . .	strain in your brain. . . .]

NOTES

1. This article is a revised and expanded version of a paper delivered at the Conference on Perspectives in Bilingual Education. Yeshiva University, 4 June, 1984.

2. The cooperation of the principal of Papa Juan XXIII, Sr. Jesús Sánchez, and that of the bilingual students at Papa Juan and Pedro Albizu Campos secondary schools was invaluable; I owe them a debt of gratitude. Thanks are also due to Jazmin Rivera for her preliminary transcription of the interviews.

3. Initial support for the research was provided by the Hunter College George N. Shuster Fund and an American Psychological Association Short Term Study Grant. It was carried out with the help of a National Endowment for the Humanities Summer Stipend and a research grant from the Professional Staff Congress of the City University of New York.

4. Although Puerto Rican teachers, journalists, and researchers consistently speak/write about "neo-ricans," interpreted to mean "new Puerto Ricans" (Irizarry 1981), that term was unknown to the students.

5. Lack of Spanish fluency may account for some of the returned migrants' reported dissatisfaction with school in Puerto Rico; 'Not only do most of the children of returned migrants hate school but a whopping 62.9% actively dislike their teachers (as compared to 13.3% of children of non-migrants)' (Underhill 1981).

6. Evidence in support of this view appeared in the comments of some 'regulares'. When asked if he would mind if Puerto Rico spoke English only in 50 years, one monolingual Spanish speaking student responded, 'Me encantaria' [I'd love it].

7. A 1981 study of 282 returned migrants (adults) conducted by the University of Puerto Rico's School of Public Health found that it took them six years to get settled (Underhill 1981).

REFERENCES

Algarín, Miguel, and Piñero, Miguel (eds.) (1975). *Nuyorican Poetry: An Anthology of Puerto Rican Words and Feelings*. New York: Morrow.

Attinasi, John T. (1979). Language attitudes in a New York Puerto Rican community. In *Bilingualism and Public Policy: Puerto Rican Perspectives*. New York: Centro de Estudios Puertorriqueños, City University of New York.

——. (1983). Language attitudes and working class ideology in a Puerto Rican barrio of New York. Unpublished manuscript.

Bonilla, Frank (1983). Manos que sobran: work, migration and the Puerto Rican in the 1980s. Paper prepared for the National Puerto Rican Coalition, December.

Casillas Alvarez., Juan (1983). Nuestro espanol es irremplazable. *Claridad*, 24–30 junio: 40.

Ferguson, Charles (1964). Diglossia. In *Language in Culture and Society;* D. Hymes (ed.). New York: Harper and Row.

Fishman, Joshua (1966). *Language Loyalty in the United States: The Maintenance and Perpetuating of Non-English Mother Tongues by American Ethnic and Religious Groups*. The Hague: Mouton.

———. (1967). Bilingualism with and without diglossia: diglossia with and without bilingualism. *Journal of Social Issues* 23, 29–38.

———, Cooper, R., Ma, R., et al. (1971). *Bilingualism in the Barrio.* Bloomington: Indiana University Press.

Flores, Juan, Attinasi, J., and Pedraza, P., Jr. (1981). *La Carreta* made a U-turn: Puerto Rican language and culture in the United States. *Daedalus* (Spring), 193–218.

Friedman, Robert (1982). In Puerto Rico or States, some kids are nowhere. *New York Daily News,* Sunday, May 2.

Ghigliotty, Julio (1983). Bilingual education said not a matter of language. *San Juan Star,* April 3.

Gumperz, John J. (1964). Linguistic and social interaction in two communities. In *The Ethnography of Communication,* J Gumperz and D. Hymes (eds.). *American Anthropologist* 66 (6, pt. II), 137–154.

———. (1976). The sociolinguistic significance of conversational code-switching. Papers on Language and Context. University of California, Berkeley.

González, José Luís (1982). Los problemas del idioma en Puerto Rico. *El Nueva Dia,* 1 de agosto, 6–9.

———. (1983). Identidad y diáspora en nuestra realidad. *El Nueva Dia,* 21 de agosto, 6–9.

Irizarry, María Antonia (1981). The attitudes of permanent and migrant Puerto Ricans determined by language use. Unpublished manuscript.

Junta de Planificación de Puerto Rico (1980). *La Población Inmigrante en Puerto Rico.* Santurce, P.R.: Junta de Planificación.

Labov, William. (1972). *Sociolinguistic Patterns.* Philadelphia: University of Pennsylvania Press.

Lambert, W. E. (1972). *Language, Psychology, and Culture.* Stanford: Stanford University Press.

Lambert, Wallace, Hodgson, R. C., Gardner, R. C., and Fillenbaum, S. (1960). Evaluational reactions to spoken languages. *Journal of Abnormal and Social Psychology* 60, 44–51.

Language Policy Task Force (1980). Social dimensions of language use in East Harlem. Working Paper 7. New York: Centro de Estudios Puertorriqueños, City University of New York.

La Viera, Tato (1985). *Am-e-Rican.* Houston, Texas: Arte Público.

McClure, Erica (1977). Aspects of code switching in the discourse of bilingual Mexican-American children. In *Linguistics and Anthropology,* Muriel Saville Troike (ed.), 93–117. Washington, D.C.: Georgetown University Press.

Morales, Carlos M. (1982). El Idioma y el Supremo Federal. *El Nueva Dia,* 27 enero, 25.

Pedraza, Pedro, Attinasi, J., and Hoffmann, G. (1980). Rethinking diglossia. Language Policy Task Force Working Paper 9. New York: Centro de Estudios Puertorriqueños.

Poplack, Shana (1979). 'Sometimes I'll start a sentence in EnglishY TERMINO EN ESPANOL': towards a typology of code switching. Working Paper 4. New York: Centro de Estudios Puertorriqueños, City University of New York.

Ramos Perea, Israel (1972). The school adjustment of return migrant students in Puerto Rican junior high schools. Unpublished Doctoral dissertation, University of Missouri at Columbia.

Rosario, Rubén Del (1983). Ser Puertorriqueño. *Claridad,* Suplemento En Rojo, 5–11 agosto, 16-17.

Sankoff, D., and Poplack, S. (1980). A formal grammar of code switching. Technical Report No. 495. Montreal: Centre de Recherches Mathematiques, Université de Montréal.

Santiago, Isaura (1984). Language policy and education in Puerto Rico and the continent. *International Education Journal* (1), 39–61.

Seda Bonilla, Eduardo (1975). Qué Somos: puertorriqueños, neorriqueños or niuyorriqueños? *The Rican: Journal of Contemporary Puerto Rican Thought* 2 (2–3), 81–107.

Tió, Salvador (1982), *Sobre la Lengua.* El Nueva Dia, 26 enero, 24.

Trudgill, Peter (1974). *Sociolinguistics: An Introduction.* New York: Penguin.

Underhill, Connie (1981). Impact of the returned migrant. *San Juan Star Magazine,* September 20, 1–5, 15.

Valdés, Guadalupe (1981). Code-switching as deliberate verbal strategy. In *Latino Language and Communicative Behavior,* R. P. Durón (ed.), 95-108. Norwood, NJ: Ablex.

Vélez, Adelina (1983). No es puertorriqueno. *El Mundo,* 24 junio.

Zentella, Ana Celia (1981). Language variety among Puerto Ricans. In *Language in the U.S.A.,* Charles Ferguson and S. Heath (eds.). London: Cambridge University Press.

———. (1985): The value of bilingualism: code switching in the Puerto Rican community. In *The Language of Inequality,* Joan Manes and Nessa Wolfson (eds.). Berlin: Mouton.

———. (1986). Language minorities and the national commitment to foreign language competency: resolving the contradiction. *ADFL Bulletin* 17 (3), April.

———. (1987). Language and female identity in the Puerto Rican community. In *Women and Language in Transition,* Joyce Penfield (ed.). Albany: S.U.N.Y. Press.

———. (1988). Language politics in the U.S.A.: the English-Only movement. In *Literature, Language and Politics in the 80's,* Betty J. Craige (ed.). Athens: University of Georgia Press.

16

The Empowerment of
Language-Minority Students

Richard Ruiz

A central and early tenet of bilingual education advocates was that inclusion of the child's language and culture in the curriculum would lead to greater school achievement. The claims for the benefit of native language instruction were broad, including not only an increase in language proficiency, but also enhancement of more general, nonlinguistic skills such as problem solving and conceptualization (Lambert, 1978; Cummins, 1979; Kessler and Quinn, 1980). More recently, this discussion has turned from a consideration of merely cognitive and academic consequences of mother tongue instruction and bilingualism to their sociolinguistic and political consequences as well. This goes beyond suggestions that being bilingual can be of some economic or commercial advantage: it entails a general reordering of prevailing societal patterns of stratification. In other words, native language instruction in schools can be an important factor in ethnic communities shedding their minority status by sharing power with the dominant group.

The focal concept in these arguments is "empowerment." In the following pages, I will try to explain the general connection between language and power, the arguments concerning school language programs and empowerment, the problems and limitations of those arguments from the perspective of a critical pedagogy, and some possibilities for the role that school language programs can play in the authentic empowerment of minority students and their communities.

LANGUAGE AND POWER

Frantz Fanon begins his book *Black Skin, White Masks* (1967) with an essay titled "The Negro and Language." He is concerned with the psychological consequences of colonialism and the role that language suppression and domination play in it: "The problem that we confront in this chapter is this: The Negro of the Antilles will be proportionately whiter—that is, he will come closer to being a real human being—in direct ratio to his mastery of the French Language" (p. 18). By "the French Language," he means to say "the French of France, the Frenchman's French, French French" (p. 20). Fanon illustrates the relation between language and power in society: not merely social position, but ontological status, can be inferred from the language one speaks. The colonializing power of language has a long history and a large literature; the overt political effects of linguistic and cultural dominance are well documented (for a recent treatment of such questions, see, for example, *Language of Inequality*, 1985, edited by Wolfson and Manes). I am more interested in exploring aspects of this relationship that are less obvious.

A major dimension of the power of language is the power to define, to decide the nature of lived experience. In social relations, the power to define determines dominance and subordination, as Moreau (1984) says: "In social discourse, the dominated are defined (collectively) as incomplete, while the dominant are singularized and defined as the incarnation of achieved human nature" (p. 46). Put another way, subordinate minority groups are those who are named and defined by majority groups. Consider that most ethnic minority communities in the United States are known by names not of their own choosing: "Asians" and "Hispanics" are lumped into categories that deny the distinctiveness of the groups they comprise; American Indian nations usually are distinguished by names ("Papago" or "Stockbridge," for example), but those names generally are not the ones by which they refer to themselves. And, when groups do try to define themselves—when Mexican Americans become "Chicanos," when Negroes become "Blacks," or Blacks propose for themselves "African Americans"—there is resistance, not just because of the inconvenience and confusion created for the rest of us, but because of a deep-felt sense that this sort of self-definition by these groups lacks legitimacy: who has given them the right to change their name?

This concern with whether a person or group is allowed the power of self-definition is closely related to another dimension of the relation of language and power: the distinction between *language* and *voice*. The link between language and voice is put forward by Giroux (1986): "Language represents a central force in the struggle for voice . . . language is able to shape the way various individuals and groups encode and thereby engage the world" (p. 59).

As much as language and voice are related, it is also important to distinguish between them. I have become convinced of the need for this distinction through a consideration of instances of language planning in which the "inclusion" of the language of a group has coincided with the exclusion of their voice. Guadalupe Valdes (1981) has conducted a series of important studies on the Spanish language classes designed for U.S. Hispanics. She finds that "a surprising number of Spanish-speaking students in the American Southwest are still being placed in beginning Spanish classes for non-speakers to help them 'unlearn' their 'bad' habits and begin anew as foreign speakers" (p. 7). She cites an attitude study of Texas Spanish teachers in which a common sentiment expressed was that "Spanish-speaking students should be provided with grammar explanations which show them why their way of speaking is wrong" (p. 6). This is a case of a language class designed to show speakers of that language that theirs is not really that language—perhaps is not really *any* language. This is similar to my personal experiences with teachers in "maintenance" bilingual education programs, where the explicit goal is to conserve the language of the child.

What I frequently find, however, is that the language of the child is rarely spoken in the classroom, much less taught in formal lessons. There are two important explanations for this. In the first place, teachers in these classrooms rarely speak the language of the child; either they have learned a textbook language that no one actually uses in everyday conversation, or they confine their speech to standard forms because of their sense of what is proper or acceptable classroom behavior. In the second place, even if they themselves speak or are familiar with the language of the child, they have appropriated the view that it is not proper language and therefore not to be encouraged in the classroom. They attain their goal of language "maintenance" to the extent that they eradicate *lonche* and replace it with *almuerzo*. One might properly ask why this is called "language maintenance."

One other case of language planning will help illustrate the distinction between language and voice. In Peru, Quechua was made an official language, "co-equal" with Spanish, in 1975. This policy was hailed at the time as an enhancement of the status of the indigenous language communities to be a significant part of the nation. The problem with Quechua's officialization was the relatively minor role that the Quechua communities themselves played in the decision and its implementation. Almost fifteen years later, there is little hope that Quechua will fulfill any substantive role as an official language, or that Quechua-Spanish bilingual programs in the Highlands will have any impact on Quechua language maintenance (Hornberger, 1988).

I have offered these examples to illustrate the distinction between language and voice. *Language* is general, abstract, subject to a somewhat arbitrary normalization; *voice* is particular and concrete. *Language* has a life of its own—it exists even when it is suppressed; when *voice* is suppressed, it is not heard—it does not exist. To deny people their language, as in the colonial situations described by Fanon (1967) and Macedo (1983), is, to be sure, to deny them voice; but, to allow them "their" language (as in the bilingual education and Peruvian cases just mentioned) is not necessarily to allow them voice. Indeed, this may be the most evil form of colonialism, because everyone, even the colonizers themselves, recognize it as just the opposite. To have a voice implies not just that people can say things, but that they are heard (that is, that their words have status, influence). Giroux (1986) argues that "schools do not allow students from subordinate groups to authenticate their problems and experiences through their own individual and collective voices" (p. 65). Nichols (1984) makes a similar point regarding adult-to-child and male-to-female speech dynamics: "Children talking with adults and women talking with men are consistently and frequently interrupted by their speaking partners, as well as ignored or unsupported when they attempted to choose the topic of conversation" (p. 25). The *language* of these situations is largely irrelevant; let us assume that everyone was speaking in his or her own conversational mother tongue. What is important is that some groups consistently impose their *voice* on others. When sociolinguists carry out their investigations of language use, they ask "Who says what to whom in what language?" When we investigate the issue of voice, we should ask, "Who says?"

The question of voice will be taken up again presently. We might anticipate my conclusion: voice is the central ingredient of critical pedagogy; without its consideration, there is no radical reform of curriculum. I would like now to turn to a recent proposal for curricular reform aimed directly at the language-minority student. My evaluation of it will be based on this concern for voice.

SCHOOL LANGUAGE AND EMPOWERMENT

Jim Cummins's 1986 article in the *Harvard Educational Review*, "Empowering Minority Students: A Framework for Intervention," has become one of the most influential works in the literature on the education of minority students. He has since expanded his ideas into the book *Empowering Minority Students* (1989). His use of the term *empowerment* is already a stock item in the lexicons of various areas within the education literature, most notably bilingual education and special education. Any treatment of the concept of empowerment in education would be incomplete without consideration of Cummins's work. Let us turn to that now.

Cummins's argument runs as follows: First, the failure of minority students is not completely, perhaps not even in major part, an academic or school matter. Instead, one should examine their subordinate status in the larger society, and the ways in which the school reinforces or reproduces that status: "Status and power relations between groups are an important part of any comprehensive account of minority students' school failure" (Cummins, 1986, p. 21). Such failure will persist so long as school reformers fail to take into account these extraschool factors. Second, school and curricular reform must involve the inclusion of the students' home cultural experiences. Here, Cummins is most concerned with four aspects of school structure: "incorporation of minority students' culture and language, inclusion of minority communities in the education of their children, pedagogical assumptions and practices operating in the classroom, and the assessment of minority students" (p. 24). To the extent that schools consistently exclude the child's home experiences from the curriculum, alienate their families and discourage their participation in the education of the children, transmit in an authoritarian way a standardized curriculum, and bias their assessment of minority children to ensure that some "problem" will be found in them, minority students will be disabled. Empowerment comes when schools are inclusionary, when their pedagogy encourages critical, independent thinking, and when they aim to find and build on a child's strengths rather than identify weaknesses. Third, and finally, in the same way that school failure is not merely a school matter, student empowerment cannot be confined to the school. There is a dynamic interrelation between home and school: real school reform and authentic student empowerment will contribute to the transformation of societal power relations as well.

This argument is significant for language-minority students because it describes deep structural reasons for school failure. The language difference of the child is no longer of primary concern; or, more precisely, particular language differences are indicators of class differences, and these are where our examination of school failure should focus. The argument is also significant because it bypasses the usual concern for cognitive or academic justifications for using the first language of these children. One might even say that Cummins's argument makes irrelevant the research on the effectiveness of various methods to use with language-minority students.

I have chosen to be critical of Cummins's work for a specific reason. Few doubt his personal commitment to the betterment of education for language-minority students or the significance of his scholarship. I judge that Cummins is one of only a handful of academics whose work consistently determines the direction of the literature in this area. It is precisely for that reason that I offer this criticism. What I will try to demonstrate is that, even for those among us who are the most sympathetic to the concerns of minority communities and who are the most conscious of the effect of our public statements, our words sometimes betray what we intend.

Let me now take up this criticism at its most central point. It has to do with the issue of voice. Note the use of "empowerment" in the following typical passages:

> Students from "dominated" societal groups are "empowered" or "disabled" as a direct result of their interactions with educators in the schools. (p. 21)

> Minority students are disabled or disempowered by schools in very much the same way that their communities are disempowered by interactions with societal institutions. (p. 24)

What disturbs me most about such usage is the passivity of the "empowered" groups. Empowerment appears to be an action performed by others on their behalf. This is put most directly in the following passage.

> Language minority students' educational progress is strongly influenced by the extent to which individual educators become advocates for the promotion of students' linguistic talents, actively encourage participation in developing students' academic and cultural resources, and implement pedagogical approaches that succeed in liberating students from instructional dependence. (p. 35)

I do not see here any action on the part of those who are to be empowered. Instead, empowerment is portrayed as a gift to the powerless. This evokes several questions. If empowerment is a gift from those in power to those out, what kind of power would they be willing to give up? Will it be of a sort that might lead to the transformation of society? Could empowerment entail another sort of acculturation, by which we change the behavior of underachieving students to conform to that of high achievers? Are higher test scores the ultimate index of empowerment? Would empowered students become critical, or merely successful?

Beyond these important questions, we should ask, what has happened to student voice? Assuming that students' language has been included in the curriculum, whose voice is heard in it if they are not active participants? How can they be characterized as "empowered" when minority communities merely wait for schools to change in particular ways?

The radical pedagogue who treats empowerment as a gift is not yet radical. Teachers do not empower or disempower anyone, nor do schools. They merely create the conditions under which people can *empower themselves*, or not. It is certainly true that teachers impart skills—literacy, numeracy, and others; but these are not in themselves power. They are tools to be used or not, and, if used, for responsible or irresponsible ends. (If the proficiency in using a standard language to which I contributed becomes a means to denigrate the experience of nonstandard speakers, that is empowerment—but I would not boast about my connection with it.)

The idea that empowerment might be construed as a gift should be a central concern in the development or evaluation of a critical transformative pedagogy. It is one anticipated by Freire (1970), in his most famous work, *Pedagogy of the Oppressed*:

Not even the best-intentioned leadership can bestow independence as a gift. The liberation of the oppressed is a liberation of men [and women], not things. Accordingly, while no one liberates himself [or herself] by his [or her] own efforts alone, neither is he [or she] liberated by others . . . The conviction of the oppressed that they must fight for their liberation is not a gift bestowed by the revolutionary leadership, but a result of their own *conscientizacão*. (pp. 53–54)

Freire avoids this problem, as well as the problem of voice, by eschewing an orientation of "inclusion." He does not suggest, as does Cummins, that the language and culture of the child should be "included" in the curriculum of the school; this would suggest that this curriculum is fundamentally sound but that it needs a few additions or modifications. Instead, for Freire, the language and culture of the child *constitute* the curriculum. The most dramatic example of this are the "generative words" he uses in adult literacy programs. These words are recorded in an initial period of observation in the village where the program is to take place. In the course of the training, these words are represented to the students as the basis for both decoding instruction and discussion. The discussion results in the development of more words, and these words eventually become themes for further study and discussion. In this way, student voice becomes the curriculum; furthermore, the discussion of themes with other students demonstrates how one's individual voice can be joined with other voices to effect social action on behalf of the community. This is the essence of what Freire calls *conscientizacão*, the development of critical consciousness. Although Freire's early work involved literacy training of peasant adults, he has gone on to show how his can be a more general pedagogy (Freire and Macedo, 1987).

Cummins can be criticized in his assumption that the school will contribute to its own transformation, with little active participation by the minority communities. Freire denies that this can happen, and asserts that the transformation of society will come when the oppressed empower themselves. We should now turn to a consideration of how this might happen, with special emphasis on language minority communities.

PRIVATIZATION AND POWER

Henry Giroux (1986) chastises radical educators because they have concentrated on developing a "language of resistance" but not a "language of possibility." By this he means that we should not only understand society, its institutions, and the power relations that result in oppressed classes, but we should devise strategies by which we can take advantage of the transformative possibilities that exist even in the worst cases. In what remains of this essay, I would like to suggest a possibility for social transformation that exists in a conservative critique of bilingual education and cultural pluralism.

This critique is put forward most elegantly by John Edwards (1984). In its broadest terms, it contends that ethnic language and cultural identification are essentially private matters. To promote them in the public sector would be chaotic and fragmenting, since there is no objective measure by which to choose the ethnicities and languages to be subsidized. Besides, this is undesirable because the interest of the state is unity and coherence, and a public cultural pluralism leads to conflict. Therefore, to the extent that programs such as public school bilingual education are to be tolerated, it is only the narrowest form of transitional program that should receive public support. This would exclude "maintenance" programs designed to preserve ethnic language and culture. Presumably, this would also preclude funding any proposals such as that by Cummins, not to mention Freire.

The conservative movement of the 1980s in the United States has placed such critiques at the basis of much public policy, including bilingual education policy. Instead of cultural pluralism, we have "cultural literacy" (Hirsch, 1987) as the guiding principle of curricular reform. This entails, among other things, a national culture and history to be appropriated by everyone as a result of public schooling. From the perspective of critical pedagogy, it means a total exclusion of student voice from the school. Such a state of affairs minimizes the prospects for the empowerment of language minority communities, if we are to believe Cummins and Freire. How can a language of possibility be fashioned from such a critique?

The key lies in the distinction between public and private life. The conservative argues for what I call the "privatization of pluralism," and makes a distinction between private pluralism and public unity. Some advocates of bilingual education see such arguments (rightly, I think) as a way to limit funding for and eventually suppress these programs. Their reaction is to increase the pressure in favor of public funding. Although I do not disagree with the effort to conserve such public school programs, I believe another strategy is advisable if language maintenance and authentic empowerment are the aims. This strategy is to be more conservative than the conservatives by developing the power of privatization.

My study of two contrasting cases has brought me to this point; I refer to them often in my classes and when I write, but it is only now that I articulate the essential lesson in them. These are the German communities of the Midwest in the latter half of the nineteenth century and the Mexican communities of the Southwest at precisely the same time. The Germans were afforded the most extensive programs of public school bilingual education in the history of the country. The public school districts in cities within the so-called German Triangle—Cincinnati, St. Louis, Milwaukee, Chicago, Indianapolis, and others—also developed formal offices of German instruction to supervise the programs. Seminaries and institutes established in part to train German teachers for both public and private schools flourished in Milwaukee and Chicago. In some school districts, as much as 70 percent of the school population took some of their instruction in German as late as 1916. This situation persisted until the beginning of World War I, when anti-German sentiment made German study unpopular. By 1920, the programs that had been so pervasive in the public schools virtually disappeared (Ruiz, 1988). This case is easily contrasted with that of the Mexicans. Not only did they not receive instruction in their own language, but their language was actively suppressed. In some districts, Mexicans were prohibited from attending public schools; when they were allowed, they were prohibited from speaking Spanish, even outside class. This situation persisted into the 1960s, when federally funded Spanish-English bilingual programs were allowed for the first time in the schools of the Southwest.

There is another important contrast to be made in these cases. Today, German communities have effectively lost their language: they are culturally but not linguistically German communities. On the other hand, in spite of much individual language loss, Spanish-speaking Mexican communities still flourish in the Southwest. How is that explained? How is it that publicly supported school programs have led to language loss, whereas linguistic discrimination has resulted in language maintenance? In large part, the explanation lies in the dynamics of privatization. The German communities had strong cultural maintenance institutions of their own—schools, churches, civic organizations—which were neglected in the period of public subsidy. When public support was suddenly withdrawn, those institutions weakened considerably. Along with that, the reversal of public sentiment toward Germans made those communities less willing to engage in activities of cultural and linguistic loyalty which would only intensify social conflict for them. The Mexicans, on the other hand, had no reason to believe that their cultural institutions would be supported outside their communities; they turned inward for support, thereby strengthening those very institutions—the church, the family, and neighborhoods—which would allow for long-term language maintenance. The difference in these two cases demonstrates the potential power of privatization.

I am not the first to suggest such a strategy for language-minority communities. Geneva Smitherman (1984) describes how traditional White education has pulled Black people away from Black language and community. She explores the possibilities for self-empowerment through the reclaiming of Black language within the Black community. Similarly, Shirley Heath (1985) makes a distinction between the *maintenance* of language, or the efforts of those outside the community to preserve the language, and the *retention* of language, whereby the community itself acts out its language loyalty. This is put most forcefully by Kjolseth (1982), an advocate of bilingual education and cultural pluralism:

> Chicano families who desire the maintenance of their ethnic language *must* exercise their control over that single domain of language use where they do have effective and continuing control: the family. Parental insistence upon the use of Spanish by themselves and their children within the private family domain is the *only* realistic hope. (p. 25)

Privatization implies two things: developing the resources readily available to minority communities to increase what the critical theorist calls their own "cultural capital," and minorities taking control of their own lives in such a way that their communities can act positively in their own interests. Such action may include pressure on the public sector for subvention of their activities, but it need not be dependent on such support. School programs that aim at these goals might very well resemble Mr. Hardcastle's English class, of which one student reported the following: "If the type of English work we have been discussing continues, then the possibility of taking control of our own lives, our own education, and becoming our own experts, is extremely exciting" (McLeod, 1986, p. 49). Privatization and "taking control" is another way of saying that the student's voice is developed and heard in the educational experience. Let me conclude by suggesting two modifications to the lexicon of critical pedagogy. First, we should understand that when we say "language," we often mean "voice." I hope I have shown how we delude ourselves into thinking that because we include the first we include the second. And second, *empowerment* may not be desirable in English because of our tendency to use it as a transitive verb; this denies both voice and agency to students and communities. A convenient one-word substitute does not come readily to mind; *appropriation* is not exactly synonymous with *taking control*. Perhaps this discussion will provoke someone to think of something suitable. The point to be made is that voice and agency are central to critical pedagogy; without them there is no such thing as "empowerment."

REFERENCES

Cummins, J. (1979). Linguistic interdependence and educational development of bilingual children. *Review of Educational Research, 49,* 222–251.

⸻ (1986). Empowering minority students: A framework for intervention. *Harvard Educational Review, 56,* 18–36.

⸻ (1989). *Empowering minority students.* Sacramento: California State Department of Education.

Edwards, J. (1984). Language, diversity and identity. In J. Edwards (Ed.), *Linguistic minorities, policies and pluralism* (pp. 277–310). Orlando, Fla.: Academic Press.

Fanon, F. (1967). *Black skin, white masks.* Translated by C. L. Markmann. New York: Grove Press.

Freire, P. (1970). *Pedagogy of the oppressed.* Translated by M. B. Ramos. New York: Continuum.

Freire, P., and Macedo, D. (1987). *Literacy: Reading the word and the world.* South Hadley, Mass.: Bergin and Garvey.

Giroux, H. A. (1986, Spring). Radical pedagogy and the politics of student voice. *Interchange, 17,* 48–69.

Health, S. B. (1985). Language policies: Patterns of retention and maintenance. In W. Connor (Ed.), *Mexican Americans in comparative perspective.* Washington, D.C.: The Urban Institute.

Hirsch, E. D. (1987). *Cultural literacy.* Boston: Houghton Mifflin.

Hornberger, N. (1988). *Bilingual education and language maintenance: A southern Peruvian Quechua case.* Providence, R.I.: Floris.

Kessler, C., and Quinn, M. (1980). Positive effects of bilingualism on science problem-solving abilities. In J. Atatis (Ed.), *Georgetown University round table on languages and linguistics 1980.* Washington, D.C.: Georgetown University Press.

Kjolseth, R. (1982). Bilingual education programs in the United States: For assimilation or pluralism? In P. R. Turner (Ed.), *Bilingualism in the southwest* (2nd. ed., rev., pp. 3–28). Tucson: University of Arizona Press.

Lambert, W. (1978). Some cognitive and sociocultural consequences of being bilingual. In J. Alatis (Ed.), *Georgetown University round table on languages and linguistics* (pp. #). Washington, D.C.: Georgetown University Press.

Macedo, D. P. (1983, Winter). The politics of emancipatory literacy in Cape Verde. *Journal of Education, 165,* 99–112.

McLeod, A. (1986, January). Critical literacy: Taking control of our own lives. *Language Arts, 63*, 37–50.

Moreau, N. B. (1984). Education, ideology, and class/sex identity. In C. Karmarae, M. Schulz, and W. M. O'Barr (Eds.), *Language and power* (pp. 43–61). Beverly Hills, Calif.: Sage Publications.

Nichols, P. C. (1984). Networks and hierarchies: Language and social stratification. In C. Kramarae, M. Schulz, and W. M. O'Barr (Eds.), *Language and power* (pp. 23–42). Beverly Hills, Calif.: Sage Publications.

Ruiz, R. (1988). Bilingualism and bilingual education in the United States. In C. B. Paulston (Ed.), *International handbook of bilingualism and bilingual education*. Westport, Conn.: Greenwood Press.

Smitherman, G. (1984). Black language as power. In C. Kramarae, M. Schulz, and W. M. O'Barr (Eds.), *Language and power*. Beverly Hills, Calif.: Sage Publications.

Valdes, G. (1981). Pedagogical implications of teaching Spanish to the Spanish-speaking in the United States. In G. Valdex, A. G. Lozano, and R. Garcia-Moya (Eds.), *Teaching Spanish to the hispanic bilingual: Issues, aims, and methods*. New York: Teachers College Press.

Wolfson, N., and Manes, J. (Eds.). (1985). *Language of inequality*. Berlin: Mouton.

V
CULTURAL DEMOCRACY AND SCHOOLING

17

Creating the Conditions
for Cultural Democracy
in the Classroom

Antonia Darder

> *But democracy, by definition, cannot mean merely*
> *that an unskilled worker can become skilled. It must*
> *mean that every "citizen" can "govern" and that*
> *society places him [or her] in a general condition to*
> *achieve this.*

—Antonio Gramsci
Selections from Prison Notebooks

Cultural democracy in the classroom cannot be discussed, within the context of a critical bicultural pedagogy, outside of the theoretical dimensions that function to position teachers with respect to their educational practice. Gramsci's words support a theory of cultural democracy that not only locates bicultural students within a historical and cultural context, but also addresses questions related to moral and political agency within the process of their schooling and the course of their everyday lives. In short, this critical view suggests that, prior to any engagement with instrumental questions of practice, educators must delve rigorously into those specific theoretical issues that are fundamental to the establishment of a culturally democratic foundation for a critical bicultural pedagogy in the classroom.

This view is also consistent with that of Freire (1970) and other critical educational theorists who emphatically express that any liberatory pedagogy cannot represent a recipe for classroom practice. Rather, it is meant to provide a set of critical educational principles that can guide and support teachers' critical engagement with the forces determining the reality of classroom life. Informed by this tradition, a critical foundation for bicultural education must not be presented in the form of models for duplication or how-to instruction manuals. One of the most important reasons for this thinking is expressed by Simon (1988), who speaks eloquently to the notion that all educational practice must emerge from the contextual relationships defined by the very conditions existing at any given moment within the classroom. Such a practice "is at root contextual and conditional. A critical pedagogy can only be concretely discussed from within a particular 'point of practice,' from within a specific time and place, and within a particular theme" (p. 1).

Hence, efforts to instrumentalize or operationalize a critical perspective outside the context in which it is to function fail to engage with the historical, cultural, and dialogical principles that are essential to a critical learning environment. In addition, this approach also ignores that, prior to the development of practice, there are cultural and ideological assumptions at work determining how educators define the purpose of education, their role, and the role of their students in the process of schooling. The belief that teachers must be provided with "canned" curriculum to ensure their success fails to acknowledge the creative potential of educators to grapple effectively with the multiplicity of contexts that they find in their classrooms and to shape environments according to the lived experiences and actual educational needs of their students.

Teacher education programs are notorious for reducing the role of teachers to that of technicians. Instead of empowering teachers by assisting them to develop a critical understanding of their purpose as educators, most programs foster a dependency on predefined curriculum, outdated classroom strategies and techniques, and traditionally rigid classroom environments that position not only students but teachers as well into physically and intellectually oppressive situations. This occurs to such a degree that few public school teachers are able to envision their practice outside the scope of barren classroom settings, lifeless instructional packages, bland textbooks, standardized tests, and the use of meritocratic systems for student performance evaluation.

Educators of bicultural students must recognize the manner in which these conditions work to disempower both teachers and students in American public schools. Teachers can then begin to refuse the role of technicians in their practice as educators as they struggle together to abandon their dependency on traditional classroom artifacts. This represents an essential step if teachers are to educate students of color to discover themselves and their potential within an environment that permits them to interact with what they know to be their world. This is particularly important, given the fact that values supporting cultural diversity, social struggle, and human rights are so often absent from the curricular materials teachers are forced to use in most public schools.

A critical bicultural pedagogy that is built on a foundation of cultural democracy represents a missing educational discourse in the preparation and practice of most public school teachers. As discussed in Chapter 3 of my book, *Culture and Power in the Classroom*, the many different forms in which the bicultural experience manifests itself in American life seldom find their way into traditional classroom settings. Instead, bicultural experiences remain, for the most part, hidden within the reinforced silence of students of color. If the voices of difference are to find a place in the everyday interactions of public schools, educators of bicultural students must create the conditions for all students to experience an ongoing process of culturally democratic life. With this in mind, this chapter will address the major questions and issues that educators face in their efforts to pave the way for a critical bicultural pedagogy.

THE QUESTION OF LANGUAGE

It is impossible to consider any form of education—or even human existence—without first considering the impact of language on our lives. Language must be recognized as one of the most significant human resources; it functions in a multitude of ways to affirm, contradict, negotiate, challenge, transform, and empower particular cultural and ideological beliefs and practices. Language constitutes one of the most powerful media for transmitting our personal histories and social realities, as well as for thinking and shaping the world (Cole & Scribner, 1974). Language is essential to the process of dialogue, to the development of meaning, and to the production of knowledge. From the context of its emancipatory potential, language must be understood as a dialectical phenomenon that links its very existence and meaning to the lived experiences of the language community and constitutes a major cornerstone for the development of voice.

The question of language must also be addressed within the context of a terrain of struggle that is central to our efforts to transform traditional educational structures that historically have failed bicultural students. In doing so, it is essential that we do not fall into totalizing theoretical traps—ignoring that human beings are in fact able to appropriate a multitude of linguistic forms and utilize them in critical and emancipatory ways. It is simplistic and to our detriment as educators of bicultural students to accept the notion that any one particular form of language (e.g., "standard" English), in and of itself, constitutes a totalizing dominant or subordinate force, as it is unrealistic to believe that simply utilizing a student's primary language (e.g., Spanish, Ebonics, etc.) guarantees that a student's emancipatory interests are being addressed. Consequently, the question of language in the classroom constitutes one of the most complex and multifaceted issues that educators of bicultural students must be prepared to address in the course of their practice.

The complexity of language and its relationship not only to how students produce knowledge but also to how language shapes their world represent a major pedagogical concern for all educational settings. In public schools, teachers can begin to address this complexity by incorporating activities based on the languages their students bring into the classroom. In this way, the familiar language can function as a significant starting point from which bicultural students can engage with the foreign and unknown elements that comprise significant portions of the required curriculum. An example of how teachers might do this with younger students is to develop language instruction and activities with their students that give them the opportunity to bring the home language into the context of the classroom. This can be done by having students and parents introduce their languages through songs, stories, games, and other such activities. Giving attention to the home language raises it to a place of dignity and respect, rather than permitting it to become a source of humiliation and shame for bicultural students. It should be noted that the introduction of different languages must also be accompanied by critical dialogues that help students examine prevailing social attitudes and biases about language differences. These discussions can assist students to consider typical discriminatory responses to such situations as when people speak with foreign accents, or when people do not understand the language being spoken. In addition, students from similar cultural and language communities can be encouraged and made to feel comfortable when they converse together in their primary language as part of the classroom experience.

Such opportunities support the development of voice, as well as affirm the bicultural experience of students of color. Bell hooks addresses this point:

> Learning to listen to different voices, hearing different speech challenges the notion that we must all assimilate—share a single similar talk—in educational institutions. Language reflects the culture from which we emerge. To deny ourselves daily use of speech patterns that are common and familiar, that embody the unique and distinctive aspect of our self is one of the ways we become estranged and alienated from our past. It is important for us to have as many languages on hand as we can know or learn. It is important for those of us who are Black, who speak in particular patois as well as standard English, to express ourselves in both ways. (hooks, 1989, pp. 79–80)

With older students, the issue of language can be addressed in more complex terms. As mentioned previously, bicultural students must find opportunities to engage in classroom dialogues and activities that permit them to explore the meaning of their lived experiences through the familiarity of their own language. But also important to their development of social consciousness and their process of concientization is the awareness of how language and power intersect in ways that include or exclude students of color from particular social relationships. Although it is paramount that bicultural students fully develop and strengthen their bicultural voices (as Puerto Ricans, Chicanos, African Americans, etc.) through their interactions with others in their own communities, it is also imperative that, in order to understand more fully the impact of language on social structures and practices, students of color enter into critical dialogues with those outside their cultural communities. Through the process of these cross-cultural dialogues, students come to better recognize for themselves the manner in which language works to define who they are, and how language as a tool can assist them to explore critically those possibilities that have remained hidden and out of their reach.

It is significant for teachers to recognize that it is more common for bicultural students to reflect on these issues and to express themselves predominantly through a *language of practice*—a highly pragmatic language that is primarily rooted in notions of common sense and concrete experiences. Although this process represents a necessary step in the empowerment of bicultural students, their transformative potential can only be extended when they are able to unite practice with theory, or when they are able to recognize themselves as critical beings who are constantly moving between concrete and abstract representations of experiences that influence how they make decisions about their actions in the world.

In order to create the conditions for students to determine their own lives genuinely within a multiplicity of discourses, teachers must introduce their students to the *language of theory*. The language of theory constitutes a critical language of social analysis that is produced through human efforts to understand how individuals reflect and interpret their experiences and, as a result, how they shape and are shaped by their world. Although it is a language generally connected to the realm of abstract thinking, its fundamental function of praxis cannot be fulfilled unless it is linked to the concrete experiences and practices of everyday life. Such language also encourages the use of more precise and specific linguistic representations of experience than is generally expected—or even necessary—in the course of everyday practice. Challenging bicultural students to engage openly with the language of theory and to understand better its impact on their lives can awaken them to the tremendous potential available to them as social agents.

At this point it is significant to note that what has been traditionally considered theoretical language has also been—almost exclusively—controlled and governed by those who have held power in academic circles, namely: elite, White males. As a result, the greatest number of formal theoretical texts considered as legitimate knowledge, reflect conservative, Eurocentric, patriarchal notions of the world. Generally speaking, these texts uniformly support assumptions that reinforce racism, classism and sexism, while written in such a way as to justify claims of neutrality and objectivity.

In their efforts to resist conservative forms of language domination, many educators disengage from all forms of theoretical language, thereby relegating the language of theory exclusively to a sphere of domination. Not surprisingly, this uncritical view comes dangerously close to being little more than a less recognized form of anti-intellectualism. The greatest danger is that it abandons the struggle for a liberatory language of theory by its refusal to challenge academic work that perpetuates all forms of domination and to assert the need for multiple forms of theoretical language rooted in culturally diverse perspectives and a variety of styles (hooks, 1989).

From another standpoint, efforts to resist the inequality and alienation reinforced by traditional uses of theoretical language can result in protective mechanisms of resistance among students of color, and this too can give rise to unintentional forms of anti-intellectualism. Given the nature of such responses, it is not unusual for bicultural students, who have suffered the negative impact of domination in their lives, to reject indiscriminately those cultural forms and social institutions that they come to associate with hostility and alienation. As a consequence, it is no simple task to challenge attitudes of anti-intellectualism in the classroom. To do so requires that teachers recognize that attitudes of resistance manifested by students of color are very often rooted in legitimate fears and subsequent responses to support community survival. In addition, these fears and responses are strongly fostered by a *legacy of resistance*, which is reinforced daily through their personal and institutional relationships. These relationships include interactions with their parents, who often harbor unspoken fears that they may lose their children forever if they should become educated. hooks describes this parental fear:

> They feared what college education might do to their children's minds even as they unenthusiastically acknowledged its importance. . . . No wonder our working class parents from poor backgrounds feared our entry into such a world, intuiting perhaps that we might learn to be ashamed of where we had come from, that we might never return home, or come back only to lord it over them. (hooks, 1989, pp. 74–75)

Also included among these interactions are relationships with many of their teachers, who themselves have never successfully moved beyond the language of practice. Consequently, it is not unusual for many teachers, when asked to engage with the language of theory, to respond by feeling almost as fearful, intimidated, and disempowered as their students. Simon (1991) addresses this *fear of theory* among teachers who are graduate students in his classes: "A fear of theory [is] more often expressed by students who have had to struggle for acceptance and recognition within the dominant institutions which define the terrain of everyday life. These are students whose lives have been lived within the prescriptive and marginalizing effects of power inscribed in relations of class, gender, ethnicity, race and sexual preference" (p. 7).

These responses by teachers are often used by teacher preparation programs around the country to justify astute arguments against the widespread use of theoretical language. More often than not, these arguments are shaped by a lack of critical engagement with the emancipatory potential of language and by a reproductive ideology that reduces students to simple objects, who are somehow mystically stripped of all dignity and voice, by expecting them to engage in disciplined critical thought and to address abstract concepts related to practice in more precise ways. These complaints are generally accompanied by a call for more visual language, more anecdotal accounts, or more how-to discussions. In essence, such requests for the predominant use of a language of practice inadvertently perpetuate a nondialectical and dichotomized view of theory and erode the teacher's potential for creative social action. If one listens carefully between the lines of this pragmatic educational discourse, it echoes a "false generosity of paternalism" (Freire, 1970) built on assumptions that arise from a lack of faith in the ability of oppressed groups to appropriate, transform, and utilize the language of theory in a liberatory fashion.

Educators in bicultural communities must grapple with their own language biases and prejudices beyond simply the issue of language differences, and work to encounter the deep frustrations and anxieties related to their fear of theory. This significant area of concern also needs to be adequately addressed by teacher preparation programs. This is particularly true for those programs that have traditionally neglected or ignored altogether this fundamental issue, as evidenced by curricula that place a greater emphasis on numerous predefined ways to teach the standard subjects rather than on exploring the complexity inherent in the human dynamics of creating meaning and producing knowledge in the classroom.

Language represents one of the most significant educational tools in our struggle for cultural democracy in the public schools. It is intimately linked to the struggle for voice, and so is essential to our struggle for liberation. Through language we not only define our position in society, but we also use that language to define ourselves as subjects in our world. Herein lies one of the most important goals for a critical bicultural pedagogy: creating the conditions for the voices of difference to find their way to the center of the dialogical process, rather than to remain forever silent or at the fringes of American classroom life.

THE QUESTION OF AUTHORITY

The question of authority represents one of the most heated areas of contention among major educational theorists in this country. This should not be surprising, for the manner in which we conceptualize authority truly represents a necessary precondition for the manner in which we define ourselves, our work, and our very lives—so much so that it is impossible to discuss cultural democracy in the classroom without addressing the issues that directly stem from this question.

In order to engage critically with the notion of authority, it is vital that teachers come to understand that authority does not automatically equal authoritarianism. Authority, within the context of a critical bicultural pedagogy, is intimately linked to the manner in which teachers exercise control, direct influence, and make decisions about what is actually to take place in their classrooms. To engage with the question of authority in a liberatory fashion clearly requires an understanding of power and how power is used to construct relationships, define truth, and create social conditions that can potentially either subordinate or empower bicultural students. Hence, authority must be understood as a dialectical "terrain of legitimation and struggle," rather than simply as an absolute, hierarchical, and totalizing force (Giroux, 1988b).

Efforts to examine the question of authority in the classroom also require teachers to address their personal contradictions related to how they formulate ideas of control, power, and authority in their own lives. This is particularly necessary given the manner in which teachers in public schools are consistently subject to administrative dictates and school conditions that undermine their power and authority. As teachers struggle together to challenge their conflicts and contradictions in this area, they are more able to build environments that support an emancipatory view of authority, stimulating their students to rethink critically their values, ideas, and actions in relation to the consequences these might have on themselves and others.

Although the question of authority is seldom discussed in liberatory terms by either conservative or liberal educators, it is essential that it be critically addressed in teacher preparation programs. As mentioned above, it is difficult for teachers to address the issue of authority if they themselves hold uncritical, conflicting, and contradictory attitudes about power and its relationship to human organization. Such attitudes are apparent in prevailing commonsense beliefs about the nature of power. While conservative educators are more likely to see power as a positive force that works to maintain order, earn respect, and "get the job done," liberals—and even many radical educators—are more prone to believe that "power corrupts" and that, despite human efforts, power ultimately leads to destruction. As a consequence, power is commonly perceived either as an absolute force for good, or else as an evil or negative force that dehumanizes and divests the individual's capacity for justice and solidarity with others. Understanding how these views of power are enmeshed in the contradictory thinking of teachers can help to shed light on the inadequacy and helplessness that so many educators express. This is of particular concern, given the fact that so many liberal and radical educators who hold negative assumptions related to power also speak to the necessity of *empowering* students, communities, and teachers alike.

The contradictory assumptions that underscore the question of authority also function to perpetuate the status quo, through the manner in which they sabotage, limit, and distort teachers' perceptions of classroom authority and their ability to alter the conditions they find in public schools. Such teachers, who do not possess a dialectical view of authority, generally lack the critical criteria to challenge attitudes, beliefs, and actions that perpetuate social injustice. In light of this, authority can be more readily understood in terms of its potential to uphold those emancipatory categories essential to the foundation of critical democratic life.

In our efforts to address this dimension, it must be explained that contradictory assumptions of authority cannot be deconstructed by simply utilizing a language of practice. The task of challenging society's contradictions requires educators to delve fearlessly into both the abstract and concrete experiences that unite to inform the theoretical realm. Through uniting their critical reflections of practice with theory, teachers come to discover the manner in which distorted views of power inform those classroom practices that reinforce undercurrents of oppression, perpetuating conditions that marginalize and alienate students of color.

The authoritarian nature of a conservative view of teacher authority is often hidden beneath the guise of traditional notions of respect, which can incorporate objective, instrumental, and hierarchical relationships that support various forms of oppressive educational practices at the expense of student voice. On the other hand, the oppressive impact of the liberal view of teacher authority, which all but disengages with questions of authority, often functions in an equally perverse manner. Hidden under the values of subjectivity, individualism, and intentionality, this view easily deteriorates into a crass relativism, asserting that all expressed values and ideas are deserving of equal time (Giroux, 1981). This is put into practice to the extent that some teachers proudly proclaim that they always consider all ideas generated by their students as equal, irrespective of personal histories, ideologies, or cultural differences—thus professing a specious notion of shared power. Although this perspective may ring true when entertained exclusively in the language of practice, theoretically it reflects an uncritical disengagement with issues related to social forms of domination and the manner in which ideas are generated and informed by particular interest that silence and oppress students from subordinate groups. Therefore, it is fraudulent to pretend that a teacher does not possess the authority and power over students to determine how the classroom will be governed; and it is an act of irresponsibility for teachers to abdicate their duty to challenge critically the oppressive nature of student ideas when these ideas constitute acts of racism, sexism, classism, or other forms of psychological violence that attack the dignity and self-worth of students of color.

Unlike traditional views on teacher authority, an emancipatory view of authority suggests that, although teachers hold knowledge that is considered to render them prepared to enter the classroom, they must come to recognize that knowledge as a historical and cultural product is forever in a creative state of partiality. And, as a consequence, all forms of discourse represent only one small piece of the larger puzzle that constitutes all possible knowledge at any given moment in time. Hence, all forms of knowledge must be open for question, examination, and critique by and with students in the process of learning. In this way, teachers actively use their authority to create the conditions for a critical transformation of consciousness that takes place in the process of the interaction of teacher, students, and the knowledge they produce together. Grounded in criteria informed by a liberatory vision of life, teachers embrace the notion of authority in the interest of cultural democracy, rather than against it.

REDEFINING FAIRNESS AND EQUALITY

If American public schools are to establish classroom environments that are culturally democratic, teachers will have to undertake a critical analysis of what has been traditionally defined as *fair-and-equal.* Just as the principles of democracy have so often been reduced to numerical head-counts and majority rule, concepts of fairness and equality have also been reduced to such quantifiable forms. Therefore, it is not unusual to hear teachers across the country express the belief that fair-and-equal is equivalent to providing the same quantity and quality of goods to all students across the board, irrespective of differences in social privilege and economic entitlement.

Clearly inherent in this perspective of fair-and-equal is the elimination of any transformative impact that these principles might have on the lives of disenfranchised students. The consequence in public schools is that students from the dominant culture who enter with major social and economic advantages receive as much—and at times even more—than students from subordinate cultures who arrive with far fewer social advantages. In an analysis of resource distribution among students in public schools, it is unquestionably apparent that poor children, who receive the least at home, receive the least from public education (Kozol, 1990). This painfully reminds us that the American educational system has little to do with cultivating equality. For if equality was, in fact, a part of the philosophical vision of education, the educational system would prioritize its resources in such a manner as to ensure that the majority of students were placed in settings where they could achieve successfully. Under such conditions, students from disenfranchised communities who require more educational opportunities by way of teacher contact, educational materials, nutritional support, and health care would receive more, while those students who arrive with greater privileges and with many more resources already in place would receive less.

Instead, what we find in most schools is the opposite. Students from the dominant culture who excel because they have been raised in homes that can provide them with the social, economic, and cultural capital necessary to meet the elitist and ethnocentric standards of American schools enjoy greater advantages and more positive regard than those from disenfranchised communities who must consistently struggle to succeed under social conditions working to their detriment. For decades it has been well documented that students from the dominant culture, who are raised in environments of privilege, score higher on standardized examinations. Hence, these students are perceived as superior when compared to most bicultural students. In addition, many of these superior students are also considered by public schools to exhibit mentally gifted abilities, while the majority of students of color are stigmatized and shamed by assignments into basic and remedial classes. This mentally gifted status has then been used as a justifiable rationale for appropriating additional resources to the already privileged—a group that just happens to include very few working-class students of color.

The consequence here is that the majority of bicultural students who are in need of greater school resources and educational opportunities find themselves in less challenging and less stimulating environments—environments that operate under the assumption that the students themselves, their parents, and their culture are to blame for their deficiency, while ignoring the deficiencies of a larger social caste system that replicates itself in public schools. Efforts by the White House in the past decade have merely functioned to make the situation worse. Plans that had been made to equalize school funding among districts have been replaced by a major reduction of funding to educational programs and an emphasis on building student motivation and self-control. Jonathan Kozol suggests that the consequences of tougher conservative rhetoric and more severe demands have led to further discrimination toward disenfranchised students:

Higher standards, in the absence of authentic educative opportunities in early years, function as a punitive attack on those who have been cheated since their infancy. Effectively, we now ask more of those to whom we now give less. Earlier testing for schoolchildren is prescribed. Those who fail are penalized by being held back from promotion and by being slotted into lower tracks where they cannot impede the progress of more privileged children. Those who disrupt classroom discipline are not placed in smaller classes with more patient teachers; instead, at a certain point, they are expelled—even if this means expulsion of a quarter of all pupils in school. (Kozol, 1990, p. 52)

Buried deep within traditional institutional views of fairness and equality is a stubborn refusal to engage with the reality of social conditions that marginalize students of color in this country. As a consequence, not only are bicultural students perceived as somehow less intelligent and therefore less deserving than middle-class students from the dominant culture, but also they are taught through their interactions with the system to perceive themselves in this way. If conditions in public schools are to change, teachers must openly challenge traditional views of fairness and equality and expose how these have functioned to reinforce notions of entitlement and privilege based on a doctrine of Social Darwinism that has proven to be incompatible with any emancipatory vision of social justice and equality.

THE USE OF MULTICULTURAL CURRICULUM

When educators first begin to think about how they can meet the needs of students of color, one of the most common places to begin is by bringing traditional cultural objects and symbols into the classroom. In fact, most multicultural curricula place a major emphasis on such cultural artifacts because they can be easily seen, manipulated, and quantified, although they ignore the more complex subjectivities of cultural values, belief systems, and traditions that inform the production of such cultural forms. Also problematic are depictions of cultural images and symbols that promote Eurocentric interpretations of cultural groups—depictions that function to dissolve cultural differences and reinforce mainstream expectations of assimilation. As a consequence, these traditional multicultural approaches operate to the detriment of students of color because they fail to respect and affirm their cultural differences and to help them understand the social and political implications of growing up bicultural in American society.

This is not to imply that bicultural students should not be exposed to curriculum that seeks to present cultural artifacts affirming their cultural traditions and experiences, but rather to emphasize that such multicultural materials and activities do not, in and of themselves, ensure that a culturally democratic process is at work. As mentioned above, this is in fact the case with most traditional efforts to promote cultural diversity. And many situations exist in which students are presented with games, food, stories, language, music, and other cultural forms in such a way as to strip these expressions of intent by reducing them to mere objects disembodied from their cultural meaning.

In order to prevent such an outcome, educators must become more critical not only of the actual curriculum they bring into the classroom, but also of the philosophical beliefs that inform their practice. First, they can begin to assess carefully their personal assumptions, prejudices, and biases related to issue of culture. Since it is far more common for teachers to think of themselves as neutral and unbiased toward all students, many racist, classist, and sexist attitudes and behaviors are most often disguised by faulty common-sense assumptions utilized extensively to assess student academic performance or classroom behavior. For example, most teachers still retain notions of culture that reflect color-blind or melting-pot assumptions and a bootstrap mentality. Simply put, these teachers believe that all people are the same in spite of race or culture, that the United States is a place where all cultures have (or should have) melted together to form one culture, and that anyone who wants to succeed *can* succeed, irrespective of social or economic circumstances.

Unfortunately these assumptions work to undermine the emancipatory potential of multicultural curricula. This is primarily because, when educators engage with issues related to cultural diversity based on these beliefs, they are unable to accurately address cultural issues related to power and dominance, as well as the impact that these forces have on the lives of bicultural students. For instance, in situations where students of color act out their resistance to cultural domination by passively refusing to participate in classroom activities or by actively disrupting the process, these student behaviors are interpreted by the majority of teachers as simply a classroom management problem—or, at most, as cause for concern about the emotional stability or well-being of the student. Seldom does it occur to most teachers who are faced with such behaviors to consider the manner in which cultural subordination and prevailing social hostility toward differences might represent the genesis of classroom resistance. Consequently, despite well-meaning efforts by teachers to intervene, their faulty assumptions generally hinder their effectiveness with bicultural students through unintentional acts of cultural invasion and further cultural subordination of students of color.

Second, in order to approach effectively the need for culturally relevant curriculum in the classroom, educators must be willing to acknowledge their limitations with respect to the cultural systems from which bicultural students make sense of their world. This requires teachers to recognize that students and their families bring to the classroom knowledge about their cultures, their communities, and their educational needs. This can best be accomplished by creating conditions for students to voice more clearly what constitutes the cultural differences they experience and to unfurl the conflicts as they struggle together to understand their own histories and their relationships with others. In addition, teachers must take the time to learn about the communities in which their students live. As teachers gain a greater understanding of students' lives outside of school, they are more able to create opportunities for classroom dialogue, which assists bicultural students to affirm, challenge, and transform the many conflicts and contradictions that they face as members of an oppressed group.

Third, educators also need to become more critical in their assessment of multicultural curricula and activities with respect to the consequences of their use in the classroom. For example, many teachers believe that making feathered headbands and teaching students about the Indians' contributions to the first Thanksgiving are effective activities for the study of Native Americans. In reality, these types of activities constitute forms of cultural invasion that reinforce stereotypical images of Native Americans and grossly distort the history of a people. Although this is a deeply problematic representation of culture for all students, it has a particularly perverse effect on students who have had little or no exposure to Native Americans other than what they have seen on television and in films, and a destructive impact on the self-esteem and identity of Native American students who are victimized by such distorted depictions of their cultural histories.

And fourth, teachers must come to realize that no multicultural curriculum, in and of itself, can replace the dialogical participation of bicultural students in the process of schooling. This is to say that even the most ideologically correct curriculum is in danger of objectifying students if it is utilized in such a way as to detach them from their everyday lives. Gramsci (1971) observes, "Thus, we come back to the truly active participation of the pupil in the school, which can only exist if the school is related to life. The more the new curricula nominally affirm and theorize the pupil's activity and working collaboration with the teacher, the more they are actually designed as if the pupil were purely passive" (p. 37). Gramsci's words support the notion that a genuine affirmation of cultural diversity in the classroom requires the restructuring of power relations and classroom structures in such a manner as to promote the *active* voice and participation of bicultural students. Through the creation of culturally democratic classroom conditions that also place bicultural voices at the center of the discourse, all students can come together to speak out about their lives and engage in dialogues that permit them to examine their cultural values and social realities. In this way, students can learn to make problematic their views of life; search for different ways to think about themselves; challenge their self-imposed as well as institutionally defined limitations; affirm their cultural and individual strengths; and embrace the possibilities for a better world through a growing sense of solidarity built on love, respect, and compassion for one another and a commitment to the liberation of all people.

CHALLENGING RACISM IN THE CLASSROOM

No matter how much a teacher might feel committed to the notion of cultural diversity, it is impossible to create a culturally democratic environment that can effectively meet the educational needs of bicultural students if that teacher is ill equipped to challenge incidences of racism when they surface in the curriculum or in student relationships. Racism results from institutionalized prejudices and biases that perpetuate discrimination based on racial and cultural differences. When educators fail to criticize discriminatory attitudes and behaviors, they permit bicultural students to suffer needless humiliation and psychological violence that negatively reinforce feelings of disentitlement and marginalization in society.

Despite attitudes to the contrary, cultural differences do not constitute the problem in public schools; rather, the problem is directly related to the responses of the dominant culture to these differences—responses that function to perpetuate social, political, and economic inequality. Instead of adopting the neutral position of most multicultural approaches, Carol Phillips suggests that educators teach students

> how to recognize when culturally and racially different groups are being victimized by the racist and biased attitudes of the larger society; how these behaviors are institutionalized in the policies and procedures of [schools] and programs; how these practices of excluding people are so mystified that well-meaning advocates for change fail to see them operating; [and] how to act against prevailing forces that perpetuate racism. (Phillips, 1988, p. 45)

The inability to address racism, as suggested by Phillips, is commonly observed in the failure of educators to address even racial slurs when they occur. A common scenario may find two or more students in a disagreement, and one or more may yell out at the other, "You nigger!" or "You greaser!" More times than not, educators who overhear such comments—unable to deal with their own discomfort—let them go by altogether, or they may tell the students to stop fighting, or that it is against the rules to call each other names. Unfortunately, despite good intentions, these approaches ignore the social circumstances that inform such behavior and the consequences for all students involved. In addition, it does nothing to assist these students and their peers to understand their actions critically, nor will it transform their relationships in any way.

Educators who strive for culturally democratic environments will need to call on their courage and inner strength to challenge the tension and discomfort they experience when confronting issues of discrimination in the classroom. Instead of looking for quick-fix methods to restore a false sense of harmony at such moments of confrontation, educators must seek to unveil the tensions, conflicts, and contradictions that perpetuate discriminatory attitudes and behaviors among their students. In a situation such as the one described above, the educator can bring students together into a critical dialogue about racial epithets and their role in perpetuating injustice. This may begin with questions about the feelings that precipitate these words: Where did they learn the words? What is the intent behind their use? What are the effects of these epithets on the victim? On the victimizer? How does this behavior relate to other forms of racism in the community? How could students engage in resolving their differences in other ways?

Dialogues such as this should be consistently introduced and encouraged among students within the context of the classroom, so that they may come to understand how their attitudes and behaviors affect others and, more importantly, so that they may come to act on behalf of all who are oppressed. Through their participation in this process, students have the opportunity to speak their feelings about race and how it relates to their lived experiences, and to become conscious of their own investment in racist attitudes and behaviors. In addition, they also learn to analyze how racism affects the conditions that exist in their communities, and to develop strategies for countering racism when they encounter it in their own lives (Giroux, 1990). For bicultural students, the dialogue must extend further. It must also assist them to identify the different ways in which their relationships with the dominant culture have conditioned them to take on contradictory attitudes and beliefs about themselves that cause them to participate unintentionally in the perpetuation of their own oppression.

THE CULTURE OF THE TEACHER

Whenever educators begin seriously to confront the complexity of teaching in bicultural communities, they also begin to question what impact the teacher's cultural background has on her or his ability to educate successfully students of color. It is an important question to consider within the context of a critical bicultural pedagogical discourse—particularly because of the profound nature of cultural belief systems and their relationship to issues of identity and social power. In addition, it brings into the arena of discussion notions of cultural differences with respect to the roles that teachers play if they are from the dominant culture, versus those who come from subordinate cultures.

As suggested earlier, in their efforts to learn about different cultural communities, teachers generally pursue materials that address the more visible or tangible aspects of cultural experience, while neglecting the deep structural values that inform the cultural worldviews of subordinate groups. In conjunction with this, teachers have been socialized to believe that by simply gathering or obtaining information on any particular subject they can come to know. From a critical bicultural perspective, learning about a culture from a book or a few seminars does not constitute knowing that culture. This is particularly true with respect to understanding the daily lived experiences of the group and the historicity of social forces that work to shape and shift how its members interact in the world. For example, someone who is not Hopi might read many books or articles about the Hopi people and yet still not know what it means to grow up as a Hopi in American society.

To even begin to comprehend the bicultural experience requires that teachers from the dominant culture invest time and energy into establishing critical dialogues with people of color if they wish to understand their communities better. Even then, these teachers must recognize and respect that their process of learning and knowing is inherently situated *outside* that cultural context, and is therefore different from the knowledge obtained from living *within* a particular cultural community. This is an essential understanding for teachers who have been raised in the dominant culture and whose cultural reference point is based on White Euroamerican values—which are the predominant values informing most American institutions. This is not to say that all Anglo-Americans conform to these values, but rather to suggest that, even in states of nonconformity, Euroamerican values represent the central reference point that individuals of the dominant culture move toward or move away from in the course of their personal and institutional relationships. This reference point also dictates the multitude of subject positions that individuals from the dominant culture assume in their lives with respect to class, gender, sexual orientation, spirituality, politics, and other ideological categories related to worldview.

The biculturation process represents an attempt to describe the dynamics by which people of color interact with the conflicts and contradictions arising when growing up in a primary culture that dictates a reference point and subject positions in conflict with those of the dominant culture. As a consequence, members from subordinate groups must find ways to cope and function within institutional environments that on the one hand generally undermine and curtail their rights to equality, and on the other hand push them to assimilate the values of the dominant culture. The different ways in which bicultural people attempt to resolve the tension created by such forces are reflected in the predominant response patterns they utilize to survive. What complicates this process further is the manner in which Euroamerican values are perpetuated through hegemonic forces of social control, while the primary values of African Americans, Latinos, Native Americans, Asians, and other subordinate groups are relegated to subordinate positions in American society.

The consequence is that very often people of color whose bicultural voices and experiences have been systematically silenced and negated are not necessarily conscious of the manner in which racism and classism have influenced their individual development, nor how they have functioned to distort perceptions of their cultural group within an Anglocentric world. Therefore, the fact that a person is bicultural does not guarantee that she or he occupies a position of resistance to such domination. In fact, under current social conditions, it is not unusual to find people of color in positions of power who ignore issues of social power and perpetuate ideas and beliefs that function to the detriment of their own people. Such prominent figures include the likes of Senator Samuel Hayakawa, who was an outspoken advocate for a national English-only initiative; Linda Chavez, a former member of the National Human Relations Commission; and Shelby Steele, the author of *The Content of Our Character*. This is also the case with the many teachers of color who have naively made attempts to assimilate into the dominant culture without critically engaging with the impact of their beliefs on their lives and work.

This perspective is offered here because it represents a reality that must be understood if educators are honestly to consider questions related to the cultural background of the teachers who educate bicultural students. It is a reality that must be acknowledged if we are to prevent falling into the trap of essentialist arguments, such as those proclaiming that only teachers of color can effectively educate students of color. Instead, what is needed is the courage, willingness, and desire to speak honestly to those issues that relate directly to how individuals define their cultural identity and how this influences their work with bicultural students. How teachers perceive the notion of cultural identity is especially important, given that the majority of educators in the United States are members of the dominant culture, and that most educators—of all cultures—have been schooled in traditional pedagogical models. Hence, the teacher's cultural background, espoused ideology, and academic preparation embody equally important areas of concern in our efforts to create conditions that are conducive to a culturally democratic life in the classroom.

If public schools are to provide successfully for the educational needs of bicultural students, they must work in collaboration with bicultural educators, students, parents, and their communities. Anything short of this effort suggests an educational process that is in danger of oppressing and disempowering students of color. This is not to imply that all teachers in bicultural communities must necessarily be teachers of color, but rather to emphasize that it is an arrogant and patronizing gesture for educators from the dominant culture to think that they can meet the needs of a culturally different community when they fail to work in solidarity with educators and other members of that community.

Efforts to establish solidarity among culturally diverse groups require relationships based on mutual respect and equality. White teachers need to abandon, willingly, unfair notions of entitlement and privilege so they may enter into relationships with people of color that support the struggle for freedom and a better world. This requires that White educators acknowledge the manner in which people of color have been historically discriminated against and subordinated to inferior positions in the society at large and the manner in which public education has perpetuated this process. They must come to see how these injustices actually exist in their own profession by the very nature of the assumptions that inform their practice. For example, it is not unusual to find bicultural/bilingual instructional aides with ten or more years of experience in the classroom working under inexperienced White middle-class teachers who know very little about the actual needs of bicultural students. Yet, when such conditions are challenged as part of a wider struggle for more bilingual/bicultural teachers, it is interesting to note the manner in which questions of social control ultimately inform the responses of many public school districts. Rather than create the conditions for well-experienced instructional aides to complete their education and receive certification, many large urban school districts have decided to import teachers from Spain. These are teachers who, in fact, are less knowledgeable of the American bicultural experience than Euroamerican educators. This illustrates only one of the ways in which a process of hegemony operates in public schools to sabotage the transformative struggles of oppressed communities and to ensure the perpetuation of the status quo. Such forms of hegemony can be understood by teachers and challenged in the course of their work.

Further, in order for bicultural students to develop both an individual and social sense of empowerment in their lives, they need to establish relationships with both White and bicultural teachers who are genuinely committed to a democratic vision of community life. When students actually experience the process of White teachers and bicultural teachers working together to address issues related to cultural differences and conflicts, they also come to better understand cultural democracy and learn to participate in cross-cultural dialogues in ways that truly respect and honor the emancipatory rights of all people.

Critical educators from the dominant culture demonstrate a spirit of solidarity and possibility when they willingly challenge both cultural values and institutional conditions of inequity despite the fact that these potentially function to their material benefit. Their refusal to accept social conditions of entitlement and privilege for themselves at the expense of oppressed groups helps to lay the groundwork for relations with people of color based on a solidarity and commitment to social justice and equality. Such educators truly recognize the need to create conditions in the classroom that empower students of color and to open opportunities that historically have remained closed to these students. Operating from this perspective, programs developed under such mandates as affirmative action and equal educational opportunity are given support as beginning efforts toward social equality, rather than seen as somehow taking away from members of the dominant culture. The way in which teachers themselves address these issues in the larger world is significant, because it usually also reflects how they relate with students of color in the course of their daily interactions with them in the classroom.

It is also essential that students of color experience a variety of teachers of color during the course of their schooling. Bicultural educators who are socially conscious bring a wealth of knowledge and experience that often resonates with the realities that students of color experience in their own lives. Many of these teachers are bilingual, understand the complexity of their students' cultural worldviews, are knowledgeable about their history and literature, are cognizant of the different styles in which students learn and communicate, are conscious of the rules of appropriate relationships and interactions among people, and know the communities from which their students come. As a consequence, bicultural teachers are generally more able to use their own learning experiences and knowledge of their cultural values to develop effective curricula that engage with issues related to cultural diversity. In addition, through their knowledge of the community, they are able to find ways in which to integrate the students' lived culture into classroom relationships. They are also more genuinely able to affirm and support the development of the bicultural voice, given their ability to engage with the lived conditions of cultural domination and resistance. Hence, it must be recognized that bicultural teachers serve vital roles as models for students of color—many of whom have seldom witnessed people of color in positions of power and influence. Most importantly, through their experiences with critical bicultural educators, bicultural students are more concretely challenged and supported as they come to redefine their possibilities within the context of American society.

RESTRUCTURING PUBLIC SCHOOLS

Critical educators of bicultural students must consider creative ways in which they can work to restructure public school environments that support experiences of culturally democratic life. The manner in which this is done must take into account not only the specific needs that bicultural students bring into the classroom, but also the needs that teachers have in order to be more effective educators. Through gaining a better understanding of the lived histories and daily lives of both students of color and their teachers, critical educators can transform classroom structures to reflect meaningful social relationships and critical pedagogical approaches that are built on the principles of cultural democracy. Just as students are critically challenged to redefine the possibilities for transforming the world, their teachers should be actively involved in such a process within the context of their own profession.

First of all, efforts by teachers to promote the development of voice, participation, social responsibility, and solidarity are strongly reflected in the way they physically structure and situate the learning environment in their classrooms. A few classroom changes that would address this concern include these examples:

- The furniture, and in particular the seating in the room, is arranged so as to permit free physical movement of students about the classroom.
- Classroom spaces promote working in groups and on collaborative projects.
- Classroom bulletin boards are generated in conjunction with the participation of students, who are encouraged to utilize materials that are meaningful to them. These forms of cultural expression are then used to stimulate dialogues about their relationship to the context of students' lives and communities.
- Curricular activities are created for students to have opportunities to converse in their home languages with each other and to introduce various aspects of their language experience to other students.

- Students are actively involved in the development of classroom rules and in making decisions about classroom activities whenever possible. In addition, they are involved in dialogues designed to help them consider the consequences of rules and decisions made with respect to themselves as individuals and the class as a whole.

It is important to note that none of these suggestions, in and of itself, constitutes *the* way to incorporate a critical bicultural pedagogy, for the manner in which a critical pedagogy evolves in any particular classroom environment must be based on the contextual conditions present. No lesson plan or curriculum should ever supersede the actual learning needs expressed by students or identified by the teacher. Learning is a contextual experience by which knowledge and meaning are produced within the complexity of a multitude of potential responses generated by students and teacher alike.

The few suggestions mentioned above focus on what teachers can do to transform the structures and relationships within their own classrooms. But outside the classroom, there is also much to be done related to the general restructuring of the working conditions that teachers find in public schools. Critical educators must explore some possible ways in which to transform these conditions so that schools may function to support their own empowerment as well as an emancipatory vision for education. Some suggestions to consider with respect to this concern are as follows:

- The development of cross-cultural teaching teams in schools with large bicultural student populations.
- The initiation of professional development opportunities for all teachers to become knowledgeable in the principles of a critical bicultural pedagogy. This would provide teachers the opportunity to better understand the bicultural experience of students and to examine together their own prejudices and biases related to issues of cultural diversity.
- A greater involvement of teachers in the development, evaluation, and selection of texts, films, and other instructional materials.
- An ongoing collaborative effort with parents and community members to transform the educational environments of public schools.
- Establishment of regular public forums within schools to discuss issues related to bicultural students, such as bilingualism, the bicultural process, the academic needs of students, parent involvement in the classroom, and so forth.

In addition, teachers must also struggle to transform the structural conditions related to both out-of-class work and class size. Much of the demoralization teachers experience is not, for the most part, a consequence of low pay; rather, it is more closely linked to the powerlessness generated by working in an environment that is fundamentally incompatible with engaging in the complexities of teaching a culturally diverse student population. In order to address this issue, public school teachers might begin by demanding that the number of students in their classrooms be limited to approximately twenty. It is not unusual to find public schools in large urban settings where teachers are assigned up to forty students, with limited assistance from an instructional aide. One of the most revolutionary actions that public school teachers can take, at this point in time, is to assume an uncompromising posture with respect to the issue of class size. It is well documented that students are more successful when they receive more individualized attention from the teacher. So completely conscious of this fact are private schools that they use as a major selling point their policy of small class size. Teacher unions and other teacher organizations need to become advocates for themselves as well as for disenfranchised students by asserting the entitlement of the latter to the rights enjoyed by students from privileged classes. Most importantly, teachers who are less burdened by the tremendous demands placed on them by large class size are more able to engage consistently and critically with the actual needs of bicultural students and issues related to cultural diversity.

Also of major importance is the struggle for the redefinition of the teacher's workday. Seldom are teachers afforded opportunities to come together on an ongoing basis to reflect and dialogue critically about the concerns they experience in their efforts to meet the needs of their students. And even more seldom do they have the time to maintain some consistent form of personal contact with parents, despite the fact that studies clearly indicate this to be a significant factor in the achievement of bicultural students (Rashid, 1981; Goldenberg, 1987; Cummins, 1986). Teachers require institutional support in their efforts to develop working relationships with their colleagues, students, parents, and the communities in which they work. This can only take place when the teacher's work is redefined more realistically to include both what teachers are required to implement daily in their classrooms and those important functions they must perform outside the classroom setting to be effective educators. But this redefinition can only take place when teachers struggle to transform the conditions of their labor within the context of a critical process that is generated by working together for a better life—not only as educators, but as workers and free democratic citizens.

BEYOND DESPAIR

Much frustration is evident in the attitudes and responses of many educators to the conditions they find in public schools. Many teachers blame the problems they experience on the increasing number of students of color. Others are acutely aware that they were insufficiently prepared by teacher education programs to meet the needs of a culturally diverse student population. Still others experience a deep feeling of personal frustration, which they attribute to their own individual failure as teachers. Whatever the manner in which teachers define the cause of their frustration, it is clear that their perceptions echo a great sense of despair and powerlessness.

It is important to note that those teachers who find themselves within public school conditions—where their voices are silenced and their opportunities to decide on curricula, texts, and other classroom requirements are limited—are most in danger of experiencing a sense of despair. Public school teachers in these environments must work together to challenge themselves and each other to move beyond the limitations that they find in these schools. In addition, they must also move beyond their own dependency on traditional classroom structures and the artifacts that support the perpetuation of their disempowerment.

For example, under such conditions as described above, teachers must initially cultivate their creative abilities to utilize commonplace materials and natural environments that can serve as ideal conditions for students to investigate the ordinary, and, through acting on it, discover their potential power to create and change their world. Given this approach, any classroom situation can potentially be converted into a critical environment as educators discover the multitude of pedagogical possibilities at their disposal. But this can only take place when educators courageously abandon old and disempowering notions of what is necessary and certain, and move beyond the boundaries of prescribed educational practice and into the realm of creativity and discovery.

As emphasized earlier, fundamental to creating the conditions for cultural democracy is a political commitment to a liberatory vision. A critical bicultural pedagogy can only emerge within a social context where teachers are grounded in a commitment to both individual and social empowerment. Hence, the smaller political endeavor of the classroom is not seen as simply an encapsulated moment in time, but rather it is consistently connected to a greater democratic political project. From this vantage point, teachers function as empowered social agents of history, who are firmly committed to collaborative struggles for transformation as they seek to change and redefine the conditions that threaten the opportunities for voice, participation, and solidarity in their schools. As teachers work in solidarity with their colleagues, parents, students, and the community, they discover their tremendous collective power, and through this process of affirmation move beyond despair. It is, in part, this critical commitment to act on behalf of freedom and social justice that also serves as a model for their students to discover their own personal power, social transformative potential, and spirit of hope.

Embodied in this emancipatory spirit of hope is also a faith in the capacity of human beings to transform the oppressive and dehumanizing conditions that disconnect, fragment, and alienate us from one another. Grounded in this struggle by a collective vision of liberation, critical educators search out creative ways to expand the opportunities for students of color to become authentic beings for themselves, in spite of the limitations of traditional curricula and prevailing social conditions. Students are encouraged to question the conflicts, contradictions, disjunctions, and partiality of standardized knowledge forms in their own lives as well. Consistently, liberatory educators support and challenge bicultural students to struggle together so that they may come to know all the possibilities that might be available to them as free citizens. For it is through this critical process of discovery and empowerment that teachers and students move in solidarity across the terrain of cultural differences to arrive at the knowledge that hidden in the complexity of these differences are many ways to be human, and many ways to struggle for a world in which we can all be free.

18

Teaching and Social Change
Reflections on a Freirean Approach
in a College Classroom

Daniel G. Solorzano

In March 1986, the Brazilian educator and social theorist Paulo Freire traveled to Southern California to hold a dialogue with educators and community organizers who were using—or who considered using—his problem-posing pedagogy. Having employed a Freirean method, I attended the meetings and decided to share my experience with other educators. This paper represents my reflections on the 1978–1979 academic year, when I used Freire's problem-posing method with a group of students at a community college.

FREIRE'S PROBLEM-POSING METHOD

Freire's (1970, 1973) method starts from the premise that all education is political and thus schools are never neutral institutions. He asserts that schools either function to maintain and reproduce the existing social order or empower people to transform themselves and/or society. Freire argues that when schools domesticate, they socialize students into accepting as legitimate the ideology and values of society's dominant class. According to Freire (1970), schools use the "banking method" to domesticate students. When this approach is taken, students are viewed as passive receptacles waiting for knowledge to be deposited by the teacher. They are taught in a narrative format whereby the teacher communicates with the students in one-way monologues. This approach can lead students to feel that their thoughts and ideas are not important enough to warrant a two-way dialogue with the teacher. Students also are dependent on the teacher for their acquisition of knowledge. Finally, teachers are seen as conduits through which the ideology and values of the dominant social class are transmitted to the students.

When schools liberate, however, students are viewed as subjects willing and able to act on their world. To create a liberating education, Freire developed the problem-posing method, in which a two-way dialogue of cooperation between the student and the teacher is the focus, content, and pedagogy of the classroom.

Freire's method includes three general phases: 1) identifying and naming the problem, 2) analyzing the causes of the problem, and 3) finding solutions to the problem (Freire 1970, 1973; Smith and Alschuler 1976).

In the naming phase, the educator enters the community or social setting. While in the community, she or he learns about the major issues and problems of the area by listening and speaking to the people and observing community life. After gathering the needed information, the educator develops generative codes. These codes are visual renditions—as in pictures, drawings, stories, articles, or films—of the significant themes for problems that have been identified. The codes are at the heart of the problem-posing process because they are used to begin critical dialogue among the participants.

In the second or analytic phase, the educator takes the codified theme and describes and analyzes the causes of the problem through dialogue with students. In the final or solution phase, students—in collaboration with the educator—find and carry out solutions to the problem.

This process of reflecting and acting on one's reality by describing and defining a problem clearly, analyzing its causes, and acting to resolve it is the key element of the problem-posing method. Students are encouraged to view issues as problems that can be resolved, not as realities to be accepted. Hence students feel that their ideas are recognized as legitimate and that the problem posed can be resolved in a constructive manner. In addition, students and teachers becomes dependent on each other for knowledge.

THE FREIREAN APPROACH IN THE COLLEGE CLASSROOM

In the fall of 1978 I taught a cross-listed course called "Directed Practice in Social Welfare" at East Los Angeles College in the Sociology and Chicano Studies departments. East Los Angeles College is located about 10 miles east of downtown Los Angeles; in 1978 nearly 20,000 day and evening students attended. About 85 percent were Chicano students, generally from working-class homes in the greater East Los Angeles area. At that time the Chicano Studies department was one of the largest in the country, offering over 50 classes each semester in the day and evening programs.

The purpose of Directed Practice was to involve students in social and political activities in the greater East Los Angeles community. As part of the course, instructors placed students as volunteers in local elementary and secondary schools or in community service agencies. The students worked in the schools or agencies for at least three hours a week and met one day a week in class to discuss their experiences with other students. Although this approach had been shown to be an enriching experience for students, I wanted to integrate a Freirean problem-posing orientation into the class.

Phase I: Naming and Posing the Problem

In Freirean style, I began the semester by engaging the students in a dialogue about how various issues affect their communities. Although such social problems as educational and occupational inequality were identified and discussed, the issue raised most frequently was the youth gang problem in the East Los Angeles neighborhoods. This emphasis was not surprising because the gang incidents were, and are, portrayed continually in newspapers, television, and social science texts as a major social problem in the Chicano Community (Heller 1966; Trujillo 1974; United States Commission on Civil Rights 1977, 1979). The importance that students placed on this issue also may have been due to the critical and economic success of Luis Valdez's 1978 play *Zoot Suit* (Wilson 1978). The play focused sensitively on the struggles of Pachuco gang youth during the early 1940s in Los Angeles.

By coincidence, in the first week of the fall 1978 semester (September 10) the *Los Angeles Times* ran the first of a three-part series on Chicanos in the mass media (Knoedelseder 1978). This article examined problems on the set of the Universal Studios film titled *Gang* (later renamed *Walk Proud*). The film depicted the story of a young Chicano gang member named Emilio—played by actor Robby Benson—who falls in love with a young white woman named Sarah. At Sarah's insistence and on discovering that his father is white (added at the insistence of Universal Pictures), Emilio leaves the gang (Knoedelseder 1978). The basic story line focused on the film's white characters helping Emilio to see the evil of his cultural (i.e., Chicano) ways. This theme of different cultures clashing was the basis for a preliminary discussion in the class. (Topical class discussions from multiple points of view were central to every stage of the process).

The initial *Los Angeles Times* articles briefly mentioned another film, *Boulevard Nights*, then in the early production phase for Warner Brothers Studios (Knoedelseder 1978; Wilson 1978). This film had a less offensive story line than *Walk Proud*. It examined intrafamily conflict: an older brother, Raymond, struggles to leave the gang and neighborhood and to become a member of a car club, while his younger brother, Chuco, remains a member of the gang.

Walk Proud and *Boulevard Nights* were not isolated releases. According to another *Times* article, these films—scheduled for 1979 release, represented two in a series of gang films which included the following: *The Warriors* (February), *On the Edge* (May), *The Wanderers* (July), *Defiance* (August), and *The Gangs of New York* (Month?) (Kilday 1978). Another movie in production titled *American Me*—specifically about a Chicano gang leader—apparently inspired the other projects (Kilday 1978).

Because of these articles, the class spent two weeks on the initial question: "What are some of the images of Chicanos in the mass media?" After reading and discussing the subsequent articles in the *Times* and collecting and discussing other visual and written materials on popular and professional Chicano stereotypes, the class decided that the negative portrayal of Chicanos in the mass media would be the main focus of the semester (see Council on Interracial Books for Children 1977; Martinez 1969; Trujillo 1974; United States Commission on Civil Rights 1977; Wilson 1978; Woll 1977). The students then posed the problem of the negative media image of Chicanos as two additional questions: "Why are Chicanos portrayed negatively in the mass media?" and "Whose interests are served by these negative portrayals of Chicanos?" To answer these questions, the class decided to conduct detailed case studies on the two Chicano gang films, *Boulevard Nights* and *Walk Proud*.

Phase II: Analyzing the Causes of the Problem

After deciding on the problem, the students began to analyze the causes. From the beginning I believed that in order for students to critically understand the nature of any social problem, they had to possess the skills necessary to gather data and have a firm grasp of the theories used to interpret the data. The class decided to gather general information related to Chicanos in the media and Chicano gangs, plus specific information on the films *Boulevard Nights* and *Walk Proud*. To complete this task, students divided into three work groups.

The first group used the library to collect more information on the images of Chicanos in the media from both a contemporary and a historical perspective. They used the *Readers Guide to Periodical Literature, Sociological Abstracts*, the *Social Science Index*, the *Los Hispanic American Periodicals Index*, and the *Chicano Periodical Index*. They also examined such Hollywood trade papers and magazines as The *Hollywood Reporter, Daily Variety*, and *American Film*. In addition, they discovered an excellent Chicano news monitoring service called *COMEXAZ* to gather background information from seven major newspapers in the southwestern United States.

A second group gathered public information data on youth gangs in East Los Angeles from the Los Angeles County Sheriff's Department and the Los Angeles City Police Department. This group also examined different sociological theories of gang and deviant behavior (see Hernandez, Haug, and Wagner 1976; Mirande 1978; Moore 1978; Morales 1972; and Trujillo 1974). They also gathered first-hand information from youths involved in gang activity. To develop a demographic profile of Chicanos, this group analyzed census data from the 1970 Census publications for the United States, California, and the Los Angeles-Long Beach Standard Metropolitan Statistical Areas (United States Bureau of the Census 1972a, 1972b, 1972c, 1973).

A third group contacted and interviewed representatives of Universal Pictures and Warner Brothers Studios for further information on *Boulevard Nights* and *Walk Proud*. The studio's public relations department gave them a standard press packet on the film's background, shooting schedule, and expected release date. Students also contacted and interviewed Chicano community and professional organizations who were working as technical and script consultants on the two films (Barrios Unidos, Project Ayudate, the Imperials Car Club, and Nosotros). With the help of these groups, students could determine each organization's role in the film's production; some of the groups served as on-site security, while others supplied more technical and professional help. Finally, students contacted and interviewed community and professional groups who were beginning to challenge the negative role of Chicanos in the media, such as the Coalition of Mexicanos/Latinos Against Defamation (Morales 1978).

For two weeks the students analyzed and synthesized the statistical and anecdotal data and the theoretical explanations of the Chicanos' social conditions in the United States, and contemporary images of Chicanos in film and television. It became apparent that the entertainment industry was not concerned with accurate portrayals of Chicano social life. For example, it appeared that the data on Chicano youth gangs were being blown out of proportion. The students' research disclosed that the proportion of Chicano youth in gangs was not the 10 percent claimed by the electronic and print media, but closer to three percent (Morales 1972, 1978). This finding led the students to question the statistics of the Los Angeles County Sheriff and the Los Angeles City Police Department and related police practices regarding Chicano youth and youth gangs in the Los Angeles area.

In addition, through the visual imagery in television, films, newspapers, magazines, and textbooks, the students concluded that Chicanos were stereotyped disproportionately in subordinate and demeaning occupational and social roles such as bandits, thieves, and gangsters. Students also found negative Latino portrayals in films and in magazine and newspaper articles dating back to the turn of the century (Council on Interracial Books for Children 1977; Lamb 1975; Martinez 1969; Trujillo 1974; United States Commission on Civil Rights 1977, 1979; Woll 1977). This popular media portrayal seemed to reinforce the social scientific image of Chicanos as stereotypic social beings whose problems could be traced to a deficient or disadvantaged culture (Heller 1966).

Phase III: Finding Solutions to the Problem

The students concluded that the Hollywood studios were not concerned with projecting a more positive image of Chicanos; their main concern was the profit that this genre of film could generate. Therefore one solution to the problem was to organize some public action against the Chicano youth gang films. The students decided that the action should achieve two goals: 1) to bring the attention of both the Chicano and the non-Chicano community to the problem of the negative portrayal of Chicanos in the media, and 2) to stop the further release of media that reinforced a negative image of the Chicano population. After discussion, the students decided to organize a boycott and an organized action. The CBS program *60 Minutes* ran a segment on Chicano gangs in East Los Angeles, titled "The West Coast Story." This program (air date December 10, 1978) was seen as a negative and inaccurate portrayal of life in East Los Angeles, and drew criticism from community and professional organizations (Morales 1978). Dr. Armando Morales, the president of the Coalition of Mexicanos/Latinos Against Defamation, lodged a formal protest with Robert Salant, the president of CBS, criticizing the program's portrayal of Chicano youth. He asked for equal time to present "the ELA gang situation on *60 Minutes* in a more balanced, objective, and factual manner" (Morales 1978). CBS denied his request (Chandler 1978).

This incident reminded the students that they would be fighting a media giant, and that at least a formal campus organization would be needed as a base of support. The student approached MECHA (Movimiento Estudiantil Chicanos de Aztlan), the Chicano student organization of the East Los Angeles College (ELAC) campus, to discuss the project. The MECHA students decided to get involved, and they established the ad hoc Gang Exploitation Film Committee to oversee and support the project.

The Gang Exploitation Film Committee approached and received the support of the MECHA Central Committee of college and high school campuses in the Los Angeles area. In February 1979, the ELAC Committee took a plan of action to MECHA's statewide conference in Sacramento and received the endorsement of the state organization (Gang Exploitation Film Committee 1979). The Committee also took the plan to local community organizations to solicit their support for the boycott. Other MECHA chapters throughout California gathered support in their own areas. During this period a February 1979 article in the magazine *American Film* titled "The Lowriders of Whittier Boulevard," confirmed our information on other scripts or ideas being considered for films, pending the financial and critical outcome of *Boulevard Nights* and *Walk Proud* (Jeffries 1979).

After examining the information collected on *Walk Proud*, the students felt that this film would be an easier target for the boycott. By default, the boycott shifted to March 21, the release date of *Boulevard Nights* (Schreger 1979). Students decided that *Boulevard Nights* symbolized a genre of films on Chicano youth gangs. They were protesting against the gang theme, and *Boulevard Nights* happened to be the first film of that genre to be released.

After a private screening of *Boulevard Nights*, Nosotros, a national Latino organization of media professionals, denounced the film one month before its opening (Warren 1979). (This organization, however, served as technical advisors in script and casting to *Walk Proud*; Nuestro 1979.)

At the opening of *Boulevard Nights* in West Los Angeles, over 100 students organized a picket line. The mayor of Los Angeles, Tom Bradley, entered the controversy by including and then deleting his name from the list of dignitaries planning to appear at the film's opening. He was to give the filmmaker a city proclamation honoring *Boulevard Nights* as "an instrument of peace" (Warren 1979). In addition, for the first three weeks of the film's run, boycotts and informational picket lines were conducted by local MECHA chapters and community organizations at theaters throughout southern and northern California. During this period television, radio, and newspaper media focused on the problems of Chicano stereotypes in the mass media. After a stabbing and shooting at a San Francisco theater showing *Boulevard Nights*, Mayor Diane Feinstein requested that the film be removed from the theater (Grant 1979a, 1979b). Gang-related incidents also caused the film to be canceled in Pomona (Landsbaum 1979).

Despite the boycott, the picket lines, and generally negative publicity, *Boulevard Nights* had a somewhat successful run. The reviews of the film were mixed: the *Los Angeles Herald Examiner* film critic called it "as Latino in flavor as a Jack-in-the-box taco" (Sagrow 1979). The *Los Angeles Times* critic was kinder, referring to the film as "entertaining and admirable as a use of the medium" (Champlin 1979). An editorial writer for the *Herald Examiner* said, "Were this a book, it might qualify as the Great Mexican-American Novel" (Castro 1979). A *Times* editorial writer called the film a "thoughtful attempt to portray a subculture that Americans have heard much about but know very little." The writer criticized the film, however, for making "no attempt to show the pathetic state of many schools in East Los Angeles . . . it's these schools that help create gang members by turning off young Chicanos with insensitive or ill–trained teachers and outmoded or irrelevant study programs, all of which contribute to high drop-out rates" (Del Olmo 1979). Another *Times* staff writer claimed, "Groups both within the film industry and on its edges are monitoring the gang films . . . there's the question of whether they'll make more . . . no one has announced another gang film." The writer also quoted a Universal Pictures spokesperson, who said, "It's possible that adverse reaction by the splinter groups may very well turn the studios sour about films relating to these groups" (Schreger 1979).

Despite the controversy, Universal Pictures released *Walk Proud* in May 1979. Without explanation, however, the film was not released in any of the major Latino media markets in the southwest United States. Furthermore, none of the other Chicano gang genre movies cited in the *American Film* article were released to the general public (Jeffries 1979).

After the action was complete, the ELAC committee went before the California MECHA organization to report on its successes and failures. It was clear that as an informational tactic, the word on negative stereotypes of Chicanos in the media had been projected to the general public in an organized and documented fashion. Many students also credited the committee with doing something positive about the release of these negative films. It was also clear, however, that *Boulevard Nights* received free publicity, and many people felt that the action brought too much attention to a "B" film. Other students argued that the committee had called negative attention to Latino actors who were only trying to showcase their professional talent, albeit in negative roles. To reinforce this point, the *Los Angeles Times* quoted a Universal Pictures senior vice-president as saying, "In the end, it may very well hurt the job market for (Hispanic) actors and technical people who work in these pictures" (Schreger 1979). The tactical question of whether to take action, or what type of action to take, must be discussed and dealt with if the problem-posing process is to be effective.

Because of the publicity and the action by the studio, the boycott was fulfilling its two major goals: first, to bring the negative image of Chicanos in the media to the attention of both the Chicano and the non-Chicano community, and second, to stop (albeit temporarily) the further release of media that reinforced a negative image of the Chicano population.

Reflections on the Problem-Posing Process

The Hollywood studios' decision to put the Chicano youth gang theme on the back burner was probably based on a sound financial decision. Though the students and the community members could not take full credit for this decision, their actions surely had some effect (see Schreger 1979).

From their interactions with a variety of people, it was apparent that the students developed commitment to and confidence in their own ideas, as well as research, organizational, and communication skills to test those ideas. They had become empowered for the "moment." In that moment they had exposed the larger community to an organized group of people who felt, acted, and succeeded in doing something they considered positive about a genre of films that reinforced the negative stereotypes of Chicano youth. As an educator I can only hope that the students' critical curiosity, their new problem-solving skills, and the related sense of empowerment remain with them as they meet other personal and social problems. If they do remain, the Freirean approach has achieved its major goal of empowering students to reflect and act on real-life problems on a sustained basis.

Moreover, to my knowledge—as of summer 1988—no major motion picture studio has released a major film exclusively on Chicano youth gangs. (Although Chicano gangs are a part of the plot, the major focus of *Colors* (1988) is on black gangs in Los Angeles.) For 10 years the image of Chicanos in major films was largely ignored or remained on the periphery, but in the recent films *La Bamba* (1987), *Born in East L.A.* (1987), *Stand and Deliver* (1988), and *The Milagro Beanfield War* (1988), the major themes and characters are Latino-oriented. The Latino characters range from the narrow in recent minor films such as *Zoot Suit* (1981). *The Ballad of Gregorio Cortes* (1982), *El Norte* (1983), and *Latino* (1985), the Latino roles have depth and range; the overall images and messages are relevant, positive, and powerful (Keller 1985). Because of the nature and number of these Latino-related films, this period should be seen as a significant benchmark in Chicano filmmaking.

Critique of the Problem-Posing Process

Several problems emerged both during and after the course. The first problem concerned student who felt uncomfortable with the critical nature of the Freirean pedagogy. As a personal policy, I do not require students to participate in activities to which they feel strongly opposed. Usually I offer alternative ways of meeting the course requirements. In this course, three students reacted negatively to Paulo Freire's radical theory and chose not to participate in any of the political activity. In preparation for each of our discussions, however, I successfully challenged them to bring to the class alternative views on the topics. These challenges supplied important learning exercises for the other students, who later would meet similar skeptics on the picket line and in the press.

A second problem concerned Freire's "action" phase. Because it is the students who decide what actions to take, their range of responses to the problem posed has included the action described in this paper, letter-writing campaigns, and discussions of the problem in class with no outside action. I believe that to understand the problem posed and to empower students, one must take action on the problem and reflect critically on the action taken. Therefore it is my responsibility as the coordinator to challenge students to resist passivity, to take a more active role in their education generally, and to address the specific social problems they have identified. In some of my courses I have failed to do this, but, as most educators know, each class has a different personality and will react to issues differently.

A third problem relates to time: I had the benefit of working with a group of students for two semesters. The action I describe in the paper might not work as effectively in a 10-week quarter or a 16-week semester.

Despite these problems, the approach described in this paper is a pedagogic method for examining critically and taking action on social problems that students view as significant. Therefore the method can be used—with modifications—in such sociology courses as social problems, social change, and race, ethnic, and gender relations.

CONCLUSIONS

When I worked on this project 10 years ago, only a small number of educators were using the Freirean method in college- and community-based settings. Since that time the number has increased modestly to include Shor's work with college students in an English curriculum (Shor 1980; Shor and Freire 1987); Fiore and Elaster (1982) and Holzman (1988) in advanced literacy; Wallerstein's (1983) work with English as a second language for adult students; Hodder (1980) in art education; Frankenstein (1983) in the mathematics curriculum; Moriarity and Wallerstein's (1980) work in teacher training and staff development; Crawford-Lange (1981) in foreign language instruction; and Alschuler (1980) in school discipline. Mackie (1981) is a good source for understanding Freirean pedagogy critically, albeit sympathetically. Freire's most recent collaborative works with Macedo and Shor on the politics of education, adult literacy, and transforming education are up-to-date references on the current state of the method (Freire 1985; Freire and Macedo 1987; Shor and Freire 1987). Also, the publication *Radical Teacher* consistently has information on Freirean pedagogy. Although I'm not sure they still exist, the newsletters *Education Liberadora* (*Liberating Education*) and *Second Thoughts* were excellent sources for people networking in the Freirean method.

Finally, Herbert Gintis (1984) states. "The political economy of learning . . . is based on the principle that learning occurs most effectively, and with the greatest positive acceptance on the part of the learners, when the educational environment empowers the powers." In this paper I have tried to show that the problem-posing approach has the potential to challenge the problem posed, and to engage, challenge, and empower the students who pose it and the educators who initiate the process.

REFERENCES

Alschuler, Alfred. 1980. *School Discipline: A Socially Literate Solution*. New York: McGraw-Hill.

Castro, Tony. 1979. "Los Angeles: A Movie Fights Back," *Los Angeles Herald Examiner*, April 6.

Champlin, Charles. 1979. "Brothers on the Boulevard." *Los Angeles Times*, March 23, Section IV, Page 1.

Chandler, Robert, 1978. Correspondence dated December 29, 1978 to Armando Morales on behalf of CBS Inc. concerning the *60 Minutes* segment "West Coast Story."

Council on Interracial Books for Children. 1977. *Stereotypes Distortions and Omissions in U.S. History Textbooks*. New York: Racism and Sexism Resource Center.

Crawford-Lange, Linda. 1981. "Redirecting Second Language Curricula: Paulo Freire's Contribution." *Foreign Language Annals* 14: 257–268.

Del Olmo, Frank. 1979. " 'Nights': A View from East L.A." *Los Angeles Times*, March 18, Section IV, Page 1.

Fiore, Kyle, and Nan Elaster. 1982. " 'Strangers No More': A Liberatory Literacy Curriculum." *College English* 44: 115–128.

Frankenstein, Marilyn, 1983. "Critical Mathematics Education: An Application of Paulo Freire's Epistemology." *Journal of Education* 165.315–339.

Freire, Paulo. 1970. *Cultural Action for Freedom*. Cambridge MA: Harvard Educational Review Monographs.

———. 1973. *Pedagogy of the Oppressed*. New York: Seabury.

———. 1985. *The Politics of Education: Culture, Power, and Liberation*. South Hadley, MA: Bergin and Garvey.

———, and Donaldo Macedo. 1987. *Literacy: Reading the Word and the World*. South Hadley, MA: Bergin and Garvey.

Gang Exploitation Film Committee. 1979. *A Reader and Information Packet on 'Gang' Exploitation Films*. Monterey Park, CA: East Los Angeles College MECHA.

Gintis, Herbert. 1984. "The Political Economy of Literacy Training." *Unesco Courier*. February, Pages 15–16.

Grant. Lee. 1979a. "Chicanos Picket 'Boulevard Nights.'" *Los Angeles Times*, March 23, Section I, Page 19.

———. 1979b. "Produce Hits 'Nights' Closing." *Los Angeles Times*, March 28, Section IV, Page 17.

Heller, Celia. 1966. *Mexican American Youth: Forgotten Youth at the Crossroads*. New York: Random House.

Hernandez, Carrol, Marsha Haug, and National Wagner, 1976. *Chicanos: Social and Psychological Perspectives*. St. Louis: Mosby.

Hodder, Geoffrey. 1980. "Human Praxis: A New Basic Assumption for Adult Education of the Future." Adult Literacy Education." *College English* 50:177–189.

Holzman 1988

Jeffries. Georgia. 1979. "The Lowrider of Whittier Boulevard." *American Film*, February. Page 58.

Keller, Gray. 1985. *Chicano Cinema: Research, Reviews, and Resources*. Binghamton, NY: Bilingual Review Press.

Kilday, Gregg 1978. "The Gang's All Here." *Los Angeles Times*, September 10, Calendar Section, Page 23.

Knoedelseder, William. 1978. "Filming 'Gang'—A West Side Story." *Los Angeles Times*, September 10, Calendar Section, Page 1.

Lamb, Blaine. 1975. "The Convenient Villain: The Early Cinema View of the Mexican American." *Journal of the West* 14:75–81.

Landsbaum, Mark. 1979. "Theater Cancels 'Boulevard' Film after Violence." *Los Angeles Times*, March 29, Section II, Page 1.

Mackie, Robert. 1981. *Literacy and Revolution: The Pedagogy of Paulo Freire*. New York: Continuum.

Martinez. Thomas. 1969. "Advertising and Racism: The Case of the Mexican-American." *El Grito: A Journal of Contemporary Mexican American Thought* 2: 3–13.

Mirande, Alfredo. 1978. "Chicano Sociology: A New Paradigm for Social Science." *Pacific Sociological Review* 21: 293–312.

Moore, Joan (with Robert Garcia, Carlos Garcia, Luis Cerda, and Frank Valencia). 1978. *Homeboys: Gangs, Drugs and Prisons in the Barrios of Los Angeles*. Philadelphia: Temple University Press.

Morales, Armando. 1972. *Ando Sangrando (I Am Bleeding): A Study of Mexican American Police Conflict*. La Puente, CA: Perspectiva.

———. 1978 Correspondence dated December 19, 1978 to Robert Salant, President of CBS Inc. on behalf of the Coalition of Mexicanos/Latinos Against Defamation concerning the *60 Minutes* segment "West Coast Story."

Moriarity, Pia, and Nina Wallerstein. 1980. "By Teaching We Can Learn: Freire Process for Teachers." *California Journal of Teacher Education* 7:39–46.

Nuestro Magazine. 1979. "Movie Industry Tries to Portray 'Gangs'?" February. Page 9.

Sagrow. Michael. 1979. "Nights on 'Boulevard' Due Today." *Los Angeles Herald Examiner*, March 23, Section B, Page 1.

Schreger, Charles. 1979. "Gang Movie Stirs Controversy." *Los Angeles Times*. March 28, Section IV, Page 14.

Shor, Ira. 1980, *Critical Teaching and Everyday Life*. Boston: South End.

Shor, Ira, and Paulo Freire, 1987. *A Pedagogy for Liberation: Dialogues on Transforming Education*. South Hadley, MA: Bergin and Garvey.

Smith, William, and Alfred Alschuler. 1976. "How to Measure Freire's Stages of Conscientizacão: The C Code Manual." Unpublished manuscript, University of Massachusetts, Amherst.

Trujillo, Larry. 1974. "La Evolucion del 'Bandido' al 'Pachuco': A Critical Examination and Evaluation of Criminological Literature on Chicanos." *Issues in Criminology* 9: 43–67.

United States Bureau of the Census. 1972a. *Census of Housing: 1970, Volume 1, Housing Characteristics for States, Cities, and Countries, Part 6, California.* Washington, DC: United States Government Printing Office.

————. 1972b. *Census of Housing: 1970. Block Statistics, Final Report HC(3)-18.* Los Angeles-Long Beach, California Urbanized Area. Washington, DC: United States Government Printing Office.

————. 1972c. *1970 Census of Population and Housing, Census Tracts.* Los Angeles-Long Beach Standard Metropolitan Statistical Area, Part 1 and 2. Washington, DC: United States Government Printing Office.

————. 1973. *Census of Population: 1970, Volume 1, Characteristics of the Population, Part 6, California-Sections 1 and 2.* Washington, DC: United States Government Printing Office.

United States Commission on Civil Rights. 1977. *Window Dressing on the Set.* Washington, DC: United States Commission on Civil Rights.

————. 1979. *Window Dressing on the Set: An Update.* Washington, DC: United States Commission on Civil Rights.

Wallerstein, Nina. 1983. *Language and Culture in Conflict: Problem-Posing in the ESL Classroom.* Reading, MA: Addison-Wesley.

Warren, Elaine. 1979. "The Politics of a Gang Film's Premiere." *Los Angeles Herald Examiner*, March 22, Section A, Page 1.

Wilson, John. 1978. "Hollywood and the Chicano." *Los Angeles Times.* September 17, Calendar Section, Page 1.

Woll, Allen. 1977. *The Latin Image in American Film.* Los Angeles: ULCA Latin American Studies Center.

19

Effective Instruction for
Language Minority Students:
The Teacher

Eugene E. Garcia

In the fervent debate over how best to educate bilingual students, one issue is often overlooked: the effectiveness of teachers. Research has focused primarily on competing types of language minority programs, and the results have been inconclusive. Over the last decade, project assessment reports have not yielded any clear-cut answers as to the effectiveness of different program types (for reviews, see August & Garcia, 1988; Baker & de Kanter, 1983; Hakuta & Gould, 1987; Troike, 1981; Willig, 1985). Thus, rather than emphasizing differential program effects, this paper focuses on teaching. I have attempted to identify those attributes which characterize "exemplary" teachers serving language minority students in the elementary school years.

A concern for the effectiveness of teachers is not new. From the earliest days of evaluating educational programs, the quality of the instructional staff has been considered a significant feature (Heath, 1982). Unfortunately, this concern has often been missing in the evaluation of programs serving language minority students. "Effectiveness" has been defined by an empirical concern regarding the significance of the use/non-use of the students' native language and the academic development of the English language (August & Garcia, 1988). Very little attention has been given to the attributes of the professional and para-professional staff who implement the programs. Researchers have typically recorded only such superficial characteristics as years of service and extent of formal educational training (Olsen, 1988). Yet, most educational researchers will grant that any instructional intervention depends for its effectiveness on the instructors who implement it.

Within the field of language minority education, there has been growing dissatisfaction with unproductive debates over the relative effectiveness of bilingual education (Hakuta, 1986; Hakuta & Garcia, 1989). This field has continually been subjected to national evaluations (most recently, Ramirez, Yuen, Ramey, & Pasta, 1991), that assess the effects of various approaches. Such studies, widely criticized for their methodological flaws, have little effect on what teachers actually do in classrooms (August & Garcia, 1988). Beginning with William Tikunoff (1983), some scholars have conducted in-depth studies of particular schools and classrooms which are "working" for language minority students (Carter & Chatfield, 1986; Garcia, 1988; Pease-Alvarez, Garcia, & Espinosa, 1991). Such an emphasis suggests that there is much to learn from programs that are serving language minority students well. Instead of searching for the "best" program by doing large-scale comparative studies, all which will likely be methodologically flawed, this new line of inquiry suggests that we search out effective programs and carefully document the attributes that make them effective.

In this "micro" spirit, the present study attempts to advance our understanding of what makes good language minority teachers. Such a study required the reliable identification of the exemplary teachers (no small task), followed by interviews with these teachers and observation of their work. In addition, interviews of school administrators and parents helped give a more comprehensive perspective on these teachers. I do not mean to suggest that all good language minority teachers need to be like the ones discussed in this work. But I do hope to describe the attributes of these effective teachers in such a way that others may use this information to better serve language minority students.

CHARACTERISTICS OF EFFECTIVE TEACHERS FOR LANGUAGE MINORITY STUDENTS

Tikunoff (1983) reported on the Significant Bilingual Instructional Features (SBIF) study, which observed 58 teachers at six sites with a variety of non-English languages. Teachers were considered "effective" on two criteria: First, teachers were nominated by members of four constituencies—teachers, other school personnel, students, and parents—as being effective. Second, their teaching produced rates of "academic learning time" (a measure of student engagement in academic tasks) at least as high as that reported in other effective teaching research.

Successful teachers of limited-English-proficient students appeared to share the following characteristics:

1. They communicated high expectations for what their students would learn, while conveying a sense of confidence in their own ability to teach.
2. Like effective teachers in general, they used "active teaching" methods found to be effective in improving students' performance on tests of reading and mathematics, including these: (a) they communicated clearly when giving directions and presenting new information; (b) they engaged students by pacing instruction appropriately, promoting involvement, and communicating their expectations for students' success in completing instructional tasks; (c) they monitored students' progress, and (d) they provided immediate feedback whenever required.
3. They used both the students' native language and English for instruction, alternating between the two languages whenever necessary to ensure clarity of instruction (but without translating directly from one language to another).

The SBIF study also reports that the successful teachers made use of information from the students' home culture so as to promote engagement in instructional tasks and contribute to a feeling of trust between children and their teachers. The SBIF researchers found three ways in which home and community culture was incorporated into classroom life: (a) teachers used cultural referents in both verbal and nonverbal forms in communicating with students; (b) teachers built their instruction upon rules of discourse from the L1 culture; and (c) values and norms of the L1 culture were respected equally with those of the school.

In more recent research which focused on Mexican-American elementary school children, I reported several findings related to instructional strategies utilized in "effective" schools (Garcia, 1988). These schools were nominated by language minority colleagues and had students scoring at or above the national average on Spanish and/or English standardized measures of academic achievement. My research characterized instruction in the effective classrooms as follows:

1. Students were instructed primarily in small groups and academic-related discourse was encouraged between students throughout the day. Teachers rarely utilized large-group instruction or more individualized (mimeographed worksheets) instructional activities. The most common activity across classes involved small groups of students working on assigned academic tasks with intermittent assistance by the teacher.
2. Teachers tended to use a technique often reported in the literature (Mehan, 1979; Morine-Dershimer, 1985) of eliciting student responses at relatively low cognitive and linguistic levels.
3. After eliciting a lesson, teachers encouraged students to take control of the discourse by inviting fellow-student interaction, usually at higher-order cognitive and linguistic levels.

Teachers in my 1988 study fulfilled general expectations reported by Hugh Mehan (1979) for regular classroom teachers and by Arnulfo Ramirez (1986) for language minority teachers. Teachers did not invite instructional interaction in other than the most communicatively simple mode (factual and truncated "answer giving"). This type of elicitation style may be particularly harmful for Hispanic students, who may not be challenged to use either their native or second language to express higher-order cognitive processes.

However, teachers in my 1988 study were clearly allowing student-to-student interaction in the child-reply component of the instructional discourse segment. Teachers encouraged and engineered general student participation once the instructional peer interaction was set in motion. This finding is particularly significant. An earlier study (Garcia, 1983) suggests that such student-to-student interaction discourse strategies enhance linguistic development. Wong-Fillmore and Valdez (1986) report that peer interaction is particularly significant for enhancing second-language oral acquisition in Hispanic children. Moreover Spencer Kagan (1986) has suggested that schooling practices which focus on collaborative child-child instructional strategies fit the social patterns of Mexican-American families. The interactional style documented in this study seems to be beneficial, both linguistically and culturally, to Mexican-American students.

My earlier study, much like the SBIF report, strongly suggests that teachers can play a significant role in English language development for language minority students. The present study attempts to extend this previous work by focusing on a case study of one school and three elementary teachers identified by their peers as "effective" instructors for Mexican-American language minority students. In doing so, we may improve our understanding of effective schooling practices for serving language minority students. As a number of educators and researchers have noted (Heath, 1982; Wilcox, 1982), education, like any other social phenomenon, is best understood when placed within a larger set of circumstances. Consequently, this case study will touch on the demographic, social, political, and pedagogical contexts. As in the classic case study, I interviewed teachers, principals, parents, and students and conducted systematic classroom observations. I have sought to bring these sources of data together to tell an informed story of effective language minority education with particular attention to the teacher.

THE SCHOOL AND COMMUNITY

Field Town School is located in central California. The school serves students and families from different socioeconomic and ethnic backgrounds; 70% are Chicano/Latino. To encourage integration of Anglos, an academic program with clear goals and expectations was developed. In addition, the school is committed to dual language and literacy development in Spanish and English for all participating students, regardless of native language or ethnic affiliation.

The school is located in a heavily agricultural area of the central California coast. Anglos and Mexicans have lived in this community since 1848, the year California was annexed to the United States. Since that time Anglos have gained a firm economic foothold in the community and have come to dominate its farming, which produces mainly apples, strawberries, and lettuce. Historically, minority populations, first Asian- and later Mexican-origin, have provided cheap labor and thereby have ensured the economic success of their Anglo employers.

The Mexican-origin population began to grow rapidly in the late 1950s as the U.S. government encouraged an influx of cheap farm labor to meet the needs of a rapidly expanding agricultural economy. The late 1960s and early 1970s were characterized by increasing interethnic turmoil over political and social inequities. Currently over half of the total Field Town population and 58% of the school-age population is of Latino origin. Latino growth is attributed to the continual flow of Mexican immigrants who are employed as farm workers. First- and second-generation Mexican Americans, who tend to work as skilled or semi-skilled laborers, also make up a sizable proportion of the total population.

The area's Anglo population is predominantly middle-class; it includes professionals, business people, and a number of people who work in agriculture but not as farm workers. Many of the Anglo families trace their roots to Slavic immigrants who came to the area during the late 19th century and early 20th century. Asians have also had a significant impact on the community: Chinese, Filipino, and Japanese laborers came to the region in successive waves. Several Japanese families have prospered in agriculture to the point of owning their own fruit-packing businesses.

Field Town School is considered one of the district's bilingual schools. The curriculum is structured so that Latino and Anglo students receive subject matter instruction in their native languages. The curriculum focuses on mastery of a specific inventory of skills that are delineated for each grade level. Students receive additional instruction in science and computers, physical education, and music from specialists who are supported by desegregation funds. The school aims to produce English-competent students by the end of sixth grade, but not to "force" students into a transition from Spanish to English.

ATTRIBUTES OF "EFFECTIVE" TEACHERS

The present study focused on three teachers—one each at the first, third, and fifth-grade levels—at the Field Town School. These teachers were consistently identified at their school and at the district level as effective teachers. Approximately 50% to 70% of their students were Spanish-dominant, the remainder being English-dominant. The findings of this study regarding teacher attributes will be divided into four distinct but interlocking domains: (1) knowledge, (2) skills, (3) dispositions, and (4) affect.

Knowledge

These teachers were all bilingual and biliterate in English and Spanish. They had the prerequisite state teacher credentials and had graduated from bilingual teacher training programs. They had an average of 7.1 years experience as bilingual teachers. These were not novices. They were also not complacent: they reported that they routinely participated in staff development efforts, either taking courses or attending workshops on techniques that they wanted to implement in their classrooms. Some of the workshops, sponsored by the school or district, were mandatory, but these teachers also participated in courses that they sought out and financed on their own. Some of these latter courses related to Spanish language development and others related to pedagogy.

These teachers were quite knowledgeable and articulate with regard to the instructional philosophies which guided them. They communicated these coherently in their interviews. They never hesitated in addressing "why" they were using specific instructional techniques and usually couched these explanations in terms of a theoretical position regarding teaching and student learning. Principals and parents also commented on these teachers' ability to communicate effectively the rationales for their instructional techniques. One principal commented, "She's always able to defend her work with her students. When she first came here, I didn't agree with all that she was doing, and sometimes I still do not agree. But she always helps me understand why she is doing what she is doing. I respect her for that. She is not a 'recipe' teacher." A parent commented with regard to her child's journal writing: "I didn't understand why she was letting ____ make all these spelling mistakes. It annoyed me. During the teacher-parent conference, she showed me the progress ____ was making. His spelling was getting better without taking a spelling test every week. I was surprised. She knows what she's doing." A parent concerned about his daughter's difficulty with English in the third grade indicated, *"Me explicó que aprendiendo en español le va a ayudar a mi hija hablar mejor el inglés. Dice bién, porque mi hijo que vino conmigo de Mexico, hablando y escribiendo en español, aprendio el inglés muy facil.*" ("She explained that learning Spanish will help my child learn English. She has a point since my older son learned Spanish first, and English was easier.") Moreover, these teachers seemed to be quite competent in the content areas. The upper elementary teacher teaching fractions had a solid and confident understanding of fractions. She did not seem to be "one step ahead of the students."

Skills

Despite their differing perspectives, the teachers demonstrated specific instructional skills. They used English and Spanish in highly communicative ways, speaking to students with varying degrees of Spanish and English proficiency in a communicative style requiring significant language switching. They rarely translated directly from one language to another, but they frequently used language switching in contexts which required it.

Of course, variations existed among these exemplary teachers. They had developed their own sets of instructional skills which they indicated led to their own effectiveness. But there were common themes:

1. *Teachers adopt an experiential stance toward instruction.* Along with many of their colleagues, these exemplary teachers had abandoned a strictly skills-oriented approach to instruction. To varying degrees they organized instruction in their classes so that children first focus on that which is meaningful to them. Early-grade teachers used an approach to reading instruction that treats specific skills in the context of extended pieces of text (e.g., an entire book, passage, or paragraph). They initiated shared reading experiences by reading to and with children from an enlarged book, pointing to each word as they read. Because most of these books rely on a recurring pattern (e.g., a repeating syntactical construction, rhyming words, repetitions), children who cannot read words in isolation are able to predict words and entire constructions when participating in choral reading activities. With time the teacher encourages students to focus on individual words, sound-letter correspondences, and syntactic constructions. The teacher also encourages children to rely on other cueing systems as they predict and confirm what they have read as a group or individually.

These teachers also used a thematic curriculum. Science and social studies themes are often integrated across a variety of subject areas. Once a theme is decided upon, usually in consultation with students, the teacher plans instruction around a series of activities that focus on that theme. For example, a unit on dinosaurs included reading books about dinosaurs, categorizing and graphing different kinds of dinosaurs, touring a museum that features dinosaur exhibits, writing stories or poems about a favorite dinosaur, and speculating on the events that led to the dinosaurs' disappearance. In the third-grade classroom, a student suggested that the class address "the stuff in the field that makes my little brother sick": pesticides. The teacher developed a four-week theme which engaged students in understanding the dangers of pesticide use in their community.

Despite the use of instructional strategies that depart from traditional skills-based approaches to curriculum and instruction, these teachers did sometimes structure learning around individual skills or discrete components. For example, the teachers devote a week or two to preparing students for standardized tests. During this time they teach skills that will be tested and they administer practice tests. Said one teacher: "I don't like testing. But we have to do it. I teach my kids how to mark the bubbles and I make sure that they take their time. We practice test-taking, but we don't take it serious."

2. *Teachers provide opportunities for active learning.* These teachers organized a good portion of class time around a series of learning activities that children pursue either independently or with others. During science and math, children work in small groups doing a variety of hands-on activities designed to support their understanding of a particular concept (e.g., classification, estimation, place value) or subject area (e.g., oceanography, dinosaurs).

Each teacher's commitment to active learning was revealed in her commitment to a studio or workshop format for literacy instruction. Instead of teaching students about reading and writing, teachers organize their program so that students actively read and write. Real reading and writing takes place in the context of a literature-based reading program and during regularly scheduled times when students write in their journals on topics of their own choosing and teachers respond to their entries. There is also time for students to engage in writer's workshop. Generating their own topics during the workshop, the students write, revise, edit, and publish their finished writings. Like adult published authors, they share their writing with others and often receive input that helps them revise and improve upon what they have written. One teacher commented, "These kids produce their own reading material and they take it home to share it with their parents. It's real good stuff. I help a little, but it's the kids that help each other the most."

3. *Teachers encourage collaborative/cooperative interactions among students.* These teachers organize instruction so that students spend time working together on a wide range of instructional activities. The two primary-grade teachers structure their day so that students work on group and individual activities (e.g., graphing, journal writing, science projects) in small heterogeneously organized groups. Teachers felt that cross-cultural interactions are much more likely to take place when students are obliged to work together to complete a single task.

Dispositions

I have classified a number of teacher attributes as "dispositions" because I find no other category that applies. They are individual characteristics which these teachers possess, characteristics which they share with successful professionals in all fields. For instance, these teachers are highly dedicated. They reported working very hard, getting to school first and being the last to leave, working weekends, and sometimes feeling completely overworked. They reported spending close to $2,000 of their own money in modifying their room and obtaining the materials their students need. They indicated that they see themselves as "creative," "resourceful," "committed," "energetic," "persistent," and "collaborative." They seek assistance from their colleagues and are ready to provide as much assistance as they receive.

Although these teachers feel they are effective, they are not complacent. They have greatly changed their instructional practices (and in some cases their philosophies) over the years: they have shifted "paradigms." These teachers, who once advocated skills-based and authoritarian modes of instruction such as "DISTAR," are now experimenting with child-centered approaches. Moving away from authoritarian modes in the classroom, teachers say they enjoy a certain degree of autonomy in their school. They feel that they are free to implement the changes that they want. In recent years, when they have wanted to implement something new in their classrooms, they have gone to their principal with a carefully thought-out rationale and have eventually enlisted his support. These teachers have been involved in change that has had an impact on other classrooms as well as their own. Along with other teachers, they have obtained support to eliminate teaming and ability grouping across subject areas in the first grade. In addition, they have taken part in a district-wide teacher-initiated movement to eliminate kindergarten testing. In short, these teachers have been involved in individual and group efforts to improve the quality of education at the school. They are highly committed to improving themselves personally as well as the education profession and the service to students in general.

Above all, they are highly confident, even a bit cocky, regarding their instructional abilities. They say such things as: "I have changed my own view on how students learn—we need to understand learning does not occur in bits and pieces. Why do teachers still insist on teaching that way?" "I know what I am doing is good for kids. Some of my colleagues say I work too hard—I say they do not work hard enough. Not that they are lazy, they just don't seem to understand how important it is to do this job right." "I know my kids are doing well, all of them. I would rather keep them with me all day than send them to someone who is supposed to help them in their 'special' needs but doesn't help them at all."

Affect

These teachers feel strongly that classroom practices that reflect the cultural and linguistic background of minority students are important ways of enhancing student self-esteem. Part of their job, as they see it, is to provide the kind of cultural and linguistic validation that is missing in Field Town, a community known for deprecating the Latino culture and Spanish language. According to these teachers, learning Spanish and learning about Latino culture benefits Anglo students as well as Latino students. In their eyes, people who learn a second language tend to be more sensitive to other cultures. It seems particularly important to learn a language that is shared by so many residents of this country. These teachers feel that being bilingual and bicultural will enrich their students' lives.

Latino culture is reflected in the content of the curriculum in various ways. The two primary-grade teachers, who organize their curriculum around a variety of student-generated themes, address cultural experiences of Latino students within the themes. For example, in a unit on monsters they may highlight Mexican legends and folktales that deal with the supernatural. In addition, these teachers use literature that reflects the culture of their Latino students. They also encourage students to share favorite stories, poems, and sayings that they have learned at home.

These teachers had high expectations for all their students. As one put it:

No "*pobrecito*" syndrome here—I want all my students to learn and I know they can learn even though they may come from very poor families

and may live under "tough" conditions. I can have them do their homework here and I can even get them a tutor—an older student—if they need
it. I understand that their parents may not be able to help them at home.
That's no excuse for them not learning.

These teachers portrayed themselves as quite demanding: they take no excuses
from students for not accomplishing assigned work and they are willing to be
"tough" on those students who are "messing around."

Most significant was the teachers' affinity toward their students. They made
such comments as: "These students are like my very own children." "I love these
children like my own. I know that parents expect me to look after their kids and to
let them know if they are in trouble." "When I walk into that classroom I know we
are a family and we're going to be together a whole year. . . . I try to emphasize first
that we are a family here. . . . I tell my students, 'You're like brothers and sisters'
and some students even call me Mom or Tia. It's just like being at home here." Each
teacher spoke of the importance of strong and caring relationships among class
members and particularly between the teacher and the students. They feel that this
provides students with a safe environment that is conductive to learning.

Parents also reported a similar feeling. They directly referred to the teachers in
the interviews as members of an extended family, as persons to be trusted, respected,
and honored for their service to their children. These teachers are often invited to
"*bautismos,*" "*bodas,*" "*fiestas de cumpleanos,*" soccer games, and family barbe-
cues. And they attended such occasions, reporting that such participation was inherently rewarding and instructive with regard to their own personal and professional
lives. Parents made comments such as these: "*La señorita ___, le tengo mucha confi-
anza, quiero que mi niño la respete como a mi*" ("I trust the teacher, I want my child
to respect her just as he respects me"); "Nunca se larga mi nina de ella, se porta
como mi hermana, siempre le puedo hablar y me gusta mucho ayudarle" ("My
daughter is 'close' to her, she's like my sister, I can always talk to her and enjoy helping her"); "I know my son is well cared for in her class, I never worry—she even calls
me when he does something good."

CONCLUSION

This case study has described attributes of teachers who are considered effective
for language minority students. These teachers are highly experienced, not
novices to teaching or to the instruction of language minority students. They are
highly skilled in communication with students, parents, and their administrative
supervisors. They think about and communicate their own instructional philosophies. They work hard to understand the community which they serve, and they
incorporate attributes of the local culture into the curriculum. They have
adopted instructional methods which are student-centered, collaborative, and
process oriented—no "worksheet" curriculum here. They collaborate with their
colleagues. They undertake activities for personal and professional growth. Most
significantly, these teachers care for their students: they are advocates. Having
"adopted" their students, they watch out for their students' welfare while at the

same time— far from accepting the *"pobrecito"* syndrome—they challenge students with high expectations. Like much research, this study raises a number of questions that merit further and more in-depth investigation. Are the attributes described here necessary for any exemplary teacher, not only those who serve children of diverse linguistic and cultural backgrounds? The most interesting questions concern the future of these teachers: Will they continue to be effective? If so, will they modify their perspectives and their instructional techniques?

Since the sample of this study was quite small, it needs to be asked whether the attributes which characterize these teachers are requisite for other effective language minority teachers. Certainly, more research specification to the education of language minority education and those who implement such education effectively is needed. I hope that the story told by this study will help stimulate such research.

REFERENCES

August, D., & Garcia, E. E. (1988). *Language minority education in the United States.* Springfield, IL: Charles C. Thomas.

Baker, K., & de Kanter, A. A. (1983). An answer from research on bilingual education. *American Education, 19*(6), 40–48.

Carter, T. P., & Chatfield, M. L. (1986). Effective bilingual schools: Implications for policy and practice. *American Journal of Education, 95*(1), 200–234.

Garcia, E. (1983). *Bilingualism in early childhood.* Albuquerque: University of New Mexico Press.

Garcia, E. (1988). Effective schooling for Hispanics. *Urban Education Review, 67*(2), 462–473.

Hakuta, K. (1986). *Mirror of language: The debate on bilingualism.* New York: Basic Books.

Hakuta, K., & Garcia, E. (1989). Bilingualism and education. *American Psychologist, 44*(2), 374–379.

Hakuta, K., & Gould, L. J. (1987). Synthesis of research on bilingual education. *Educational Leadership, 44*(6), 38–45.

Heath, S. B. (1982). Ethnography in education: Defining the essentials. In P. Gilmore & A. A. Glatthorn (Eds.), *Children in and out of school* (pp. 131–163). Washington, DC: Center for Applied Linguistics.

Kagan, S. (1986). Cooperative learning and sociocultural factors in schooling. In *Beyond language: Social and cultural factors in schooling language minority students* (pp. 231–298). Los Angeles, CA: Evaluation, Dissemination, and Assessment Center, California State University, Los Angeles.

Mehan, H. (1979). *Learning lessons.* Cambridge: Harvard University Press.

Morine-Dershimer, G. (1985). *Talking, listening and learning in elementary classrooms.* New York: Longman.

Olsen, L. (1988). *Crossing the school house border: Immigrant students and the California public schools.* San Francisco: California Tomorrow.

Pease-Alvarez, C., Garcia, E., & Espinosa, P. (in press). Effective instruction for language minority students: An early childhood case study. *Early Childhood Research Quarterly.*

Ramirez, A. (1986). *Bilingualism through schooling.* Albany: State University of New York Press.

Ramirez, J. D., Yuen, S. D., Ramey, D. R., & Pasta, D. J. (1991). *Final report: Longitudinal study of immersion strategy, early-exit and late-exit transitional bilingual education programs for language-minority children.* San Mateo, CA: Aguirre International.

Tikunoff, W. J. (1983). *Compatibility of the SBIF features with other research instruction of LEP students.* San Francisco: Far West Laboratory (SBIF-83-4.8/10).

Troike, R. C. (1981). Synthesis of research in bilingual education. *Educational Leadership, 38*(6), 498–504.

Wilcox, K. (1982). Ethnography as a methodology and its application to the study of schooling: A review. In G. Spindler (Ed.), *Doing the ethnography of schooling* (pp. 381–395). New York: Holt, Rinehart, and Winston.

Willig, A. C. (1985). A meta-analysis of selected studies on effectiveness of bilingual education. *Review of Educational Research, 55,* 269–317.

Wong-Fillmore, L., & Valdez, C. (1986). Teaching bilingual learners. In M. C. Wittrock (Ed.), *Handbook of research on teaching* (3rd ed., pp. 684–685). New York: Macmillan.

20

Promoting the Success of Latino Language-Minority Students: An Exploratory Study of Six High Schools

Tamara Lucas
Rosemary Henze
Ruben Donato

In "Effective Schools for the Urban Poor," Ron Edmonds states: "All children are eminently educable, and the behavior of the school is critical in determining the quality of the education. . . ." (1979, p. 20). This way of thinking diverges from often-cited "deficit" models of education, which account for student failure by reference to certain cultural, linguistic, and socioeconomic factors in students' backgrounds, thus making a liability out of difference. Language-minority (LM) students in particular have often been blamed for their underachievement in U.S. schools.[1] By considering them "difficult" or culturally and linguistically "deprived," schools have found it easy to absolve themselves of responsibility for the education of these students. Edmonds, on the other hand, places the responsibility for quality education squarely in the hands of the schools.

This assignment of responsibility for language-minority students has had a complex legal history. In 1973 the Supreme Court held, in the *Lau v. Nichols* decision, that public schools had to provide an education comprehensible to limited-English-proficient (LEP) students.[2] In an attempt to equalize educational opportunities for LEP students in U.S. schools, the Court stated: "Basic English is at the very core of what public schools teach. Imposition of a requirement that, before a child can effectively participate in the education program, he must already have acquired those basic skills is to make a mockery of public education" (*Lau v. Nichols*, 1973).

The *Lau* decision has had a powerful impact on the education of language-minority students. It marked the beginning of a national interest in educational equity for LM students and provoked policymakers throughout the country to respond to the special needs of this growing student population. After 1974, under pressure from the federal government, many states began to push school districts to develop programs for LM students. California, for example, passed a bill in 1976 mandating bilingual education in its public schools.[3] School districts in California with large numbers of LEP students were required by the state to demonstrate how they were going to serve those students. For the most part, however, school districts focused on LEP students in elementary schools and ignored the schooling of secondary LEP students.

However, secondary schools do enroll many students whose English proficiency is limited. For example, poor economic conditions in Mexico have caused large numbers of Mexican students to arrive in the Southwest, with or without their families. Political unrest and war have brought thousands of refugees to the United States from such countries as El Salvador, Nicaragua, Guatemala, Vietnam, Cambodia, Laos, and Afghanistan. Students of all ages often arrive with little or no knowledge of English. Because of wartime conditions in their countries, many students have had interrupted schooling and thus come unprepared not only in English, but also in content knowledge, basic study skills, and knowledge of school culture. Providing effective schooling for these students is particularly challenging at the secondary level, when students are expected to possess a wealth of implicit and explicit knowledge about how to be a student.

On the other hand, many immigrant students arrive in the United States with strong educational backgrounds; for example, those who have attended "*Secundaria*" in Mexico may have had higher levels of math than their U.S.-born peers. Secondary LM students, in other words, are extremely diverse, bringing with them educational, social, academic, and cultural experiences that may differ widely from those of members of the host culture. To assure academic success, schools must attend to this diversity through special programs and practices, and through increased sensitivity to students' needs. High drop-out rates, low standardized test scores, poor attendance records, and the small numbers of students going on to post-secondary education all attest to the failure of most high schools to meet the needs of this student population (See Arias, 1986; Brown & Haycock, 1984; Espinosa & Ochoa, 1986; Gingras & Careaga, 1989; Medina, 1988; Orfield, 1986; Orum, 1988; Rumberger, 1987; U.S. General Accounting Office, 1987).

Because we believe that schools are responsible for the quality of education students receive, and that, given a good education, all students can achieve, we are interested in what makes some schools more successful than others. During the past fifteen years, some educational researchers have turned away from attempting to explain school and student failure and have focused instead on explaining success, producing a body of research known as the "effective schools" literature. This work, most of which comes from studies conducted in urban elementary schools, provides some insight into the attributes of successful schools, including strong leadership; high expectations of students; school-wide staff development; parent involvement and support; recognition of students' academic success; district support; collaborative planning; collegial relationships; and sense of community (Edmonds, 1979; Purkey & Smith, 1983).

The research on effective schools is not without its detractors, however. Critics have pointed to shortcomings in the literature, citing, for example, lack of generalizability to any but elementary schools; lack of attention to the variety of student populations and community contexts; an over-emphasis on attributes and lack of sufficient attention to complex processes and interrelationships; and a top-down strategy for school improvement growing out of the "implementation of attributes" approach (See Carter & Chatfield, 1986; Rosenholtz, 1985; Rowen, Bossert, & Dwyer, 1983; Stedman, 1987; Wilson & Corcoran, 1988).

One of the most frequent criticisms is that the effective schools literature has given little attention to what makes some schools more successful than others with language-minority students. Jennifer Bell (1989) has offered several reasons for this lack of attention. First, since most of the effective schools studies were conducted in schools which were predominantly Black and White in composition, LM students were not a major factor in overall student achievement. Second, with certain exceptions, most researchers did not consider language to be an important factor in student achievement. Third, the diversity of LM students was generally considered too difficult to account for in research design. Furthermore, since the public has been so sharply divided over bilingual instruction, research on LM students in the schools has focused primarily on the role of language in instruction rather than on the effectiveness of the whole school.

Recently, however, some studies have focused on effective schooling for language-minority students. Thomas Carter and Michael Chatfield (1986) reported on characteristics of three effective bilingual elementary schools, emphasizing processes over structures and attributes. The schools they described were characterized by such factors as: a well-functioning total system producing a school climate that promotes positive student outcomes; positive leadership, usually from the formal leaders; high staff expectations for students and instructional programs; strong demand for academic performance; denial of the cultural deprivation argument and stereotypes that support it; and high staff morale.

Bruce Wilson and Thomas Corcoran (1988) report on a number of middle and secondary schools that are successful with "at risk" students, which they define as students from poor and minority backgrounds (p. 130). Since some of the schools had sizable numbers of Latino and Asian students, we can assume that some of them were language-minority students, although the authors do not discuss the language backgrounds or English proficiency of students. The common elements of these successful schools include a positive attitude toward the students, a willingness to question conventional practices, a strong and competent leadership, a highly committed teaching staff, high expectations and standards, and an emphasis on high achievement in academics.

A number of studies have examined effective instructional practices for language-minority students in elementary bilingual programs (Ramírez, 1988; Tikunoff, 1985; Wong-Fillmore, McLaughlin, Ammon, & Ammon, 1985). However, there is little research of any kind at the secondary level, and little at either the elementary or secondary level that looks beyond effective classroom instruction to the broader issues involved in effective schooling for LM students. In a critique of the ways in which the "effective schools formula" has been applied, Stedman (1987) argues for a reconceptualization of the effective schools literature, focusing on "detailed descriptions of school organization and practice" (p. 217) and on providing "concrete guidance about what to do to make a school effective" (p. 218). Ways in which good schools foster cultural pluralism need to be documented, Stedman writes, and secondary schools need to be given more attention.

The exploratory study reported here intends to narrow these gaps in the existing research and to extend our knowledge about effective schooling. The study is based on information gathered at six secondary schools that have been recognized by local, state, or federal agencies for their success in providing a quality education for LM students, not only through effective classroom instruction but also through whole-school approaches. Because previous research, such as that described above, has primarily focused on successful instructional practices for LM students, our discussion will focus its attention on the whole school rather than on classroom practices per se.

It is important to point out that there is of course no formula or prescription for success; no single combination of variables will produce an effective school. Educators cannot simply adopt the features of these six schools and expect their institutions to become successful with LM students overnight. Schools can, however, begin to work toward such success by following the lead of these schools in ways that are appropriate and realistic for their particular school settings.

We believe that the most critical element in determining whether educators can work toward success for all students is the belief that all students can succeed. In 1979, Edmonds argued that the degree to which we effectively teach "the children of the poor" depends more on our political persuasions than on the information we gain from educational research. He asserted that we already know more than enough to successfully teach all students, and that the question is whether we *want* to teach all students. Recently, Shirley Jackson (1989) made a similar assertion. Yet many educators still appear uncertain as to whether schools can significantly influence the achievement and attainment of poor and minority youths, often claiming that parents do not support their children's educational efforts and implying that therefore schools cannot be blamed for failing to educate these children (Suro 1990). In contrast, we hope that by presenting case studies of "living examples of success" (Carter & Chatfield, 1986, p. 229), we will not only encourage educators to believe that *all* students can succeed, but also provide them with concrete knowledge of what schools can do to help them.

BACKGROUND

In 1988, an initiative was undertaken by the Southwest Center for Educational Equity, at the request of and in collaboration with the Arizona Department of Education and representatives of six Arizona school districts, to develop strategies for Arizona high schools to serve language-minority students.[4] In surveying the literature on effective schooling, we realized that little was known about successful schooling for LM students at the secondary level. To gather information for the Arizona High School Initiative, we therefore conducted an exploratory study of schools promoting the achievement of this student population. We visited five high schools in California and one in Arizona that had large populations of Latino students and that had been recognized by local, state, and/or federal agencies for excellence.[5] Because the needs of different groups of LM students vary, and because we wanted to increase comparability of student populations across schools, we decided that schools working successfully with Latino LM students in particular would be the focus of this part of the initiative.[6]

METHODS

Selection of Case Study Schools

The selection of case study schools was complicated by the lack of consensus about what constitutes an "effective" or "successful" school. After much deliberation over which criteria were the most relevant, we decided to take a two-pronged approach to site selection, using both qualitative and quantitative criteria. First, we sought nominations from a variety of people familiar with secondary schools with large numbers of language-minority students, consulting with educators at state, county, and district levels and asking them to recommend schools that they believed were successful with those students (Wilson & Corcoran, 1988). We then contacted the principals of the recommended schools to determine whether they had received any formal recognition from local, state, or federal agencies for their instructional programs for LM students and whether they could provide us with some quantitative evidence of their success—for example, average daily attendance rates, drop-out rates, numbers of Latino LM students going on to post-secondary education, and standardized test scores that compared favorably with other minority schools. While we recognize that "effectiveness is a construct, an abstraction" (Wilson & Corcoran, 1988, p. 26) and that this process did not capture the full range of possible indicators of success, we believe it enabled us to select six schools which are taking identifiable, positive steps to educate LM students.

Data Collection

Data were collected at five school sites in California and one in Arizona.[7] Two to four project staff members visited each site for three days, thus providing multiple perspectives and allowing for intensive collection of information. The combined data from all six schools consisted of audiotapes and notes from structured interviews with 1 superintendent, 2 district-level bilingual program directors, 6 principals, 6 assistant principals, 5 school-level project and program directors, 15 counselors, 52 teachers and aides, and 135 students; 124 student questionnaires (35 from newcomers and 89 from non-newcomers); 54 classroom observations; schoolwide observations of the 6 schools; and various records and documents for each school, including policies regarding LM students, special program descriptions, transcripts for students who were interviewed, and other written information that interviewees gave us. Because we wanted above all to facilitate communication, we allowed students to use either English or Spanish for interviews and questionnaires, depending upon their preference. Students whose proficiency in English was very limited would not have been able to participate had they not been given the opportunity to use Spanish. Because the study sought to understand what contributes to the success of high school LM students, we were primarily interested in obtaining information from school staff who worked extensively and effectively with these students. Assistant principals, counselors, and teachers were selected to be interviewed if they 1) worked with large numbers of Latino LEP students, and 2) were recommended by others (administrators, counselors, teachers, students) as being especially effective with, and/or knowledgeable about, these students.

At each school, we asked a counselor, or in some cases a program director, to select students for us to interview. We requested six Latino students in each of four groups—high achievers, average achievers, students who had been doing poorly but had now improved, and students who had immigrated within the last two years. We also asked that students be non-native speakers of English. Though we succeeded in interviewing an average of 24 Latino LM students at each school, the distinctions among high achievers, average achievers, and "turnarounds" were not at all clear. For purposes of analysis, therefore, we grouped students only as newcomers or non-newcomers. Both groups included students from grades nine through twelve.

Sixty-one percent of the students interviewed were born in Mexico. The newcomers had arrived in the United States between the ages of fourteen and eighteen, while the non-newcomers were students born in the United States and students who had entered the United States in the early and middle grades. According to the student questionnaire, 72.5 percent of the students spoke Spanish at home, while 39 percent used Spanish at school. Ninety-eight percent of the students' fathers worked in labor- or service-related jobs, while 90 percent of the mothers worked as housewives or in service-related jobs.

In the aggregate, then, the Latino students we interviewed came from working-class backgrounds. However, they represented a tremendous range of educational and cultural experiences, from those whose entire education had been in the United States to those who had attended school in several different countries before coming here. Some students, according to the questionnaire, had had interruptions of several years in their schooling due to political unrest in their countries, while others had attended continuously. Factors such as these, combined with the different cultural identities of Mexicanos, Chicanos, Nicaragüenses, and other groups, made it clear that there is no such thing as a "typical" Latino student, and that a school successful with this population would have to be sensitive to differences in students' experiences and backgrounds.

Data Analysis

Data analysis was a recursive process which began with the design of the study. The design, influenced by previous research on effective schooling, determined who would be interviewed and what other types of data would be collected. The questions used in interviews were formulated as new issues emerged from the data. Categories for analysis, inspired at first by the effective schools literature, were continually shaped as we interviewed, observed, and gathered documents at each site. Once information-gathering had ended, intensive analysis proceeded from within-site analyses to cross-site analyses:

1.   Each person who visited a site wrote a report of the data that she or he collected from interviews, observations, and serendipitous encounters. These reports brought together all of the data collected by each researcher into one organized and accessible whole. Reports included information about the school context (community, school board, student body composition and ethnicity, language census), types of Latino LM students enrolled at the school,

what seemed to be working based on what was reported and what we saw, and what improvements were suggested to better meet the needs of the students.

2. All individual reports about each school were then synthesized into one case study report per school to provide "a well-grounded sense of the local reality" in that setting (Miles & Huberman, 1984, p. 151).

3. The six case studies were then analyzed in order to compare perceived realities

In this process, we developed both concrete descriptions of what we observed and categories or themes derived from the data and informed by other studies of effective schooling (see Merriam, 1988). This process resulted in highlighting eight features that existed across sites, as noted in the introduction. Although each school is unique, the eight features represent commonalities in the ways the schools were promoting success for language-minority students. Most of the study findings are derived from interviews with staff members and students—particularly when the same or similar features were mentioned by a large number of people in different schools—and from our informed observations. In many cases, the language of the findings reflects words or phrases we heard repeatedly. What we were told in interviews was also confirmed and concretized through classroom and school-wide observation and consultation of school records and documents.

FINDINGS

School Profiles

Five of the six schools were relatively large, with 1,700 to 2,200 students. All had minority White populations, and in all but the smallest school, Latino students constituted the largest single group—more than one-third of the school population. The four schools with the larger proportions of non-White students (Nogales, Overfelt, Sweetwater, and Newcomer) also had larger proportions of non-White staff. In none of the schools, however, was the ethnicity of the staff comparable to the student population; in all of them, a much larger proportion of staff than students was White. The percentage of students participating in a school lunch program—a rough measure of their socioeconomic status—varied considerably among the six schools. At Anaheim and Artesia, fewer than 25 percent of the students received such aid, at Overfelt and Sweetwater, about 33 percent did so, and at Nogales and Newcomer 80 percent did so. Thus, socioeconomic status of students is not a feature shared by these schools overall, although as noted earlier, the Latino students whom we interviewed were largely working class.

Key Features that Promote the Success of Language-Minority Students

Through the exploratory case studies and the analysis across cases, eight features emerged which we believe to be the most important in promoting the success of language-minority students at the six schools we visited. A more concise version of these eight features appears in Table 20.1.

TABLE 20.1 Features of High Schools that Promote the Achievement of
Language-Minority Students

1. *Value is placed on the students' languages and cultures* by:
   Treating students as individuals, not as members of a group
   Learning about students' cultures
   Learning students' languages
   Hiring bilingual staff with similar cultural backgrounds to the students
   Encouraging students to develop their primary language skills
   Allowing students to speak their primary language except when English develop-
   ment is the focus of instruction or interaction
   Offering advanced as well as lower division content courses in the students' primary
   languages
   Instituting extracurricular activities that will attract LM students

2. *High expectations of language-minority students are made concrete* by:
   Hiring minority staff in leadership positions to act as role models
   Providing a special program to prepare LM students for college
   Offering advanced and honors bilingual/sheltered classes in content areas
   Making it possible for students to exit ESL programs quickly
   Challenging students in class and providing guidance to help them meet the chal-
   lenge
   Providing counseling assistance (in the primary language if necessary) to help stu-
   dents apply to college and fill out scholarship and grant forms
   Bringing in representatives of colleges and minority graduates who are in college to
   talk to students
   Working with parents to gain their support for students going to college
   Recognizing students for doing well

3. *School leaders make the education of language-minority students a priority.* These
   leaders:
   Hold high expectations of LM students
   Are knowledgeable of instructional and curricular approaches to teaching LM stu-
   dents and communicate this knowledge to staff
   Take a strong leadership role in strengthening curriculum and instruction for all stu-
   dents, including LM students
   Are often bilingual minority-group members themselves
   Hire teachers who are bilingual and/or trained in methods for teaching LM students

4. *Staff development is explicitly designed to help teachers and other staff serve language-minority students more effectively.* Schools and school districts:
   Offer incentives and compensation so that school staff will take advantage of available staff development programs
   Provide staff development for teachers and other school staff in:
   —effective instructional approaches to teaching LM students, e.g., cooperative learning methods, sheltered English, and reading and writing in the content areas
   —principles of second-language acquisition
   —the cultural backgrounds and experiences of the students
   —the languages of the students
   —cross-cultural communication
   —cross-cultural counseling

TABLE 20.1 *Continued*

5. *A variety of courses and programs for language-minority students is offered.* The programs:
   Include courses in ESL and primary language instruction (both literacy and advanced placement) and bilingual and sheltered courses in content areas
   Insure that the course offerings for LM students do not limit their choices or trap them in low-level classes by offering advanced as well as basic courses taught through bilingual and sheltered methods
   Keep class size small (20–25 students) in order to maximize interaction
   Establish academic support programs that help LM students make the transition from ESL and bilingual classes to mainstream classes and prepare them to go to college

6. *A counseling program gives special attention to language-minority students* through counselors who:
   Speak the students' languages and are of the same or similar cultural backgrounds
   Are informed about post-secondary educational opportunities for LM students
   Believe in, emphasize, and monitor the academic success of LM students

7. *Parents of language-minority students are encouraged to become involved in their children's education.* Schools can provide and encourage:
   Staff who can speak the parents' languages
   On-campus ESL classes for parents
   Monthly parents' nights
   Parent involvement with counselors in planning their children's course schedules
   Neighborhood meetings with school staff
   Early morning meetings with parents
   Telephone contacts to check on absent students

8. *School staff members share a strong commitment to empower language-minority students through education.* This commitment is made concrete through staff who:
   Give extra time to work with LM students
   Take part in a political process that challenges the status quo
   Request training of various sorts to help LM students become more effective
   Reach out to students in ways that go beyond their job requirements, for example, by sponsoring extra-curricular activities
   Participate in community activities in which they act as advocates for Latinos and other minorities

---

1. Value is placed on the students' languages and cultures.
Rather than ignoring barriers to equality and perpetuating the disenfranchisement of minority students, the principals, administrators, counselors, teachers, and other support staff at the schools we visited celebrated diversity. They gave language-minority students the message that their languages and cultures were valued and respected, thus promoting the self-esteem necessary for student achievement. They communicated this sense of value and respect in a number of concrete ways, translating the ideal into an everyday reality.

First, the ability to speak a language in addition to English was treated as an advantage rather than a liability. A number of White and Latino teachers and counselors who were not native speakers of Spanish had learned the language. Some spoke it well enough to understand some of what their students said; others had learned it well enough to teach bilingual content classes. Students commented in interviews that they appreciated efforts made by teachers to speak Spanish and were pleased to see that the teachers valued their language. One student noted that "when teachers are bilingual, it makes our learning easier. They treat us equally." Another described the school as "*una amiga bilingüe*" (a bilingual friend).

Although these high schools made English literacy a primary goal, they also encouraged students to enhance their native language skills in classes for those students who spoke Spanish. Four of the six high schools we visited offered Spanish courses for Spanish speakers. Of these, three of them offered both literacy skills instruction and advanced courses in Spanish. Advanced Placement (AP) Spanish classes at these schools gave native-Spanish-speaking students the opportunity to capitalize on their native language to obtain college credit. The principal at Nogales High School, where 89 percent of the students were Latino, had gone even further in demonstrating the value placed on Spanish. All students at this school were required to take five years of language instruction—four in English and one in Spanish. Students who passed a proficiency test in Spanish were free to take another language to fulfill the fifth year requirement; others had to take Spanish for Spanish speakers or Spanish as a second language, whichever was appropriate.

A less formal but no less effective way that educators showed respect for the students' language was to allow them to speak their native language when English language development was not the focus of instruction. Their philosophy was that nothing was gained from stifling a young person's desire to communicate in his or her primary language. Throughout the campuses of the high schools we visited, students were free to speak Spanish with each other and with school staff. The use of their native language was not restricted to informal settings. Five of the schools provided content courses in Spanish, thus giving students the opportunity to progress through the content areas while developing their English skills. They were not required to postpone taking advanced content courses until they were fluent in English.

Besides showing respect for students' native language, staff in these schools also celebrated the students' cultures. Perhaps the most transparent and readily accessible aspects of culture are customs, holidays, and overtly stated values. While many schools give lip service to these aspects of culture, for example, by celebrating *Cinco de Mayo* and serving tacos on that day, the schools we visited affirmed the customs, values, and holidays of the language-minority students' countries in deeper and more consistent ways throughout the year.

Teachers, for example, made it their business to know about their students' past experiences. Some had visited Mexican schools to better understand their students' previous educational experiences. A group of teachers from one school had observed mathematics teaching in a Mexican school. One of them said that understanding how Mexican students were taught math in Mexico made teaching them easier. He could say to students, "This is the way most of you were taught how to divide in Mexico. And that's OK. This is another way of doing it." Without denigrating what they had learned in Mexico, he would ask which way was easiest for them.

In addition, while faculty and staff were sensitive to the importance of students' language and cultures, they did not treat students simply as members of an undifferentiated ethnic group. They recognized students' individual strengths, interests, problems, and concerns rather than characterizing them by reference to stereotypes. The assistant principal at one school said, "Basically, Hispanic kids are no different from other kids; they want to learn. Those who fall by the wayside are those whose needs aren't being met. Who wants to fail everyday?"

Faculty and staff also knew that there is no such thing as a generic Latino LM student. Rather, people from Mexico, Nicaragua, El Salvador, Guatemala, Cuba, and other Spanish-speaking countries were known to have different histories and customs and to speak different varieties of Spanish. Mexican immigrants, Mexican Americans, and Chicanos were also recognized as different from one another, and variation among Mexican immigrants based upon socioeconomic background and educational attainment level was acknowledged. When asked to describe the Latino students at the school, one teacher responded with five categories: those who are "well off, well educated, not disenfranchised; the migrant kids who have little education; children born here of parents who have immigrated here; limited-English-proficient students who have been here ten to twelve years but have lived in insular communities and had no education in Spanish; and then Central Americans."

Respect for students' languages and cultures was communicated through support programs as well as academic programs. In some schools, special programs provided tutorial and counseling assistance. Teachers and Latino students were paired in mentoring and advocacy activities, thus increasing the sense among faculty of a personal connection with the students. Extracurricular programs involved activities that were relevant to Latino cultures. In one school, students could take a PE class called *Bailes*, in which they learned and performed dances from different regions of Mexico. In another, a student-run group published a monthly newspaper in Spanish called *El Mitotero*. Begun by a teacher, the paper was quickly "taken over" by the students themselves. They formed a committee and organized a formal club with officers and by-laws, which was then recognized by the school's student association. According to the teacher who started it, the paper is "very culturally-oriented—if you understand Spanish, you might understand the words, but if you are not familiar with the local Mexican culture, you will probably miss a lot of the 'double meanings' and cultural references." One issue of the newspaper was devoted to a debate about bilingual education. The newspaper staff interviewed students and teachers and then presented both pro and con sides of the debate, the former written in Spanish and the latter in English.

A final and important way in which these high schools showed respect for the students' cultures and languages was through their staffing. Faculty members who spoke the native languages of the language-minority students in the school and shared similar cultural backgrounds not only used this skill and knowledge to improve instruction for them, but also served as role models and advocates for these students. Comments of several faculty reflect their awareness of the roles they were playing. For example, the principal at Nogales High School said:

> When we hire teachers, we try to look for the best teachers, number one, but number two and most importantly, we try to get teachers that relate to our type of kids, and number three, if we can get teachers that are from this

area, that are teachers that have graduated from this high school, teachers that have had to go through these problems, the growing-up problems, the educational problems from here, and have gone out and have become successful, then we have provided role models for our kids that are essential. I think probably that's one of the reasons I'm principal. We've had all kinds of principals, but I think that the community itself has tried to hire administrators that, number one, relate to our community, and number two, have been here [for a long time]. The majority of the administration from this district is from here.

A teacher at another school said, "The students are very proud and the teachers support that. It's okay to speak Spanish, to be Mexican, not to know English." He believes that students at the school feel supported by the fact that teachers speak Spanish "in public." One student had come to him and reported with some incredulity, "Mr. W. [an Anglo] spoke Spanish to me in class!" The head counselor at the same school said:

> Parents and students see us [Latinos] in leadership positions, not just in the cafeteria or as janitors. People in the school understand problems in the community and have lived it themselves. . . . For example, I understand if a student has to stay home all week to take care of kids. . . . Parents come in because I speak Spanish and can understand their problems. I'm not from a middle-class, elite, intellectual background.

A counselor at a third school said, "I have a sensitivity to these students that comes from my family background. I'm third generation here. I know what it is to leave your roots and live in a system different from that of your parents. Maybe that's why I have an urgency to push college." Students also referred to their teachers and others at the schools as role models. When asked to tell us about a faculty member who was particularly effective, one student commented, "Ms. V. has been a good role model. She speaks many languages and inspires me." Another student said, "Mr. A. encourages students to break stereotypes by being good in chemistry, physical science, and physics."

2. High expectations of language-minority students are made concrete.
Throughout the schools we visited, people recognized the importance of high expectations for Latino LM students. Such expectations form the foundation for the program features we describe. One principal put it this way: "I firmly believe that what you give to the best kids, you give to all," while taking into account special needs and equity issues. The professional staff members in the six schools we visited not only held high expectations of their students but had also taken concrete actions to demonstrate those expectations and to help students accomplish what was expected. Some of these actions already have been mentioned. For example, when students see people like themselves who have become teachers, counselors, and principals, they learn that professions like these are attainable.

Recognizing that language-minority students do not have information that mainstream students possess, school counselors who understood students' languages and cultures helped them plan their high school programs, find information about different colleges, apply to college, fill out financial aid forms, and apply for scholarships. Counselors also communicated with parents to gain their support for their children to apply for college, understanding that if going to college is a new idea to the student, it is probably completely unfamiliar, perhaps even threatening, to the parents. As one female student noted, "At first my parents weren't wanting me to go to college, but Mrs. C [the counselor] convinced them that it was okay." College and university representatives were brought to the high school to talk with students. Former graduates of similar backgrounds who had gone to college were invited back to the high school to share their experiences and to encourage others to follow in their path.

In classes, teachers challenged students with difficult questions and problems. Complex ideas and materials were made more accessible to LM students through visuals, board work, group work, reading aloud, and clear and explicit class expectations. Teachers did not talk down to limited-English-proficient students in "foreigner talk," but spoke clearly, with normal intonation, explaining difficult words and concepts as needed.

In all the schools we visited, student success was recognized publicly. In one high school, achievement in a particular class was recognized through a ritual in which the principal came to the class and congratulated the student. In another school, LM students who did well in particular areas (for example, most improved or perfect attendance) were recognized at a monthly "Student of the Month" luncheon during which teachers who had nominated the students presented certificates to them and spoke briefly about the students' accomplishments. Several high schools had special assemblies for students on the honor roll, where parents were invited and recognized while the students received certificates. "It makes you want to try harder when you get an award," noted one student. Latino LM students received these forms of recognition just as other students did.

3. School leaders make the education of language-minority students a priority.
Strong instructional leadership has been cited as a key ingredient of effective schools (Carter & Chatfield, 1986; Purkey & Smith, 1983). Effective school leaders, usually principals, are described as actively coordinating curriculum; monitoring students' academic progress; having a clear mission for the school which they communicate to staff, students, and parents; holding high expectations for student achievement and promoting the same among faculty and staff. In the high schools we visited, the principals were, in addition, sincerely committed to educating LM students and knowledgeable about effective teaching approaches for this population. All but one of the principals were bilingual minority-group members themselves. Although each had a unique leadership style, they all demonstrated a strong commitment to raising the achievement levels of minority students, including LM students. Sweetwater's principal, a Latino himself, said:

> One of our major roles in this community is to develop a sense of confidence that we can compete in all areas, not just athletics, that we can go out there and be just as good as anybody else. I guess if I had a wish, I would like for the kids in the school to absolutely believe and know in their hearts that they are as good as anybody on this planet.

Steps taken by this principal to support the success of language-minority students illustrate the types of leadership that we found in these schools. Sweetwater's principal was given the authority by the district to make virtually all decisions at the school, including hiring teachers of his choice. He had initiated several changes in the education program for language-minority students. For example, all remedial classes were eliminated so that LM students would not receive "watered-down versions of content." When he came to the school, he discovered that bilingual classes were "remedial," that the school offered bilingual life science rather than biology and bilingual math rather than algebra. He quickly set out to "amend" the situation. Sections of physics, chemistry, and calculus were added along with summer sessions of geometry; the requirements for athletic participation were raised; the number of bilingual staff was increased from eight to thirty-three; the bilingual program was expanded to include advanced courses such as economics, biology II, and honors chemistry as well as lower division bilingual courses.

Although now credited with raising standardized test scores, tightening discipline, and raising the morale of students and teachers, the principal (and staff who supported his changes) encountered opposition from some staff members from the very beginning. When he eliminated the "remedial" classes in the school, for example, some teachers felt he was unrealistic; they argued that students were going to be lost in algebra. The principal recalled telling them that "students perform as well as they're expected . . . [and that] students in remedial classes in junior high school are still in remedial classes in the twelfth grade, often performing worse as time [goes] on." He believes students "will learn more in a classroom filled with students of mixed abilities than in a class composed solely of students with minimal math skills." He provided calculators for students, justifying their placement in basic algebra when others would think them more suited for remedial math: "If they're going to fail remedial math, why not have them fail basic algebra?"

We found that good leadership can and does come from program directors, department chairpersons, and teachers in high schools as well as from principals. In some schools, these individuals had taken on strong leadership roles vis-à-vis the education of LM students. At Artesia High School, for example, a separate ESL department had been formed, and it was the chair of this department who advocated most strongly for the education of LEP students. The principal at this school played a less active role in this area, though the previous principal, it should be noted, had been very active in making changes for the LM population. This example of a leader who is not a principal serves as a reminder that the strength for change does not necessarily have to come from the top. Though a strong principal who is deeply committed to the needs of LM students is certainly desirable, the principal is not the only person who can make a difference. Teachers, program coordinators, and department chairs can also take it upon themselves to be leaders in the education of LM students.

4. Staff development is explicitly designed to help teachers and other staff serve language-minority students more effectively.
As Lisa Delpit writes, "It is impossible to create a model for the good teacher without taking issues of culture and community context into account" (1988, p. 291). Teachers who are expert in the instruction of mainstream students are not necessarily effective instructors of language-minority students. For this reason, professional development

was a high priority for school administrators, teachers, and other professional staff at these schools. Teachers at Nogales High School in Arizona, for example, were encouraged to get an ESL or bilingual endorsement. Teachers received a salary bonus if they held such an endorsement and incorporated ESL or bilingual methods into their curriculum plan. In addition, staff at this school and others we visited received professional development through in-service workshops and conferences. Teachers received training in the principles of second language acquisition and effective instructional approaches for teaching language-minority students, such as sheltered content,[8] cooperative learning, and reading and writing in the content areas. Teachers and other staff learned about students' cultural backgrounds and experiences. Counselors became informed about cross-cultural counseling strategies. Professional staff worked to develop their ability in the native languages of their students, enabling them to communicate more effectively with LM students and their parents.

Most important, *all* teachers and other professional staff were encouraged to participate in professional development of the sort described here, not just those who taught specific classes for this special student population. It appeared that all school staff took responsibility for teaching these students. No one expressed the attitude that one group of teachers would "take care" of LM students and that the others therefore did not need to "worry" about them. In fact, one principal had set a policy prohibiting bilingual teachers from teaching bilingual classes the entire day. He believed that bilingual teachers should teach mainstream as well as bilingual classes so they would not forget what they were preparing LM students to do.

At Anaheim High School, a five-year plan developed to improve the achievement of Latino students included a strong emphasis on staff development and teacher empowerment. When the current principal first came to Anaheim High School in 1983, she convened the ten department heads, and together they examined the effective schools literature to establish a commonality of language and philosophy before instituting changes. These teachers developed a school plan. According to the principal, "[Empowering the teachers] was the best thing I could have done. I had ten advocates for change, and the plan was theirs, not mine. . . . You can force compliance, but you can't force commitment." Later, the principal and ten department heads shared the process they had gone through with all the teachers. One of the teachers who went through the process reflected, "There is an overall drive to help kids. That's one of the unique things about Anaheim High School. That mood was set by Mrs. C., and the turn-around is now being seen." At Anaheim, staff development was conceived of as teacher-motivated, rather than the traditional top-down process. A small cadre of teachers, with the support of the principal, made it their business to learn what could be done to improve the quality of education at their school and later served as models and teachers for the rest of the staff. A similar process occurred at Artesia High School, where a strong staff development program had been developed partly as a result of the school's participation in the state's School Improvement Program.

5. A variety of courses and programs for language-minority students is offered.
Too often LM students are placed and kept in a limited selection of low-level high school courses with the rationale that their English is not proficient enough to allow them to cope with more advanced classes. Often these classes are overfilled, leaving

students with few opportunities to interact with the teacher adequately (Brown & Haycock, 1984). Yet LM students, like all students, do best when they have the opportunity to take a wide range of courses, including advanced courses that challenge them intellectually.

In these high schools, those who did not yet speak or write fluent English nonetheless were given the opportunity to progress in content courses appropriate to their academic level. Educators in these high schools did not assume that English proficiency matched content knowledge or cognitive skills. They recognized the fine but critical line between programs that failed to prepare LM students for college and those that facilitated their transition to an English language curriculum while providing continuing academic challenge through a variety of bilingual and sheltered courses. If, for instance, a student from Mexico had passed fundamental math and algebra in her country and had limited proficiency in English, she was able to take a geometry class taught in Spanish or one that used sheltered English methods. Advanced-Placement Spanish offered strong Spanish speakers the opportunity to receive college credit for studying Neruda and Cervantes, just as native-English-speaking students could receive advanced credit for studying Wordsworth and Hawthorne. Bilingual economics and bilingual honors chemistry allowed those who possessed the required content-area background to move beyond basics, doing advanced work in these areas while developing their English language competence. In addition to offering a wide range of courses to LM students, two of the schools also had special programs to facilitate their transition to mainstream classes, and another had a program to identify those who qualified for participation in the school's GATE (Gifted and Talented) program.

Special programs were also in place in all the high schools to promote LM students' academic and social growth. These programs had the net effect of extending learning time through before- and after-school activities, a feature which Wilson and Corcoran believe may be the "critical difference between a mediocre school and an excellent one" (1988, p. 58). In an advocate program, teachers were paired with students as tutors and advocates. BECA (Bilingual Excellence in Cognitive Achievement) provided tutoring, career planning, and multicultural awareness for both limited and fluent English-speaking Latino students at one high school. UCO (University and College Opportunity) encouraged and prepared underrepresented minority students in another high school to go to college. The Tanner Bill Program (or "SAT program," as it was known in one school) had a similar goal, though it targeted Latino students in particular. AVID (Advance Via Individual Determination) was a college-prep program for disadvantaged students in one high school that included one class specifically geared to LEP students. These are only a few of the special programs that either targeted or included LM students. A more complete listing appears in Table 20.2 along with names of the schools where the programs were offered.

6. A counseling program gives special attention to language-minority students.
In our interviews with students, one question asked them to identify the teacher or other staff member who had helped them the most. Many students referred to counselors as being key to their adjustment to the new environment and to their clarification of future goals. "At the beginning of the year," said one student, "I wasn't into

TABLE 20.2 Courses, Programs, and Activities for Language-Minority Students at Six High Schools

Academic Courses and Programs

—*ESL:* focus on English language development.

—*Transitional ESL/Booster courses:* for students who have completed the ESL sequence but need some extra help in order to succeed in mainstream English classes.

—*Sheltered English content classes:* content classes with English language development built in (includes advanced classes).

—*Spanish-language content courses:* content classes taught in Spanish (includes advanced classes).

—*Spanish for Spanish speakers:* basic literacy and advanced Spanish skills.

—*Math and reading labs (computer-assisted instruction):* work on basic skills at individual pace.

Support Programs

Some of these programs serve only Latino and/or LM students; most include but are not limited to Latino LM students. Some focus on helping students develop advanced skills; others focus on more basic skills.*

—*Advocate Program:* Teachers volunteer to be paired with students, act as advocates and tutors. (Nogales)

—*BECA (Bilingual Excellence in Cognitive Achievement):* tutoring, career planning, multicultural awareness for Latino LM students. (Overfelt)

—*UCO (University and College Opportunity Program):* to encourage and prepare underrepresented minorities to go to college. Students are assigned to a special counselor, go on field trips to colleges. (Overfelt)

—*AVID (Advance Via Individual Determination):* college-prep program for disadvantaged students of all ethnic backgrounds. Uses peer and college tutors. One class in the program is specifically geared to LM students. (Sweetwater)

—*SAT Program, funded by the Tanner Bill:* for Latino students who have potential for academic success. Teachers are specially trained, classes are small (25 students), teachers act as mentors for 10–12 students, parents are involved. (Anaheim)

—*MESA (Math, Engineering, Science Achievement):* college-prep program for disadvantaged students of all ethnic backgrounds with emphasis on science and math. (Overfelt)

—*PLATO (Programmed Logic for Automatic Teaching Operations):* This computer-based dropout program allows students to attend school part of the day and work part-time. They use computers for individualized instruction, get career and college counseling. Students can receive regular diploma. (Sweetwater)

—*High-Risk Program:* for students who have failed a class or two and/or have attendance problems. Students are assigned to work with mentor teachers who have had training to participate. All participate voluntarily.

—*Chapter I program:* for students in low socioeconomic brackets who have scored below the 36th percentile on the CTBS or equivalent. Focuses on basic math and language arts and the use of computers; 20 students per class. (Anaheim)

Extracurricular Activities

—*Bailes*—a group of students who learn and perform dances from different regions of Mexico. (Anaheim)

—*La Prensa Latina*—a student journalism group that produces a Spanish-language newspaper called *El Mitotero*. (Sweetwater)

—*International Club*—a student group that sponsors events to increase intercultural awareness. (Artesia)

—*Celebration of cultural events and holidays* such as *Cinco de Mayo* by the whole school.

—*MECHA (Movimiento Estudiantil Chicano de Atzlán)*—a group that represents the interest of Chicano, Mexican-American, and Mexican students on college and high school campuses. (Sweetwater)

—*Sports:* soccer and baseball are emphasized over football.

*Schools where these programs were operating are listed in parentheses.

school. Then I talked to Mrs. B [a counselor] and got into it. My mom said she was proud of me." In the schools we visited, there was at least one bilingual Latino counselor who was able to communicate effectively with newcomers as well as with longer term residents, and who understood the sociocultural backgrounds of the students. This person was also well informed about post-secondary educational opportunities for language-minority students—scholarships, fellowships, grants—and could guide the students in getting and filling out the appropriate forms. He or she could also communicate with parents about students' successes and problems in school and the value of a college or university education.

One case we heard of involved a twelfth-grade student who lived with her aunt and uncle because her parents were in Mexico. The parents were reluctant to let their daughter, who had been accepted at a reputable college, move away from the family. The counselor took it upon herself to call the parents and talk it over with them, eventually convincing them of the wisdom of letting their daughter take this opportunity. In a school with no bilingual counselor who cared as much as this one did, this student—and presumably others like her—would have missed her opportunity and become another statistic of the low college attendance of minority students.

Simply having one or more bilingual counselors on the staff who are sensitive to students' cultures does not necessarily mean that LM students have access to that counselor, however. In talking with counselors and students, we learned about the importance of having an effective method of assigning students to counselors. Schools used a variety of methods, including assignment by class level, alphabetical order, special needs, and various combinations of these. Those that were most effective made sure that language-minority students were assigned to a counselor who could communicate with them, was knowledgeable of post-secondary opportunities for language-minority students, and was sincerely committed to helping all students succeed in school and beyond.

In the better counseling programs, case loads were relatively low, and bilingual Latino counselors were specifically designated for Latino LM students. At Sweetwater, in order to encourage counselors to guide all students toward post-secondary education, the procedures used to evaluate counselors took into account the test scores of the students with whom they worked, the number of students who applied to college, and the number of students who received college/university grants and scholarships. The head counselor said that four or five years before, they had realized that some people on the counseling staff were doing a much better job than others. They all sat down together and decided that helping students get money for college and go to college would be the priorities of the staff. The approach was later adopted for the whole district. It is a competitive approach, but "we work together. A counselor might say, 'What did you do that I didn't?'" At Artesia High School several Latino LM students indicated that their counselors worked with them on future plans, made sure they were doing well in classes, and advised them about the courses to take so they would have the option of going to a university. A College Aspiration Partnership Program (CAPP), developed by the counseling department at this high school, paired the school with several colleges and universities in the surrounding area. Language-minority students met with representatives of these institutions to learn the requirements for entry and procedures for applying for scholarships and other student support funds.

At Newcomer High, which unlike the other schools serves immigrant students for only a year before they make the transition to regular high schools, college counseling is not as large a component of the counselors' roles as helping students, many of them refugees, deal with the emotional and physical traumas they have experienced in leaving war-torn countries and coming to the United States. The counselors there, two of whom speak Spanish and one of whom speaks Chinese, see themselves as nurturers and facilitators of cultural adjustment. One of them described her roles: "I wear many hats; at times I'm a mother, a referral service to agencies, and I may have to be a comedian when needed." A student, commenting on her first day at the school, said, "*Para mi no fué tan extraño. La señora S. me presentó a los compañeros.*" ("For me it wasn't so strange. Mrs. S. introduced me to friends.") It is the counselor's job, as well as that of teachers, to acquaint students with the expectations of the school system, particularly those areas that differ from one culture to another. Students learn, for instance, that in most U.S. classrooms student participation—including asking questions of the teacher—is expected and desired and that one shows respect to Anglo teachers by making eye contact while they are speaking. In addition to dealing with cross-cultural issues, counselors at Newcomer had to be experts at referring students to appropriate agencies for medical or psychological traumas which could not be handled at the school.

We realize that for schools which are only now beginning to see an increase in language-minority and LEP populations, it may be difficult to find qualified counselors who share the students' linguistic and cultural backgrounds. Until such counselors are found and hired, however, it is advisable to at least have a counselor who speaks the students' native language, who has been trained in cross-cultural counseling techniques, and who can bring to students' attention special funding and scholarship opportunities.

7. Parents of language-minority students are encouraged to become involved in their children's education.
The parent participation feature was the least developed component of the high schools we visited. The principals, counselors, and teachers at all of the schools commented that more needed to be done to increase the schools' interaction with the parents of LM students. Yet they had taken steps to encourage parents to take an active part in their children's education. Several schools had Parent Advisory Committees that met monthly and included parents of LM students. These committees typically reached out to other parents for assistance with parent-sponsored multicultural activities. Some schools regularly sent newsletters to parents in their native languages.

Newcomer High School held a parent night once a month. Students and teachers in the school worked together to plan presentations about various aspects of the school's education program, including ways parents could help their children be better students. When we visited the high school, students were being prepared in their reading class to present to parents a play that dramatized some ways of "monitoring and motivating one's child," the topic for that month's meeting. The play was to be performed in Spanish, Chinese, Burmese, Vietnamese, Tagalog, and English. Afterwards, students would read several poems to parents—"Exile" by Pablo Neruda; "The Truth" by a student; and "The Road Not Taken" by Robert Frost. Finally, students would sing "The Impossible Dream."

The Tanner Bill program for Latino students at Anaheim High School required that the teachers and parents of participating students meet twice a month. In addition, the program coordinator held evening meetings several times a year in the neighborhoods of the students in the program. Representatives of colleges and universities in the area attended these meetings to inform parents of the college programs offered by their institutions, the entry requirements, and the scholarships and other support services available to language-minority students. Generally, the college and university representatives who attended spoke the parents' native language(s).

Nogales and Anaheim held early morning pancake breakfasts and invited parents to attend before they went to work; 800 people had attended Anaheim's most recent breakfast when we visited the school. Nogales also held monthly student-of-the-month breakfasts for parents and students in which a student in each department was honored, as well as an Honors Assembly each quarter in which parents were asked to stand up and be recognized with their children. More than 750 people attended the most recent Honors Assembly. Overfelt High School had a full-time community liaison who spoke Spanish and offered ESL classes for parents on the school campus. Parents of Overfelt students had also come out on weekends to paint the school. Several schools contacted parents by telephone to check on students who were absent or to inform parents when a student had become ill and was returning home. The person making the contact spoke the parents' native language.

Although we did not interview parents, comments from students indicated that many Latino parents were very supportive of their children's education. The language barrier, lack of familiarity with the U.S. educational system, and their own lack of educational experience made it difficult for some parents to help directly with homework; however, they encouraged their children in other ways to pursue the education they had not had the opportunity to receive. One student reported, "For my mom, the only thing is school. She said I could do anything; 'All I want is for you to finish school.' She pushes that I get educated. She herself dropped out and got married and regrets it. I dropped out too for awhile; it tore my mom and me apart." The theme of "becoming somebody" is a strong thread in the students' talk about their parents and their own goals for the future. "My dad is always telling me to work and study, to be somebody," said one. "*Quiero seguir estudiando para llegar a ser alguien en la vida*" ("I want to keep studying so that I can become somebody in life"), said another. These comments by students attest to the strong desire among these Latino parents to do whatever they are able to do to gain a good education for their children. The schools we visited were working hard to find ways of making the schools accessible to parents.

8. School staff members share a strong commitment to empower language-minority students through education.
The most fundamental feature of all, and the most difficult to describe in concrete terms, is the commitment we heard about from most if not all of the school staff and students we interviewed. This commitment goes beyond the value the staff places on students' languages and cultures and beyond the high expectations staff members hold for language-minority students. One can value the language and culture of a student and expect that student to be successful, yet still remain passive when it comes to promoting that student in the world. Commitment and empowerment of

students involve staff members reaching out, giving extra time to further the goals of a few students, and taking part in a political process that challenges the status quo. In the words of Jim Cummins, "minority students can become empowered only through interactions with educators who have critically examined and, where necessary, challenged the educational (and social) structure within which they operate" (1989, p. 6).

Such commitment manifested itself in various ways at the schools we visited. Teachers and other staff at the schools were described as having students' best interests at heart and giving extra time and energy after school and during lunch or preparation time to counsel as well as teach them. For example, the Coordinator of Special Projects at Overfelt High School said that he had found the teachers there to be very eager to learn how to work effectively with language-minority students. He said that they considered it "a very serious endeavor" to be sensitive to the needs of such students, and that they frequently requested training of various sorts to help them become more effective. At all of the schools, students mentioned teachers who had given them special help and attention, often crediting them with providing personal counseling as well as academic support. Typical student comments included the following: "The teachers here don't just teach; they care about you" and "Teachers stay after school to explain what we didn't understand."

Activities at these schools promoted participation and empowerment of Latino students outside the classroom as well. Through participation in MECHA[9] groups, Latino clubs, Spanish language newspapers, soccer teams, and other activities sponsored and advised by school staff, Latino students developed awareness and knowledge of their cultures and language as well as a sense of community and cooperation with other Latino and non-Latino students. School staff involved in these activities took their commitment beyond the classroom to help develop students as whole people. Through the *Ballet Folklorico* group at Anaheim, for example, students not only learned and performed various Mexican dances, but also learned about the different regions in Mexico where dances originated, and presented this information in performances as well. They thus deepened their own and others' knowledge and understanding of Mexican culture and history.

Besides their work in the school setting to promote the achievement and success of Latino and other language-minority students, staff at these schools also participated in various community activities, attended meetings, and held positions in their communities through which they acted as advocates for Latinos and other minorities. An assistant principal at Nogales High School, a Latino from the community, had been the mayor of Nogales. A teacher and MECHA advisor at Sweetwater High School, also a Latino, was elected to the City Council of National City in 1989. The principal at Anaheim High School described her work to develop an advocacy base in the community through her ongoing participation in a variety of community events and activities. She had gotten support from Anaheim graduates in the community, some business people, and many parents—both Latino and Anglo—by participating in community activities herself. Some of these people had spoken out at school board meetings, advocating programs and services that were crucial to the success of the district's language-minority students. Sensitive to the fact that the way certain issues are discussed can trigger negative reactions and therefore interfere with the achievement of desired goals, she worked to communicate effectively with different audiences. Above all, she said, "I have not been naïve in thinking I can do it all by myself; I spent the first year getting a sense of who supported the equity issues that I'm concerned with."

It was evident at these schools that teachers, counselors, administrators, and other staff were highly committed to promoting the success of language-minority students in school and beyond. Besides promoting the achievement of such students, they acknowledged the educational and social structures that surround the students and challenged these structures in productive ways through concrete actions such as those described above. By taking their advocacy into the community, those who held elective offices and participated in community groups challenged negative attitudes and policies that may have been creating obstacles to the improvement of education for minority groups. Those who initiated and sponsored activities to expand LM students' knowledge and understanding of their own cultures and languages helped them develop a sense of identity and community that knowledge of their own backgrounds could provide. Those who were putting their extra energy into helping students with their academic work were fighting to raise the low achievement records of language-minority students. This commitment and accompanying action provided the framework within which the attributes and processes we have described above were developed and carried out.

CONCLUSION

The eight features we have described appeared to be key to the success of language-minority students at the schools we visited. While the study was exploratory in nature, we believe it provides educators with a working model of effective education for language-minority students at the secondary level. These eight features can be thought of as a set of general recommendations, or perhaps as a checklist against which to compare other schools or programs.

Many of the key features we have described mirror features in the effective schools literature. The notions of high expectations, parent involvement, strong leadership, and staff development are common threads throughout the many studies that have been conducted. In addition, those studying schools with large numbers of minority and bilingual students found, as we did, that support services, a positive attitude toward students, and commitment to helping students achieve were crucial factors in the overall success of the schools. In these areas, our report offers further confirmation that, in order to be successful with language-minority students, high schools must place a high priority on services and attitudes that go beyond academic instruction.

But this study makes several additional contributions. The first of these is the focus on secondary schools with large numbers of LM students. Second, wherever possible, general features across schools have been operationalized through concrete examples of practices in particular schools. Much of the effective schools literature lists general attributes, but does not take the next step in describing ways of actually carrying out these broad manifestos. We have tried to provide not only food for thought but also suggestions for concrete action. Third, we have emphasized an integrated approach to secondary programs for language-minority students. The schools we visited provided strong academic preparation for these students in three areas—content knowledge and understanding, English language skills, and primary language skills. They also helped students develop their pride and identity as individuals, as members of ethnic groups, and as participants in a multicultural society by showing respect for students' languages and cultures, holding high expectations of students and acting upon them in concrete ways, guiding them in preparing for their futures, encouraging their parents to become involved in their schooling, and promoting student empowerment in school and in the larger community. This multifaceted approach manifested itself at all levels of the curriculum and throughout academic, support, and extracurricular programs at these schools.

Finally, this study strongly suggests that the diversity among students cannot simply be ignored. While the schools recognized the importance of integrating language-minority students with mainstream students and of providing equally challenging instruction for all students, they did not try to minimize differences among mainstream and Latino students or among Latino students themselves. Approaches to schooling that value linguistic and cultural diversity and that promote cultural pluralism were welcomed and explored whenever possible (see Stedman, 1987). Students' languages and cultures were incorporated into school programs as part of the effort to create a context in which all students felt valuable and capable of academic success (see Cummins, 1989).

Though this study was exploratory in nature, we hope the findings will guide further research. Many more secondary schools with large numbers of language-minority students need to be visited for longer periods of time to determine whether the features which emerged in the six schools we studied apply to other similar schools. The features themselves need to be examined in greater depth so that educators can understand them more fully and apply them in appropriate contexts. For example, a study of parent involvement in language-minority student schooling should include extensive interviews with parents themselves as well as with students and school staff. Longitudinal studies of secondary schools with large numbers of language-minority students could increase our understanding of the processes schools go through in providing and maintaining effective schooling for such students. Schools with different populations of students also need to be examined—for example, students of different ethnic and language backgrounds, students who have lived in the United States for various lengths of time, students who are immigrants, refugees, and native-born citizens. Nevertheless, the study has extended our knowledge of what makes schooling work for a rapidly growing segment of the school population. We hope that this working model will also provide inspiration and a sense of possibility to educators who are seeking an effective response to the needs of secondary language-minority students.

NOTES

The authors wish to extend their thanks to all of the staff and students at the schools we visited. We greatly appreciated the hospitality and friendliness with which we were received and the unique perspectives which people took the time to describe to us in interviews. We also want to thank our colleagues Marie Mayen, Leticia Perez, Huynh Dinh Te, William Tikunoff, Sau-Lim

Tsang, Betty Ward, and Harriet Doss Willis for their work on various stages of this project and their support throughout. The information reported here was collected as part of a plan for providing technical assistance to Arizona secondary schools. The technical assistance project was conducted by the South-west Center for Educational Equity, which is funded by the U.S. Department of Education, Office of Elementary and Secondary Education, under Title IV of the Civil Rights Act of 1964. The contents of this article do not necessarily reflect the views or policies of the Department of Education.

1. We will use the phrase "language-minority (LM) students" to refer to those who come from families where a language other than English is spoken. Such students may or may not speak English fluently.

2. We will use the phrase "limited-English-proficient (LEP) students" to refer specifically to those language-minority students who are not yet fluent in English.

3. California State Department of Education, Assembly Bill 1329, 1976. In 1982, AB-1329 was revised as AB-507.

4. The Southwest Center for Educational Equity is funded by Title IV of the U.S. Department of Education to assist school districts in California, Arizona, and Nevada in their desegregation efforts in the areas of race, gender, and national origin.

5. Awards and recognition included a California Department of Education Distinguished School Award, a city Commendation Award, nomination as an exemplary school for the National Secondary School Recognition Program, an award for the academic achievement of the school's graduates attending a university in the state, a U.S. Department of Education Excellence in Education Award, and selection as one of the "77 Schools of the Future" by *Omni* magazine.

6. The term *Latino* is used here because it is the term that the majority of people we interviewed used to describe their own ethnicity, when speaking on a broader level than their individual countries of origin.

7. Anaheim High School, Anaheim, CA; Artesia High School, Lakewood, CA; Newcomer High School, San Francisco, CA; Overfelt High School, San Jose, CA.

8. The term *sheltered content* refers to an approach to teaching content classes for LEP students in English in which the development of English language skills is emphasized along with content area development. Teachers use whatever means they can to make the content comprehensible and meaningful to the students: for example, simplified speech, vocabulary work, visuals, hands-on activities, and highly structured lessons (see Northcutt & Watson, 1986).

9. MECHA, or *Movimiento Estudiantil Chicano de Atzlán*, represents the interests of Chicano and Mexican-American students.

REFERENCES

Arias, B. (1986). The context of education for Hispanic students: An overview. *American Journal of Education, 95*, 26–57.

Bell, J. (1989, February). *Merging the research on effective instruction for LEP students with effective schools' research and practice.* Paper presented at the Annual Conference of the California Association for Bilingual Education, Anaheim, CA.

Brown, P. R., & Haycock, K. (1984). *Excellence for whom?* Oakland, CA: The Achievement Council.

Carter, T. P., & Chatfield, M. L. (1986). Effective bilingual schools: Implications for policy and practice. *American Journal of Education, 95*, 200–232.

Cummins, J. (1989). *Empowering minority students.* Sacramento: California Association of Bilingual Education.

Delpit, L. D. (1988). The silenced dialogue: Power and pedagogy in educating other people's children. *Harvard Educational Review, 58,* 280–298.

Edmonds, R. (1979, May 5). Effective schools for the urban poor. *Educational Leadership, 37*(1), 15–27.

Espinosa, R., & Ochoa, A. (1986). Concentration of California Hispanic students in schools with low achievement: A research note. *American Journal of Education, 95,* 77–95.

Gingras, R. C., & Careaga, R. C. (1989). *Limited-English-proficient students at risk: Issues and prevention strategies.* Silver Spring, MD: National Clearinghouse for Bilingual Education.

Jackson, S. (1989, May). Luncheon address, Symposium on Excellence in Mathematics and Science Achievement: The Gateway to Learning in the 21st Century. Sponsored by the Southwest Center for Educational Equity, San Francisco.

Lau v. Nichols, 414 U.S. 563, 566 (1973).

Levin, H. M. (1987). Accelerated schools for disadvantaged students. *Educational Leadership, 44*(6), 19–21.

Medina, M. (1988). Hispanic apartheid in American public education. *Educational Administration Quarterly, 24,* 336–349.

Merriam, S. B. (1988). *Case study research in education: A qualitative approach.* San Francisco: Jossey-Bass.

Miles, M. B., & Huberman, A. M. (1984). *Qualitative data analysis: A sourcebook of new methods.* Beverly Hills, CA: Sage.

Northcutt, L., & Watson, D. (1986). *SET: Sheltered English teaching handbook.* San Marcos, CA: AM Graphics and Printing.

Orfield, G. (1986). Hispanic education: Challenges, research, and policies. *American Journal of Education, 95,* 1–25.

Orum, L. S. (1988). *The education of Hispanics: Status and implications.* Washington, DC: National Council of La Raza.

Purkey, S. C., & Smith, M. S. (1983). Effective schools: A review. *The Elementary School Journal, 83,* 428–452.

Ramírez, D. (1988, April). *A comparison of structured English, immersion, and bilingual education programs: Results of a national study.* Paper presented at the Annual Meeting of the American Educational Research Association, New Orleans.

Rosenholtz, S. J. (1985). Effective schools: Interpreting the evidence. *American Journal of Education, 93,* 352–388.

Rowen, B., Bossert, S.T., & Dwyer, D.C. (1983). Research on effective schools: A cautionary note. *Educational Research, 12*(4), 24–31.

Rumberger, R. W. (1987). High school dropouts: A review of issues and evidence. *Review of Educational Research, 57,* 101–121.

Stedman, L.C. (1987). It's time we changed the effective schools formula. *Phi Delta Kappan, 69,* 215–224.

Suro, R. (1990, April 11). Education secretary criticizes the values of Hispanic parents. *The New York Times,* pp. A1, B8.

Taylor, S. J., & Bogdan, R. (1984). *Introduction to qualitative research methods* (2nd ed.). New York: Wiley.

Tikunoff, W. (1985). *Applying significant bilingual instructional features in the classroom.* Rosslyn, VA: National Clearinghouse for Bilingual Education.

U.S. General Accounting Office. (1987). *School dropouts: Survey of local programs* (GAO/HRD-87-108). Washington, DC: GPO.

Wilson, B.L., & Corcoran, T.B. (1988). *Successful secondary schools.* New York: Falmer Press.

Wong-Fillmore, L., McLaughlin, B., Ammon, P., & Ammon, M.S. (1985). *Learning English through bilingual instruction. Final Report to the National Institute of Education.* Berkeley: The University of California.

21

Education and the Mexican American: Eleuterio Escobar and the School Improvement League of San Antonio

Mario Garcia

An illiterate cannot defend himself, his community or his country.

—*Eleuterio Escobar* (autobiography)

The Mexican-American Generation regarded educational reform as its most important social issue. The League of United Latin American Citizens (LULAC), of course, attacked de facto school segregation in the courts. At the community level, other Mexican Americans pressured authorities for improvements in the Mexican schools. Education, as LULAC leaders stressed, was the key to integration and social mobility. Hence, the battle over the schools was a logical arena of protest, especially for the aspiring lower middle class. The schools symbolized, on the one hand, Anglo institutions of authority and control and yet, on the other, the promise of upward mobility if Mexican Americans could help change their direction. As sociologists Piven and Cloward correctly argue, "people experience deprivation and oppression within a concrete setting, not as the end product of large and abstract processes, and it is the concrete experience that molds their discontent into specific grievances against specific targets."[1] Lacking access, for the most part, to political offices and unlike Mexican-American workers who could strike and unionize to express their discontent, lower-middle class Mexican Americans as community leaders focused on school issues as a natural forum for their social protest. Schools affected their children's chances for the American dream as well as serving as a community issue bringing together all sectors of the barrio. This chapter examines the politics of educational reform in San Antonio initiated by Eleuterio Escobar and the School Improvement League.

Escobar and the league, composed of a small number of dedicated community leaders, from 1934 to 1956 carried on a persistent crusade to improve conditions for thousands of Mexican-American children in the west-side barrio of San Antonio. While other Mexican-American leaders of this period sought social reforms through the courts, politics, or labor struggles, Escobar and the league took on the local school board and organized a grassroots resistance to a legacy of educational injustice.

ELEUTERIO ESCOBAR

Eleuterio Escobar came to educational reform out of his own life experiences. Born in 1894 in Laredo, Texas, to working-class parents, Escobar faced educational discrimination and segregation growing up in south Texas. Years later he wrote:

> When I first attended school (in Pearsall), I was segregated along with other children with a Spanish surname. There were three elementary schools. One for Anglos made of permanent construction with several acres of play ground, one for Mexican Americans, a dilapidated one room frame building to serve first, second, and third grades. During these years I attended school in and out and some years after I never saw that any of my mates ever reached the sixth grade. The other school was for colored children.[2]

Most Mexican-American children worked on ranches performing a variety of tasks. The combination of limited and inferior schools as well as poverty produced, as Escobar observed, "a great number of families in which their sons, parents and grandparents were completely illiterate and many of them died in frustration, poor and without enjoying equal educational rights." Escobar, himself, never went much beyond the third grade and at age thirteen became the male head of the house after his father died. He and his mother worked at a ranch close to Charlotte, Texas. As a farmhand, Escobar received forty cents a day. Later as a foreman, he noted numerous working alongside their parents instead of attending school. "Man he remembered, "were making nearly as much as some grown people." Determined to rise above his position, Escobar abandoned fieldwork small savings established in 1912 a bicycle repair and rental shop in Pearsall. However, the big city attracted him and he soon left to become a traveling salesman working out of San Antonio. Selling quilts and blankets, Escobar traveled throughout south Texas.[3]

Escobar succeeded as a salesman despite his customers' from town to town he observed the inferior conditions under Mexicans lived and worked. Most customers could not to his receipts. They could only make their mark. Families dated and congested shacks. Children rarely went to school and when they did received a limited education in segregated facilities.[4] As economist Paul Taylor would later note, the Anglo establishment of south Texas would finance and provide only restricted education for Mexican-American children since farmers needed them to reproduce the agricultural labor force.[5] Nevertheless, Escobar was always received warmly and with much hospitality by his Mexican-American clientele despite their difficult lot. They saw Escobar not just as a merchant but as a friend. "Being in their homes I could see clearly what these people were up against," he wrote in his autobiography:

> I believe that with twenty thousand dollars in those days I would never have learned what I learned just for the price of trying to make a living.

This touched me very much, because I had to go through their experience and I could feel their suffering because I am one of those unfortunates who was denied an equal education, and my human and constitutional rights were denied and infringed by our highest state and school officials. Their frustration and suffering caused mothers to shed many tears. I said to my God, "God if I ever am in a position to help these unfortunate children in my humble way, I am going to do it."[6]

In 1918, after the United States entered World War I, Escobar enlisted in the infantry and saw service in Europe. He returned one year later and again traveled as a salesman. He wanted his own business and with credit opened the San Antonio Mercantile Company with his friend and partner, Antonio Martínez. They worked hard to satisfy their Mexican customers, and Escobar's retail business flourished during the Roaring Twenties. In 1924 he left Martínez with the business and formed the Escobar Furniture Company in the west-side barrio of San Antonio. With his wife, whom he had married the previous year, Escobar again succeeded in his enterprise. "Since this was the only furniture store owned by a Mexican American," he remembered, "it attracted the attention of the vast Mexican American colony." Besides acquiring his store, Escobar purchased property on the west side. "Everything went well," he later wrote, "until 1929 when the depression broke out." He could now barely pay his creditors, and his own customers and tenants defaulted on their payments. As the depression deepened, Escobar—like most everyone else—struggled to survive.[7]

Yet, more fortunate than others, Escobar in both good and bad times participated in community life. In 1927 he had helped organize the Mexican Casino in San Antonio, composed of about sixty Mexican-American and mexicano businessmen and professionals. The casino served as a social and cultural center and apparently also sponsored charitable work.[8] Escobar joined the Knights of America, one of the predecessors to LULAC. As a representative of the Knights, Escobar attended the 1929 Corpus Christi conven in youth the San Antonio merchant promoted athletic activities for Mexican-American boys by providing baseball equipment and converting some of his property into a baseball diamond that came to be called Escobar Field.[9] Although educational reform as an organized activity would in time become Escobar's primary civic activity, he did not come to it in a vacuum. Along with other Mexican-American political novices, Escobar evolved politically. At the height of the depression, he and a few other Mexican-American leaders, including prominent civic leader Alonso Perales, organized to participate in electoral politics. The depression, plus increased racial tensions, spurred them in this direction. In 1930, for example, some Texas Democrats had unsuccessfully attempted to ban Mexican Americans from primaries by arguing that Mexicans were not whites but Indians.[10] Lack of effective Mexican-American political representation in San Antonio also encouraged electoral politics. "At that time Mexican-Americans did not have a voice in the city, county, or state governments," Escobar later explained, "and the only representatives that we had were a few policemen, street sweepers, and garbage collectors." Composed predominantly of business and professional men, many of whom had never participated in electoral politics, the Association of Independent Voters selected Escobar as its president.[11] The association stressed the endorsement of candidates who possessed no prejudices against "people of Latin descent," who would deal with Mexican Americans on an equal basis with Anglos, and who would provide fair representation on juries and in governmental affairs.[12]

Unfortunately, the association soon divided on whether it should endorse state candidates, especially for governor, or just local ones. Irreparably split, the association collapsed. Escobar and other founders abandoned it and, according to Escobar, "the Association of Independent Voters . . . died . . . of natural causes."[13] In a postmortem, Alonso Perales optimistically noted that despite the association's demise it was only the initial phase of a more concerted Mexican-American political movement in San Antonio. The challenge was to maintain unity among the people. "This is the problem," Perales told Escobar, "and you and I will have to study this issue and see what we can do."[14]

EDUCATIONAL STRUGGLES DURING THE GREAT DEPRESSION

Escobar's political evolution led him to the cause that would come to occupy much of his active civic life: the campaign to provide educational opportunities for Mexican-American children. Deprived of an education himself, although self-taught, Escobar fervently embraced this struggle.[15] Escobar witnessed the increasing poverty of Mexican Americans in depression-ridden San Antonio and believed that only increased educational opportunities could alter such an uninspiring future. He wrote:

In 1933 . . . the economic and educational situation was desperate. Thousand[s] of San Antonio families in order to survive were compelled to work shelling pecans for very low wages. Some of them were making as low as 15 cents a day. This made it very difficult for the family to feed, clothe, and educate the children.[16]

Few possessed a chance for a better life. The 1931 San Antonio city directory, for example, listed only five Spanish-surnamed lawyers. In addition, the difficulty with English plus lack of knowledge concerning their civil rights handicapped many Mexican Americans and mexicanos. Still, parents coveted education for their children and cried for help. "Many mothers swallowed their tears," Escobar recalled, "some were imploring with their cries for human justice. Others murmured with trembling voices, 'My children are not attending school.' "[17]

Escobar and other Mexican-American leaders concluded that only education could lift Mexican Americans out of poverty. Consequently, they organized to improve the schools in San Antonio's west side. In early 1934 Escobar worked as a member of LULAC Council No. 16 and became chair of the council's Committee for Playground and School Facilities. The committee at first engaged in what some scholars term "action research": documenting the unsuitable nature of the Mexican schools with the intent of affecting public policy. Escobar astutely understood that his most formidable strength would be documentation not rhetoric.[18]

Over a period of weeks and months, mostly through Escobar's research in school and municipal records, the committee compiled an impressive array of data about the depressed and inadequate state of west-side schools. Escobar focused on the inequities surrounding the Mexican schools and compared them to the Anglo schools in other parts of San Antonio. An almost equal number of students attended both types of schools. The west-side schools contained 12,334 students while 12,224 studied in the non-Mexican schools. However, the students on the west side were cramped into only 11 schools, while 28 schools serviced the other sections. The Mexican schools contained less physical space and grounds: 23 acres for the 11 west-side schools to 82 acres for the other schools. Two-hundred and fifty-nine rooms were contained in west-side schools, while 368 rooms were in the other schools. The average number of students per room on the west side came to 48, while the average in the other sections was 23. Two-hundred and eighty-six teachers taught in the Mexican schools while 330 taught in the Anglo ones. The school board averaged a direct cost of $24.50 per pupil on the west side, while spending an average of $35.96 per pupil elsewhere. Finally, Escobar observed that west-side schools contained 34 temporary frame rooms, while only 10 such rooms could be found in other schools.[19]

As the comparative data indicated, overcrowdedness posed the biggest problem for west-side schools: too many children and not enough facilities. The 11 schools had 259 rooms with a capacity for 9,065 pupils; yet 12,334 students were already attending. Crockett School, for example, had 1,430 students, but room for only 1,050. Barclay School with a capacity for 1,120 received 1,717 students. Navarro School had 1,822 with a total capacity for 1,330. And Brackenridge Memorial School hosted 2,004 children but could comfortably accommodate only 1,435. In all, the 11 schools had an excess of 3,269 students.[20]

Additional research revealed particular problems among individual schools. The committee reported that in Brackenridge Memorial, 14 children not yet registered but attending classes had to stay in the school auditorium due to lack of rooms. "They wait their turn until there is room for them," the committee observed, "and they are then permitted to be registered and to attend regularly." In the Barclay School, 53 fifth-graders were found in one room with only 40 desks. To accommodate all of them, the teacher sat 26 children 2 to a chair. At the Sidney Lanier Junior High School, administrators assigned the cafeteria, auditorium, library, dining rooms, and cooking and sewing rooms as classrooms.[21]

Bulging with students, the west-side schools had to resort to only half-day classes for many of the children. The committee discovered that about 1,000 first-graders attended school only half-day on double shifts. "For this reason," it noted, "it takes these children twice as long to complete a grade." With not enough room for them, as many as 6,000 school-age children on the west side did not attend any school. "Occasional inquiries have been made of children on the streets," the committee recorded, "and they say they are not in school because there is no room for them."[22]

The committee concluded that a direct link existed between overcrowded conditions and the discriminatory appropriation of funds for west-side schools by the school board. Besides providing less money per pupil to west-side schools, the school board did not spend the entire amount of monies apportioned for the Mexican schools. The total income for these schools based on both state contributions and property taxes came to $799,152.00. Yet the total expenditures for the 11 schools amounted to only $422,203.48. A surplus of $376,948.52 remained that the school board chose to spend elsewhere despite the poor conditions of the west-side schools.[23]

Utilizing these data, Escobar and the committee proposed that much more could be done by the school board to alleviate overcrowded and inadequate conditions for Mexican-American children. The committee was not prepared to directly challenge the de facto segregated status of the Mexican schools, but it called for at least making them equal to Anglo schools. It suggested a minimum of 5 new elementary schools with a total of between 82 and 94 rooms to service an additional 3,269 students. At least one more junior high was also needed. The construction of these new schools could easily be financed within the existing school board budget. The committee pointed out the contradiction of the school board's ability to finance the construction of new schools and facilities in Anglo neighborhoods but not in the west side. This money would be better utilized, the committee reasoned, in meeting the congested west-side school problems.[24]

Besides documenting the uneven development of the Mexican schools, the committee organized the ideological arguments for remedying the situation. Justice, for one, demanded that these educational inequities be corrected. It was not just for Mexican-American school children to be deprived of a good education. Educational reform would breed sound citizenship, which would benefit the entire San Antonio community. The committee contradicted malicious rumors that its proposed reforms were intended to foster self-segregation. Rather, these reforms were practical corrections to deplorable conditions harming more than just Mexican-American children. Twenty-five percent of the schoolchildren in the west side were Anglos, "and they are being discriminated the same as the others." The committee insisted that it fought for all children regardless of race, color, or creed. Finally, and perhaps more important, good and equal education for Mexican-American children was not only a moral issue but a constitutional one. Under the law, Mexican Americans were entitled to such education. The committee concluded that 82 additional rooms in the form of 5 new school buildings were needed by the opening of the new school year.[25]

Their data collected and their arguments sharpened, the LULAC committee headed by Escobar presented its case to the school board. The board listened and agreed to review the west-side situation but at the same time became defensive. Escobar and the committee attended various other meetings only to receive no response or delays.[26] On one occasion, R. S. Menefee, the president of the board, even suggested that the only reason behind the committee's proposal to build new schools consisted of Escobar's hopes to profit from selling his west-side property to the board. The committee quickly rebuffed Menefee, and Escobar reminded the board that the committee's sole desire was to achieve a good education for west-side children. The problem lay not with the committee but with the board's refusal to upgrade the west-side schools and instead spending money intended for them elsewhere. Escobar noted that mothers in the west side loved their children as much as mothers in other districts and "are interested in seeing that their children get their just due at the hands of this Board."[27] Supporting Escobar, attorney Alonso Perales appeared before the board and categorically denied Menefee's unfounded allegations. "The truth is," Perales stressed, ". . . that each and every member of Council No. 16 of the League of United Latin American Citizens is sincerely and honestly interested in the welfare of all our school children." Escobar had been selected to chair LULAC's committee on education not because he owned west-side property but because of his leadership qualities and his willingness to spend the time gathering the facts of the case. Perales charged that it had been Menefee who had first raised the issue of Escobar's property by offering to buy it if Escobar dropped the proposal for improving west-side schools.[28]

To appease the committee and to neutralize the issue of west-side reforms, the board announced the immediate authorization of an additional school for the west side. However, this amounted only to purchasing 15 abandoned frame rooms from the Peacock Military Academy and moving them to the west side, where the board declared the completion of Lorenzo de Zavala School. Not deceived, the committee denounced the board's action as a deliberate attempt to mislead public opinion. "The said frame dwellings are inadequate and unsafe," the committed declared.[29] Perales reiterated that 88 new rooms were needed and that these had to be in permanent and fire-proof structures: "We do not want shacks."[30] Besides its meager effort in "establishing" Zavala School, the board proposed a survey of west-side school conditions by a University of Texas committee. Escobar sensed delay but hoped that the outside investigation would prove productive. He welcomed this concession and promised to provide the survey committee with his own data.[31]

Dissatisfied with the school board's response and fearful of losing momentum, the committee solicited public support to achieve its objectives. It appealed for endorsements from other organizations and invited them to the committee's meetings. It shared its data on west-side schools with other interested parties.[32] Escobar encouraged supporters to send letters to the school board concerning the west-side issue. "Your effort in their behalf," Escobar explained, "will mean happiness for thousands of school children who are not attending full sessions now for lack of space."[33] Escobar also personally contacted a variety of both Mexican-American and Anglo organizations, labor unions, and many in San Antonio's religious community. In all, the committee claimed support from seventy-three civic, social, labor, and religious organizations. Mexican-American groups endorsing the committee included the Alianza Hispano-Americana, the Baptist Good Will Center, the Democratic Club, Federación Obrera Latino-Americana, Home of Neighborly Service, Cámara Mexicana de Comercio, Mexican Ministries Alliance, Mexican Protestant Social Workers, Order Hijos de América, Sociedad Benito Juárez, Unión de Barberos Latino-Americanos, Unión de Empleados y Dependientes, Unión de Jornaleros, and Unión de Panaderos.[34]

With strong community support, especially among Mexican Americans, Escobar went above the heads of the school board by appealing directly for school relief to State Superintendent of Public Instruction, L. A. Woods.[35] Woods agreed to investigate the west-side conditions and would inspect the area himself. "I assure you," he promised Escobar, "that I am not going to be a party in hurting the Latin-American children of San Antonio."[36] Capitalizing on Woods's favorable response, the committee mobilized to host Woods at a mass rally where it could impress upon the state superintendent the urgency of school reform and of the community's support for it. Scheduled for October 24, 1934, at Sidney Lanier Junior High School, the evening meeting was hailed as an opportunity to hear Woods's proposals for relieving the congested school conditions. Besides asking Woods, the committee invited other prominent speakers including the Reverend C. Tranchese, a leading Mexican-American religious leader and the pastor of Our Lady of Guadalupe; James Tafolla, president of LULAC Council No. 2 of San Antonio; Orlando F. Gerodetti, president of LULAC Council No. 16; Ermilio R. Lozano, president general of LULAC; Alonso Perales; local attorney Carl Wright Johnson; Mrs. María Hernández, secretary of Orden Caballeros de América; Carlos E. Castañeda, librarian-historian at the University of Texas and superintendent of the San Felipe School District in Del Rio, Texas; P. H. Dickson, a member of the state legislature; and Franklin Spears, also of the state legislature. Escobar, of course, would likewise speak.[37] In his autobiography, Escobar recalled the problem of adequate seating for the many families expected. From his store, he lent the arrangements committee 2,500 chairs. As the ceremony commenced, Escobar observed thousands of people marching into the outdoor meeting place. "That was the most impontant [sic], impressive and emotional scene that I have ever seen," he wrote. Escobar estimated the audience to be between 10,000 and 13,000. La Prensa had announced before the meeting that it would be the largest ever held by Mexicans in San Antonio.[38]

During the speeches, the crowd interrupted each speech with rounds of applause. Attorney Johnson drew an enthusiastic response when he stated, "There is no question about it that those West Side children are being deprived of an adequate education by our state school board officials and are victims of abuse and discrimination and these injustices should be corrected." Finally, Superintendent Woods addressed the meeting. He praised for their interest in the schools and did not deny the charges concerning the west-side schools. He concluded: "I promise after I investigate, that I will see to it that your school children's problems will be corrected." The crowd was ecstatic and so was Escobar.[39]

One week later, Escobar informed supporters that he had received a letter from Woods in which the superintendent agreed to support the committee's efforts. Woods conceded the truthfulness of the committee's depiction of the west-side schools. He noted that both the president of the San Antonio School Board and the local superintendent of schools admitted the deficiencies of the Mexican schools. However, the situation could be remedied by utilizing some $900.000 in bond money available to the district. If the school board refused to do this and instead spent it elsewhere, Woods suggested that the committee resort to the courts to prohibit such action. "Frankly," he told Escobar, ". . . I am of the opinion that the first thing the school board should do is to remedy the terrible school conditions that exist in the westside, and I believe that if you continue your work the Board will concede your just demands." A delighted Escobar welcomed Woods's opinion as the first moral victory of the school campaign and believed that with the superintendent's intervention the struggle would go forward.[40]

Taking full advantage of Woods's letter, Escobar sent a summary of it along with supporting data to some of the city's leading Anglo leaders. To Escobar's surprise, many of them, including the mayor, responded with letters of support. Still, despite such favorable response to the committee, the school board refused to deal with Escobar. Board President Menefee told a reporter that he saw no necessity of working with LULAC since the board was moving on its own to make reforms. "(If) we could be free of outside intervention," Menefee was quoted as saying, "we could make the correction much easier." A disappointed Escobar now believed that as long as he headed LULAC's school committee, Menefee would have nothing to do with it. Escobar offered to resign.[41]

THE SCHOOL IMPROVEMENT LEAGUE

Escobar's offer of resignation was also indicative of internal strains within LULAC. On at least two occasions, Escobar had complained about the unwillingness of various LULAC members to support wholeheartedly the school campaign.[42] These tensions plus the reluctance of the school board to negotiate with Escobar led Council No. 16 to appoint a new school committee excluding Escobar. The council also designated the new committee without first conferring with the various organizations supporting the school issue. Insulted and angered, representatives of these other groups denounced the council's actions and moved to organize their own school committee with Escobar as its president. Informed of such action, Escobar approved it and agreed to head the alternative committee. Named La Liga Pro-Defensa Escolar (the School Improvement League), the Liga quickly claimed the support of more than seventy organizations representing approximately 75,000 persons. With such response, the Liga now spearheaded the struggle for better schools and superseded the LULAC committee, which self-destructed.[43]

Early in 1935 the Liga mobilized support from Anglo politicians. Most of San Antonio's representatives to the state legislature, undoubtedly sensitive to increasing political activism by Mexican Americans, endorsed the Liga as did two members of the school board who publicly admitted the depressed school conditions on the west side. Confident of both community and political backing, the Liga moved to pressure the school board by initiating a bill introduced by Representative J. Franklin Spears that would reduce a San Antonio School Board member's term from six to two years. The Liga believed that much of the problem with the school board concerned board members feeling immune from public pressures due to their long terms.[44] Board members apparently felt less sensitive to Mexican-American pressures because of exceedingly low turnout of voters, including Mexican Americans, for school board elections. The bill passed the house but stalled in the education committee of the senate. To impress upon that committee, especially Senator Ernest Fellbaum of San Antonio, the level of community support for the bill, the Liga encouraged supporters to send telegrams to Fellbaum. "Our organization composed of more than five hundred members requests you support bill number three forty-six shortening term members School Board," the Sociedad De La Unión informed Fellbaum.[45] Over 200 telegrams reached Fellbaum and the committee. In addition, Liga members headed by Escobar attended a public hearing sponsored by the education committee. Escobar once again revealed the deplorable school conditions for Mexican-American children. Legislators questioned Board President Menefee, who under pressure conceded the Liga's arguments and promised to upgrade the Mexican schools. He would recommend the construction of at least 2 new schools and the addition of 50 new rooms. Additional property on the west side would also be purchased for school playgrounds. Menefee further agreed to hire sufficient teachers for the west-side schools. With Menefee's concessions, the education committee shelved the bill.[46]

Not willing to relax its campaign after the Austin hearings, Escobar and the Liga sought to solidify community support and to establish an information network. It commenced publication of a bilingual newspaper, *The Defender* (*El Defensor De La Juventud*) to keep both its Spanish-speaking and Anglo supporters informed of Liga activities and issue. *The Defender* reinforced the arguments for the citizens of San Antonio to support the movement for better schools. It was their duty as parents, as taxpayers, and as concerned citizens interested in the welfare of youth. It was the moral thing to do. The Liga reiterated that it would maintain pressure on the school board until Mexican-American children received justice.[47] In its English-language section, *The Defender* also appealed to concerned Anglo citizens for support. Besides its community newspaper, the Liga utilized other methods to reach out to the public. In March 1935 it announced plans for a large fiesta at the Municipal Auditorium. Escobar obtained as headliner Mexico's foremost composer and singer, Agustín Lara. Held on April 10, the fiesta proved a success. The Liga mixed entertainment with consciousness raising by publishing a fiesta program containing data about the school problem. In addition, Carlos Castañeda from the University of Texas explained the Liga's role and objectives. The fiesta attracted large numbers of people and raised more than $700 for the Liga. Other community events sponsored by the Liga included athletic field days for the children of the west side.[48]

The Liga received its most important success, however, a few months later in July 1935, when the University of Texas survey committee completed its report of west-side school conditions. It confirmed the findings of the earlier LULAC research and recommended construction of new schools plus additions to existing ones in the west side. The school board accepted the recommendations and together with Menefee's previous pledges authorized the building of 3 new elementary schools during the next three years in addition to maintaining Zavala School with its wooden barracks.[49] Yet these concessions, after over a year's struggle, would only partially improve west-side conditions. Unfortunately, the Liga, affected by the economic pressures of the depression, found it difficult to maintain momentum. Moreover, the dawn of World War II completely set aside the school campaign and ended the first chapter of the School Improvement League.

THE POSTWAR STRUGGLES

The war over, a still-committed Escobar believed it propitious to launch another protest movement concerning west-side school conditions. The school board had made some additional modifications but had done nothing substantial to relieve congestion on the west side while the number of school-age children increased. On sound personal economic footing after the war, Escobar now plunged back into the school struggle. In August 1947, representatives from more than thirty Spanish-speaking organizations along with certain Anglo supporters reconstituted the School Improvement League with Escobar as its president. "Before the war we fought a bitter campaign in order to obtain a mere dole of four schools of varied and inadequate construction from the San Antonio School Board," Escobar reminded delegates. "With the onset of the war all of our efforts were then enlisted in behalf of victory. Our campaign for educational justice remained dormant."[50] The war had been won and Mexican Americans intensified their demands for opportunities equal to those of other Americans.

The league's ideological argument for quality education was enhanced by the experience of the war. "Our fight to preserve our way of life from the endangering and hostile forces of the world has ended victoriously," the league stressed, "and we now face the task of rebuilding our own community." The war, by enlisting Mexican-American efforts in the struggle to preserve American democracy, had accelerated the acculturation of Mexican Americans. Consequently, the league more intensively defended Mexican-American children not as "Latin Americans," "México-Texanos," or "Indo-Latinos" but as Americans. "If in the trenches of Europe and the Pacific we were equal and we demonstrated our loyalty and love for the Stars and Stripes," the league noted, "then in civic life we also desire equality." The league sought no special privileges, just equality: "We simply want the same opportunity given our children in education as the equal duty that was given them to figh[t] and die for our country."[51]

Having reorganized the league, Escobar sought to capture media attention, revitalize the issue of the west-side schools, and once again put the school board on the defensive. He astutely accomplished this by focusing attention on the "fire traps"— the temporary wooden buildings—housing many west-side children during school hours. In interviews with local newspapers, Escobar charged that the lives of more than 2,000 schoolchildren were being endangered by having to attend classes in these buildings. "In the event of fire any one of these school buildings would result in our children dying like rats," he told the *San Antonio Evening News*.[52] Drawn to the sensationalism of this story, the same newspaper published photographs that supported Escobar's charges. One revealed an abandoned pecan shelling plant reconverted to classrooms at Sidney Lanier High School. Another showed an old abandoned wooden church serving as a music hall for the same school. Still a third exposed two worn outdoor tables at Zavala School that substituted for a cafeteria. Escobar reminded readers that the entire Zavala School consisted of old frame buildings that should be condemned. Already a fire in 1945 had destroyed part of Zavala.[53] Asked to comment on Escobar's charges, Superintendent of Schools Thomas B. Portwood declined to debate the School Improvement League in the media. The league exploited this publicity by announcing that it would not be satisfied until such wooden structures were replaced by permanent ones and additional schools built in the westside. "We don't want any more shacks," Escobar insisted.[54]

To effectively argue, as in the 1930s, that it spoke for the Mexican-American community, the league again concentrated on obtaining broad public support. Many of the older Mexican-American organizations once more enthusiastically endorsed the league, as did certain Anglo welfare and religious groups. In addition, younger Mexican Americans, many of them "veteranos" recently returned from the war, received their political baptism by joining the league. The league expanded its support base even more in the postwar period by securing the formal encouragement of the Catholic hierarchy in San Antonio through the Archdiocesan Office for the Spanish Speaking. More than eighty organizations ratified the league's objectives.[55]

Public support was also solicited by the re-establishment of an information network. Besides its own newspaper and reliance on sympathetic publications such as the *San Antonio Light* and the Spanish-language *La Prensa*, the league this time made use of radio as a consciousness-raising and information-disseminating tool.

Several San Antonio radio stations, especially Spanish-language ones, offered free radio time. For example, Raul Cortez, owner of KCOR, allowed Escobar fifteen minutes each Monday at 1 p.m. for the league's program. KITE through its daily afternoon program "La Voz de México" (The Voice of Mexico) granted the league fifteen minutes each day.[56] Reaching thousands of people on a daily basis, the league used radio to further four basic objectives. First, it strongly counseled parents to keep their children in school in spite of difficult school conditions and the economic hardships faced by families. The situation was underscored by the large number of migrant farmworking families who resided in the city during the nonharvest season, but who left during the picking season to utilize all family members, including children, as a working unit. These parents were told that by not keeping their children in school they irrevocably harmed them. "The money that your children can earn in one year of farmwork," the league stressed to parents, "cannot justify ruining their futures by a lack of education."[57] Second, the league used radio to socialize Mexicans in San Antonio, especially parents, to the league's educational philosophy. Education raised children from a state of ignorance and made them better sons and daughters as well as future parents and citizens. It prepared them to cope with life. Education was both a human and a constitutional right. Mexican-American children were entitled as U.S. citizens to an education and no one could deny them that opportunity. Third, through the air the league informed parents about its activities and of basic facts concerning the schools. Escobar estimated that about 80 percent of Mexicans in San Antonio did not know their educational rights. Some did not know at what age their children could attend school or what school district they belonged to. Finally, Escobar used time on English-language broadcasts to reach Anglos and convince them of the league's cause.[58]

To justify additional schools and facilities as well as to educate the public about the west-side school problem, the league once again engaged in "action research." It formed a special research committee to compile data.[59] Although the basic inequities between Mexican schools and Anglo ones had not changed, the committee discovered that the disparities of resources had widened. Overcrowded conditions still plagued west-side schools. The league estimated that 11 west-side elementary schools did not possess adequate classroom space for over 7,000 students. In some cases, 50 or more students occupied one classroom. "The state law requires that there shall be no more than 35 students to each teacher," Escobar observed, "but on the West Side there are more than that—in West Side classrooms, in some instances, 65 to 75 pupils per teacher." Overcrowded conditions forced many children to attend only half-day classes. In 5 elementary schools alone more than 1,800 students were restricted to half-day classes. Thousands of others attended schools out of their district for lack of space. Those fortunate enough to attend were not only cramped in classrooms but did not have proper recreational areas. While 25 elementary schools in Anglo sections contained over 70 acres of recreational space to serve 9,225 students, on the west side 4 elementary schools, as an example, only possessed 13 acres of playgrounds to care for 4,087 students. Escobar calculated that over 15,000 west-side school children had unsuitable playgrounds.[60]

Overcrowded and confined in space, many of the Mexican schools also represented firetraps. More than 2,000 children occupied temporary frame rooms. The league stressed the dangers of this condition by arranging an on-site inspection of these facilities by the San Antonio Fire Department accompanied by league members and representatives of the school board. In its report, the fire department substantiated the league's concerns. Of Zavala School, the report read: "buildings are situated within 20 feet of each other, thus creating an exposure hazard to all buildings." And of the one-story wooden annex at Sidney Lanier, it noted; "Wallpaper is rotten and loose. This constitutes a very serious fire hazard." The fire chief recommended immediate evacuation of the annex. The Lanier music hall—the old wooden church—had no fire extinguishers. Even west-side schools built of brick, such as J. T. Brackenridge, possessed no fire extinguishers.[61] "Imagine a city that lays claim to be counted as modern," the league chastised San Antonio, "having to admit that hundreds of its little people are closeted for hours daily in school buildings which have been proved to be positive fire traps!"[62]

The league concluded its postwar survey of school conditions by formally petitioning the school board on November 12, 1947, for changes. Escobar and league officers demanded the immediate elimination of the worst aspects of the west-side schools and the commencement of a new school construction program. League spokesman Manuel Castañeda stressed to the board that crowded classrooms and congested playgrounds retarded the intellectual and physical health of children. "The combination of these two evils, namely stunted mental growth and inferior physical conditions," he warned, "in turn creates fertile conditions for the existence of warped social complexes, vice, and inevitable juvenile delinquency and criminality."[63] The league insisted that all temporary wooden buildings—the firetraps—be vacated and replaced by permanent structures. It also called for acquisition of new playground acreage for west-side schools. Escobar noted that these immediate changes would pose no undue financial burdens on the board since, according to his research, it possessed more than adequate and unused building funds. The league called for the construction of the following specific items: 6 to 8 new elementary schools, 1 junior high school, 1 senior high school, and 1 vocational school.[64]

Receiving the league's demands, School Board President Harry Rogers thanked the league for coming to the board rather than to the newspapers. Yet unwilling to concede past board failures concerning the west side, Rogers defensively insisted that the board already had initiated its own improvements for schools in the area. These included condemned property adjoining some schools, such as Sidney Lanier, that could be purchased by the board for new buildings and playgrounds. As for the wooden buildings, Rogers concluded that they could not be closed immediately. "Would you rather we close these 'firetraps' and have more half-day sessions?" he challenged league members. "Yes," responded Castañeda, "They're nothing but firetraps." "Well," reacted Rogers, "these firetraps have been there for 25 years and we've never had a child burned to death." Despite the heated exchange and Rogers's display of insensitivity, both sides agreed to appoint subcommittees and negotiate league demands. The league had won round one by forcing the board to consider their petition and accept negotiations. Assuming the moral high ground, the league gained additional public sympathy. "Apologies for existing conditions as well as vague promises of improvement are out of order," the *San Antonio Express* criticized the board. "There is work to be done, for which the entire community must share responsibility even as it will share the benefits of the achievement. How about ditching the talk—and getting on with the job."[65]

In its follow-up meeting with the board's subcommittee, the league presented specific proposals for immediate action on the firetraps and over-crowded conditions. They included the abandonment of the old pecan shelling plant used as a schoolroom annex at Sidney Lanier; the purchase of the city block south of Sidney Lanier and the construction of a new annex composed of classrooms and a gymnasium; the building of a new Zavala School to replace the barracks; the authorization of a new elementary school on 20 acres at the intersection of Barclay and Arizona streets; the addition of 8 new classrooms to Brackenridge School; and the acquisition of 4 sites for new elementary schools. Faced with the league's pressure plus public concern over the firetraps, the school board acquiesced to some of these demands. It would acquire the city block south of Sidney Lanier and build additional classrooms and a gymnasium. The old pecan shelling plant at Lanier would be closed and students temporarily transferred to other schools. A new Zavala School would replace the barracks. However, Zavala students would remain in the frame buildings until the new school became available on adjacent property. Brackenridge School would acquire 8 new classrooms. Finally, the board, in subsequent action, approved construction of 2 new elementary schools at a total cost of $400,000. An elated but cautious Escobar informed the Mexican-American community that this success was only the beginning of a new struggle over the schools. Much still remained to be done.[66]

Escobar's cautiousness was not unwarranted. Although the board in principle agreed to most of the league's initial demands, it procrastinated in fulfilling them. Instead, it accelerated new school construction in Anglo neighborhoods or in nonpopulated suburbs where they hoped to entice new housing developments.[67] Dissatisfied with the board's slow response to reforms plus believing that the public did not fully appreciate the magnitude of the west-side school problem, Escobar and the league gathered and presented additional evidence. More than 10,000 students did not have access to adequate schooling. Of those attending school, over 7,000 were cramped "like sardines" in fewer than 200 classrooms. West-side schools averaged more than 40 pupils per room, while those in other sections averaged fewer than 30. At Collins Garden School, for example, 901 students attempted to learn in 25 rooms averaging 32 to 39 per room. The league estimated that even with the construction of the proposed 4 new elementary schools on the west side they would still not be able to accommodate all of the school-age children. Critically affected were the hundreds of first and second graders who attended only half-day classes. In 4 west-side schools alone with a total of 3,621 students, almost 1,500, or 41 percent, went to half-day sessions due to lack of space. When the *San Antonio Light* reported that some educators did not believe half-day classes retarded students since all they lost was recreation time, Escobar countered: "If half-day classes do not retard education why don't these educators put all children on half-day classes so that all children will receive equal education, instead of picking on underprivileged children?"[68]

The league called further attention to the deplorable facilities provided to west-side children. Some schools possessed limited or no cafeterias. At both the Sam Houston and Hood schools no cafeterias had ever been built in twenty years. The children ate off the floor. At Sidney Lanier a cafeteria with a seating capacity of 120 serviced a student body of over 1,700.[69] Many students had to eat their lunches on the school grounds. "This creates a problem of sanitation since food particles are dropped on the yard which attract rats, mice, roaches, and flies."[70] The Lanier Senior and Junior High School library, for example, only could accommodate 125. Of course, the use of wooden classrooms continued to plague the west side. Despite the board's pledge to eliminate the firetraps, many still functioned as classrooms. Out of 67 such rooms in all San Antonio elementary schools 55 were located on the west side. The barracks courted disaster. In 1948 another fire broke out in one of Zavala's frame buildings that fortunately injured no students. Two years later, a third fire at Zavala engulfed and destroyed two classrooms along with two offices and a library. No permanent classrooms had as yet been built by the school board. Miraculously, the fire occurred on a weekend with no students in attendance.[71] Calling Zavala a "possible funeral pyre," Escobar castigated the board for its "criminal negligence": "We hope that it will not be necessary to see that two or three hundred children are burned to death before we see to it that the School Board does something to correct completely this menacing situation." Escobar and the league insisted on the completion of the projects already agreed upon plus at least one more elementary school and one junior high school.[72]

Seemingly unable to get action from the school board despite persistent and confrontational attendance at board meetings, the league appealed again to public opinion. It utilized its radio program to disseminate information and to request funds and volunteers. In 1948 the league mobilized support for the election of lawyer Gus García to the school board. Several thousand Mexican Americans went to the polls and elected García.[73] In addition, Escobar attempted to duplicate the 1934 mass rally. The highlight of this demonstration would be to show photographic evidence of decaying west-side school conditions. "This [sic] slides will show once and for all that our children have not only been deprived of equal school facilities, advantages and opportunities," a league leaflet read, "but that no amount of money would ever be able to repay them for the tremendous loss in morale and physical wellbeing that they have had to suffer."[74] With the meeting scheduled for August 31, 1948, Escobar hoped to use the occasion, as in 1934, to appeal to State Superintendent Woods for school relief. Labeling Superintendent Portwood a "menace" to the welfare of children in San Antonio, Escobar called on Woods to authorize a survey of west-side school conditions.[75] Escobar likewise invited members of the school board: "Mr. President, and everyone of you ladies and gentlemen are invited to attend that meeting, so that you can see in pictures the way that you have neglected, abused and punished helpless children."[76]

Three thousand people attended the rally and heard main speaker Carlos Castañeda decry the fact that schools attended by Mexican Americans in Texas were in worse shape in 1948 than they had been in 1934. "The inferior schools are not a matter of discrimination or segregation but a plain case of social injustice and a violation of the state school law," Casteñeda charged.[77] The league displayed photographic slides that, among other things, revealed pictures of a dead dog that had lain in front of the Brackenridge cafeteria for three days before being removed, of children eating on the ground at Zavala, and of a young boy at Lanier practicing his music in a bathroom for lack of proper space. Although Woods could not attend, Escobar nevertheless used the rally to urge him once more to intervene in San Antonio.[78]

Woods this time did not intervene. However, faced with the league's persistence and its ability to solicit public sympathy, the board itself proposed a survey of the west side. In 1949 it authorized Dean T. H. Shelby, head of the Extension Department of the University of Texas, to head the study. Escobar attacked the survey as incomplete, but the Shelby Committee did note that San Antonio faced an acute shortage of facilities at the same time that its school-age population was expanding. The committee went further and recommended that a minimum of $15 million would have to be expended within five years if the city was going to realistically confront its educational problems. The Shelby Committee's report, however, found little support among school board members. Historically biased against upgrading the west-side schools due to their perception of the "limited educational needs" of the Mexican Americans, the majority of the board desired to spend as little as possible on the Mexican schools and instead use its funds for the equally expanding Anglo neighborhoods. Board President Rogers in early 1950 established still another survey in the hope of soliciting a lower price tag. Rather than staffed by academicians, this committee consisted of citizens approved by the board. The Citizens' Survey Committee would study not just the west side but all San Antonio's schools and propose changes. Rogers suggested that one of these might be a $5 million bond issue. Chaired by Superintendent Portwood, the committee included nine members but only one Mexican American: Bennie Cantú of the Mexican Chamber of Commerce.[79]

Following four months of investigation, the Citizens' Survey Committee issued its report at a special board meeting. It surprised Rogers by advising a $9.2 million bond issue to cover the construction over five years of new schools and improvements and additions to old ones in all parts of San Antonio. For the west-side schools, the committee recommended a new 24-room Zavala School as well as new classrooms and additions at other schools plus cafeteria improvements. It further supported the building of a new junior high school on the west side and the expansion of Sidney Lanier High School. However, the committee chose not to target specific expenditures to particular projects. It believed that this would better be served by the board.[80] Prepared to address the committee's report, the league stacked the board meeting with between 50 and 75 members. "The West Side School Improvement League," one reporter observed, "took to the floor at the outset of the open discussion and held the floor almost the entire evening." Spokesman Richard Sánchez replied that the league found the report satisfactory except for its "discrepancies in the western part of the city." Sánchez proposed 3 new elementary schools and supported a bond issue, but only if the amount adequately met school needs. When Sánchez and other league members discussed individual schools on the west side, including the firetraps, they drew the ire of President Rogers. "We will not destroy good sound buildings because a few individuals do not know the difference between a good school and a bad one," he angrily addressed the league. Rogers added that, rather than constantly criticizing the board, Escobar and his followers should go out and support the bond issue. And, in a direct attack on the league that exposed Rogers's biases, he concluded: "We can't keep building schools for transients who go to school only three months out of the nine." Not intimidated, league members forced one committee member to admit that even under the report's recommendations some frame rooms would still be utilized on the west side. The board member received catcalls from league partisans when he defended the barracks by insisting that Zavala was the safest school in the district.[81]

The league countered the Citizens' Survey Report by issuing its own based on its most recent research. It found the citizens' report incomplete and incorrect and noted that its recommendations would only partially solve the problems. "We have lived on the Westside and we know the people, their hopes and aspirations," Escobar addressed the citizen's committee. "We feel that we speak for these people in warning you that your report and your request is not ample, and that in a very short time the citizens of San Antonio will again be called on to rectify some of the mistakes which are being made." Escobar observed that the citizens' report called for the construction of new schools in certain northern, eastern, and southern sections of the city where league research revealed nearly two vacant classrooms. Some schools in these predominantly Anglo neighborhoods, instead of being used as schools, were being occupied by administrative offices. Three such buildings could accommodate close to a thousand students. "Why does the Board propose to build more school rooms in some sections of town, when there is a total of 57 vacant rooms already in these schools?" inquired Escobar. On the other hand, minority neighborhoods cried out for new schools and improvements. Escobar pointed out that the survey overlooked black requests for a much-needed vocational school in the eastern portion of San Antonio. On the west side, Escobar stressed that the survey had completely failed to provide for such needs as adequate playground space, cafeteria facilities, auditoriums, and additional classrooms. Escobar concluded by insisting that the board commit a certain percentage of the bond money for specific proposals, especially on the west side. Board member Gus García believed that at least $3 million of the $9 million bond issue was needed for west-side schools. The league promised to endorse the bond issue, but only if the board reciprocated by allocating certain monies for west-side needs.[82]

Shortly before the bond election, both the School Improvement League and the local branch of the NAACP requested at a board meeting that the board agree to allocate specific portions of the bond to the Mexican and black schools within the district. Attorney Alonso Perales supported these requests by introducing a letter from Archbishop Robert E. Lucey calling attention to the inadequate school facilities in the poorer parts of the city. Undaunted, President Rogers responded that much was already being done in these neighborhoods and that he could not agree to the pledge desired by Escobar and the NAACP. "This board is not going to be pushed around," he told Escobar. The league president replied; "You talk like you own the school board. I say the (Citizen Survey) committee's report is a lot of misinformation."[83] Faced with a recalcitrant board, the league refused to endorse the bond issue but did not counsel supporters on how to vote. The league declared that it would not campaign against the bond measure and that it would leave the decision up to the voters. In a small turnout, the $9.3 million bond issue passed. A satisfied board asserted that although it was not bound by the citizens' survey it would comply with most of its recommendations. Accordingly, it approved new plans for a permanent Zavala School plus other construction and improvements outlined for the west-side schools.[84]

CONCLUSION

Relentless in its campaign against the school board, the league continued its struggle into the 1950s. Unfortunately, it never fully achieved its objectives of equal and adequate educational facilities and opportunities for Mexican-American children. Yet, as with many poor community movements, it succeeded in forcing the issue of the west-side schools on the school board and on the conscience of San Antonio. Through its dedication to cause and by a display of keen organizational skills, the league also gained some concrete results. The new schools and improvements first promised and partially reaffirmed following the 1950 bond issue were in time completed. In 1952 the Zavala firetraps—long the symbol of the league's struggle—were finally torn down and a new permanent structure opened its doors.[85] Because of the league more Mexican-American children could attend school. The league continued to function, although less actively until at least 1956. By then not only were other community organizations engaged in educational issues, but Mexican Americans in San Antonio were achieving a greater voice within the educational structures of the city as teachers, administrators, and representatives to the school board. A legacy of inferior education had not been eliminated, but the league had commenced the movement by Mexican Americans to gain control over educational resources and to assert the rights of their children as U.S. citizens to equal schooling with other Americans. This movement would expand in later decades to include not only the desegregation of Mexican schools as a means to equal education but also the need to restructure curriculums to account for the bilingual, bicultural traditions of Mexican Americans. As if to crown Escobar's and the league's pioneering efforts, a new junior high school was dedicated in 1958 in the name of Eleuterio Escobar: "This gesture of recognition that I gladly accept," Escobar noted at the dedication,

> is really due not to my efforts alone, but to the efforts of all of you—the groups, friends, and organizations—who, side by side with the School Improvement League, joined in the struggle for educational emancipation until the rights of our children were recognized and respected with equality and justice.[86]

NOTES

1. Frances Fox Piven and Richard A. Cloward, *Poor People's Movements: Why They Succeed, How They Fail* (New York, 1977), p. 20.

2. Eleuterio Escobar, Final Autobiography, 1894–1958 (typescript) in Eleuterio Escobar Collection, box 1, fld. 1e, Rare Books and Manuscript Collection, Mexican American Archives, Benson Latin American Library, University of Texas at Austin. Both his parents' families had lost land to the incoming Anglos by the turn of the century. Hereinafter, all documents cited are from Escobar Collection.

3. *Ibid.*

4. *Ibid.*

5. Taylor, *An American-Mexican Frontier.* Also see Montejano, *Anglos and Mexicanos.*

6. Escobar Autobiography.

7. *Ibid.*

8. The casino lasted until 1931; see *La Prensa* (San Antonio). Oct. 30 1927. Miscellaneous Newspapers folder.

9. Escobar Autobiography, In the early 1930s, Escobar and other Mexican-American businessmen and professionals also sponsored the Hispano League for amateur baseball players.

10. See clipping from *San Antonio Evening Express*, July 25, 1930, in Miscellaneous Newspapers.

11. Escobar Autobiography.

12. See correspondence and documents of Association of Independent Voters in box 1; hereinafter referred as Association. See flyer "A Los Ciudadanos, México-Americanos, Jan. 22. 1932," Miscellaneous Newspapers. See unsigned to Escobar, San Antonio, June 11, 1932; Walter Tynan to Escobar, Aug. 23, 1932; Hart McCormick to Association, July 28, 1932; flyer: "Mensaje Del. Lie. Alonso S. Perales"; and see sample ballot: "Ejemplo de la Boleta," in Association, Box 1.

13. Escobar Autobiography.

14. Alonso S. Perales to Escobar, Managua, Nicaragua, Nov. 22, 1932, in Miscellaneous Incoming Mail & Telegrams, 1929–1969 and undated in box 1.

15. Escobar Autobiography.

16. See "Preliminary Notes to Autobiography," box 1. On the Depression in San Antonio see García, "The Making of the Mexican-American Mind," and Julia Kirk Blackwelder, *Women of the Depression: Caste and Culture is San Antonio, 1929–1939* (College Station, Tex., 1984).

17. See fld. id. "A Revised Autobiographical Draft."

18. Escobar Autobiography.

19. See Escobar to A. B. Stevens, San Antonio, May 4. 1934, in folder "Escobar Archives," box 1; see pamphlet "More and Better Schools for the Western Section," in "Escobar Archives," box 1.

20. See incomplete document dated 1934 in fld. 3, box 2, and "More and Better Schools."

21. Undated document but apparently written in 1934 in "Escobar Archives," box 1.

22. See Board of Education documents, Oct. 23, 1934, in fld. 3, box 2, and undated document apparently written in 1934 in "Escobar Archives," box 1. Conditions in the Mexican schools in other parts of Texas were no better. In El Paso, for example, 41 percent of the Mexican children only attended half-day school in 1934. In one school there existed an average of 61.4 pupils per room. *See LULAC News*, Dec. 1936, pp. 3–6.

23. "More and Better Schools."

24. Undated document apparently written in 1934 in fld. 3, box 3; see Escobar to Honorable Board of Trustees, San Antonio Independent School District, April 9, 1934, in "Escobar Archives," box 1, and "More and Better Schools."

25. Undated document apparently written in 1934 in fld. 3, box 2; also undated documents, "Escobar Archives," box 1. See "La Verdadera Situación Escobar," in "Escobar Archives," box 1; "More and Better Schools"; undated document apparently written in 1934 in "Escobar Archives," box 1; and president, LULAC Council 16, and Escobar to the Honorable Board of Trustees, San Antonio Independent School District. n.d., 1934, in "Escobar Archives," box 1.

26. See Escobar to R. S. Menefee, president, San Antonio Board of Education, April 9, 1934; Gregory Salinas to Menefee, April 12. 1934; same to same, April 30, 1934; president, LULAC Council 16, to Menefee, May 1, 1934; same to Honorable Board to Trustees, May 5, 1934; unsigned to same, May 5, 1934; president, LULAC Council, to Menefee, May 24, 1934, all in "Escobar Archives," box 1.

27. Escobar to Board, San Antonio, May 17, 1934, in "Escobar Archives," box 1.

28. See Perales statement, San Antonio, May 15, 1934, in "Escobar Archives," box 1.

29. "More and Better Schools."

30. Perales statement, May 15, 1934, in "Escobar Archives," box 1.

31. Escobar to Dr. B. F. Pittinger, San Antonio, Nov. 17, 1934, and Escobar to Dr. Marberry, San Antonio, Nov. 17, 1934, in "Escobar Archives," box 1.

32. Escobar to W. O. W. Juárez. San Antonio, Sept. 4, 1934, in "Escobar Archives," box

1; see form letter in both Spanish and English written by Escobar, San Antonio, Sept. 28, 1934. "Escobar Archives," box 1.

33. See Escobar form letter, San Antonio, Oct. 19, 1934, "Escobar Archives," box 1.

34. See list of contacts in *ibid.*: form letter, Sept. 28, 1934, and Escobar to H. C. Bell, San Antonio, Oct. 13, 1934; also see Escobar to James Tafolla Jr., San Antonio, Nov. 1, 1934, in "Escobar Archives," box 1. For a list of sponsoring organizations see clipping from *La Prensa*, Oct. 21, 1934, in Miscellaneous Newspapers.

35. Eugenio Salinas to R. S. Menefee, San Antonio, Aug. 15, 1934, "Escobar Archives," box 1.

36. L. A. Woods to Escobar, Austin, Sept. 17, 1934, "Escobar Archives," box 1.

37. Escobar form letter, Oct. 18, 19, 1934. "Escobar Archives," box 1; see program, Oct. 21, 1934, in fld. 3, box 2.

38. Escobar Autobiography; Escobar to José Rendón, San Antonio, Nov. 7, 1934, "Escobar Archives," box 1; *La Prensa*, Oct. 24, 1934, Miscellaneous Newspapers.

39. Escobar Autobiography.

40. Escobar to Reverend Pedro Reyna, San Antonio, Nov. 10, 1934, "Escobar Archives," box 1.

41. Same to Respectable Auditorio, San Antonio, Dec. 14, 1934, "Escobar Archives," box 1.

42. Same to Dr. O. Gerodetti, San Antonio, April 4, 1934, "Escobar Archives," box 1, and same to C. E. Castañeda, San Antonio, Sept. 4, 1934, in fld. 1, box 3.

43. See Escobar Autobiography; "Minutes & List of Founding Members & Organizations of the School Improvement League, 1934," in fld. 1, box 2; "Liga Pro-Defensa Escolar Acto Primordial," in fld. 2, box 2; and Pedro Hernández to Dr. Orlando Gerodetti. San Antonio, Dec. 5. 1934, and "Refitación a un Informe Dado Por El Concilio No. 16 de los LULACS," in "Escobar Archives," box 1. Escobar officially resigned from being president of the LULAC Committee and from Council 16 on March 16, 1935; see Escobar to Gerodetti, San Antonio, March 16, 1935, "Escobar Archives," box 1.

44. See R. L. Reoder to Escobar, Austin, Jan. 28, 1935, fld. 2, box 3, and *La Prensa*, Jan. 7, 1935, Miscellaneous Newspapers; see *The Defender of the Youth*, Feb. 16, 1935, Miscellaneous Newspapers.

45. A. Barrera to Ernest Fellbaum, San Antonio, Feb. 4, 1935, fld. 2, box 3; see additional telegrams in fld. 2, box 3.

46. *El Defensor de la Juventud*, Feb. 16, 1935, pp. 1–6, in Miscellaneous Newspapers.

47. *Ibid.*, p. 1.

48. *El Defensor*, March 9, 1935, p. 1; Escobar to Agustín Lara, San Antonio, March 5, 1935, fld. 3, box 3; same to same, April 16, 1935, fld. 2. box 3; same to same, May 6, 1935, fld. 3, box 3; Fiesta program, fld. 13, box 4; Carlos E. Castañeda to Escobar, Del Rio, March 27, 1935, fld. 2, box 3; J. Tafolla, Sr. to Santos S. López, San Antonio, June 8, 1935, fld. 2, box 3: and *San Antonio Evening News*, June 11, 1935, Miscellaneous Newspapers.

49. *La Prensa*, July 21, 1935, in Miscellaneous Newspapers.

50. Escobar Autobiography; Escobar radio transcript, undated, fld. 9, box 5; "Informe del Presidente Escobar—Jan. 27, 1948," fld. 6, box 5; *ABC*, Sept. 1948, p. 3. fld. 12, box 4; Escobar radio transcript KIWW, Jan. 11, 1950, fld. 8, box 5: Articles of Incorporation of School Improvement League, Oct. 7, 1947, fld. 1, box 4. During the war, Escobar invested in wholesale silver craft manufacturing through his own company, the EECO Silver Craft Factory. He also represented certain Mexican oil interests that required manufactured equipment from Texas.

51. *ABC*, Sept. 1947, pp. 3–14, fld. 2, box 4.

52. *San Antonio Evening News*, Sept. 2, 1947; p. 1, in Escobar Scrapbook, 1947–50.

53. *Ibid.*, Sept. 3, 1947, p. 1; Escobar radio transcript, KIWW, Feb. 15. 1950, fld. 8, box 5.

54. *San Antonio Light*, Aug. 20, 1947, in Scrapbook.

55. See affiliation cards, 1947–48, in box 2; *ABC*, Sept. 1947; Escobar to Dwight Allison San Antonio, Dec. 29, 1947, fld. 4, box 3.

56. Escobar speech to General Assembly to League, Aug. 27, 1947, fld. 3, box 5.

57. League radio transcript. undated, fld. 5, box 5.

58. Elpidio Barrera radio transcript, Oct. 1947, KCOR, fld. 5, box 5; League radio transcript, undated, fld. 9, box 5; transcript of Escobar speech at San Fernando School, Nov. 26, 1947, fld. 3, box 5; Escobar radio transcript, KMAC, undated, fld. 9, box 5.

59. Transcript of Escobar address to League, Aug. 22, 1947, fld. 3, box 5; and Escobar to Honorable C. Ray Davis, San Antonio, Sept. 10, 1947; same to Arthur Fenster-Maker, San Antonio, Sept. 10, 1947; Thomas B. Portwood to Escobar. San Antonio, Oct. 13, 1947; James T. Shea to Escobar, San Antonio, Oct. 15, 1947, all in fld. 4, box 3.

60. See undated report, appears to be 1947, in fld. 8, box 6; *San Antonio Evening News*, Aug. 25, 1947, in Scrapbook; Escobar-Henry B. González report, undated appears to be 1947, fld. 4, box 6; Manuel Castañeda radio transcript, KIWW. Sept. 11, 1947, fld. 5, box 5; transcript of Escobar address to League, Dec. 8, 1947, fld. 5, box 5; and *ABC*, Sept. 1947, p. 2.

61. See report of Fire Prevention Bureau, Nov. 1, 1947, fld. 3, box 4.

62. League radio transcript, KMAC, undated, appears to be 1947, fld. 9, box 5.

63. As quoted in *San Antonio Express*, Nov. 13, 1947. in Scrapbook.

64. *Ibid.*; also see "Comité de Delegados de la Liga Pro-Defensa Escobar en la presentación de su Petición Oficial ante el Consejo Escobar," Nov. 12, 1947, fld. 2, box 4; Escobar radio transcript, KCOR, Nov. 17, 1947, fld. 5, box 5; transcript of Escobar speech, San Fernando School, Nov. 26, 1947, fld. 3, box 5; transcript of Escobar speech, Jan. 27, 1948, fld. 6, box 5; and Escobar radio transcript, KCOR, Nov. 25, 1947, fld. 5, box 5.

65. *Express*, Nov. 13, 15, 1947, in Scrapbook.

66. Transcript of Escobar speech, undated, appears to be 1947, fld. 7, box 5; Escobar to School Board Committee, San Antonio, Dec. 1, 1947, fld. 5, box 5; *Evening News*, Nov. 26, 1947; *Light*, Dec. 10, 1947; *Express*, Dec. 17, 1947, in Scrapbook and transcript of Escobar speech, undated, fld. 9. box 5; Escobar radio transcript, KCOR, Dec. 15, 1947, fld. 5, box 5.

67. Escobar to Board of Trustees, San Antonio, Nov. 28, 1947, fld. 4, box 3; Escobar to Board, undated, but appears to be Dec. 1947, fld. 8, box 4.

68. League radio transcript, KIWW, Jan. 18, 1950, fld. 8, box 5; *Evening News*, Nov. 22, 1949. p. 102, Miscellaneous Newspapers; Escobar radio transcript, KIWW, April 26, 1950, fld. 8, box 5; undated report, fld. 5, box 6; undated report, fld. 14, box 4; *Light*, March 29, 1948, Miscellaneous Newspapers; undated document in "Escobar Archives," box 1; *Light*, March 29, 1948, Miscellaneous Newspapers; Escobar speech, undated but appears to be 1948, fld. 14, box 4.

69. League radio transcript, KIWW, Feb. 15, 1950, fld. 8, box 5; "Growth and Development of Sidney Lanier School According to Enrollment, Buildings and Grounds Since 1923–1950," Feb. 13, 1950. fld. 2, box 6.

70. "Growth and Development at Sidney Lanier."

71. Undated document, fld. 5, box 6; *Express* , Jan. 8, 1950; *La Prensa*, Jan. 8, 1950; Jan. 10, 1950, in Miscellaneous Newspapers.

72. See undated clipping from *Express*, Miscellaneous Newspapers; *ibid.*, Jan. 15, 1948, Miscellaneous Newspapers. 73. Manuel Castañeda radio transcript, KCOR, April 5, 1948, fld. 6, box 5; Escobar radio transcript, KCOR, April 5, 1948, fld. 6, box 5; newspaper clipping, Miscellaneous Newspapers.

74. League flyer, fld. 14, box 4.

75. Escobar to Woods, San Antonio, Aug. 12, 1948, fld. 5, box 3.

76. As quoted in Escobar to Elpido Barrera, San Antonio, Aug. 3, 1948, fld. 5, box 3.

77. Newspaper clipping, Escobar Scrapbook. During the war Castañeda had served as regional director of the Fair Employment Practice Commission in the Southwest.

78. Escobar to Woods, San Antonio, Sept. 4, 1948. fld. 5, box 3.

79. *San Antonio*, Jan. 12, 1950, in Scrapbook; *La Prensa*, April 30, 1950, p. 3, in Scrapbook; "School Survey of the University of Texas," in fld. 5, box 6; Gus García to Survey Committee of the San Antonio Independent School District, n.d., fld. 2, box 4; see news clipping, Jan. 12, 1950, Scrapbook.

80. *Light*, April 5, 1959, Scrapbook; Report of the Citizens' School Survey Committee, May 17, 1950, fld. 6, box 6.

81. *Express*, May 23, 1950, Scrapbook; *Light*, May 23, 1950, Scrapbook.

82. See league report. n.d., fld. 7, box 6; García radio transcript, KIWW, Sept. 21, 1950, fld. 8, box 5; league report, fld. 7, box 6.

83. *Express*, June 15, 1950, Scrapbook; *Evening News*, June 15, 1950, p. 1–A. Scrapbook.

84. *Evening News*, June 16, 1950, p. 8, Miscellaneous Newspapers; *La Prensa*, June 18, 1950, p. 1, Scrapbook; *Express*, June 20, 1950, Scrapbook.

85. News clipping, Jan. 23, 1950, Miscellaneous Newspapers.

86. Escobar to Ed. W. Ray, San Antonio, Dec. 30, 1958, fld. 8, box 3; news clipping, 1959, Miscellaneous Newspapers. Escobar died on May 10, 1970.

VI
LATINOS AND
HIGHER EDUCATION

22

Racism in Academia:
The Old Wolf Revisited

María de la Luz Reyes
John J. Halcón

In this article, the authors modify and use the metaphor of "a wolf in sheep's clothing" as the theme in uncovering racism aimed at Chicanos in higher education. The authors, who are new to the academic profession, as are many Chicanos in the field, discover that the old wolf, racism, is as active in academia as in their previous educational settings. In elementary and secondary schools the wolf's disguises include educational tracking, low expectations, and negative stereotypes. Chicanos who have overcome these obstacles and who are attempting to break into the faculties and administrations of U.S. higher education institutions are finding the wolf in a new wardrobe. The authors identify the various disguises used to hide racism by higher education faculties and administrations.

A Chicano candidate was being interviewed for a tenure-track faculty position. The small conference room, with a seating capacity of twelve, was filled beyond its limits. Extra chairs were brought in as faculty from various departments sat elbow to elbow. Just a week before, it had been impossible to round up four warm bodies to interview a White male candidate applying for another faculty position in the School of Education.

At the head of the table, in a dark pinstriped suit, sat the invited candidate. He smiled as he waited for another question. At the center of the table, an older Anglo professor leaned forward, brushed back his thinning white hair, adjusted his glasses, and peered at the waiting candidate.

"Dr. Fuentes,[1] I see here in your vita that you have a bachelor's degree in Chicano Studies, a specialization in bilingual education, your publications deal mostly with minority issues, and you have been keynote speaker at two Chicano commencements."

"Yes, that's correct," replied Dr. Fuentes.

"Well, Dr. Fuentes, I have a problem with these things."

"What's the problem?" queried Dr. Fuentes.

"Frankly, I am concerned that if we hire you, you will be teaching separatism to our impressionable young administrators. . . ."

The blood rushed to the candidate's face, and the anger in his eyes was difficult to conceal. The audience grew silent.

●   ●   ●

As minorities, we know from personal experience that racism in education is vigorous and pointed. We realize that, in spite of bona fide college degrees, our credentials are challenged by pervasive racist attitudes, and our efforts toward full incorporation into academic positions in institutions of higher education (IHEs) are hampered by layers of academic stratification. We find that, even with earned Ph.D.s, the academic road is the beginning of another Sisyphean climb. If current patterns of minority hiring persist, the best we can expect is to occupy positions outside the mainstream ranks, those most peripheral to the hub of governance and power.

Not long ago, as graduate students, we believed that successful completion of our graduate programs would be our license to "play in the big leagues." In our naïveté, we assumed that attainment of our advanced degrees would mark the end to our "language problems," our experiences with educational tracking, low expectations, negative stereotyping, use of tests to denote our ranking and placement in the system, and a myriad of other institutional obstacles. In a sense, we assumed—or maybe hoped—that the frequent encounters with racism which we experienced in schools were confined to the lower echelons of the educational ladder. We believed that our Ph.D.s paved the way to an egalitarian status with mutual respect among professional colleagues, where the new rules of competition would be truly based on merit. We were wrong. Instead, we find that even in academia, we face the same racism under different conditions—the old wolf in new clothing.

The racism experienced by Chicanos in academia is not new. Chicano scholars have characterized it as "academic colonialism" (Arce, 1978; Ornelas, Ramirez, & Padilla, 1975). Many Chicano writers blamed this form of racism for their inability to penetrate the elitist, White, male-dominated system which excluded them from full and significant participation (Arvizu, 1978; Candelaria, 1978; Casso & Roman, 1975; Valverde, 1975). But to those of us new to academe, the manifestations of racism at the professorial level appear new. This sense of newness may be attributed to the fact that the majority of racial incidents are generally associated with the experiences of minorities at elementary, secondary, and baccalaureate levels. The very idea that racism could exist among the *educated* elite is disconcerting to new academicians of color, and might come as a surprise to aspiring novices looking in from the outside.

In the early 1970s, some believed that there were only about one hundred Chicano Ph.D.s in the United States (C. de Baca, 1975). The most recent data indicate that full-time Hispanic faculty (including Cubans, Chicanos, Puerto Ricans, and South Americans) in higher education institutions as of Fall, 1983 numbered 7,356 (*Digest of Education Statistics,* 1985-86 and 1987). There is no specific breakdown for Chicanos provided in these data, but the fact is clear that today we have more Hispanic academics than ever before.

From personal observations and from what we have learned through our interactions with other Hispanics in academe, we believe that for the first time there exists a noticeable number of over-qualified, under-employed Hispanic Ph.D.s unable to gain access to faculty positions in IHEs. Ten to fifteen years ago we might not have been able to name ten Chicano Ph.D.s; today many of us can easily name six to ten Hispanic Ph.D.s unable to obtain academic positions. This observation is at once ironic and paradoxical: we are considered the elite and best-educated members of a minority community that is still struggling desperately to graduate its members from high school, and yet, rather than finding a payoff at the end of the educational tunnel, we find a dark path draped in full academic regalia—for aspiring Chicano academics, this is indeed a sobering and humbling reality.

As Chicano academics, we have personally met or have come to know about a large number of Chicano Ph.D.s, through a loose, informal network across the country. This network provides information about the experiences of other Chicano academicians from which we have collected examples of racism in IHEs. This essay is an attempt on the part of two Chicanos to describe incidents of racism in IHEs that we, and other Chicano colleagues, have experienced.

DEFINITION OF RACISM

Dube's (1985) definition of racism provides a useful framework for our discussion of racism in academia. He describes three types of racism: overt, covert, and reactive. This paper will focus on the overt and covert forms found in academia. According to Dube, overt racism is based on the notion that some races are inherently superior to others. It is the most easily identified form, "open and up-front" (p. 88), and publicly displayed like that of the Ku Klux Klan, for example. In contrast, covert racism stems from a more subtle philosophy, "at times taking the form of superior virtue . . . believed to be common only to virtuous 'races'" (p. 88). Although not easy to identify, it has negative consequences for minorities.

In our experiences within educational systems, we find that examples of these two types of racism occur regularly. In some cases, long and well-established patterns of behavior are so entrenched that they function as standard operating procedures. In the following pages we will discuss manifestations of these types of racism primarily as they affect Chicano academics.

Overt Racism

Overt racism at IHEs usually occurs in isolated events such as the interview described at the beginning of this article. Although "open and up-front," overt racism is usually not exhibited publicly beyond the campus. It is most common in situations where minorities are being considered for positions occupied primarily by Whites, as in the case of minorities vying for tenure-track faculty positions at predominantly White colleges and universities.

A recent series of incidents comes to mind. Five Chicano Ph.D.s applied for various faculty positions at a southwestern college located in a community with a 40 percent Chicano constituency. Over the course of a year and a half, they each surfaced as finalists and were interviewed for tenure-track positions. The strong pool of Chicano candidates resulted from active recruitment efforts by Chicano faculty who wanted to improve academic opportunities for other Chicanos.

Some faculty and school deans were surprised to learn that five Chicano applicants had been invited to interview, especially since the dean of arts and sciences had reported that previous faculty recruitment efforts had yielded "no qualified minorities." Although the number of candidates seemed significant compared to previous searches, it was small when compared to the twenty-five to thirty-five White candidates interviewed during the same period. Chicano candidates drew a large number of faculty spectators to their interviews, while non-minority applicants went virtually unnoticed—even in the departments to which they had applied. On at least two occasions, one department chair in education reported at a faculty meeting that only two faculty members had attended the interviews for the math and science education candidates (two White males). Given the predominance of White faculty across the campus, the seemingly frequent and obvious presence of Chicanos within a relatively short span of time prompted one school dean to remark, "What do they think this is, Taco University?" That racial slur resurfaced each time another Chicano was to be interviewed.

Optimistically, one might believe that the faculty came to meet and listen to the candidate, but that was not the case. Instead, many appeared to attend the interviews chiefly to find fault with the candidate or to offer their reasons for not hiring the candidate. In one case some faculty members came with copies of previously circulated petitions, attempting to halt the search on the grounds that they did not agree with the job description used in the national search. No formal objection to the job description had been made before the search committee let it be known that a Chicano had emerged as the top candidate.

The tragedy was that those overt racist tactics were successful—none of the five Chicanos were hired. According to personal accounts from the candidates in subsequent communications, they were told they were rejected on the basis of "inexperience," "lack of sufficient qualifications," or "incompatibility" with the faculty in the departments in which they had applied. Four of the five positions were left vacant, and in the fifth, a White male who had served as an adjunct instructor was hired on a temporary basis. A year later, one of the Chicano applicants was hired, but only after a series of confrontations between minority faculty and the administration, as well as pressure from Chicano and Black students and from members of the Hispanic community.

Covert Racism

Covert racism is the most pervasive form of racism in higher education. Because of its elusive nature, however, covert racism is ignored by those who have never experienced it, and denied by those who contribute to it. As discussed previously, our interactions with other Chicanos in academe have allowed us to compile typical examples of covert racism in higher education. We have organized those examples under the following categories: tokenism, the type-casting syndrome, the "one-minority-per-pot" syndrome, the "brown-on-brown" research taboo, and the hair-splitting concept. Below we discuss each category, examining closely the implications for Chicano academics.

Tokenism.   The civil rights movement of the 1960s ushered the way for Executive Order 11246, the federal blueprint for affirmative action (Holmes, 1975). This Department of Labor regulation required that all federal contractors and subcontractors take affirmative action in all employment activity, assuring equal opportunity to job applicants and barring discrimination on the basis of "race, color, religion, sex, or national origin." For Hispanics, this order opened up new opportunities. They found themselves appointed to important positions in both private and public agencies. During the same period, fellowships to pursue graduate degrees at universities across the country, especially in education, became available primarily through the Ford Foundation and Title VII of the Elementary and Secondary Education Act. Those funding sources and others like them allowed a larger number of Hispanics, who might not otherwise have afforded it, to pursue higher education.

In the mid-1970s, when minority quota systems were being implemented in many nonacademic agencies, the general public was left with the impression that Chicano or minority presence in professional or academic positions was due to affirmative action, rather than to individual qualifications or merit. But that impression was inaccurate. Generally, IHEs responded to the affirmative action guidelines with token positions for only a handful of minority scholars in nonacademic and/or "soft" money programs. For example, many Blacks and Hispanics were hired as directors for programs such as Upward Bound, Talent Search, and Equal Opportunity Programs (EOP) (Valverde, 1975). Other minority faculty were hired for bilingual programs and ethnic studies programs, but affirmative action hirings did not commonly extend to tenure-track faculty positions. The new presence of minorities on college campuses, however, which occurred during the period when attention to affirmative action regulations was at its peak, left all minority professionals and academics with a legacy of tokenism—a stigma that has been difficult to dispel.

Actual gains in academic faculty positions due to affirmative action regulations could not have been anything but minuscule. As early as 1975, Peter Holmes, then Director of the Civil Rights Commission, reported at the National Institute on Access to Higher Education for the Mexican American that the spirit of the affirmative action regulations was based on the notion of an "availability pool." This concept was interpreted such that the regulations applied *only* in situations where it could be proven that there were significant numbers of available minorities in the respective employment areas. Since the number of Hispanics with Ph.D.s constituted less than 1 percent of available persons in many academic fields at that time (*Minorities in Higher Education*, 1984), Holmes believed it was impossible for higher education institutions to comply with the regulations (see also "Discrimination in Higher Education," 1975). The University of California at Berkeley, for example, negotiated an affirmative action plan with the former Department of Health, Education, and Welfare, and mutually identified *only three* departments where projected goals for minority hiring were required under affirmative action regulations (Holmes, 1975).

Despite the minimal gains for minorities in tenure-track positions, we continue to be plagued with the assumption that we are mere tokens and have been hired without the appropriate credentials, experience, or qualifications. The legacy of tokenism and its negative implications has led to a current situation, in which unspoken pressure is put on minority academics to continually prove that they are as good as White academics. Tokenism has also had the effect of reducing minority-occupied positions to a subordinate status, providing an easy excuse to ignore or minimize our presence and our efforts.

The Typecasting Syndrome. A byproduct of tokenism is the typecasting syndrome. This is an underlying attitude or belief that Hispanics can only, or should only, occupy minority-related positions, such as those in bilingual education, Chicano Studies, foreign languages (Spanish), or student support services such as EOP.

An actual case of this typecasting syndrome occurred recently to a Chicana colleague during the negotiation of her contract with a state university on the West Coast. Two tenure-track positions were announced at the university where she applied for a faculty position. One position was in the teacher education program with a rank of associate professor, and the other position was in the bilingual education program at the assistant professor level. Although her qualifications and experience were equally strong in both areas, she applied for the teacher education position, because she had recently been promoted to associate level and because she recognized the need for integrating minority scholars into the mainstream programs. Much to her surprise, she received an invitation to interview for both the teacher education position and the bilingual position, without having applied for the latter.

When the interviews were completed, she was informed that she was the top candidate for both positions and that the university would make her an offer. A couple of weeks later, the dean called to offer her the bilingual position because "they believed that it was her main area of expertise" and that it was "where she would be most happy." She was quite aware that the position in teacher education meant breaking through an all-White faculty, while the position in bilingual education would have confined all Hispanics to the same unit. As a result, she refused the offer for the bilingual position, reminding the dean that she had not applied for it, and that since she was the top candidate in both positions, she should be allowed to select the position she preferred.

The negotiations slowed as she was informed of a "new policy" requiring candidates to "update" all college transcripts, provide proof of earned doctorate degree, and proof of good teaching evaluations from previously taught classes. She learned from the other Chicanos at the university that the "new" requirements were familiar tactics intended to discourage her from accepting the position. It took the threat of legal action to convince the Dean to offer her the associate level position in teacher education.

Arce (1978) and Olivas (1986) argue that this practice of specialized minority hiring for minority slots "is a more formal co-optation of Hispanic concerns . . . which relieves the institution of the need to integrate throughout their ranks" (Olivas, 1986, p. 14). The worst part for the few Chicanos in academia is that the typecasting syndrome segregates them in ethnically related professions. Arciniega and Morey (1985), for example, reported that in 1983 only 3.5 percent of the California State University faculty were Hispanic, and that the majority of those were in ethnic studies departments.

Another negative consequence of the typecasting syndrome is that often the only avenues for Hispanic promotion are in ethnically related fields. A recent report entitled, "The Status of Chicanos/Latinos at the University of California" (Gordon, 1988) bears this out. A coalition of Hispanic faculty members from the U.C. system complained in the report that there were only three Chicanos/Latinos in high-level academic administrative positions, and they reported that "there are no, repeat no, Chicano or Latino academic deans or department heads outside of ethnic or Chicano

Studies" (Fields, 1988, p. A17). If this is the case at the University of California system, in a state with 6.6 million Hispanics (Fields, 1988), it is not likely that Hispanic academics are faring much better in other states where their numbers are smaller.

Typecasting is indeed pervasive, and is simply another form of stereotyping that prevents Chicanos from becoming fully integrated into all areas of academia. The larger social consequences of confining minorities to the outer fringes of academia includes severely limiting White students' access to ethnically diverse points of view—resulting in a shallow education from a monocular perspective (Fishman, 1975). In an increasingly pluralistic society, this practice has the added effect of depriving White students of social skills necessary for mutual respect and co-existence with other cultural groups. The alarming increase in racial incidences involving White college students against minorities (Farrell, 1988a, b, c, d; McCurdy, 1988; Williams, 1987) is ample evidence of this deprivation.

The "One-minority-per-pot" Syndrome. Many colleges and universities operate under an unwritten quota system that manifests itself as reluctance to hire more than one minority faculty member per department. We refer to this practice as the "one-minority-per-pot" syndrome. Two or three minority faculty may be hired for ethnic studies, bilingual education, or foreign languages, but too often departments of education, sociology, history, English, or psychology, for example, seldom hire more than one minority per department.

We believe that implicit in this practice is a deep-seated belief that minorities are not as qualified as nonminorities. This conviction stems from an unspoken fear that the presence of more than one minority faculty member in a mainstream, traditional department might reduce the department's academic reputation. We have participated in faculty meetings in which the subject of additional faculty has been discussed. In these meetings, the suggestion that minority candidates be considered has generally evoked pat responses along these lines: "We don't want to hire anyone because of their ethnicity, we want *fully qualified* candidates" (see Blum, 1988a; Heller, 1988), or "This isn't a position for bilingual education," or "We hired a minority last year." Typically, consideration of minority candidates occurs only when there is pressure applied to diversify the faculty.

Scott Heller (1988) offers evidence of the deeply ingrained belief among faculty that hiring minorities reduces the caliber of the faculty already on board. In one college president's attempt to discover the reasons for the institution's inability to hire Black faculty, several faculty members revealed their reservations in private interviews when they "questioned whether affirmative action hiring wasn't tantamount to lowering academic standards" (p. A16). In a seeming contradiction, these same faculty members welcomed a pool of candidates that included minorities. Apparently, an applicant pool that includes minorities is considered by White faculty as evidence of a "good faith effort" in hiring and integrating minorities—even if minorities are not ultimately hired.

The "one-minority-per-pot" concept applies to administrators as well as faculty. Recently, a Chicano colleague of ours applied for an associate deanship at his institution. Prior to completing his application, he was forewarned by the academic vice president that he was not likely to be considered for the position. According to our colleague, the vice president told him that "there were already three other Chicano administrators at the college." Recognizing the futility of his effort, the candidate withdrew his name from consideration.

Another familiar theme closely associated with the "one-minority-per-pot" syndrome is the practice of requiring additional documentation from minorities above and beyond the standard curriculum vitae, transcripts, and letters of recommendation. For example, it is not uncommon for minorities to be required to submit copies of their dissertations, evaluations of their teaching, bibliographies from their published papers, and copies of funded proposals. Since it is usually minorities who are singled out to provide additional documentation and the requests are usually made *after* they have become top candidates, there is adequate ground for suspecting that covert racism is at work. The intent of this tactic is to discourage minority candidates from accepting faculty positions. Both points were illustrated previously in the case of our Chicana colleague who was offered a position for which she had not applied. For minority academics, this particular practice has the simultaneous effect of publicly demeaning their professional reputations while chipping away at their self-esteem.

Additionally, the limitation on minority hiring that is part of the "one-minority-per-pot" syndrome has the effect of restricting the career goals and aspirations of Hispanics and other minority faculty. We believe that the lack of minority faculty in academic departments today (Blum, 1988a, b; Fields, 1988; *Higher Education Research Institute*, 1982; Harvey, 1987; *Minorities and Strategic Planning at the University of Colorado*, 1987) is more likely the result of this unwritten quota system than it is of the lack of available candidates in some hypothetical pool.

The "Brown-on-Brown" Research Taboo. As Hispanic academics, our research interests often stem from a recognition that we have endured racial discrimination and from a compelling need to lend a dimension of authenticity to the prevailing theories about our communities. Said another way, we want to provide our own perspectives regarding prevailing negative assumptions about our values, culture, and language. This explains our interest in such topics as dropouts, bilingual education, second-language literacy, Chicano literature, and the education of minority students. Our interest in these research areas is also motivated by a concern for assisting our community in improving its second-rate status in the educational, economic, and political arenas. Tired of reading about ourselves in the social science literature written by nonminorities, we want to speak for ourselves, to define, label, describe, and interpret our own condition from the "inside out." We feel strongly about providing a balance to the existing literature and research on Chicanos.

Our efforts, like those of other minority scholars, often meet with covert disapproval by our White colleagues, who judge the quality and validity of our scholarly work, our research, and our publications (Blum, 1988a, b). Quite often, our research interests are dismissed as minor or self-serving. The general perception is that minority-related topics do not constitute academic scholarship—as was the case in the incident described in the introduction—and that they are inappropriate and narrow in scope. The assumption is that minority researchers cannot be objective in their analyses of those problems which are so close to their life experiences. In this regard we have to agree with Kushner and Norris (1980–1981) who suggest that the devaluing of minority research interests deprives minorities of the "dignity of contributing to theorizing about their worlds" (quoted in Lather, 1986, p. 264).

The perception that "brown-on-brown" research is somehow not valuable pervades academic circles. This paternal attitude from a White, male-dominated profession is a double standard that lends full credibility to Whites' conducting research on White populations, but discredits minority academics' research on minority issues. White-on-White research is accorded legitimacy, but "brown-on-brown" research is questioned and challenged at the same time that many White social scientists are establishing their professional careers as experts on minority issues. What appears to be at the heart of the objection to "brown-on-brown" research is not the credibility of our research, but an unspoken objection to a potential undermining of White expertise on minority issues.

Many minorities believe that another objection to "brown-on-brown" research is that the traditional Eurocentric perspective used to evaluate their scholarship puts nontraditional research at a disadvantage because predominantly White male academics lack the appropriate cultural perspectives from which to judge its real merit (O'Neale in Blum, 1988a; Wilson in Blum, 1988b). The problem of judging minority scholarship may also be exacerbated by the high concentration of minority academics in education, the arts, and the humanities, "where the evaluation of research is more subjective than in such fields as engineering or the natural sciences" (Wilson in Blum, 1988b, p. A17).

Referring to women in academia who share experiences similar to those of ethnic minorities, especially regarding the devaluing of their research, Simeone (1987) states:

> While the system employs the rhetoric of merit, its determination is far from objective. Even if there were agreement on the most important criteria, for example, agreement on means of assessment and actual performance would be difficult to reach. The process which is constructed to sort out the mediocre and the merely good at each level may be sorting factors other than merit, as well. Some of these may include political or social affiliations, intellectual perspective, or perceived congeniality (p. 28).

The devaluing of minority research in promotion and tenure decisions is difficult to prove. Yet many Hispanics, Blacks, and Native Americans cite cases from their research during promotion and tenure reviews (see Blum, 1988b, and Fields, 1988). A recent example is that of a Black woman in the English Department at Emory University, who lost a three-year battle to overturn her denial of tenure (Blum, 1988a). She was the only Black woman in the department, and her expertise was in Black literature. The scholar in question and her supporters claim that the decision to deny her tenure was based on institutional racism that devalues scholarship by minorities on ethnically related subjects. On the other hand, both the committee on tenure who reviewed her case and university administrators claim that the decision was based on "her weakness as a scholar" (p. A15). Several students and faculty who were interviewed did not discount racism as a factor. A member of the committee stated, ". . . it's a kind of covert or unconscious racism deflected into the belief that a certain specialty or a certain journal that is outside of established fields is not good enough" (Baker in Blum, 1988a, p. A17).

The devaluing of "brown-on-brown" research stems from the values undergirding institutions of higher education, which reflect culturally monolithic systems. These systems judge the quality of scholarship from the normative perspective of their own cultural group. As a result, the work of those individuals who depart from those standards is deemed inferior (Ramirez, 1988). The obvious consequence, then, of the tenure and promotion processes based on White males' definition of research and scholarship is that few minorities make the grade.

The Hairsplitting Concept. This last type of covert racism is rather elusive, but it is no less real. We describe the hairsplitting concept as a potpourri of trivial technicalities, or subjective judgment calls, which prevent minorities from being hired or promoted. When minorities have met all the academic criteria, jumped the hurdles, and skipped through all the specified hoops, the final decision is based on highly subjective and arbitrary points. At times, these decision border on paternalism, with White males defining and deciding what is best for us, as in the case cited earlier of the Chicana professor being told in which department she would be most happy. At times minority candidates are second-guessed and eliminated, not on the basis of their qualifications, but on the personal opinions of the decisionmakers (Heller, 1988). A minority candidate, for example, might not get a position because the committee might assume that she or he would not be happy in a predominantly White community (Wilson in Blum, 1988; Fields, 1988; Heller, 1988). Decisions that are publicly acclaimed as objective are, in fact, highly subjective. Politics, personality, and even intellectual orientation almost always color decisions and serve to exclude those who are different (Candelaria, 1978; Ramirez, 1988; Simeone, 1987).

Hairsplitting practices are a dangerous because the exclusion of Chicanos is justified by minor, arbitrary, and inconsequential factors that prevent them from reaping the benefits of their education. What appears to be consistent in the application of hairsplitting practices is that often when White-dominated selection committees feel threatened by a minority candidate, they base their selection decision on an arbitrary, hairline difference favoring the White candidate. When IHEs use arbitrary hairsplitting practices as grounds for their final decisions, the unspoken rule seems to be that it is better to support the candidate who best reflects the status quo.

Each of the above forms of covert racism has contributed to the current status of Chicanos in academia and, in part, explains the dearth of minority academicians. We have discovered a painful truth: it is difficult to escape the tentacles of racism, which touched our earlier educational experiences. The sad reality is that the "old wolf" is still around, now dressed in token assumptions, the typecasting syndrome, the one-minority-per-pot syndrome, the brown-on-brown research taboo, and the hairsplitting tactics.

SOME RESPONSES TO RACISM

Chicanos, like other minority academics, find ways to cope with racism. In talking with other Chicanos, we have identified four prevalent responses to racism: give in, give up, move on, or fight back.

Chicanos in the "give in" group play the academic game at all costs. They yield easily to the demands to assimilate. In some cases, they attempt to divest themselves of all obvious cultural traits. At the same time, they work diligently at mainstreaming their research interests, and steer clear of minority-related issues. Individuals in this group might even deny racism, explaining the dearth of minority academics simply from a "pick-yourself-up-by-your-bootstraps" philosophy. They behave as if they were convinced that the key to success in academia is simply a matter of hard work and that politics, personal preferences, and subjectivity have little to do with merit. A few in this group succeed in infiltrating the system and blending well in their academic settings. Others give in completely, but despite their full conversion, they encounter rejection by those in the system who continue to perceive them as outsiders, or "tokens." Chicanos who deal with racism in this manner may feel alienated and out of touch with the Hispanic community at large. Indeed, their own Chicano community may have little respect for them and may perceive them as sell-outs.

Chicanos in the "give up" group are usually found in institutions and departments where displays of racism are overt. These Chicanos tend to struggle against academic racism at all costs. Most of their energies are used to combat injustices instead of pursuing scholarship. These individuals tend to become so demoralized that racism destroys both their spirit and their self-esteem. The lack of a support network to assist them to survive and succeed in such an academic environment makes it almost impossible to tolerate any direct or subtle attack.

These individuals soon experience "burnout" as they see the futility of their efforts to change the system. At times, the direct or underlying hostility and alienation that these individuals experience have a disabling effect that gradually leads to a self-fulfilling prophecy regarding their academic potential. Repeated invalidation of their work serves to convince them that their efforts are substandard and their work inferior. Instead of hanging on, they give up—becoming disillusioned or convinced that they "don't have what it takes" to be an academic, that academia is not suited to their ultimate priorities, or that they "don't need the hassles." These Chicanos may leave academia altogether, and they may not return.

Chicano academics who cope with institutionalized racism by moving on to greener pastures compose the "move on" group. Individuals in this group maintain a strong affiliation with their community and feel a strong sense of responsibility to improve the status of other Chicanos in the larger community. They neither assimilate easily, nor readily ascribe to mainstream perspectives. As a result of their strong cultural awareness and assertiveness, they may often be perceived by their White peers as "arrogant." These individuals recognize manifestations of racism in the academy and fully understand that as minority academics they are in "tenuous-track" positions. They are realists. And, although they clearly fight against racism, they learn how to "pick their fights," realizing that taking on every minority issue can render them totally ineffective. They carefully evaluate their situations, looking at such factors as the key players, their support networks, and the odds of succeeding in their institutions. When they recognize that the price of the struggle is not worth their efforts *in that particular environment*, they move on. They do so instead of seriously jeopardizing their careers, damaging their self-esteem, and exhausting all their energies in futile struggles. Although few find the ideal university, many of these Chicanos eventually find the "best fit" for them.

Finally, Chicano academics in the "fight back" group respond in two ways, one of which is similar to the response of the "move on" group. That is, they fight back but recognize their limitations and the importance of succeeding in the system. They do so—not because institutions of higher education are perfect systems—but because they recognize that if institutional racism is to be eradicated, they must participate in the decisionmaking arenas controlled by tenured faculty, and where the key decisions for admission and full incorporation are made. They understand that this must be done from the inside out. So they persevere. They learn to play the game, without compromising either their integrity or their ethnicity. They comply with the rules only insofar as issues related to scholarship will earn them tenure. They may temporarily limit their involvement with the Chicano community in order to attain tenure. Once they are tenured, however, many redirect their attention to minority concerns and minority-related research that will help improve the condition of their community. A characteristic of Chicanos in this group is an unwavering tenacity and resilience that enables them to continue their efforts even when they encounter stiff opposition. Chicanos in this group often join together to plan effective strategies for combatting racism and demanding equity. Their fight against racism motivates them to surpass the limited expectations the dominant community has for them as minorities.

Another response of Chicanos in the "fight back" group is to exert every effort to prove the oppressor wrong, regardless of the consequences. These Chicanos often sacrifice their academic careers to effect a significant change that will pave the way for other Chicano academics. They are generally politically astute and know how to mobilize the minority community behind certain issues. They are often perceived as the martyrs and prophets of the community, who appear to be filled with a kind of reckless zeal to right injustices. As a result, they may pay the price of being excluded from academia altogether.

The different responses to racism that we have observed are often variations of these above four themes. For example, an individual may respond to racism in any of these four ways, depending on the specific circumstances. The most critical dividing line in these responses lies between the coping strategies that ultimately separate Chicano academics from their community and the those that allow Chicanos to maintain close ties with their community.

CONCLUSIONS

Discriminatory policies and the manifestations of racism in educational institutions have changed very little over the years. In spite of the changing demographics that indicate a dramatic rise in the Hispanic population, and in spite of the new focus on recruitment and retention of minorities by educational institutions, Chicano academics today are generally experiencing many of the same kinds of racial prejudices experienced by those who preceded them into the academy a generation ago. Forms of tokenism, typecasting, limitations on minority hiring, devaluing of Chicano research, and hairsplitting practices are prevalent manifestations of racism in academia. Each of these factors contributes to maintaining the small number of Chicano academics currently in IHEs, and to the inability of a growing number of Chicano Ph.D.s to break into the system. The latter are experiencing the disillusionment of being over-qualified, under-employed, or unemployed. They are in a Catch-22 situation: unable to get an academic job because they lack university teaching and publishing experience, and unable to acquire that experience because they cannot get an academic position. To our knowledge, no surveys have been conducted to determine the actual count, but we know that a good number of unemployed potential Chicano academics exist because the network is small, and we know many of them. This is a disturbing reality for members of a minority community who work hard to convince their youth that education is the great social equalizer that generally brings with it a guaranteed economic return.

How can we eliminate or reduce racism in academia? Eradicating institutional racism in academia will not be an easy task. Hispanic Ph.D.s (which includes Cubans, Chicanos, Puerto Ricans, and Central and South Americans) compose a mere 2.1 percent of all doctorate degrees (*Minorities in Higher Education*, 1987). Of those, Chicano academics in universities across the country represent an even smaller number. Further, we know from experience that unless the dominant majority recognizes the value of a culturally diverse professoriate, we cannot expect them to take the lead in eliminating precisely the kind of racism they tacitly condone.

On the other hand, we cannot change the system alone. Chicano academics will have to form coalitions and join forces with other Hispanic, Black, Native American, and Asian academics who share similar experiences. Together we must work at dispelling the myth of tokenism that surrounds minority hiring. We must press for an end to the typecasting syndrome, to the limit on minority hiring by certain departments, and to hairsplitting practices. We must promote instead the idea that departments should be rewarded when they can demonstrate diversity among their faculty, and at the same time, we must lobby and press for a reexamination of the criteria for review, promotion, and tenure; for a redefinition of scholarship; and for inclusion of so-called "minority journals" among those classified as premier journals.

Minority academics will have to work at convincing their institutions that minority faculty are the *key* to recruitment, retention, and promotion of other minorities, both students and faculty. They will have to press for *full incorporation* and *integration* into the various branches of the institution, not just in minority slots. Anything less than that will render them powerless to assist other minorities to move successfully through the academic hurdles. Without minority role models at all levels of the educational structure, but especially in the centers of power—the ranks of tenured professors—it will be difficult to convince young Hispanic, Black, and Native American students that they can benefit from higher levels of education.

As minority academics, we realize that we need an exceptional amount of ability, drive, dedication, and discipline to meet the requirements for academic advancement and the added demands of serving as role models for minority students. One way to compensate and to make allowances for this extra work is to exert pressure to have universities assign some weighted value to minority contributions of this type. We believe Valverde (1975) had a good idea in arguing that universities should give Chicanos (and other minorities) their "full measure by ascribing proportional value to such characteristics as language, ethnic perspective, cultural knowledge, diversity of ethnic mix in the network of people, and the power to attract other minority students into higher education" (p. 110).

To accomplish these goals, we will have to be each other's biggest fans; that is, we must seize and even create opportunities for publicly recognizing the qualifications and the contributions made by members of our own ethnic group and other minorities. We must go out of our way to promote minority scholars, to highlight their expertise, to disseminate minority publications among our non-minority colleagues, to suggest ways in which they can integrate minority perspectives into their classes and use books written by, or which include articles written by, minority scholars. We must push for diversification of the curriculum.

We recognize that it will take courageous leadership among minority academics to effect changes in the current situation and that the burden of initiating those changes lies squarely on our shoulders. No one else has the vested interest that we have. No one else can do it for us. We must tackle it ourselves because it is obvious that non-minority academic leaders are ambivalent about the role of minorities in higher education. On one hand, they pay lip service to the diversification of faculty on their campuses, but on the other hand, they do nothing to bring that about. Once we fully understand this and once we understand how institutions have excluded us from full participation, we can join forces with other people of color, set priorities, and harness our energies to combat racism in academia. If we fail to do this, we will find ourselves a generation from now still facing the same "old wolf" . . . in yet another fleecy robe.

NOTE

1. In the tradition of ethnographic field work and because of politically sensitive settings for other minorities, pseudonyms for actual persons and institutions are used throughout the essay to protect their identities and to maintain confidentiality. Accounts are based on actual interviews (May, 1986). The incidents reported in this article were either experienced by us personally or were reported to us by others.

REFERENCES

Arce, G. (1978). Chicano participation in academe: A case of academic colonialism. *Grito del Sol: A Chicano Quarterly*, 3, 75–104.

Arciniega, T., & Morey, A. I. (1985). *Hispanics and higher education: A CSU imperative.* Long Beach, CA: Office of the Chancellor.

Arvizu, S. F. (1978). Critical reflections and consciousness. *Grito del Sol: A Chicano Quarterly*, 3, 119–123.

Bayer, A. E. (1973). *Teaching faculty in academe: 1972–73.* American Council on Education, Research Report 8(2). Washington, DC: American Council on Education.

Blum, D. E. (1988a, June 22). Black woman scholar at Emory U. loses 3-year battle to overturn tenure denial, but vows to fight on. *The Chronicle of Higher Education*, pp. A15–A17.

———. (1988b, June 22). To get ahead in research, some minority scholars choose to "play the game." *The Chronicle of Higher Education*, p. A17.

C. de Baca, F. (1975). White House perspective. In H. J. Casso & G. D. Roman (Eds.), *Chicanos in higher education.* Albuquerque: University of New Mexico Press.

Candelaria, C. (1978). Women in the academy. *Rendezvous: Journal of Arts and Letters*, 13(1), 9–18.

Casso, H. J., & Roman, G. D. (Eds.). (1975). *Chicanos in higher education.* Albuquerque: University of New Mexico Press.

Digest of education statistics, 1985–86, and 1987. Washington, DC: U.S. Department of Education Office of Educational Research and Improvement.

Discrimination in higher education. (1975, Spring). *Civil Rights Digest,* 7(3), 3-21.

Dube, E. (1985). The relationship between racism and education in South Africa. *Harvard Educational Review, 55,* 86–100.

Ferrell, C. S. (1988a, January 27). Black students seen facing "New Racism" on many campuses. *The Chronicle of Higher Education* pp. Al, A37–A38.

Farrell, C. S. (1988b, January 27). Stung by racial incidents and charges of indifference, Berkeley to become model integrated university. *The Chronicle of Higher Education,* pp. A37–A38.

Ferrell, C. S. (1988c, February 17). Rising concerns over campus racial bias market at Northern Illinois University. *The Chronicle of Higher Education,* pp. A37–A38.

Ferrell, C. S. (1988d, February 24). Students protesting racial basis at U. of Massachusetts end occupation on campus building after 5 days . *The Chronicle of Higher Education,* p. A41.

Fields, C. M. (1988, May 11). Hispanics, state's fastest-growing minority, shut out of top positions at U. of California, leader says. *The Chronicle of Higher Education.* pp. A9–A10.

Fishman, J. (1975). *An international sociological perspective of bilingual education.* Keynote address. National Associations of Bilingual Education Conference, San Antonio, Texas.

Gordon, L. (1988, June 14). Second report criticizes UC on its policy towards hiring Latinos. *Los Angeles Times* p. 3

Harvey, W. B. (1987, May/June). An ebony view of the ivory tower. *Change,* 19(3), 46–49.

Heller, S. (1988, February 10). Some colleges find aggressive affirmative action efforts are starting to pay off, dispute scarcity of candidates. *The Chronicle of Higher Education,* p. A12.

Higher Education Research Institute, Inc. (1982). *Final report of the commission on the higher education of minorities.* Los Angeles: Jossey-Bass, Inc.

Holmes, P. (1975). The ineffective mechanism of affirmative action plans in an academic setting. In H. J. Casso & G. D. Roman (Eds.), *Chicanos in Higher Education* (pp. 76–83). Albuquerque: University of New Mexico Press.

Kushner, S., & Norris, N. (1980-81). Interpretation, negotiation and validity in naturalistic research. *Interchange,* 11(4), 26–36.

Lather, P. (1986). Research as praxis. *Howard Educational Review, 56,* 257–277.

McCurdy, J. (1988, June 8). Nullification of Latino student's election sparks melee at UCLA. *The Chronicle of Higher Education,* p. A23.

Minorities and strategic planning at the University of Colorado. (1987). Boulder: Office of the Associate Vice President for Human Resources.

Minorities in higher education. Third Annual Status Report. (1984). Washington, DC: American Council on Education.

Minorities in higher education. Sixth Annual Status Report. (1987). Washington, DC: American Council on Education.

Olivas, M. A. (1986). Research on Latino college students: A theoretical framework and inquiry. In M. A. Olivas (Ed.), *Latino college students* (pp. 1–25). New York: Teachers College Press.

Ornelas, C., Ramirez, C. B., & Padilla, F. V. (1975). *Decolonizing the interpretation of the Chicano political experience.* Los Angeles: UCLA Chicano Studies Cancer Publications.

Professional women and minorities: A Manpower data resource service. (1984). Washington, DC: Scientific Manpower Commission.

Ramirez, A. (1988). Racism toward Hispanics: The culturally monolithic society. In P. A. Katz & D. A. Taylor (Eds.), *Eliminating racism profiles in controversy* (pp. 137–157). New York: Plenum Press.

Simeone, A. (1987). *Academic women working towards equality.* South Hadley, MA: Bergin & Garvey.

Valverde, L. (1975). Prohibitive trends in Chicano faculty employment. In H. J. Casso & G. D. Roman (Eds.), *Chicanos in higher education* (pp. 106–114). Albuquerque: University of New Mexico Press.

Williams, A. A. (1987, Oct. 12). Advice/Dissent. *Colorado Daily.*

23

The Quest for Paradigm:
The Development of Chicano Studies
and Intellectuals

Carlos Muñoz, Jr.

More than a decade has passed since the first Chicano Studies program was created in 1968, and much has been published on the experience of people of Mexican descent in the United States. As practitioners in the field of Chicano Studies, however, we have not yet made an effort to assess the state of our research in a systematic and critical manner vis-à-vis the original objectives defined during the late 1960s or at the time of the founding of this association (NACS) in 1973. For any assessment of our research to be meaningful, however, I think it imperative that it be placed in historical perspective and within the context of the development of academic intellectuals of Mexican descent in the United States and, most importantly, in the relationship to the question of the role of Chicano Studies and Chicano intellectuals in both the university and in our respective communities.

We are all aware of the fact that until very recently there has not been any "critical mass" of scholars of Mexican descent in institutions of higher education in the United States. As a people we have not had the benefit of our own institutions of higher learning as has been the case with the black experience. With all the limitations of the Negro colleges, those institutions did make a significant contribution to the development of a black bourgeoisie and, more to the point, an intelligentsia that was able to establish a black intellectual tradition long before a few of our own were able to gain access to white colleges and universities. Prior to the sixties, many of those few who gained such access did it with the direct assistance of individual clergy from primarily the Catholic and Protestant churches, although the Mormon church also played a role. Many of the few who eventually became teachers or academics were products of religious and private institutions of higher education. The G.I. Bill and the civil rights movement made it more possible for youth of Mexican descent to attend public institutions of their choice. The end result was that prior to the creation of Chicano Studies programs there were only a handful of academics of Mexican descent in institutions of higher education. Four of them gained importance in the development of Chicano Studies as a new field of study and research.

First there was the late George Sánchez who, during the 1930s, was the first to wage battle against the racism of white schooling in general and the first to issue a critique of society from the perspective of oppressed Mexican people in the United States. In his classic study of New Mexico, *The Forgotten People,* he concluded that "in the march of imperialism a people were forgotten, cast aside as the byproduct of territorial aggrandizement" and made it clear that he did not divorce his scholarship from his commitment to his people. As he put in the preface to that study:

> It has been found necessary and desirable throughout . . . to point out faults and weaknesses in various sectors of the present situation. . . . The deficiencies are revealed and criticized with impersonal detachment and with all the scientific objectivity permitted to one who, at the same time, seeks emotional and mental identification with the mass of the people. . . . In this nation there is not excuse for human misery and . . . good intentions cannot substitute for good deeds (Sánchez, 1940, viii).

Not only was Sánchez a distinguished academician whose research had been oriented to confronting the social inequities faced by his people, but he also directly participated in the politics of his community. Throughout his academic career at the University of Texas at Austin he was an outspoken community leader and in 1941 served as the national president of the League of United Latin American Citizens (LULAC). Prior to his death in 1972, he lent his support for the creation of the Mexican American Studies Center at the Austin campus.

Américo Paredes has also been important to the development of Chicano Studies research. His research has been aimed at capturing a history of resistance and struggle on the part of Mexican people in the United States through his study of Texas Mexican folklore and music. From his classic study, *With His Pistol in His Hand,* published in 1958, until his more recent study, *A Texas Mexican Cancionero,* his work reflects the dedication he has had for his people and a concern for critical interpretation of the Chicano experience. He was instrumental in the establishment of the Mexican American Studies Center at the University of Texas at Austin in 1970 and served as its first director.

Julián Samora has been another whose work has been important to the development of our field. He was the first scholar of Mexican descent to focus his research on the problem of political leadership in a Chicano community. In particular his doctoral dissertation, completed in 1954, took a critical look a the process of cooptation of Chicano politicians by white power structures. He has devoted his scholarly career to researching the Chicano experience that eventually compelled him to establish the Mexican American Studies Center at the University of Notre Dame and contribute to the creation of a Mexican American Studies publication series through the University of Notre Dame Press.

We must not ignore another important scholar of Mexican descent who, although having never pursued an academic career, has through his independent research and writing made crucial contributions to our field. I refer to Ernesto Galarza. His work has resulted from many years of active participation in governmental affairs and the labor movement. His work as a farm worker organizer during the 1950s became the background for his first book *The Merchants of Labor,* a study that contributed heavily not only to our understanding of the Bracero experience but also to the termination of that exploitative program, a program he described in the following terms:

> The bracero system might have been a higher stage in American civilization as slavery was in Roman. If so, the affluent society, imperial in its own fashion, could ponder its good luck. It had only to reach out across the border down Mexico way to tap a reservoir of millions . . . who longed to toil as managed migrants for a reason . . . (Galarza, 1964, 259).

Sánchez, Paredes, Samora, and Galarza individually or collectively not only contributed to the training of young scholars of Mexican descent but touched a chord among those of us of the 60's generation searching for a "new" activist-oriented scholarship that could result in the kind of research we envisioned as necessary and useful to the struggle for Chicano liberation. We, however, were caught up in the politics of our times, a politics of mass protest that gave rise to an ideology of "cultural nationalism," an ideology that stressed a *Mexican* identity and rejected assimilationist and integrationist strategies that had been advocated by the older generation of activists. We therefore did not immediately give them the proper recognition they deserved. Instead we criticized them for their assimilationist and reformist bias and stance, and we did not attempt to understand the nature of the politics of their times. Américo Paredes has offered valuable insight into the politics of his generation. As he put in his *A Texas Mexican Cancionero,*

> . . . conditions in the majority culture must be taken into account in any attempt to assess the work of the activists of the post-World War II period. Mexican-Americans were ready for a change, but the United States was not. Post-World War II attitudes . . . resembled those of the late tens and twenties; the decade of the 1950s was a period of conformity and superpatriotism. We must keep this fact in mind to understand why the Mexican-American activists of the period surrounded their efforts with an aura of super-Americanism. . . . The principle of the Melting Pot was in full force during the fifties, fortified by the anti-communism fervor of the times. Under such circumstances. Mexican Americans of this period had to cope with an aggravated problem of identity . . . (Pavedes, p. 158).

As I have shown in a forthcoming work, the politics of assimilation and integration during the politics of their times were indeed, upon careful and critical evaluation, a progressive politics (Muñoz, forthcoming). For prior to the sixties, especially during the twenties and thirties, the nativist racist ideology that permeated the dominant white culture promoted an attitude that Mexicans were not assimilable because of their Indian blood and origins. The concern on the part of earlier generations of Mexican activists had therefore been to promote the counter ideology of the "melting pot," which held that the origins of the dominant culture were not simply rooted in English or German Protestant culture, but in fact were derived from various distinct immigrant cultures that had made United States society unique in the world. By placing Mexicans in the framework of the melting pot, they believed our people would eventually gain access to the rewards of "American democracy." Although the activists of that period emphasized the Spanish or white aspect of Mexican identity, they did not generally withhold criticism of dominant institutions for their policies of systematic exclusion and their oppression of Mexican people. Many struggled for the desegregation of schools and public facilities.

The work done by these four scholars has been important to the development of Chicano Studies as a new field of study and research and, most importantly, to the establishment of a Mexican academic intellectual tradition in the United States. We need to understand, however, that Chicano Studies was a generational phenomenon of the sixties and that it was defined in the process of the struggles of those times. The movement for Chicano Studies and the Chicano student movement were originally one and the same, as student activists of the 60's perceived the establishment of Chicano programs at institutions of higher education as a means of placing the resources of those institutions at the disposal of those engaged in the struggles for political and social change in their respective communities.

An examination of proposals for Chicano Studies in Texas, New Mexico, and California reflects an antiassimilationist thrust and the general objective of using such programs as means to provide direct Chicano access to institutions of higher education, to legitimize the existence of Chicano culture through the creation of curricula designed to teach students about the Mexican experience in the United States, and to prepare students to become community leaders and knowledgeable activists in community struggles for social change. *El Plan de Santa Bárbara* is one of the documents that spells out the objectives of Chicano Studies in a coherent and clear manner. It has become an historic document which provides us with insight into the politics of the Chicano intellectual generation of the sixties. The Plan was prefaced with a militant manifesto that declared in part:

> For the Chicano the present is a time of renaissance, of renacimiento. Our people and our community, el barrio and la colonia, are expressing a new consciousness and a new resolve. . . . We pledge our will to move . . . forward toward our destiny as a people . . . against those forces which have denied us freedom of expression and human dignity. For decades Mexican people in the United States struggled to realize the "American Dream" and some—a few—have. But the cost, the ultimate cost of assimilation, required turning away from el barrio and la colonia. In the meantime, due to the racist structure of this society, to our essentially different lifestyle, and to the socioeconomic functions assigned to our community by Anglo-american society—capitalist entrepreneur—the barrio and colonia remain exploited, impoverished, and marginal. . . . Culturally, the word Chicano, in the past a pejorative and class-bound adjective, has now become the root idea of a new cultural identity for our people . . . [it] signals a rebirth of pride and confidence . . . we believe that higher education must contribute to the formation of a complete man who truly values life and freedom (pp. 9–11).

Basically, *El Plan de Santa Bárbara* was a blueprint for the creation and institutionalization of various Chicano programs that could promote access to institutions of higher education. It outlined a strategy and a step-by-step process delineating how those programs could be implemented under the direct control of Chicanos. To some extent it was similar to other proposals for Chicano programs throughout the Southwest, but it differed in that it did offer a substantial framework for Chicano Studies research and for the formation of a new kind of intellectual, one who could see research in the following terms:

> The role of knowledge in producing powerful social change, indeed revolution, cannot be underestimated . . . research will not only provide Chicanos with action-oriented analysis of conditions, it will also aid significantly in politically educating the Chicano community . . . it will help measurably in creating and giving impetus to that historical consciousness . . . Chicanos must possess in order successfully to struggle as a people toward a new vision of Aztlan (p. 78).

What was being called for, although not articulated as such, was the development of organic intellectuals of Mexican descent within the university, i.e., the kind of academic who would be an integral part of his community and actively participate in the Chicano Movement, do research critical of society, and simultaneously contribute to the shaping of a Chicano consciousness. The Plan went on to underscore the importance of research to Chicano liberation.

> The systematic character of the racist relationship between gabacho society and Chicanos will not be altered unless solid research becomes the basis for Chicano political strategy and action. Rigorous analysis of conditions must be undertaken, issues identified, and priorities determined as Chicanos adopt strategies and develop tactics for the purpose of realigning our community's structural relationship to gabacho society . . . (ibid.).

The plan was the product of a three-day statewide conference held at the University of California, Santa Barbara campus, during the month of April, 1969, and was to some extent a followup to the first annual national Chicano Youth Liberation Conference sponsored by the Crusade for Justice in Denver, Colorado, where "El Plan de Aztlán" had been proclaimed a month earlier. Aware of the crucial importance of research to the successful implementation of the goals of Chicano Studies, a group from the Santa Barbara conference, all in the disciplines of history and the social sciences, began to raise important questions as to the nature of research in the university. Specifically, some of us saw the need to critically examine the question of the role of Chicano academic intellectuals in the Chicano Movement and to question in a fundamental and critical way the various assumptions and perspectives of the dominant paradigms of our respective disciplines. Soon after the conference several of the participants founded a journal for Chicano Studies at the University of California, Los Angeles (UCLA) which was to become the vehicle for the achievement of those objectives. The journal was named *Aztlán: Chicano Journal of the Social Sciences and the Arts*. The first issue appeared in the spring of 1970, a year after the

Santa Barbara conference, with the manifesto from "El Plan de Aztlán." The stated purpose of the journal was to "promote an active quest for solutions to the problems of the barrios of America" and to "focus scholarly discussion and analysis on Chicano matters as they relate to the group and to the total American society" (p. vi). The articles in this first issue were prefaced by a poem about Aztlán by Alurista, one of the first poets produced by the Chicano student movement. The editors of the journal were all graduate or undergraduate students and members of "El Movimiento Estudiantil Chicano de Aztlán" (MECHA) at UCLA. The chief editor, Juan Gómez-Quiñones, in addition to being a graduate student, was also an instructor in the department of history at UCLA at the time. He had been one of the prime movers of the Santa Barbara conference and a member of the editorial group that produced the Plan de Santa Bárbara. The articles in the first issue dealt with the question of culture and identity, Chicano history, the Chicano Movement, and a Chicano worker strike in 1933.

The second issue of *Aztlán* included a paper I had delivered as a graduate student in the 1970 annual meeting of the American Political Science Association wherein I called for a "Chicano Perspective of Political Analysis." As a member of the Santa Barbara group I was concerned with the need to go beyond the question of negative stereotypes and myths about Chicanos perpetuated by social science. It had been my feelings at the time that a primary factor for the lack of understanding about the Chicano dilemma in American society could be attributed to the fact that what had been written about Chicanos had been largely based on "a dominant Anglo perspective which has been predicated on the cultural values and norms of the dominant society" (Muñoz, 1970, 21). I argued that it was imperative for those of us concerned with research on the Chicano experience to critically examine the paradigms of the various disciplines that had developed from the dominant ideological perspectives. I concluded my paper with the following words:

> The Chicano scholar must realize that it is not enough to write critiques pointing out the stereotypes and myths that social science has perpetuated about Chicanos. The crisis that confronts his people is too great and profound and it compels him to develop new paradigms of research and analysis that will adequately deal with the problem of poverty, alienation, and political powerlessness. He now, more than ever, must commit himself to the emancipation of his people. For he does not have the luxury of remaining in the ivory tower nor to engage in "objective" analysis while his people are in the throes of crisis. The challenge before the Chicano scholar is to develop a Chicano perspective of political analysis. A perspective that will assure that his research will be oriented toward the needs of his community (Muñoz, ibid., 24).

In the third issue of *Aztlán*, Juan Gómez-Quiñones carried forth the argument for the need to develop a new paradigm for Chicano history.

> The paradigm should reveal, historically, the interrelations between culture and economic role, group personality configurations, mechanisms of social control, and the accumulating weight of historical experiences—all of

which form the historical context. With such a paradigm one can begin to investigate the pressures, structural characteristics, and events that combine to produce the Chicano community of today. . . . Chicano history is, and must continue to be, innovative . . . because it calls for a reconceptualization of history and the role of history in society. This means the use of new methods of inquiry and a reconstruction and reinterpretation of available sources . . . a union of history as discipline and history as action on behalf of a community in its struggle for survival. . . . It is not the listing of "important" names and contributions of "Mexican Americans" to the development of "this great country" . . . but must realistically reflect the historical context of the Chicano community vis-à-vis other oppressed groups in U.S. society. . . . Chicano history involves more than the creation of a new discipline or area of study . . . It involves the *self definition* (his emphasis) of a people (Gómez-Quiñones, 1971, 2, 39).

Others outside the Santa Barbara group called for a new paradigm for the study of the Chicano experience. Octavio Romano, one of the founders of *El Grito: Journal of Mexican-American Thought*, the first Chicano journal, founded in 1968, and the first to criticize the role of social science in the perpetuation of negative stereotypes and myths about Chicanos, called for a paradigm to be based on the following criteria:

All that is necessary at this point is an historical perspective and a paradigm by which to articulate that perspective. . . . [T]he eight point paradigm that follows seems most useful at present . . . First, Chicanos do not view themselves as traditionally unchanging vegetables, . . . but rather as creators of systems in their own right, for they have created cooperatives, mutualist societies, political blocks . . . Second, Chicanos view themselves as participants in the historical process . . . Third, . . . this population . . . constitutes a pluralistic people. Fourth, Chicanos see in their historical existence a continuous engaging in social issues . . . Fifth, the concept of the illiterate Mexican American must go . . . Sixth, the Chicano must be viewed as capable of his own system of rationality . . . Seventh, intellectual activity has been part and parcel of Chicano existence . . . and Eighth, as a population whose antecedents are Mexican, the bulk of Chicano existence has been oriented to a symbiotic residence within ecosystems (Romano, 1970, 13–14).

What was to be the new paradigm? Among those of the Santa Barbara group and others who generally adhered to the principles of the Plan de Santa Bárbara there was some difference of approach. The problem posed by the question was perceived differently by those who were committed to the development of Chicano Studies outside of existing academic units and those committed to doing research on the Chicano experience from within traditional disciplines. There were those few who were junior faculty members in traditional departments who believed research from a Chicano perspective could be done within the confines of such departments. Others believed it was essential to be either in the newly formed Chicano Studies departments or programs or in interdisciplinary academic programs they perceived as more fruitful to the development of an alternative paradigm. Some deemed it essential that Chicanos become faculty in traditional departments in order to maximize Chicano access to the resources of the university. Others believed that being faculty in traditional departments would compel them to do the kind of research called for by those departments in order to eventually be promoted to tenure. Furthermore, having to teach traditional courses, it was believed by some, would greatly hinder their efforts to develop Chicano Studies curricula and do meaningful Chicano Studies research.

Those committed to the development of a Chicano Studies paradigm began to conceptualize the Chicano experience in the context of Chicanos as a colonized people. We were influenced by the writings of Fanon, Memmi, Carmichael, Blauner, the analysis of the Black Panther party of blacks as a neocolony in the United States, and various Latin American scholars who had developed analyses of internal colonialism within their countries (Frank, Nun, Gonzales-Casanova, Stavenhagen). George Sánchez had been the first to write about Chicanos as a colonized people in his classic study of New Mexico published in 1940. He did not develop his analysis in the context of a theoretical framework, but did lay the foundation for its development.

The framers of the Plan de Santa Bárbara, familiar with the work of these writers, made reference to Chicanos as a colonized people. The analysis derived from the literature on colonialism and the black experience made more sense to us than did any other interpretations of Third World people in the United States offered by social scientists and historians who reflected the biases of the dominant paradigms. We launched the effort to develop a body of literature on the Chicano internal colonial experience. In a paper delivered at a symposium on the urban crisis, I challenged the work of Edward Banfield and referred to Chicano communities as internal colonies (Muñoz, 1970). In an article published in the third issue of *Aztlán*, Tomas Almaguer, then a student activist at the University of California, Santa Barbara campus, argued the need to study the Chicano experience within the context of a process of colonization (Almaguer, 1971). Then three of us committed to the principles of the Plan de Santa Bárbara wrote an article wherein we developed a theoretical framework based on our interpretation of the "Barrio as Internal Colony." We presented the work as a collective effort and a preliminary step in the development of a paradigm for Chicano Studies. We defined the internal colony framework in the following terms:

> The crucial distinguishing characteristic between internal and external colonialism does not appear to be so much the existence of separate territories corresponding to metropolis and colony, but the legal status of the colonized. According to our usage, a colony can be considered "internal" if the colonized population has the same formal legal status as any other group of citizens, and "external" if it is placed in a separate legal category. . . . Chicano communities in the United States are internal colonies, since they occupy a status of formal equality, whatever the informal reality may be. . . . [I]nternal colonialism means that Chicanos as a cultural/racial group exist in an exploited condition which is maintained by a number of mechanisms . . . [and] a lack of control over those institutions which affect their lives. . . . [It] results in the community finding its culture and social

organization under constant attack from a racist society (Barrera, Muñoz, Ornelas, 1972, 483, 485).

Historian Rudy Acuña, one of the few faculty who participated in the Santa Barbara conference, then published what was to become the first book-length study of the Mexican experience in U.S. society from a Chicano perspective. He made internal colonialism the framework for his interpretation.

Central to the thesis of this monograph is my contention that the conquest of the Southwest created a colonial situation in the traditional sense with the Mexican land and population being controlled by an imperialistic United States . . . I contend that this colonization . . . is still with us today. Thus, I refer to the colony, initially, in the traditional definition of the term and later . . . as an internal colony (Acuña, 1973, 3).

Guillermo Flores, a former MECHA activist and a graduate student at the time at Stanford University, linked the analysis of Chicanos as an internally colonized people with a Marxist theoretical framework in his article on "Race and Culture in the Internal Colony: Keeping the Chicano in His Place":

There is considerable overlap between monopoly capitalism and internal colonialism within the U.S. . . . [T]he utilization of the Chicano and other racial minorities as a carefully regulated colonial labor force contributed to the capital formation and accumulation processes necessary for the development of modern capitalism's monopoly stage (Flores, 1973, 190).

By 1973 a significant amount of literature had been generated based on the various internal colony analyses and many in Chicano Studies programs throughout the United States used it as the key literature in their courses. Internal colonialism became the "model" for Chicano Studies research and many perceived it as the alternative to the dominant paradigm of the social sciences and history. Juan Gómez-Quiñones put it in these words:

A modified colonial framework allows us to relate factors that heretofore have been kept separate . . . The status of the Chicano as a minority-territorial enclave is analogous to other colonial cases in different parts of the world. The aspects that this situation produces and the actions that it engenders, are important in the historical formation of the community and in its historical patterns. Some of these aspects are the caste-like social-economic relations, institutional hostility and neglect, and movements of resistance and assertion (Gómez-Quiñones, 1971, 5–6).

In spite of the popularity of the internal colonial concept, we perceived that the "model" was still in its embryonic stages and was far from becoming a viable paradigm. Two symposia were organized to discuss the status of the "model" in 1973 where we engaged in self-criticism and probed the further refinements we deemed necessary for it to become more meaningful and applicable to the kind of research we believed was needed by the Chicano Movement. The first of the symposia was held at the University of California, Irvine, and the second at UCLA. At the Irvine symposium, there was a general feeling that the "model" was vulnerable to becoming academically rigid thus redirecting Chicano research into a respectable and legitimate direction acceptable to the university but not necessarily conducive to the struggle for Chicano liberation. At the UCLA symposium we reached general agreement that in order to assure the internal colonial analysis remained meaningful to its original objectives it should take a Marxist approach. In this regard I argued that the "colonial model can be a transition from a cultural-racial interpretation of the problems of the Chicano to a class analysis of the Chicano experience" (García, 1974, 27).

THE FORMATION OF NACS

Both symposia raised the question of the role of the Chicano academic intellectual in the Chicano Movement in critical terms. How were those in Chicano Studies or those doing research on the Chicano experience going to prevent their work from becoming purely abstract or coopted by the dominant paradigms? What was to be done to ensure that Chicano research in general, and the internal colonial analysis in particular, was applied to the needs of the community and the Chicano Movement? Whereas the literature on Chicanos and internal colonialism had reached a certain amount of respectability within Chicano Studies circles, it was not considered good scholarship by those in traditional departments of the university, both Chicano and white. Those of us involved in Chicano caucuses in the various social science associations therefore formed the National Caucus of Chicano Social Scientists and agreed to the need to form a national association of Chicano social scientists that could become the mechanism whereby these concerns could be collectively dealt with by Movement scholars throughout the country. Such an association was perceived by some of us as the crucial foundation for the development of a Chicano Studies paradigm. We believed it could join together a community of Chicano scholar-activists— organic intellectuals—dedicated to pursuing the same basic objectives.

The National Caucus of Chicano Social Scientists held a meeting at the New Mexico Highlands University in May of 1973 for the purpose of creating a national association. The meeting was attended by approximately fifty people, most of whom were graduate students and a handful who were junior faculty, recent Ph.D.s, or at the dissertation stage. We focused our attention on the nature and direction of Chicano social science research and the structure of the proposed association. Agreement was reached that traditional social science research was to be discouraged within the proposed association in favor of more critical analysis as afforded by the internal colonial and Marxist class analysis. The question of the role of Chicano academic intellectuals was heavily discussed. We agreed that Chicano social science research should fall under the following criteria:

(1) Social Science research by Chicanos must be more problem-oriented than traditional social science . . . scholarship cannot be justified for its own sake: It must be a committed scholarship that can contribute to Chicano liberation. (2) . . . research projects must be *interdisciplinary* in

nature . . . traditional discipline(s) . . . serve . . . to fragment our research in a highly artificial manner, and obscure the interconnections among variables that operate to maintain the oppression of our people. (3) . . . research and action should exist in a dialectical relationship . . . in order to bridge the gap between theory and action, Chicano social scientists must develop close ties with community action groups. (4) Chicano social science must be highly *critical* . . . of American institutions . . . (5) . . . We must study the Chicano community . . . within the context of those dominant institutional relationships that affect Chicanos . . . research has to do with the relationship between class, race, and culture in determining the Chicano's historical experience (Caucus newsletter, 1973, 2).

The proposed association would set the example and the direction for Chicano research as outlined above. Its task would be to establish communication among Chicano scholars across geographic and disciplinary lines, encourage the development of new social theories and models, struggle for the recruitment of Chicanos into all graduate levels of social science institutions, and attempt to generate funds for research by Chicanos that met the objectives of the association. Membership in the association was to be on the basis of participation in interdisciplinary local and regional collective research units called "focos." It was agreed the name of the association would be the National Association of Chicano Social Scientists (NACS) and that it would hold annual meetings where the work of each foco would be presented. At the 1977 annual meeting held at the University of California, Berkeley, the association changed its name to the National Association for Chicano Studies.

By the time of the founding of NACS, however, the concept of internal colonialism began to lose much of its original thrust. It became clear that, at least as we had applied it to the Chicano experience, there was no true consensus to make it *the* paradigm for Chicano Studies research. For if we agree with Thomas Kuhn that a paradigm defines "the entire constellation of beliefs, values, techniques, etc., shared by the members of a given community" of scholars, then we were not even close (Kuhn, 1970, 175).

The initial basis for the founding of NACS had been a general agreement about the failure of the dominant paradigms of the social sciences to meaningfully address themselves to a proper interpretation of the Chicano experience and the desire to develop an organization that could be in tune with the need to do interdisciplinary research of import to the Chicano Movement, e.g., that could contribute to Chicano liberation, specifically, to encourage the development of alternative modes of analysis that could be applied to the resolution of problems in the Chicano community. The founding of NACS, however, took place at a time when the nationalist-oriented student movement was already in decline. The politics of "Chicanismo" or "cultural nationalism" were being questioned in critical terms by those of us who saw Marxism as the alternative paradigm that needed to be applied to Chicano research and political action. The first analyses developed of Chicanos as an internally colonized people had been directly the result of our participation in the student movement, the Santa Barbara conference, or the various Chicano struggles of the late sixties addressing the quest for Chicano identity and culture as a means for liberation. Internal colonialism had been meaningful as a concept that offered an alternative interpretation of the Chicano experience that stressed racism and directly related to our task of interpreting the Chicano movement as a struggle for decolonization and antiassimilation.

By 1973, the time of the founding of NACS, most of us who had earlier applied the concept of internal colonialism had engaged in self-criticism of our own work. Mario Barrera, for example, placed the origins of the concept in critical perspective at the UCLA symposium on internal colonialism prior to the founding of NACS.

> I think there is truly no colonial model as such . . . we tend to fall into the habit of using and talking about the colonial model . . . there's rather a concept . . . that some of us have tried to use in order to try to understand the experience of the Chicano, Puerto Rican, black and native American. . . . There is no one interpretation of colonialism . . . when it started to be used . . . to refer to the experience of national minorities here [it] was really used in a kind of polemic against liberal interpretations of the experience of these minority groups. I think the fact that it began in that kind of context influenced its direction, its central themes . . . [it] still represents that kind of dialogue (Proceedings, 1973).

It had become clear in most of our minds that Marxist theory and class analysis offered much in the way of potential contributions to the development of a truly alternative paradigm for Chicano Studies. Within the NACS constituency at that time, however, there was much diversity of thought as to the validity of Marxist methodology and theory in the reinterpretation of the Chicano experience. Many remained committed to a research focused on the question of culture vis-à-vis the ideological framework of the Plan de Santa Bárbara. Others agreed that class analysis should be incorporated into the internal colonial framework, while still others became convinced that the question of paradigm was best addressed by limiting it to a classical Marxist-Leninist framework of class struggle. One of those with the latter perspective was Gilbert González, a participant in the Santa Barbara conference in 1969 who rejected internal colonialism on the following grounds:

> The theory of the internal colony model . . . focuses attention upon the national question. . . . However, it is full of dangers and idealistic assumptions which are inherent in non-Marxist as well as anti-Marxist works. It does not place into proper perspective the questions of class and racial (and ignores sexual) exploitation. In the long run the contradictions of the theory are such that it would be of little use in the destruction of racism and exploitation. For one truly interested in the liberation of oppressed peoples (for example, whites in Appalachia) the internal colony model is an incorrect, ineffective, and ultimately counterrevolutionary theory (González, 1974, 160–161).

González and others holding to classical Marxist-Leninist schools of thought critiqued the concept of internal colonization as positing a "racial war" as opposed to a "correct theory" of class struggle.

Another critique of the internal colonial concept was made by Fred Cervantes in a paper delivered at the annual NACS meeting in Austin in 1975. According to him, the concept was limited because it did not truly place the "realities of contemporary Chicano history and politics" in proper context (Cervantes, 1975, 16). According to this critique, the oppression of Chicanos was due to a "legacy of colonialism rather than as an example of internal colonialism" because Chicanos in American society were in reality a "post-colonial minority" (ibid.).

The limitations of the internal colonial concept, as outlined by those of us who first applied it to the Chicano experience and our critics, made it clear that a paradigm that could result in the further definition of Chicano Studies could not be restricted to the type of analysis that concept generated. The concept was of great significance in that it was the first concrete effort to radically depart from the dominant paradigms and free Chicano research to some extent from dependence on the theories and methodologies of the traditional academic disciplines. The limitations of the concept notwithstanding, it has contributed significantly to our collective development as Chicano academic intellectuals and to Chicano Studies as a new field of study and research.

The concept of internal colonialism, however, never achieved legitimacy in the university in the context that we applied it during the early seventies. In the minds of white academics and those scholars of Mexican descent removed from the struggles for Chicano Studies who perpetuate the myth of "objective" and "value-free" research, the concept was simply a polemic or political ideology that had little to offer in the way of scholarship. Academic Marxists held a similar attitude since the concept did not neatly fit into any of their paradigms. In contrast, those of us who applied the concept to our research and interpretations of the Chicano experience viewed our quest for paradigm as inseparable from the Chicano struggle for in our minds just as the Chicano Movement had directly challenged the dominant institutions of the State for their failure to meet the needs of our people and communities, we perceived Chicano Studies as a challenge to the dominant paradigms that had either failed to properly interpret or that altogether ignored the Chicano experience. Both the Chicano struggle and Chicano Studies were movements aimed at altering the nature of the status quo, the former being concerned with changing existing power relationships and the latter with challenging the perspectives, models, and theories that had legitimized those relationships. In a very real sense we were engaged in the process that Thomas Kuhn has described as follows:

> This genetic aspect of the parallel between political and scientific development should no longer be open to doubt . . . political revolutions aim to change political institutions in ways those institutions themselves prohibit. . . . Like the choice between competing institutions, that between competing paradigms proves to be a choice between incompatible modes of community life (Kuhn, 1970, 93, 94).

The consequence has been that most Chicano Studies research produced thus far reflects a scholarship rooted in the dominant paradigms of the established disciplines. Collectively speaking, we have yet to liberate ourselves from those disciplines to the extent we are free to seriously and critically ponder the theoretical and methodological questions that need to be examined in any effort to develop a new paradigm or discipline. We continue to refer to ourselves as historians, political scientists, sociologists, etc., as opposed to consciously making the effort to underscore the interdisciplinary nature of Chicano Studies research.

Why is this the case? The answer lies in the structure of the university. We remain victimized by it and are powerless to control our collective intellectual development. Our survival as faculty is dependent upon how well we meet the criteria for excellence in scholarship as defined by the dominant paradigms. We are not in the position whereby we can profoundly influence the graduate training of Chicano students since we have as yet not established a single Chicano Studies Ph.D. program anywhere in the country that is under our full control and gives us the opportunity to produce Chicano organic intellectuals. In short, Chicano Studies scholarship has not yet been legitimized although Chicano scholars as individuals have.

If we critically evaluated the research that has been produced thus far in accordance with the criteria defined by El Plan de Santa Bárbara and the founders of this association some no doubt would consider most of it as not legitimate Chicano Studies research. The development of any field of study, however, must be placed in the context of a process of intellectual development that takes place not in a vacuum but that originates from the larger societal situation that in turn influences the political consciousness of intellectuals. The quest for paradigm is therefore a continuous process and one that is never ending. The restrictions placed on our research by the structure of the university can be overcome and have been, as the fruit of our collective labor is beginning to show, and there is evidence that a critical Chicano scholarship is alive and well. Many of us are finally at the stage of producing works that have for many years been in the process of intellectual and political percolation.

The state of Chicano Studies research is a healthy one, for in spite of the pessimistic forecasts about the future of our programs that have been made since the 1970s, a small but significant number of us have survived in the university. Sánchez, Paredes, Samora, and Galarza established a Mexican intellectual tradition of critical inquiry and advocacy in this society, and we of the generation of the sixties have built on it and will preserve it.

REFERENCES

Acuña, Rodolfo. 1972. *Occupied America: The Chicano's Struggle Toward Liberation*. San Francisco: Canfield Press.

Almaguer, Tomás. 1971. "Toward the Study of Chicano Colonialism." *Aztlán: Chicano Journal of the Social Sciences and the Arts*, Spring, 1971, pp. 7–21.

Barrera, Mario; Carlos Muñoz, Jr.; and Charles Ornelas. 1972. "The Barrio as Internal Colony." In Harlan Hahn, ed., *People and Politics in Urban Society*, pp. 465–498. Los Angeles: Sage Publications.

Cervantes, Fred A. 1977. "Chicanos as a Post-Colonial Minority: Some Questions Concerning the Adequacy of the Paradigm of Internal Colonialism." In Reynaldo Flores Macias, ed., *Perspectivas en Chicano Studies*. Proceedings of the Third Annual Meeting of the National Association of Chicano Social Scientists. Los Angeles: NACS.

Chicano Coordinating Council on Higher Education. 1969. *El Plan de Santa Bárbara: A Chicano Plan for Higher Education*. Oakland: La Causa Publications.

Flores, Guillermo V. 1973. "Race and Culture in the Internal Colony: Keeping the Chicano in His Place." In Frank Bonilla and Robert Girling, eds., *Structures of Dependency*, pp. 189–223. Stanford: Institute of Political Studies.

Galarza, Ernesto. 1964. *The Merchants of Labor*. Santa Barbara: McNally & Loftin.

García, Mario. 1974. "A report on the UCLA Symposium on Internal Colonialism and the Chicano." *La Luz*, April, 1974, p. 27.

Gómez-Quiñones, Juan. 1971. "Toward a Perspective on Chicano History." *Aztlán*, Fall, 1971, pp. 1-49.

González, Gilbert G. 1974. "A Critique of the Internal Colonial Model." *Latin American Perspectives*, Spring, 1974, pp. 154-161.

Kuhn, Thomas. 1970. *The Structure of Scientific Revolutions*. Chicago: University of Chicago Press.

Muñoz, Carlos, Jr. *Youth and Political Struggle: The Chicano Student Generation*. Forthcoming.

———. 1970. "On the Nature and Cause of Tension in the Chicano Community: A Critical Analysis." Paper prepared for delivery at the Invitational Research Symposium on Urban Problems, Institute of Government and Public Affairs, UCLA, April 2, 1970.

———. 1970. "Toward a Chicano Perspective of Political Analysis." *Aztlán*, Fall, 1970, pp. 15–26.

National Caucus of Chicano Social Scientists Newsletter, 1977. In Reynaldo Flores Macias, ed., *Perspectivas en Chicano Studies*. Proceedings of the Third Annual Meeting of the National Association of Chicano Social Scientists, pp. 215–216. Los Angeles: NACS.

Paredes, Américo. 1976. *A Texas Mexican Cancionero*. Urbana: University of Illinois Press.

Romano, Octavio Ignacio, V. 1970. "Social Science, Objectivity, and the Chicanos." *El Grito: Journal of Contemporary Mexican-American Thought*, Fall, 1970, pp. 4–16.

Samora, Julián, and James Watson. 1954. "Subordinate Leadership in a Bicultural Community: An Analysis." *American Sociological Review*, August, 1954, pp. 413–421.

Sánchez, George. 1940. *The Forgotten People*. Albuquerque: University of New Mexico Press.

Symposium on Internal Colonialism and the Chicano. 1973. Unpublished proceedings of symposium at UCLA. Author's files.

24

Confronting Barriers to the
Participation of
Mexican American Women
in Higher Education

Melba J. T. Vasquez

Problems for ethnic minorities and women are still pervasive in general and especially on the nation's campuses despite gains made in the last two decades (Women's
Equity Action League Educational and Legal Defense Fund, Note 1). In particular,
educational status for Mexican American women, or Chicanas (for the purposes of
this article, the term "Chicana" will be synonymous with Mexican American and
is defined as a female American citizen of Mexican ancestry), remains low. The
United States Commission on Civil Rights (1978) reported a March 1976 study that
revealed that while 32% of all Mexican American men who entered college completed a degree, only 15% of all Mexican American women did so. In comparison,
approximately 50% of every nonminority who enters college completes a degree.
Moreover, fewer Chicanos than nonminorities enroll in college after high school
graduation (*Chronicle of Higher Education*, 1975). Clearly, while both male and female Chicanos are at an educational disadvantage, Chicanas fare less well.

There is a strong ethos in this country that suggests that education is a means
to socioeconomic mobility and independence. Yet, the figures that reflect the educational attainment of Chicanas at all levels (undergraduate, graduate, and faculty)
in higher education are bleak (Escobedo, 1980). Hence, the effectiveness of higher
education for Chicanas may be improved if we learn more about why a large proportion of students do not participate fully in higher education.

The purpose of this article is to identify the barriers that contribute to the low
numbers of undergraduate Chicanas in higher education as well as to identify practical measures to minimize Chicana students' chances of dropping out. The research
literature in the area of Chicana academic achievement is extremely limited. Thus,
many issues, hypotheses, or generalizations will be extrapolated from the general
literature on attrition and retention as well as from the meager research on women,
Mexican Americans, and other ethnic minority groups in higher education. First,
the effects of sex-role restrictions on Chicanas will be discussed. Then the myths
about the effects of culture and language on academic achievement will be critiqued. It seems important to address and clarify the negative stereotypic myths that

have been perpetuated by studies that have utilized a pathological model of cultural deficit to account for low educational achievement and whose interpretations of data are biased. The deleterious effects of low economic status as well as sources of financial support in college will also be discussed. The notion of environmental fit and the stress from alienation and isolation for Chicanas in all-white institutions will be addressed. The inappropriate use of traditional admissions criteria and the importance of motivation, expectations, and self-esteem to mediate barriers to success for Chicanas are final considerations.

SEX DIFFERENCES

Does sex-role socialization restrict participation of Chicana women in higher education? Stereotyped attitudes about role definitions for women (e.g., childbearers) and role definitions for men (e.g., the "machismo" image) in traditional Latin cultures are examples of sex-role factors suggested to restrict educational aspirations and levels of achievement for Chicanas. While the traditionally high value placed on *La Familia* has its positive rewards (Keefe, Padilla, and Carlos, 1978), Mexican American women, often first-generation college students, experience role conflict as they attempt to balance the relative rewards and costs of marriage and children with an education and, ultimately, a career.

In their study on Chicanos in higher education on four California campuses, for example, Munoz and Garcia-Bahne (Note 2) found sex differences for academic performance. Forty-two percent of the males compared to 30% of the females in their sample reported that they had been on academic probation at some time. Chicanas received superior grades than Chicanos in high school and in college. Yet, figures reported earlier reflect the relatively low rates of persistence to graduation for Chicanas.

Women and men in general are found to differ in their educational and intellectual development (Maccoby & Jacklin, 1974). One would assume that different needs and role expectations for men and women would result in differences in academic performance. Cope and Hannah (1975) concluded that the variable of sex in predicting withdrawal from college is a complex one. They reported that most studies investigating sex as a variable related to attrition found more men withdrawing than women, but when an adequate follow-up study including reentry and transfer was conducted, only slightly different variations in the attrition rate for men and women were found. While women tended to graduate on schedule more often than men, men were more likely to complete degree requirements eventually.

More information about sex differences in academic performance was reported by Astin (1971, 1977). In a presentation of selectivity data for 2,300 American colleges, Astin reported that women received higher grades than men in both high school and in college. He found that the academic performance of the female freshman surpasses that of the average male freshman, even when they were matched on high school grades and aptitude test scores, a finding similar to that of Munoz and Garcia-Bahne (Note 2) for Chicanas. Despite their superior academic performance, women were more likely to drop out of college after the freshman year.

Astin reported similar conclusions in his later (1977) study. He found that although women earned higher grades than men, they were less likely to persist in college and to enroll in graduate or professional school. Moreover, women's aspirations for higher degrees declined, while men's aspirations increased during the undergraduate years.

The socialization process that often perpetuates or reinforces roles for girls and women results in a serious limitation of choices for them. Russo (1976) points out the psychological constraints that sex-role socialization, and particularly the "motherhood mandate," has on women. Dixon (1975) described the very real limitations that marriage and children have on the pursuit of an education. Women who were high school seniors in 1965 were interviewed in 1971. Of those who had started college, 75% of the married women with children had dropped out of school, compared with 52% of married men with children, 22% of single women, and 27% of single men. Sex-role restrictions thus limit the actualization of potential that women have.

Apparently, while women—both Chicana and non-Chicana—perform better academically, persistence to graduation is lower compared to men within respective ethnic groups. The social, economic, and cultural factors common to all women exert great influence on educational attainment. The extent to which cultural elements, in addition, influence the educational attainment of Chicanas is difficult to determine. Because she is often the first generation to enter higher education, the Chicana often experiences stresses resulting from sex-role conflicts. Because of the traditionally high value placed on the Chicano family, the struggle between pursuit of education and the traditional roles of wife and mother may cause many Chicanas to doubt the pursuit of an education. They have often seen their own mothers dedicate their lives to the home and children. Chicanas must thus receive support in dealing with those conflicts and stresses.

CULTURE AND LANGUAGE

What are the effects of the Mexican American culture and the use of Spanish language on Chicanas' academic performance? While we should not underestimate the possible effects on Chicanas of traditional sex-role restrictions, interpretation of the research regarding the effects of culture on Mexican Americans in general is fraught with difficulties. In a review of vocational education research of minority group needs, Hamilton (1975) concluded that the research was generally based on a social pathology model of cultural deficit and on stereotypes of cultural disadvantage without identifying positive attributes. Martinez (1977) points out that "psychological formulations that adequately explain the behavior of Anglos within the Anglo culture may not necessarily explain the behavior of Chicanos within the Chicano culture" (p. 11). The concept of cultural relativism—that human behavior can be understood only if it is viewed within the cultural context in which it occurs—sensitizes people to the importance of careful interpretation of various studies. Unfortunately, many discussions imply that identification with the values, attitudes, behaviors, and language of the Chicano culture is a liability to educational achievement and that acculturation—the process of "giving up" of one's subculture and adapting to the values, attitudes, and behaviors of the majority culture—should be the guiding philosophy of educational programming and interventions (Heller, 1968; Madsen, 1964; Schwartz, 1971). As Escobedo (1980) points out, the deficit model fails to examine the environmental impact on individuals that limits educational resources.

In a review of several studies negatively relating cultural factors to educational achievement and personality adjustment, for example, Ramirez (1971) concludes that socioeconomic variables are central to the issue. Being "educationally disadvantaged" refers to those environmental deficiencies that are detrimental to an individual's performance in education regardless of ethnic or racial status. Low socioeconomic status, a negative family environment, and limited exposure to cultural and intellectual resources may be properly considered indications of a disadvantaged situation. However, while these conditions may be associated with a portion of the Mexican American population for economic and social reasons, they should not be construed as arising from the group's culture per se (National Board on Graduate Education, 1976; Ryan, 1971).

Language is a culturally related factor that may be a disadvantage if a child does not understand English. The relationship of bilingualism and academic achievement has been recognized as a problem by educators. The National Center for Education Statistics (1978) reported, for example, that "language-minority persons" had lower grade attainment for age and a higher dropout rate. Persons of Hispanic origin were found to be even more disadvantaged than language-minority persons in general. These findings were based on an analysis of data from the nationwide survey of income and education (SIE), conducted in the spring of 1976, by the Bureau of the Census. However, it is suggested by Long and Padilla (Note 3) that bilingualism, itself, is not the problem. Rather, additional factors result in "dual-cultural deprivation." Those factors may include educational deprivation, which is related to low socioeconomic status, which in turn is related to a large proportion of the bilingual population.

Long and Padilla (Note 3), recognizing that little research had concentrated on assessing the role of bilingualism in the academic achievement of college-age students, surveyed successful (Ph.D. recipients) and unsuccessful (dropouts) Chicano graduate students at the University of New Mexico. They found that 94% of the successful students but only 7% of the unsuccessful students reported coming from a bilingual background; most of the unsuccessful students reported that English was the only language in their childhood homes. Long and Padilla concluded that the finding of the high rate of bilingualism in the sample of successful Spanish American students implied that these students may have been better able to interact readily with members of both their own culture and that of the dominant American culture. They further suggested that these individuals may simply be better adjusted members of both cultures; hence, their tendencies to be more successful. The lack of bilingual background of the unsuccessful student may reflect a tendency in the homes to reject their Spanish American background, and the ensuing conflict may lead to a general maladjustment.

The reports of several studies have, in fact, challenged the assumption that acculturation is a cure-all and that identification with one's culture is damaging (Henderson and Merritt, 1968; Ramirez, 1971; Ramirez and Castañeda, 1974; Cordova, Note 4; Long and Padilla, Note 3). A more appropriate philosophy—that of cultural democracy—maintains that identification with one's ethnic group is, in fact, a necessary ingredient of academic success and psychological adjustment. Researchers have begun to indicate that active participation in two or more cultures may, in fact, provide the basis for a more flexible and sophisticated psychological adjustment (Henderson and Merritt, 1968; Ramirez and Castañeda, 1974; Cordova, Note 4; Ramirez, Castañeda, and Cox, Note 5).

Thus, while some studies imply that Chicano culture and use of the Spanish language are barriers to educational attainment (National Center for Educational Statistics, 1978; Schwartz, 1971), others propose a positive relationship between a bilingual, bicultural identity and academic success, psychological adjustment, and social flexibility (Henderson and Merritt, 1968; Ramirez and Castañeda, 1974; Cordova, Note 4; Long and Padilla, Note 3). Other factors, such as low socioeconomic status resulting in limited exposure to cultural and intellectual resources, may partially account for low academic performance and attainment of Mexican American men and women.

EFFECTS OF SOCIOECONOMIC STATUS ON ACADEMIC PERFORMANCE OF CHICANAS

Perhaps one of the primary barriers to higher education for Chicanas is the effect of low socioeconomic status. Mexican American women in particular are at the lowest levels of occupational, educational, and financial indices (Vasquez, 1978; Vasquez and Banning, Note 6), and a large portion of the Mexican American population falls in the lower social class (Carter, 1970; U.S. Commission on Civil Rights, 1971). Various indices of social class and their relationship to academic performance have been investigated. Socioeconomic status (SES), as measured by parents' education, occupation, and income, mediates a large number of academic values, attitudes, opinions, and patterns of behavior. The findings frequently reported are that the lower the level of parental education, occupational position, and income, the lower the academic performance. Students from higher SES backgrounds tend to obtain higher grades and persist in college (Astin, 1971, 1975; Astin, Astin, Bisconti, and Frankel, 1972; Cope and Hannah, 1975; Pantages and Creedon, 1978; Vasquez, 1978).

Vasquez (1978), for example, examined factors that influenced and mediated grade point average, persistence, and attrition of Chicana and Anglo University of Texas women. The results of a discriminant analysis showed that socioeconomic status was one of three major variables that contributed to differences between the "successful" and "nonsuccessful" groups. Descriptive data showed that both Anglo and Chicana students who were persisters also had higher parental educational, occupational, and income levels. For the total sample, Chicanas generally reflected lower SES levels than Anglo women.

The process of socialization means that children acquire many of the hopes and expectations of their parents within the social class; they also acquire verbal and auditory skills that have an effect on their ability to adjust to the academic and social demands of college (Cope and Hannah, 1975; Anderson and Johnson, Note 7). Poverty causes stress, particularly in the family structure which has been cited to be the most important facet of life for Chicanos (Cuellar and Moore, 1970). Poor people are also the victims of discrimination in schools and other environments. Thus

poverty and discrimination may combine to limit the development of predispositions, habits, knowledge, and experiences that promote academic achievement for
Mexican American students (Hernandez, 1973).

Hernandez concluded in a review of two studies that SES is not as significant a
predictor for achievement for Mexican American students as for the general population. In an extensive study of Chicanos at four California universities, Munoz and
Garcia-Bahne (Note 2) found no significant differences between college grade point
average and socioeconomic standing of the family. In a study investigating the
sociocultural determinants of Mexican American high school students, Anderson
and Johnson (Note 7) found that when achievement motivation was controlled, the
previously discovered relationship between SES and grades almost disappeared.
These studies suggest that while social and economic indices do relate to academic
performance, achievement motivation of Mexican American students mediates the
otherwise deleterious effects of SES. However, since need achievement is supposedly
one of the attitudinal factors negatively affected by low SES, the question of why
some low SES students acquire achievement motivation and others do not remains.

The extent of academic preparation for Chicanos is a related issue that should
be explored. Mexican American students in general, and women in particular, are often "tracked" into taking non-college preparatory courses. The National Academy
of Sciences (1977) made visits to 29 engineering campuses with active programs to
increase minority student enrollment and found insufficient preparation in mathematics and the physical sciences as one of several reasons for attrition among minority engineering students. Basic study skills are often lacking in minority students who
otherwise have the academic potential to succeed in higher education.

While it seems that the academic performance of many students is adversely affected by factors associated with low SES (e.g., stereotypic societal messages, lack of
resources, inadequate preparation, different academic values and attitudes, patterns
of behavior), other students prevail despite those negative associations. Perhaps the
ambition to better oneself mediates the usual disadvantaged situation of the Chicano
student from the low SES family. How that ambition is acquired despite negative environmental limitations remains a question, particularly for Chicanas. Yet, many
more Chicanos who have potential to succeed are adversely effected. It may well be
important to focus energies on alleviating the poverty cycle in which so many Mexican American families find themselves. The negative effect of poverty on academic
performance is just one of the deleterious consequences of the stresses of poverty.

FINANCIAL SITUATION

Related to low economic status is the resultant problem of financial support in
school. Financial situation has a greater impact on Chicano students than on majority students. The U.S. Bureau of the Census (1970) reports that Mexican American
families earn about 70% as much income as nonminority families (Table 266, U.S.
Bureau of the Census). In a comprehensive study, the National Board on Graduate
Education (1976, pp. 77–81) reported that Chicanos anticipate a much lower median parental contribution toward the cost of college ($194 per year) compared to
white students ($1,145 per year). These figures are alarming in view of the fact that

Astin (1975) concluded that receiving support from parents for college expenses generally enhances the student's ability to complete college (except for women from high-income brackets).

While Munoz and Garcia-Bahne (Note 2) found no differences between college grade point average and socioeconomic status (using parental educational and occupational levels), they did find a negative relationship between family income and dropping out of school. Low family income had a detrimental effect on the Chicano college student's chances of completing college.

Financial concerns do indeed predominate as major problem areas for minority students, as evidenced by reports of a needs assessment conducted at the University of Texas (Baron, Valdez, Vasquez, and Hurst, Note 8) and one conducted at Colorado State University (Vasquez and Banning, Note 6). These two studies found that the area of greatest concern to minority students was that of finances. For the Texas study, those students reporting inadequate income also reported significantly higher mean concerns for 58 of the 63 items on the survey. The extent to which financial aid and other student assistance programs have compensated for disparities in financial circumstances remains unclear. Minorities in general place greater reliance on scholarships, workstudy programs, and loans in financing their undergraduate education, in contrast to nonminority students who receive more parental assistance.

The way in which various types of financial aid affects student performance was investigated by Astin (1975). He concluded that scholarships or grants are associated with small increases in student persistence rates; participation in workstudy programs also appears to enhance student persistence. Reliance on loans, on the other hand, is associated with decreased persistence among men in all income groups while the effects are highly variable among women. Reliance on savings or other assets also appears to decrease the students' chances of finishing college. We can thus hypothesize that one of the barriers to higher educational participation for Mexican American women is primarily the lack of funds and secondarily the common necessity of students to rely on loans. We could conclude that activities designed to make scholarships and grants more available to Chicanas might enhance tendency to enter and remain in school.

GEOGRAPHIC LOCATION, SIZE OF HIGH SCHOOL, AND "CULTURE SHOCK" PHENOMENON

A Chicana student's hometown location and size are also factors in academic performance. In a review of three studies, Summerskill (1974) concluded that higher attrition rates were found among students from rural homes than among students from cities or towns. Astin (1975) and Cope (1972) found that growing up in a small town was most consistently related to dropping out. "Out of state" students were "underachievers"; students from cities with populations of more than 100,000 were "overachievers." However, in their review of several studies, Cope and Hannah (1975) found conflicting results: some studies indicated that school size makes no difference or that students from smaller high schools do better in college, whereas others showed that students from larger, more urban high schools performed better. The location and size of home communities in themselves probably do not determine a student's academic performance. Yet, variation in quality of secondary schools and in the number and range of the cultural and educational activities among different cities and towns may be influential.

The "culture shock" phenomenon may account in part for the difficulty many Chicana students encounter, especially at large all-white universities. Students report alienation and isolation as a result of being the only minority student in a class of 300 students or in a large residence hall. Astin (1975) and Cope and Hannah (1975) concluded that the "fit" between the size and nature of the student's hometown and the college is important to student academic performance, particularly persistence. Indeed, many students report preferring to return to smaller colleges or community colleges in order to feel more comfortable. Establishment of effective cultural programs, organizations, and other student services can help offset the alienation that Chicana students experience.

ADMISSIONS CRITERIA

The use of traditional admissions criteria as a barrier to the participation of minorities has been recognized by many. Very few studies have attempted to investigate the possible differential relationship of admissions criteria to college grade point average and persistence for Mexican American students, and this author was not able to locate any studies that identified differences for Chicanas. The few studies that have been completed report dissimilar and occasionally contradictory results, possibly due to differences in methodology, selected variables, and populations (Cole and Hanson, 1973; Dalton, 1974; Goldman and Hewitt, 1976; Goldman and Richards, 1974; Sedlacek and Brooks, 1976; Thomas and Stanley, 1969).

Generally, studies reported that the use of admission test scores and high school grades work disproportionately against minority groups. Goldman and Hewitt (1976), for example, found that the accuracy of college grade point average prediction by the combined use of high school grade point average and SAT scores was considerably weaker for black and Chicano students than for white or Asian students in their sample. Goldman and Hewitt (1976) concluded that "if a given *predicted* grade point average were used to select college applicants, then proportionately fewer Black and Chicano applicants would be admitted than would actually surpass this grade point average criterion" (p. 116).

Some researchers conclude that high school achievement is a better predictor than admissions tests scores for minorities. Yet, high school achievement is a less effective predictor of college grades for minority students than for nonminorities (Dalton, 1974). Others who found test scores to be better predictors of academic success than high school achievement also caution that they are not as predictive for minority students as for majority students (Cole and Hanson, 1973; Thomas and Stanley, 1969). Obviously, the conflicting findings are likely due to problems and differences in methodology. For example, studies that do find the traditional predictors valid for ethnic minorities use subjects who are largely unrepresentative of the larger number of minority students with the potential to do college work, since minority students attracted to higher education tend to be relatively homogeneous on the admissions criteria.

Clearly, university admissions offices that continue to use the traditional criteria prevent many Chicana students and other minorities who have college potential from even entering school. Admissions and other counseling personnel should thus be aware of the lack of predictability of such criteria for Chicanas and other groups.

MOTIVATION, SELF-EXPECTATIONS, AND SELF-ESTEEM

As indicated earlier, motivation is one of the identified variables that mediate barriers to the participation of Chicanas in higher education. Personal commitment to either an academic or occupational goal has been identified as one of the single most important determinants of persistence in college. Cope and Hannah (1975) concluded that the commitment to finish college resulting partly from the motivational climate of the family was far more important than having enough money. The literature is conflicted regarding the aspirations, expectations, and motivational climate for Mexican Americans and their families to attend college. Some studies that utilize the pathological model of cultural deficit reported low educational aspirations and expectations (Heller, 1968; Madsen, 1964); others suggested that aspirations and expectations were just as strong for Mexican American students and their parents as for their Anglo counterparts when socioeconomic status and educational circumstances were controlled (Anderson and Johnson, Note 7; Ulibarri, Note 9). A study by Moerk (1974) found that while aspirations were high, expectations to attend college, in reality, were relatively lower.

One of the most recent studies on Chicanos in higher education by Munoz and Garcia-Bahne (Note 2) found that 55% of the Chicano students in their sample from four California universities began thinking of attending college during the 10th grade or later, and more than 26% did not consider the possibility until 12th grade or later. In contrast, the vast majority of Anglo students had planned to attend college during their elementary or junior high school years. This finding implied differences in the *development* of aspirations and expectations to attend college.

In order to have positive expectations for oneself, one must first experience positive feelings and perceive oneself to be skillful in interacting in the Anglo world, such as the generally all-white institutions of higher education. Self-esteem and one's image is developed primarily from two sources: (a) feedback about one's personal worth and competence, and (b) from cultural feedback about the *legitimacy* of a person's primary reference group (Zimbardo, 1979). The negative stereotypes about Chicanas, in particular, convey "illegitimate" messages about our primary reference group. It is not surprising, then, that actual expectations for Chicanas may be lower and that the development of expectations to attend college occurs later. Clearly, it is crucial that Mexican American women with potential to succeed in college receive strong doses of encouragement from parents as well as other significant people in their lives, such as teachers, in order to deter the negative messages from society about their primary reference group. Overt as well as covert, subtle patterns of prejudice and discrimination often result in negative internalized messages about one's general worth as a woman, as a member of an ethnic minority group, and, in most cases, as a member of the low economic group in this country.

First-generation Chicana college students in particular must inoculate themselves against the crippling effects of being a "triple minority" by establishing a sense of pride in their origins, history, and group identity as well as in their abilities. Parents and teachers have been found to be influential. In a study evaluating the effects of school desegregation by court-ordered busing on the subsequent dropout rate of majority and minority students, for example, Felice and Richardson (Note 10) found that the more favorable expectations of teachers at higher socioeconomic-climate schools produced lower minority dropout rates. The National Academy of Sciences (1977) conducted a study of retention of minority students in engineering and reported that the amount of personal contact among students, faculty, and staff was an important variable in a retention program. Using a discriminant analysis to determine the variables that best discriminated between the "successful" and "nonsuccessful" groups of Chicana university students, Vasquez (1978) found that "mother encouragement to do well in school" was one of the most important. Given the oppression that Mexican American women experience as a "triple minority," self-expectations and self-esteem may be relatively low, or at best develop more positively at a later time than most non-Chicana students. These negative effects can be mediated by positive contact, support, and encouragement from parents, teachers, and other significant individuals in their lives.

In conclusion, several barriers to the participation of Chicanas in higher education have been identified. Sex-role socialization as well as negative messages in society about the Mexican American culture result in conflicts and low self-expectations. Some of the literature (Heller, 1968; Madsen, 1964; Schwartz, 1971) implied that identification with the Chicano culture is a liability to educational achievement. The reports of other studies (Henderson and Merritt, 1969; Ramirez, 1971; Ramirez and Castañeda, 1974; Cordova, Note 4; Long and Padilla, Note 3) challenged the view that identification with one's culture is damaging. It seems, in fact, that identification with one's ethnic group is a necessary ingredient of academic success as well as psychological adjustment.

Low socioeconomic factors result in social and economic disadvantages and oppressions. Many Chicanas thus experience severe limitations in the development of predispositions, habits, knowledges, and experiences that promote academic achievement. Yet, many Chicanas from those backgrounds persevere despite those disadvantages (Hernandez, 1973). Achievement motivation seems to mediate the otherwise deleterious effects of low socioeconomic status (Anderson and Johnson, Note 7). Cope and Hannah (1975) expressed belief that personal commitment either to an academic or occupational goal was one of the single most important determinants of persistence in college.

Mexican American parents often cannot afford to finance education, and difficulty with financial sources for education is also a barrier that often results in the inability to continue or delay in acquisition of a college education. Scholarships, grants, and work-study were described as the sources of support that enhance student persistence; but loans often decrease students' chances of finishing college, possibly because of stresses that students may experience at the thought of continuing to acquire debts.

Because the all-white environment of a university institution may be so different and oppressive compared to that of the Chicana, the lack of "fit" may result in the "culture shock" phenomenon which results in isolation and alienation. Establishment of effective student services, cultural programs, and organizations can help offset the deleterious effects that Chicanas otherwise experience.

Admissions criteria, such as standardized test scores and high school achievement, are not as predictive for Chicanas and other ethnic minority groups as they are for nonminorities. Thus, admissions offices that continue to use the traditional criteria prevent many potentially successful Chicana students from entering the university.

Many barriers thus account for the relatively low participation of Mexican American women in higher education. Support for women and strong identification with the positive aspects of one's culture seem particularly important for Mexican American women who must struggle with sex-role conflicts as well as innoculate themselves against the patterns of prejudice and discrimination that often otherwise result in negatively internalized messages about one's worth as a woman, as a member of an ethnic minority group, and, in many cases, as a member of the low economic group in this country.

Mexican American women are often first-generation college students. The development of expectations to attend college occurs later for Mexican American students than for nonminority students (Munoz and Garcia-Bahne, Note 2). It is thus crucial that Mexican American women with potential to succeed in college be strongly encouraged by parents, teachers, and other significant people in their lives. Vasquez (1978), in an attempt to identify variables that best discriminated between "successful" and "nonsuccessful" groups of Chicana university women, found that "mother encouragement to do well in school" was one of the most important. Felice and Richardson (Note 10) found that more favorable expectations of teachers at higher socioeconomic climate schools accounted for lower minority dropout rates. Positive expectations and encouragement from significant people clearly effect academic persistence of Mexican American students. More research is needed to determine the relative meaningfulness of encouragement from different sources for different populations. For example, is mother encouragement similarly impactful for Mexican American males, or is sex-role identification an important variable? Is encouragement and affirmation from nonminority teachers differentially effective for Chicana students from different backgrounds?

Confronting the barriers that exist for Mexican American women is a responsibility of all individuals who are in positions to offer support as well as impact the environments in which those barriers occur. Only through those efforts will Mexican American women be able to experience more accessibility to higher education, a right purported to exist for all Americans on an equal basis.

NOTES

1. Women's Equity Action League Educational and Legal Defense Fund. *Facts about women in higher education*, 1977. Available from author, 733 15th Street, N.W., Suite 200, Washington, D.C. 20005.

2. Munoz, D., and Garcia-Bahne, B. *A study of the Chicano experience in higher education*. Final report for the Center for Minority Group Mental Health Programs, National Institute of Mental Health, Grant No. NN24597-01, University of California, San Diego, 1978.

3. Long, K. K., and Padilla, A. M. *An assessment of successful and unsuccessful college*

students. Paper presented at the American Association for the Advancement of Science. Regional Meeting, Colorado Springs, 1969.

4. Cordova, I. R. *The relationship of acculturation, achievement, and alienation among Spanish-American sixth grade students.* Paper presented for the Conference on Teacher Education for Mexican Americans, New Mexico State University, ERIC: CRESS, 1969.

5. Ramirez, M., III, Castañeda, A., and Cox, B. G. *A biculturalism inventory for Mexican American college students.* Unpublished manuscript, University of California, Santa Cruz, 1977.

6. Vasquez, M. J., and Banning, J. H. *Needs assessment service utilization and factors of success for minority students: Research findings.* Paper presented at the National Association of Student Personnel Association, Region IV West Conference, Omaha, Nebraska, 1979.

7. Anderson, J. G., and Johnson, W. H. *Sociocultural determinates of achievements among Mexican American students.* Paper presented at the National Conference of Educational Opportunities for Mexican Americans, ERIC Clearinghouse on Rural Education and Small Schools, New Mexico State University, 1968.

8. Baron, A., Valdez, J., Vasquez, M. J., and Hurst, J. C. *Assessing the concerns of minority students: Process and outcome.* Paper presented at the 60th National Association of Student Personnel Administrators Conference, Kansas City, Missouri, 1978.

9. Ulibarri, H. *Educational needs of the Mexican American.* Paper presented at the National Conference of Educational Opportunities for Mexican Americans, ERIC Clearinghouse on Rural Education and Small Schools, New Mexico State University, 1968.

10. Felice, L. G., and Richardson, R. L. *The effects of busing and school desegregation on majority and minority student dropout rates: An evaluation of school socioeconomic composition and teachers' expectations.* ERIC Dialog File 1, 1976.

REFERENCES

Astin, A. W. *Predicting academic performance in college: Selectivity data for 2,300 American colleges.* New York: The Free Press, 1971.

———. *Preventing students from dropping out.* San Francisco: Jossey-Bass, 1975.

———. *Four critical years: Effects of college on beliefs, attitudes, and knowledge.* San Francisco: Jossey-Bass, 1977.

Astin, H. S., Astin, A. W., Bisconti, A. S., and Frankel, H. H. *Higher education and the disadvantaged student.* Washington, D. C.: Human Service Press, 1972.

Carter, T. *Mexican-Americans in the school: A history of educational neglect* Princeton, N.J.: College Entrance Examination Board, 1970. *Chronicle of Higher Education.* 1975, 11(7), whole.

Cole, N. S., and Hanson, G. R. *Assessing students on the way to college: Technical report for the American College Testing Assessment Program* (Vol. 1). Iowa City: The American College Testing Program, 1973.

Cope, R. G. Are students more likely to drop out of large colleges? *College Student Journal,* 1972, 6(2), 92–97.

———, and Hannah, W. *Revolving college doors: The causes and consequences of dropping out, stopping out, and transferring.* New York: Wiley-Interscience, 1975.

Cuellar, A., and Moore, J. W. *Mexican-Americans.* New York: Prentice-Hall, 1970.

Dalton, S. Predictive validity of high school rank and SAT scores for minority students. *Educational and Psychological Measurement,* 1974, 34, 367–370.

Dixon, R. Women's rights and fertility. *Studies in Family Planning,* 1975, 17, 1–20.

Escobedo, T. H. Are Hispanic women in higher education the nonexistent minority? *Educational Researcher,* October, 1980.

Goldman, R. D., and Hewitt, B. N. Predicting the success of black, Chicano, Oriental, and white college students. *Journal of Educational Measurements* 1976, 13(2), 107–117.

———, and Richards, R. The SAT prediction of grades for Mexican-Americans versus Anglo-American students at the University of California, Riverside. *Journal of Educational Measurement*, 1974, 11, 129–135.

Hamilton, D. *Vocational education research and development for ethnic minority students.* Washington, D. C.: National Academy of Sciences, National Research Council, 1975.

Heller, C. S. *Mexican-American youth: Forgotten youth at the crossroads.* New York: Random House, 1968.

Henderson, R. W., and Merritt, C. B. Environmental backgrounds of Mexican-American children with different potentials for school success. *Journal of Social Psychology*, 1968, 75, 101–106.

Hernandez, N. G. Variables affecting achievement of middle school Mexican-American students. *Review of Educational Research*, 1973, 43(1), 1–41.

Keefe, S. E., Padilla, A. M., and Carlos, M. L. The Mexican American extended family as an emotional support system. In J. M. Casas and S. E. Keefe (Eds.), *Family and mental health in the Mexican American community.* Los Angeles: Spanish Speaking Mental Health Research Center, UCLA, Monograph No. 7, 1978.

Maccoby, E. E., and Jacklin, C. N. *The psychology of sex differences.* Stanford, Cal.: Stanford University Press, 1974.

Madsen, W. *Mexican-Americans of South Texas: Case studies in cultural anthropology.* New York: Holf, Rinehart & Winston, 1964.

Martinez., J. L., Jr. (Ed.). *Chicano psychology.* New York: Academic Press, 1977.

Moerk, E. L. Age and epogenic influences on aspirations of minority and majority group children. *Journal of Counseling Psychology*, 1974, 21, 294–298.

National Academy of Sciences, *Retention of minority students in engineering.* Washington, D.C.: National Research Council, 1977.

National Board on Graduate Education. *Minority group participation in graduate education.* Washington, D.C.: National Academy of Sciences, 1976.

National Center for Education Statistics. *The educational disadvantage of language-minority persons in the United States.* Washington, D.C.: National Center for Educational Statistics, 1978.

Pantages, T. J., and Creedon, C. F. Studies of college attrition: 1950–1975. *Review of Educational Research*, 1978, 48(1), 49–102.

Ramirez, M., III. The relationship of acculturation to educational achievement and psychological adjustment in Chicano children and adolescents: A review of the literature. *El Crito*, 1971, 4(4), 21–28.

———, and Castañeda, A. *Cultural democracy, bicognitive development and education.* New York: Academic Press, 1974.

Russo, N. F. The motherhood mandate. *Journal of Social Issues*, 1976, 32(3), 143–153.

Ryan, W. *Blaming the victim.* New York: Vintage Books, 1971.

Schwartz, A. J. A comparative study of values and achievement: Mexican-American and Anglo youth. *Sociology of Education*, 1971, 44, 438–462.

Sedlacek, E., and Brooks, G. C., Jr. *Racism in American education: A model for change.* Chicago: Nelson Hall, Inc., 1976.

Summerskill, J. Dropouts from college. In N. Sanford, *College and character: A briefer version of the American college.* New York: John Wiley & Sons, 1974.

Thomas, C. L., and Stanley, J. C. Effectiveness of high school grades for predicting college grades of black students: A review and discussion. *Journal of Educational Measurement*, 1969, 6, 203–215.

U.S. Bureau of the Census. *Characteristics of the population*, 1970 (Vol. 1). Washington, D.C.: U.S. Government Printing Office, 1973.

U.S. Commission on Civil Rights, *The unfinished education: Outcomes for minorities in the five southwestern states* (Mexican American Education Study, Report II). Washington, D.C.: U.S. Government Printing Office, 1971.

U.S. Commission on Civil Rights. *Social indicators of equity for minorities and women.* Washington, D.C.: U.S. Government Printing Office, 1978.

Vasquez, M. J. *Chicana and Anglo university women: Factors related to their performance, persistence and attrition.* Unpublished dissertation, University of Texas, Austin, 1978.

Zimbardo, P. G. *Psychology and life* (10th ed.). Glenview, Ill.: Scott, Foresman & Co., 1979.

25

Research on Latino
College Students:
A Theoretical Framework
and Inquiry

Michael A. Olivas

THE CONDITION OF HISPANIC EDUCATION

In 1982 Hispanic children attended schools that were more segregated than in 1970. Data[1] showing dramatic national and regional trends reveal that a high percentage of Hispanic students now attend schools in which minority children are the majority of the student body. More than two-thirds of all Hispanic students are enrolled in public schools in which 50 percent of the enrollment is minority. Understandably, many Hispanic families feel that desegregative racial assignments without regard to a child's linguistic competence will dilute bilingual programs and render both desegregation and bilingual education ineffective (Arias, 1980).

Hispanic students are far less likely than majority students to complete high school or graduate with their age group. Attention rates, which tend to understate the extent of dropout, show that 1978 high school completion rates for Mexican Americans who were twenty-five years or older were 34.3 percent compared to 67.1 percent for non-Hispanics over twenty-five. Hispanic students who did remain in school fell behind until 24 percent of the fourteen-to twenty-year-olds were enrolled two grades behind their classmates. Only 9 percent of the Anglo students were two years behind their same-age peers.

Moreover, bilingual education programs remain inadequate in most states, both in the diagnosis of linguistic competence and in the provision of bilingual curricula and personnel. Tests and other instruments have not been widely used to measure the cognitive abilities and English-speaking abilities of linguistic-minority children. However, even when Hispanic children are diagnosed as "limited-English" or "non-English proficient," fewer than half are enrolled in bilingual programs. Further, few classrooms have Hispanic teachers: In 1976, less than 3 percent of all public school employees were Hispanic, with nearly as many Hispanic service workers (custodians) as Hispanic teachers. Until the number of Hispanic educators is increased, bilingual programs and school systems will continue to be unresponsive to bilingual children's needs.

The failures of school systems to meet the needs of Hispanic communities are mirrored in postsecondary institutions. Here, issues of limited access, discriminatory employment practices, and high attrition disproportionately affect Hispanic students. Although there is a public perception that Hispanic enrollments have increased greatly in recent years, the reality is very different. Hispanic students have neither entered a broad range of institutions nor dramatically increased their numbers throughout the system. For example, from 1970 to 1984, full-time Hispanic undergraduate students increased only from 2.1 percent of the total to 3.5 percent. Even more dramatic is the decline of the percentage of Hispanic high school graduates attending college, from 35.4 percent in 1975 to 29.9 percent in 1980. It thus becomes clear that Hispanic matriculation has not shown the growth one would have expected from affirmative action, governmental, or institutional programs and efforts to increase minority-student enrollments.

While these figures reveal that Hispanic entry into postsecondary institutions has not been deep, distribution data show that access also has not been widespread. Hispanics are concentrated in the less prestigious and less well funded institutions, and, indeed, in very few four-year institutions. In 1984, only 23 percent of white full-time students attended two-year colleges, while fully 46 percent of Hispanic students attended such institutions. This uneven distribution of Hispanics within the system indicates that a large cadre of Hispanic students seeking a full-time, traditional learning experience is doing so in institutions established for part-time commuter students. While two-year institutions have increased Hispanic access, they suffer from the inherent problems of student transfers, part-time faculty, commuter programs, and funding patterns. Moreover, Hispanic students do not even enjoy full access into open-door institutions: A mere twenty-one colleges in the mainland United States enroll 24 percent of all mainland Hispanic students; when the thirty-four Puerto Rican institutions are included, these fifty-five colleges collectively enroll 43 percent of all U.S. Hispanic students. Additionally, unlike other minority students who benefit from historically black or tribal colleges, Hispanic students do not have access to a network of traditionally Hispanic colleges. Therefore, Hispanic students are disproportionately concentrated in fewer than 2 percent of the more than 3,100 colleges and universities in the country and in institutions that lack historical missions to serve Hispanic students.

To note that the leadership of these schools is non-Hispanic is an understatement. In the summer of 1985, there were six Hispanic four-year-college presidents and twenty Hispanic two-year-college presidents. A survey of two-year-college trustees revealed that only .6 percent were Hispanic, while a study of postsecondary coordinating boards found 1.1 percent of the commissioners to be Hispanic. At another level of leadership, there is little evidence to suggest that significant leadership will be drawn from faculty ranks, because only 1.4 percent of all faculty (and 1.1 percent of all tenured professors) are Hispanics, including faculty members in Spanish and bilingual education departments. With many Hispanics employed in special assistant or affirmative action and equal-employment-opportunity staff capacities, even fewer will hold important policymaking positions. Confronted with these data,

/

one is forced to concede that Hispanics have not entered American institutions of higher education in any significant fashion.

RESEARCH ON HISPANIC STUDENTS

Any comprehensive review of research findings can only conclude that little is known about Hispanic students. As a result, program-evaluation researchers measure Hispanic children with instruments and methodologies evolved from studies of majority students. More often than not, such studies predictably find evidence that educational programs are not accomplishing the goal of improving Hispanic student performance. In questioning the value of research on Mexican American children, Carter and Segura (1979) have noted:

> Little had been written about the interaction of cause and effect among the three important variables—the school, the social system, and the Mexican American subcultural group. The available literature, however, clearly demonstrated that Mexican Americans often do poorly in school, drop out early, speak Spanish, and are poor. These four factors are usually seen as causal and circular: Chicanos do poorly in school because they are poor, speak Spanish, and are culturally Mexican; or Mexican Americans are poor, speak Spanish, and carry a traditional folk culture because they do poorly in school. Most research slighted the socioeconomic influence; the nature and outcomes of school programs, policies, and practices; and the more recent considerations of school social climate. There was little analysis of school intervention in the apparently self-perpetuating cycle of poverty-school-failure-poverty. (p. 7)

Although their criticisms addressed research on Chicanos in the southwestern United States, the authors might well have noted that, by the same token, research on Puerto Ricans and other Latinos has ignored them or blamed them for the condition of their education.

The research findings on elementary and secondary Hispanic students have been summarized by several commentators and do not merit detailed repetition here. However, the bulk of this literature falls into two conceptual categories: studies that blame Hispanics for their own school failures and studies that articulate a deficiency model of minority education, a model of remediation, or one of compensation. In the first view, minority communities are themselves to blame for not encouraging their children to do better in school and for not providing a more learner-centered home environment. In the second, a corollary view is offered to explain why these children do not act like children from the middle class and therefore require remedial efforts to overcome their cultural deprivation.

This record of poor evidence on Hispanic elementary and secondary student characteristics has severely limited research on Hispanic college populations. In particular, the K–12 attrition rates and disproportionate Hispanic attendance at two-year institutions create major problems for population validity and college entrance measures, which most frequently have been normed on Anglo or black cohorts. Breland (1981), for instance, has noted: "Although a few studies have been made of Hispanic groups, these are not sufficient to allow for any sound generalizations. Hispanics are often grouped with blacks to construct a minority population. Given the possibility of important linguistic influences, it seems essential that more studies be made—both in prediction and in internal analysis—for groups having had substantially different linguistic and cultural experiences" (p. 49).

Our understanding of Hispanic college students is not significantly increased by the available student literature. A major summary of research on college students published in 1973 reported no studies on Hispanic students (Feldman & Newman, 1973). This book is the first on Hispanic college students. However, one unpublished study of Chicano students in the University of California and California State University systems does suggest a methodologically and conceptually appropriate approach to understanding Hispanic undergraduates—that of analyzing the stress encountered. The research, updated in this book and originally reported in *A Study of the Chicano Experience in Higher Education* (Muñoz & García-Bahne, 1977), employed three instruments, two of which were designed specifically to test the minority experience in majority institutions. The first was a structured interview format, adapted from a study of black students in white colleges. The second was a general demographic questionnaire designed to test language and family characteristics. Finally, a standardized test to measure stress, the College Environmental Stress Index (CESI), was administered. The results revealed that:

1. Chicanos and Chicanas reported greater stress levels than did their Anglo counterparts;
2. Anglo men and women were very similar regarding the intensity of stress they perceived;
3. Chicanos and Chicanas reported vast differences regarding the intensity of stress experienced, with Chicanas scoring higher at every level;
4. There were significant differences between Anglo women and Chicanas, which suggest that socioeconomic and cultural differences were more influential than their gender identity; and
5. Chicanas reported greater stress scores than did Chicano men, Anglo men, and Anglo women. In spite of their higher stress scores, however, Chicanas did not appear to have a higher attrition rate than Chicanos. Furthermore, Chicanas performed academically at a higher level than did Chicanos. Primary support systems for Chicanas seemed to be Chicano campus organizations and Chicana discussion groups. Chicanas and Chicanos were significantly more similar than any other groups in ranking events from most to least stressful, although they differed considerably with respect to the intensity of stress perceived (Muñoz & García-Bahne, 1977, pp. 9–18, 131–132).

While these findings do not surprise Hispanic educators, they reveal a marginalization of the students within a system that accommodates them only reluctantly, and they suggest the extent to which K–12 systems alienate Hispanic students—even the elite who graduate from high school and attend college. It seems clear that much work is needed on Hispanic student characteristics and achievement. The disappointing quality of Hispanic data in longitudinal and large-scale sample projects is indicative of the nescience of scholars and the consequent lack of research paradigms in this important area.

RESEARCH ON FINANCE

One area of Hispanic education on which significant attention has been focused, indirectly if not directly, is school finance research. As evidenced by the school finance litigation brought by Chicano litigants in *Serrano* and *Rodríguez* (*Serrano v. Priest*, 1971; *San Antonio Independent School District v. Rodríguez*, 1973), school finance equity considerations remain important to Hispanic educators and communities. The passage of Proposition 13 in California, however, has called into question the appropriateness of Senate Bill 90, the post-*Serrano* school finance mechanism, as have the more recent developments in the Los Angeles desegregation case.

In 1970, Coons, Clune, and Sugarman (1970, pp. 356–357) concluded that most minority children live in the wealthiest school districts, as measured by rankings of total assessed property value. However, a reanalysis of total-assessed-value data with assessed-value-per-pupil measures shows opposite results (Domínguez, 1977). In such a situation, it is necessary to establish ground rules in equity issues. The phrasing of fiscal inequities is extremely important; major efforts are required to review school finance decisions, summarize the equity implications, survey the technical considerations, and propose models of equitable school finance.

Another necessary K–12 finance initiative is bilingual education cost-index construction: Major data required include analyses of categorical programs, such as bilingual education, as well as more careful analyses of implementation of legal mandates. In California, for instance, bilingual programs include formula-based expenditures from the Educationally Disadvantaged Youth Program, Bilingual-Bicultural Programs (under A.B. 1329), Economic Impact Aid Program, and six additional state and federal programs. With proposed federal regulations for bilingual education meeting enormous resistance, it is urgent that realistic cost projections, personnel requirements, and assessment tools be developed. Additional federal initiatives to merge categorical programs into block grants will require better data on alleged cost savings and reduced overhead than those that exist at present.

There are four debates in higher-education finance that have major equity implications for Hispanics in higher education: two-year colleges, financial-aid packaging, financing graduate studies, and returns on schooling. While each of these is of obvious concern to majority students as well, the demographic condition and underrepresentation of Hispanics in higher education make these issues crucial for Hispanics. Although major technical and conceptual problems remain in analyzing these areas, more researchers have been investigating the problems, leading to greater clarity in these equity issues.

The resolution of the question "Do community colleges get their fair share of the funds?" is critical to Hispanic students because they are disproportionately enrolled in the two-year sector; in addition, there was a significant decline in Hispanic enrollment in the California community college system, due to the state's fiscal condition. Once again, the demographics of Hispanic enrollments make the study vital to an understanding of the underlying equity issues: If the distribution of Hispanic students throughout the postsecondary system is skewed into one sector, and that sector receives less than its "fair share" compared to the four-year sector, then there are serious questions of access and equity (Nelson, 1978, 1980). Two-year-college financing issues have two major dimensions: whether two-year institutions receive less money per student (or per student measure, as a full-time equivalent [FTE] formula), and whether students in two-year colleges receive less financial assistance than do their four-year counterparts. There are serious data deficiencies and major conceptual disagreements on both dimensions, and much work needs to be done in these areas.

Researchers employing different data sets or methodologies reach different conclusions in redistribution debates. The same is true in subsidy debates. Nelson and Breneman (1979) summarized the results of these arguments and categorized three intersectoral models: institutional spending per student, rates of state subsidies per sector, and comparisons of resources actually spent on a two-year student's education relative to those spent on a four-year-college student. In reviewing the conflicting results, the authors are persuaded that "community college students have approximately the same volume of resources spent on them and receive about as much subsidy as their counterparts at senior public institutions" (p. 33). They were particularly impressed by the arguments advanced by James, who reanalyzed 1966–67 data from a 1971 Carnegie Commission study—data that had shown only slight intersectoral disparities in favor of senior colleges. James measured subsidies (instructional costs minus tuition) and found evidence that two-year-college students "cost more and pay less" than do senior-college students (cited in Nelson, 1979). Hyde (1979) and Augenblick (1978) have concluded the opposite.

The short summary here of this complex debate obviously does not do justice to the topic. However, despite Nelson and Breneman's assertions that "the absence of serious expenditure differentials at least moves the burden of proof onto critics of the current funding patterns" (1979, p. 22), it is unclear whether the studies or the reanalyses of data warrant such an assertion. Several major issues have yet to be resolved; most importantly, the major studies have employed data that are not current. Indeed, the major data sets analyzed by Nelson and Breneman in 1979 dated back to 1964 and 1966–67. Since that time, the number of community colleges has increased considerably: The period between 1966 and 1974 saw more than one new public two-year college open each week, more than doubling the existing number of institutions—from 408 to 901. Even though the number of private two-year colleges declined, the total number of community colleges grew from 685 in 1966 to 1,151 in 1975. Further agreement needs to be reached on how to account for capital expenditures. Two concerns should be paramount. First, capital expenditures are frequently administered by separate state agencies and bond authorities, so the construction costs and bond-repayment expenses vary even within state systems. Second, public two-year colleges rarely have dormitory facilities, in itself a measure of "opportunity" and a major consideration in any discussion of intersectoral equity.

FTE data are not an accurate measure for intersectoral comparisons because the two-year-college sector enrolls proportionately more part-time students than do senior colleges. For example, of the sixty largest colleges in the country, only one two-year college (Miami-Dade) enrolls more full-time than part-time students. Conversely, of the sixty, only six senior colleges enroll more part-time than full-time students. This difference, reflecting both comprehensive institutional missions and lack of residential facilities, means that an FTE measure in a two-year college is likely to be three or four students taking one course each (to equal twelve); the FTE measure in a senior college is likely to be one student taking twelve hours. The economies of scale become clear when the administrative costs (bursar, admission, financial aid, registrar, and so forth) are calculated to account for the increased number of registrants. Institutions are extraordinarily complex, with certain programs supporting other less popular or more expensive courses. This cross-subsidizing makes intersectoral comparisons difficult, particularly if technical or professional curricula are measured.

The debate on intersectoral subsidies has a counterpart in financial-aid awards: Do two-year colleges receive their "fair share" of student financial assistance? A study by Lawrence Gladieux (1975) answered "no" concerning campus-based programs—Supplemental Educational Opportunity Grants (SEOGs), National Direct Student Loans (NDSLs), and, to a lesser extent, the College Work Study Program (CWSP). He attributed this "underutilization" to a number of causes but found few systemic reasons for the pattern. He labeled the phenomenon an "enigma" and suggested that the community colleges themselves were not as entrepreneurial as senior colleges and that they were penalizing themselves by not placing more attention on the financial-aid function. Nelson, however, with more recent data, found less underutilization in the campus-based programs and found a "fair share" in Basic Educational Opportunity Grants (BEOGs). Further, she was critical of the "half-cost limitation," the differential treatment of veterans' benefits, and the data from which she drew her conclusions (Nelson, 1978). More attention by researchers to these intersectoral financial-aid patterns would enlighten the larger debates of distribution in the system and clarify our understanding of the effects of disproportionate Hispanic enrollments in the two-year sector.

Although both Gladieux and Nelson found a measure of underutilization in campus-based loan programs for two-year colleges, disaggregated packaging data for Hispanic freshmen tell a different story. In an analysis of 1972–73 financial-aid awards, Wagner and Rice (1977) found Hispanic students' packages to have a 10 percent higher proportion of loans—the only portion of packages that has to be repaid. In the first recent packaging study of Hispanic students, I found near-exclusive reliance upon grants by freshmen and concluded that need-based programs worked well but that the reliance upon grants portended problems. The data problems are particularly severe in this type of study, as are conceptual issues of "need" and appropriateness of packaging configurations. While there is no generally accepted "norm" for packaging financial assistance, Hispanics should have no more reimbursable aid in their packages than do majority students.

One possible reason for this finding may be the difficulty Hispanic families (and most low-income families) encounter in applying for assistance and in negotiating complex financial-aid applications. The financial-aid deadlines, for example, fall well before income tax returns are due, and poor families—who may or may not be required to file federal income tax forms—frequently miss deadlines for all nonreimbursable programs. Loans, however, can often be secured late in the admissions process, if students can negotiate the complex lending procedures. In this scenario, any first-come-first-served procedure would limit even the loan access for late filers.

Moreover, poor families have to negotiate even more basic problems, such as whether financial aid will negatively affect public-assistance eligibility (it does, particularly for commuter students) or whether they can document their income, which frequently is paid in cash, with poor records (Mudrick, 1980).

These considerations, as well as the greater price elasticities of disadvantaged populations, should pose substantial questions for proponents of higher tuition/increased aid strategies. Even acknowledging the information barriers that all applicants (but particularly disadvantaged applicants) encounter, Nelson and Breneman (1979) conclude: "Our analysis suggest that a higher tuition/higher aid strategy, the pricing policy traditionally supported by economists on efficiency grounds, is also the more equitable" (p. 33). Information theorists dispute this claim, as would those persons who saw rescissions across the board in BEOG payments for 1979–80. Congress disregarded the legislative reduction formula required by Title IV, initiating what became a series of trade-offs that disproportionately affected low-income students. The same is likely to happen again in Gramm–Rudman cutbacks.

A third consideration in Hispanic finance would be the manner in which Hispanic graduate students finance their studies. Data from the National Research Council (NRC) show that white and Hispanic students employ considerably different methods of financing this burden (NRC, 1980). The most evident disparity is the more obvious availability of teaching and research assistantships to white doctoral students. These patterns hold importance not only because of the basic issues of sustenance and living expenses but for informal and formal professional reasons. Assistantships are mainstream apprenticeship activities, involving graduate students in major teaching or research responsibilities with faculty mentors and departments.

Other data corroborate the need for further research on Hispanic graduate-education financing. NRC data for 1978 show that Hispanic doctoral students took an average of 10.2 years after the B.A. to complete the doctorate, with a total registered time of 6.3 years; for whites, it was 8.9 and 6.2 years, respectively (NRC, 1979). For Hispanics in 1979, the total time to the doctorate was 10 years, with a total registered time of 6.5 years; for whites it was 9.1 and 6.2 years, respectively (NRC, 1980). Thus, while the time in graduate school was similar, Hispanics took approximately one year longer, suggesting a longer time in the work force or a leave pattern different from that of whites.

Fellowship provisions are significant but largely unexplored. There is anecdotal evidence, for instance, that Title VII fellows become marginalized in elite universities and have difficulty securing intramural funding when the fellowships expire—usually during the dissertation-writing stage. The Ford Foundation doctoral fellowships were consolidated into a postdoctoral program, while the Graduate and Professional Opportunities Program (Title IX) fellowships to Hispanics have declined appreciably from 1978. There has not been any major change in Hispanic graduate enrollments or degrees since 1976, when the National Board on Graduate Education (1976) noted, "Mexican and Puerto Rican Americans appear to have the lowest [graduate] participation rates relative to other ethnic and minority groups" (p. 45).

A fourth area, returns on education to Hispanics, suggests itself in response to economists who argue that tangible benefits are more important than the less empirical "assumed-social-good" rationale advanced by many. Data in this area are particularly problematic. Refugee and immigration patterns, heterogeneity of the

Hispanic work force, and historical exclusion from postsecondary education make research into educational returns difficult and cloud the equity issues. Therefore, studies have found unaccounted-for discrimination in pay differentials for Chicano workers, as well as higher returns on college investment to Chicano males than to Anglo males, even with lower absolute income for Chicanos. Although it is important for economists to sharpen these arguments, it is not clear whether Hispanics attempt to maximize their earning potential by attending college. Educational aspirations are a tangle of motivations, not all of them economic. Nonetheless, many Hispanic educators will need to address "returns on education" as a concern in increasing Hispanic participation in higher education.

GOVERNANCE RESEARCH

It is governance, particularly in the form of school boards or boards of trustees, that constitutes "the system" of education in the United States. State and local boards determine educational policy for school systems, while state coordinating or governing bodies and trustee boards determine higher education policy. Neither sector has been particularly responsive to the concerns of Hispanic parents or students, and the theoretical model of internal colonialism is premised largely upon such a system of unresponsiveness. While it is difficult to disentangle the electoral and political components of such a situation from the precise research questions posed by the condition, it is important to note that the history of Hispanic education has been one of struggle against insensitive government agencies and school boards, those organizations responsible for governing education systems. Whether this struggle has manifested itself in the form of litigation, political action, or legislation, the focus has continued to be upon sensitizing larger governance structures.

As on the institutional level, Hispanics have not historically had access to these structures: Few minorities are appointed or elected to school boards or to trustee boards. These boards and commissions are not "representative," however the norm may be defined. A 1978 study, for example, found only 1.1 percent (5 of 463) of state postsecondary commission members to be Hispanic, although the legislation requires the commissions to be "broadly and equitably representative of the general public" (Salazar & Martorana, 1978, table 2). Commission and board appointments constitute a major representative device in a democracy and are a significant policy arena, particularly as federal education policy shifts to a decentralized block-grant approach and as large amounts of federal financial aid are coordinated through states.

While a sense of history should inform all educational-governance research, in minority education most of the historical context has been a belated acknowledgment of racism and of slavery's effect upon the schooling of black children. Following the *Adams v. Califano* (1977) litigation, statewide boards have been involved in "desegregation" of public higher education. Because society tends to perceive desegregation solely in terms of black access into white institutions, the fate of historically black public colleges is uncertain. White and black colleges have been merged in order that the hybrid have no racial identity. While the lack of historically Hispanic colleges means that Hispanic students have little to fear from the *Adams* litigation, there is the danger of Hispanic student equity issues being ignored in *Adams* states with large black and Hispanic populations. This occurred in Texas, for instance, where the first Office for Civil Rights (OCR) study mandated by *Adams* did not examine Chicano access but instead concentrated upon the state's two public black colleges. No analysis of Chicano enrollment patterns, disproportionate community college attendance, or lack of Chicano faculty and staff was performed—although at the time, no Texas senior college had ever had a Chicano president. OCR has not exacted much from Texas institutions, and it is clear that little progress will result from the tepid plan (Martínez, 1983).

There has been little scholarly inquiry into the effects of racist immigration statutes on Asians, the systematic discrimination that continues against Native Americans, or exclusionary schooling policies affecting Hispanic children. The indicia of these practices are evident in minority educational achievement today, yet major historical analyses of minority schooling are rare. Nonetheless, legal decisions and administrative actions frequently turn upon the litigants' analyses of history, whether in quantifying school attendance zones, in measuring Hispanic children's historical access into bilingual educational programs, or even in arguing that Mexican Americans are to be included in desegregation plans.

These examples present persuasive evidence that Hispanics have not controlled the political or organizational structures of education but have been held in subordinate positions by school systems and post-secondary secondary institutions. The victories of a few Hispanic parents or educators has not increased the quality of education for Hispanic students, and in several key indices, Hispanic educational conditions appear to have worsened. Moreover, the ascendancy of an Hispanic elite has been accomplished at great cost to these individuals, who frequently are ghettoized by majority policymakers and perceived pejoratively as compromisers by Hispanic communities. Although additional evidence of such structural discrimination is readily apparent, a theoretical explanation is essential for understanding how this condition could persist, even when major federal resources have been brought to bear upon school systems enrolling disadvantaged children. In fact, these resources have scarcely altered the patterns of governance, and a retreating federal commitment to education equity is evident.

HISPANIC EDUCATION AND INTERNAL COLONIALISM

In analyzing "academic colonialism," Arce (1978) noted that "the most prominent feature of the Chicano experience with higher education is its peripheralness relative to the overall academic enterprise." Arce developed a taxonomy of Chicano-Academe Contact Patterns within his framework of academic colonialism, modeled after Orlando Fals Borda's "colonialismo intelectual," a theory of marginalization in a South American context. In Arce's view, *academic colonialism* is

the selective imposition of intellectual premises, concepts, methods, institutions, and related organizations on a subordinate group and/or the unselective and uncritical adoption and imitation of the intellectual premises, concepts, methods, institutions, and organizations of other groups, with the

selection processes not being in the control of the subordinate group. Inherent in this definition is the monopolizing of the resources for academic
enterprise (colleges and universities, foundation and government funding
agency review boards, journals and other publishing outlets, etc.) by the
dominant group and the provision of only limited and controlled access to
these resources to the subordinate minority. (p. 77)

Within this scheme, there are six patterns that evolve from the subordinate Chicano role in higher education: structural accommodation and realignment, conscious
assimilation, nationalist exhortative, affirmative action, independent transformational, and interdependent analytical. These patterns fall along axes of ideology and
degree of infiltration within institutions, as shown in table 25.1.

   In the structural accommodation/realignment and conscious assimilation patterns, Hispanic students are docile and peripheral to the institution. In the first
typology, these students do not become involved in mainstream or ethnic activities on
campus. They become marginalized, are likely to have high attrition rates, and if they
do succeed in graduating, will in all likelihood have been average or below-average
students in less demanding major fields of study. In the conscious assimilation pattern,
Hispanic students are more likely to become involved in college activities but tend to
shun ethnic identification or involvement. This Anglicization is a strong influence em-
anating from the college setting, and students who feel no sense of Hispanic community or whose families were not politicized are likely to be found in this category.

   In the cooptive ideological categories, two major conservative practices prevail.
Within the nationalist exhortative pattern, the singling out of outstanding Hispanics
to serve as role models is combined with a tendency toward a romanticized reconstruction of history. The affirmative action pattern is more formal cooptation of Hispanic concerns manifested by specialized minority hiring to fill minority slots, which
relieves the institutions of the need to integrate throughout their ranks. These responses to internal colonization are understandable, for curricula and instruction are
sorely in need of Hispanic perspectives and revision, while existing job discrimination has excluded many Hispanics from any substantial employment in education.
The danger, though, is clear when *Cinco de Mayo* festivities substitute for more extensive curriculum revision and when hiring is limited to affirmative action, bilingual
education, or creating token positions.

   The final two patterns exist primarily in theory, for they require an extraordinary combination of people, resources, and timing to exist and mature. As this model
suggests, the system of structural discrimination present in American education
makes progressive educational movements for minorities almost impossible. The independent transformational pattern is feasible only in a historically Hispanic institution, only three of which exist in the mainland United States, or in community-based
organizations and alternative schools. Such alternatives to mainstream institutions
and school systems probably have their best analogues in tribally controlled community colleges (which receive government funds) or in quasi-academic units such as
research or training divisions in Hispanic community-based organizations. The second progressive approach, the interdependent analytical pattern, links Hispanic academics across institutional or disciplinary lines. Examples include the National
Chicano Council on Higher Education, the Special Interest Group on Hispanic Re-

Table 25.1:   Chicano-Academe Contact Patterns

	Institutional Relationship	
Ideology	Separated	Integrated
Marginal	Accommodation/realignment	Conscious assimilation
Cooptive	Nationalist exhortative	Affirmative action
Progressive	Independent transformational	Interdependent analytical

Source: Adapted from Arce, 1978, p. 101.

search of the American Educational Research Association, and similar collaborative intellectual exchange mechanisms. The focus is on intellectual self-development and solidarity with other Hispanic academics, which may be practiced through visiting appointments, professional meetings, caucuses, or other informal means.

As is evident in these patterns, marginalization is a major feature of Hispanic participation in higher education, confirmed most notably in attrition and underparticipation data. Those who do enter the system do so in a peripheral, nonthreatening manner; more radical participation is extremely rare and unlikely to generate its own resources or continuation. Observers on the scene of Hispanic education will recognize these patterns not as rough approximations but as strikingly accurate portrayals of the condition. While they are essentially pessimistic compare to the Brazilian and Chilean experiences detailed in Paulo Freire's (1973) notion of *conscientizacao*, these categories reflect an accurate ideological and operational reality.

Arce's work complements the larger labor-market-segmentation theory developed by Chicano scholar Mario Barrera. In particular, Barrera's (1979) explication of an internal colonial model extends the Arce thesis. Because the model has been most frequently employed to explain labor discrimination, academic job discrimination against Hispanic educators is powerfully illuminated. Barrera uses University of California hiring practices as evidence of structural discrimination, concluding that in most organizations, structural discrimination against Chicanos consists of labor repression, wage differentials, occupational stratification, reserve labor pools, and peripheral buffer-role policies. Bonilla and Campos (1981) have analyzed a similar colonial exploitation of Puerto Ricans, noting that "the root problems of educational inequity for Puerto Ricans remain unresolved and largely unaddressed" (p. 164). These economic analyses suggest a circularity in defining Hispanic educational inequality: Hispanics are undereducated because they have been historically exploited, and their poverty precludes them from further education. While this circle could conceivably surround many discrete American groups, none except Native Americans can claim such a long and misunderstood history of exclusion and underparticipation. However defined or measured, Hispanics' participation in education is proportionate neither to their percentage of the U.S. population nor to their percentage of the school-age population. Although several scholars have questioned the validity of work within the internal colonialism framework (Muñoz, 1983), it has not been critically employed in the study of education, where it holds much promise.

While the foregoing discussion established the condition and described theories of Hispanic underparticipation, the measurement and understanding of root causes are crude and preliminary. The final section suggests a possible agenda for research on the condition of Hispanic education, focusing on structural, demographic, and historical means of inquiry, and introduces the articles that follow.

SUMMARY AND RESEARCH RECOMMENDATIONS: LATINOS IN HIGHER EDUCATION

At present, we can lay claim to only rudimentary knowledge about Hispanics in education and the socioeconomic and political forces that characterize the internal colonial status of Hispanics in American society. As Barrera (1979) has conceded, "for the foreseeable future, the politics of the Chicano community can be expected to revolve around both class and colonial divisions in a complex manner whose outlines we can only dimly perceive in the current period of confusion and redefinition" (p. 219). He might also have included Puerto Ricans and other Latinos, because population statistics aggregate Spanish-origin data; and even Cubans, perceived to be the least disadvantaged Hispanic group, find themselves victims of anti-Spanish-language and antirefugee hysteria. While popular hysteria and anti-immigration attitudes are the most extreme forms of negative behavior toward Hispanics, institutional practices that methodically exclude Hispanic participation present a far more serious and systemic barrier.

A research agenda for examining institutional attitudes requires two major foci: examination of *structural* phenomena and analysis of *individuals* within institutions. As detailed earlier, even when the data are inadequate and the methodologies frequently inappropriate, the condition of education for Hispanics remains poor relative to Anglo or other minority populations. This condition, manifested in several important, though indirect, indices, suggests an inquiry into organizational features. For instance, measuring Hispanic participation in school, despite its seeming simplicity, has not been done well: Schools are understandably reluctant to report their attrition rates accurately, particularly when funding formulas are based on attendance figures. Despite school finance litigation, complex appropriations and fiscal procedures often render school expenditure data incomparable. Sheer measurement difficulties, therefore, have presented researchers and policymakers with an incomplete picture of important school features. The debate concerning community college financing is a postsecondary example of the structural debate: How can intersectoral-equity arguments be mounted when there is no agreement on what an FTE expenditure represents in a two-year or senior college?

At the individual level, we know precious little about Hispanic students, in large part because survey methodologies have been inadequate in measuring Hispanic community characteristics. For instance, the National Assessment of Educational Progress (1977) has severe regional restrictions and poorly designed questions on language usage, while the Survey of Income and Education (1980) has the flaws of minority census data. Even the greatly improved minority information from the High School and Beyond data have been badly analyzed: A recent HSB study on minority students in private and Catholic secondary schools noted that "no distinction is possible in the present research between Cuban, Puerto Rican, and Mexican Hispanics" (Greeley,

1981, p. 8) when the data were able to be disaggregated. Indeed, the study indicated that 30 percent of Hispanic private school students were Cuban, a fact that would severely limit public policy implications for Mexican and Puerto Rican children.

NOTE

1. Data cited in this chapter, where not otherwise indicated are from the National Center for Education Statistics special tabulations. I thank Samuel Peng and Jeffrey Owings from NCES for their assistance and support.

REFERENCES

Adams v. Califano, 430 F. Supp. 118 (D.D.C. 1977).

Aday, L. (1980). Methodological issues in health care surveys of the Spanish heritage population. *American Journal of Public Health*, 70, 367–374.

Admissions Testing Program. Unpublished 1979–80 SAT data.

Aguirre, A. (1979). The sociolinguistic situation of bilingual Chicano adolescents in a California border town. *Aztlán: International Journal of Chicano Studies Research*, 10, 55–67.

Allsup, C. (1977). Education is our freedom: The American GI forum and the Mexican American school segregation in Texas, 1948–1957. *Aztlán: International Journal of Chicano Studies Research*, 8, 27–50.

American Institutes for Research in the Behavioral Sciences. (1979). *Evaluation of the impact of ESEA Title VII Spanish/English bilingual education programs*. Palo Alto, CA: AIR.

Andes, J. (1974). *Developing trends in content of collective bargaining contracts in higher education*. Washington, DC: Academic Collective Bargaining Information Service.

Applied Management Sciences. (1980). *Study of the impact of the Middle Income Student Assistance Act (MISAA)*. Silver Spring, MD: AMS.

Arce, C. (1978). Chicano participation in academe: A case of academic colonialism. *Grito del Sol: A Chicano Quarterly 3*, 75–104.

Arias, B. (1980). Issues in tri-ethnic desegregation. Paper presented at the meeting of the American Educational Research Association, Boston.

Aspira. (1976). *Social factors in educational attainment among Puerto Ricans in U.S. metropolitan area*, 1970. New York: Aspira.

Astin, A. (1975). *The myth of equal access in public higher education*. Paper presented at the meeting of the Southern Education Foundation.

Augenblick, J. (1978). *Issues in financing community colleges*. Denver, CO: Educational Commission of the States.

Augenblick, J., & Hyde, W. (1979). *Patterns of funding, net price and financial need for postsecondary education students*. Denver: ECS.

Barrera, M. (1979). *Race and class in the Southwest*. Notre Dame, IN: University of Notre Dame Press.

Beck, M. (1976). *The analysis of Hispanic texts*. New York: Bilingual Press.

Berdahl, R. (1971). *Statewide coordination of higher education*. Washington, DC: American Council on Education.

Bonilla, F., & Campos, R. (1981, Spring). A wealth of poor: Puerto Ricans in the new economic order. *Daedalus*, 133–176.

Boshier, R. (1972). The effect of academic failure on self-concept and maladjustment indices. *Journal of Educational Research*, 65, 347–351.

Breland, H. (1981). *Assessing student characteristics in admissions to higher education.* New York: College Entrance Examination Board.

Bridge, G. (1978). Information imperfections: The Achilles' heel of entitlement plans. *School Review,* 86, 504–529.

Brown, G., Rosen N., Hill, S., & Olivas, M. (1980). *The condition of education for Hispanic Americans.* Washington, DC: National Center for Education Statistics.

Brunner, S., & Gladieux, L. (1979). *Student aid and tuition in Washington State.* Washington, DC: College Entrance Examination Board.

Burbules, N. (1979) *Equity, equal opportunity, and education.* Stanford, CA: Institute for Finance and Governance.

———, & Sherman, A. (1979) *Equal educational opportunity: Ideal or Ideology?* Stanford, CA: Institute for Finance and Governance.

Cárdenas, J. (1976). *Bilingual education cost analysis.* San Antonio, TX: Intercultural Development Research Associates

Carter, T. (1970). *Mexican Americans in school.* New York: College Entrance Examination Board.

———, & Sergura, R. (1979) *Mexican Americans in school: A decade of change.* New York: College Entrance Examination Board.

Catteral., J., & Thresher. T. (1979). *Proposition 13: The campaign, the vote, and the immediate aftereffects for California schools* Stanford, CA: Institute for Finance and Governance.

Condition of Education, 1977, 1984. (1979, 1985). Washington, DC: National Center for Education Statistics.

Conlisk, J. (1977). A further look at the Hansen-Weisbrod-Pechman debate. *Journal of Human Resources,* 10, 147–163.

Conrad, C., & Cosand, J. (1976). *The implications of federal higher education policy.* Washington, DC: American Association for Higher Education.

Coons, J., & Sugarman, S. (1978). *Education by choice.* Berkeley, CA: University of California Press.

———, Clune, W., & Sugarman, S. (1970). *Private wealth and public education.* Cambridge, MA: Harvard University Press.

Crain, R., & Mahard, R. (1978). *The influence of high racial composition in Black College attendance and achievement test performance.* Santa Monica, CA: RAND

Cronbach, L., Yalow, E., & Schaefer, G. (1979). *Setting cut scores in selection: A mathematical structure for examining policies.* Stanford, CA: Institute for Finance and Governance.

Dill, D. (1979). Teaching in the field of higher education: Politics of higher education courses. *Review of Higher Education,* 2, 30–33.

Domínguez, J. (1977). School finance: The issues of equity and efficiency. *Aztlán: International Journal of Chicano Studies Research,* 8, 175–199.

Drake, S. (1977). *A study of community and junior college boards of trustees.* Washington, DC: American Association of Community and Junior Colleges.

Durán, R. (1983). *Hispanics' education and background.* New York: College Entrance Examination Board.

Education Commission of the States. (1978). Summary of State regulations. *Higher Education in the States,* 6, 125–148.

Educational Testing Service. (1979). *Principles, policies, and procedural guidelines regarding ETS products and service.* Princeton, NJ: ETS.

Epstein, N. (1977). *Language, ethnicity, and the schools.* Washington, DC: Institute for Educational Leadership.

Estrada, L. (1979). A chronicle of the political, legislative and judicial advances in bilingual education in California. In R. Padilla (Ed.), *Bilingual education and public policy in the United States* (pp. 77–108). Ypsilanti, MI: Eastern Michigan University.

Fals Borda, O. (1970). *Ciencia propia colonialismo intelectual.* Mexico City: Editorial Nuestro Tiempo.

Feldman, K., & Newman, T. (1973). *The impact of college on students.* San Francisco: Jossey-Bass.

Fernández, E. (1975). *Comparison of persons of Spanish surname and persons of Spanish origin in the United States.* Washington, DC: U.S. Bureau of the Census.

Finn, C. (1978). *Scholars, dollars and bureaucrats.* Washington, DC: Brookings Institution.

Fishman, J. (1966). *Language loyalty in the United States.* The Hague: Mouton.

Flores, F., et al. (1977). Right to undocumented children to attend public schools in Texas. *Chicano Law Review,* 4, 61–93.

Flores, R. (1978). *The economic of a college education to Mexican American.* Papers presented at the meeting of the Southwestern Social Science Association, San Diego, CA.

Franssinetti, A. (1978). La mariginalidad en América Latina: Una bibliografía comentada. *Revista Mexicana de Sociología,* 15, 221–331.

Freire, P. (1973). *Education for critical consciousness.* New York: Seabury Press.

García, J. (1979). Bilingual education program fiscal accountability. In R. Padilla (Ed.), *Bilingual education and public policy in the United States* (pp. 229–224) Ypsilanti. MI: Eastern Michigan University.

García, J. (1976). *Cost analysis of bilingual, special, and vocational public school programs in New Mexico.* Unpublished doctoral dissertation, University of New Mexico.

García, J. (1980). *Ethnic identity and background traits: Explorations of Mexican-origin populations.* La Red/The Net, 29, 2.

General Accounting Office. (1980). *The National Institute of Education should further increase minority and female participation in its activities.* Washington, DC: GAO.

Gladieux, L. (1975). *Distribution of federal student assistance: The enigma of two-year colleges.* Washington, DC: College Entrance Examination Board.

Gladieux, L., & Byce, C. (1980). *As middle-income student aid expands, are low-income students losing out?* Unpublished manuscript, College Entrance Examination Board.

Gladieux, L., & Wolanin, T. (1976). *Congress and the colleges..* Lexington, MA: Health.

Golub, L. (1976). Evaluation design and implementation of a bilingual education program. *Education and Urban Society,* 10, 363–384

Greeley, A. (1981). *Minority students in Catholic secondary schools.* Unpublished manuscript, National Opinion Research Center, Chicago.

Guerrero, M. (1979). Substantive due process for resident aliens. *Aztlán: International Journal of Chicano Studies Research,* 10, 31–54.

Gutierrez, F., et al. (1979). *Spanish-language radio in the southwestern United States.* Monograph Series. Austin, TX: University of Texas.

Halstead, D. K. (1974). *Statewide Planning in Higher Education.* Washington, DC: U.S. Government Printing Office.

Hansen, J., & Gladieux, L. (1978). *Middle-income students: A new target for financial aid.* Washington, DC: College Entrance Examination Board.

Hanson, W., & Weisbrod, B. (1969). *Benefits, costs and finance and finance of public higher education.* Chicago: Markham.

Haro, C. M. (1977). *Mexicano/Chicano concerns and school desegregation in Los Angeles.* Los Angeles: Chicano Studies Research Center Publications.

Hayes-Bautista, D. (1980). Identifying "Hispanic" populations: The influence of research methodology upon public policy. *American Journal of Public Health,* 70, 353–356.

Heffernan, J. (1973). The credibility of the credit hour. *Journal of Higher Education,* 44, 62–72.

Henderson, E., & Long, B. (1971). Personal-social correlates of academic success among disadvantaged school beginners. *Journal of School Psychology,* 9, 101–113.

Hernández, J. (1975). La migración Puertorriquena como factor demográfico: Solución y problema. *Revista Interamericana,* 4, 526–534.

———, Alvirez, D., & Estrada, L. (1973). Census data and the problem of conceptually defining the Mexican American population. *Social Science Quarterly,* 53, 671–687

Hernández, N. (1973). Variables affecting achievement of middle school Mexican-American students. *Review of Educational Research,* 43, 1–39.

Hyde, W. (1979). *Equity of the distribution of student financial aid.* Denver, CO: Education Commission of the States.

Jackson, G. (1979). *Community colleges and budget reduction.* Stanford, CA: Institute for Finance and Governance.

Johnson, J. (1979, April 12). Hispanic "label" protested. *Washington Post,* p. C4.

Katz, D., & Weiner. F. (1979). *Proposition 13 and the public schools: The first year.* Stanford, CA: Institute for Finance and Governance.

King, L. (1975). *The Washington lobbyist for higher education.* Lexington, MA: Health.

Klees, S. (1974). *The role of information in the market for education services.* Occasional paper in the Economic and Politics of Education. Stanford, CA: Stanford University press.

Korman, F., & Valenzuela, N. (1973). Patterns of mass media use and attitudes about mass media among selected Anglo and Chicano opinion leaders. *Aztlán: International Journal of Chicano Studies Research,* 4, 335–342.

Levin, B., et al. (1972). *Paying for Public schools: Issues of school finances in California.* Washington, DC: Urban Institute.

Levin, H. (1979). *Educational vouchers and social policy.* Stanford, CA: Institute for Finance and Governance.

———. (1977). Postsecondary entitlements: An exploration. In N. Kurland (Ed.), *Entitlement studies* (pp. 1–51). Washington , DC: National Institute of Education.

Locks , N., Pletcher, B., & Reynolds, D. (1978). *Language assessment instruments for limited-English-speaking students: A needs analysis.* Washington, DC: National Institute of Education

López, R. W., Madrid-Barela, A., & Macías, R. (1976). *Chicanos in higher education: status and issues.* Monograph No. 7. Los Angeles: Chicano Studies Center Publications, University of California, Los Angeles.

Lowry, I. (1980). *The Science and politics of ethnic enumeration.* Paper presented at the meeting of the American Association for the Advancement of Science.

McGuinness, A. (1975). *The changing map of postsecondary education.* Denver, CO: Education Commission of the States.

McGuire, J. (1976). The distribution of subsidy to students in California public higher education. *Journal of Human Resources,* I, 35–37.

Machlis, P. (1973). The distributional effects of public higher education in New York City. *Public Finance Quarterly,* 35–37.

Martínez, J. (1977). *Chicano psychology.* New York: Academic Press.

Martínez, O. (1978). Chicano oral history: Status and prospects. *Aztlán: International Journal of Chicano Studies Research,* 9, 119–131.

Martínez. R. (1983, December 2). Testimony before the U.S. House postsecondary subcommittee. Houston, Texas.

Martínez, V., & Lara, M. (1978). "Who gets in?" *Self-Determination Quarterly Journal,* 2, 17–25.

Martorana, S., & Nespoli, L. (1978). *Regionalism in American postsecondary education: Concepts and practice.* University Park, PA: Pennsylvania State University.

Mexican American Legal Defense and Educational Fund. (1980). *Law school admissions study.* San Francisco: MALDEF.

Millard, R. (1976). *State boards of higher education..* Washington, DC: Higher Education.

Morris, L. (1970). *Elusive equality.* Washington, DC: Howard University Press.

Mudrick, N. (1980). *The interaction of public assistance and student and student financial aid.* Washington, DC: College Entrance Examination Board.

Muñoz, C. (1983). The quest for paradigm: The development of Chicano studies and intellectuals. In *History, Culture, and Society: Chicano Studies in the 1980s* (pp. 19–36). Ypsilanti, MI: Bilingual Press.

———, & Rodríguez, P. (1977). Origen, distributión y eficiencia del gasto educativo en México. *Revista del Centro de Estudios Educativos, 7,* 1–54.

Muñoz, D., & Garcia-Bahne, B. (1977). *A study of the Chicano experience in higher education.* Washington, DC: National Institute of Mental Health.

National Assessment of Educational Progress. (1977). *Hispanic student achievement in five learning areas.* Denver: NAEP.

National Board of Graduate Education. (1976). *Minority participation in graduate education.* Washington, DC: NBGE

National Institute of Education. (1979). *Survey information systems.* NIE Project 400–79–9920.

National Institute of Education. (1977). *Women and minorities in education R&D.* Washington, DC: NIE.

National Research Council. (1980). *Summary report 1979, doctorate recipients from United States universities.* Washington, DC: NRC.

National Research Council. (1979). *Summary report 1978, doctorate recipients from United States universities.* Washington, CD: NRC.

Navy BOOST. (1980). Washington, DC: NRTC.

Navy ROTC Bulletin, 1981. (1980). Washington, DC: NROTC.

Nelson, S. (1980). *Community colleges and their share of student financial assistance.* Washington, DC: College Entrance Examination Board.

———. (1979). *Community college finance in California: Equity implications in the aftermath of Proposition 13.* Unpublished manuscript, Brookings Institution.

———. (1978). *The equity of public subsidies for higher education: Some thoughts on the literature.* Denver, CO: Education Commission of the States.

———, & Breneman, D. (1979, December). *An equity perspective on community college finance.* Paper presented at the meeting of the UK/US Conference on Collective Choice in Education.

Newman, M. (1978). A profile of Hispanics in the U.S. work force. *Monthly Labor Review, 101,* 3–14.

Nielsen, F., & Fernández, R. (1981). *Hispanics and the High School and Beyond data.* Unpublished manuscript, National Opinion Research Center, Chicago.

Ogbu, J. (1978). *Minority education and castle.* New York: Academic Press.

Olivas, M. (1979). *The dilemma of access.* Washington, DC: Howard University Press.

———. (1981). *Financial aid: Access and packaging policies.* Stanford, CA: IFG.

———. (1982). Hispanics in higher education: Status and issues. *Educational Evaluation and Policy Analysis, 4,* 301–310.

———. (1982). Information inequities: A fatal flaw in parochiaid plans. In E. Gaffney (Ed.), *Government's role in non-public education* (pp. 133–152). Notre Dame, IN: University of Notre Dame Press.

———. (1983). Research and theory on Hispanic education: Students, finance, and governance. *Aztlán: International Journal of Chicano Studies Research, 14,* 111–146.

———, & Hill, S. (1980). Hispanic participation in postsecondary education. In Brown et al., (pp. 117–216).

Olmedo, E. (1977). Psychological testing and the Chicano: A reassessment. In J. Martínez (Ed.), *Chicano psychology.* New York: Academic Press.

Olmedo, E., & Padilla, A. (1978). An empirical and construct validation of a scale of acculturation for Mexican Americans. *Journal of Social Psychology, 105,* 781–790.

Pacheco, A. (1980). *Educational vouchers and their implications for equity.* Stanford, CA: Institute for Finance and Governance.

Padilla, A. (1979). Critical factors in the testing of Hispanic Americans: A review and some suggestions for the future. In *Testing, Teaching, and Learning.* Washington, DC: National Institute of Education.

———. (1979). *Bilingual education and public policy in the United States.* Ypsilanti, MI: Eastern Michigan University.

Panel for the Review of Laboratory and Center Operations. (1978). *Report to NIE.* Washington, DC: National Institute of Education.

Pechman, J. (1970). The distributional effects of public higher education in California. *Journal of Human Resources,* 361–370.

Peñalosa, F. (1970). Toward an operational definition of the Mexican American. *Aztlán: International Journal of Chicano Studies Research,* 1, 1–12.

Peterson, G. (1972). *The regressivity of the residential property tax.* Washington, DC: Urban Institute.

Pfeffer, L. (1974). Aid to parochial schools: The verge and beyond. *Journal of Law and Education,* 3, 115–121.

Poston, D., & Alvírez, D. (1973). On the cost of being a Mexican American worker. *Social Science Quarterly,* 53, 697–709.

Roaden, A., & Worthen, B. (1976). Research assistantship experiences and subsequent research productivity. *Research in Higher Education,* 5, 141–158.

Salazar, J. L. (1977). *State 1202 commission member characteristics and positions on issues of importance to postsecondary education.* Unpublished doctoral dissertation, Pennsylvania State University.

Salazar, J. L., & Martorana, S. (1978). *State postsecondary education planning (1202) commissions: A first look.* University Park, PA: Pennsylvania State University.

San Antonio Independent School District v. Rodríguez, 411 U.S. 1 (1973).

Serrano v. Priest, 487 P.2d 1241 (1971).

Siegel, J., & Passell, J. (1979). *Coverage of the Hispanic population of the United States in the 1970 census.* Washington, DC: U.S. Bureau of the Census.

Southern Regional Education Board. (1980). *Black and Hispanic enrollment in higher education, 1978.* Atlanta, GA: SREB.

Survey of Income and Education. (1980). *Characteristics of Hispanic postsecondary students.* Washington, DC: NCES.

Troike, R. (1978). *Research evidence for the effectiveness of bilingual education.* Rosslyn, VA: National Clearinghouse for Bilingual Education.

U.S. Bureau of the Census. (1980). *Conference on census undercount.* Washington, DC: U.S. Bureau of the Census.

U.S. Commission on Civil Rights. (1974). *Counting the forgotten.* Washington, DC: USCCR.

———. (1978). *Improving Hispanic unemployment data.* Washington, DC: USCCR.

Valdez, A. (1979). The role of mass media in the public debate over bilingual education. In R. Padilla (Ed.), *Bilingual education and public policy in the United States* (pp. 175–188). Ypsilanti, MI: Eastern Michigan University.

Wagner, A., & Rice, L. (1977). *Student financial aid: Institutional packaging and family expenditure patterns.* Washington, DC: College Entrance Examination Board.

Windham, D. (1970). *Education, equality and income redistribution.* Lexington, MA: Heath.

———. (1980). *The benefits and financing of American higher education: Theory, research, and policy.* Stanford, CA: IFG.

Zimmerman, D. (1973). Expenditure-tax incidence studies, public higher education, and equity. *National Tax Journal,* 26, 65–70.

Notes on Contributors

Gloria Anzaldúa is a well known feminist cultural critic and author.

John J. Attinasi is Director of the Bilingual Education Program and professor of Education and Linguistics at California State University, Long Beach.

Mario Barrera is professor of Ethnic Studies at the University of California at Berkeley.

Antonio Darder is an associate professor of Education at The Claremont Graduate School, Center for Educational Studies.

María de la Luz Reyes is a professor of Education at California State University, Monterey Bay.

Denise de la Rosa Salazar is a policy analyst and organizational consultant.

Adela de la Torre is Director of the Mexican-American Studies and Research Center at the University of Arizona.

Ruben Donato is an associate professor at the College of Education, Texas A & M University.

Juan Flores is associate professor in the Department of Latin American and Caribbean Studies at City College and in Sociology and Cultural Studies at the CUNY Graduate Center.

Mario Garcia is professor of History and Chicano Studies at the University of California, Santa Barbara.

Eugene E. Garcia is the Dean of the Graduate School of Education at the University of California, Berkeley and former Director of the U.S. Office for Bilingual Education and Minority Language Affairs.

Martha E. Gimenez is associate professor of Sociology at the University of Colorado at Boulder.

Gilbert G. Gonzalez is professor of Chicano/Latino Studies and Social Sciences at the University of California, Irvine.

Henry Gutíerrez is an assistant professor in the department of Social Sciences at San José State University.

Héctor R. Cordero Guzmán is a sociologist and affiliated with Centro de Estudios Puertorriquenos, Hunter College.

John J. Halcón is an assistant to the Provost at California State University, Monterey Bay.

Rosemary Henze is an education specialist associated with ARC Associates in Oakland, California.

Tamara Lucas conducts research on language-minority students in the United States.

Donaldo Macedo is the graduate program director of Bilingual and ESL Studies at the University of Massachusetts, Boston.

Arturo Madrid is Norine R. and T. Frank Murchison Distinguished Professor of the Humanities, Trinity University.

Carlos Muñoz, Jr. is a professor of Chicano Studies at the University of California, Berkeley.

Michael A. Olivas is professor of law at the University of Houston Law School and director of the Institute of Higher Education Law and Governance.

Rafael Peréz-Torres is a sociologist affiliated with the Centro de Estudios Puertorequeños, Hunter College.

Sonia M. Pérez was a policy analyst for the National Council of La Raza in Washington, D.C. At the time her article was originally published.

Richard Ruiz is an associate professor at the University of Arizona.

George I. Sánchez, considered the pioneer in bilingual/bicultural education, was a professor at the University of Texas, Austin until his death in 1972.

Gonzalo Santos holds a Ph.D. in sociology from the State University of New York, Binghamton.

Guadalupe San Miguel, Jr. is an education historian currently teaching at the University of Houston.

Daniel G. Solorzano is assistant professor of Education at the University of California, Los Angeles.

Rodolfo Torres is a professor of Public Policy and Comparative Latino Studies at California State University Long Beach.

Melba J.T. Vasquez is a psychologist in independent practice in Austin, Texas.

George Yúdice is an assistant professor of romance languages at Hunter College, CUNY.

Ana Celia Zentella teaches Black and Puerto Rican Studies at Hunter College, CUNY.